# MINORITY SHAREHOLDERS' REMEDIES

# Minority Shareholders' Remedies

ELIZABETH J. BOROS

CLARENDON PRESS · OXFORD
1995

*Oxford University Press, Walton Street, Oxford* OX2 6DP
*Oxford New York*
*Athens Auckland Bangkok Bombay*
*Calcutta Cape Town Dar es Salaam Delhi*
*Florence Hong Kong Istanbul Karachi*
*Kuala Lumpur Madras Madrid Melbourne*
*Mexico City Nairobi Paris Singapore*
*Taipei Tokyo Toronto*
*and associated companies in*
*Berlin Ibadan*

*Oxford is a trade mark of Oxford University Press*

*Published in the United States*
*by Oxford University Press Inc., New York*

*British Library Cataloguing in Publication Data*
*Data available*

*Library of Congress Cataloging in Publication Data*
*Boros, Elizabeth J.*
*Minority shareholders' remedies/Elizabeth J. Boros.*
*p. cm.*
*Includes bibliographical references.*
*1. Minority shareholders—Legal status, laws, etc.—Australia.*
*2. Stockholders' derivative actions—Australia. 3. Remedies (Law)—*
*Australia. 4. Minority stockholders—Legal status, laws, etc.—*
*Great Britain. 5. Stockholders' derivative actions—Great Britain.*
*6. Remedies (Law)—Great Britain. I. Title.*
*K1344.B67 1995*
*346.41'0926—dc20*
*[344.106926] 95–637*
*ISBN 0–19–825975–1*

1 3 5 7 9 10 8 6 4 2

*Typeset by Cambrian Typesetters, Frimley, Surrey*
*Printed in Great Britain on acid-free paper by*
*Bookcraft Ltd., Midsomer Norton, Avon*

# *Preface*

The problems faced by a minority shareholder in a listed public company may be very different from those encountered by a shareholder in a two-person company. The means available to remedy those problems will frequently also be quite different. This book identifies situations which commonly give rise to conflict between the interests of majority and minority shareholders in different types of company, and examines the various means by which these situations can be addressed.

Minority shareholders' remedies is an area which has developed quite profoundly in recent years. The contribution of the courts has been especially notable in two areas: the development of the 'oppression' or 'unfair prejudice' remedy, particularly in the context of disputes arising out of a breakdown in the relations between quasi-partners; and the resolution of the conflicts of interest associated with the compulsory acquisition of minority shareholdings remaining after a takeover. At the same time, there has been a growing trend for shareholders to try to regulate the internal governance of the companies in which they invest by non-litigious means. In closely-held companies, this has been reflected in the use of shareholders' agreements and specially drafted articles. In listed companies, there has been greater activism by shareholders concerning the governance of companies in which they invest, particularly by institutional shareholders.

Despite the increasing importance of Europe in shaping United Kingdom company law, and the less significant but nevertheless discernible influence of North American developments in Australia, company law in England and Australia has continued to develop in similar directions. However, minority shareholder complaints often arise in slightly different contexts in the two countries, and a comparison of how these problems are dealt with in different jurisdictions not only fills gaps which would otherwise exist in the treatment of a particular topic, but frequently also reveals an emerging pattern or underlying principle.

The law is stated as at 8 March 1995.

E. J. B.

# *Acknowledgments*

I am grateful to Professor L. S. Sealy of Gonville & Caius College Cambridge for his invaluable advice and comments, and to Graham Kirkwood and Peter and Catherine Boros for their encouragement and support. I also thank The Shell Company of Australia Limited, the Committee of Vice-Chancellors and Principals of the Universities of the United Kingdom which administers the Overseas Research Awards Scheme, and the Trustees of the W. M. Tapp Fund at Gonville & Caius College Cambridge for their generous financial sponsorship of the research which formed the basis for this book.

I thank the Australian Stock Exchange Limited, and The Controller of HMSO and the Central Statistical Office for kindly allowing the reproduction of their tables of share ownership of listed companies in Australia and the United Kingdom respectively.

I received assistance in gathering information for this book from numerous sources. Especial thanks are due to the Association of British Insurers, the Australian Investment Managers' Association, the Institutional Fund Managers' Association, the Institutional Shareholders' Committee, J. B. Were & Son, Korn/Ferry Carré Orban International, Pensions & Investment Research Consultants Limited, Pro-Ned Australia, Pro-Share, the Legal Division of Shell International Petroleum Company Limited, the Panel on Takeovers and Mergers, The Australian Shareholders' Association, The National Association of Pension Funds Limited, Mr Bruce Dyer of Monash University, Ms Belinda Fehlberg of Melbourne University, Mr M. J. Heffernan of the Australian Stock Exchange Limited and Mr Henry Bosch AO.

I was very fortunate to have had access to the resources of, and the help of the librarians at the Squire Law Library in Cambridge, and the law libraries of the University of Adelaide, the University of Melbourne and the Institute of Advanced Legal Studies. Sincere thanks must also go to the partners and librarians at Blake Dawson Waldron in Melbourne.

I also wish to thank my publishers for all their help.

Melbourne                                                                                    E. J. B.
24 May 1995

# Contents

*Table of Abbreviations*                                        viii
*Table of Cases*                                                  xi
*Table of Statutes*                                           xxxvii

**PART I  THE PROBLEM**

  1:  Introduction                                                 3
  2:  Common Complaints of Minority Shareholders                   5

**PART II  PREVENTION**

  3:  Self-help in Listed Companies                               13
  4:  Self-help in Quasi-partnership and Joint Venture
      Companies                                                   63
  5:  Self-help in Other Companies                               107

**PART III  REMEDY**

  6:  The Oppression/Unfair Prejudice Remedy                     111
  7:  Winding Up                                                 166
  8:  Common Law Relief                                          183
  9:  Application of Litigious Remedies to Identified
      Complaints                                                 218
 10:  Compulsory Acquisition                                     260

**PART IV  CONCLUSIONS**

 11:  Overview and Conclusions                                   319

*Index*                                                          331

# Abbreviations

| | |
|---|---|
| ABI | Association of British Insurers |
| ABS | Australian Bureau of Statistics |
| AIMA | Australian Investment Managers' Association |
| ASA | Australian Shareholders' Association |
| ASC | Australian Securities Commission |
| ASX | Australian Stock Exchange |
| CA 1985 (UK) | Companies Act 1985 (This Act is referred to in general terms as United Kingdom legislation. However, it does not extend to Northern Ireland or apply to companies registered or incorporated in Northern Ireland or outside Great Britain, except where otherwise expressly provided). |
| CA | Court of Appeal (England) |
| CA BC | Court of Appeal, British Columbia (Canada) |
| CA NI | Court of Appeal, Northern Ireland |
| CA NSW | Court of Appeal, New South Wales (Australia) |
| CA NT | Court of Appeal, Northern Territory (Australia) |
| CA NZ | Court of Appeal, New Zealand |
| CA Ontario | Court of Appeal, Ontario (Canada) |
| CASAC | Companies and Securities Advisory Committee (Australia) |
| City Code | City Code on Takeovers and Mergers (UK) |
| CL (Aust) | Corporations Law (Australia) |
| CS (IH) | Court of Sessions (Inner House) (Scotland) |
| CSO | Central Statistics Office (UK) |
| Full Ct, Qld | Full Court of the Supreme Court of Queensland (Australia) |
| Full Ct, SA | Full Court of the Supreme Court of South Australia |
| Full Ct, WA | Full Court of the Supreme Court of Western Australia |
| Full Ct, Vic | Full Court of the Supreme Court of Victoria (Australia) |
| Full Ct, Tas | Full Court of the Supreme Court of Tasmania (Australia) |
| Full Fed Ct | Full Federal Court (Australia) |
| HC | High Court of Australia |
| HL | House of Lords |
| IA 1986 (UK) | Insolvency Act 1986 (This Act is referred to in general terms as United Kingdom legislation, However, see |

| | |
|---|---|
| | Part XIX of this Act regarding its extension to Scotland, Northern Ireland and other territories). |
| ISC | Institutional Shareholders' Committee |
| Listed company | This expression is used in its widest sense to include companies whose share capital has been admitted to the Unlisted Securities Market, as well as listed companies in the strict sense. |
| Ltd. | Limited. When appearing at the end of a company's name, this denotes that the liability of members is limited. In England it also indicates that the company is not public (see plc), whereas in Australia, when used on its own, it indicates that the company is not a proprietary company (see Pty. Ltd.). |
| NAPF | National Association of Pension Funds |
| NCSC | National Companies and Securities Commission (Australia). This was the predecessor of the ASC. |
| Petition/Petitioner | In the discussion of the unfair prejudice and winding-up remedies, the applicant for relief is, for convenience, described as the 'petitioner'. This reflects the initiating proceeding for such applications in the Chancery Division in England. In Australia, the form of application depends upon the court to which it is made. |
| PIRC | Pensions Investments Research Consultants |
| plc | public limited company. The name of a public company must end with these words in England. |
| PC | Privy Council |
| PRO NED | Promotion of Non-Executive Directors |
| Pty. Ltd. | Proprietary Limited. These are the last two words of the name of a proprietary company in Australia (see also Ltd.) |
| SCC | Supreme Court of Canada |

Abbreviations of journal names are the same as those used in the Index to Legal Periodicals.

# Table of Cases

## AUSTRALIA

ABT Holdings Pty Ltd, Re (1979) 4 ACLR 40 . . . . . . . . . . . 252
ACM Gold Ltd, Re (1992) 7 ACSR 231; 10 ACLC 573 . . 282, 310, 311
ANZ Executors & Trustees Ltd v Humes Ltd (1989) 15
  ACLR 392 . . . . . . . . . . . . . . . . . . . . . . . . 271, 307
ANZ Executors & Trustee Company Ltd v Qintex Australia
  Ltd (Recs and Mgrs apptd) [1991] 2 Qd R 360 (Full Ct. Qld) . . . 102
AWA Ltd v Daniels (1992) 7 ACSR 759; 10 ACLC 933 . . . . . 28, 241
Abeles v Fuller Holdings Pty Ltd (1977–1978) ACLC
  40–329 . . . . . . . . . . . . . . . . . . . . . . . . . 113
Abraham v Tunalex Pty Ltd (1987) 5 ACLC 888 . . . . . . . . . 210
Allen v Atalay (1993) 11 ACSR 753; 12 ACLC 7 . . . . . . . . . 213
Aloridge Pty Ltd v West Australian Gem Exporters Pty Ltd
  (1995) 15 ACSR 645; 13 ACLC 196 . . . . . . . . . . . . . . 190
Amalgamated Pest Control Pty Ltd v McCarron (1994) 13
  ACSR 42; 12 ACLC 171 . . . . . . . . . . . . . . . . . . 73, 82
Ardlethan Options Ltd v Easdown (1915) 20 CLR 285 (HC) . . . . . 73
Arnotts Ltd v Campbell Investment (Aust) Pty Ltd (1993) 9
  ACSR 675 (CA NSW) . . . . . . . . . . . . . . . . . . . . 95
Asia Oil & Minerals Ltd, Re (1986) 5 NSWLR 42 . . . . . . . . . 282
Associated Products & Distribution Pty Ltd v Sunkist
  Holdings Ltd (1967) 41 ALJR 61 (HC) . . . . . . . . . . . . . 97
Associates Tool Industries Ltd, Re (1963) 5 FLR 55 . 117, 119, 232, 322
Augold NL, Re [1987] 2 Qd R 297 . . . . . . . . . . . . . 247, 248
Austamax Resources Ltd, Re (1985) 10 ACLR 194; 4 ACLC
  76 . . . . . . . . . . . . . . . . . . . . . . . . . . 282, 286
Australasian Venezolana Pty Ltd, Re (1962) 4 FLR 60 . . . . . . . 241
Australian Agricultural Company v Oatmont Pty Ltd (1992)
  8 ACSR 255; 10 ACLC 1220 (CA NT) . . . . . . . . . . . . . 187
Australian Consolidated Press Ltd v Australian Newsprint
  Mills Holdings Ltd (1960) 105 CLR 473 (HC) . . . . . . . . . 264, 267
Australian Fixed Trusts Pty Ltd v Clyde Industries Ltd (1959)
  59 SR (NSW) 33 . . . . . . . . . . . . . . . . . . . . . 38
Australian Foundation Investment Company Ltd, Re [1974] VR
  331 . . . . . . . . . . . . . . . . . . . . . . . . . . 290
Australian Marinas (A'asia) Pty Ltd, Re [1975] VR 372 . . . . . . . 252
Australian Securities Commission v Gallagher (1993) 10
  ACSR 43; 11 ACLC 286 (Full Ct, WA) . . . . . . . . . . . . . 241

*Table of Cases*

Australian Securities Commission *v* Marlborough Goldmines Ltd
(1993) 177 CLR 485 (HC) . . . . . . . . . . . . . . . . . . . . . 286
Australian Securities Commission *v* Multiple Sclerosis Society
of Tasmania (1993) 10 ACSR 489; 11 ACLC 461 . . . . . . . . . 137,
138, 224, 225, 298

BDC Investments Ltd, Re (1988) 13 ACLR 201; 6 ACLC 1196 . . . 282
BWN Industries Pty Ltd *v* Downey (1993) 11 ACSR 777; 11
ACLC 1191 . . . . . . . . . . . . . . . . . . . . . . . . . . . . 201
Back 2 Bay 6 Pty Ltd, Re (1994) 12 ACSR 614; 12 ACLC 253 . . . 163
Bagot Well Pastoral Co Pty Ltd, Re; Shannon *v* Reid (1992)
9 ACSR 129; 11 ACLC affd sub nom Re Bagot Well
Pastoral Co Pty Ltd (1993) 61 SASR 61 . . . . . . 156, 157, 224, 231,
232, 236, 244, 251
Baily *v* Mandala Private Hospital Pty Ltd (1987) 12 ACLR 641;
6 ACLC 43 . . . . . . . . . . . . . . . . . . . . . . . . . . 228, 229
Bain & Company Nominees Pty Ltd *v* Grace Bros Holdings
Ltd (1983) 1 ACLC 816 . . . . . . . . . . . . . . . . . . . . . . . 304
Bancorp Investments Ltd *v* Primac Holdings Ltd (1984) 9
ACLR 263; 3 ACLC 69 . . . . . . . . . . . . . . . . . . . . . . . . 304
Bank of Adelaide, Re the (1979) 22 SASR 481 (Full Ct, SA) . . 282, 309
Barrack Mines Ltd *v* Grants Patch Mining Ltd [1988] 1 Qd R
606 (Full Ct, Qld) . . . . . . . . . . . . . . . . . . . . . . . . 247, 248
Bernhardt *v* Beau Rivage Pty Ltd (1989) 15 ACLR 160; 7
ACLC 639 . . . . . . . . . . . . . . . . . . . . . . . . . . . . 169, 179
Biala Pty Ltd *v* Mallina Holdings Ltd (No 2) (1993)
11 ACSR 785; 11 ACLR 1 082 affd sub nom Dempster *v*
Mallina Holdings Ltd (1994) 15 ACSR 1 (Full Ct,
WA) . . . . . . . . . . . . . . . . . . . . . . . . . . . . . 190, 192, 198,
214, 237, 238, 241, 247, 322
Blue Metal Industries Ltd *v* R. W. Dilley [1970] AC 827
(PC) . . . . . . . . . . . . . . . . . . . . . . . . . 265, 267, 276, 308
Bodaibo Pty Ltd, Re (1992) 6 ACSR 509; 10 ACLC 351 . . . . 156, 158
Bond Corporation Holdings Ltd, Re (1991) 5 WAR 143 . . . . 285, 286
Bountiful Pty Ltd, Re (1994) 12 ACLC 902 . . . . . . . . . . . . 158
Bride *v* Commissioner for Corporate Affairs (1989) 1 ACSR
36; 7 ACLC 1202 . . . . . . . . . . . . . . . . . . . . . . . . . 249
Brierley *v* Dextran Pty Ltd (1990) 3 ACSR 455; 9 ACLC
30 . . . . . . . . . . . . . . . . . . . . . . . . . . . . . . . 270, 276
Bright Pines Pty Ltd, Re [1969] VR 1002 (Full Ct, Vic) . . . . 116, 117,
118, 119, 135, 231
Broadcasting Station 2GB Pty Ltd, Re [1964–5] NSWR
1648 . . . . . . . . . . . . . . . . . . . . . . . . . . 116, 117, 232

Broken Hill Proprietary Co Ltd *v* Bell Resources Ltd (1984)
8 ACLR 609; 2 ACLC 157 . . . . . . . . . . . . . . . . 213
Brooks *v* Burns Philp Trustee Co Ltd (1969) 121 CLR 432
(HC) . . . . . . . . . . . . . . . . . . . . . . . . . 87, 97, 98
Brooks (William) & Co Ltd, Re [1962] NSWR 142 . . . . 113, 176, 178
Buche *v* Box Pty Ltd (1993) 31 NSWLR 368 . . . . . . . . . . . 230
Buckland *v* Johnstone (1991) 5 ACSR 404; 9 ACLC 1193 . . . . . . 90
Bulfin *v* Bebarfald's Ltd (1938) 38 SR (NSW) 423 . . . . . . . . 290, 304

CAC (NSW) *v* Drysdale (1978) 141 CLR 236 . . . . . . . . . . . . 35
Campaign Holdings Pty Ltd, Re (1989) 15 ACLR 762; 8 ACLC 64 . 297
Carrier Australasia Ltd *v* Hunt (1939) 61 CLR 534 (HC) . . . . . . . 70
Catto *v* Ampol Ltd (1989) 16 NSWLR 342 . . . . . . . . 276, 295, 312
Cescastle Pty Ltd *v* Renak Holdings Ltd (1991) 6 ACSR 115;
9 ACLC 1333 . . . . . . . . . . . . . . . . . . . . . . 248
Chase Corporation (Australia) Pty Ltd *v* North Sydney
Brick and Tile Co Ltd (1994) 14 ACSR 586; 12 ACLC 997 . . . . 134
Checker Holdings Pty Ltd, Re (1985) 3 ACLC 565 . . . . . . . . . 169
Chequepoint Securities Ltd *v* Claremont Petroleum NL
(1986) 11 ACLR 94; 4 ACLC 711 . . . . . . . . . . . . . . . 304
Chevron (Sydney) Ltd, Re [1963] VR 249 . . . . . . . . . . . . . 285
City Meat Co Pty Ltd, Re (1984) 8 ACLR 673; 2 ACLC 149 . . 117, 243
Claremont Petroleum NL, Re (1989) 1 ACSR 494; 8 ACLC 56
affd [1990] 2 Qd R 31 (Full Ct, Qld) . . . . . . . . . . . 247, 248
Claremont Petroleum NL, Re (No. 2) (1990) 2 ACSR 84;
8 ACLC 548 . . . . . . . . . . . . . . . . . . . . . . . 249
Colarc Pty Ltd *v* Donarc Pty Ltd (1991) 4 ACSR 155 . . . . . . 203, 228
Commonwealth Bank of Australia *v* Friedrich (1991) 5
ACSR 115; 9 ACL 946 . . . . . . . . . . . . . . . . . . . 240
Compaction Systems Pty Ltd, Re [1976] 2 NSWLR 477 . . . . . . . 92–3
Coogan (W) & Co Pty Ltd, Re (1993) 10 ACSR 461; 11 ACLC
388 . . . . . . . . . . . . . . . . . . . . . . . . . . . 286
Coombs *v* Dynasty Pty Ltd (1994) 14 ACSR 60; digested
(1994) 12 ACLC 915 . . . . . . . . . . . . . 146, 227–8, 232, 255
Crumpton *v* Morrine Hall Pty Ltd [1965] NSWR
240 . . . . . . . . . . . . . . . . . . . . . . 72, 90, 207, 301
Cumberland Holdings Ltd *v* Washington H Soul Pattinson
& Co Ltd (1977) 2 ACLR 307 (PC) . . . . . . . . . . . . . . 169

Dalkeith Investments Pty Ltd, Re (1984) 9 ACLR 247; 3 ACLC
74 . . . . . . . . . . . . . 87, 132, 141, 146, 156, 176, 227, 229
Dalley (M) & Co Pty Ltd, Re (1968) 1 ACLR 489 . . . . 118, 119, 133–4,
135–6, 138, 224

Dalley (M) & Co Pty Ltd *v* Sims (1968) 120 CLR 603 (HC) . . . . . .		92
Darvall *v* North Sydney Brick & Tile Co Ltd (No 2) (1987)
	16 NSWLR 212 . . . . . . . . . . . . . . . . . . . . . . . . . . . .		215
Darvall *v* North Sydney Brick & Tile Co Ltd (No 4) (1988)
	14 ACLR 474; 6 ACLC 1095 . . . . . . . . . . . . . . . . . . .		73
Darvall *v* North Sydney Brick & Tile Co Ltd (1989) 16
	NSWLR 260 (CA NSW) . . . . . . . . . . . . . . . . . . . .		280
Davidson *v* Smith (1989) 15 ACLR 732 . . . . . . . . . . . .		102, 103
Davies *v* Davies (1919) 26 CLR 348 (HC) . . . . . . . . . . . . . .		98
Dempster *v* Biala Pty Ltd (1989) 1 WAR 266 (Full Ct,
	WA) . . . . . . . . . . . . . . . . . . . . . . . . . . . . . . . .		190, 213
Dempster *v* Mallina Holdings Ltd (1994) 15 ACSR 1
	(Full Ct, WA) . . . . . . . . . . . . . . . .		192, 214, 237, 241, 322
Deniliquin Corp Ltd, Re (1994) 12 ACSR 623; 12 ACLC
	261 . . . . . . . . . . . . . . . . . . . . . . . . . . . . . . . . . .		294
Dernacourt Investments Pty Ltd, Re (1990) 20 NSWLR 588 .		115, 133,
								135, 233, 251
Devereaux Holdings Pty Ltd *v* Pelsart Resources NL (No 2)
	(1985) 9 ACLR 956 . . . . . . . . . . . . . . . . . . . . . . .		304
Direct Acceptance Corporation Ltd, Re (1987) 5 ACLC
	1037 . . . . . . . . . . . . . . . . . . . . . . . .		283, 285, 287, 311
Dividend Fund Incorporated (in liq.), Re [1974] VR 451 . . . . . . .		73
Doncon *v* Doncon & Ors (1990) 2 ACSR 385; 8 ACLC 860 . . .		228, 229


Eastment (FT) & Sons Pty Ltd *v* Metal Roof Decking
	Supplies Pty Ltd (1977) 3 ACLR 69; (1977–78) CLC 40–368 (CA
	NSW) . . . . . . . . . . . . . . . . . . . . . . . . . . . . . . . .		286
East West Promotions Pty Ltd, Re; Cheetham *v* McCoy (1986)
	10 ACLR 222; 4 ACLC 84 . . . . . . . . . . . . . . . . . .		169, 232
Eastern Petroleum Australia Ltd *v* Horseshoe Lights Gold
	Pty Ltd (1985) 9 ACLR 980; 3 ACLC 594 . . . . . . . . . . . . .		214
Eddy *v* W. R. Carpenter Holdings Ltd (1985) 10 ACLR
	316; 4 ACLC 101 . . . . . . . . . . . . . . . . .		274, 276, 278, 279
Edman *v* Ross (1922) 22 SR (NSW) 351 . . . . . . . . . . . . . .		246
Elkington *v* Shell Australia Ltd (1993) 32 NSWLR 11 (CA
	NSW) . . . . . . . . . . . . . . . . . . . . . . . .		274, 276, 307
Elkington *v* Vockbay Pty Ltd (1993) 10 ACSR 785; 11 ACLC
	591 . . . . . . . . . . . . . . . . . . . . . . . . . . . . . .		276, 280
Enterprise Gold Mines NL, Re (1991) 3 ACSR 531 rusd sub nom
	Jenkins *v* Enterprise Gold Mines NL (1992) 6 ACSR 539; 10
	ACLC 136 . . . . . . . .		137–8, 139, 158, 161–2, 228, 231, 237, 320
Equiticorp Finance Ltd (in liq.) *v* Bank of New Zealand
	(1993) 32 NSWLR 50 (CA NSW) . . . . . . . . . . . . . . . .		306

Eromanga Hydrocarbons NL *v* Australis Mining NL & Ors
 (1988) 14 ACLR 486; 6 ACLC 906 . . . .  189, 190, 192, 201, 202, 228

FAI Insurances Ltd *v* Urquhart (No 2) (1986) 11 ACLR 38 . . . . .  186
Farrow *v* Registrar of Building Societies [1991] 2 VR
 589 . . . . . . . . . . . . . . . . . . . . . . . .  190, 191–2
Feiersinger *v* Transfield (Australia) Pty Ltd (Unrep 3
 November 1988 NSW) . . . . . . . . . . . . . . . . . . . . . 97
Felton *v* Mulligan (1971) 124 CLR 367 (HC) . . . . . . . . . . 97, 98
Ffrost & Co Pty Ltd, Re [1993] 1 Qd R 1 . . . . . . . . . . . . 76, 78
Fischer *v* Easthaven Ltd [1964] NSW 261 . . . . . . . . . . . . 72, 90
Fowlers Vacola Manufacturing Co Ltd, Re [1966] VR 97 . . . . . .  294
Fraser *v* NRMA Holdings Ltd (1994) 14 ACSR 656; 12 ACLC 855
 affd (1995) 15 ACSR 590; 13 ACLC 132 (Full Fed Ct) . . . . . .  78,
                                                      278, 290, 304
Fulloon *v* Radley [1992] 2 Qd R 290 . . . . . . . . . . . . . . . 189
Furs Ltd *v* Tomkies (1936) 54 CLR 583 (HC) . . . . . . . . . . .  198

GPI Leisure Corporation Ltd *v* Herdsman Investments Pty
 Ltd (Unrep 24 November 1989 NSW) . . . . . . . . . . . . . . 96
Gambotto *v* WCP Ltd (1992) 8 ACSR 141; 10 ACLC 1046
 on App WCP Ltd *v* Gambotto (1993) 30 NSWLR 385 (CA
 NSW) rvsd sub nom Gambotto *v* WCP Ltd . . . . . . . . . . 298, 300
Gambotto *v* WCP Ltd (1995) 16 ACSR 1; 13 ACLC 342
 (HC) . . . .  208, 209, 226, 227, 277, 280, 289, 297, 298, 303, 304, 314
Garden Mews – St. Leonards Pty Ltd *v* Butler Pollnow Pty
 Ltd (1984) 9 ACLR 91 . . . . . . . . . . . . . . . . . . . . .  190
Gazelle Constructions Pty Ltd, Re (1984) 10 ACLR 140; 2 ACLC
 680 . . . . . . . . . . . . . . . . . . . . . . . . . . . . . 285
Gibson *v* Opalspectrum Pty Ltd (Unrep 10 November 1994
 Federal Court NSW) . . . . . . . . . . . . . . 247, 248, 249–50, 250
Glandon Pty Ltd *v* Strata Consolidated Pty Ltd (1993) 11
 ACSR 543; 11 ACLC 895 (CA NSW) . . . . . . . . . . . . . . 280
Glass *v* The Pioneer Rubber Works of Australia Ltd [1906]
 VLR 754 . . . . . . . . . . . . . . . . . . . . . . . . . . . 70
Grant *v* John Grant & Sons Pty Ltd (1950) 82 CLR 1
 (HC) . . . . . . . . . . . . . . . . . . . . . . . . . . . . . 73
Group Four Industries Pty Ltd *v* Brosnan (1992) 59 SASR
 22 (Full Ct, SA) . . . . . . . . . . . . . . . . . . . . . 240, 242

Hannes (JD) *v* M. J. H. Pty Ltd (1992) 7 ACSR 8; 10
 ACLC 400 (CA NSW) . . . . . . . . . . . . . . . . . . . 229, 232
Harrison (Saul D) & Sons plc, Re [1994] BCC 475 (CA) . . . . . . 232

Hawkesbury Development Co Ltd *v* Landmark Finance Pty
    Ltd [1969] 2 NSWR 782 (No 2) . . . . . . . . . . . . . . . . .    186
Heron *v* Port Huon Fruitgrowers' Co-operative Association
    Ltd (1992) 30 CLR 315 (HC) . . . . . . . . . . . . . . . . . .    71
Holdings (J&E) Pty Ltd *v* Bourke (1994) 13 ACSR 83 . . . . . . .    225
Holt *v* Cox (1994) 15 ACSR 313 . . . . . . . . . . . . . . . . 143, 144
Hooker Investments Pty Ltd *v* Email Ltd (1986) 10 ACLR
    443 . . . . . . . . . . . . . . . . . . . . . . . . . . . . . .    189
Howard Smith Ltd *v* Ampol Petroleum Ltd [1974] AC 821
    (PC) . . . . . . . . . . . . . . . . . . . 87, 189, 201, 228, 244
Hunter Resources Ltd, Re (1992) 7 ACSR 436; 10 ACLC
    538 . . . . . . . . . . . . . . . . . . . . . . . . . . . 298, 313
Hurley *v* BGH Nominees Pty Ltd (1982) 31 SASR 250 . . . . . . .    190
Hurley *v* NCSC (1993) 11 ACLC 443 . . . . . . . . . . . . . . .    241

Independent Quarries Pty Ltd, Re (1993) 12 ACSR 188; 12
    ACLC 159 . . . . . . . . . . . . . . . . . . . . . . . . . . .    123
Inge *v* Inge (1990) 3 ACSR 63; 8 ACLC 943 . . . . . . . . . . . .    96
Ingleburn Horse and Pony Club Ltd, Re [1973] 1 NSWLR
    641 . . . . . . . . . . . . . . . . . . . . . . . . 116, 117, 118
Intercapital Holdings Ltd *v* MEH Ltd (1988) 13 ACLR 595;
    6 ACLC 1068 . . . . . . . . . . . . . . . . . . . . . . . 247, 248
International Harvester Co of Australia Pty Ltd, Re [1953] VLR
    669 (Full Ct, Vic) . . . . . . . . . . . . . . . . . . . . . .    309

Jax Marine Pty Ltd, Re [1967] 1 NSWR 145 . . . . . . . . . . . .    285
Jeffery (G) (Mens Store) Pty Ltd, Re (1984) 9 ACLR 193; 2
    ACLC 421 . . . . . . . . . . . . . 133, 136, 141, 244, 253, 305
Jenkins *v* Enterprise Gold Mines NL (1992) 6 ACSR 539; 10
    ACLC 136 (Full Ct, WA) . . . . . 137–8, 139, 158, 228, 231, 237, 320

Kalblue Pty Ltd, Re (1994) 12 ACLC 1057 . . . . . . . . . . . .    167
Kingston *v* Keprose Pty Ltd (1987) 11 NSWLR 404 (CA
    NSW) . . . . . . . . . . . . . . . . . . . . . . . . . . . 264, 271
Kingston *v* Keprose Pty Ltd (No 2) (1987) 12 ACLR 599; 6
    ACLC 111 . . . . . . . . . . . . . . . . . . . . . . . . . . .    275
Kinsela *v* Russell Kinsela Pty Ltd (in liq.) (1986) 4 NSWLR
    722 (CA, NSW) . . . . . . . . . . . . . . . . . . . . . . . .    197
Kizquari Pty Ltd *v* Prestoo Pty Ltd (1993) 10 ACSR 606; 11
    ACLC 568 . . . . . . . . . . . . . . . . 146, 156, 158, 253, 305
Knightswood Nominees Pty Ltd *v* Sherwin Pastoral
    Company Ltd (1989) 15 ACLR 151; 7 ACLC 536 . . . . . . . . .    249
Kornblums Furnishings Ltd, Re [1982] VR 123 . . . . . . . . . .    139

Kraus *v* J. G. Lloyd Pty Ltd [1965] VR 232 . . . . . . . . . . . 188, 193

Landmark Corporation Ltd, Re [1968] 1 NSWR 759 . . . . . . . . 285
Leaney *v* Olmstead Pty Ltd (1994) 12 ACLC 520 . . . . . . . . . . 122
Legal & General Life of Australia Ltd *v* A. Hudson Pty Ltd
    (1985) 1 NSWLR 314 (CA NSW) . . . . . . . . . . . . . . . . 144
Linter Textiles Corporation Ltd (Recs and Mgrs apptd), Re
    [1991] 2 VR 561 . . . . . . . . . . . . . . . . . . . . . . . . . 286
Lorenzi *v* Lorenzi Holdings Pty Ltd (1993) 12 ACSR 398 . . . . 81, 228

Maas *v* McIntosh (1928) 28 SR (NSW) 441 . . . . . . . . . . . . 189
Magill *v* Santina Pty Ltd (in liq.) [1983] 1 NSWLR 517 (CA
    NSW) . . . . . . . . . . . . . . . . . . . . . . . . . . . . . . . 72
McConochie *v* Derrawee Pastoral Co Pty Ltd (1994) 15
    ACSR 126 . . . . . . . . . . . . . . . . . . . . . . . . . . . . 144
McEwan *v* Dick (1985) 9 ACLR 1011; 3 ACLC 671 . . . . . . . . . 86
McFarlane *v* Daniell (1938) 38 SR (NSW) 337 . . . . . . . . . . . 86
McGuire *v* Ralph McKay Ltd & Ors (1987) 12 ACLR 107
    (Full Ct, Vic) . . . . . . . . . . . . . . . . . . . . . . . . . . 228
McWilliam *v* L. J. R. McWilliam Estates Pty Ltd (1990) 20
    NSWLR 703 . . . . . . . . . . . . . . 133, 135, 244, 245, 253, 305
Medefield Pty Ltd, Re (1977) 2 ACLR 406; (1977–78) ACLC
    40–325 . . . . . . . . . . . . . . . . . . . . . . . 210, 212, 321
Melcann Ltd *v* Super John Pty Ltd (1994) 13 ACLC 92 . . . . . 295, 296
Menard *v* Horwood and Company Limited (1922) 31 CLR
    20 (HC) . . . . . . . . . . . . . . . . . . . . . . . . 152, 175, 177
Mercantile Mutual Life Insurance Co Ltd & Ors *v* Actraint
    No 85 Pty Ltd (No 2) (1990) 52 SASR 506 . . . . . . . . . . 264, 275
Metal Manufacturers Pty Ltd *v* Lewis (1988) 13 NSWLR 315
    (CA NSW) . . . . . . . . . . . . . . . . . . . . . . . . . . . . 240
Meyer *v* Douglas Pty Ltd, Re [1965] VR 638 . . . . . . . . . . . 122
Miles *v* The Sydney Meat Preserving Co Ltd (1913) 17 CLR
    639 (PC) . . . . . . . . . . . . . . . . . . . . . . . . . . . . . 242
Mincom Pty Ltd *v* Murphy [1983] 1 Qd R
    297 . . . . . . . . . . . . . . . . . . . . 119, 176, 177, 178, 179
Morgan *v* 45 Flers Avenue Pty Ltd (1986) 10 ACLR 692; 5
    ACLC 222 . . . . . . 124, 126, 133, 140, 153, 175, 176, 225, 236, 243
Morley *v* Statewide Tobacco Services Ltd [1993] 1 VR
    423 . . . . . . . . . . . . . . . . . . . . . . . . . . . . . 240, 242

Nankivell *v* Benjamin (1892) 18 VLR 543 . . . . . . . . . . . . . 186
National Roads & Motorists' Association *v* Parker (1986) 6
    NSWLR 517 . . . . . . . . . . . . . . . . . . . . . . . . . . . 188

Newman (TC) (Qld) Pty Ltd *v* D. H. A. Rural (Qld) Pty
  Ltd [1988] 1 Qd R 308 . . . . . . . . . . . . . . . . . . . . .   228
New South Wales Medical Defence Union Ltd *v* Crawford
  (1993) 31 NSWLR 469 (CA NSW) . . . . . . . . . . . . . . . .   72
Ngurli Ltd *v* McCann (1953) 90 CLR 425 (HC) . . .   200, 201, 202, 206,
                                                              209, 229
Nicron Resources Ltd *v* Catto & Ors (1992) 8 ACSR 219; 10
  ACLC 1186 . . . . . . . . . . . . . .   199, 204, 286, 292, 312, 313
Niord Pty Ltd *v* Adelaide Petroleum NL (1990) 54 SASR 87 . . . .   122
Nordic Bank plc *v* International Harvester Australia Ltd
  [1983] 2 VR 298 (Full Ct, Vic) . . . . . . . . . . . . . . . . .   285
North Sydney Brick & Tile Co Ltd *v* Darvall & Anor (1986)
  5 NSWLR 681 (CA NSW) . . . . . . . . . . . . . . . . . .   266, 269
Norths Ltd *v* McCaughan Dyson Capel Cure Ltd (1988) 12
  ACLR 739; 6 ACLC 320 . . . . . . . . . . . . . . . . . . . . .   72
Norvabron Pty Ltd (No 2), Re (1986) 11 ACLR 279; 5 ACLC
  184 . . . . . . . . . . . . . . . .   126, 127, 132, 144, 146, 157, 176


Oswald *v* Bailey (1987) 11 NSWLR 715 (CA NSW) . . . . . . . . . .   74
Overton Holdings Pty Ltd, Re [1985] WAR 224 . . . . . . . .   158, 236


Pacific Fisheries Ltd, Re (1909) 26 WN (NSW) 127 . . . . . . . . .   114
Parker *v* National Road and Motorists' Association (1989) 1
  ACSR 227 affd (1993) 11 ACSR 370; 11 ACLC 866 (CA
  NSW) . . . . . . . . . . . . . . . . . .   160, 164–5, 192, 232, 234, 237
Permanent Building Society (in liq.) *v* Wheeler (1994) 11
  WAR 187 . . . . . . . . . . . . . . . . . . . . . . . . . . . .   241
Permanent Trustee Australia Ltd *v* Perpetual Trustee Co
  Ltd (1994) 15 ACSR 722; 13 ACLC 66 . . . . . . . . . . . .   214, 238
Peters' American Delicacy Co Ltd *v* Heath (1939) 61 CLR
  457 (HC) . . . . . . . .   74, 84, 193, 194, 203, 204, 206, 209, 301–3
Pheon Pty Ltd, Re (1986) 47 SASR 427 . . . . . . . . . . . . . .   289
Phosphate Co-operative Co of Aust Ltd *v* Shears & Anor
  (No 3) [1989] VR 665 . . . . . . . . . . . . . . . . . . . .   288, 289
Pitt (Richard) & Sons Ltd, Re (1979) 4 ACLR 459
  (Full Ct, Tas) . . . . . . . . . . . . . . . . . . . . . . . .   136, 222
Premier Gold NL *v* Ocean Resources NL (1994) 15 ACSR
  695; 12 ACLC 931 . . . . . . . . . . . . . . . . . . . . . . .   214
Prime Group Holdings Ltd, Re (1994) 13 ACSR 357; 12 ACLC
  308 . . . . . . . . . . . . . . . . . . . . . . . . . . . . . .   297


QIW Retailers Ltd *v* Felview Pty Ltd [1989] 2 Qd R 245 . . . .   148, 176

Quest Exploration Pty Ltd, Re (1992) 6 ACSR 659 . . . . . . . . . 157
Quinlan *v* Vital Technology Australia Ltd (1987) 5 ACLC
  389 . . . . . . . . . . . . . . . . . . . . . . 247, 248

Ramsay Health Care Ltd *v* Elkington (1992) 7 ACSR 73; 10
  ACLC 421 . . . . . . . . . . . . . . . . . . . . . 412
Rees' Application, Re [1972] QWN 47 . . . . . . . . . . . . . . 273
Reid House Pty Ltd *v* Beneke & Ors (1986) 5 ACLC 451 . . . . . . 135
Rema Industries and Services Pty Ltd *v* Coad; Re Taspac
  Thermoforming Pty Ltd (1992) 7 ACSR 251; 10 ACLC
  530 . . . . . . . . . . . . . . . . . . . . . . 240, 242
Residues Treatment and Trading Co Ltd *v* Southern
  Resources Ltd (1988) 14 ACLR 375 . . . . . . . . . . . . . 304
Residues Treatment and Trading Co Ltd *v* Southern
  Resources (No 4) (1988) 51 SASR 196 (Full Ct, SA) . . . . . . . 189,
                       201–2, 209, 228
Reuthlinger *v* MacDonald [1976] 1 NSWLR 88 . . . . . . . . . . . 97
Roberts *v* Walter Developments Pty Ltd (1992) 10 ACLC
  804 . . . . . . . . . . . . . . . . . . . . . . 232, 243
Roberts *v* Walter Developments Pty Ltd (No 2) (1992) 10
  ACLC 1734 . . . . . . . . . . . . . . . . . . . . 155, 156
Rural Industries Co-operative Society Ltd *v* Porky Pigs Pty
  Ltd (1988) 12 ACLR 794; 6 ACLC 383 . . . . . . . . . . . . 170

Saddington (PW) & Sons Pty Ltd, Re (1990) 19 NSWLR 674 . . . . . 92
Sanford *v* Sanford Courier Services Pty Ltd (1986) 10 ACLR
  549; 5 ACLC 394 . . . . . . . . . . 143, 156, 157, 231, 232, 234, 243
Scarel Pty Ltd *v* City Loan & Credit Corporation Pty Ltd
  (1988) 12 ACLR 730; 6 ACLC 219 . . . . . . . . . . 190, 192, 214
Shears *v* Chisholm (1992) 9 ACSR 691 . . . . . . . . . . . . 192, 193
Shears *v* Phosphate Co-operative Company of Australia Ltd
  (1988) 14 ACLR 747; 7 ACLC 812 . . . . . . . . 100, 133, 226, 233
Shine Fisheries Ltd, Re (1994) 12 ACSR 627; 12 ACLC
  233 . . . . . . . . . . . . . . . . . . . . 199, 292, 295, 296
Simon *v* HPM Industries Pty Ltd (1989) 15 ACLR 427; 7
  ACLC 770 . . . . . . . . . . . . . . . . . . . . . 73, 90
Southern Resources Ltd, Re (1989) 15 ACLR 770 affd sub nom
  Southern Resources Ltd *v* Residues Treatment and
  Trading Co Ltd (1990) 56 SASR 455 (Full Ct, SA) . . . . . . 214, 229
Spargos Mining NL, Re (1990) 3 WAR 166 . . . 119, 123, 137, 139, 155,
                159, 161, 162, 164, 236, 237, 320, 329
Spicer *v* Mytret Pty Ltd (1984) 8 ACLR 711; 2 ACLC 214 . . . . . 118

Starr (John J) (Real Estate) Pty Ltd *v* Robert R. Andrew
  (A'asia) Pty Ltd (1991) 6 ACSR 63; 9 ACLC 1372 . . . . .    124, 131,
                                                               169, 225
Stenhouse Australia Ltd *v* Phillips [1974] AC 391 (PC) . . . . . . . . 87
Stockbridge Ltd, Re (1993) 9 ACSR 637; 11 ACLC 201 . .   282, 310, 311
Straw Products Pty Ltd, Re [1942] VLR 222 . . . . . . . . . . .    113
Strang Patrick Stevedoring Pty Ltd *v* James Patrick & Co
  Pty Ltd (1993) 32 NSWLR 583 . . . . . . . . . . . . . . . .    144
Swane *v* Swane Bros Pty Ltd (1992) 10 ACLC 904 . . . .   251, 253, 305
Sypkes Securities *v* Jeugny Pty Ltd (1991) 4 ACSR 668 . . . . . . .   252

TNT Ltd *v* NCSC (1986) 11 ACLR 59; 4 ACLC 624 . . . . . .   269, 307
Theseus Exploration NL *v* Mining and Associated Industries
  Ltd [1973] Qd R 81 . . . . . . . . . . . . . . . . . . . . . .   210
Thorby *v* Goldberg (1964) 112 CLR 597 (HC) . . . . . . . . .   101, 102
Thornett *v* Federal Commissioner of Taxation (1938) 59
  CLR 787 (HC) . . . . . . . . . . . . . . . . . . . . .   294
Tinios *v* French Caledonia Travel Service Pty Ltd (1994) 13
  ACSR 658; 12 ACLC 622 . . . . . . . . . . . . . . . . . .   248, 249
Tivoli Freeholds Ltd, Re [1972] VR 445 . . . . . . . . . .   113, 114, 117

US Masters Ltd, Re (1991) 4 ACSR 462 . . . . . . . . . . . .   282
United Service Insurance Co Ltd (in liq.) *v* Lang (1935) 35
  SR (NSW) 487 . . . . . . . . . . . . . . . . . . . . . .   71
Unity APA Ltd *v* Humes Ltd (No 2) [1987] VR 474 . . . . . . .   247, 248

Vrisakis *v* Australian Securities Commission (1993) 9 WAR
  395 . . . . . . . . . . . . . . . . . . . . . . . . . . . .   241

Waipuna Investments Pty Ltd, Re [1956] VLR 115 . . . . . . . . .   113
Wallace Dairy Co Ltd, Re [1980] VR 588 . . . . . . . . . . .   282, 309
Wallington *v* Kokotovich Constructions Pty Ltd (1993) 11
  ACSR 759; 11 ACLC 1207 . . . . . . . . . . . . . .   155, 169, 228
Warrick Howard (Aust) Pty Ltd, Re (1982) 7 ACLR 441 . . . .   254, 255
Wayde *v* New South Wales Rugby League Ltd [1985] 1 NSWLR
  86 (CA NSW); (1985) 10 ACLR 87; 3 ACLC 799 (HC) . . . . . .   122,
                        132, 133, 134, 135, 136, 142, 226, 231, 233
Webb Distributors (Aust) Pty Ltd & Ors *v* The State of
  Victoria & Anor (1993) 179 CLR 15 (HC) . . . . . . . . . . . .   73
Whitehouse *v* Carlton Hotel Pty Ltd (1987) 162 CLR 285
  (HC) . . . . . . . . . . . . . . . . . . . . . . . . . . .   87, 228
Williams *v* United Dairies Ltd (1968) 10 ACLR 406; 4 ACLC
  275 . . . . . . . . . . . . . . . . . . . . . . . . . . . .   276

Winthrop Investments Ltd *v* Winns Ltd [1975] 2 NSWLR
666 (CA NSW) . . . . . . . . . . . . . .       196, 200, 202, 209, 229
Wondoflex Textiles Pty Ltd, Re [1951] VLR 458 . . . . . . . .     113, 114
Woodroofe Ltd *v* M. S. McLeod Ltd (1984) 37 SASR
269 . . . . . . . . . . . . . . . . . . . . . . . . . . . . . . .     73
Wright, Marriage of (1979) 29 FLR 10  . . . . . . . . . . . . . .     98

Zempilas *v* J. N. Taylor Holdings Ltd (in liq.) (No 6) (1991)
5 ACSR 28 . . . . . . . . . . . . . . . . . . . . . . . . . . .     190
Zephyr Holdings Pty Ltd *v* Jack Chia (Australia) Ltd & Ors
(1988) 14 ACLR 30; 7 ACLC 239 . . . . . . . . . . . . . . .     135, 236


# CANADA

British America Nickel Corporation Ltd *v* O'Brien [1927]
AC 369 (PC) . . . . . . . . . . . . . . . . . . . . . . . .     204, 291
Bowater Canadian Ltd and R. L. Cain Inc, Re (1987) 62 OR (2d)
752 (CA Ontario) . . . . . . . . . . . . . . . . . . . . . . . . .     78
Burland *v* Earle [1902] AC 83 (PC) . . . . . . . . . . . . . . .     95, 195

Cook *v* Deeks [1916] 1 AC 554 (PC)  . . . . . . . . . .     195–6, 197, 200

Dad's Cookie Co (BC) Ltd, Re (1969) 7 DLR (3d) 243 . . . . . . .     276

Esso Standard (Inter-America) Inc *v* J. W. Enterprises Inc
and Morrisroe (1963) 37 DLR (2d) 598 (SCC)  . . . . . . . . . .     273

Johnston *v* West Fraser Timber Co Ltd (1981) 29 BCLR 379
revsd (1982) 37 BCLR 360 (CA BC)  . . . . . . . . . . . . .     127, 222

Labatt (John) Ltd and Lucky Lager Breweries Ltd, Re (1959) 20
DLR (20) 159 . . . . . . . . . . . . . . . . . . . . . . . . . .     277

Manning *v* Harris Steel Group Inc (1989) 63 DLR (4th) 125
(CA BC) . . . . . . . . . . . . . . . . . . . . . . . . . .     274, 277
Martello & Sons Ltd, Re [1945] 3 DLR 626 (CA
Ontario)  . . . . . . . . . . . . . . . . . . . .     113, 152, 175, 177

Rathie *v* Montreal Trust Co [1953] 4 DLR 289 (SCC) . . . . . . . .     306
Ringuet *v* Bergeron (1960) 24 DLR (2d) 449; [1960] SCR 672
(SCC) . . . . . . . . . . . . . . . . . . . . . .     91, 93, 96, 100, 102, 103

Sayvette Ltd, Re (1975) 65 DLR (3d) 596 . . . . . . . . . . . . . 276
Shoppers City Ltd and M. Loeb Ltd, Re (1968) 3 DLR (3d)
35 . . . . . . . . . . . . . . . . . . . . . . . . . . . . . 274, 316

## IRELAND

Nash *v* Lancegaye Safety Glass (Ireland) Ltd (1958) 92 Ir
LTR 11 . . . . . . . . . . . . . . . . . . . . . . . . . . . 202, 228
Newbridge Sanitary Steam Laundry Ltd, Re [1917] 1 IR 67 . . . . . 113

## NEW ZEALAND

Ashburton Veterinary Club Incorporated *v* South Island
Dairy Association Ltd (1991) 5 NZCLC 67,296 . . . . . . . . . 226
Ashby Bergh & Co Ltd, Re (1988) 4 NZCLC 64,131 . . . . . . . . 233

Berlei Hestia (NZ) Ltd *v* Fernyhough [1980] 2 NZLR 150 . . . . . 102

Cockle *v* Carlingford Nominees Ltd (1989) 4 NZCLC
65, 120 . . . . . . . . . . . . . . . . . . . . . . . . . . 274
Coleman *v* Myers [1977] 2 NZLR 225 (CA NZ) . . . . . . . . . . . 280
Cotterall *v* Fidelity Life Assurance Co Ltd (1987) 3 NZCLC
100,054 . . . . . . . . . . . . . . . . . . . . . . . . . . . . 252
Curtis *v* J. J. Curtis & Co Ltd [1984] 2 NZLR 267 (CA NZ) . . . . . 73

Deans, Re [1986] 2 NZLR 271 . . . . . . . . . . . . . . . . . 274, 275

Federated Fashions (NZ) Ltd, Re (1981) NZCLC 98, 109 . . . . . 251

Great Outdoors Co Ltd, Re The (1984) 2 NZCLC 99,260 . . . . . . 222

Hall (F) & Sons Ltd, Re [1939] NZLR 408 (CA NZ) . . . . . . 152, 175

Kuwait Asia Bank EC *v* National Mutual Life Nominees Ltd
[1991] 1 AC 187 (PC) . . . . . . . . . . . . . . . . . . . . . 35

Lusk *v* Archive Security Ltd (1991) 5 NZCLC 66, 979 . . . . . . . . 169

Metropolitan Life Assurance Co of NZ Ltd *v* Triple M Ltd
(1984) 4 NZCLC 96, 274 . . . . . . . . . . . . . . . . . . . . 289

Plaza Fabrics (Tauranga) Ltd *v* National Airlines Co Ltd
(1991) 5 NZCLC 67, 288 . . . . . . . . . . . . . . . . . . . . 275

Rongo-ma-tane Farms Ltd, Re (1987) 3 NZCLC 100, 145 . . 146, 147,
152, 169

Shadgett *v* Appellor Fisheries Ltd (1992) 6 NZCLC
68,166. . . . . . . . . . . . . . . . . . . . . . . . . . . . . . . 146
Shalfoon *v* Cheddar Valley Co-operative Dairy Co Ltd
[1924] NZLR 561 . . . . . . . . . . . . . . . . . . . . . . . . 91
Sheldon, Re (1987) 3 NZCLC 100,058 . . . . . . . . . . . . . 276, 277
Southland Woollen-Mills Ltd, Re [1929] NZLR 289 . . . . . . . . 114

Thomas *v* H. W. Thomas [1984] 1 NZLR 686 (CA
NZ). . . . . . . . . . . . . . . . . . . . . 132, 134, 141, 226, 244, 253
Tullamore Holdings Ltd *v* The Selby Shoe Company Ltd
(1986) 3 NZCLC 99,759 . . . . . . . . . . . . . . . . . . . . 163, 232

Vuynovich *v* Vuynovich [1988] 2 NZLR 129 (CA NZ) affd
[1989] 3 NZLR 513 (PC) . . . . . . . . . . . . . . . . 152, 170, 171

Waitikiri Links Ltd, Re (1989) 4 NZCLC 64,922 . . . . . . . . . 243
Woodlands Ltd *v* Logan [1948] NZLR 230 . . . . . . . . . . . . 70

## SOUTH AFRICA

Benjamin *v* Elysium Investments 1960 (3) SA 467 . . . . . . . . . 322

Sammel *v* President Brand Gold Mining Co Ltd 1969 (3) SA
629 . . . . . . . . . . . . . . . . . . . . . . . . . . . . . . . . 278

## UNITED KINGDOM

A. & B. C. Chewing Gum Ltd, Re [1975] 1 WLR 579 . 117, 174, 221, 223
Abbey Leisure, Re [1989] BCLC 619; (1989) 5 BCC 183 revsd
[1990] BCC 60 and sub nom Virdi *v* Abbey Leisure Ltd
[1990] BCLC 342 (CA) . . . . 142, 144, 145, 146, 147, 148, 169, 180–2
Addlestone Linoleum Co, Re (1887) 37 Ch D 191 (CA) . . . . . . 73
Adelaide Electric Supply Co Ltd *v* Prudential Assurance Co
Ltd [1934] AC 122 (HL) . . . . . . . . . . . . . . . . . . . . 80
Admiralty Commissioners *v* Valverda [1938] AC 173 (HL) . . . . . . 98

Allen *v* Gold Reefs of West Africa Ltd [1900] 1 Ch 656
    (CA) . . . . . . . . . . . . . . . .    74, 84, 203–4, 208, 209, 210, 301
Anglo-Austrian Printing and Publishing Union, Re; Isaac's Case
    [1892] 2 Ch 158 . . . . . . . . . . . . . . . . . . . . . . . . . .    70
Anglo-Continental Supply Company Ltd, Re [1922] 2 Ch. 723 . . . .    309
Associated Provincial Picture Houses Ltd *v* Wednesbury
    Corporation [1948] 1 KB 223 (CA) . . . . . . . . . . . . . . . .    244
Attwood *v* Lamont [1920] 3 KB 571 (CA) . . . . . . . . . . . . . .    87
Atwool *v* Merryweather (1867) LR 5 Eq 464 n . . . . . . . . . .    197


BSB Holdings Ltd, Re [1993] BCLC 246; [1992] BCC
    915 . . . . . . . . . . . . . . . . . . . . . . . . . .    125, 126, 234
Bagshaw *v* Eastern Union Railway Co (1849) 7 Hare 114,
    affd (1850) 2 Mac & G 389 . . . . . . . . . . . . . . . . . . .    189
Baillie *v* Oriental Telephone & Electric Co Ltd [1915] 1 Ch
    503 (CA) . . . . . . . . . . . . . . . . . . . . . . . . . . . .    304
Baily *v* British Equitable Assurance Co [1904] 1 Ch 374
    (CA) revsd sub nom British Equitable Assurance Co Ltd
    *v* Baily [1906] AC 35 (HL) . . . . . . . . . . . . .    70, 88, 89, 90
Baku Consolidated Oilfields Ltd, Re [1944] 1 All ER 24 . . . . . .    113
Baltic Real Estate Ltd (No 1), Re [1993] BCLC 498 . . . . . . . .    125
Bamford *v* Bamford [1970] Ch 212 (CA) . . . . . .    197, 199, 200, 201,
                                                        202, 203
Bank of Bombay *v* Suleman Somji (1908) 99 LT 62 (PC) . . . . . .    246
Barrett *v* Duckett Unrep 27 July 1994 (CA) . . . . . .    175, 191, 192, 322
Barry Artist Ltd, Re [1985] 1 WLR 1305 . . . . . . . . . . . . . .    92
Baum, ex parte; Re Baum (1878) 7 Ch D 719 (CA) . . . . . . . .    100
Beattie *v* E and F Beattie Ltd [1938] Ch 708 (CA). . . . . . .    68, 70, 71
Bellador Silk Ltd, Re [1965] 1 All ER 667 . . . . . . . . . . . .    116, 154
Bennett *v* Bennett [1952] 1 KB 249 (CA) . . . . . . . . . . . . .    98
Bentley-Stevens *v* Jones [1974] 1 WLR 638 . . . . . . . . . .    211, 212
Binney *v* Ince Hall Coal and Cannel Co (1866) 35 LJ Ch 363 . . . .    189
Bird Precision Bellows Ltd, Re [1984] Ch 419, affd [1986] Ch
    658 (CA) . . . . . . . . . . . . . . . . . .    64, 143, 153, 157, 255
Blériot Manufacturing Air Craft Co Ltd, Re (1916) 32 TLR 253 . .    113
Blue Arrow plc, Re [1987] BCLC 585; (1987) 3 BCC
    618 . . . . . . . . . . . . . . . . . . .    76, 139–40, 235, 254
Boswell & Co (Steels) Ltd, Re; (Re a Company No 001567 of
    1987 (1989) 5 BCC 145 . . . . . . . . . . . . . . . . . . . . .    144
Boulting *v* Association of Cinematograph, Television and
    Allied Technicians [1963] 2 QB 606 (CA) . . . . . . . . . . . .    197

Bovey Hotel Ventures Ltd, Re Unrep, 31 July 1981 . . 132, 133, 231, 232
Bransfield Engineering Ltd, Re (1985) 1 BCC 99,409 . . . . . . . . 169
Bratton Seymour Service Co Ltd *v* Oxborough [1992] BCLC
   693; [1992] BCC 471 (CA) . . . . . . . . . . . . . . . . . 73
Brazilian Rubber Plantations & Estates Ltd, Re [1911] 1 Ch 425 . . 239
Breckland Group Holdings Ltd *v* London & Suffolk
   Properties Ltd [1989] BCLC 100; (1988) 4 BCC 542 . . . . . 106, 193
British and American Trustee and Finance Corp Ltd and
   Reduced *v* Couper [1894] AC 399 (HL) . . . . . . . . . . . . . 294
British Equitable Assurance Co Ltd *v* Bailey [1906] AC 35
   (HL) . . . . . . . . . . . . . . . . . . . . . . . . . . . . 70, 204
British Murac Syndicate Ltd *v* Alperton Rubber Co Ltd
   [1915] 2 Ch 186 . . . . . . . . . . . . . . . . . . . . . . . 88, 90
Britoil plc, Re [1990] BCC 70 (CA) . . . . . . . . . . . . . . . . 276
Brown *v* British Abrasive Wheel Co Ltd [1919] 1 Ch
   290 . . . . . . . . . . . . . . . . . . . . . . . 204, 299, 300, 306
Browne *v* La Trinidad (1887) 37 Ch D 1 (CA) . . . . . . . . . . . . 71
Bugle Press Ltd, Re [1961] Ch 270 (CA) . . . . 208, 272, 273, 274, 300
Burr *v* Harrison; Re Saul D. Harrison & Sons plc [1994] BCC
   475 (CA) . . . . . . . . . . . . . . . . . . . . . . . . . 132, 142
Bushell *v* Faith [1970] AC 1099 (HL) . . . . . . . . . 81–2, 88, 106, 321

Cade (JE) & Son Ltd, Re [1992] BCLC 213; [1991] BCC
   360 . . . . . . . . . . . . . . . . . . . . 130, 136, 168–89, 223
Cane *v* Jones [1980] 1 WLR 1451 . . . . . . . . . . . . . . . . . . 92
Cape Breton Co *v* Fenn (1881) 17 Ch D 198 (CA) . . . . . . . . . . 190
Carlton Holdings Ltd, Re [1971] 1 WLR 918 . . . . . . . . . . 265, 275
Carrington Viyella plc, Re (1983) 1 BCC 98,951 . . . . . . . . . . 120
Carruth *v* Imperial Chemical Industries Ltd [1937] AC 707
   (HL) . . . . . . . . . . . . . . . . . . . . . . . . . 79, 291, 296
Castleburn Ltd, Re [1991] BCLC 89; (1989) 5 BCC 652 . . . . . 142, 144
Charnley Davies Ltd (No 2), Re [1970] BCLC 760; [1990] BCC
   605 . . . . . . . . . . . . . . . . . . . . 137, 225, 233, 235, 238
Charterbridge Corporation Ltd *v* Lloyds Bank Ltd [1970]
   Ch 62 . . . . . . . . . . . . . . . . . . . . . . . . . . . 233, 306
Chemicals (DR) Ltd, Re; Re a Company (No 005134 of 1986)
   (1989) 5 BCC 39 also reported as Re a Company (No
   005134 of (1986); ex parte Harries [1989] BCLC
   383 . . . . . . . . . . . . . . . . 64, 87, 140, 143, 157, 227, 231
Chez Nico (Restaurants) Ltd, Re [1992] BCLC 192; [1991] BCC
   736 . . . . . . . . . . . . . . . . . . . . . . . . 265, 279, 280

City Equitable Fire Insurance Co Ltd, Re [1925] Ch 407
(CA) . . . . . . . . . . . . . . . . . . . . . . . . . . 239, 240, 241
City Property Investment Trust Corporation Ltd, Petitioners
1951 SLT 371 . . . . . . . . . . . . . . . . . . . . . . . . 288
Clemens v Clemens Brothers Ltd [1976] 2 All ER 268 . . . . . . 211–12,
227, 321
Coltness Iron Company Ltd, Petitioners 1951 SLT 344 . . . . . . . 289
Company, Re a (No 002567 of 1982) [1983] 1 WLR
927 . . . . . . . . . . . . . . . . . . . . . . . . 148, 176, 178, 180
Company, Re a (No 004475 of 1982) [1983] Ch
178 . . . . . . . . . . . . . . . . . . . . . . 128, 133, 253, 305
Company, Re a (No 002612 of 1984) [1985] BCLC 80;
(1984) 1 BCC 99,262 . . . . . . . . . . . . . . . . . . . 162, 232
Company, Re a (No 002612 of 1984) [1985] 2 BCC 99,453
affd (1986) 2 BCC 99,495 and sub nom re Cumana Ltd
[1986] BCLC 430 (CA) . . . . . . . . . 120, 157, 228, 232, 255, 257–8
Company, Re a (No 00477 of 1986) [1986] BCLC 376; (1986)
2 BCC 99,171 . . . . . . . . . . . . . . . . . 129, 132, 168, 255
Company, Re a (No 003160 of 1986) [1986] BCLC 391;
(1986) 2 BCC 99,276 . . . . . . . . . . . . . 122, 129, 132, 168
Company, Re a (No 007623 of 1984) [1986] BCLC 362;
(1986) 2 BCC 99,191 . . . . . . . . . . . 87, 120, 143, 144, 181, 256
Company, Re a (No 005287 of 1985) [1986] 1 WLR
281 . . . . . . . . . . . . . . . . . . . . . . . 125, 220, 232
Company, Re a (No 007828 of 1985) [1986] 2 BCC 98,951 . . . . . 122
Company, Re a (No 008699 of 1985) [1986] BCLC 382; 2
BCC 99,024 . . . . . . . . . . 128, 137, 226, 232, 233, 252, 253, 280
Company, Re a (No 00596 of 1986) [1987] BCLC 133; (1986)
2 BCC 99,063 . . . . . . . . . . . . . . . . . . . . . . . . 163
Company, Re a (No 1761 of 1986) [1987] BCLC 141 . . . . . . . . 127
Company, Re a (No 003843 of 1986) [1987] BCLC 562; (1987)
3 BCC 624 . . . . . . . . . . . . . . . . . . . 130–1, 179, 255
Company, Re a (No 004175 of 1986) [1987] 1 WLR 585 . . . . . . . 163
Company, Re a (No 005136 of 1986) [1987] BCLC 82 also
reported as Re Sherborne Park Residents Co Ltd (1986)
2 BCC 99,528 . . . . . . . . . . . . . . . . 164, 189, 201, 202, 228
Company, Re a (No 007281 of 1986) [1987] BCLC 593 . . . . . . . 124
Company, Re a (No 003096 of 1987) [1988] 4 BCC 80 . . . . . . 144, 176
Company, Re a (No 00370 of 1987); Ex parte Glossop [1988] 1
WLR 1068 . . . . . . . . . . . . . . 120, 121, 168, 232, 244, 245
Company, Re a (No 005134 of 1986); Ex parte Harries [1989]
BCLC 383 also reported as Re D. R. Chemicals Ltd (1989)
5 BCC 39 . . . . . . . . . . . . . . . 64, 87, 140, 143, 157, 227, 231

Company, Re a (No 006834 of 1988); Ex parte Kremer [1989]
BCLC 365; [1989] BCC 218 . . . . . . . . . . . . . 142, 143, 144, 147
Company, Re a (No 00789 of 1987) (Nuneaton Borough
AFC Ltd) (1989) 5 BCC 792 also reported as Re a Company
(No 00789 of 1987); Ex parte Shooter [1990] BCLC
384 . . . . . . . . . . . . . . . . . . . . . . . . . 120, 157–8, 225
Company, Re a (No 005686 of 1988); Ex parte Schwarcz (No
2) [1989] BCLC 427 also reported as Re Ringtower Holdings
plc (Re a Company No 005686 of 1988 (No 2)) (1989)
5 BCC 82 . . . . . . . . . . . . . . . . . 149–50, 151, 225, 255
Company, Re a (No 001363 of 1988); Ex parte S-P [1989]
BCLC 579; (1989) 5 BCC 18 . . . . . . . . . . . . . . . . . 176
Company, Re a (No 00314 of 1989) [1991] BCLC 154; [1990]
BCC 221 . . . . . . . . . . . . . . . . . . 138, 139, 169, 174, 251
Company, Re a (No 00789 of 1987); Ex parte Shooter [1990]
BCLC 384 also reported as Re a Company No
00789 of 1987 (Nuneaton Borough AFC Ltd) (1989) 5
BCC 792 . . . . . . . . . . . . . . . . . 120, 156, 157–8, 225
Company, Re a (No 00330 of 1991); Ex parte Holden [1991]
BCLC 597; [1991] BCC 241 . . . . . . . . . . . . . . . . . 146, 147
Company, Re a (No 002470 of 1988); Ex parte Nicholas
[1991] BCLC 480 affd [1992] BCC 895 and sub nom
Nicholas *v* Soundcraft Electronics Ltd [1993] BCLC 360
(CA) . . . . . . . . . . . . . . . . . . . . . . . . 126, 173, 233
Company, Re a; Ex parte Burr [1992] BCLC 724 also reported
as Re Saul D Harrison & Sons plc [1994] BCC 475 affd sub
nom Burr *v* Harrison; Re Saul D Harrison & Sons plc
[1994] BCC 475 (CA) . . . . . . . . . . . . . . . . . 132, 142, 232
Company, Re a (No 004502 of 1988); Ex parte Johnson [1992]
BCLC 70; [1991] BCC 234 . . . . . . . . . . . . . . . . . . 164
Company, Re a (No 008126 of 1989) [1992] BCC 542 also
reported as Re Hailey Group Ltd [1993] BCLC 459 . . 124, 162, 165
Company, Re a (No 001126 of 1992) [1994] 2 BCLC 146;
[1993] BCC 325 . . . . . . . . . . . . . . . . . . . . . . 125, 164
Company, Re a (No 003061 of 1993); Safinia *v* Comet
Enterprises Ltd [1994] BCC 883 . . . . . . . . . . . . . . . . 163
Crossmore Electrical & Civil Engineering Ltd, Re [1989]
BCLC 137; (1989) 5 BCC 37 . . . . . . . . . . . . . . . . . 164
Crown Bank, Re (1890) 44 Ch D 634 . . . . . . . . . . . . . . 114
Crowther (John) Group plc *v* Carpets International plc [1990]
BCLC 460 . . . . . . . . . . . . . . . . . . . . . . . . . . . 101
Cumana Ltd, Re [1986] BCLC 430 (CA) see Re a Company (No
002612 of 1984) [1985]

Cumbrian Newspapers Group Ltd *v* Cumberland and
  Westmorland Herald Newspaper and Printing Co Ltd
  [1987] Ch 1 . . . . . . . . . . . .    70, 75, 76, 78, 79, 82, 89, 106, 321
Currie *v* Cowdenbeath Football Club [1992] BCLC 1029 . . . . . .    163
Cuthbert Cooper & Sons Ltd, Re [1937] Ch 392 . . . . . . . . . .    115

Dafen Tinplate Co Ltd *v* Llanelly Steel Co (1907) Ltd [1920]
  2 Ch 124 . . . . . . . . . . . . . . . . . . . . . . . . . . .    204, 299
Daniels *v* Daniels [1978] Ch 406 . . . . . . . . . . . . . . . .    197, 239
Davis and Collett Ltd, Re [1935] Ch 693 . . . . . . . . . . . .    113
Davstone Estates Ltd's Leases; Manprop Ltd *v* O'Dell
  [1969] 2 Ch 378 . . . . . . . . . . . . . . . . . . . . . . . . .    87
Dawson International plc *v* Coats Paton plc 1988 SLT 854,
  affd 1989 SLT 655 . . . . . . . . . . . . . . . . . . . . . . .    102
Devlin *v* Slough Estates Ltd [1983] BCLC 497 . . . . . . . . . . .    67
Dorchester Finance Co Ltd *v* Stebbing [1989] BCLC
  498 . . . . . . . . . . . . . . . . . . . . . . . . . . . . . .    241
Dorman Long & Co Ltd, Re [1934] Ch 635 . . . . . . . . . .    286, 289
Duomatic Ltd, Re [1969] 2 Ch 365 . . . . . . . . . . . . . . . . .    92

Ebrahimi *v* Westbourne Galleries Ltd [1973] AC 360
  (HL) . . . . .    64, 65, 112, 113, 114, 132, 137, 139, 142, 145, 152, 166,
                    167, 168, 171, 174, 175, 211, 212
Edwards *v* Halliwell [1950] 2 All ER 1064 (CA) . . . . . . . . .    185, 187
Elder *v* Elder & Watson Ltd 1952 SC
  49 . . . . . . . . . . . . . . . . . . . . . .    115, 117, 118, 135, 255
Eley *v* Positive Government Security Life Assurance Co Ltd
  (1876) 1 Ex D 88 (CA) . . . . . . . . . . . . . . . . . . . . .    68, 72
Elgindata Ltd, Re [1991] BCLC 959 . . . . . . .    149, 151, 232, 238, 239
Elgindata Ltd (No 2), Re [1992] 1 WLR 1207 (CA) . . . . . . . .    164
Elliott *v* Richardson (1870) LR 5 CP 744 . . . . . . . . . . .    99, 100
Elliott *v* Wheeldon [1993] BCLC 53; [1992] BCC 489 (CA) . . . . .    280
English, Scottish & Australian Chartered Bank, Re [1893] 3 Ch
  385 (CA) . . . . . . . . . . . . . . . . . . . . . . . . . . .    286, 294
Estmanco (Kilner House) Ltd *v* Greater London Council
  [1982] 1 WLR 2 . . . . . . . . . . . . . . . . . . . .    192, 193, 195
Everite Locknuts Ltd, Re [1945] Ch 220 . . . . . . . .    276, 277, 279
Expanded Plugs Ltd, Re [1966] 1 WLR 514 . . . . . . . . . . . . .    64

Fargro Ltd *v* Godfroy [1986] 1 WLR 1134 . . . . . . . . . . . . .    190
Faure Electric Accumulator Co, Re (1888) 40 Ch D 141 . . . . . .    239
Ferguson *v* Maclennan Salmon Co Ltd [1990] BCC 702
  (CS(IH)) . . . . . . . . . . . . . . . . . . . . . . . . . . . .    163

Fildes Bros Ltd, Re [1970] 1 WLR 592 . . . . . . . . . . 64, 114, 141
Fischer (George) (Great Britain) Ltd v Multi-Construction
 Ltd [1995] BCC 310 (CA) . . . . . . . . . . . . . . . . . . 235
Five Minute Car Wash Service Ltd, Re [1966] 1 WLR 745 . . . 117, 238
Foss v Harbottle (1843) 2 Hare 461; 67 ER 189 . . . . . . 69, 158, 185,
187, 188, 189, 192, 195, 198, 199, 201, 202, 213, 214, 215, 236, 237, 248,
328, 329

Gaiman v National Association for Mental Health, Re [1971]
 Ch 317 . . . . . . . . . . . . . . . . . . . . . . . . . . 298
Galbraith v Merito Shipping Co Ltd 1947 SC 446 . . . . . . . . . 114
Gammack, Petitioner 1983 SLT 246 . . . . . . . . . . . . . . 176
Gething v Kilner [1972] 1 WLR 337 . . . . . . . . . . . . . 233, 280
Ghyll Beck Driving Range Ltd, Re [1993] BCLC 1126 . . . . . 155, 156
Gorwyn Holdings Ltd, Re (1985) 1 BCC 99,479 (CA) . . . . . . . 128
Greenhalgh v Arderne Cinemas Ltd [1946] 1 All ER 512
 (CA) . . . . . . . . . . . . . . . . . . . . . . . . . . 80, 151
Greenhalgh v Arderne Cinemas Ltd [1951] Ch 286 . . . . . . 200, 204,
205, 206, 210, 211, 212, 226
Greenhalgh v Mallard [1943] 2 All ER 234 (CA) . . . . . . . . 93, 95
Greenwell v Porter [1902] 1 Ch 530 . . . . . . . . . . . . . 95, 103
Grierson, Oldham & Adams Ltd, Re [1968] Ch
 17 . . . . . . . . . . . . . . . . . . . 274, 275, 276, 277, 287
Guinness plc v Saunders [1990] 2 AC 663 (HL) . . . . . . . . . . 92

Hailey Group Ltd, Re [1993] BCLC 459 also reported as Re a
 Company (No 008126 of 1989) [1992] BCC 542 . . . . . 124, 162, 165
Hall v Dyson (1852) 17 QB 785; 117 ER 1481 . . . . . . . . . . . 100
Halt Garage (1964) Ltd, Re [1982] 3 All ER 1016 . . . . . . . . . . 233
Harman v BML Group Ltd [1994] 1 WLR 893 (CA) . . . . . . 83, 220
Harmer (H.R.) Ltd, Re [1959] 1 WLR 62 (CA) . . . 117, 118, 119, 134,
155, 225, 322
Harrison v Thompson [1992] BCLC 833; [1992] BCC 67;
 affd [1993] BCLC 784; [1992] BCC 962 (CA) . . . . . . . . . . 164
Haven Gold Mining Co, Re (1882) 20 Ch D 151 (CA) . . . . . . . 113
Hayes v Bristol Plant Hire Ltd [1957] 1 WLR 499 . . . . . . . . . . 69
Hellenic & General Trust Ltd, Re [1976] 1 WLR 123 . . . 282, 284, 285,
286, 287, 309, 311
Hickman v Kent or Romney Marsh Sheepbreeders'
 Association [1915] 1 Ch 881 . . . . . . . . . . . . . . . . . . 68
Hinde (Fras) & Sons Ltd, Re The Times 23 April 1966 . . . . . . . 275
Hoare & Co Ltd, Re (1933) 150 LT 374 . . . . . . . . . . 274, 275, 305
Hogg v Cramphorn Ltd [1967] Ch 254 . . . . . . 194, 197, 199, 200, 203

Holders Investment Trust Ltd, Re [1971] 1 WLR 583 . .     61–2, 204, 291, 292, 294, 295

Home Treat Ltd, Re [1991] BCLC 705; [1991] BCC 165 . . . . . . .     92

Horsley v Weight Ltd, Re [1982] Ch 442 . . . . . . . . . . . . .     197

Houldsworth v City of Glasgow Bank (1880) 5 App Cas 317 (HL) . . . . . . . . . . . . . . . . . . . . . . . . . . . . .     73

House of Fraser plc v ACGE Investments Ltd [1987] AC 387 (HL) . . . . . . . . . . . . . . . . . . . . . . .     80, 293, 294

Howie v Crawford [1990] BCLC 686; [1990] BCC 330 . . . . . . . .     143

Hydrosan Ltd, Re [1991] BCLC 418; [1991] BCC 19 . . . . . . .     252

Hyman v Hyman [1929] AC 601 (HL) . . . . . . . . . . . . . . . .     98


Imperial Chemical Industries Ltd, Re [1936] Ch 587 . . . . . . . .     296


Jaber v Science & Information Technology Ltd [1992] BCLC 764 . . . . . . . . . . . . . . . . .     123, 130, 154, 161, 163

James v Buena Ventura Nitrate Grounds Syndicate [1896] 1 Ch 452 (CA) . . . . . . . . . . . . . . . . . . . . . . . . . . .     74

Jaybird Group Ltd v Greenwood [1986] BCLC 319 . . . . . . . . .     191

Jermyn Street Turkish Baths Ltd, Re [1971] 1 WLR 1042 (CA) . . . . . . . . . . . . . . . . . . . . . . . . . . .     117, 122

Jesner v Jarrad Properties Ltd [1993] BCLC 1032; [1992] BCC 807 (CS(IH)) . . . . . . . . . . . . . . . . . . . .     134, 153, 172

Jessel Trust Ltd, Re [1985] BCLC 119 . . . . . . . . . . . . . .     289, 290

Jones v Sherwood Computer Services plc [1992] 1 WLR 277 (CA) . . . . . . . . . . . . . . . . . . . . . . . . . . . .     144

Jones (William) & Sons Ltd, Re [1969] 1 WLR 146 . . . . . . . . .     294


K/9 Meat Supplies (Guildford) Ltd, Re [1966] 1 WLR 1112 . . .     64, 115

Kaye v Croydon Tramways Co [1898] 1 Ch 358 (CA) . . . . . . . .     304

Kenyon Swansea Ltd, Re [1987] BCLC 514; (1987) 3 BCC 259 . . . . . . . . . . . . . . . . . . . . . . . . . . . . .     128, 221

Kitson & Co Ltd, Re [1946] 1 All ER 435 (CA) . . . . . . . . . .     114

Kregor v Hollins (1913) 109 LT 225 (CA) . . . . . . . . . . . . .     102


Lagunas Nitrate Co v Lagunas Syndicate [1889] 2 Ch 392 (CA) . . . . . . . . . . . . . . . . . . . . . . . . . . . . .     239

Lee Panavision Ltd v Lee Lighting Ltd [1992] BCLC 22; [1991] BCC 620 (CA) . . . . . . . . . . . . . . . . . . . . .     101

Leicester Club and Country Racecourse Company; ex parte Cannon, Re (1885) 20 Ch D 629 . . . . . . . . . . . . . . . . .     69

Leigh Estates (UK) Ltd, Re [1994] BCC 292 . . . . . . . . 62, 204, 292

Lifecare International plc, Re [1990] BCLC 222; (1989) 5 BCC
755 . . . . . . . . . . . . . . . . . . . . . . . . . . . . 278

Little Olympian Each-Ways Ltd, Re [1994] 2 BCLC 420; also
reported as Supreme Travels Ltd *v* Little Olympian Each-
Ways Ltd [1994] BCC 947 . . . . . . . . . . . . . . . . . 124, 165

Little Olympian Each-Ways Ltd, Re [1994] BCC 959 . . . . . . . . 165

Lo-Line Electric Motors Ltd, Re [1988] Ch 477 . . . . . . . . . . . 35

London School of Electronics Ltd, Re [1986] Ch 211 . . . 152, 153, 157,
171, 175, 231, 255

Lucas (T.) & Co Ltd *v* Mitchell [1972] 1 WLR 938 . . . . . . . . . 87

Lundie Brothers Ltd, Re [1965] 1 WLR 1051 . . . . . . . . . . . 117

MB Group plc, Re [1989] BCLC 672; (1989) BCC 684 . . . . . . . 289

McGuinness *v* Bremner plc 1988 SLT 891, affd 1988 SLT
898 n . . . . . . . . . . . . . . . . . 137, 139, 162, 175, 233, 320

MacConnell *v* E. Prill & Co Ltd [1916] 2 Ch 57 . . . . . . . . . . . 304

MacDougall *v* Gardiner (No 2) (1875) 1 Ch D 13
(CA) . . . . . . . . . . . . . . . . . . . . . . . . 67, 187, 203

Mackenzie & Co Ltd, Re [1916] 2 Ch 450 . . . . . . . . . . . . . 295

MacKie *v* HM Advocate (Unrep HC of Justiciary 16
February 1994) . . . . . . . . . . . . . . . . . . . . . . . 58, 59

Macro (Ipswich) Ltd, Re [1994] 2 BCLC 354; [1994] BCC
781 . . . . . . . . . . . . . . . . 54, 127, 156, 157, 220, 234, 238

Malleson *v* National Insurance and Guarantee Corpn [1894]
1 Ch 200 . . . . . . . . . . . . . . . . . . . . . . . . . . 74

Marx *v* Estates and General Investments Ltd [1976] 1 WLR
380 . . . . . . . . . . . . . . . . . . . . . . . . 165, 188, 191

Mason *v* Harris (1879) 11 Ch D 97 (CA) . . . . . . . . . . . . . 198

Mason *v* Provident Clothing and Supply Co Ltd [1913] AC
724 (HL) . . . . . . . . . . . . . . . . . . . . . . . . . . 86

Menier *v* Hooper's Telegraph Works (1874) LR 9 Ch App
350 . . . . . . . . . . . . . . . . . . . . . . . . . . . 195, 200

Meyer *v* Scottish Textile and Manufacturing Co Ltd,
Scottish Co-operative Wholesale Society Ltd 1954 SC
381 . . . . . . . . . . . . . . . . . . . . . . . . 121, 143, 211

Milgate Developments Ltd, Re [1993] BCLC 291; (1991) BCC 24 . 164

Minster Assets plc, Re [1985] BCLC 200; (1984) 1 BCC 99,299 . . . 289

Moffatt *v* Farquhar (1878) 7 Ch D 591 . . . . . . . . . . . . . . . 73

Molineaux *v* London, Birmingham and Manchester
Insurance Co Ltd [1902] 2 KB 589 (CA) . . . . . . . . . . . . . 70

Moorgate Mercantile Holdings Ltd, Re [1980] 1 WLR 227 . . . . . 304

Mountforest Ltd, Re [1993] BCC 565 . . . . . . . . . . . . . .　161, 162
Multinational Gas and Petroleum Co v Multinational Gas
　　and Petrochemical Services Ltd [1983] Ch 258 . . . . . . . . . .　197
Murray's Judicial Factor, Petitioner, Re [1993] BCLC 1437;
　　[1992] BCC 596 (CS(IH)) . . . . . . . . . . . . . . . . .　141, 252

National Bank Ltd, Re [1966] 1 WLR 819 . . . . . . . . . . .　309, 315
National Bank of Wales Ltd, Re [1899] 2 Ch 629 . . . . . . . . . .　239
New British Iron Co, Re; Ex parte Beckwith [1898] 1 Ch 324 . . . . .　70
Newtherapeutics Ltd v Katz [1990] BCC 362 . . . . . . . . . . . .　70
Nicholas v Soundcraft Electronics Ltd [1993] BCLC 360;
　　also reported as Re a Company (No 002470 of 1983);
　　Ex parte Nicholas [1992] BCC 895 (CA) . . . . . . . .　126, 173, 233
Nidditch v The Calico Printers' Association Ltd 1961 SLT
　282 . . . . . . . . . . . . . . . . . . . . . . . . . . . . . . . .　277
Noble (R.A.) & Sons (Clothing) Ltd, Re [1983] BCLC
　273 . . . . .　117, 132, 133, 134, 141, 153, 171, 172, 175, 231, 232, 321
Norman v Theodore Goddard [1991] BCLC 1028; [1992]
　BCC 14 . . . . . . . . . . . . . . . . . . . . . . . . . .　240, 241
Northern Counties Securities Ltd v Jackson & Steeple Ltd
　[1974] 1 WLR 1133 . . . . . . . . . . . . . . . . . . . . . . . . .　92
Northern Engineering Industries plc, Re [1993] BCLC 1151;
　　[1993] BCC 267, affd [1994] 2 BCLC 704;
　　[1994] BCC 618 (CA) . . . . . . . . . . . . . . . . . .　80, 293, 294
North-West Transportation Co Ltd v Beatty (1887) 12 App Cas
　589 (PC) . . . . . . . . . . . . . . . . . . . . . . .　95, 194, 196, 197
Nuneaton Borough Association Football Club Ltd, Re [1989]
　BCLC 454 (1989) 5 BCC 792 (CA) . . . . . . . . . . . . . . .　122
Nurcombe v Nurcombe [1985] 1 WLR 370 (CA) . . . . .　188, 190, 231

OC (Transport) Services, Re [1984] BCLC 251 . . . . . . . . . . .　157
Old Silkstone Collieries Ltd, Re [1954] 1 Ch 169 (CA) . .　289, 294, 295
Opera Photographic Ltd, Re [1989] 1 WLR 634 . . . . . . . . . . .　83
Othery Construction Ltd, Re [1966] 1 WLR 69 . . . . . . . . . .　173
Overend & Gurney Co v Gibb (1872) LR 5 HL 480 . . . . . . . .　239

Pavlides v Jenson [1956] Ch 565 . . . . . . . . . . . . . . .　197, 239
Payne v The Cork Company Ltd [1900] 1 Ch 303 . . . . . . . . . .　98
Pender v Lushington (1877) 6 Ch D 70 . . . .　68, 95, 100, 187, 194, 202
Pennell v Venida Investments (Unrep 25 July
　1974) . . . . . . . . . . . . . . . . . . . .　211, 212, 227, 321
Pepe v City and Suburban Permanent Building Society
　[1893] 2 Ch 311 . . . . . . . . . . . . . . . . . . . . . . . . . .　74

Perfectair Holdings Ltd, Re [1990] BCLC 423; (1989) 5 BCC
837 . . . . . . . . . . . . . . . . . . . . . . . . . . . 169
Peveril Gold Mines Ltd, Re [1898] 1 Ch 122 (CA) . . . . . . . . . 98
Phillips v Manufacturers' Securities Ltd (1917) 116 LT
290 (CA) . . . . . . . . . . . . . . . . . . . . . 262, 298, 305
Posgate & Denby (Agencies) Ltd, Re [1987] BCLC 8; (1986) 2
BCC 99,352 . . . . . . . . . . . 96, 132, 136, 142, 162, 168, 255, 256
Press Caps Ltd, Re [1948] 2 All ER 638 . . . . . . . . . . . . 277, 279
Press Caps Ltd, Re [1949] Ch 434 (CA) . . . . . . . . . . . . . 276
Prudential Assurance Co Ltd v Chatterley-Whitfield
Collieries Co Ltd [1949] AC 512 (HL) . . . . . . . . . . . . . 294
Prudential Assurance Co Ltd v Newman Industries Ltd (No
2) [1981] Ch 257; revsd [1982] Ch 204 (CA) . . 54, 164, 188, 190, 192,
198, 235, 322
Puddephatt v Leith [1916] 1 Ch 200 . . . . . . . . . . . . . . 96, 100
Pulbrook v Richmond Consolidated Mining Co (1878) 9
Ch D 610 . . . . . . . . . . . . . . . . . . . . . . . . . 69
Punt v Symons & Co Ltd [1903] 2 Ch 506 . . . . . . . . . . 84, 88, 90
Putsman v Taylor [1927] 1 KB 637 . . . . . . . . . . . . . . . 86


Quickdome Ltd, Re [1988] BCLC 370; (1988) 4 BCC 296 . . . . . . 122
Quin & Axtens Ltd v Salmon [1909] AC 442 (HL) . . . . . . . 69, 193


R v The Mariquita and New Granada Mining Company
(1858) 1 El & El 289; 120 ER 917 . . . . . . . . . . . . . . . 246
R v Merchant Tailors' Company (1831) 2 B & Ad 115; 109
ER 1086 . . . . . . . . . . . . . . . . . . . . . . . . 246
Rackham v Peek Foods Ltd, Re [1990] BCLC 895 . . . . . . . . . 101
Rank Radio and Television Ltd, Re, The Times 19 November
1963 . . . . . . . . . . . . . . . . . . . . . . . . . . . 312
Rankin & Blackmore Ltd, Petitioners 1950 SLT 160 . . . . . . . . 289
Ratners Group plc, Re [1988] BCLC 685; (1988) 4 BCC 293 . . . . 296
Rayfield v Hands [1960] Ch 1 . . . . . . . . . . . . . . 68, 69, 71
Read v Astoria Garage (Steatham) Ltd [1952] Ch 637 (CA) . . . . . 70
Red Rock Gold Mining Co Ltd, Re (1889) 61 LT 785 . . . . . . . . 113
Regal (Hastings) Ltd v Gulliver [1967] 2 AC 134 n (HL) . . . . 196, 197
Richmond Gate Property Co Ltd, Re [1965] 1 WLR 335 . . . . . . . 69
Ringtower Holdings plc, Re; (Re a Company (No 005686 of 1988)
(No 2) (1989) 5 BCC 82; also reported as Re a Company
(No 005686 of 1988); Ex parte Schwarcz (No 2) [1989] BCLC
427 . . . . . . . . . . . . . . . . . . . . . . . . 149–50, 225

Russell *v* Northern Bank Development Corpn Ltd [1992]
  BCLC 431; [1991] BCC 517 (CA NI); revsd [1992] 1
  WLR 588 (HL) . . . . . . . . . . .   64, 84, 85, 87, 88, 95, 97, 106, 321
Rutherford, Petitioner; Re Lawrie & Symington Ltd [1994]
  BCC 876 . . . . . . . . . . . . . . . . . . . . . . . . . .   163

Saltdean Estate Co Ltd, Re [1968] 1 WLR 1844 . . . . . . . .   80, 293, 294
Salton *v* New Beeston Cycle Co (No 1) [1899] 1 Ch 775 . . . . . . . .   70
Savoy Hotel Ltd, Re [1981] Ch 351 . . . . . . . . . . . .   282, 290, 309
Scott *v* Frank F. Scott (London) Ltd [1940] Ch 794 (CA) . . . . . . .   73
Scottish Co-operative Wholesale Society Ltd *v* Meyer
  [1959] AC 324 (HL) . . . . . .   117, 119, 120, 121, 126, 127, 137, 138,
                                                       156, 231, 234, 258

Scottish Insurance Corp Ltd *v* Wilsons & Clyde Coal Ltd
  [1949] AC 462 (HL) . . . . . . . . . . . . . . . . . . . . .   294
Seaton *v* Grant (1867) LR 2 Ch App 459 . . . . . . . . . . . . .   189
Shaw (John) & Sons (Salford) Ltd *v* Shaw [1935] 2 KB 113 (CA) . .   193
Sherborne Park Residents Co Ltd, Re (1986) 2 BCC 99,528 also
  reported as Re a Company (No 005136 of 1986) [1987]
  BCLC 82 . . . . . . . . . . . . . . . . .   164, 189, 201, 202, 228
Shuttleworth *v* Cox Brothers and Co (Maidenhead) Ltd
  [1927] 2 KB 9 (CA) . . . . . . . . . . . . . . . .   204, 233, 300, 301
Sidebottom *v* Kershaw, Leese & Co Ltd [1920] 1 Ch 154
  (CA) . . . . . . . . . . . . . . . . . . . . . . .   204, 208, 299
Simo Securities Trust Ltd, Re [1971] 1 WLR 1455 . . . . .   264, 266, 267
Singer Manufacturing Co *v* Robinow 1971 SC 11 . . . . . . . .   282, 309
Smith *v* Croft [1986] 1 WLR 580 . . . . . . . . . . . . . . . . .   232
Smith *v* Croft (No 2) [1988] Ch 114 . . . . . . . . .   186, 189, 191, 199
Snelling *v* John G. Snelling Ltd [1973] QB 87 . . . . . . . . . . . .   94
Southern Foundries (1926) Ltd *v* Shirlaw [1940] AC 701
  (HL) . . . . . . . . . . . . . . . . . . . . . . . . . . . .   89
Sovereign Life Assurance Co *v* Dodd [1892] 2 QB 573
  (CA) . . . . . . . . . . . . . . . . . . . . . . . . . . .   284
Stephen (Robert) Holdings Ltd, Re [1968] 1 WLR 522 . . . . . . .   297
Stewarts (Brixton) Ltd, Re [1985] BCLC 4 . . . . . . . .   126, 234, 322
Sticky Fingers Restaurant Ltd, Re [1992] BCLC 84; [1991] BCC
  754 . . . . . . . . . . . . . . . . . . . . . . . . . . . . .   83
Suburban Hotel Co, Re (1867) 2 Ch App 737 . . . . . . . . . . .   113
Supreme Travels Ltd *v* Little Olympian Each-Ways Ltd
  [1994] BCC 947; also reported as Re Little Olympian
  Each-Ways Ltd [1994] 2 BCLC 420 . . . . . . . . . . . . . . .   124
Sussex Brick Co Ltd, Re [1961] Ch 289 . . . . . . . . . . . . .   274

Tett *v* Phoenix Property and Investment Co Ltd [1986]
  BCLC 149 (CA) . . . . . . . . . . . . . . . . . . . . . . 73
Thomson *v* Drysdale 1925 SC 311 . . . . . . . . . . . . . . . . 113
Thorn EMI plc, Re [1989] BCLC 612; (1988) 4 BCC 698 . . . . . . 296
Tiessen *v* Henderson [1899] 1 Ch 861 . . . . . . . . . . . . 290, 304
Tottenham Hotspur plc, Re [1994] 1 BCLC 655 . . . . . . . . . . 221

Unisoft Group Ltd (No 1), Re [1993] BCLC 528; [1992] BCC
  494, affd [1993] BCLC 1292; [1994] BCC 11 (CA) . . . . . . . . 165
Unisoft Group Ltd (No 2), Re [1993] BCLC 532 . . . . . . . . . . 165
Unisoft Group Ltd (No 2), Re [1994] BCC 766 . . . . . . . . . 35, 125
Unisoft Group Ltd (No 3), Re [1994] 1 BCLC 609 . . . . . 35, 125, 130

Vatcher *v* Paull [1915] AC 372 (PC) . . . . . . . . . . . . . . . 193
Virdi *v* Abbey Leisure Ltd [1990] BCLC 342; also reported
  as Re Abbey Leisure Ltd [1990] BCC 60 (CA); see also
  Re Abbey Leisure [1989] BCLC 619; (1989) 5 BCC 183 . . . 144, 145

Walker *v* London Tramways Company (1879) 12 Ch D 705 . . . . . . 84
Walker *v* Standard Chartered Bank plc [1992] BCLC 535 (CA) . . 54, 95
Wallersteiner *v* Moir (No 2) [1975] QB 373 (CA) . . . . . . . . 164, 192
Watts *v* Midland Bank plc [1986] BCLC 15 . . . . . . . . . . . . 190
Weller (Sam) & Sons Ltd, Re [1990] Ch 682 . . . . 121, 132, 133, 168,
                                                 231, 232, 243, 245
Welton *v* Saffery [1897] AC 299 (HL) . . . . . . . . . . . . . . 85, 95
Wessex Computer Stationers Ltd, Re [1992] BCLC 366 . . . . . . . 173
Westbourne Galleries Ltd, Re [1970] 1 WLR 1378 on appeal
  [1971] Ch 799 (CA) revsd sub nom Ebrahimi *v* Westbourne
  Galleries Ltd [1973] AC 360 (HL) . . . . . . . . . . 117, 128, 129
Western Manufacturing (Reading) Ltd, Re [1956] Ch 436 . . . . . 276
Wheal Buller Consols, Re (1888) 38 Ch D 42 . . . . . . . . . . . . 70
Whitchurch Insurance Consultants, Ltd, Re [1993] BCLC 1359 . . . . 83
White *v* Bristol Aeroplane Co Ltd [1953] Ch 65 (CA) . . . . . . 80, 81
Whyte, Petitioner 1984 SLT 330 . . . . . . . . . . . . . . . . 162, 232
Wilson *v* Jones (1867) LR 2 Exch 139 . . . . . . . . . . . . . . 188
Wilsons & Clyde Coal Company *v* Scottish Insurance Corpn
  1948 SC 360 . . . . . . . . . . . . . . . . . . . . . . . . . 295
Wood *v* Odessa Waterworks Company (1889) 42 Ch D
  636 . . . . . . . . . . . . . . . . . . . . . . . . . . . . . 73

X Y Z Ltd, Re a Company (No 004377 of 1986) [1987] 1 WLR
  102 . . . . . . . . . . . . . . . . 64, 142, 143, 144, 147, 148, 149

*Table of Cases*

## UNITED STATES

Dodge *v* Ford Motor Co 204 Mich 459; 170 NW 668 (1919) . . . . .    242

Weinburger *v* UOP Inc 457 A 2d 701 (1983) . . . . . . . . . . . . .    303

## WEST INDIES

Loch *v* John Blackwood Ltd [1924] AC 783 (PC) . . . . . . . .   113, 178

# Table of Statutes

## AUSTRALIA

Australian Securities Commission Act 1989 (Cth)
s 50 . . . . . . . . . . . . . . . . . . . . . . . . . . . . 213

Close Corporations Act 1989 (Cth)
s 60 . . . . . . . . . . . . . . . . . . . . . . . . . . . . 326
Companies Code: Companies Act 1981 and Companies
([Name of State]) Code
s 125 . . . . . . . . . . . . . . . . . . . . . . . . . . . 75
s 128 . . . . . . . . . . . . . . . . . . . . . . . . . . . 75
s 320 . . . . . . . . . . . . . . . . . . . . . . . . 119, 131, 235
(NSW) ss 2(a) . . . . . . . . . . . . . . . . . . . . 133
s 361(1)(k) . . . . . . . . . . . . . . . . . . . . . . . 73
s 413 . . . . . . . . . . . . . . . . . . . . . . . . . . . 75
s 574 . . . . . . . . . . . . . . . . . . . . . . . . . . . 213
(5)(6) . . . . . . . . . . . . . . . . . . . . . . . . . . 214
Companies and Securities Legislation (Miscellaneous
Amendments) Act 1983 (Cth)
s 89 . . . . . . . . . . . . . . . . . . . . . . . . . . . . 119
Corporate Law Reform Act 1994 (Cth) . . . . . . . . . . . . . . 242
Corporations Law
s 9 . . . . . . . . . . . . . . . . . . . . . . . 3, 173, 247, 268
ss 11, 12 . . . . . . . . . . . . . . . . . . . . . . . . . . 268
s 53(c) . . . . . . . . . . . . . . . . . . . . . . . . . . . 136
s 60(1) . . . . . . . . . . . . . . . . . . . . . . . . . 34, 103
s 111 AD . . . . . . . . . . . . . . . . . . . . . . . . . 7
AK . . . . . . . . . . . . . . . . . . . . . . . . . . . 7
s 116 . . . . . . . . . . . . . . . . . . . . . . . . . . . 3, 6
s 117(2) . . . . . . . . . . . . . . . . . . . . . . . . . . 114
s 161, 162 . . . . . . . . . . . . . . . . . . . . . . . . . 186
s 171(2) . . . . . . . . . . . . . . . . . . . . . . . . . . 95
s 172(1)(c) . . . . . . . . . . . . . . . . . . . . . . . . . 75
(2) . . . . . . . . . . . . . . . . . . . . . . . . . . 74, 75
(8) . . . . . . . . . . . . . . . . . . . . . . . . . . 74
s 175 . . . . . . . . . . . . . . . . . . . . . . . . . . 67, 142
s 176 . . . . . . . . . . . . . . . . . . . . . . . . . . . 5
(1) . . . . . . . . . . . . . . . . . . . . . . . . . . 84

*Table of Statutes*

(2)(3) . . . . . . . . . . . . . . . . . . . . . . . . . . . . . . . . 75
s 180(1) . . . . . . . . . . . . . . . . . . . . . . . 67, 70–1, 72, 142
    (a)–(c) . . . . . . . . . . . . . . . . . . . . . . . . . . . . . 71
    (3) . . . . . . . . . . . . . . . . . . . . . . . . . . . . . . . . 74
    (5) . . . . . . . . . . . . . . . . . . . . . . . . . . . . . . . . 71
s 184 . . . . . . . . . . . . . . . . . . . . . . . . . . . . . . 122, 313
s 186 . . . . . . . . . . . . . . . . . . . . . . . . . . . . . . 118, 136
s 195 . . . . . . . . . . . . . . . . . . . . . . . . . . . . . . . . 291
    (3)(4) . . . . . . . . . . . . . . . . . . . . . . . . . . . . . . 297
    (7) . . . . . . . . . . . . . . . . . . . . . . . . . . . . . . . . 291
s 197 . . . . . . . . . . . . . . . . . . . . . . . . . . 77, 224, 294
    (2) . . . . . . . . . . . . . . . . . . . . . . . . . . . . . . 77, 78
    (3) . . . . . . . . . . . . . . . . . . . . . . . . . . . . . . . . 78
    (4)(5) . . . . . . . . . . . . . . . . . . . . . . . . . . . . . . . 79
    (8) . . . . . . . . . . . . . . . . . . . . . . . . . . . . . . . . 81
s 198 . . . . . . . . . . . . . . . . . . . . . . . 77, 78, 224, 294
    (2) . . . . . . . . . . . . . . . . . . . . . . . . . . . . . . 77, 78
    (3) . . . . . . . . . . . . . . . . . . . . . . . . . . . . . . . . 78
    (4)–(6) . . . . . . . . . . . . . . . . . . . . . . . . . . . . . . 79
    (8) . . . . . . . . . . . . . . . . . . . . . . . . . . . . . . . . 78
s 199 . . . . . . . . . . . . . . . . . . . . . . . 77, 78, 224, 294
    (2) . . . . . . . . . . . . . . . . . . . . . . . . . . . . . . 77, 78
    (3) . . . . . . . . . . . . . . . . . . . . . . . . . . . . . . . . 78
    (4)(5) . . . . . . . . . . . . . . . . . . . . . . . . . . . . . . . 79
s 200 . . . . . . . . . . . . . . . . . . . . . . . . . . . . . . . . 75
s 205 . . . . . . . . . . . . . . . . . . . . . . . . . . . . . . . . 215
s 212 . . . . . . . . . . . . . . . . . . . . . . . . . . . . . 123, 224
s 227 . . . . . . . . . . . . . . . . . . . . . . . . . . . . . . . . 82
s 232 . . . . . . . . . . . . . . . . . . . . . . . . . 103, 213, 238
    (1) . . . . . . . . . . . . . . . . . . . . . . . . . . . . . . . . 216
    (2) . . . . . . . . . . . . . . . . . . . . . . . . . . . . . . . . 35
    (4) . . . . . . . . . . . . . . . . . . . . . . . . . . . . . . 35, 242
    (5) . . . . . . . . . . . . . . . . . . . . . . . . . . . . . . . . 35
s 237 . . . . . . . . . . . . . . . . . . . . . . . . . . . . . 195, 245
s 239 . . . . . . . . . . . . . . . . . . . . . . . . . . . . . . . . 43
s 243 ZF . . . . . . . . . . . . . . . . . . . . . . . . . . . . . . 199
s 246 . . . . . . . . . . . . . . . . . . . . . . . . . . . . . . . . 214
s 247 . . . . . . . . . . . . . . . . . . . . . . . . . . . . . . . . 246
s 251 . . . . . . . . . . . . . . . . . . . . . . . . . . . . . . . . 83
s 253 . . . . . . . . . . . . . . . . . . . . . . . . . . . . . 246, 298
    (4) . . . . . . . . . . . . . . . . . . . . . . . . . . . . . . . . 298
s 255 . . . . . . . . . . . . . . . . . . . . . . . . . . . . . . . . 92
s 256 . . . . . . . . . . . . . . . . . . . . . . . . . . . . . . 94, 95

s 259(1) . . . . . . . . . . . . . . . . . . . . . . . . . . . . . 246
s 260 . . . . . . . . . . . . . . . . . . . . . . . . . . . . 119, 121
   (1)(a)(ii) . . . . . . . . . . . . . . . . . . . . . 80, 119, 224
   (4) . . . . . . . . . . . . . . . . . . . . . . . . . . . 154, 177
   (5) . . . . . . . . . . . . . . . . . . . . . . . . . . . 122, 231
      (b) . . . . . . . . . . . . . . . . . . . . . . . . . 131
s 315 . . . . . . . . . . . . . . . . . . . . . . . . . . . . . . 245
s 319 . . . . . . . . . . . . . . . . . . . 217, 247, 251, 252, 279
s 411 . . . . . . . . . . . . . . . . . . . . . . . . . . . 75, 263
   (1) . . . . . . . . . . . . . . . . . . . . . . . . . . . . 283
     (A)–(C) . . . . . . . . . . . . . . . . . . . . . . . . 283
   (2) . . . . . . . . . . . . . . . . . . . . . . . . . . . . 284
   (3) . . . . . . . . . . . . . . . . . . . . . . . . . . . . . 75
   (4)(a)(ii) . . . . . . . . . . . . . . . . . . . . . . . . . 283
   (10) . . . . . . . . . . . . . . . . . . . . . . . . . . . . 283
   (13) . . . . . . . . . . . . . . . . . . . . . . . . . . . . 288
   (17) . . . . . . . . . . . . . . . . . . . . . . . 308, 310, 311
      (b) . . . . . . . . . . . . . . . . . . . . . . . . . 310
s 412(1)(a) . . . . . . . . . . . . . . . . . . . . . . . . . . . 287
      (ii) . . . . . . . . . . . . . . . . . . . . . . . . . 288
     (b) . . . . . . . . . . . . . . . . . . . . . . . . . . . 287
   (2) . . . . . . . . . . . . . . . . . . . . . . . . . . 287, 288
   (3) . . . . . . . . . . . . . . . . . . . . . . . . . . . . 289
   (4) . . . . . . . . . . . . . . . . . . . . . . . . . . . . 287
   (5) . . . . . . . . . . . . . . . . . . . . . . . . 287, 288, 311
   (6)–(8) . . . . . . . . . . . . . . . . . . . . . . . . . . 284
s 414 . . . . . . . . . . . . . . . . . 266, 267, 270, 271, 272, 281
   (2) . . . . . . . . . . . . . . . . . . . . . . . . . . . . 267
   (3) . . . . . . . . . . . . . . . . . . . . . . . . . . . . 275
   (7)–(8) . . . . . . . . . . . . . . . . . . . . . . . . . . 267
   (10) . . . . . . . . . . . . . . . . . . . . . . . . . . . . 267
s 461 . . . . . . . . . . . . . . . . . . . . . . . . . . . . . . 167
   (e) . . . . . . . . . . . . . . . . . . . . . . . . 167, 176, 234
   (f)(g) . . . . . . . . . . . . . . . . . . . . . . . 154, 167, 175
   (k) . . . . . . . . . . . . . . . . . . . . . . . . . 113, 167
s 462 . . . . . . . . . . . . . . . . . . . . . . . . . . . . . . 172
s 467(2) . . . . . . . . . . . . . . . . . . . . . . . . . . . . 173
   (4) . . . . . . . . . . . . . . . . . . . . . . . . . . . . 176
s 563A . . . . . . . . . . . . . . . . . . . . . . . . . . . . . . 73
s 588G . . . . . . . . . . . . . . . . . . . . . . . . . . . 35, 240
   J . . . . . . . . . . . . . . . . . . . . . . . . . . . . . 35
s 592 . . . . . . . . . . . . . . . . . . . . . . . . . . . . . . 240
s 609 . . . . . . . . . . . . . . . . . . . . . . . . . . . . . . 268

(2) . . . . . . . . . . . . . . . . . . . . . . . . . . 268
s 615 . . . . . . . . . . . . . . . . . . . . . . 38, 39, 266
s 633 . . . . . . . . . . . . . . . . . . . . . . . . . 266
s 635(a) . . . . . . . . . . . . . . . . . . . . . . . . 271
s 648 . . . . . . . . . . . . . . . . . . . . . . . 279, 288
s 649 . . . . . . . . . . . . . . . . . . . . . . . . . 270
s 672(3) . . . . . . . . . . . . . . . . . . . . . . . . 304
s 701 . . . . . . . . . . . . . . . 263, 268, 271, 273, 281
(2) . . . . . . . . . . . . . . . . . . . . . . . . . 271
    (a)(b) . . . . . . . . . . . . . . . . . . . . . . 271
(6) . . . . . . . . . . . . . . . . . . . . . . . . . 275
(7)(8) . . . . . . . . . . . . . . . . . . . . . . . 271
(9) . . . . . . . . . . . . . . . . . . . . . . . . . 270
s 702 . . . . . . . . . . . . . . . . . . . . . . . . . 263
s 703 . . . . . . . . . . . . . . . . . . . . . . . 263, 271
ss 704–5 . . . . . . . . . . . . . . . . . . . . . . . . 278
s 710 . . . . . . . . . . . . . . . . . . . . . . . . . 271
s 730 . . . . . . . . . . . . . . . . . . . . . . . . . 269
s 750 . . . . . . . . . . . . . . . . . . . . . . . 246, 278
s 995 . . . . . . . . . . . . . . . . . . . . . . . . . 278
s 999 . . . . . . . . . . . . . . . . . . . . . . . . . 278
s 1052 . . . . . . . . . . . . . . . . . . . . . . . . . 7
s 1069(1)(K) . . . . . . . . . . . . . . . . . . . . . . 38
s 1324 . . . . . . . . . . . . . . . 213, 214, 237, 238, 242
(6)(7) . . . . . . . . . . . . . . . . . . . . . . . 214
(10) . . . . . . . . . . . . . . . . . . . . . . . . 213
s 1325(3) . . . . . . . . . . . . . . . . . . . . . . . . 213
Part 1.2 DIV 2 . . . . . . . . . . . . . . . . . . . . . 268
    DIV 5 . . . . . . . . . . . . . . . . . . . . . . 268
Part 3.2A . . . . . . . . . . . . . . . . . . . . . 195, 245
Part 6.3–4 . . . . . . . . . . . . . . . . . . . . . 268, 269
7 . . . . . . . . . . . . . . . . . . . . . . . . . 39
Part 9.4A . . . . . . . . . . . . . . . . . . . . . . . 269
    4B . . . . . . . . . . . . . . . . . . . . . . . . 35
Schedule 1—Table A
art 4(3) . . . . . . . . . . . . . . . . . . . . . . . . 81
Crown Lands Act (Northern Territory)
s 38A . . . . . . . . . . . . . . . . . . . . . . . . . 187

Federal Court of Australia Amendment Act 1991 (Cth) . . . . . . . 190

Income Tax Assessment Act 1936 (Cth)
S 80G . . . . . . . . . . . . . . . . . . . . . . . . . 307

Division 7 . . . . . . . . . . . . . . . . . . . . . . . . . . . . 243

Partnership Act 1892 (NSW)
s 24 . . . . . . . . . . . . . . . . . . . . . . . . . . . . . . . . 324
ss 28–30 . . . . . . . . . . . . . . . . . . . . . . . . . . . . . . 324
ss 32, 33 . . . . . . . . . . . . . . . . . . . . . . . . . . . . . . 325
s 46 . . . . . . . . . . . . . . . . . . . . . . . . . . . . . . . . 324
Partnership Act 1891 (QLD)
s 27 . . . . . . . . . . . . . . . . . . . . . . . . . . . . . . . . 324
ss 31–3 . . . . . . . . . . . . . . . . . . . . . . . . . . . . . . . 324
ss 35, 36 . . . . . . . . . . . . . . . . . . . . . . . . . . . . . . 325
s 48 . . . . . . . . . . . . . . . . . . . . . . . . . . . . . . . . 324
Partnership Act 1891 (SA)
s 24 . . . . . . . . . . . . . . . . . . . . . . . . . . . . . . . . 324
ss 28–30 . . . . . . . . . . . . . . . . . . . . . . . . . . . . . . 324
s 32, 33 . . . . . . . . . . . . . . . . . . . . . . . . . . . . . . 325
s 46 . . . . . . . . . . . . . . . . . . . . . . . . . . . . . . . . 324
Partnership Act 1891 (TAS)
s 5 . . . . . . . . . . . . . . . . . . . . . . . . . . . . . . . . . 324
s 29 . . . . . . . . . . . . . . . . . . . . . . . . . . . . . . . . 324
ss 33–5 . . . . . . . . . . . . . . . . . . . . . . . . . . . . . . . 324
ss 37, 38 . . . . . . . . . . . . . . . . . . . . . . . . . . . . . . 325
Partnership Act 1958 (VIC)
s 6 . . . . . . . . . . . . . . . . . . . . . . . . . . . . . . . . . 324
s 28 . . . . . . . . . . . . . . . . . . . . . . . . . . . . . . . . 324
ss 32–4 . . . . . . . . . . . . . . . . . . . . . . . . . . . . . . . 324
ss 36, 37 . . . . . . . . . . . . . . . . . . . . . . . . . . . . . . 325
Partnership Act 1895 (WA)
s 6 . . . . . . . . . . . . . . . . . . . . . . . . . . . . . . . . . 324
s 34 . . . . . . . . . . . . . . . . . . . . . . . . . . . . . . . . 324
ss 39–41 . . . . . . . . . . . . . . . . . . . . . . . . . . . . . . 324
ss 43, 44 . . . . . . . . . . . . . . . . . . . . . . . . . . . . . . 325
Partnership Ordinance 1963 (ACT)
s 5 . . . . . . . . . . . . . . . . . . . . . . . . . . . . . . . . . 324
s 29 . . . . . . . . . . . . . . . . . . . . . . . . . . . . . . . . 324
ss 33–5 . . . . . . . . . . . . . . . . . . . . . . . . . . . . . . . 324
ss 37, 38 . . . . . . . . . . . . . . . . . . . . . . . . . . . . . . 325

Trade Practices Act 1974 (Cth) . . . . . . . . . . . . . . . . . . 304
s 52 . . . . . . . . . . . . . . . . . . . . . . . . . . . . . . . . 278

# CANADA

Ontario Business Corporations Act 1982
ss 245–8 . . . . . . . . . . . . . . . . . . . . . . . . . . . . . 216

# NEW ZEALAND

Companies Act 1993
ss 165–8 . . . . . . . . . . . . . . . . . . . . . . . . . . . . 159
s 178 . . . . . . . . . . . . . . . . . . . . . . . . . . . . . 250

# SOUTH AFRICA

Close Corporations Act No 69 1984 . . . . . . . . . . . . . . . . .. 325

# UNITED KINGDOM

Companies Act 1862
s 79(5) . . . . . . . . . . . . . . . . . . . . . . . . . . . . 113
s 82 . . . . . . . . . . . . . . . . . . . . . . . . . . . . . . 98
s 91 . . . . . . . . . . . . . . . . . . . . . . . . . . . . . . 99
Companies Act 1928
s 50 . . . . . . . . . . . . . . . . . . . . . . . . . . . . . 263
Companies Act 1948
s 20(1) . . . . . . . . . . . . . . . . . . . . . . . . . . . 69, 70
s 184(1) . . . . . . . . . . . . . . . . . . . . . . . . . . . . 82
s 210 . . . . . . . . . . . . . . . . . . . . . . . . . . . 6, 119
Companies Act 1980 . . . . . . . . . . . . . . . . . . . . . 121, 159
s 75 . . . . . . . . . . . . . . . . . . . . . . . . . . . . . 119
Companies Act 1985
s 1(3) . . . . . . . . . . . . . . . . . . . . . . . . . . . . . 3
s 3A . . . . . . . . . . . . . . . . . . . . . . . . . . . . . 114
s 5 . . . . . . . . . . . . . . . . . . . . . . . . . 74, 75, 224
s 8 . . . . . . . . . . . . . . . . . . . . . . . . . . . 67, 142
s 8A . . . . . . . . . . . . . . . . . . . . . . . . . . . . 327
s 9 . . . . . . . . . . . . . . . . . . . . . . . . . . . . 5, 84
s 14 . . . . . . . . . . . . . . . . . . . . . . . . . . . . 142
(1) . . . . . . . . . . . . . . . . . . . . . . . . . . . 67, 68
s 16 . . . . . . . . . . . . . . . . . . . . . . . . . . . . . 74

| | |
|---|---|
| s 17 | 74, 77 |
| (2)(3) | 75 |
| s 22(2) | 122, 313 |
| s 35(2)(3) | 186 |
| ss 89–95 | 40 |
| s 111A | 73 |
| s 118 | 3 |
| s 125 | 77, 294 |
| (5) | 76, 77 |
| (7) | 78 |
| s 127 | 79, 224 |
| (2)(3) | 79 |
| s 136 | 291 |
| (3) | 297 |
| (5)(6) | 297 |
| s 137 | 291 |
| s 138(1)(2) | 291 |
| s 139–41 | 291 |
| s 203(3)(4) | 272 |
| s 204 | 39 |
| (5)(6) | 272 |
| s 232 | 43 |
| s 238–9 | 245 |
| s 251–3 | 245 |
| s 303 | 81 |
| s 309 | 34 |
| s 312–13 | 195, 245 |
| s 319 | 34, 45, 195, 245 |
| s 320 | 34, 195, 245 |
| s 321–2 | 34 |
| ss 330–6 | 34 |
| s 337 | 195 |
| s 338–46 | 34 |
| s 359 | 123, 224 |
| s 368 | 139 |
| s 369 | 246 |
| s 371 | 83 |
| s 378(2)(3) | 298 |
| s 380 | |
| (4)(c) | 94 |
| (5) | 94 |
| s 381 | |
| A–B | 93 |

C . . . . . . . . . . . . . . . . . . . . . . . . . . . . . . . . . 93
    (2) . . . . . . . . . . . . . . . . . . . . . . . . . . . . . . 93
s 383 . . . . . . . . . . . . . . . . . . . . . . . . . . . . . 246
s 425 . . . . . . . . . . . . . . . . . . . . . . . . . . . 75, 283
    (1)–(3) . . . . . . . . . . . . . . . . . . . . . . . . . . . 283
s 426 . . . . . . . . . . . . . . . . . . . . . . . . . . . . . . 75
    (2)(3) . . . . . . . . . . . . . . . . . . . . . . . . . . . . 287
    (4) . . . . . . . . . . . . . . . . . . . . . . . . . . . . . 289
    (5) . . . . . . . . . . . . . . . . . . . . . . . . . . . . . 287
    (7) . . . . . . . . . . . . . . . . . . . . . . . . . . . . . 288
s 427A . . . . . . . . . . . . . . . . . . . . . . . . . . . 75, 283
s 428(7) . . . . . . . . . . . . . . . . . . . . . . . . . . . . 265
s 429(8) . . . . . . . . . . . . . . . . . . . . . . . . . . . . 265
s 430
    (3)(4) . . . . . . . . . . . . . . . . . . . . . . . . . . . . 265
    C(1) . . . . . . . . . . . . . . . . . . . . . . . . . . . . . 275
    (4) . . . . . . . . . . . . . . . . . . . . . . . . . . . . . 276
    (5) . . . . . . . . . . . . . . . . . . . . . . . . . . . 265, 269
    D . . . . . . . . . . . . . . . . . . . . . . . . . . . . . . 265
    E(1)–(3) . . . . . . . . . . . . . . . . . . . . . . . . . . . 272
    (4) . . . . . . . . . . . . . . . . . . . . . . . . . . . . . 271
    (6)–(8) . . . . . . . . . . . . . . . . . . . . . . . . . . . 272
    F . . . . . . . . . . . . . . . . . . . . . . . . . . . . . . 266
s 459 . . . . . . . . . . . . . . . . . . . . . . . . . 119, 228, 265
    (2) . . . . . . . . . . . . . . . . . . . . . . . . . . . 122, 231
ss 460–1 . . . . . . . . . . . . . . . . . . . . . . . . . . 121, 123
s 741 . . . . . . . . . . . . . . . . . . . . . . . . . . . . . . 34
    (1)(2) . . . . . . . . . . . . . . . . . . . . . . . . . . . . 103
Part XIIIA . . . . . . . . . . . . . . . . . . . . . . . 263, 266, 279
Part XVII . . . . . . . . . . . . . . . . . . . . . . . . . . 121, 159
Sch 6 Part 1 . . . . . . . . . . . . . . . . . . . . . . . . . . . 43
Companies Act 1989
    s 128 . . . . . . . . . . . . . . . . . . . . . . . . . . . . . 327
    s 145 . . . . . . . . . . . . . . . . . . . . . . . . . . . . . 168
Sch 19 para 11 . . . . . . . . . . . . . . . . . . . . . 121, 168, 235


Financial Services Act 1986
    s 172 . . . . . . . . . . . . . . . . . . . . . . . . . . . . . 263
Sch 12 . . . . . . . . . . . . . . . . . . . . . . . . . . . . . 263


Income and Corporation Taxes Act 1988
    s 413 . . . . . . . . . . . . . . . . . . . . . . . . . . . . . 307

Insolvency Act 1968
  s 122(1)(g) . . . . . . . . . . . . . . . . . . . . . . . . . . . 113, 167
  s 124 . . . . . . . . . . . . . . . . . . . . . . . . . . . . . . 172, 173
  s 125 . . . . . . . . . . . . . . . . . . . . . . . . . . . . . . 176
  s 127 . . . . . . . . . . . . . . . . . . . . . . . . . . . . . . 147
  s 214 . . . . . . . . . . . . . . . . . . . . . . . . . . . . . . 34
    A . . . . . . . . . . . . . . . . . . . . . . . . . . . . . 240

Joint Stock Companies Winding-up Act 1848
  s 5(8) . . . . . . . . . . . . . . . . . . . . . . . . . . . . . 113

Partnership Act 1890
  s 24 . . . . . . . . . . . . . . . . . . . . . . . . . . . . . . 324
  ss 28–30 . . . . . . . . . . . . . . . . . . . . . . . . . . . . 324
  ss 32, 33 . . . . . . . . . . . . . . . . . . . . . . . . . . . . 325
  s 46 . . . . . . . . . . . . . . . . . . . . . . . . . . . . . . 324

Restrictive Trade Practices Act 1976 . . . . . . . . . . . . . . . . 95
Restrictive Trade Practices Act 1977 . . . . . . . . . . . . . . . . 95

# Regulations and Statutory Instruments

## AUSTRALIA

Corporation Regulations 1990 SR 1990 No 455

    reg 5.1.01 . . . . . . . . . . . . . . . . . . . . . . . . . . . . . . . 288

    reg 7.12.05–06 . . . . . . . . . . . . . . . . . . . . . . . . . . . . 59

    sch 5

        cl 25 . . . . . . . . . . . . . . . . . . . . . . . . . . . . . . . . 43

        cl 29 . . . . . . . . . . . . . . . . . . . . . . . . . . . . . . . . 43

    sch 8 . . . . . . . . . . . . . . . . . . . . . . . . . . . . . . . . . . 288

        Pt 3 cl 3 . . . . . . . . . . . . . . . . . . . . . . . . . . . . . . 288

## UNITED KINGDOM

Supply of Goods (Exclusion of Implied Terms) Order 1982

    SI 1982 No 1771 . . . . . . . . . . . . . . . . . . . . . . . . . . . 240

The Companies (Table A to F) Regulations 1985 SI 1985 No 805

## UNITED STATES

Employee Retirement Income Security Act 1974 . . . . . . . . . . . 36

# PART I

# *The Problem*

# Introduction

This book considers the position of minority shareholders under English and Australian law. It identifies the most common complaints expressed by minority shareholders, examines the relief which is available both in the courts and by self-help measures, and applies these two forms of relief to the identified complaints.

For the purposes of cataloguing minority shareholders' complaints, companies have been divided into three broad types:[1]

(1) listed public companies;
(2) quasi-partnership and joint venture companies; and
(3) a residual category of companies.

Both the susceptibility of shareholders to particular oppressive practices, and the means available to remedy or prevent them vary according to the nature of the company. The nature of minority shareholders' complaints and the companies in which they occur are examined in Chapter 2.

The first avenue of relief examined is self-help, and is covered in Chapters 3–5. This is directed primarily at prevention rather than cure. Depending on the relative negotiating strengths of the parties the minority shareholders may be able to secure the adoption of a structure which minimizes the potential for oppression. The form which such structural changes may take depends upon the type of company. For example, institutional shareholders in listed companies may collectively have sufficient power to secure measures such as the appointment of non-executive directors to the board, whereas, in quasi-partnership and joint venture companies, shareholders may use devices such as shareholders' agreements, weighted voting and class rights to protect their position.

The second avenue of relief discussed is recourse to the courts, and is covered in Chapters 6–10. Rather than the usual chronological approach to analysing the various available remedies, the discussion in Chapters 6–9

---

[1] Companies falling into the first category will necessarily be public. Whether companies of the latter two types are officially classified as 'public' or 'private' is not critical to the following discussion, and is influenced by the differing methods of classification adopted in the United Kingdom and Australia. Cf. ss. 1(3) and 118, CA 1985 (UK) which contain an inclusive definition of public company with ss. 9 and 116, CL (Aust) which instead adopt an inclusive definition of proprietary company, with public companies forming the residual category.

focuses on the evolving role and interpretation of the statutory remedy against unfairly prejudicial conduct. The view advanced in this book is that intervention by the courts under this remedy is grounded on departure from the parties' legitimate expectations, and that the nature of the company helps to define the ambit of the parties' legitimate expectations in a particular case. The residual roles of the winding-up remedy and the relief which is available at common law are addressed against this background. Chapter 10 examines the specific issue of compulsory acquisition of minority shareholdings, and the attitude of the courts to the various means which may potentially be used for this purpose.

Conclusions are drawn in Chapter 11 as to the extent to which, by a combination of litigation and self-help, the common complaints of minority shareholders are currently capable of remedy or prevention.

This book is confined to prevention measures or remedies which lie in the hands of shareholders. It does not, therefore, deal with the statutory powers of investigation and institution of proceedings which are vested in England in the Secretary of State for Trade and Industry and in Australia in the Australian Securities Commission.

# Common Complaints of Minority Shareholders

One of the pillars of company law is the principle of majority rule. Both at the level of the board of directors and the company in general meeting, company decisions are generally[1] decided by a simple majority vote. But while the concept of majority rule is fundamental, it carries with it the potential for abuse of power. This book is concerned with the position of minority shareholders where the company's controllers are taking advantage of their more powerful position to oppress the minority.

At the outset, it is necessary to draw certain distinctions, both as to the nature of minority shareholders' complaints and as to the nature of the company in which they occur. Indeed, these two factors are interrelated, since the nature of the company will determine whether and to what extent minority shareholders are affected by particular forms of conduct.

At one end of the spectrum of company types is the listed public company. Here risk bearing and management are separated, and most shareholder complaints therefore relate to dissatisfaction with management. They may stem from disagreements over policy matters, charges of inefficiency or negligence, or, more seriously, that the controllers are profiting at the expense of the company. The one advantage that minority shareholders in listed companies have when faced with these situations is that in many cases they will be able to avoid the problem by selling their shares.

Nevertheless, there are some situations where disposal of their shares will not be a satisfactory option. For example, the conduct of the controllers may have depressed the value of the shares, the minority may not wish to dispose of their stake for personal or strategic reasons, or a sale may not be viable because the shares were purchased as part of an indexed fund.[2] The aggrieved shareholders will then have to look to other remedies.

At the other end of the spectrum are corporate quasi-partnerships.

---

[1] Special majorities may be prescribed for certain decisions either by the articles or by statute. For example a three-quarters majority is prescribed by statute in respect of a resolution altering the articles of association: s. 9, CA 1985 (UK), s. 176, CL (Aust).

[2] See Chapter 3 Section 3(1)(d).

These companies are generally formed on the basis that decisions will be reached by consensus rather than a strict application of majority rule, and it is usually as a consequence of a breakdown in the personal relationship between the participants that one party takes advantage of a controlling position to oppress the other. Thus, although complaints may relate, for example, to bad management or self-interested conduct, such conduct has a much more personal effect on the minority than in a listed company. Further, there is a greater potential for the oppressive conduct to take other forms. A reversion to strict majority rule consequent upon a breakdown of relations may result in the frustration of the minority shareholder's expectations as to his or her rights and obligations. Foremost among these is usually an expectation of participation in management. Exclusion from this role may have particularly serious consequences. First, an isolated minority shareholder in a small private company may well have little or no say in the running of the business of the company. Secondly, at least until recently,[3] it has been rare for private companies to pay dividends. Instead, most of the profits have been applied towards directors' remuneration, with any surplus going to reserves. The excluded shareholder may therefore suddenly be placed in the position of receiving no return on his or her investment.

Both excluded quasi-partners and minority shareholders in other unlisted companies share the disadvantage of illiquidity. There are two facets to this grievance. First, there is usually no established market place and hence no readily ascertainable market price for their shares. Secondly, it is usual for the articles of association of private companies to impose restrictions on the transfer of shares.[4] The effect of this may be to give the oppressors the power to prevent the transfer of the shares to a third party without placing any corresponding obligation either on them or on the company to purchase the shares. Illiquidity therefore compounds[5] the effect of any oppressive conduct by controllers. It may for example become particularly significant where it is combined with a low dividend policy, since it will make it virtually impossible for a shareholder to replace his or her investment in the company with one which produces greater income.

The converse problem is compulsory acquisition. In a quasi-partnership

---

[3] This practice was formerly driven by taxation considerations.

[4] In Australia, in order for a company to be incorporated as a proprietary company its memorandum or articles must contain provisions which restrict the right to transfer shares: s. 116, CL (Aust).

[5] See J. A. C. Hetherington and M. P. Dooley, 'Illiquidity and Exploitation: A Proposed Statutory Solution to the Remaining Close Corporation Problem' (1977) 63 *Va L Rev* 1, and cf. F. H. Easterbrook and D. R. Fischel, 'Close Corporations and Agency Costs' (1986) 38 *Stan L Rev* 271, at 274–275. See also D. Prentice, 'Protection of Minority Shareholders, Section 210 of the Companies Act 1948' [1972] *Current Legal Problems* 124, at 129.

or joint venture company, the exclusion of a minority shareholder from management participation may, when combined with pre-emption provisions in the company's articles, result in *de facto* compulsory acquisition. In addition, there are specific procedures in both jurisdictions which enable a substantial majority shareholder to acquire the shares of a dissenting minority, subject to certain safeguards. The approval requirements for these procedures mean that they will seldom be applicable to quasi-partnership companies. Rather they are more likely to be invoked in order to remove the few remaining minority shareholders after a takeover of a public company which has been substantially successful. Whether or not relief is sought against compulsory acquisition will often depend upon the price to be paid for the minority's shares.

Finally, one overriding complaint of shareholders in all types of company is lack of information. But again, this complaint takes different forms according to the nature of the company. There are numerous sources of information available to shareholders in listed companies. These include the Stock Exchange, the financial Press, analysts' forecasts, computerized data bases and other subscription services. In Australia, there are also continuous disclosure obligations and periodic reporting requirements on certain unlisted companies.[6] Shareholders may obtain information regarding these companies from the Australian Securities Commission. But, as all the information sources referred to above are external to the company, they may not reveal evidence of mismanagement or fraud until a very late stage. Further, for personal investors, the costs of gaining access to this information may be disproportionate to the value of their investment. As regards other companies, the company itself is the primary source of information. Thus for quasi-partners, access to information is usually not an issue. However, for excluded quasi-partners and for shareholders in other unlisted companies, information may be very difficult to obtain. Thus, lack of information may be a complaint in its own right, but it also has the effect of exacerbating the effect of the other complaints.

Figure 2.1 lists 10 recurring complaints of minority shareholders, and catalogues them according to the nature of the company in which they are likely to arise. Compiling a 'top 10' list of common complaints necessarily involves a degree of arbitrariness. The list in Figure 2.1 is based in part on one compiled by Stedman and Jones,[7] and has been refined by reference to

---

[6] Broadly, where a lodged or deemed prospectus relates to the company's securities, where the company's securities were issued as consideration for an acquisition under a takeover scheme or a compromise or arrangement, or where the company has issued debentures to which s. 1052, CL (Aust) applies. See further ss. 111AD–111AK, CL (Aust).

[7] G. Stedman and J. Jones, *Shareholders' Agreements* (2nd edn., London, Longman Group UK Ltd, 1990) at 108.

FIGURE 2.1 Common Complaints of Minority Shareholders Catalogued According to the Nature of the Company.

LEGEND

Complaints which are commonly expressed by shareholders in listed companies

Complaints which are commonly expressed by shareholders in quasi-partnership companies

Complaints which are commonly expressed in other companies

| COMPLAINT | COMPANY TYPE |
|---|---|
| Disregard of rights granted by statute or by the articles | |
| Alteration of the articles | |
| Dilution of equity stake or voting rights* | |
| Self-interested transactions by controllers** | |
| Negligent or inefficient management | |
| Little or no participation in profits | |
| Limited access to information about the company's affairs | |
| Illiquidity | |
| Exclusion from management | |
| Compulsory acquisition | |

\* In some (but not necessarily all) cases this will overlap with the next category.

\*\* Such conduct may take many forms. Some recurring examples are: diversion of corporate opportunity to another business which the directors also control, entering into a transaction with the company on terms favourable to themselves, paying themselves excessive remuneration, causing the company to abandon legal proceedings against them and frustrating a takeover offer which would threaten their position.

the problems which emerge from reported cases, Press reports and concerns expressed by shareholder interest groups.

This book examines the action which can be taken by minority shareholders who are affected by one or more of these identified complaints.

# PART II

---•---

# *PREVENTION*

## ⤳ 3 ⤶

# *Self-help in Listed Companies*

1. Introduction                                                                                  15

2. Historical Developments in Corporate Governance                                               21
   (1) United Kingdom                                                                            21
       (a) Changing responses to corporate sector
           under-performance                                                                     21
       (b) Fall-out of the 1980s                                                                 22
       (c) Institutional Shareholders' Committee initiatives                                     22
       (d) The Cadbury Code                                                                      22
       (e) Enforcement                                                                           23
   (2) Australia                                                                                 24
       (a) Australian Investment Managers' Association                                           25
       (b) Corporate Practices and Conduct                                                       25
       (c) Enforcement                                                                           26
   (3) Non-executive directors                                                                   27
       (a) Ideological objections                                                                27
       (b) Practical objections                                                                  29
       (c) Reform proposals                                                                      30

3. Influences on Institutional Activism                                                          31
   (1) Incentives                                                                                31
       (a) The size of collective institutional shareholdings                                    31
       (b) Recession                                                                             31
       (c) Social pressure                                                                       31
       (d) Indexing                                                                              31
   (2) Disincentives                                                                             32
       (a) Cost-benefit                                                                          32
       (b) Competition                                                                           32
       (c) Conflicts of interest                                                                 32
       (d) Short-term horizons                                                                   33
       (e) Potential liability as a shadow director                                              34
       (f) Disincentives relating specifically to voting                                         36
           (i) Practical obstacles                                                               36
           (ii) Legal obstacles                                                                  37
               (A) Who can vote?                                                                 37
               (B) Section 1069(1)(k) Corporations Law                                           38
               (C) Takeover legislation                                                          38

4. Institutional Activism and Identified Complaints          39
   (1) Dilution of equity stake or voting rights              39
       (a) Pre-emption rights                                 40
       (b) Shares with differential voting rights             40
   (2) Self-interested transactions by controllers            42
       (a) Management buy-outs                                42
       (b) Scrip dividends                                    43
       (c) Executive remuneration                            43
           (i) Disclosure                                     43
           (ii) Term                                          45
           (iii) Linkage to company performance               45
           (iv) Total remuneration                            46
           (v) Remuneration committees                        47
       (d) Other related party transactions                  48
   (3) Negligent or inefficient management                    48
       (a) Structure and composition of the board            49
       (b) Appointment and removal of directors              50
   (4) Dividend policy                                        52
   (5) Information about the company's affairs                52
   (6) Other complaints                                       53

5. Implications for Other Shareholders                        55
   (1) Pre-emption rights                                     55
   (2) Dividend policy                                        56
   (3) Access to information                                  56
       (a) Continuous disclosure obligations                 56
       (b) Annual general meetings                            60
       (c) Frequency of reporting                            61
   (4) Resolution of conflicts between institutions and other
       shareholders                                           61

## SUMMARY

*In listed companies, it will often be the case that all shareholders are minority shareholders. However, a distinction can be drawn between institutional shareholders and other categories of minority shareholder. Because of the size of collective institutional shareholdings, and because of the sophistication of institutions as investors, self-help options are available to them which have the potential to overcome most commonly expressed complaints.*

*External influences on institutional shareholders mean that they are more likely to exert their influence to seek structural changes or adherence to general guidelines, rather than becoming involved in issues which are specific to a particular company, and that they may not vote against management if their 'behind the scenes' pressure is unheeded.*

*To the extent that institutions are active as shareholders, this activism generally also benefits other shareholders. However, in some cases it operates to their disadvantage. The most significant disadvantage to other shareholders is in terms of access to information. The preferential position of the institutions means that different channels of communication have developed between them and the companies in which they invest. Not only do other shareholders not have access to these channels, but their existence weakens the statutorily enshrined methods of communication, namely the general meeting and the annual report and accounts.*

## 1. INTRODUCTION

A preliminary question of definition arises in listed companies as to which shareholders should be classified as 'minority' shareholders. This is because factual as opposed to legal control may be achieved with a smaller shareholding than 51 per cent.[1] Rather, as described by Berle and Means, the holder of a substantial minority of the shares in a company with otherwise widely dispersed share ownership may, as a result of shareholder apathy and solicitation of proxies, be able to procure a majority of votes at a general meeting, and so have what has been called 'minority control'.[2] Alternatively, where no one shareholder has a substantial minority interest, control may lie with the management.[3] However, there is no sharp dividing line between these two situations.

In larger listed companies it may be the case that all shareholders can be classified as 'minority' shareholders in the sense that none of them has either legal or factual control.[4] On the basis of Berle and Means' analysis, these companies could be regarded as examples of management control. However, this may be to oversimplify the situation by ignoring the typical profile of the modern listed public company.

In the United Kingdom, there has been a transformation in the constituency of shareholders in listed companies in the last 50 years. In 1945, shareholders were primarily personal or individual investors. Now,

---

[1] A. A. Berle and G. C. Means, *The Modern Corporation and Private Property* (revised edn., New York, Harcourt, Brace & World Inc, 1968).

[2] Ibid., at 75–8. See also C. Harris and N. Tait, 'The Club No One Wants To Join' *Financial Times*, 4 April 1988, at 30.

[3] Berle and Means, op. cit., at 78–84.

[4] A Korn/Ferry International survey, *Boards of Directors Study UK (1991)*, found that in 40% of companies with sales in excess of £500m and in 21% of companies with sales between £150m and £500m there were no institutional shareholders with a minimum 5% shareholding.

driven largely by the growing role of pension and superannuation plans, increasing proportions of shares are being held by institutional share-holders.[5] The combined holdings of the two largest institutional investors (pension funds and insurance companies) increased from 16.4 per cent in 1963 to 52 per cent in 1990. During the same period, there was a corresponding drop in individual holdings from 54 per cent to 20.3 per cent.[6] As Figure 3.1 illustrates, the combined holdings of pension funds and insurance companies stabilized at 51–52 per cent over the succeeding three years, with total institutional shareholdings over the same period consistently exceeding 60 per cent.

Until recently, empirical information regarding the beneficial ownership of Australian companies has been prepared using varying samples, making direct comparisons difficult. Nevertheless, the data evidences a parallel trend towards increasing share ownership by institutions.[7] Since March 1991, empirical information has been prepared by the Australian Stock Exchange[8] on a quarterly basis. These statistics show combined institutional shareholdings reaching a peak of 42.6 per cent in December 1991, and decreasing slightly but steadily since then to 38.8 per cent in March 1994. The combined holdings of life insurance companies and superannuation funds for those periods were 28.2 per cent and 23.3 per cent respectively. These figures are illustrated in Figure 3.2.[9]

Thus, although the broad trends in the two jurisdictions over the last 30 years are similar, a significant difference between them is that institutions control well over half of the shares in companies in the United Kingdom,

[5] The factors contributing to the growth of institutional shareholders and the implications of this change raise many issues other than the minority protection question with which this book is concerned. See further J. H. Farrar and M. Russell, 'The Impact of Institutional Investment on Company Law' (1984) 5 *Company Lawyer* 107.

[6] Source: Central Statistical Office, *Share Ownership: The Share Register Survey Report, end 1993*, (London, HMSO, 1994). Note, however, the CSO qualification that: 'The apparent trends in these series is affected, particularly for the earlier data, by sampling errors and varying degrees of success in the identification of nominee holdings'.

[7] See E. L. Wheelwright and J. Miskelly, *Anatomy of Australian Manufacturing Industry* (Sydney, Law Book, 1967), at 3 and 18, Campbell Committee, *Australian Financial System: Final Report of the Committee of Inquiry* (Canberra, AGPS, 1981), at 552 and G. J. Crough, *Financial Institutions and the Ownership of Australian Corporations*, Research Monograph Number 12 (University of Sydney, Transnational Corporations Research Project, January 1981).

[8] The statistics are prepared by M. J. Heffernan, based on the Australian Bureau of Statistics Australia National Accounts–Financial Accounts–Catalogue 5232.0.

[9] Note, however, that the Australian Bureau of Statistics has subsequently revised some of the raw data constructs which were used by Mr Heffernan to calculate the share ownership figures. The revision would have the effect of redistributing approximately 10 percentage points of the total for 'Households' into the total for 'Rest of World', but would not affect the other categories or the general trends for the 'Household' and 'Rest of World' sectors. See also: ASX submission to *Institutional Investor Inquiry: Parliamentary Joint Committee on Corporations and Securities*, (Australia, 1994), at 430–1.

FIGURE 3.1 Beneficial Share Ownership of UK Listed Companies 1963–1993

| Beneficial Owner | % of total equity owned, 31 December | | | | | | | | |
|---|---|---|---|---|---|---|---|---|---|
| | 1963 | 1969 | 1975 | 1981 | 1989 | 1990 | 1991 | 1992 | 1993 |
| Pension funds | 6.4 | 9.0 | 16.8 | 26.7 | 30.6 | 31.6 | 31.3 | 35.1 | 34.2 |
| Insurance companies | 10.0 | 12.2 | 15.9 | 20.5 | 18.6 | 20.4 | 20.8 | 16.7 | 17.3 |
| Unit trusts | 1.3 | 2.9 | 4.1 | 3.6 | 5.9 | 6.1 | 5.7 | 6.2 | 6.6 |
| Banks | 1.3 | 1.7 | 0.7 | 0.3 | 0.7 | 0.7 | 0.2 | 0.5 | 0.6 |
| Other financial institutions | 11.3 | 10.1 | 10.5 | 6.8 | 2.7 | 2.3 | 2.3 | 2.5 | 3.1 |
| Individuals | 54.0 | 47.4 | 37.5 | 28.2 | 20.6 | 20.3 | 19.9 | 20.4 | 17.7 |
| Other personal sector | 2.1 | 2.1 | 2.3 | 2.2 | 2.3 | 1.9 | 2.4 | 1.8 | 1.6 |
| Public sector | 1.5 | 2.6 | 3.6 | 3.0 | 2.0 | 2.0 | 1.3 | 1.8 | 1.3 |
| Industrial & commercial cos | 5.1 | 5.4 | 3.0 | 5.1 | 3.8 | 2.8 | 3.3 | 1.8 | 1.5 |
| Overseas | 7.0 | 6.6 | 5.6 | 3.6 | 12.8 | 11.8 | 12.8 | 13.1 | 16.3 |
| Total | 100.0 | 100.0 | 100.0 | 100.0 | 100.0 | 100.0 | 100.0 | 100.0 | 100.0 |

Source: Share Register Survey 1993. Central Statistical Office. Crown Copyright. 1994. Reproduced by the permission of the Controller of HMSO and the Central Statistical Office.

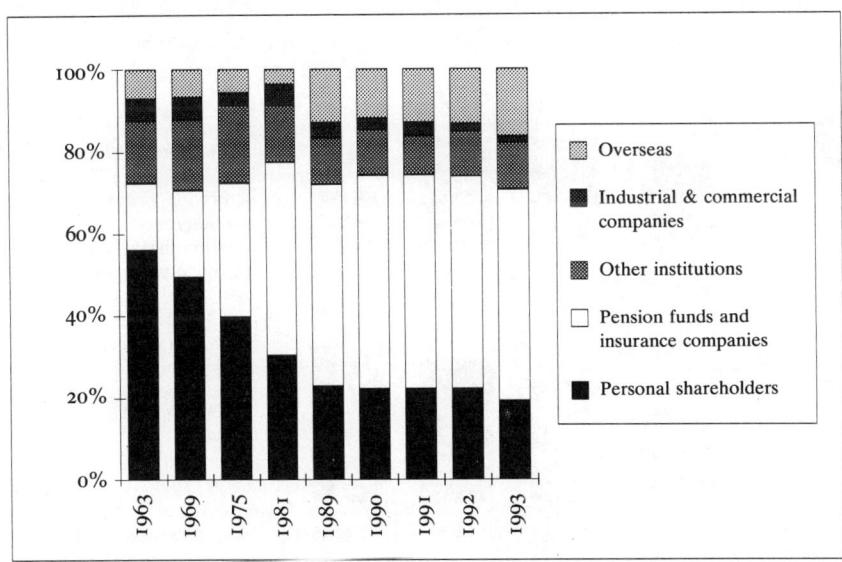

In the above chart, the category of 'personal shareholders' incorporates both individual and other personal sector holdings. The category of 'other institutions' comprises banks, other financial institutions, unit trusts and public sector holdings.

FIGURE 3.2 Share Ownership of Australian Listed Companies 1991–1994

| Beneficial Owner | % of total equity owned, 31 March | | | |
|---|---|---|---|---|
| | 1991 | 1992 | 1993 | 1994 |
| Private Corporate Trading Entities | 16.6 | 13.5 | 10.1 | 6.5 |
| Banks | 3.0 | 3.0 | 2.8 | 2.2 |
| Non-Bank Financial Intermediaries | 1.9 | 1.5 | 1.2 | 0.8 |
| Life Insurance and Superannuation | 26.4 | 27.2 | 25.6 | 23.3 |
| Other Financial Institutions | 6.3 | 6.6 | 6.9 | 10.3 |
| Government | 2.6 | 1.9 | 2.9 | 2.2 |
| Rest of World | 21.7 | 19.2 | 18.7 | 19.8 |
| Households | 21.6 | 27.1 | 31.9 | 34.9 |
| Total | 100.0 | 100.0 | 100.0 | 100.0 |

Source: M. J. Heffernan, Chief Economist/Lawyer, Australian Stock Exchange Limited, Adjusted Ownership of Shares, based on Australian Bureau of Statistics ('ABS') Australia National Accounts—Financial Accounts. For details of adjustments made to ABS figures see ASX submission to Institutional Investor Inquiry: Parliamentary Joint Committee on Corporations and Securities (Australia, 1994) at 442–4.

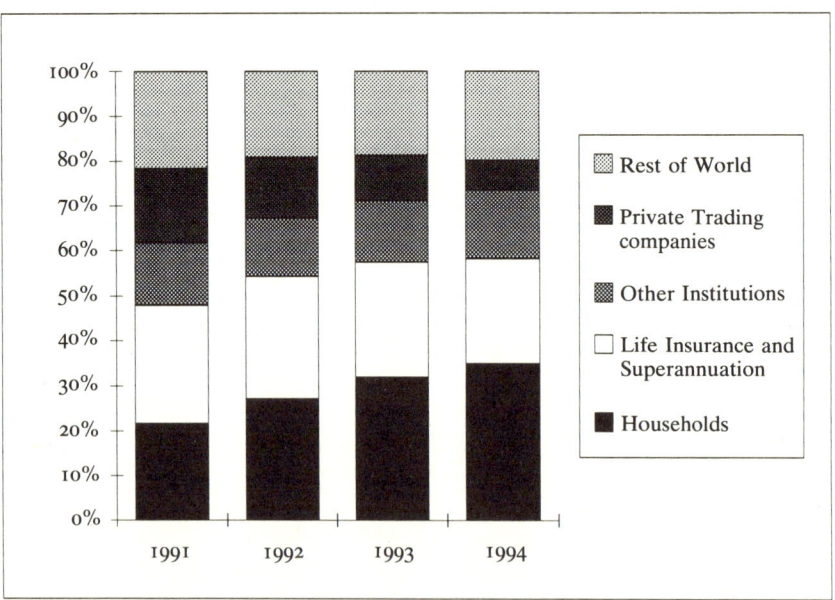

In the above chart, the category of 'other institutions' is made up of banks, non-bank financial intermediaries, other financial institutions and government holdings.

whereas the percentage of shares held by institutions in Australian companies is substantial (at just under 40 per cent), but significantly lower: see Figure 3.3. However, whereas in the United Kingdom, the proportion of companies held by the major institutional investors (pension funds and insurance companies) hardly varies as between large and small listed companies,[10] institutional shareholdings in Australia are concentrated in larger blue chip companies.[11] In these larger listed companies, the proportion of institutional investment may well approach the levels seen in the United Kingdom.

The implications of this statistical information are that, collectively institutional shareholders will have either minority control or, in many cases, actual majority control of the companies in which they invest.[12] The collective voting power of the institutional shareholders means that they may be able to protect themselves (and consequently other shareholders as well) from abuse of power by the directors or other shareholder complaints. Even though in Australia the combined shareholdings of individuals in listed companies are comparable with those of institutions, the relatively small size of individual holdings tends to make collective action infeasible.[13] The size of institutional holdings in particular companies and the sophistication of institutions as investors set them apart from other categories of minority shareholders and, in particular, from individual shareholders.

The remainder of this chapter is divided into four sections. Section 2 provides some historical background on developments in corporate governance. Section 3 examines the factors which may affect the extent to which institutional shareholders use their influence in the companies in which they invest. The issues where institutional shareholders are active are described in section 4. Finally, section 5 explores the implications of institutional activism for non-institutional minority shareholders, most of whom (in number if not in size of holdings) are individual or personal investors.

---

[10] CSO, *The Ownership of Company Shares: Share Register Survey Report, end 1992* (London, HMSO, 1994) at 16.

[11] J. Hill, 'Institutional Investors and Corporate Governance in Australia' in T. Baums *et al.*, (eds) *Institutional Investors and Corporate Governance* (Berlin, Walter de Gruyter, 1994), at 590 and I. M. Ramsay and M. Blair, 'Ownership Concentration, Institutional Investment and Corporate Governance: An Empirical Investigation of 100 Australian Companies' (1993) 19 *Melb U L Rev* 153, at 186.

[12] See further P. L. Davies, 'Institutional Investors in the United Kingdom' in Baums (ibid), at 270.

[13] A survey by the ASX, *Australian Shareownership Survey 1994* found that 52.2% of share portfolios held by individuals had a total value of $A10,000 or less and 33.2% were of $A5,000 or less. As to the problems of collective action, see ASX Discussion Paper, *Differential Voting Rights*, November 1993, at 6. Note also the qualification in n. 9 above.

FIGURE 3.3  Ownership of Listed Company Shares in the United Kingdom and Australia as at
31 December 1993

| Beneficial Owner | % of total equity owned | |
| --- | --- | --- |
| | United Kingdom | Australia |
| Institutional Shareholders | 63.1 | 38.6 |
| Personal Shareholders | 19.3 | 35.8 |
| Trading Companies | 1.5 | 6.2 |
| Overseas | 16.3 | 19.4 |
| Total | 100.0 | 100.0 |

Sources: As for figures 3.1 and 3.2, except that for the purposes of comparison, categories of
institutional shareholder have been amalgamated, and Australian data is for December 1993.

## United Kingdom

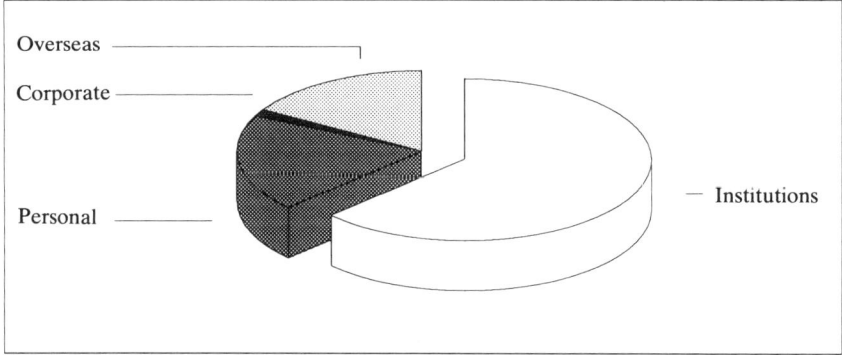

## Australia

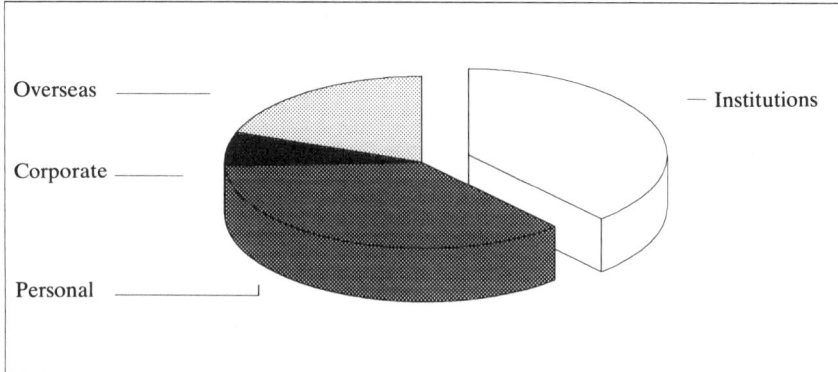

## 2. HISTORICAL DEVELOPMENTS IN CORPORATE GOVERNANCE

### (1) United Kingdom

#### (a) Changing responses to corporate sector under-performance

The role of institutional investors in corporate governance came to prominence in the United Kingdom in 1973 as the implications of the expansion of institutional shareholding became apparent. Earlier, the conventional wisdom had been that if shareholders were dissatisfied with management they should sell their shares.[14] But this became less tenable as the size of their investments compared to the size of the market meant that they were often effectively locked in.[15] In the course of that year, the Company Affairs Committee of the Confederation of British Industry and a Government White Paper[16] both expressed support for the view that institutional shareholders should take a leading role in monitoring the management of the companies in which they invested. Also in that year the Institutional Shareholders' Committee ('ISC') was formed as an umbrella body covering insurance companies, pension funds, unit trusts, and investment trusts, with the expectation that it might act as a focus for concerted action in relation to poorly governed companies.[17]

A complementary development during this period was the establishment in 1982 of PRO NED which, as its name suggests, is an organization which promotes the appointment of non-executive directors.[18] In April 1987[19]

---

[14] J. Charkham, *Corporate Governance and the Market for Companies: Aspects of the Shareholders' Role* Bank of England Discussion Paper Number 44, November 1989, at 12–13 and J. W. Barnard, 'Institutional Investors and the New Corporate Governance' (1991) 69 *NCL Rev* 1135, at 1150.

[15] *Company Law Reform* Cmnd. 5391 (1973) para. 62.

[16] *The Responsibilities of the British Public Company* Final Report of the CBI Company Affairs Committee chaired by Lord Watkinson 19 September 1973 paras 27–33 and *Company Law Reform*, ibid.

[17] J. Charkham, 'The Bank and corporate governance: past, present and future' (1993) 33 *Bank of England Quarterly Bulletin* 388. The constituent bodies of the ISC are Association of British Insurers, Association of Investment Trust Companies, Association of Unit Trusts and Investment Funds, British Merchant Banking and Securities Houses Association and The National Association of Pension Funds Ltd.

[18] PRO NED's initial sponsors were the Bank of England, British Institute of Management, British Merchant Banking and Securities Houses Association, British Bankers' Association, Confederation of British Industry, ECI Ventures Limited, Institutional Shareholders' Committee, London Stock Exchange and 3i plc. PRO NED has since become a commercial enterprise, having being bought out by a partnership of PRO NED Management and Egon Zehnder International.

[19] For a description of PRO NED's activities in the intervening years, see Charkham, above n 17.

PRO NED published a Code of Recommended Practice on non-executive directors which was commended by the chairman of the London Stock Exchange to all public companies.

### (b) Fall-out of the 1980s

During the boom years and the intense takeover activity of the 1980s, the discussion of the role of institutional investors in corporate governance appeared to lose its momentum, and bodies such as the ISC lay dormant. However, in the late 1980s, the testing effect of the recession on management, a string of corporate collapses and dissatisfaction at excessive directors' remuneration put corporate governance back on the agenda.

### (c) Institutional Shareholders' Committee initiatives

In 1988, a new lease of life was injected into the ISC.[20] The Committee's first area of concern was management buy-outs.[21] The focus of the ISC subsequently expanded to more structural changes, and in 1991 it published statements of best practice on the role and duties of directors and the responsibilities of institutional shareholders. These were followed in 1992 by a suggested form of disclosure by companies of their research and development expenditure.

### (d) The Cadbury Code

Against this background came the formation in May 1991 of the Committee on the Financial Aspects of Corporate Governance under the chairmanship of Sir Adrian Cadbury (the 'Cadbury Committee'). The Committee was set up by the Financial Reporting Council, the London Stock Exchange and the accountancy profession, prompted by the lack of confidence in Britain in financial reporting and in the value of audits.[22] It followed a series of collapses of companies which had received clean audit reports shortly before their downfall. On 1 December 1992 it published its final report and set out its core recommendations in a Code of Best Practice ('the Cadbury Code'). In light of its terms of reference, the Committee's recommendations focused on the control and reporting functions of boards and the role of auditors. They built on the guidelines of PRO NED and the ISC (both of which have since been revised to include

---

[20] See C. Wolman, 'Forum for resolving City rows with industry revived' *Financial Times* 29 October 1988, at 6.      [21] See discussion below, section 4(2)(a).

[22] It consists of representatives of investment institutions, the CBI, the Stock Exchange, academics, accountants, and lawyers.

additional matters covered in the Cadbury Code). The key recommendations are:

(1) division of responsibilities at the head of a company (usually by separate persons holding the positions of chairman and chief executive);[23]

(2) appointment of a minimum of three non-executive directors, the majority of whom are independent,[24] for fixed terms[25] and by a formal appointment procedure;[26]

(3) availability of independent professional advice for directors at the company's expense;[27]

(4) establishment of an audit committee composed of at least three non-executive directors[28] and a remuneration committee composed wholly or mainly of non-executive directors;[29]

(5) disclosure of the remuneration of the chairman and the highest-paid director, broken down into constituent parts with an explanation of the calculation method of performance-related pay,[30] and relevant information regarding stock options, stock appreciation rights and pension contributions;

(6) limitation of directors' service contracts to three years (unless there is shareholder approval);[31] and

(7) reporting by the directors on the effectiveness of the company's system of internal control,[32] and that the business is a going concern[33] with supporting assumptions or qualifications as necessary.[34]

### (e) Enforcement

Various attempts[35] have been made in the United Kingdom to enact legislation dealing specifically with the appointment of non-

---

[23] Cadbury Code para. 1.2.
[24] Cadbury Code paras 1.3 and 2.2. The minimum of 3 non-executive directors flows from the audit committee requirement.    [25] Cadbury Code para. 2.3.
[26] Cadbury Code para. 2.4.    [27] Cadbury Code para. 1.5.
[28] Cadbury Code para. 4.3; Final Report para. 4.35. Cf., Draft Report para. 4.29 which fell short of prescribing a minimum number of non–executive directors.
[29] Cadbury Code para. 3.3.    [30] Cadbury Code para. 3.2.
[31] Cadbury Code para. 3.1.
[32] This requirement was activated for companies with accounting periods beginning on or after 1 January 1995 after the publication on 22 December 1994 of guidance for directors on the internal control statement.
[33] This requirement was activated for companies with accounting year ends from December 1994 after the publication on 7 November 1994 of guidance for directors and auditors on the going concern statement.    [34] Cadbury Code paras 4.5 and 4.6.
[35] E.g., various abortive private members' bills brought by Sir Brandon Rhys Williams including: Bill 38 1977 and Bill 52 1988–9.

executive directors and establishment of audit committees but have been unsuccessful.[36]

The Cadbury Report recommends instead that listed companies state in their annual report and accounts whether they comply with the Code and identify and give reasons for any areas of non-compliance.[37] It also recommends that certain specified aspects of the compliance statement which are capable of objective verification be reviewed by the company's auditors prior to publication. These recommendations have been given force by the London Stock Exchange which has made them continuing obligations of listing for United Kingdom companies.[38]

The listing rule came into effect in 1993 and this self-regulatory approach, which relies to a large extent on institutional shareholders to influence company practice,[39] has had some impact.[40]

However, the City Group for Small Companies has published an alternative code aimed at listed companies with market capitalizations below £250 million which, among other things, reduces the number of non-executives on a board from three to two, and does not require smaller companies to split the roles of chief executive and chairman.[41]

The Cadbury Committee saw the publication of the Code as a stage in an ongoing process of development, and recommended the establishment of a new committee by June 1995 to review the working of the Code.

#### (2) Australia

Corporate governance developments in Australia have in several respects followed a similar pattern to those in the United Kingdom. Thus, an institutional shareholders' association was formed in 1984 but disintegrated through lack of interest and the competing interests of members.[42] Spectacular corporate failures in the late 1980s highlighted the advantages of institutions playing a greater role in management and united them on a

---

[36] See Sir Arthur Knight, 'The Aims and Objectives of Corporate Bodies' in K. Midgley, (ed.) *Management Accountability and Corporate Governance* (London, The Macmillan Press Ltd, 1982), at 11.

[37] Final Report para. 3.7.

[38] Stock Exchange Listing Rule para. 12.43(j). Unlisted Securities Market companies are now also required to include a similar rule in their general undertaking to the Stock Exchange.

[39] Cadbury Committee Final Report para. 6.16.

[40] See discussion below, section 4(3)(a).

[41] 'Cadbury code rules are toned down for smaller companies' *The Independent*, 10 May 1994, at 27.

[42] E. Fry, 'Shareholders form watch-dog club' *Australian Financial Review* 4 October 1990, at 1 and 8. P. E. Moody, 'A more active role for institutional shareholders' *The Banker*, February 1979, at 49 also emphasizes that normally the competition between institutions militates against concerted action.

wider range of issues.[43] And, in 1989, PRO-NED Australia began operations,[44] one of its main objectives being to widen the pool from which directors were sought.[45]

### (a) Australian Investment Managers' Association

In October 1990 institutional investors began discussing the formation of an institutional shareholders club. In February 1991, the Australian Investment Managers' Group, now known as the Australian Investment Managers' Association ('AIMA') was formed. At last count, it had a membership of 53, including the major fund managers and several of the largest self-managed corporate superannuation funds.[46]

### (b) Corporate Practices and Conduct

In a separate development the Bosch Committee[47] produced a discussion paper entitled *Corporate Practices and Conduct* in June 1990, and published the final version of the paper in May 1991. The paper made broadly similar recommendations to those emanating from the United Kingdom regarding board structure and non-executive directors. In addition, it contained more detailed discussion of the role of the board of directors and directors' duties and recommended that public companies should develop, publish and enforce codes of ethics.

The AIMA responded to this initiative by writing to the chairmen of the top 150 Australian companies asking them to state in their annual reports

[43] Perhaps the defining event in the formation of AIMA was when Bond Corporation became involved in the Bell companies in Western Australia. See the evidence of Mr Hall to the Joint Committee on Corporations and Securities, *Role of institutional investors in Australia's capital markets*, Official Hansard Report, 18 May 1994, at 8.
[44] Founding Patrons: AMP Society, Australian Institute of Company Directors, Australian Stock Exchange Ltd., The BHP Company Ltd., BP Australia Ltd., Coca–Cola Amatil Ltd., National Australia Bank Ltd. Founding Sponsors: AIDC Limited, Australian Chamber of Commerce and Industry (formerly Confederation of Australian Industry), Australian Chamber of Manufactures, Australian Society of Certified Practising Accountants, Chamber of Manufactures of New South Wales, Reserve Bank of Australia, Rothmans Holdings Ltd. There are now also several additional sponsors.
[45] See further: G. Pease and K. McMillan, *The Independent Non–Executive Director* (Melbourne, Longman Professional, 1993), at 5; M. Gilchrist, 'Headhunting a Different Class of Director' *Business Review Weekly*, 26 November 1993, at 83.
[46] Evidence of Mr Hall to the Joint Committee on Corporations and Securities, above n 43, at 3.
[47] The committee was chaired by Mr Henry Bosch AO and consisted of the Australian Merchant Bankers Association, Australian Society of Certified Practising Accountants, Australian Stock Exchange Ltd., Business Council of Australia, Law Council of Australia (Business Law Section), the Australian Institute of Company Directors, The Institute of Chartered Accountants in Australia and the Securities Institute of Australia.

that they supported the principles formulated by the Bosch Committee and confirming that their companies would follow them. It also stated that its members would give preference in their investment decisions to those corporations which complied with the principles in the paper. The AIMA subsequently joined the Bosh Committee, and contributed to the second edition of *Corporate Practices and Conduct* which was published in 1993.

The second edition contained new sections on participation by share-holders (particularly institutional shareholders) in corporate governance, dealing with boardroom dissent and the role of company accountants and auditors.

Although the thrust of these recommendations is very similar to those of the Cadbury Committee, several points of distinction should be noted:

(1) the Bosch Committee recommends that the board contain a majority of non-executive directors a minimum of two of whom are truly independent;

(2) the recommendations regarding audit committees are aimed only at public company boards of sufficient size and refer to the committee having 'at least a majority of independent non-executive directors';

(3) there is no equivalent of the Cadbury Code requirement for directors to report on the effectiveness of the company's system of internal controls or that the company is a going concern;

(4) the Cadbury Committee's final report recommends that information about the relevant interests of directors should be disclosed in the directors' report. A proposal along these lines was put forward in the exposure draft of the second edition of *Corporate Practices and Conduct* but attracted strong opposition, and was removed from the final report.[48]

### (c) Enforcement

Korn/Ferry's survey in 1993 found that while 46 per cent of all respondents said they had adopted the principles contained in *Corporate Practices and Conduct*, only 28 per cent of them (that is, 13 per cent overall) made a statement to that effect in either the annual report or any other public document.[49] Further, the publication of *Corporate Practices and Conduct* does not appear to have had a major impact on board structure and composition in Australia.[50]

---

[48] H. Bosch, 'Cadbury report new findings' *Company Director*, February 1993, at 23.
[49] Korn/Ferry International and Australian Institute of Company Directors, *Boards of Directors in Australia 13th Study 1994*, at 12.
[50] See discussion below, section 4(3)(a).

Giving evidence to the inquiry into the role of institutional investors in Australia's capital markets in May 1994, Mr Hall on behalf of the AIMA stated that there had been a marked decline in reported adherence to *Corporate Practices and Conduct*, and considered that the process of structural reform in corporate governance had stalled.[51]

Australian Stock Exchange ('ASX') listing rules require listed companies to state in their annual reports whether they have an audit committee and, if they do not, to provide a statement explaining why.[52] However, at the time of writing, there is no formal requirement to comply with any other aspect of *Corporate Practices and Conduct* nor indeed with any other guidelines, nor to disclose the level of compliance.

Changing the listing requirements to ensure a minimum quota of non-executives has been mooted in Australia, but was not pursued.[53] In September 1994 the ASX issued a discussion paper seeking views on the introduction of a listing rule comparable to that of the London Stock Exchange. If introduced, it is envisaged that the rule would apply to annual reporting periods ending on or after 30 June 1996.[54]

### (3) Non-executive directors

A common feature of corporate governance reform proposals in both jurisdictions is the appointment of greater numbers of non-executive directors, with the expectation that they will not only bring a diversity of skills to the boards which they join, but will also monitor the conduct of the executives. This approach has been criticized on both ideological and practical levels.

#### (a) Ideological objections

The Cadbury Code sparked controversy in the United Kingdom for being divisive in expecting non-executive directors to monitor the performance of the board within a unitary board structure.[55] Much of this debate has its origins in the draft Fifth Company Law Directive[56] which was first

---

[51] Above n 43, at 6.      [52] ASX Listing Rule 3C(3)(i).

[53] The House of Representatives Standing Committee on Legal and Constitutional Affairs recommended in para. 5.5.22 of its report *Corporate Practices and the Rights of the Shareholders* (28 November 1991) that ASX listing rules be amended to require every listed company to establish an audit committee with the chairman and a majority, or all, of the members being non-executive directors. Similar recommendations were made by the Senate Standing Committee of the same name in the *Company Directors' Duties* (Canberra, AGPS, November 1989), ¶ 8.15.

[54] ASX Discussion Paper, *Disclosure of Corporate Governance Practices by Listed Companies*, (September 1994), at 2.

[55] See two articles by Sir Owen Green, 'Why Cadbury leaves a bitter taste' *Financial Times*, 9 June 1992, at 19; and 'A simple aim and a single board' *Director*, April 1994, at 38.

[56] OJ 1972 No. C 131/49.

published by the European Commission in 1972. Article 21a of the Directive provides for a mandatory distinction between executive and non-executive directors and for there to be either a majority of non-executive directors on the boards of public companies, or two separate boards, for management and for supervision. The Directive also requires employee involvement in company decision-making.[57] The Directive has been controversial in the United Kingdom and has also failed to obtain approval from a majority of member States.[58]

A related theme to these objections is that filling the board with non-executive directors will be detrimental to company performance. The Institute of Directors has added its voice to these critics, saying that the Code is too prescriptive and limiting, and is stifling business enterprise.[59]

This issue has not caused the same degree of divisiveness in Australia. Indeed, *AWA Ltd.* v. *Daniels*[60] expressly acknowledges the monitoring role of non-executive directors and the implications of this for directors' duties. However, similar arguments to those made in the United Kingdom regarding the importance of the calibre and mix of directors and the need for the board to act cohesively as a group and to place greater emphasis on company performance and less emphasis on issues of conformance have been made in a publication of the Independent Working Party into Corporate Governance entitled *Strictly Boardroom*.[61] On the other hand, that document does advocate the establishment of audit committees comprised entirely of non-executive directors, with the chairman of the committee and the majority of its members also independent of the company, on the basis that the best way for a board to be able to focus

[57] The draft Directive has been the subject of much controversy which raises issues beyond the scope of this book, but possibly also explains why in the UK, by contrast with the US, shareholder involvement in corporate governance has not taken the form of shareholder advisory panels. The current version is published in OJ 26 C 240, 9 September 1983, at 2–38, as amended in 1989. Amendments relating to barriers to take-overs were made in 1991. For an overview of the progress of the draft 5th Directive see J. H. Farrar *et al.*, *Farrar's Company Law* (3rd edn., London, Butterworths, 1991), at 29–31 and references cited; and J. P. Charkham, *Keeping Good Company: A Study of Corporate Governance in Five Countries* (Oxford, Clarendon Press, 1994), at 279. The issue has recently been revived by the Labour party. See P. Hosking, 'Labour drives for worker directors' *The Independent*, 25 September 1994, at 1. For selected views of the issues raised by the debate see K. Midgley, (ed.) *Management Accountability and Corporate Governance* (London, The Macmillan Press Ltd, 1982) *passim*. For a critical examination of the operation of shareholder advisory committees as they operate in the US see Barnard, above n 14.

[58] DTI Consultative Document 'Amended Proposal for a Fifth Directive on the Harmonisation of Company Law in the European Community,' (January 1990), ¶ 15.1.

[59] 'Crunch time for Cadbury body' *The Observer*, 20 February 1994, and R. Thomson, 'Bosses lay into Cadbury rules' *The Independent*, 8 May 1994, Business on Sunday, at 1.

[60] (1992) 7 ACSR 759; 10 ACLC 933.

[61] The Independent Working Party into Corporate Governance, *Strictly Boardroom: Improving Governance to Enhance Company Performance* (The Business Library, Melbourne, 1993).

on performance is for it to be confident that its conformance duties are being properly handled.[62]

## (b) Practical objections

Other commentators have criticized the reliance on independent non-executive directors to prevent a recurrence of the excesses of the 1980s on practical grounds.

They point out that despite formal independence from the companies to which they are appointed, non-executives are not socially independent. A survey of the United Kingdom's largest companies conducted in 1991 found that 70 per cent of companies relied on the 'old boy' network for appointing independent directors.[63] In Australia, Korn/Ferry's 1994 study found that the selection process for non-executive directors was: 35 per cent by informal input by directors, 33 per cent on the recommendation by a major shareholder, 14 per cent following the recommendation of a nomination committee and 10 per cent by executive search.[64]

Further, even in the minority of companies which have professionalized their selection procedure, non-executives are still appointed by management and are dependent upon management for their tenure as directors.

An additional factor militating against their willingness to monitor energetically is that most outside directors are chief executive officers of other public companies and are unlikely to monitor more energetically than they believe they should be monitored by their own boards.[65]

There is also the question of what are the realistic expectations of a person who spends a relatively small amount of time on company affairs. Surveys have found that non-executive directors in the United Kingdom spend approximately 15 days per year on the affairs of the company on whose board they sit.[66] In Australia, the average is 22 days.[67] (Footnote 67 appears on p. 30).

---

[62] Ibid., at 61.

[63] See the illuminating description of the appointment process by Sir Adrian Cadbury, 'Owners and Investors' in *Creative Tension?* (London, NAPF, 1990), at 31–2, and 'Statutory support for the Cadbury Code?' *Management Accounting*, July/August 1993, at 4. See also B. G. M. Main, 'The Nominations Process and Corporate Governance—A Missing Link?' (1994) 2 *Corporate Governance Research Papers* 161.

[64] Above n 49, at 9. The other effect of the smaller business community in Australia is that there is a tendency for a small number of people to take on a large number of appointments. In 1994 a survey found that there were 40 directors holding 5 or more board seats each, and 9 holding 10 or more board positions: A. Ferguson, 'Life gets tough for the super directors' *Business Review Weekly*, 12 September 1994, at 50.

[65] R. J. Gilson and R. Kraakman, 'Reinventing the Outside Director: An Agenda for Institutional Investors' (1991) 43 *Stan L Rev* 863, at 875.

[66] A survey by Merton Associates, *Non Executive Directors of plcs, Performance Survey September 1991: Greater Authority and Accountability for Non Executive Directors in Corporate Governance in the 1990s*, at 27, found that 69% of non-executive directors spend

One of the Cadbury Code's more outspoken critics is Sir Owen Green. He has consistently opposed the Code's emphasis on non-executive directors and notes that 1993 (a year of significantly increased compliance with the Code) witnessed more dramatic setbacks or failures and an increase in the controversy on directors' pay.[68]

### (c) Reform proposals

A common theme in both practical and ideological objections to current proposals regarding the appropriate role of non-executive directors is the tension inherent in a board with shared goals but at the same time consisting of the watchers and the watched.[69]

Reform proposals have therefore taken as their premise that non-executive directors can perform a useful monitoring function, but that the system needs to be changed to break their link with management and make them dependent on shareholders.[70] However, a further common feature of the proposals is their focus on institutional shareholders, at the potential expense of the interests of the other categories of shareholder.[71] This issue is examined in greater detail in section 5 below. But first it is necessary to examine the incentives and disincentives to institutions using their influence in the companies in which they invest, and the issues in respect of which they tend to be most active.

between 10 and 20 days per year. The 1991 Korn/Ferry International survey, (above n 4) revealed a reasonable fluctuation in the amount of time spent on the company's affairs, with the most common being between 13 and 20 days for companies with sales over £500m and between 10 and 12 days in respect of companies with sales between £150m and £500m. Similar results were obtained by PRO NED in March 1989: *Non-Executive Directors: A Survey of Fees and Related Facts* at 7–8.

[67] Korn/Ferry, (above n 49), at 11.

[68] Sir Owen Green, 'A simple aim and a single board', above n 55.

[69] M. Bishop, 'Watching the boss' *The Economist*, 29 January 1994, Corporate Governance Survey.

[70] E. B. Rock, 'The Logic and (Uncertain) Significance of Institutional Shareholder Activism' (1991) 79 *Geo LJ* 445; Gilson and Kraakman, above n 65, at 881; J. C. Coffee, Jr., 'Institutional Investors as Corporate Monitors: Are Takeovers Obsolete?' in J. H. Farrar, (ed.) *Takeovers, Institutional Investors and the Modernization of Corporate Laws* (Auckland, Oxford University Press, 1993) and Davies, above n 12, at 281–2.

[71] As to the disadvantages of too close a relationship developing between institutions and management see Bishop, above n 69; and Hill, above n 11, at 602–3, who gives the example of the alliance between AMP and Westpac.

## 3. INFLUENCES ON INSTITUTIONAL ACTIVISM

### (1) Incentives

#### (a) The size of collective institutional shareholdings

The proportion of shares collectively held by institutions operates as a stimulus for activism, since it makes selling a less viable option. In cases where the price of stock has been diminished by poor governance there are likely to be losses on sale, and difficulty in finding a substitute investment.

#### (b) Recession

In buoyant economic conditions the differing objectives of institutional investors are more likely to come to the fore,[72] thus reducing the scope for collective action. In addition, when companies are operating profitably there is likely to be little inducement to interfere with management.

#### (c) Social pressure

The passive stance taken by institutions in the corporate collapses of the 1980s has attracted widespread criticism, particularly in Australia.[73] However, the more cynical may query whether this stigma may be as temporary as the influence of the recession.

#### (d) Indexing

It is sometimes argued that the growing popularity of index-tracking funds will encourage institutional activism, since if a fund has acquired its shares as part of a basket of shares or 'indexed fund', the act of selling and reinvesting out of the index or in other shares within the index distorts the whole point of indexing.[74] However, other commentators have pointed out[75] that since such funds compete on their low running costs, their managers are unlikely to be attracted by a strategy which involves expenditure on monitoring.

---

[72] See T. Jackson, 'The Institutions Get Militant' *Financial Times*, 11 June 1991, at 18.
[73] Hill, above n 11, at 597–8.
[74] 'Indexing assumes that an investor is diversified throughout an entire community of shares . . . and that, over time, the performance of the entire index, left untouched, will outperform managed funds. Indexing permits an investor to eliminate research costs and transaction costs attendant to selective trading': Barnard, above n 14, at 1152.
[75] Davies, above n 12, at 280 and J. C. Coffee, Jr., 'Liquidity Versus Control: The Institutional Investor as Corporate Monitor' (1991) 91 *Colum L Rev* 1277.

## (2) Disincentives

### (a) Cost-benefit

Although the overall proportion of shares held by institutions is high, this is in most cases composed of a wide spread of small shareholdings. Further, the only measure which the clients of institutional shareholders use to assess their performance is financial. As a result, if companies are delivering financial returns, it is often considered not to be cost effective for institutions to be involving themselves in the governance of each company in their portfolios.

### (b) Competition

The market in which institutional shareholders operate is highly competitive. Institutions may therefore be reluctant to raise a matter openly, in case this causes their competitors to sell down their holdings and consequently depress the value of the holding of the active shareholder. These competitive influences also make the task of forming and maintaining a coalition against the best efforts of management difficult.[76]

Another consequence of the competitive market is the 'free rider' problem. Institutional shareholders may be reluctant to bear the cost of conduct which benefits all shareholders equally.

### (c) Conflicts of interest

Many of the companies in which institutional shareholders invest are also clients of the institutions.[77] This situation may arise, for example, where a pension fund is established by a company or where a fund manager is a subsidiary of a merchant bank of which the company is a client.[78] Conflicts may be compounded where companies and institutional shareholders have common directors or where the trustees of a fund are also directors of the company.

Fund managers in such situations may be unwilling to jeopardize their ability to obtain or retain the management of the company's business by opposing board proposals. Conflicts may also be indirect, in the sense that a fund manger may fear that it will lose business from the corporate

---

[76] Davies, above n 12, at 277–8, N. Cohen, 'When the time comes for shareholders to stand up and be counted' *Financial Times*, 6 April 1992, at 12; and P. Syvret and A. Deans, 'Tactical win to Goodman' *Australian Financial Review*, 11 August 1994, at 23.

[77] A. Bernoth, 'Tarnished handshakes' *Sunday Times* 21 August 1994.

[78] Charkham, above n 57, at 286.

community generally if it is perceived as an 'activist'.[79] Another risk in being perceived to be 'activist' is that it may put an end to the flow of soft information that management provides to 'friendly' securities analysts and institutions.[80]

### (d) Short-term horizons

There has been considerable criticism of institutional investors on the grounds of short termism.[81] The underlying theme is that in order for companies to be successful and internationally competitive, they require shareholders who will make a long-term commitment. The institutions are said to fall short of this ideal by being overeager to sell shares in under-performing companies and by favouring the takeover market for the punishment of poor management.[82] Further, it is argued[83] that the institutions encourage short-termist management by placing pressure upon companies to deliver dividends[84] without regard to overall profitability. Pay structures for executives are said to exacerbate this tendency by granting bonuses where profits exceed planned growth in a single year or where a company's earnings per share are increased above a specified threshold over periods of one to three years.[85]

On the other hand, it is recognized that fund managers are also the victims of short-termism in that their performance is assessed on a quarterly basis,[86] and the level of competition in the market causes investors to chase returns.[87] This then feeds back into a short-term investment horizon.[88]

The charges of 'short-termism' levelled at the institutions are addressed

---

[79] Coffee, above n 75.

[80] B. S. Black, 'Shareholder passivity reexamined' (1990) 89 *Mich L Rev* 520, at 602.

[81] See, e.g., J. Charkham, *Corporate governance and the market for control of companies*, Bank of England Panel Paper No 25, March 1989 and above n 14; Institute for Public Policy Research, *Industrial Policy Paper No. 3: Takeovers and Short-termism in the UK* (London, IPPR, 1990) and S. Hoyle, 'Shaken to task' *Australian Financial Review*, 13 September 1994, at 18.

[82] S. Holberton, 'Short-termism: myth or reality?' *Financial Times*, 11 February 1991, at 4, and Jackson, above n 72.

[83] See, e.g., C. Leadbeater, 'Lilley warns of dangers in deal-making culture' *Financial Times*, 25 October 1990, at 8.

[84] See N. Cohen 'Warning on Automatic Dividend Increases' *Financial Times*, 16 December 1991, at 5. See also 'A Policy for Dividends' *Financial Times*, 11 March 1992, at 18.

[85] S. Holberton, 'Why the ideal board remains so elusive' *Financial Times*, 4 July 1990, at 10 and Korn/Ferry, Carré/Orban International, *Boards of Directors Study UK (1994)* at 37.

[86] See Charkham, above n 14, at 12.

[87] Life Insurance Federation of Australia submission to *Institutional Investor Inquiry*, above n 9, at 246.

[88] Charkham, above n 57, at 291 who considers that the influence of performance measurement of fund managers on short-termism may be exaggerated.

in various policy statements. For example, the ISC publication on the responsibilities of institutional shareholders[89] advocates a more extensive dialogue between institutional shareholders and management, with the expectation that where a company has kept its shareholders informed of its long-term plans, confidence and understanding will develop, making it less likely that a hostile takeover bid will succeed.

Complaints by companies that they are discouraged from spending on research and development by shareholders who would rather see money spent on bigger dividends or on acquisitions are addressed in the ISC's publication on disclosure of research and development expenditure which sets out the information which would be useful to institutional investors to enable them to assess a company's long-term growth potential.[90]

The AIMA has sought to tackle the other side of this issue, by releasing a position paper entitled 'Understanding Investment Performance Measurement'[91] which seeks to encourage survey organizations to place greater emphasis on longer-term horizons, and to measure other parts of the investment process, such as the investment objectives and strategy of the fund.

It remains to be seen what impact these measures will have on future institutional investment patterns.[92]

### (e) Potential liability as a shadow director

Companies legislation in both jurisdictions includes a shadow director or 'person in accordance with whose directions or instructions the directors . . . are accustomed to act' within the definition of director for certain purposes.[93] In England, liability for wrongful trading[94] can be imposed on shadow directors. Thus, they may be liable to make a

---

[89] ISC *The Responsibilities of Institutional Shareholders in the UK*, December 1991.

[90] In a break from the previous tradition of ISC initiatives originating in the ABI, the ISC proposed the guidelines after it was approached by the Electrical Equipment Association: see N. Cohen, 'Institutions tackle "short-termism" ' *Financial Times*, 30 April 1992, at 8.

[91] 17 May 1994.

[92] Comparing the period 1963–7 with that of 1973–7 the Committee to Review the Functioning of Financial Institutions, chaired by Sir Harold Wilson, Cmnd. 7937, 1980 (paras 7.13 and 7.18) found that the average holding period for insurance companies and pension funds fell from 24 years to 8 years in the case of insurance companies and 6 years for pension funds (although rising to 10 years and 11 years respectively in 1978), that for investment trusts the period halved from 10 to 5 years and for unit trusts the period was less than 3 years. See also A. Simpson, 'Balancing Power with Responsibility' *Investors Chronicle*, 24 September 1993, at x.

[93] Section 741, CA 1985 (UK); s. 60(1), CL (Aust).

[94] Section 214, IA 1986 (UK). Other provisions which apply to shadow directors include s. 309, CA 1985 (UK) (duty to have regard to the interests of employees), and ss. 319, 320–2 and 330–46, CA 1985 (UK) (which concern contracts with and loans to directors).

contribution to the company's assets if the company goes into insolvent liquidation and it is established that at some time before liquidation they knew or ought to have known that there was no reasonable prospect of avoiding insolvent liquidation.

A comparable provision regarding insolvent trading applies in Australia,[95] which potentially attracts civil and criminal penalties[96] as well as a liability to compensate the company[97] if:

(1)  the company incurs a debt when it is insolvent, or becomes insolvent as a result of incurring the debt;

(2)  there are reasonable grounds for suspecting that the company is insolvent or would so become insolvent; and

(3)  the director was aware that those grounds existed, or a reasonable person in a like position in a company in the like circumstances of that company would have been so aware.

Other relevant provisions in the Corporation Law are the codified directors' duties to act honestly, with reasonable care and diligence and the prohibition on making improper use of company information.[98] Contravention of these provisions again potentially attracts civil and criminal penalties.[99]

The shadow director provisions in the Australian legislation are not made specifically applicable to particular statutory provisions. Rather, they apply unless a contrary intention appears. They have been held to apply to the codified directors' duties,[100] and although there are no specific decisions on this question they would appear to be applicable to the insolvent trading provisions.

However, the shadow director provisions have been interpreted to apply only where the shadow director has influence over the whole board[101] or, at the very least, a governing majority of it.[102] It has also been held that the words 'accustomed to act' must refer to acts over a period of time and as a regular course of conduct.[103] Although the consequences of being a shadow director are potentially significant, most institutional activism would be very unlikely to attract the provisions.

---

[95]  Section 588G, CL (Aust).

[96]  Part 9.4B, CL (Aust).

[97]  Section 588J, CL (Aust).

[98]  Sections 232(2),(4) and (5), CL (Aust).

[99]  Above n 96.                    [100]  *CAC (NSW)* v. *Drysdale* (1978) 141 CLR 236.

[101]  *Re Lo-line Electric Motors Ltd.* [1988] Ch 477 at 489 and *Kuwait Asia Bank EC* v. *National Mutual Life Nominees Ltd.* [1991] 1 AC 187 (PC).

[102]  *Re Unisoft Group Ltd. (No. 3)* [1994] 1 BCLC 609, also reported as *Re Unisoft Group Ltd. (No. 2)* [1994] BCC 766.                    [103]  Ibid.

## (f) Disincentives relating specifically to voting

Many of the disincentives described above, and in particular the factors of cost-benefit (judged against short-term horizons and liquidity requirements) and conflicts of interest are equally relevant in inhibiting institutional shareholders from exercising voting rights.

In 1991, the ISC conducted a survey of the voting practices of its members, and found that insurance companies were the only institutional investors to use their votes on a regular basis on mundane issues as well as contentious ones.[104] Since then, there has been a trend towards slightly greater use by institutions of voting rights. A separate survey by the ISC on the extent to which the top 20 institutional holdings were voted in 20 major public companies in 1993 found that on average 34 per cent of all shares were voted, compared with the figure of 20 per cent in a similar survey conducted three years earlier.[105]

The view of virtually all interested parties and commentators is that it would be desirable for institutions to make greater use of their voting rights, and the case for following United States developments regarding compulsory voting and confidential ballots has been debated.[106]

However, in addition to the general disincentives to voting there are both practical and legal obstacles which operate specifically in relation to voting which need to be addressed.

### (i) *Practical obstacles*[107]

Practical obstacles take several forms. There is the administrative task of keeping track of the meeting-dates and proposed resolutions in a diversified portfolio. In cases where funds are managed externally, there are the additional factors of keeping track of the extent to which the discretion to vote has been delegated and obtaining instructions. The short notice-periods for shareholder meetings mean that it is usually impossible for the managers to obtain instructions from trustees in time if instructions are required. Even where these obstacles are overcome, the vast majority of investors cast their votes by proxy, which means that often they are not brought into play unless a poll is called for.

---

[104] 11 out of 13 insurance companies surveyed said that they voted at all times. This compared with only one out of 7 merchant banks, one out of 13 unit trusts and 10 out of 35 investment trusts. No clear trend emerged amongst the pension funds, with 20% stating they voted at all times and 23% saying they never voted.

[105] ISC, *Report on Investigation of Use of Voting Rights by Institutions*, July (1993) UK.

[106] See further regarding compulsory voting for funds covered by the Employee Retirement Income Security Act 1974 ('ERISA') the submission by Corporate Governance International Pty. Ltd. to the *Institutional Investor Inquiry*, above n 9, at 545 ff.

[107] See further: Simpson, above n 92.

One development which helps to overcome the practical problem of keeping track of all the company meetings is the establishment of proxy voting services. NAPF has established a proxy voting service which tracks all the companies in the FT-SE 100 index, prepares reports on matters to be voted at each general meeting, states whether the matter is considered contentious and whether it conforms with NAPF guidelines on best practice in corporate governance.[108]

An alternative source of voting advice in Britain is Pensions Investments Research Consultants ('PIRC') which was founded in 1986 by a consortium of local authorities as an ethical issues research organization for pension funds. It offers a proxy voting service covering the top 250 companies ahead of their annual meetings, analysis of corporate governance issues, and specific advice to clients on how to vote at shareholders meetings.[109] PIRC's advice not only reflects the principles of the Cadbury Code, but also monitors environmental reporting, political donations, directors' remuneration and the 'insulation' of directors, whereby executive directors are not required to retire regularly for re-election by shareholders.[110]

The first Australian proxy advice service, Independent Shareholder Services (ISS Australia), was established in August 1994.[111] It provides coverage of the top 50 companies, but aims to expand over time to the top 200. It analyses proposals in detail and provides preliminary reports based on interim announcements but, unlike its United States sponsor, it does not provide a firm recommendation on which way to vote.[112]

### (ii) Legal obstacles

### (A) Who can vote?

Where a fund is managed externally, there is a trend towards making specific provision on the subject of voting in the fund management agreement.[113] However, although this removes the practical uncertainty as to who has the power to exercise the vote, it does not specifically address

---

[108] N. Cohen, 'Investors urged to behave like owners' *Financial Times*, 7 May 1992, Pension Fund Investment Survey at VIII.

[109] R. Northedge, 'Private clients turn to ethical adviser' *The Daily Telegraph*, 5 October 1994, at 31.

[110] PIRC voting guidelines 1994, para. 2.3.

[111] By the Partners Group, Corporate Governance International and International Shareholder Services Inc.

[112] I. Ries, 'Shareholders put on muscle' *Australian Financial Review*, 27 October 1994, at 72.

[113] E.g., under cl. 12 of the AIMA standard investment agreement the trustee retains the ability to give directions to the investment manager, but in the absence of any direction authorizes the manager to exercise or direct the custodian regarding the right to vote attached to shares in the portfolio as the manager sees fit.

the legal uncertainty which affects moneys held on trust, such as superannuation funds and unit trusts, which is whether trustees have the power to delegate the discretion as to how to vote to the investment manager, in light of the primary duty of the trustee to supervise the trust and the trust fund at all times.[114]

In Australia, there are two further legal obstacles which affect the ability of institutions to vote in some circumstances.

### (B) Section 1069(1)(k) Corporations Law

This section applies to public unit trusts (also called prescribed interest schemes) and requires an approved trust deed to contain covenants requiring the trustee or representative to obtain approval from a majority of unit holders before voting in respect of the election of directors. This provision was inserted to overcome the decision in *Australian Fixed Trusts Pty. Ltd.* v. *Clyde Industries Ltd.*[115] Industry participants have tended to regard section 1069(1)(k) as requiring the holder's consent to be obtained after the relevant company has issued a notice of the meeting for the election of directors,[116] which in many cases makes obtaining consent in time for the meeting a practical impossibility. The Australian Securities Commission ('ASC') has indicated that it will grant relief from this section in certain circumstances, but the exemption does not apply if the trustee or manager or their associates are entitled to more than 10 per cent of the voting shares.[117] Both the section and the limited ASC exemption have been criticized,[118] and consideration is being given to removing this legislative restriction.

### (C) Takeover legislation

There are two aspects of the takeover legislation which may inhibit collective institutional activism, the mandatory offer requirement and the obligation to disclose substantial shareholdings.

In broad terms, section 615 of the Corporations Law prohibits a person acquiring shares in a company if the acquisition would lead to the person becoming entitled to more than 20 per cent of the voting shares in

---

[114] See further G. J. Jones, 'Delegation by Trustees: A Reappraisal' (1959) 22 *Mod L Rev* 381, D. Harding, 'Do Institutional Investors in Australia have a Fiduciary Responsibility to Vote?' *Proxy Voting Conference Convened by the AIMA and the Institute of Corporate Managers, Secretaries and Administrators Ltd.*, 7 September 1994, at 14–16, and J. H. Farrar 'Legal restraints on Institutional Investor Involvement in Corporate Governance', (December 1993) published as part of the AIMA submission to the *Institutional Investor Inquiry*, above n 9, at 367 ff.                              [115] (1959) 59 SR (NSW) 33.
[116] ASC submission to *Institutional Investor Inquiry*, above n 9, at 565.
[117] ASC Policy Statement 55.
[118] See e.g., Harding, above n 114, at 9 and I. Ries, 'Directors face more pressure' *Australian Financial Review*, 11 February 1994, at 40 and back page.

the company, unless that person makes a takeover offer.[119] For the purpose of determining 'entitlement' to shares, the holdings of associates are included. The definition of associate extends to those with whom the person has an understanding for controlling the board or the affairs of the body corporate. There is accordingly a risk that collective action will involve more than 20 per cent of the voting shares.[120] However, section 615 only inhibits collective action if the institution wishes to acquire shares.

Part 6.7 of the Corporations Law requires a 'substantial shareholder' of a listed public company to disclose its interest to the company within two business days of acquiring the interest and to serve a copy of the disclosure notice on the Stock Exchange. A 'substantial shareholding' arises when a person is 'entitled' to not less than 5 per cent of the relevant class of shares. 'Entitlement' is calculated in the same way as for the purposes of section 615,[121] and accordingly may be triggered by collective institutional action.[122]

## 4. INSTITUTIONAL ACTIVISM AND IDENTIFIED COMPLAINTS

The incentives and disincentives outlined above mean that institutions are more likely to exercise their influence to implement universal guidelines for best practice rather than to address issues which are specific to a particular company. The following discussion examines the extent to which institutional activism has in practice addressed the complaints outlined in Chapter 2.

### (1) Dilution of equity stake or voting rights

Institutional shareholders have consistently opposed proposals with the potential to reduce their stake or influence within a company and which consequently make it easier for management to insulate itself against a takeover.[123] Such proposals may, for example, take the form of an issue of shares which is not first offered to existing shareholders on a *pro rata* basis,

---

[119] See further, Ch. 10 section 2(1)(b)(ii).

[120] Cf., Rule 9.1 of the City Code on Takeovers and Mergers regarding mandatory offers in the UK. Note 2 to Rule 9.1 states that the Panel does not normally regard the action of shareholders voting together on particular resolutions as constituting them as a group acting in concert, although a voting agreement may indicate the existence of a concert party.

[121] Cf., s. 204 CA 1985 (UK), (the equivalent 'concert party' provision regarding reporting requirements for substantial shareholders) which applies only to agreements which include provision for the acquisition of shares, and in pursuance of which shares are in fact acquired.

[122] See further D. Harding, 'Institutional Investor Voting—Acting Independently' *AIMA Newsletter*, October 1994, at 10.

[123] See Davies, above n 12, at 274–5.

issues of non-voting shares or conversely of super-voting shares. Each of these examples is considered in greater detail below.

### (a) Pre-emption rights[124]

Disapplication of pre-emption rights became a controversial issue[125] in the United Kingdom in 1986 and 1987 when companies tried to raise money overseas.[126] In response to concern about dilution of shareholders' interests, the investment committees of the Association of British Insurers ('ABI') and the National Association of Pension Funds ('NAPF') reissued guidelines on the circumstances in which their members would consent to a disapplication of their statutory pre-emption rights.[127] In an effort to resolve the conflicting interests of the parties involved, the London Stock Exchange convened a pre-emption group which included representatives of institutional investors and companies. The group recommended guidelines which were subsequently agreed by both the ABI and the NAPF,[128] and which influenced Stock Exchange Listing Rules.[129]

### (b) Shares with differential voting rights

The issue of non-voting equity shares arouses strong reactions in institutional shareholders because of its potential to entrench management and so operate as a takeover defence. This issue split the Jenkins Committee, the majority taking the view that a legislative ban on non-voting shares would be too drastic a step.[130] Although opposing a ban on issuing shares with differential voting rights, the committee recommended that non-voting or restricted voting shares be clearly labelled as such.[131] Nevertheless, opposition by institutions to the creation of equity shares which do not carry full voting rights has been maintained,[132] and it would appear that on a practical level this opposition has been largely successful.

---

[124] Pre-emption rights, in this context, refers to the right of existing shareholders to have the first opportunity to subscribe for any new issue of shares in a company.

[125] See generally: 'Pre-emption Rights' (1987) *Bank of England Quarterly Bulletin* 545; and Davies, above n 12, at 274–5.

[126] N. Bunker, 'Pre-emption rights "still on agenda" ' *Weekend Financial Times*, 4 May 1989, at XIV.

[127] See ss. 89–95, CA 1985 (UK).

[128] The guidelines confine disapplication of rights to a maximum of 5% of the company's issued share capital in any one year, with a rolling limit of 7.5% in any 3-year period.

[129] See further Davies, above n 12, at 274–5.

[130] Jenkins Committee, *Report of the Company Law Committee*, Cmnd. 1749, (1962) paras 123–40 (UK). See also the Note of Dissent at 207.

[131] Listing Rules, App. 1 to Ch. 13, r. 2 and r. 3 require that the words 'non-voting', 'limited voting' or 'restricted voting' appear in the designation of such shares.

[132] ISC, above n 90, at 5.

In June 1993, there were only 50 United Kingdom companies (with a total market capitalization of £13,535.2 million) which had differential voting rights,[133] and Weinberg observes that 'there are no instances in recent years of a company seeking a listing for any new class of non-voting equity capital.'[134] Conversely, there are recent examples of non-voting shares being enfranchised.[135]

In Australia, ASX Listing Rule 3K(2) incorporates the one share one vote rule for listed companies. However this rule has been put to the test in recent times. In 1990, in response to '[c]hanges of practice on overseas stock exchanges, the introduction of Exempt Foreign Company status, privatization proposals and an application by The News Corporation Limited ('News Corp.') to be allowed to issue limited voting shares', the ASX sought views on the desirability of enabling companies to issue ordinary shares with no voting rights.[136] As a result of that process, the ASX determined that, as a general rule, such shares were inappropriate for listed companies,[137] although exceptions have been made for companies such as co-operative building societies and to enable governments to retain a golden share in privatized utilities.[138]

News Corp. again stimulated debate on the question of differential voting rights in late 1993, this time with a proposal to issue super-voting shares. The original proposal (for a 1-for-10 issue of non-transferable super-voting shares with 25 votes per share)[139] was strongly opposed by the AIMA[140] and was subsequently revised so that the shares would be transferable and the block of super voting shares restricted to 40 per cent of total voting rights.[141] The revised scheme also included a proposed

---

[133] London Stock Exchange, 'Non-voting and restricted voting shares in UK companies' *Stock Exchange Quarterly*, April–June 1993, at 12.

[134] M. A. Weinberg, (Consulting Ed.) *Weinberg & Blank on Take-overs and Mergers* (5th edn, London, Sweet & Maxwell, 1990, looseleaf) para. 3–805. See also Davies, above n 12, at 274.

[135] H. Davidson, 'Regent Street truce begins to crack' *Sunday Times*, 16 May 1993, Business Section at 5.

[136] ASX Discussion Paper *Appropriate Voting Rights for Equity Securities*, (October 1990), at 3.

[137] ASX Discussion Paper, *Differential Voting Rights*, (November 1993), at 2.

[138] I. Ries, 'Super vote a Murdoch winner' *Australian Financial Review*, 13 October 1993, at 27 and back page.

[139] I. Ries, 'Takeover rules concern in News' super vote sidestep' *Australian Financial Review*, 2 November 1993, at 24 and back page.

[140] B. Dunstan, 'An ASX bombshell' *Australian Financial Review*, 11 November 1993; at 1 and 23; S. Hoyle and N. Tabakoff, 'Managers urge inquiry on News super-voting issue' *Australian Financial Review*, 12 November 1993, at 27; and M. Furness, 'Big funds united against News plan' *The Australian*, 12 November 1993 at 17. Cf., S. Fridman, 'The News Corporation Super Shares Proposal: Crime of the Century or Tempest in a Teapot' (1994) 4 *Australian Journal of Corporate Law* 184.

[141] N. Chenoweth, 'Murdoch all set to claim a super win' *Australian Financial Review*, 22 November 1993, at 1 and 22.

amendment to News Corp.'s articles amending the threshold for launching a takeover bid from 20 per cent of ordinary shares to 20 per cent of voting shares.[142] Nevertheless, opposition to the scheme by the AIMA[143] and two of the largest investment institutions[144] persisted, and despite a further modification to the plan which would have restricted takeover bidders to offering equal prices for super and ordinary shares,[145] the proposal to issue super-voting shares was ultimately withdrawn.[146]

In the end, News Corp. gained support for an issue and listing of non-voting shares, but with a dividend premium of at least 20 per cent over the ordinary shares.[147]

## (2) Self-interested transactions by controllers

### (a) Management buy-outs

In 1988 when the ISC was revived in Britain,[148] its first area of concern was management buy-outs. Working in co-operation with the Panel on Takeovers and Mergers, it produced guidelines addressing ways in which the inevitable conflicts of interest might be reduced and the provision of sufficient advice and information to shareholders might be ensured. The main features of the guidelines are that proposed management buy-outs are unlikely to be favourably received unless they are supported by independent non-executive directors of long standing who have taken independent financial advice, and that in most cases the offeror should not be advised by the company's previous advisers.[149]

[142] Ibid. See further regarding the takeover requirements Ch. 10 section 2(1)(b)(ii).

[143] N. Chenoweth, 'Appeal to Lavarch on News super shares' *Australian Financial Review*, 23 November 1993, at 20.

[144] I. Ries, 'Big guns open fire on Murdoch's super shares' *Australian Financial Review*, 30 November 1993, at 52 and 24.

[145] N. Chenoweth, 'News Corp. waters down super shares proposal' *Australian Financial Review*, 1 December 1993, at 22.

[146] N. Chenoweth and T. Dodd, 'Murdoch yields on super shares' *Australian Financial Review*, 9 December 1993, at 1. The incident sparked the formation of an Expert Panel of Inquiry, which reported in March 1994 that it would be premature to introduce super-voting shares in Australia because there are insufficient safeguards for minority shareholders and that policy issues concerning the role of shareholders in monitoring the performance of company management would first need to be addressed, but that super voting shares should not be prohibited out of hand: Report by Expert Panel of Inquiry into Desirability of Super Voting Shares for Listed Companies, *Super Voting Shares*.

[147] S. Bartholomeusz, 'News Corp.'s prefs spring surprise in painless birth' *The Age*, 4 November 1994, at 21 and N. Chenoweth, 'Prefs listing seals Murdoch control' *Australian Financial Review*, 4 November 1994, at 34.

[148] See C. Wolman, 'Forum for resolving City rows with industry revived' *Financial Times*, 29 October 1988, at 6.

[149] Concern regarding management buy-outs is reiterated in the ISC's subsequent publication: *The Role and Duties of Directors—A Statement of Best Practice* 18 April 1991 (revised August 1993).

## (b)  Scrip dividends

Another issue of potential conflict of interest which has caused sufficient concern for some institutional shareholders to make a general statement of their position, is scrip dividends. An ABI Investment Committee statement on this topic seeks to ensure that shareholders are not disadvantaged when given the option of taking scrip in lieu of a cash dividend.[150]

## (c)  Executive remuneration

Institutional activism regarding executive remuneration has been on several levels: disclosure of its make-up, opposition to long-term contracts which make dismissal of under-performers expensive, and attempts to tie remuneration more closely to performance. It has, however, shied away from influencing absolute levels of remuneration. Each of these initiatives is examined in greater detail below.

### (i)  Disclosure

Regulatory provisions in both jurisdictions require the notes to the accounts to disclose the total emoluments received by the directors, and to list in bands (of £5,000 in England and of $A10,000 in Australia) the number of directors whose total income falls within each band.[151] In Australia, listed companies must provide comparable information in respect of executive officers whose total income exceeds $A100,000.[152] In England the emoluments received by the chairman, and by the highest paid director (if they exceed those of the chairman) must also be disclosed in certain circumstances.[153] There is an additional right in Australia for 10 per cent of the total number of members or members collectively holding at least 5 per cent in value of the company's issued shares to obtain an audited statement of the total emoluments and other benefits received by each of the directors of the company or its subsidiary.[154]

In addition to these requirements, the Cadbury Code recommends that companies give separate figures for pension contributions and performance-related pay elements for the board, the chairman and, if different, the

---

[150] See ABI Investment Committee statement, 3 May 1990.
[151] Section 232 and sch. 6 pt 1, CA 1985 (UK); Corporations Regs, sch. 5, cl. 25 (Aust). Exempt proprietry companies are excluded from this obligation in Australia. See further F. Micallef, 'Disclosure of Directors' and Executives' Remuneration Required by Schedule 5 and Employee Share Ownership Plans' (1994) 12 *Company & Sec LJ* 465.
[152] Corporations Regs 1991, sch. 5 cl. 29 (Aust).
[153] Above n 151.                                    [154] Section 239, CL (Aust).

highest paid director. It also requires companies to report on the basis for measuring performance.[155] Institutional shareholders have lobbied for compliance with this aspect of the Code,[156] and companies are providing more information than in the past.[157] However, there are examples of disclosure regarding bonus schemes which blandly stated that they were 'based on earnings per share'[158] or on 'individual management and professional contributions to the group and to competitive market conditions',[159] without offering any further information.[160] Similarly, disclosure of option plans in many cases does not give sufficient information to enable shareholders to see how much directors are being paid.[161] Attempts by the Accounting Standards Board's Urgent Issues Task Force to address this issue have been hampered by legal advice that the body does not have power to issue a directive on disclosure of share options.[162] The body has, however, called for companies to disclose specified information regarding options, and has said that if the cost of the options has been calculated, it must also be shown.[163]

Institutional shareholders in Australia have also sought[164] additional and more detailed disclosure of the various components of remuneration packages and information about how board remuneration committees determine executive pay levels,[165] so that the true level of remuneration and the relationship between company performance and remuneration can be ascertained. To date, this has not produced results in terms of the information disclosed in companies' annual reports and accounts.

---

[155] Cadbury Code para. 3.2.

[156] See e.g. V. Houlder, 'Chairman paid £375,000 after governance rethink' *Financial Times*, 29 September 1993, at 28 and P. Rodgers, 'Pension funds want full disclosure of boardroom pay' *The Independent*, 10 December 1994, at 16.

[157] PIRC Corporate Governance Service, *Meeting the Cadbury Challenge? A Summary of Trends Towards Compliance with the Cadbury Committee Report on Corporate Governance*, July 1993, at 13. Cf., 'How to pay top executives' *Financial Times*, 8 April 1992, at 18.

[158] R. Cowe, 'Bosses stick to their tradition of big cheques and little explanation' *The Guardian*, 21 April 1994, at 14.

[159] R. Cowe, '£1m pay packets for Warburg bosses' *The Guardian*, 1 June 1994, at 12.

[160] A report by *Company Reporting* found that under 4% of British companies show how executives' bonuses are calculated: A. Edgecliffe-Johnson, 'Companies fall short on directors' pay disclosure' *The Daily Telegraph*, 30 December 1994, at 23. See also PIRC, above n 157 at 13–14.

[161] 'Investors mount pressure in bid to secure details of directors options' *The Irish Times*, 3 June 1994, supplement at 4.

[162] R. Cowe, 'Call for companies to come clean over directors' share option deals' *The Guardian*, 19 May 1994, at 16.

[163] Ibid. See also P. Ryland, 'A piece of Cadbury melts' *Investors Chronicle*, 22 April 1994, at 6.

[164] See P. Griffin, 'Executive Rewards versus Shareholder Benefits—everyone a winner or a zero sum game?' Conference Paper, *Executive Rewards Conference*, Australian Investment Managers' Group and Australian Institute of Company Directors, Melbourne, 9 June 1994.

[165] S. Hoyle, 'Call for transparency on top salaries' *Australian Financial Review*, 6 June 1994, at 25.

## *(ii) Term*

Before the Cadbury Report, five-year contracts were common.[166] The Cadbury Code recommends limiting service contracts to three years (unless shareholders' approve otherwise),[167] and after publication of the report this became the norm. One of Britain's larger institutions, PosTel (the Post Office and British Telecom pension fund) has lobbied with some success in favour of rolling contracts of two years or less, to limit the compensatory payments to poorly-performing directors who are forced to resign.[168] Nevertheless, a survey carried out in October 1994 found that four out of 10 were on three-year rolling contracts, and that in the 80 FT–SE 100 companies which responded to the survey more than half the chief executives and almost half of the other directors had such contracts.[169] Further, the fact that many of the senior managers of the giant pension funds are themselves on three year rolling contracts has operated as a disincentive to other institutional investors adopting PosTel's high profile stance.[170]

## *(iii) Linkage to company performance*

Pressure to link employee share plans and executive share option schemes more closely to long-term company performance has come from organizations representing both individual and institutional shareholders. Guidelines for schemes which promote those objectives have been formulated by virtually all relevant shareholder organizations,[171] and have

---

[166] 'Executive pay' *Financial Times*, 25 June 1994, at 24. This is the maximum period allowed without attracting the shareholder approval requirements in s. 319, CA 1985 (UK).

[167] Final Report para. 4.41.

[168] N. Buckley *et al.*, 'Argyll shortens rolling contracts to two years: PosTel campaign gathers pace as NAPF consults members on corporate governance' *Financial Times*, 20 July 1994, at 23, P. Montagnon, 'Survey of Pension Fund Investment (12): The focus shifts to boardroom pay—Corporate Governance' *Financial Times*, 27 April 1994, at VII, and M. Waller, 'Rolling contracts inquiry' *The Times*, 22 July 1994. Cf., s. 237 CL (Aust).

[169] R. Cowe, 'Pay survey shows good life goes on for bosses' *The Guardian*, 18 October 1994, at 18, citing the results of a survey by Bacon & Woodrow.

[170] 'A racket in need of reform' *The Economist*, 27 August 1994, at 45, and A. Bernoth, 'Tarnished handshakes' *Sunday Times*, 21 August 1994, although there are nevertheless reports of behind the scenes pressures by other institutions on remuneration committees regarding the high levels of pay-offs: J. Ashworth, 'Shareholders squeeze golden handshakes' *The Times*, 12 August 1994.

[171] Organizations which have formulated guidelines include the Investment Fund Managers Association, ABI, NAPF and UK Shareholders Association in the UK and the AIMA and ASA in Australia, both of whom have recently reissued guidelines in conjunction with the Australian Institute of Company Directors. See further N. Cohen, 'Owners work harder' *Financial Times*, 24 March 1992, at 17; 'Shareholders of the Nation, Unite!' *Investors Chronicle*, 8 April 1994, at 12; and J. MacLeay, 'Golden perks under fire' *The Australian*, 30 March 1994, at 38.

resulted in many schemes being dropped or amended.[172] However, private opposition by institutions to schemes which, for example, do not contain sufficiently high performance criteria, does not always translate into a vote against the scheme.[173] A further criticism which has been made of the NAPF and ABI guidelines, is that by generally limiting options for managers to four times cash remuneration, the guidelines in fact inhibit the linking of pay to performance.[174]

### (iv) Total remuneration

The area where institutional activism has been least successful has been in curbing the overall amount which directors are paid.[175] Concern has been expressed that directors' remuneration has in recent times increased at levels higher than the rate of inflation, but also that increases have been unrelated to performance.[176] Individual shareholders who have sought to challenge executive pay rises have been defeated by proxies held by the directors.[177] Not only do conflicts of interest inherent in the inter-relationship between companies and institutions operate as a disincentive against institutions taking action on this front,[178] but some fund managers also do not see a great deal of advantage in challenging excessive

[172] A. White, 'Not such a great idea, St George' *Australian Financial Review*, 16 December 1992, at 15; M. Corrigan, 'Shareholders query staff option plan' *Australian Financial Review*, 22 February 1994, at 20.

[173] Evidence of Mr Easterbrook to the *Joint Committee on Corporations and Securities*, above n 43, at 54.

[174] B. G. M. Main, 'Reflections on Institutional Guidelines on Top Executive Pay' *University of Edinburgh Working Paper* (September 1994) to be published in *The Review of Policy Issues*. See also I. M. Ramsay, 'Directors and Officers' Remuneration: The Role of the Law' [1993] *J Bus L* 351. But cf., the ABI's more recent guidelines, 'Long term remuneration for senior executives', 25 May 1994.

[175] This issue has attracted political attention in Britain as a result of large pay increases awarded to directors of privatized utilities and, in particular, a 71% pay increase awarded to the chief executive of British Gas. A task force known as the Greenbury Committee has recently been set up in Britain by the Confederation of British Industry, in conjunction with the Stock Exchange, the ABI, the NAPF and the Institute of Directors to address this issue: P. Bassett, 'City taskforce launched to control directors' pay' *The Times*, 17 January 1995, at 1. This issue has also prompted action by PIRC: R. Corzine and W. Lewis, 'British Gas braced for shareholder unrest over chief's pay' *Financial Times*, 8 April 1995, at 1.

[176] A study by the London School of Economics released in December 1992 found that the average pay of directors had risen by 20% a year since 1983, and that increases were virtually unrelated to company performance: J. Hurst, 'In the UK, it's cash with class' *Australian Financial Review*, 28 April 1993, at 4. But cf., B. G. M. Main *et al.*, 'Total Board Remuneration and Company Performance' *University of Edinburgh Working Paper* (August 1994) whose study of directors' emoluments includes share options granted over the period 1982–9, and who conclude that due to such options, there is a statistically significant connection between boardroom pay and company performance.

[177] L. Wood, 'CBA directors take a pasting over pay rises' *Australian Financial Review*, 29 October 1992, at 38.

[178] P. J. Dunstan, 'The Corporate Governance Agenda: Crucial Issues for Directors in the 1990s' (1991) 1 *Australian Journal of Corporate Law* 145.

remuneration, since the actual impact of a scheme on shareholders' wealth may be negligible.[179] Another substantial disincentive is the fact that many of the senior managers of the institutions are themselves on generous remuneration packages.[180] The legislative response to this issue in Australia[181] has been to require that shareholder disclosure be made and approval obtained for remuneration paid to company directors or employees (among others) by public companies or their 'child entities' which is not 'reasonable'. However, in the absence of a definition of reasonableness, this requirement seems unlikely to have any practical impact.

### (v) Remuneration committees

Where institutions have been more successful is in encouraging company boards to form remuneration committees. In Korn/Ferry's 1994 United Kingdom survey, 98 per cent of companies reported having a remuneration committee, virtually all with a non-executive majority as recommended by the Cadbury Code.[182] The percentage of companies in Korn/Ferry's 1994 Australian survey which reported having a remuneration committee was 48 per cent, the typical composition of which was 4 members, three of whom were non-executive,[183] although a different survey[184] confined to the top 100 Australian companies obtained the much higher figure of 73 per cent of respondent companies.

However, far from curbing increases in directors' remuneration, a study by Main and Johnston on the 1990 reports of 220 large publicly held companies which reported having a remuneration committee found that those companies were associated with higher levels of pay.[185]

Perhaps more significantly,[186] Main and Johnston's research found that the existence of a reported remuneration committee made no positive impact on the incentive structure of pay.

---

[179] Mirador survey commissioned by the Australian Institute of Superannuation Trustees, (May 1994), at 93, and L. Buckingham, 'Boom time on the boards' *The Guardian*, 18 June 1994, at 40.

[180] Bernoth and 'A racket in need of reform', see above n 170.

[181] Pt. 3.2A, CL (Aust).

[182] Korn/Ferry, above n 85, at 21.

[183] Korn/Ferry, above n 49, at 12 and 18.

[184] By the AIMA, ASX and the Business Council of Australia conducted in October 1993: AIMA Media Release (4 November 1993).

[185] B. G. M. Main and J. Johnston, 'Remuneration Committees and Corporate Governance' (1993) 23 *Accounting and Business Research* 351. See also by the same authors 'Deciding on Top Pay by Committee' *Personnel Management* (July 1992), at 32, which found that chief executives whose pay was determined by remuneration committees were paid 18% more than colleagues at companies without such arrangements.

[186] There is some uncertainty among commentators as to whether holding down pay levels is the function of the remuneration committee. Main and Johnston 'Remuneration Committees and Corporate Governance', ibid., at 358 and Charkham, above n 57, at 276.

Again, the reasons for these statistics are not hard to find. Most non-executive directors are chief executives or executive directors of other companies, and as a consequence are unlikely to recommend anything that might adversely affect their own remuneration, or show the remuneration packages received by their boards in a bad light.[187] In addition, the increasing practice of obtaining advice from external consultants can lead to a system in which the 'going rate' spirals upwards.[188]

### (d) Other related party transactions

In the context of forgiveness of executive debt arising out of share option schemes, there are recent examples of strong opposition by individual shareholders which has been rendered nugatory by institutional shareholders voting in favour of the proposals.[189]

In a similar vein, it was not institutional shareholders but rather Mr Gruzman who led a notable and ultimately successful campaign against Coles Myer Ltd. for greater disclosure of the company's dealing with entities related to the directors.[190]

### (3) Negligent or inefficient management

Institutions have consistently stated that they do not wish to become involved in management or business policy.[191] The reasons for this are not hard to find. As Davies points out:[192] 'Such interventions involve not only the likelihood of a bruising confrontation with the existing management, but also much greater commitments of time and energy in analysing the company's problems and in helping to devise a solution.' Instead, institutional involvement on this front is generally directed towards influencing board structure and composition. Exceptions exist where the investor is locked in (for example in a medium-sized company) or where the company is seeking more capital.[193]

[187] Montagnon, above n 168.

[188] Montagnon, ibid., and S. Wright, *Two Cheers for the Institutions* (London, Social Market Foundation, 1994).

[189] Evidence of Mr Hall, above n 43, at 18–23. See also A. Cornell, 'No sharing between rivals' *Australian Financial Review*, 28 January 1994, at 21.

[190] I. McIlwraith, 'Coles to report on related-party dealings to ASX' *Australian Financial Review*, 17 November 1992, at 20; and M. Gill, 'Gruzman claims scalp in Coles–Myer battles' *Australian Financial Review*, 9 August 1993, at 21.

[191] See, e.g., ANZ submission to *Institutional Investor Inquiry*, above n 9, at 181.

[192] Davies, above n 12, at 277.

[193] Davies, ibid.

## (a) Structure and composition of the board

Institutional shareholders in the United Kingdom have put their weight behind the Cadbury Code and pressured companies to comply with it.[194] Since the listing rule came into effect requiring disclosure of the extent of compliance with the Code, a noticeably higher percentage of companies have taken steps to divide power at the head of the company[195] to appoint an increasing proportion of non-executive directors to their boards,[196] and to establish audit[197] and remuneration committees.[198]

In Australia, the response to *Corporate Practices and Conduct* has been more muted. There has been a significant increase in the number of companies with a non-executive chairman.[199] However, figures regarding the appointment of non-executive directors[200] and establishment of board committees[201] have been relatively static. This is despite the fact that, when surveyed,[202] many fund managers (although not all) commented on the importance to them of a balance of executive and non-executive

---

[194] P. Stiles and B. Taylor, 'Benchmarking Corporate Governance: The Impact of the Cadbury Code' (1993) 26 *Long Range Planning* 61 and 'Non-Executive Directors' *Financial Times* 5 March 1992, at 40. See also Cadbury Committee Final Report para. 6.16.

[195] The percentage of companies responding to Korn/Ferry's surveys which split the roles from 1988 to 1993 inclusive were: 75%, 68%, 70%, 75%, 85%, 86%. However, the chairman was a full-time executive who played the leading role in 22% of companies splitting the roles in 1993. Sources: Holberton, above n 85, and Korn/Ferry, above n 4, at 15, n 85, at 16–17, and n 49, at 7. Note also that the movement has not all been in one direction: see R. Morrison, 'Two views on a split personality' *Financial Times*, 4 October 1991, at 17, N. Cohen, 'Buxton seeks to reassure Barclays shareholders' *Financial Times*, 1 May 1992, at 17, 'Taylor to combine Textiles roles' *Financial Times*, 4 March 1993, at 11; 'Clutterbuck comes to the head' *Financial Times*, 17 December 1992, at 15, and N. Cohen, 'Marshall "might quit" if curbed' *Financial Times*, 23 January 1993, at 5.

[196] The ratio of executives to non-executives went from 64:36 in 1988 to 59:41 in 1990. In 1993, 60% of the larger listed companies in the UK had as many or more non-executive directors on the board. Among smaller listed companies, 51% had as many or more non-executive directors as executives on the board, compared with 35% the previous year. Sources: 'Composition of company boards' *Bank of England Quarterly Bulletin*, May 1988, at 242, Korn/Ferry, above nn 4 and 85.

[197] In 1993, all but 2% of companies responding to Korn/Ferry's survey had an audit committee, over 90% with a non-executive majority. This compared with 41% in 1990: above nn 4 and 85.

[198] See discussion above section 4(2)(c)(v).

[199] The increase was from 67% of respondents in 1983 to 86% in 1993: Korn/Ferry, above n 49.

[200] Korn/Ferry's survey results for the past 10 years have found that Australian boards typically have 8 directors, 2 executive and 6 non-executive: Korn/Ferry, above n 49. But cf., the ASX finding that a significant proportion of the smaller listed companies have only 3 or 4 directors, with typically no more than one non-executive director: ASX Discussion Paper, above n 54, at 13.

[201] In Korn/Ferry's 1994 survey (above n 49) the percentage of companies with an audit committee dropped from 69% in 1992 to 67% in 1993.

[202] Mirador survey, above n 179. at 87 ff.

directors on the board, expressing a preference for independent non-executive directors and separation of the roles of chairman and chief executive.

The slow pace of change in this regard may be partly because Australian boards have traditionally included non-executive directors, and indeed, non-executive directors have been in the majority on the boards of larger companies. Further, there has been a substantial increase in the number of companies establishing audit and remuneration committees over the last 10 years, if not over the last two to three years.[203] However, the effectiveness of these committees must be questioned, since in the overwhelming majority of companies there are no formal terms of reference for such committees, written minutes of their meetings or reviews of board performance.[204]

### (b) Appointment and removal of directors

The financial press contains numerous reports of ousters of top executives, particularly where companies are facing financial difficulties.[205] Perhaps the most notable of these in the United Kingdom[206] have been the replacement of the chairmen of Barclays[207] and BP.[208] Another significant exit was the departure from the board of Lonrho of Mr Rowland.[209] In the case of BP, the ouster was followed by a split in the roles of chairman and chief executive.[210] Although in some cases there was collective action on the part of the institutions,[211] in others there has rather been an accumulation of pressure from individual institutions, senior executives and non-executive directors.[212] And indeed, this is representative of the

---

[203] In Korn/Ferry's 1983 survey 20% of companies reported having these committees: above n 49.

[204] AIMA media release, above n 184.

[205] See Jackson, above n 72; A. Hill, 'Institutions force resignations of Savage chairman and chief executive' *Financial Times*, 26 November 1990, at 17, and J. Plender, 'Tougher at the Top' *Financial Times*, 28–9 September 1991, at 7, and 'Shareholder Revolt!' *Best of Business Week*, 29 May 1991, at 34.

[206] Even more momentous was the removal of the Chairman of General Motors in the United States: See M. Dickson, 'Revolution behind closed doors' *Financial Times*, 13 April 1992, at 10. Further, 1993 saw the ouster of bosses at IBM, Kodak and Westinghouse: 'Blessed are the peacemakers' *The Economist*, 5 February 1994, at 81.

[207] See R. Peston, 'Barclays Chairman to Stand Down' *Financial Times*, 25–6 April 1992, at 1 and C. Lorenz, 'Knives are out in the boardroom' *Financial Times*, 1 May 1992, at 11.

[208] D. Lascelles, 'Horton is ousted as chairman of British Petroleum' *Financial Times*, 26 June 1992, at 1.

[209] A. Brummer, 'Lonrho shows case for new Cadbury role' *The Guardian*, 5 November 1994, at 38.

[210] In Barclays, the pressure from institutions to split the roles continued: R. Rudd, 'Institutional concern over a top banker's dual role' *Financial Times*, 6 August 1992, at 19.

[211] Hill, above n 205.

[212] See Jackson, above n 72, and Plender, above n 205.

pattern of influence. Although institutional shareholders have combined in the ISC to publicize their collective wisdom as to the composition of boards and improved channels of communication, the ISC is no longer[213] seen as a medium for taking collective action on behalf of institutional shareholders regarding specific issues in particular companies.[214] Nor is collective action by institutions wide-spread even on an *ad hoc* basis.[215] For example, in what has been described as 'probably the most public and fierce of all recent boardroom battles'[216] Norwich Union's (£600,000) efforts to replace the board received financial support from only one other shareholder, and other institutions 'needed active hand-holding to maintain their voting support throughout the affair'.[217] Rather, such influence as is being exerted on companies in this regard is usually by non-executive directors and by institutions acting independently.[218]

However, in Australia, several institutions acted collectively and publicly to pressure changes in the board composition of Goodman Fielder.[219] There is also Australian evidence of activism by independent directors to effect boardroom change. An example is provided by the battle between the independent directors and majority shareholders in Fosters Brewing Group Ltd. as to the pace of reconstruction. The independent directors' stance galvanized both small and large shareholders who overwhelmingly gave their mandate at the general meeting.[220]

Although individual shareholders have played their part in the high profile ousters of directors of under-performing companies it is less common for them to have any input in the choice of replacement directors. Independents may offer themselves as candidates for a board position.[221] However, they are seldom successful,[222] unless they obtain institutional

---

[213] Cf., the role which was originally envisaged for the ISC when it was first established in 1973: Wilson Committee, above n 92 para. 912.

[214] Discussion with Messrs Regan and Crowshaw, Investment Committee, ABI, 9 April 1992.

[215] See N. Cohen and M. Urry, 'Institutions demand fair shares for all' *Financial Times*, 30 April 1992, at 23.                         [216] Cohen, above n 76.

[217] Ibid. See also A. Blair, 'A coalition versus a dictator' *Financial Times*, 27 May 1992, at 13.

[218] P. E. Moody, 'A more active role for institutional shareholders' *The Banker*, February 1979, at 49.

[219] P. Syvret, 'Goodman—behind the board bloodbath' *Australian Financial Review*, 15 December 1993, at 1 and 20.

[220] See further I. Ries, 'Why Elliott will remember Foster's independents' day' *Australian Financial Review*, 14 November 1991, at 72.

[221] I. McIlwraith, 'McPherson's board to face music' *Australian Financial Review*, 9 October 1992, at 60, T. Kaye, 'Minority three rate their own chances as slim' *Australian Financial Review*, 22 December 1992, at 18.

[222] R. Webb, 'McPherson's board survives' *Australian Financial Review*, 9 November 1992, at 20, B. Dunstan, 'Time to reshuffle the election deck' *Australian Financial Review*, 25 January 1993, at 40.

backing.[223] Institutions are approached from time to time by companies seeking their advice on the appointment of directors. However, they acknowledge that they may not be best placed to suggest names (as opposed to commenting on structural issues), partly because they do not really want to become involved, and also because they really only know of mainstream company directors.[224]

## (4) Dividend policy

The various types of institutional investor have different obligations in terms of paying out benefits to their investors. As a consequence, there is evidence that institutions may sometimes place pressure upon companies to deliver dividends, without regard to the company's particular financial plans.[225]

## (5) Information about the company's affairs

It is in respect of obtaining information about the affairs of the companies in which they invest that institutions have made the greatest use of their substantial shareholdings.

A United Kingdom study published in 1991 found that three-quarters of chief executives spend 10 or more days a year with institutional investors and a third spend 20 days or more.[226] Kellaway[227] describes the changing practices of relations with institutional investors in the following terms:

Increasingly, companies are side-stepping the broker and dealing with institutions direct. Most now hold three meetings on their results day: adding one for institutions to the traditional bashes for journalists and stockbrokers, in addition to a relentless schedule of individual meetings and visits. The big institutional investors like Legal & General have teams of analysts which might make some 500 visits to companies each year while its senior management would expect an annual lunch or dinner with the companies' top management to discuss strategy.[228]

---

[223] For a successful lobbying campaign by one individual shareholder (Mr Doug Shears) to obtain institutional backing for board appointments see e.g.: P. Syvret, 'Shears' group spreads word' *Australian Financial Review*, 31 August 1994, at 23, P. Syvret, 'Countdown to compromise' *Australian Financial Review*, 8 September 1994, at 25.

[224] Mirador survey above n 179, at 151.

[225] See N. Cohen 'Warning on Automatic Dividend Increases' *Financial Times*, 16 December 1991, at 5. See also 'A Policy for Dividends' *Financial Times*, 11 March 1992, at 18.

[226] Korn/Ferry, above n 4. The average number of days has been increasing in recent years and is estimated to have averaged 15 days in 1990 compared with 12 days a year in 1987.

[227] L. Kellaway, 'All the fun of the share' *Financial Times*, 26 April 1989, at 21.

[228] See also Professor Sir James Ball, 'Financial Institutions and their role as shareholders' in *Creative Tension?* above n 63, at 25.

Institutions in both the United Kingdom and Australia have expressed the desirability of establishing effective channels of communication with the boards of the companies in which they invest, as a supplement to the formal methods of communication of the annual report and accounts and attendance at general meetings. This dialogue is said to enable shareholders to gain a better appreciation of the long-term management objectives and to focus the attention of management on the expectations of shareholders. It is claimed to assume a special importance when there is a takeover bid.[229]

At the same time, institutions acknowledge that such contacts should not include the transmission of price-sensitive information,[230] except in the exceptional case that there are compelling reasons for a board to consult institutional shareholders on issues which are price sensitive, but this should only be done with the consent of the institutions, since it will involve a corresponding obligation upon shareholders both to keep such confidences and to suspend their ability to deal in the company's shares.[231]

### (6) Other complaints

It will be noted that the complaints of disregard of rights granted by statute or by the articles and alteration of the articles identified in Chapter 2 have been omitted from the above discussion. This is because once they occur they can generally only be remedied by means of litigation, whereas this chapter is concerned with self-help measures (although action directed at other complaints, such as the appointment of non-executive directors, or indeed direct lobbying by institutions prior to the event may prevent complaints of this kind arising).

Also omitted from the above discussion is any mention of compulsory acquisition. In listed companies, this is most likely to arise in the context of a takeover where the offeror uses one of the available methods of compulsory acquisition to acquire 100 per cent ownership of the target

---

[229] P. Griffin, 'Institutional Investors in Australia: A Shareholders' Perspective' *Corporate Governance and Australian Competitiveness: The Role of Institutional Investors Conference organised by the AIMG and the Business Council of Australia*, 11 November 1993, at 14–15 and Institutional Shareholders' Committee, above n 89.

[230] Ibid. See also B. Dunstan, 'What's this Code Really Worth?' *Australian Financial Review*, 30 May 1991, at 15, and B. Dunstan, 'Fund managers to dob in the cheats' *Australian Financial Review*, 20 February 1992, at 15.

[231] This stance begs the question as to what extent institutional investors who are in possession of inside information but who fail to use it for the benefit of those on whose behalf they invest may be liable to their clients for breach of fiduciary duty. See further B. A. K. Rider, 'The Fiduciary and the Frying Pan' [1978] *Convey* 114. Note, however, that not all institutional investors owe fiduciary obligations to their investors. In some cases the relationship may be purely contractual. See Pennington, *The Law of the Investment Markets* (BSP Professional Books, Oxford, 1990), at 6–7.

company. Individual shareholders will find themselves in the position of dissenting minority shareholders more frequently than institutional shareholders. In any event the only remedies available to a dissenting minority in this situation are litigious ones, which are discussed in detail in Chapter 10.

However, since one of the themes explored in this chapter is the special role of institutional shareholders in corporate governance, it is interesting to note the judicial response to instances where litigation has been instituted by or at the instigation of institutional shareholders with the expressed aim of benefiting shareholders generally. The most notable case in this category is *Prudential Assurance Co., Ltd.* v. *Newman Industries Ltd. (No. 2)*.[232]

In this case Prudential, which held 3 per cent of the shares in Newman Industries, sought to bring a derivative action against two of the directors claiming that they had defrauded the company of over £400,000. At first instance[233] the plaintiffs succeeded. However, the Court of Appeal allowed the appeal in part and declined to encourage the active role taken by the plaintiff in corporate governance, saying,[234]

We were invited to give judicial approval to the public spirit of the plaintiffs who, it was said, are pioneering a method of controlling companies in the public interest without involving regulation by a statutory body. In our view the voluntary regulation of companies is a matter for the City. The compulsory regulation of companies is a matter for Parliament. We decline to draw general conclusions from the exceptional circumstances of the present case. But the results of the present action give food for thought.

Arguably the court's views were coloured by its reluctance to become involved in matters of internal management[235] and the relative cost of the proceedings when compared with the amount of damages that could have been recovered.[236]

The comments of the Court of Appeal in *Prudential*'s case can be contrasted with the neutral account in Ferris J's judgment in *Re Northern Engineering Industries plc*[237] of the fact that an objection to a reduction of capital was brought by the Commercial Union companies, both on their own behalf and 'at the prompting of the Association of British Insurers, on behalf of members of the association who invest in securities.'[238]

---

[232] [1982] Ch. 204 at 221 (CA).  [233] [1981] Ch. 257.
[234] Above n 232, at 224.  [235] Ibid., at 221.  [236] Ibid., at 224.
[237] [1993] BCLC 1151; [1993] BCC 267.
[238] See also the influence of the Cadbury Code in the references to the desirability of splitting the positions of chairman and chief executive in *Walker* v. *Standard Chartered Bank plc* [1992] BCLC 535, at 538, per Dillon LJ (CA); and *Re Marco (Ipswich) Ltd.* [1994] 2 BCLC 354, at 407; [1994] BCC 781, at 835.

## 5. IMPLICATIONS FOR OTHER SHAREHOLDERS

In most cases, the interests of institutional and individual shareholders will coincide, and individual shareholders will benefit from the activism of the institutions and effectively obtain a 'free ride'. Conversely, where the various disincentives outlined above deter institutional activism, individual shareholders are left to lobby on their own behalf.

There are, however, some instances where institutional activism may operate to the detriment of individual shareholders. Primary among these is the institutions' preferential access to information. Other shareholders may also be disadvantaged by institutional pressure for dividends and activism regarding pre-emption rights.

### (1) Pre-emption rights

As discussed above,[239] institutional investors have been influential in the drafting of Stock Exchange guidelines identifying the circumstances in which they will be prepared to consent to disapplication of their pre-emption rights. There is room for differences of opinion as to whether pre-emption rights are equally advantageous to individual and institutional shareholders.[240] But whatever the merits of that debate, pre-emption rights may operate *indirectly* to the detriment of individual shareholders because of underwriting arrangements for rights issues:[241]

Most rights issues are underwritten, typically by those same institutions which are also the major shareholders in those companies. The maintenance of arrangements that involve underwriting by the institutions on attractive terms can, it is argued, fortify their interest in preserving pre-emption rights intact. Where a rights issue is underwritten by a company's shareholders, it is sometimes argued that underwriting commission is not a real cost to the shareholders as a whole, even though it appears real enough to the company's financial management. Nevertheless, within the body of shareholders, it must be recognised that there are winners and losers, with the smaller shareholders who are not invited to underwrite bearing the cost of the commissions payable to the larger shareholders who do underwrite.[242]

---

[239] At nn 124–9 and accompanying text.

[240] See N. Bunker, 'Pre-emption rights "still on agenda" ' *Financial Times*, 4 May 1989, at XIV, P. Stephens, 'Study on share privileges set up' *Financial Times*, 5 May 1989, at 12 and a letter to the *Financial Times* from S. Hester 23 February 1989, at 27.

[241] 'Pre-emption Rights' *Bank of England Quarterly Bulletin*, November 1987, at 545 and at 548.

[242] For similar comments in the Australian context see: Evidence of Mr Hall, above n 43, at 12.

Other practical features of the way in which renounceable rights issues are structured have been highlighted by the Australian Shareholders' Association ('ASA') as disadvantaging small shareholders, namely an absence of protection for shareholders who allow their rights to lapse, lack of assistance in selling unmarketable parcels of rights, and very short periods in which renounceable rights issues may be taken up. The ASA has also proposed solutions to these perceived disadvantages, and has called for companies to structure these issues in the interests of all shareholders, even at the cost of slightly higher underwriting commissions.[243]

### (2) Dividend policy

As mentioned above,[244] the pay-out obligations of institutions may lead them to place pressure on companies to maintain dividend levels, irrespective of the company's financial position and future plans. This may be disadvantageous to the company in the long term.

### (3) Access to information

One remaining area where institutional activism provides no direct benefit to individual shareholders and indeed may work against their interests is in relation to access to information.[245]

### (a) Continuous disclosure obligations

Stock Exchange listing rules attempt to ensure equal access by all shareholders to information. Thus in the United Kingdom under the Stock Exchange Listing Rules (the '*Yellow Book*'), there is a continuing obligation[246] on listed companies to notify the Company Announcements Office of the Stock Exchange without delay of any major new developments in its sphere of activity which are not public knowledge and which may lead to substantial movements in the price of its listed securities or significantly affect its ability to meet its commitments, as well as all relevant information concerning a change in the company's financial condition or in the performance of its business or expectation of its performance where knowledge of the change is likely to lead to substantial movement in the price of its listed securities.

The London Stock Exchange has publicly censured London International Group for briefing analysts on its results, while leaving small

---

[243] ASA, Position Paper: *Renounceable Rights Issues*, July 1994.

[244] Section 4(4).

[245] See generally N. Ryder and M. Regester, *Investor Relations* (London, Hutchinson Business Books, 1988).

[246] *The Listing Rules*, Ch. 9, especially paras 9.1 and 9.2.

shareholders to fend for themselves,[247] and has since addressed this issue in a guidance drafted by a working group which included Stock Exchange member firms, analysts, investors and listed companies.[248] The guidance states that 'companies should not disclose significant data, least of all financial information such as sales and profit figures, to selected groups rather than to the market as a whole.'[249] With respect to questions from analysts the guidance states:[250]

Analysts can play a constructive role in assisting the market in its understanding and valuation of companies. Companies are encouraged to assist analysts where possible in forming a view of their activities and trading prospects. Companies should, however, have a firm policy about the extent to which analysts' questions should be answered. For example, companies can explain information already in the public domain or discuss the markets in which they operate. They should decline to answer analysts' questions where individually or cumulatively the answers would provide price sensitive information. If analysts' comments or views appear inaccurate (because they are based, for example, on a mistaken view of sales growth) companies can consider what public information is available to be drawn to their attention.

The London Stock Exchange guidance instead advocates focusing on broader issues, stating:[251] 'Even within these constraints, there is plenty of scope for companies to hold a useful dialogue with their shareholders and other interested parties about their prospects, business environment and strategy (particularly in the medium and long term).'

The guidance is broadly consistent with the recommendations of the Cadbury Report that boards must 'ensure that any significant statements concerning their companies are made publicly and so are equally available to all shareholders'.[252] The Cadbury Report also states that 'it is important that companies should communicate their strategies to their major shareholders and that their shareholders should understand them'.[253] However, as Finch points out,[254] the danger in this pronouncement is that it endorses differential treatment of shareholders and impliedly rules out communications of strategy with individual shareholders.

These Stock Exchange initiatives are complemented by the active

---

[247] 'Stopping the insider dealer' *Sunday Times*, 16 May 1993, Business Section at 2.
[248] London Stock Exchange, *Guidance on the dissemination of price sensitive information*, (February 1994). See also ProShare's shareholders' charter on best practice in investor relations.     [249] Ibid., para. 10.     [250] Ibid., para. 24.
[251] Ibid., para. 10.     [252] Cadbury Report para. 6.13.
[253] Cadbury Report para. 6.15.
[254] V. Finch, 'Board Performance and Cadbury on Corporate Governance' [1992] *J Bus L* 581, at 587.

enforcement of insider dealing legislation.[255] Further, the emphasis on
equal access to information is reinforced in the takeover context in the
City Code on Takeovers and Mergers, the principal goal of which is
'to ensure fair and equal treatment of all shareholders in relation to
takeovers'.[256] Thus, it is stated[257] that: 'During the course of an offer, or
when an offer is in contemplation, neither an offeror, nor the offeree
company, nor any of their respective advisers may furnish information to
some shareholders which is not made available to all shareholders.' This
general obligation is supplemented by a specific rule[258] which states that:
'[i]nformation about companies involved in an offer must be made equally
available to all shareholders as nearly as possible at the same time and in
the same manner.'

In recognition of the practice of both bidder and target companies
meeting with major institutions as a standard feature of a bid, a note to the
rule[259] permits meetings between directors of companies involved in a
takeover (or their advisers) and selected shareholders to take place. But
this is subject to the proviso that no material new information is
forthcoming. There will inevitably be a grey area in determining whether
new information is or is not material.[260] However, the rule is enforced by
the requirement[261] that a representative of the financial adviser or
corporate broker of the companies concerned should be present at the
meeting, and that the representative should be responsible for confirming
to the Takeover Panel no later than noon on the following day that no
material new information had been forthcoming at the meeting.

In Australia, a comparable continuous obligation exists under the listing
rules,[262] which requires listed companies to notify the ASX immediately of
any information concerning the company which a reasonable person would
expect to have a material effect on the price or value of securities of the
company.[263] Further, the listing rules in both countries state[264] that
information that is required to be notified to the Company Announcements
Office must not be given to a third party before it has been so notified.[265]
The United Kingdom rules specifically require companies to make arrange-

---

[255] See *MacKie* v. *HM Advocate*, discussed in greater detail below at n 270 and
accompanying text.                                           [256] Introduction, para. 1(a).
   [257] General Principle 2.      [258] Rule 20.1.      [259] Note 3 to rule 20.1.
   [260] See e.g., the Statement of the Takeover Panel 1992/11 regarding the takeover offer by
Petrocon Group plc for James Wilkes plc.                          [261] In Note 3.
   [262] Listing Rule 3A.
   [263] There is, however, an exclusion for confidential information in certain circumstances.
   [264] *The Listing Rules*, para. 9.7 (UK); ASX Listing Rule 3J(l)(f).
   [265] Exceptions exist in the case of confidential information in certain situations. Alternative
publication obligations apply where the Company Announcements Office is not open for
business: *The Listing Rules*, paras 9.4, 9.6 and 9.15 (UK); ASX Listing Rules 3A(l) and
3J(l)(e).

ments for notifications to the Company Announcements Office so that any announcement to a meeting of holders of listed securities is made no earlier than the time at which the information is published to the market.[266]

The practice of institutions dealing in a company's stock after a briefing by the company appears has been acknowledged in Australia, but appears not to have been publicly condemned or acted upon by regulators.[267]

The information differential between institutional and individual shareholders, and the potential for institutions to sell their holdings, with possible detrimental effects on individuals is acknowledged by the AIMA as the catalyst to the formation of the organization.[268] Indeed, the informational advantages of institutional investors are enshrined in the Corporations Law exemption from mandatory disclosure requirements for institutional investors so that, for example, a prospectus is not required for capital raising if the investor is a life insurance company, the trustee of a government superannuation fund or a superannuation or investment fund with assets of at least $A10 million.[269]

As *MacKie*'s case shows,[270] analyst briefing sessions may disadvantage individual shareholders even when no unpublished price-sensitive information is disclosed. This case concerned a charge of insider dealing against an analyst who attended a routine meeting with the chairman of a company. In the result, the conviction was quashed on the basis of lack of corroboration. Of equal interest is the undisputed evidence that after attending the meeting, the analyst revised his view of the company's future growth potential, and that he altered his assessment of the company from 'hold' to 'top slice'. In response to this downgrading, many of the broker's clients sold their shares in the company.

As the Wilson Committee points out:[271]

. . . the shareholder who has an opportunity to meet and assess management and to discuss the meaning of published information with them can form a better view of a company than the shareholder who has no such opportunity and can thereby be put, or at least appear to be put, at a market advantage even if no information is exchanged which is technically price-sensitive.[272]

---

[266] *The Listing Rules*, para. 9.7.
[267] L. G. Cox, 'Institutional Ownership in a Changing World: Is there a Need for a Segmented Market?' *Corporate Governance & Australian Competitiveness*, above n 229. See also Evidence of Mr Cameron to the Joint Committee on Corporations and Securities, above n 43, at 93–4.
[268] B. Pheasant, 'AIMG moves to help restore our credibility' *Australian Financial Review*, 15 July 1993, at 27.
[269] Regs 7.12.05 and 7.12.06, Corporations Regs (Aust).
[270] *MacKie* v. *HM Advocate* unreported decision of the High Court of Justiciary, Scotland, 16 February 1994.                                    [271] Above n 92, para. 905.
[272] See also the Cadbury Report paras 4.54 and 6.13.

### (b) Annual general meetings

In the United Kingdom, insider dealing reforms, the Stock Exchange guidance, and the consequent cut-back on private briefings have led some fund managers to suggest that the annual general meeting be revamped as a forum for announcing news.[273] Similarly, in Australia, Dunstan has suggested[274] that it would constitute a real improvement if investment managers produced a standard question, on notice, to all chairmen of all major listed companies for annual general meetings. The question might deal with the variation in sales and profits compared with the same quarter in the previous year and with the actual budget for the period, seek an estimate of the half-yearly result, and an indication of whether the current dividend could be maintained. This, he suggests, would send all shareholders away from the annual meeting with up-to-date information.

However, the experience of annual general meetings during the recession provides little encouragement for the prospects for reform along these lines. Rowdy meetings prompted by the corporate collapses of the late 1980s and early 1990s led instead to attempts by companies to limit discussion. In the United Kingdom, Hanson proposed, among other things, to curb discussion at its annual general meetings, but was forced to back down after a high-profile campaign by PIRC.[275]

In Australia, the ASC issued a report clarifying the conduct of meetings and the members' right to speak.[276] This sparked publications by the Australian Institute of Company Directors, whose concern was disruptive shareholders,[277] and the ASA, who rejoined with complaints of failure to answer questions put in writing prior to the meeting, exclusion of journalists, holding of meetings at inappropriate times, and, in remote locations, failure to allow questions to be directed to the appropriate person, curtailing the opportunity for shareholders to ask questions and inadequate records and follow-up of questions asked at meetings and responses.[278] A truce appears to have been called in the form of a joint publication by the two organizations which seeks to address all these issues.[279]

---

[273] 'The annual general farce' *The Economist*, 12 March 1994, at 88. See also the Wilson Committee, above n 92, para. 906, and Charkham, above n 81, at 7.

[274] B. Dunstan, 'Company reports leave investors short-changed' *Australian Financial Review* 18 June 1991, at 19.

[275] 'Reluctant owners' *The Economist*, 29 January 1994, Corporate Governance Survey at 16.

[276] ASC, *Chairperson's Conduct of Meetings and Members' Right to Speak at Meetings*, (1992) 3 *ASC Digest*, SPCH 154.

[277] *Rights and Responsibilities of Shareholders at General Meetings*, (December 1993).

[278] *The Conduct of Annual General Meetings*, (January 1994).

[279] *The Conduct of Annual General Meetings—Code of Best Practice* (September 1994).

## (c) Frequency of reporting

Listed companies in both jurisdictions are required by listing rules to prepare half-yearly reports.[280]

One response to the information differential between individual and institutional shareholders has been calls both in the United Kingdom and in Australia for quarterly reports.[281]

It remains to be seen whether any of these proposals will be implemented. For the present, access to information by individual shareholders depends upon their financial resources. Individual shareholders can inform themselves of the main stories through the financial media. More detailed information is available, for example through various forms of subscription service, but shareholder access to this type of information depends upon how much they are prepared to spend.

### (4) Resolution of conflicts between institutions and other shareholders

There is a tension which is acknowledged in the ISC's document on the responsibilities of institutional shareholders,[282] namely that institutional investors have conflicting (or in the ISC's terms 'overriding') obligations to those on whose behalf they invest.

Although there is widespread acceptance of the proposition that the size and importance of institutional shareholdings carries with it an obligation to use that power responsibly, there is seldom any detailed discussion of the priority to be given to the various interest groups involved. The ISC's statement that the interests of those on whose behalf the institutions invest prevail over the responsibilities which are a corollary of ownership is potentially challenged by the case of *Re Holders Investment Trust Ltd.*,[283] a case concerning a proposed reduction of capital by

---

[280] *The Listing Rules*, para. 12.46 ff. (UK), ASX LR 3B and App. 3 (Aust). Mining companies in Australia are subject to separate quarterly disclosure requirements. In Australia, the Corporations Law has been amended to require half-yearly accounts to be prepared by 'disclosing entities' (defined more widely than listed companies) and to be audited or reviewed by an auditor: Corporate Law Reform Act 1994, sch. 1.

[281] The ASC recommended the introduction of quarterly reporting in its response to a report by the Companies and Securities Advisory Committee ('CASAC'), *Report on an Enhanced Statutory Disclosure System* (September 1991). The CASAC, although acknowledging the merit of quarterly reporting, did not recommend a statutory requirement for them. Similar sentiments were expressed in the Cadbury Report paras 4.55–6 which also considered quarterly reporting, but noted that it would involve additional costs and recommended instead that interim reports should be expanded to increase their value to users. See also L. Burr, 'The Board/Institutional Shareholders Relationship—A Necessary Step Forward' *Australian Institute of Company Directors First Asia–Pacific Corporate Governance Conference*, 24 May 1993. [282] Above n 89.

[283] [1971] 1 WLR 583.

cancellation of a company's preference shares. The trusts held 90 per cent of the preference shares and 52 per cent of the company's equity capital. Based on the interests of the trusts and having regard to their large holdings of the equity capital of the company, the trustees voted in favour of the reduction. It was held that in voting as members of the class of preference shareholders, the trustees should have voted *bona fide* in the best interests of the class as a whole, an issue to which it was held that the trustees did not address their minds.

One interpretation of this case is that the trustees were required to give priority to the interests of the class as a whole over the interests of the trust, and hence the beneficiaries on whose behalf the trust was investing. However, Harding has pointed out[284] that although shareholders must not vote in a manner which amounts to a fraud on a minority or would be oppressive or unfairly prejudicial, they do not have fiduciary obligations towards the company and other shareholders. He argues that the question which Megarry J had to decide in *Holders'* case[285] was whether a reduction of capital was fair. In that context, Megarry J's approach was to discount the votes of the trustee which stood to gain through its interests in the ordinary capital, rather than to impose an overriding obligation on shareholders to vote in the best interests of the class.[286]

---

[284] Harding, above n 114.                                          [285] Above n 283.
[286] Some support for this approach can be found in the recent case of *Re Leigh Estates (UK) Ltd.* [1994] BCC 292. See further Ch. 10.

# ━━○ 4 ○━━
# Self-help in Quasi-partnership and Joint Venture Companies

1. Introduction                                                           64

2. The Articles of Association                                            66
   (1) Enforceability                                                     67
       (a) Outsider rights                                                67
           (i) England                                                    68
           (ii) Australia                                                 70
       (b) Remedies                                                       72
   (2) Alteration                                                         74
       (a) Restrictions on alterability                                   74
       (b) Class rights                                                   75
           (i) Statutory provisions                                       75
           (ii) Remedies                                                  79
           (iii) What amounts to an alteration                            79
       (c) Weighted voting                                                81
       (d) Quorum requirements                                            83
       (e) Alteration and separate contracts                              83
           (i) Contracts not to alter the corporate constitution          84
           (ii) External contracts based on the corporate
                constitution                                              88

3. Shareholders' Agreements                                              90
   (1) Comparison with articles                                          91
       (a) Parties                                                       91
       (b) Privity of contract                                           93
       (c) Alterability                                                  94
       (d) Confidentiality                                               94
       (e) Enforceability                                                95
           (i) Voting agreements                                         95
           (ii) Available remedies                                       96
           (iii) Conflict with statute                                   97
               (A) Contracts not to alter the articles                   97
               (B) Restraining the transferability of property           97
               (C) Ousting the jurisdiction of the court                 97
               (D) Vote purchasing                                       99
   (2) Fetter of directors' discretion                                   101

4. Application to Identified Complaints                          104
    (1) Alteration of the articles                              104
    (2) Dilution of equity stake or voting rights               104
    (3) Self-interested transactions by controllers             104
    (4) Negligent or inefficient management                     104
    (5) Participation in profits                                104
    (6) Information about the company's affairs                 105
    (7) Illiquidity                                             105
    (8) Exclusion from management                               105
    (9) Compulsory acquisition                                  105
    (10) Other complaints                                       105

## SUMMARY

*In order for shareholders to protect themselves against the recurring complaints identified in Chapter 2, recourse will generally be required to both the articles of association and shareholders' agreements. Each have their limitations and their benefits. The articles have the advantage that they bind the company and future members. However, a shareholders' agreement will be necessary in certain situations, for example: to confer a right other than 'qua member', to grant a right of veto over alterations to the articles without creating a separate class of shares, to preserve confidentiality, and to create rights and obligations between only some of the members. Although it is possible to include the company as a party to a shareholders' agreement and thereby bind it to the agreement's terms, Russell's case[1] shows that care must be taken to ensure that this does not involve the company in a contract not to alter its articles.*

## 1. INTRODUCTION

The term 'quasi-partnership',[2] although deprecated by Lord Wilberforce in *Ebrahimi* v. *Westbourne Galleries Ltd.*,[3] is used here for convenience as a short-hand expression to describe an organization which in its form and its

---

[1] *Russell* v. *Northern Bank Development Corpn. Ltd.* [1992] 1 WLR 588 (HL).

[2] For examples of the use of this expression in the winding-up context see *Re K/9 Meat Supplies (Guildford) Ltd.* [1966] 1 WLR 1112, *Re Expanded Plugs Ltd.* [1966] 1 WLR 514 and *Re Fildes Bros. Ltd.* [1970] 1 WLR 592. It has also been used in the context of unfair prejudice petitions: see *Re Bird Precision Bellows Ltd.* [1984] Ch. 419, affd. [1986] Ch. 658, *Re XYZ Ltd. (Re a Company (No. 004377 of 1986))* [1987] 1 WLR 102 and *Re a Company (No. 005134 of 1986; Ex parte Harries* [1989] BCLC 383, also reported as *Re D. R. Chemicals Ltd. Re a Company (No. 005134 of 1986))* (1989) 5 BCC 39.

[3] [1973] AC 360 at 379 (HL).

dealing with the outside world operates as a company, but which functions along partnership lines as far as the internal relations of the participants are concerned. Its typical features were identified by Lord Wilberforce as:[4]

(1) an association formed or continued on the basis of a personal relationship involving mutual confidence;
(2) an agreement or understanding that all or some of the shareholders shall participate in the conduct of the business; and
(3) restriction on the transfer of the members' interest in the company.

The definition of a 'joint venture company' is more elusive[5] and indeed, quasi-partnerships may be regarded as a subset of joint ventures. However the term 'joint venture company' is used in this context not to encompass this overlap, but to describe a company where, although the relationship between the participants is purely commercial, all parties nevertheless actively contribute to the company, be it in the form of management skills, time, capital, contacts or in some other way.

These two types of company are discussed in the same chapter because they share two important features. First, by virtue of their contribution to the company, the minority shareholders have broadly similar bargaining power to that of the majority participants[6] and are therefore able to take appropriate steps to protect themselves from oppressive conduct. Secondly, the participants have alternative legal structures available to them as media through which to conduct their businesses,[7] but have chosen to adopt the corporate form. The reasons for this will vary from one company to another. Some of the main advantages of the corporate form are:[8]

---

[4] Ibid. This was in the context of granting a winding-up order on the just and equitable ground.

[5] See e.g. S. Corcoran and J. C. Tucker, 'Joint Venturers as Fiduciaries' (1989) 2 *Corp & Bus, LJ* 34 who note that the only thing the authorities appear to agree upon with respect to the meaning of 'joint venture' is that the term is not a technical one.

[6] See Linklaters & Paines and C. Nightingale, *Joint Ventures* (London, Longman Group UK Ltd., 1990) at 3–4.

[7] M. Chesterman, *Small Businesses* (2nd edn., London, Sweet & Maxwell, 1982) suggests as alternatives: limited partnership, unlimited company, quoted company, co-operative society, trust or combinations of these forms. For a detailed discussion of the advantages and disadvantages of incorporation see also R. P. Burrow and A. J. Shipwright, 'To Incorporate or Not?' (1980) 124 *Solic J* 123, R. M. Walters, 'To Incorporate or Not to Incorporate—That is the Question' [1977] *Brit Tax Rev* 34, T. L. Hazen, 'The Decision to Incorporate' (1979) 58 *Neb L Rev* 627, T. Hadden, *Company Law and Capitalism* (2nd edn., London, Weidenfeld and Nicolson, 1977) and Companies and Securities Law Review Committee, *Forms of Legal Organization for Small Business Enterprises*, Discussion Paper No. 1, 1984 (Australia).

[8] Companies and Securities Law Review Committee, *Report to the Ministerial Council of Forms of Legal Organisation for Small Business Enterprises* September 1985, (Australia). Cf., the reasons given by small firm owners for choosing to incorporate: see J. Freedman, 'Small Business and the Corporate Form: Burden or Privilege?' (1994) 57 *Mod L Rev* 555.

(1) limited liability of members;[9]
(2) favourable taxation treatment;
(3) the ability to create a floating charge; and
(4) corporate personality and perpetual succession which enable purchasing, holding, conveying or dealing with property in the company's own name, the employment of controllers or members (thereby providing benefits such as superannuation, redundancy pay, and unfair dismissal claims), and the right to sue and be sued in the corporate name.

Companies legislation was originally framed to meet the needs of large-scale enterprises with outside shareholders and is in many cases ill-adapted to quasi-partnership and joint venture companies. In particular, the features of majority rule, free transferability of shares, perpetual existence, and the demarcation of roles of shareholder and director may be out of step with the expectations of the participants.[10] But, having made that choice, the company is sufficiently flexible as a business medium that the participants can take steps to regulate their rights and powers in such a way as to avoid many of the common complaints of minority shareholders.

These self-help measures may take the form of provision in the articles of association and may include class rights and weighted voting rights. The parties may also decide to enter into a separate shareholders' agreement. It is proposed to highlight[11] the benefits and disadvantages of the various alternative measures, and then to consider the extent to which a combination of these approaches can reduce the vulnerability of minority shareholders to the complaints identified in Chapter 2.

## 2. THE ARTICLES OF ASSOCIATION

In England and in Australia, the constitution of a company is contained in its memorandum and articles of association. Of these two documents, it is the articles which govern the internal administration of the company and which set out the rights and obligations of the shareholders and directors. The companies legislation does not prescribe the subject-matter to be

[9] Although this is often qualified by the requirement of finance providers for personal guarantees and possibly security.
[10] See W. J. Sandars, 'Small Businesses—Suggestions for Simplified Forms of Incorporation' [1979] *J Bus L* 14.
[11] See further, L. S. Sealy, 'The Enforcement of Partnership Agreements, Articles of Association and Shareholder Agreements' in P. D. Finn, (ed.) *Equity and Commercial Relationships* (Sydney, The Law Book Co. Ltd., 1987) at 89.

covered by the articles. Rather it provides a model set of articles which will apply to the extent that it is not modified or excluded.[12] Thus for parties wishing to override corporate assumptions which are inappropriate to their business relationship or to express their expectations in greater detail, the articles offer an obvious medium. Further, the advantage of the articles over a shareholders' agreement is that the companies legislation gives contractual effect to the articles so that its provisions automatically bind subsequent members without the need for actual execution of them by each member.[13] To be weighed against this advantage, however, are two serious disadvantages. The first is the uncertainty which surrounds the enforceability of provisions of the articles, and the second is their susceptibility to alteration.

## (1) Enforceability

A shareholder seeking to enforce the terms of the articles of association always faces the risk that the court will interpret what appears to be a personal right as a right belonging to the company,[14] or that relief will be declined on the ground that the court will not interfere in the internal management of the company.[15] A related difficulty, and one which may raise particular problems in the context of this discussion, is that the enforceability of the terms of the articles may also depend upon whether a member is suing in that capacity or as an outsider.

### (a) Outsider rights

This issue arises in a slightly different way in England as compared with Australia.

---

[12] Section 8, CA 1985 (UK); s. 175, CL (Aust). It has been proposed in Australia that Table A be repealed, and that the default internal management rules instead be set out in the legislation, but that companies would still be able to choose to have articles of association and to displace the legislative provisions: Corporations Law Simplification Program, *Forming a Company: Proposal for Simplification* December 1994. This proposal is not as far-reaching as recent reforms in New Zealand which replace the memorandum and articles of association with an optional constitution and which change the relationship between shareholders and between the company and each shareholder to one which is statutorily based. See further D. O. Jones, *Company Law in New Zealand: A Guide to the Companies Act 1993* (Wellington, Butterworths, 1993) at 20–1.

[13] Section 14(1), CA 1985 (UK); s. 180(1), CL (Aust).

[14] See further Ch. 8, section 1.

[15] *MacDougall* v. *Gardiner (No. 2)* (1875) 1 Ch. D 13 (CA) and *Devlin* v. *Slough Estates Ltd.* [1983] BCLC 497. As to the difficulty in distinguishing personal and corporate rights see C. R. Baxter, 'The Role of the Judge in Enforcing Shareholder Rights' (1983) *Cambridge LJ* 96 and 'Irregular Company Meetings' [1976] *J Bus L* 323.

### *(i) England*

Section 14(1) of the Companies Act 1985 provides as follows:

Subject to the provisions of this Act, the memorandum and articles, when registered, bind the company and its members to the same extent as if they respectively had been signed and sealed by each member, and contained covenants on the part of each member to observe all the provisions of the memorandum and of the articles.

Despite some initial uncertainty, it now seems settled[16] that this section gives the terms of the articles of association contractual effect, both as between the company and each member,[17] and also between the members of the company. However, there is some doubt as to the extent to which the statutory contract may be used to enforce what have been called 'outsider' rights.

The orthodox view is that the articles are given contractual effect only in so far as they confer rights or obligations on a member in that capacity. The authority often cited for this view is *Eley* v. *Positive Government Security Life Assurance Co. Ltd.*[18] where the plaintiff was held to be unable to enforce a provision in the articles that he should be the company's solicitor. In the subsequent case of *Hickman* v. *Kent or Romney Marsh Sheep-Breeders' Association*[19] Astbury J regarded *Eley*'s case[20] as illustrating a principle that '. . . no right merely purporting to be given by an article to a person, whether a member or not, in a capacity other than that of a member, as, for instance as a solicitor, promoter, director, can be enforced against the company'.[21] Subsequent cases have also applied the distinction between 'outsider' and '*qua* member' rights. Thus the Court of Appeal in *Beattie* v. *E. and F. Beattie Ltd.*[22] held that a director who was in dispute with a company was unable to enforce an article which provided for disputes to be referred to arbitration because the dispute was between the company and the appellant in his capacity as a director.

But the distinction between '*qua* member' and 'outsider' rights is easier to state than to apply. It appears that the concept of '*qua* member' rights is flexible and will depend to some degree upon the nature of the company. For example, an expansive interpretation has been given to '*qua* member'

---

[16] *Hickman* v. *Kent or Romney Marsh Sheep-Breeders' Association* [1915] 1 Ch. 881.
[17] *Rayfield* v. *Hands* [1960] Ch. 1 and *Pender* v. *Lushington* (1877) 6 Ch. D 70.
[18] (1876) 1 Ex. D 88 (CA).            [19] Above n 16.          [20] Above n 18.
[21] Above n 16 at 900. But as Sealy points out, (L. S. Sealy, *Cases and Materials in Company Law* (5th edn., London, Butterworths, 1992) at 91), *Eley*'s case was decided on the narrower ground that Eley was not initially a member of the company.
[22] [1938] Ch. 708 (CA).

rights in quasi-partnership companies.[23] Thus, in *Rayfield* v. *Hands*[24] a provision in the articles requiring the directors to purchase a departing member's shares was held to be a contract or quasi-contract between the members and not between the members and directors and was therefore held to be enforceable.

This flexibility leads to uncertainty. But even more difficult to reconcile with the orthodox view are the cases where the courts have given a very expansive interpretation to '*qua* member' rights without reference to the nature of the company and in circumstances which are difficult to reconcile with Astbury J's framework. For example, it has been held that a director who is also a shareholder may bring an individual action to prevent his exclusion from acting as a director,[25] and that the terms of the articles concerning remuneration of a managing director have contractual effect.[26] In a similar vein, in *Quin & Axtens Ltd.* v. *Salmon*[27] the directors were able to obtain an injunction restraining the company from acting inconsistently with an article which stated that certain resolutions required the consent of two named directors.

Based on cases such as *Quin & Axtens Ltd.* v. *Salmon*,[28] Wedderburn has argued that every member has the right to have the company's business conducted in accordance with the articles and can therefore indirectly enforce outsider rights.[29] This issue has attracted considerable academic debate, into which it is not proposed to enter here.[30] Rather the purpose of

[23] See also discussion below at nn 43–7 and accompanying text.
[24] Above n 17, applying *Re Leicester Club and Country Racecourse Company; Ex parte Cannon* (1885) 30 Ch. D 629. For discussions of this case see K. W. Wedderburn [1958] *Cambridge LJ* 148 and L. C. B. Gower, 'The Contractual Effect of Articles of Association' (1958) 21 *Mod L Rev* 401 and '*Rayfield* v. *Hands*—A Postscript and a Drop of Scotch' (1958) 21 *Mod L Rev* 657.
[25] *Pulbrook* v. *Richmond Consolidated Mining Co.* (1878) 9 Ch. D 610 and *Hayes* v. *Bristol Plant Hire Ltd.* [1957] 1 WLR 499.
[26] *Re Richmond Gate Property Co. Ltd.* [1965] 1 WLR 335, noted by K. W. Wedderburn, 'Contractual Rights Under the Articles of Association—An Overlooked Principle Illustrated' (1965) 28 *Mod L Rev* 347. [27] [1909] AC 442 (HL). [28] Ibid.
[29] K. W. Wedderburn, 'Shareholders' Rights and the Rule in *Foss* v. *Harbottle*' [1957] *Cambridge LJ* 194.
[30] Wedderburn's thesis has received support from R. Gregory, 'The Section 20 Contract' (1981) 44 *Mod L Rev* 526. Different views again are expressed by G. D. Goldberg, 'The Enforcement of Outsider-Rights under Section 20(1) of the Companies Act 1948' (1972) 35 *Mod L Rev* 362 and 'The Controversy on the Section 20 Contract Revisited' (1985) 48 *Mod L Rev* 158, G. N. Prentice, 'The Enforcement of "Outsider" Rights' (1980) 1 *Company Lawyer* 179, R. R. Drury, 'The Relative Nature of a Shareholder's Right to Enforce the Company Contract' [1986] *Cambridge LJ* 219, C. Baxter, 'The Role of the Judge in Enforcing Shareholder Rights' [1983] *Cambridge LJ* 96 and 'Irregular Company Meetings' [1976] *J Bus L* 323, R. J. Smith, 'Minority Shareholders and Corporate Irregularities' (1978) 41 *Mod L Rev* 147, N. A. Bastin, 'The Enforcement of a Member's Rights' [1977] *J Bus L* 17 and M. Blackman, 'The Company Contract: Lord Wedderburn and the Enforcement of "Outsider Rights" ' (1992) 109 *South African Law Journal* 225. For a summary of the views expressed by several of these authors see L. C. B. Gower, *Gower's Principles of Modern Company Law* (5th edn., London, Sweet & Maxwell, 1992) at 287 and Sealy, above n 21 at 96.

the discussion is to highlight some of the complications inherent in using the articles of association as a medium for expression of the members' expectations.

In England, to the extent that the orthodox view is applied, it has considerable practical importance, since it may preclude the enforcement[31] by directors of provisions in the articles relating to such matters as board-meeting procedure, directors' remuneration, and provisions designed to ensure that a particular person will remain as the company's governing director for life or until a specific age or resignation.[32]

The position is ameliorated slightly by the fact that in some cases the courts have adopted a different technique to enforce outsider rights by finding that the parties' conduct evidences an implied contract incorporating certain terms of the articles. Thus, effect has been given to provisions in the articles dealing with such matters as the duration of appointment of directors, their entitlement to remuneration, or imposing a requirement to subscribe for qualification shares.[33] But even this technique does not provide a complete solution. First, it may be unclear whether the terms of the articles are incorporated as at the time of contracting, or on the basis that they may be varied from time to time.[34] Further, as the decision in *Beattie*'s case indicates,[35] the courts will not imply a collateral contract of this kind in every case.[36]

### (ii) Australia

In Australia, section 180(1) of the Corporations Law provides:

---

[31] By legal proceedings, cf., *Woodlands Ltd.* v. *Logan* [1948] NZLR 230.

[32] G. D. Goldberg, 'The Controversy on the Section 20 Contract Revisited' (1985) 48 *Mod L Rev* 158.

[33] As regards share qualification articles, see: *Re Anglo-Austrian Printing and Publishing Union; Isaacs' Case* [1892] 2 Ch. 158, *Salton* v. *New Beeston Cycle Co. (No. 1)* [1899] 1 Ch. 775, and *Molineaux* v. *London, Birmingham and Manchester Insurance Co. Ltd.* [1902] 2 KB 589 (CA). As regards directors' remuneration and term of office see *Re New British Iron Co.; Ex parte Beckwith* [1898] 1 Ch. 324, *Glass* v. *The Pioneer Rubber Works of Australia Ltd.* [1906] VLR 754 and *Read* v. *Astoria Garage (Streatham) Ltd.* [1952] Ch. 637 (CA).

[34] Cf., *Bailey* v. *British Equitable Assurance Co.* [1904] 1 Ch. 374 (CA) with *British Equitable Assurance Co. Ltd.* v. *Bailey* [1906] AC 35 (HL). Note also the 2–2 split in the High Court of Australia in *Carrier Australasia Ltd.* v. *Hunt* (1939) 61 CLR 534. See further, M. J. Trebilcock, 'The Effect of Alterations to Articles of Association' (1967) 31 *Convey* 95 and L. Trotman, 'Articles of Association and contracts' in J. H. Farrar, (Ed) *Contemporary Issues in Company Law* (Auckland, CCH (New Zealand), 1987) at 31.

[35] Above n 22. See also *Re Wheal Buller Consols* (1888) 38 Ch. D 42 where it was held that a director was not bound to comply with a share qualification provision in the articles because it was imposed on him in his capacity as a director.

[36] This is reinforced by the more recent cases of *Cumbrian Newspapers Group Ltd.* v. *Cumberland and Westmorland Herald Newspaper and Printing Co. Ltd.* [1987] Ch. 1 and *Newtherapeutics Ltd.* v. *Katz* [1990] BCC 362.

Subject to this Law, the constitution of a company has the effect of a contract under seal:

(a) between the company and each member;

(b) between the company and each eligible officer; and

(c) between a member and each other member;

under which each of the above-mentioned persons agrees to observe and perform the provisions of the constitution as in force for the time being so far as those provisions are applicable to that person.

Eligible officer is defined[37] to mean a director, the principal executive officer or a secretary of the company.

Not only does this section remove any doubt[38] that there is a deemed contract based on the articles between the parties mentioned in paragraphs (a) and (c), but the express creation of a contract between the company and each eligible officer is intended to reverse the effect of cases such as *Beattie*'s case[39] by enabling the enforcement of the articles by a director irrespective of whether he or she is a member.

However, section 180(1) introduces its own uncertainties. First, it is unclear what is meant by the words 'so far as those provisions are applicable to that person'. Hambrook[40] argues that the section may not produce a different result on the facts of *Beattie*'s case, since the arbitration article in that case referred to disputes involving 'members' and the company but section 180(1)(b) merely allows an officer to enforce those provisions of the memorandum and articles which are applicable to that officer. Section 180(1)(b) would, however, reverse the result of *Browne* v. *La Trinidad*[41] where a director who was not a member was held unable to sue to prevent a company from dismissing him, even though his term of office prescribed by the articles had not expired.

A further feature of the section is that it does not create a contract between each member and each eligible officer. Therefore, an expansive view of '*qua* member' rights based on the quasi-partnership nature of the company would still be required in order for a director/member to enforce pre-emption rights drawn in terms similar to those in *Rayfield* v. *Hands*.[42]

---

[37] Section 180(5), CL (Aust).
[38] For cases predating the introduction of s. 180(1) in its present form see *Heron*. v. *Port Huon Fruitgrowers' Co-operative Association Ltd.* (1922) 30 CLR 315 at 338 ff. (HC) and *United Service Insurance Co. Ltd. (in liq.)* v. *Lang* (1935) 35 SR (NSW) 487 at 492–3.
[39] Above n 22.
[40] J. P. Hambrook (Chapter Ed., ch. 2.4) *Australian Corporation Law* (Sydney, Butterworths, 1991, looseleaf service) ¶2.4.0155.
[41] (1887) 37 Ch. D 1 (CA).      [42] Above n 17.

Australian courts have interpreted the concept of '*qua* member' rights according to the nature of the company in various contexts.[43] Thus, it has been held that the right of a shareholder in a home-unit company to enjoyment of a building was a right enjoyed in the capacity of member.[44] Conversely, in *Norths Ltd.* v. *McCaughan Dyson Capel Cure Ltd.*,[45] which concerned an article of the Australian Stock Exchange, a much more restrictive interpretation was adopted. The article provided for disputes to be referred to the board for settlement. Given the nature of the ASX it was held that the statutory contract would apply only to a dispute connected with '. . . the way in which the association is being administered or . . . a situation where a dispute between two members may professionally affect the whole body'.[46] Accordingly, it was held that the ASX was not empowered to entertain a dispute between members as to whether the plaintiff had validly terminated a sub-underwriting agreement with the defendant. The uncertainty inherent in this approach is well illustrated by *New South Wales Medical Defence Union Ltd.* v. *Crawford*[47] where each member of the New South Wales Court of Appeal took a different view as to whether there was an extrinsic contract of insurance based on the articles or only a deemed contract in the form of the articles of association.

Finally, section 180(1) would not alter the outcome of cases such as *Eley*'s case[48] where the 'outsider' would not come within the definition of eligible officer.[49]

Aside from the vexed question of the enforceability of 'outsider' rights, the other impediment to enforcement of the statutory contract concerns the available remedies.

## (b) Remedies

Although the articles have contractual effect, not all contractual remedies are available to enforce them. The remedies of declaration and injunction

---

[43] See H. A. J. Ford and R. P. Austin, *Ford's Principles of Company Law* (6th edn., Sydney, Butterworths, 1992) para. 1719 and Sealy, above n 11 at 99. But cf., Trotman, above n 34, at 38.

[44] *Magill* v. *Santina Pty. Ltd. (in liq.)* [1983] 1 NSWLR 517 (CA NSW), which decision drew on comments by H. A. J. Ford, *Principles of Company Law* (2nd edn., Sydney, Butterworths, 1978) ¶223 regarding the cases of *Fischer* v. *Easthaven Ltd.* [1964] NSWR 261 and *Crumpton* v. *Morrine Hall Pty. Ltd.* [1965] NSWR 240.

[45] (1988) 12 ACLR 739; 6 ACLC 320.           [46] Ibid., at 745.

[47] (1993) 31 NSWLR 469 (CA NSW).           [48] Above n 18.

[49] See further: Ford and Austin, above n 43 para. 1711, F. H. Callaway in a commentary on an essay by L. S. Sealy, above n 11, at 115, and the explanatory memorandum which accompanied the change in statutory wording, para. 223.

are available where personal membership rights are at stake.[50] However, the remedy of rectification is not available.[51] And in Australia it is not clear whether damages are available as a remedy where a member is seeking to enforce the statutory contract against the company.[52] The source of the uncertainty is *Houldsworth* v. *City of Glasgow Bank*.[53] In that case a shareholder had been induced to purchase shares in the company by fraudulent misrepresentation. When the company became insolvent, the shareholder was forced to pay calls on his shares. The House of Lords held that it was inconsistent with the plaintiff's position as a shareholder to maintain a claim in damages against the company for misrepresentation.[54] This principle has since been applied in respect of other companies which were in liquidation to preclude a claim for damages for breach of the statutory contract.[55] However, it would appear that a member can claim damages if the company is solvent. In *Moffatt* v. *Farquhar*[56] Malins V-C directed an inquiry as to damages where directors refused to register share transfers and were held to have acted in excess of their powers and in *Ardlethan Options Ltd.* v. *Easdown*[57] the Australian High Court appeared to condone the recovery of damages.[58]

---

[50] See e.g. *Wood* v. *Odessa Waterworks Company* (1889) 42 Ch. D 636 and *Darvall* v. *North Sydney Brick & Tile Co. Ltd. (No. 4)* (1988) 14 ACLR 474; 6 ACLC 1095 regarding the mode and payment of dividends, *Woodroofe Ltd.* v. *M. S. McLeod Ltd.* (1984) 37 SASR 269 regarding the mode of appointment of directors, *Grant* v. *John Grant & Sons Pty. Ltd.* (1950) 82 CLR 1 (HC) and *Curtis* v. *J. J. Curtis & Co. Ltd.* [1984] 2 NZLR 267 (CA NZ) regarding pre-emption rights. See further regarding enforcement of pre-emption rights *Tett* v. *Phoenix Property and Investment Co. Ltd.* [1986] BCLC 149 (CA), A. Borrowdale, 'The Effect of Breach of Share Transfer Restrictions' [1988] *J Bus L* 307 and P. Luxton, 'Share Transfer Restrictions and the Relative Nature of Property Rights' [1990] *J Bus L* 14.

[51] *Scott* v. *Frank F. Scott (London) Ltd.* [1940] Ch. 794 (CA) and *Bratton Seymour Service Co. Ltd.* v. *Oxborough* [1992] BCLC 693; [1992] BCC 471 (CA). But see *Simon* v. *HPM Industries Pty. Ltd.* (1989) 15 ACLR 427; 7 ACLC 770 where Hodgson J said, obiter, that a court may be able to give a remedy in the nature of specific performance ordering that a party vote in favour of a special resolution to make appropriate alterations to the articles of association to rectify any defect. The court may also be prepared to sever invalid parts of an article, giving effect to the remainder if the ordinary tests for severance are satisfied: *Amalgamated Pest Control Pty. Ltd.* v. *McCarron* (1994) 13 ACSR 42; 12 ACLC 171.

[52] The availability of damages has recently been assured by statute in England: s. 111A, CA 1985 (UK).

[53] (1880) 5 App Cas 317 (HL).

[54] For a debate as to the basis of the decision in *Houldsworth*'s case see the correspondence between J. A. Hornby and L. C. B. Gower in (1956) 19 *Mod L Rev* at 54, 61 and 185.

[55] *Re Addlestone Linoleum Co.* (1887) 37 Ch. D 191 (CA), *Re Dividend Fund Incorporated (in liq.)* [1974] VR 451 and *Webb Distributors (Aust.) Pty. Ltd. & Ors.* v. *The State of Victoria & Anor.* (1993) 179 CLR 15 (HC). In *Webb*'s case, the High Court did not express a view on the correctness of *Houldsworth*'s case, but reached its decision that damages could not be claimed against a company in liquidation on the basis that the principle in *Houldsworth*'s case had been incorporated into s. 360(1)(k) of the Companies Code. That section has since been repealed and replaced by s. 563A CL (Aust) which postpones payments of debts owed to members in that capacity until satisfaction of debts to or claims by persons otherwise than as members. [56] (1878) 7 Ch. D 591. [57] (1915) 20 CLR 285 (HC).

[58] See further Hambrook, above n 40, ¶2.4.0175.

## (2) Alteration

The contract created by statute is stated to be subject to the provisions of the legislation. These other provisions give the company power to alter the articles by special resolution. The terms of the articles therefore provide no guarantee of protection to a shareholder who does not have a sufficiently large shareholding to block a special resolution, namely more than 25 per cent.

### (a) Restrictions on alterability

That is not to say that there are no constraints upon the power of amendment. The legislation in the United Kingdom and Australia provides that, in the absence of agreement in writing, no member is bound by an alteration to the memorandum or articles which requires the member to subscribe for more shares or increases the member's liability to the company.[59] The Australian legislation[60] extends this limitation to an alteration which increases or imposes restrictions on a member's right to transfer shares.[61] Further, shareholders have the ability to challenge alterations, both at common law and under statutory minority protection provisions.[62]

But there are also certain self-help measures which may be taken. Although it is not permissible for a company to limit the statutory power to alter its articles by prescribing a different method of alteration either in the articles or in a separate agreement,[63] certain devices may be adopted to limit the potential for alteration. A provision which could have been inserted in the articles may instead be included in the memorandum,[64] and it is then possible to prohibit or to prescribe a particular procedure

---

[59] Section 16, CA 1985 (UK); s. 180(3), CL (Aust).

[60] Section 180(3), CL (Aust).

[61] It has also been stated that an alteration cannot operate retrospectively against non-consenting owners of paid-up shares: *James* v. *Buena Ventura Nitrate Grounds Syndicate* [1896] 1 Ch. 456 at 466 (CA). However, reservations were expressed regarding this statement by Lindley MR in *Allen* v. *Gold Reefs of West Africa Ltd.* [1900] 1 Ch. 656 at 674 (CA) in light of decisions such as *Pepe* v. *City and Suburban Permanent Building Society* [1893] 2 Ch. 311. But see *Oswald* v. *Bailey* (1987) 11 NSWLR 715 (CA NSW).

[62] See Ch. 8 section 4(3) and Ch. 9 section 3.

[63] *Malleson* v. *National Insurance and Guarantee Corpn.* [1894] 1 Ch. 200, *Allen* v. *Gold Reefs of West Africa Ltd.*, above n 61, *Peters' American Delicacy Co. Ltd.* v. *Heath* (1939) 61 CLR 457 (HC). See discussion below section 2(e).

[64] Since the provisions of the memorandum can be altered by special resolution (s. 17, CA 1985 (UK); s. 172(2), CL (Aust)), of itself, the only additional protection provided by the insertion of a provision in the memorandum rather than the articles is a statutory right in certain cases to apply to the court to cancel the alteration: ss. 5 and 17(3), CA 1985 (UK); s. 172(8), CL (Aust).

for its alteration or omission.[65] In Australia, an alternative exists to including additional clauses in the memorandum. Instead, it can be provided in the memorandum that a special resolution altering the articles does not have effect until a further requirement specified in the memorandum has been complied with.[66] The legislation gives as examples of such further stipulations: a requirement for a higher majority, the approval of a particular person,[67] or the fulfilment of a particular condition.[68] However, a serious limitation on entrenchment via the memorandum in Australia (by either method) is that it appears that the provision must be inserted at the time of incorporation of the company.[69]

A more flexible technique for imposing additional requirements on the alteration of the articles over and above the requirement of the passing of a special resolution, is to confer special rights on a class of members.

### (b) Class rights

#### (i) *Statutory provisions*

The creation of class rights can provide a valuable method of protection for rights such as[70] an entitlement to receive a dividend, certain voting rights, the right to appoint a nominee director to the board, or even to block a takeover or an amendment of the articles without the holder's consent.[71] Class rights may be contained either in the memorandum or the articles, in the terms of issue of the shares or in a separate contract.[72]

---

[65] Section 17(2)(b) CA 1985 (UK); ss. 172(2) and (3) CL (Aust). If a provision is entrenched in this way, it can only be altered if the memorandum so provides and the procedure is followed, or a scheme of arrangement is propounded and approved by the court under ss. 425–7A, CA 1985 (UK); s. 411–3, CL (Aust). See Ch. 10 section 3. In England (but not in Australia) in cases where an alteration is effected under such an express provision there is no right to apply to the court under s. 5, CA 1985 (UK) for the alteration to be cancelled. There remains the possibility, however, of applying to the court on the basis that the alteration is unfairly prejudicial: s. 17(2), CA 1985 (UK); s. 172(2), CL (Aust).

[66] Section 176(2), CL (Aust).      [67] See discussion of class rights below.
[68] Section 176(3), CL (Aust).

[69] Under s. 172(1)(c), CL (Aust) the only provision which may be 'inserted' in the memorandum (as opposed to being altered or omitted) is 'any other provision with respect to the objects of the company or any provision with respect to the powers of the company'. However, if a wide interpretation is given to 'powers', it may be possible to extend the scope of the insertion power. See further Hambrook, above n 40 ¶2.4.0060.

[70] Cf., the view taken prior to *Cumbrian Newspapers Group Ltd. v̇. Cumberland and Westmorland Herald Newspapers and Printing Co. Ltd.*, above n 36, by L. C. B. Gower, *Gower's Principles of Modern Company Law* (4th edn., London, Stevens & Sons, 1979) at 562–3 that class rights related only to dividends, return of capital, or voting of that class.

[71] As in the case of 'golden shares'. See further J. H. Farrar *et al.*, *Farrar's Company Law* (3rd edn., London, Butterworths, 1991) at 228 and references there cited.

[72] In Australia s. 200, CL requires that the rights of preference shareholders be set out in certain respects in either the memorandum or articles. For a detailed discussion see J. Cotton, 'Class Rights Under the Code: A Consideration of Sections 125 and 128' (1986) 4 *Company & Sec LJ* 227 at 242 ff.

In *Cumbrian Newspapers Group Ltd.* v. *Cumberland and Westmorland Herald Newspapers and Printing Co. Ltd.*[73] Scott J divided rights or benefits contained in articles into three different categories:

(1) rights or benefits which are annexed to particular shares, for example, dividend rights and rights to participate in surplus assets on a winding up;

(2) rights or benefits conferred on individuals not in the capacity of members or shareholders of the company but for ulterior reasons connected with the administration of the company's affairs or the conduct of its business, such as the appointment of a particular member as president of the company, that is, outsider rights; and

(3) an intermediate category of rights or benefits which, although not attached to any particular shares are nevertheless conferred on the beneficiary in the capacity of member or shareholder of the company, for example, giving to a named shareholder the right to subscribe for a certain fraction of further shares issued by the company in the future, or a right of pre-emption over the shares held by other members, or a power to appoint one or more directors to the board of the company.

His Lordship held that rights falling within the first and third categories were 'rights attached to a class of shares' for the purposes of the special provisions in the companies legislation dealing with class rights. Essentially, to be a class right enjoyed *qua* member, ownership of at least some shares is necessary.[74] Scott J's approach has been applied in Australia in *Re A. Ffrost & Co. Pty. Ltd.*[75]

Where class rights exist, the legislation provides a default procedure which in most cases[76] requires the consent of three quarters of the members of the class, either in writing or in the form of a resolution passed at a meeting of class members by a three-quarters majority,[77] before class rights can be altered. More commonly, the members will prescribe a

---

[73] Above n 36.

[74] Ibid., at 16–17. Cf., *Re Blue Arrow plc* [1987] BCLC 585; (1987) 3 BCC 618 where the alteration of a class right dealing with the power to remove the president was held not to be a variation of class rights, since holding the position of president was unrelated to any shareholding.  [75] [1993] 1 Qd. R 1.

[76] One exception exists in England where class rights are set out in the memorandum but neither the memorandum nor contemporaneously issued articles provide a variation of rights procedure. In this case, s. 125(5), CA 1985 (UK) provides that the rights may be varied only if all the members of the company agree.

[77] The Australian legislation requires the sanction of a special resolution, whereas the United Kingdom legislation specifies an extraordinary resolution.

special procedure before such rights can be altered, such as the consent of a specified proportion of the members of the class, or a particular kind of resolution. Where such a variation of rights clause is contained in the memorandum or articles, statutory provisions in both jurisdictions give effect to it,[78] so that class members' rights can be varied only in accordance with that clause.

Once the requisite class consent has been obtained, the procedure for effecting the alteration depends on the instrument by which the class rights were conferred. If conferred by the articles, they may be altered by special resolution. If conferred by the memorandum, then the position varies according to the jurisdiction.

In England, the rights may be altered only by the kind of resolution thereby provided, or in the absence of such a provision, with the consent of all the members of the company.[79]

In Australia, the statutory drafting leaves some uncertainty as to the procedure to be followed regarding class rights contained in the memorandum. A literal interpretation of the statutory provisions is that the statutory power of variation supplies the power to alter the memorandum and that only the class rights variation procedure need be complied with. However, against this interpretation, commentators have argued[80] that class consent should not in itself be sufficient. Rather they suggest that the company should also have to resolve to implement the variation by altering the class rights provision, otherwise the class itself would have total control over its dividend and other rights. Relying on the words 'the company may' which preface the variation of rights clause, they suggest that once class consent has been obtained, a variation of rights clause in the memorandum may be altered by ordinary resolution of the company in general meeting.[81]

Where a variation of rights clause is contained in the memorandum it may declare class rights to be unalterable, and this prohibition on variation is enforced by the legislation.[82] In Australia, the legislation also gives effect to such a declaration of inalterability where it is contained in the

---

[78] Section 125, CA 1985 (UK); ss. 197, 198, 199, CL (Aust).

[79] Section 125(5), CA 1985 (UK).

[80] Cotton, above n 72, at 230–2, J. O'Donovan and G. W. O'Grady 'Company Deadlocks: Prevention and Cure' (1982) 1 *Company & Sec LJ* 67 at 75–6 and J. P. Hambrook, (Chapter Ed., Ch. 2.6) *Australian Corporation Law* (Sydney, Butterworths, 1991, looseleaf service) ¶2.6.0095.

[81] Similar questions arise as regards the procedure following class consent for variations of class rights which are not in the memorandum or the articles: see Cotton, ibid., at 231.

[82] Section 17, CA 1985 (UK); ss. 197(2), 198(2), and 199(2), CL (Aust). In these circumstances the only possibility for variation is under a scheme of arrangement, see above n 65, or by court order under the unfair prejudice remedy.

articles.[83] Further, in most cases, the same protection is accorded to variation of rights clauses as to the substantive rights themselves.[84]

There is, however, a feature of the Australian legislation which makes it unclear how far *Cumbrian's* case is applicable in the Australian context. In *Cumbrian Newspapers Group Ltd.* v. *Cumberland and Westmorland Herald Newspaper and Printing Co. Ltd.*[85] Scott J held that the rights accorded to the plaintiff company[86] were rights attached to a class of shares. Rather than interpreting the reference in the legislation to '. . . a company whose share capital is *divided* into shares of different classes'[87] as referring to the situation where there are distinct classes of shares,[88] Scott J stated that '. . . for the purposes of section 125, the share capital of a company is . . . divided into shares of different classes, if shareholders, *qua* shareholders, enjoy different rights'.[89] Since the plaintiff was the only shareholder accorded such rights, the effect of this decision was that the plaintiff's consent was required for the variation of those rights.

Some support for the applicability of this approach in Australia can be found in *Re A. Ffrost. & Co. Pty. Ltd.*,[90] where Ryan J relied on *Cumbrian's* case for his finding that special rights conferred on a governing director were class rights, even though they were not formally designated as such. However, against this view, it should be noted that the Australian class right protection provisions distinguish between companies where the share capital is divided into classes and those where the shares are all of one class but rights are nevertheless attached to shares.[91] The former provision applies where rights are attached to shares 'included' in a class. On a literal interpretation of this statutory scheme,[92] rights such as those

---

[83] Section 197(2), s. 198(2), s. 199(2), CL (Aust). But cf., the Editors of the *Australian Corporations & Securities Law Reporter* (Sydney, CCH, 1991, looseleaf service) ¶42–160 who observe that since this power is not stated directly, there is doubt as to whether the articles can be made unalterable. See further Cotton, above n 72, at 233–4.

[84] Section 125(7), CA 1985 (UK); s. 197(3), s. 198(3), s. 199(3), CL (Aust). There are slight variations between the provisions in the two jurisdictions. See further R. R. Pennington, *Company Law* (6th edn., London, Butterworths, 1990) at 224. Note also s. 198(8), CL (Aust) which deems the allotment of shares or the division of shares into classes to be a variation of class rights, unless the same rights are attached to all shares.

[85] Above n 36.

[86] Namely, rights of pre-emption, rights in respect of unissued shares and the right to nominate a director provided its shareholding exceeded 10%.

[87] Emphasis added.

[88] Cf., Gower, above n 70, at 562–3 and *Re Bowater Canadian Ltd. and R. L. Crain Inc.* (1987) 62 OR (2d) 752 (CA Ontario).          [89] Above n 36, at 22.

[90] Above n 75.

[91] Section 198, CL (Aust). A further section (s. 199, CL) applies where a company has no share capital but its members are divided into classes and have 'special rights'.

[92] But cf., *Fraser* v. *NRMA Holdings Ltd.* (1995) 15 ACSR 590; 13 ACLC 132 (Full Fed Ct) where it was held that NRMA Ltd. was a member included in a class of members for the purposes of s. 199(2), CL (Aust) (which applies to companies without a share capital) even

enjoyed by the plaintiff in *Cumbrian*'s case may be regarded as falling within the legislative provisions which apply where the shares are all of one class but rights are attached to shares, rather than within the provisions relating to companies whose capital is divided into classes. The effect of this would be that only the consent of the holders of three-quarters of the issued shares in the company would be required to vary those rights and no special consent need be obtained from the holders of the shares which enjoy the rights.

### (ii) Remedies

In addition[93] to the usual remedies available to minority shareholders, both common law and statutory, an express right is accorded to members of the affected class[94] with the specified percentage shareholding[95] to apply to the court within a certain period[96] after a variation of class rights to disallow the variation if it is satisfied that it would unfairly prejudice the members of the class.[97] This remedy pre-dates the statutory protection against variation of class rights and at least as extensive relief could be granted under the more general remedy against unfairly prejudicial conduct. This appears to be contemplated by the Australian unfair prejudice remedy[98] which expressly applies to a resolution or proposed resolution of a class of members.

### (iii) What amounts to an alteration

Apart from the technical complexity of the class rights protection provisions, the most substantial limitation on the protection offered by class rights to minority shareholders is the restrictive construction which is generally adopted to the question of what actually constitutes an alteration

where there was no formal division of the members into different classes, with the result that NRMA Ltd.'s consent was required to remove its right to share in any surplus on a winding-up. See also C. A. Carracher, '*Cumbrian Newspapers Group Ltd.* v. *Cumberland Westmorland Herald Newspaper and Printing Co. Ltd.*' (1989) 12 *Sydney L Rev* 262.

[93] In *Carruth* v. *Imperial Chemical Industries Ltd.* [1937] AC 707 at 765 (HL) Lord Maugham said, obiter, that the specific statutory provision did not exclude an alternative remedy.

[94] Although Farrar, above n 71, at 233 notes that there is a gap in the legislation as no reference is made in s. 127, CA 1985 (UK) to the ability to apply to the court where class rights are set out in the memorandum and the memorandum and articles do not contain a variation of rights clause.

[95] In the UK the figure is 15% of the issued shares of the relevant class: s. 127(2), CA 1985 (UK). In Australia it is 10%: s. 197(4), s. 198(4), s. 199(4), CL (Aust).

[96] In the UK the period is 21 days: s. 127(3), CA 1985 (UK). In Australia it is 28 days: s. 197(5), s. 198(5), s. 199(5), CL (Aust).

[97] In Australia, this remedy is not of great benefit where there is only one class of shares because the court may only grant relief if the alteration would unfairly prejudice 'the shareholders' of the company: s. 198(6), CL (Aust), rather than the shareholders whose shares have special rights.    [98] Section 260(1)(a)(ii), CL (Aust).

of class rights. A distinction has been drawn between rights and the enjoyment of those rights, so that if class rights are the same in substance but merely commercially less valuable, there is no alteration.

An example of this approach can be seen in *Adelaide Electric Supply Co. Ltd.* v. *Prudential Assurance Co. Ltd.*[99] where the House of Lords held that the change of the place of payment of the dividend on a preference share from England to Australia did not vary the rights of the preference shareholder, even though the Australian pound was worth less than the English pound. A similar approach was taken in *Greenhalgh* v. *Arderne Cinemas Ltd.*[100] where the subdivision of a class of ten shilling shares into two-shilling shares was held not to vary the rights of a holder of existing two shilling shares, although this multiplied the voting power of the former ten shilling shareholders by five and thereby removed Greenhalgh's power to block a special resolution.

It has also been held that a reduction of capital which involves repayment of paid-up capital on preference shares which have a prior right to return of capital on a winding up does not fall within a variation of rights article. Rather it is regarded as a fulfilment of rights.[101] Listed companies will often reduce the effect of this provision by use of the Spens formula, namely a provision in the articles which states that in the event of a reduction of capital, preference shareholders are to receive at least the market value of their shares, and gives preference shareholders voting rights on the special resolution required to approve the reduction. In unlisted companies a valuation formula can achieve a similar effect.[102]

It is possible to define what will amount to a variation of rights so as to extend the ambit of class rights protection to matters which would otherwise be interpreted only to affect the enjoyment or as a fulfilment of the rights. This was successfully achieved in *Re Northern Engineering Industries plc*[103] by a provision in the articles which deemed a reduction of capital to amount to a variation of the rights of any class of shareholders. That case can be contrasted with *White* v. *Bristol Aeroplane Co. Ltd.*[104] where a clause in the articles which required class consent not only when rights were 'altered' but also when they were 'affected, modified, dealt with or abrogated in any manner' was held not to achieve this end.

---

[99] [1934] AC 122 (HL).

[100] [1946] 1 All ER 512 (CA).

[101] *Re Saltdean Estate Co. Ltd.* [1968] 1 WLR 1844, *House of Fraser plc* v. *ACGE Investments Ltd.* [1987] AC 387 (HL). See further R. Levy, 'Is a Separate Meeting of Preference Shareholders Necessary on a Reduction of Capital?' (1987) 5 *Company & Sec LJ* 262.

[102] See S. Lindsay, 'The Position of Preference Shareholders in a Reduction of Capital' (1987) 5 *Company & Sec LJ* 77 at 91.            [103] [1994] BCC 618 (CA).

[104] [1953] Ch. 65 (CA).

In *White*'s case, the company had issued both ordinary and preference shares. It proposed to issue further ordinary shares and also further preference shares ranking equally with the existing ones. The issue would vastly increase the relative voting strength of preference shareholders who were also ordinary shareholders. But the Court of Appeal held that this would not be to alter, affect, modify or abrogate the substance of the rights of the original preference shareholders. They would still be entitled to one vote per share, and so the company did not need the separate class consent of the preference shareholders for the new issue. Evershed MR did, however, envisage[105] a situation where class rights might be altered without a literal variation of the memorandum or articles and so require the consent of the class of shareholders affected. His Lordship referred, without expressing any view on it, to an example mentioned in argument of a resolution doubling the voting power of the ordinary stockholders without altering any of the other privileges or rights attached to any class. If followed, this dictum may lead to a re-evaluation of earlier cases which limited alterations requiring consent to literal alterations.[106]

In Australia, the result of *White*'s case has been reversed by section 197(8) of the Corporations Law which deems the allotment of preference shares ranking equally with existing preference shares to be a variation of the rights attached to existing preference shares unless it was expressly authorized when the existing preference shares were allotted. Further, article 4(3) of Table A provides that, 'The rights conferred upon the holders of the shares of any class issued with preferred or other rights shall, unless otherwise expressly provided by the terms of issue of the shares of that class, be deemed to be varied by the creation or issue of further shares ranking equally with the first-mentioned shares'.[107]

## (c) Weighted voting

A further option for protecting the articles of association from alteration is to provide for weighted voting rights. This device was used in *Bushell* v. *Faith*[108] to prevent the directors being removed from office by a simple majority of members.[109] There were three shareholders who each held 100 shares. The articles included a provision that on a resolution at a general meeting for the removal of any director from office, any shares held by that director should carry the right to three votes. The defendant was therefore

---

[105] Ibid., at 76–7.
[106] See further Pennington, above n 84, at 228–9. More recent cases where allotments of shares have been successfully challenged as infringing shareholders' personal rights suggest that such a re-evaluation is occurring. see Ch. 8 section 4(c) and Ch. 9 section 4.
[107] See *Lorenzi* v. *Lorenzi Holdings Pty. Ltd.* (1993) 12 ACSR 398.
[108] [1970] AC 1099 (HL).
[109] Under the precursor to s. 303, CA 1985 (UK).

able to cast 300 votes and outvote the other two shareholders. At first instance, Ungoed-Thomas J held that the article was invalid as infringing the statutory right of the shareholders to remove a director from office by ordinary resolution. But, although the statutory right is expressed to apply notwithstanding anything in the articles, the validity of the article was upheld by the Court of Appeal and by the House of Lords.[110]

The facts of this case raise difficult questions.[111] On the one hand, a strong argument may be made that a technical device which, as Lord Reid said, was 'obviously designed to evade section 184(1) of the Companies Act, 1949 [*sic*]'[112] should not be permitted to circumvent the clear intention of a statutory provision, whereas if a provision in the articles had instead stated that the plaintiff could not be removed as a director it would have been invalid. On the other hand, the policy of the legislation is questionable. In a quasi-partnership company it is usually the expectation of the members that they will also be directors and removal of a director pursuant to the statutory provision contrary to this expectation provides grounds for relief under the unfair prejudice provision and/or the basis for a winding-up order.[113] The indiscriminate application of the legislation, irrespective of the nature of the company, provides some justification for the House of Lords allowing shareholders to express their expectations by indirect means. The equivalent provision in Australia has no application to proprietary companies,[114] so that the use of weighted voting clauses in those companies should be unobjectionable. An example of weighted voting being used to provide a more general veto power in such a company is *Amalgamated Pest Control Pty. Ltd.* v. *McCarron*,[115] where a clause in the company's articles gave the permanent governing director a weighted vote at any general meeting equivalent to 26 per cent of the total votes available, and accordingly prevented any special resolution being passed without the director's approval.

In order to be effective, such weighted voting rights must themselves be entrenched, and this can be done by applying the weighted voting rights to the clause which creates the rights. In England, such provisions will also be protected by variation of class rights provisions.[116]

---

[110] Lord Morris of Borth-y-Gest dissenting.

[111] For criticism of the decision see C. M. Schmitthoff, Editorial [1970] *J Bus L* 1, D. Prentice, 'Removal of Directors from Office' (1969) 32 *Mod L Rev* 693 and J. G. Collier [1970] *Cambridge LJ* 41. But cf., B. J. Cartoon, 'The Removal of Company Directors' [1980] *J Bus L* 17 who supports the decision.          [112] Above n 108 at 1105.

[113] See Ch. 6–8.

[114] Section 227, CL (Aust). See P. Redmond, *Companies and Securities Law: Commentary and Materials* (2nd edn., Sydney, The Law Book Company Ltd., 1992) at 274–5.

[115] Above n 51.

[116] *Cumbrian*'s case, above n 36, at 17. See text accompanying nn 85–92 regarding the Australian position.

### (d) Quorum requirements

An even simpler technique than weighted voting rights is to insert into the articles of association a quorum requirement for shareholders' meetings that a particular shareholder be present, so that absence from the meeting amounts to the exercise of a power of veto. There have been some doubts as to the effectiveness of this technique, as courts have on several occasions been prepared to make an order convening a meeting[117] where minority shareholders have absented themselves as a means of frustrating the wishes of the majority.[118] However, these cases have concerned purely numerical quorum requirements, rather than provisions designed to protect a particular shareholder, and can be contrasted with the recent case of *Harman* v. *BML Group Ltd.*[119] Here, there were five shareholders, one of whom (Blumenthal) held 'B' shares. All were directors. Blumenthal was a minority shareholder, but under a shareholders' agreement, he was entitled to remain in office as a director of the company for as long as he owned the B shares, and a shareholders' meeting would be inquorate unless a B shareholder or proxy was present. Blumenthal became concerned that two other directors (who together held a majority of the shares) were stealing from the company. Blumethal and two other shareholders removed the two alleged offenders as directors on a show of hands. The two removed directors attempted to requisition a further meeting but Blumenthal refused to attend. At first instance, Paul Baker QC ordered a meeting to be held at which any two members, not necessarily including the B shareholder would constitute a quorum. This decision was reversed by the Court of Appeal who considered it inappropriate to invoke section 371 to override Blumenthal's class right to be present in the quorum.[120]

### (e) Alteration and separate contracts

The question then arises whether the susceptibility of the articles to alteration can be restricted by the more direct means of a shareholders' agreement. In answering this question, two separate situations should be distinguished:

---

[117] Under s. 371, CA 1985 (UK). The corresponding Australian section is s. 251, CL (Aust).

[118] See e.g. *Re Opera Photographic Ltd.* [1989] 1 WLR 634, *Re Sticky Fingers Restaurant Ltd.* [1992] BCLC 84; [1991] BCC 754 and *Re Whitchurch Insurance Consultants Ltd.* [1993] BCLC 1359.

[119] [1994] 1 WLR 893 (CA).

[120] See further, C. A. Riley, 'Vetoes and Voting Agreements: Some Problems of Consent and Knowledge' (1993) 44 *Northern Ireland Legal Quarterly* 34 at 41.

(1) where a company contracts not to alter the corporate constitution, contrary to the statutory power of alteration; and

(2) where the company alters its constitution in such a way as to facilitate a breach of a separate contractual obligation.

### (i) Contracts not to alter the corporate constitution

Under the companies legislation in both the United Kingdom and Australia, the articles of association may be altered by special resolution.[121] Where a provision in a company's articles specifies a different method of alteration from that prescribed by statute or prohibits its alteration, contrary to the statutory power, that provision is invalid.[122]

Prior to the recent case of *Russell* v. *Northern Development Corporation Ltd.*[123] the authorities were inconclusive as to whether a contract outside the articles not to alter the terms of the articles was equally invalid.[124] The case which considered this issue most directly was *Punt* v. *Symons & Co. Ltd.*[125] Here, the company entered into an agreement with its founder, Mr Symons, clause 6 of which provided that: 'The company shall not at any time alter or attempt to alter the clauses of the articles of association relating to the appointment of the vendor as governing director as originally framed, or do or suffer anything to be done in contravention of the provisions contained in these clauses respectively.' The relevant clauses appointed Mr Symons as governing director with wide powers, and granted the trustees the ability to exercise those powers after his death. After Mr Symons' death the company sought to amend the relevant articles so as to deprive the trustees of their powers. The trustees' action for an injunction to restrain the meeting based on clause 6 of the agreement failed for the reason that '. . . the company cannot contract itself out of the right to alter its articles'.[126]

In fact, the injunction was granted on an alternative ground,[127] and it was therefore unnecessary for the court to consider the validity of the contract. However, Byrne J appeared to treat the contract as valid when he speculated, obiter, that it might be enforceable by other remedies.[128]

---

[121] Section 9, CA 1985 (UK), s. 176(1), CL (Aust).

[122] *Walker* v. *London Tramways Company* (1879) 12, Ch. D 705, *Allen* v. *Gold Reefs of West Africa Ltd.*, above n 61, and *Peters' American Delicacy Co. Ltd.* v. *Heath*, above n 63, at 479 *per* Latham CJ and at 503 *per* Dixon J (HC).                [123] Above n 1.

[124] For a detailed examination of the state of authorities prior to *Russell*'s case see E. Ferran, 'The decision of the House of Lords in *Russell* v. *Northern Bank Development Corporation Limited*' [1994] *Cambridge LJ* 343 at 354–7 and B. J. Davenport, 'What did *Russell* v. *Northern Bank Development Corporation Ltd.* decide?' (1993) 109 *Law Q Rev* 553.

[125] [1903] 2 Ch. 506.                                    [126] Ibid., at 511.

[127] In their capacity as shareholders, the trustees were able to obtain the injunction on the ground that the directors had issued shares for the improper purpose of securing the passing of the amendments.                [128] Above n 125, at 514.

This issue was, however, squarely addressed in *Russell* v. *Northern Bank Development Corporation Ltd.*[129] *Russell's* case concerned the power granted by statute to alter the memorandum by ordinary resolution in order to increase the company's share capital, rather than the power to amend the articles. However, the House of Lords considered that the relevant principles were the same.

The facts were that the four shareholders and the company had entered into an agreement which provided in clause 3 that 'No further share capital shall be created or issued in the company . . . without the written consent of each of the parties hereto'. In considering the validity of this term, Lord Jauncey of Tullichettle (with whom the other Law Lords agreed) drew a distinction between (on the one hand) an agreement between shareholders as to how they would exercise their voting rights on a resolution to alter the company's constitution and (on the other hand) an agreement by the company that its capital would not be increased without the consent of each of the shareholders.[130] His Lordship cited *Welton* v. *Saffery*[131] as authority that the former type of agreement is valid and enforceable.[132] By contrast, the company's undertaking was held to be 'as obnoxious as if it had been contained in the articles of association and therefore . . . unenforceable as being contrary to the [statutory power of amendment]'.[133]

This distinction was overlooked by two of the three members of the Northern Ireland Court of Appeal.[134] The distinction was, however, made by Kelly LJ. His Lordship held the agreement to be invalid, substantially on the ground that the company was a party to it, but considered that the result would have been different if only the shareholders had entered into an agreement in similar terms, saying,[135] 'I find it difficult to understand why, if a voting restriction clause was intended, that it did not state in

---

[129] Above n 1.

[130] See P. Finn, 'Shareholder Agreements' (1978) 6 *Austl Bus L Rev* 97 at 101–2 and Sealy, above n 11, at 108–9, who have argued that an agreement by some or all of the shareholders that they will not alter the articles is enforceable, and there should be no objection to shareholders contracting in these terms. [131] [1897] AC 299 (HL).

[132] Cf., G. Shapira, 'Voting Agreements and Corporate Statutory Powers' [1993] 109 *Law Q Rev* 210 and J. Savirimuthu, 'Thoughts on Russell—killing private companies with kindness?' (1993) 14 *Company Lawyer* 137, both of whom argue that Lord Davey's dictum in *Welton* v. *Saffery* was taken out of context.

[133] Cf., Ferran, above n 124, who argues trenchantly that '[a] rule that can often be circumvented by those who have the time to arrange their affairs appropriately, and the resources to pay for the advice that will enable them to do so, is lacking in merit'. Shapira and Savirimuthu, both ibid., make similar observations See also C. M. S. McGlynn, 'The constitution of the company: mandatory statutory provisions v private agreements' (1994) 15 *Company Lawyer* 301 who points out that Articles 33–35 of the amended proposal for a Fifth Company Law Directive, OJ (1988) C240, 9 September 1983, would qualify the extent to which shareholders can exercise their voting rights as they please.

[134] *Russell* v. *Northern Bank Development Corporation Ltd.* [1992] BCLC 431; [1991] BCC 517 (CA NI), Lord Hutton LCJ and MacDermott LJ.

[135] Ibid., at 453; 536.

terms that the shareholders agreed to vote against any resolution brought to increase the authorised share capital which had not been agreed to in writing by all the shareholders'.

By contrast, Lord Hutton LCJ who formed the other member of the majority, appeared to base his decision that the agreement constituted an unlawful fetter on the company's statutory power to increase capital on the duration of the agreement.[136] His Lordship considered that an agreement made on the eve of the meeting would have been valid, whereas an agreement designed to be binding for a lengthy period was unlawful. With respect, it is submitted that the time at which the agreement was entered into should not be determinative of its validity. Indeed, if anything the policy arguments in favour of enforcing a formalized agreement should outweigh those favouring an *ad hoc* arrangement.

The dissenting member of the court, MacDermott LJ, similarly failed to draw any distinction regarding the enforceability of a contract based on whether or not the company was a party. His Lordship regarded the agreement as enforceable on the basis that the shareholders had entered into a personal voting agreement which fettered their own individual freedom to support or oppose a share increase resolution but did not fetter the company's ability to increase its capital.

However, if we assume the validity of the distinction drawn by Kelly LJ and by Lord Jauncey, it is necessary to consider why the appeal was allowed. It was because Lord Jauncey regarded the company's undertaking as severable from that of the shareholders,[137] leaving the agreement enforceable as between the shareholders.

Lord Jauncey analysed clause 3 of the agreement as involving two agreements. The first was personal to the shareholders and was an agreement only to exercise their voting powers in relation to the creation or issue of shares in the company if they and the company had agreed in writing. The second was an agreement by the company that its capital would not be increased without the consent of each of the shareholders and it was this second agreement which was severed.[138]

The usual conditions for severance are a threshold requirement of the 'blue pencil' test, and the additional test that severance must not alter the nature of the contract.[139]

---

[136] Ibid., at 442; 526–7.

[137] See L. S. Sealy, 'Shareholders' Agreements—An Endorsement and a Warning from the House of Lords' [1992] *Cambridge LJ* 437 regarding this aspect of the decision.

[138] The same approach was taken by the Supreme Court of New South Wales in *McEwan v. Dick* (1985) 9 ACLR 1011; 3 ACLC 671 in order to save part of a contract which breached a statutory provision prohibiting a company giving financial assistance in connection with a purchase of its shares.

[139] *McFarlane* v. *Daniell* (1938) 38 SR (NSW) 337 at 345, *Putsman* v. *Taylor* [1927] 1 KB 637 at 639–40, *Mason* v. *Provident Clothing and Supply Co. Ltd.* [1913] AC 724 at 745 (HL),

The shareholders' agreement in *Russell*'s case was drafted in such a way that in order to remove the company's promise from clause 3, the blue pencil test required the company's name to be removed altogether as a party to the agreement. The next question is therefore whether severing the company from the contract changed the nature of the contract, that is, whether the agreement was essentially a shareholders' voting agreement, or whether the fact that the company was a party was integral to it.

It may well have been possible to regard the contract as essentially a shareholders' voting agreement if its only operative clause had been clause 3. However, the agreement went on in clause 4 to prescribe a pre-emption procedure for transfers of shares.[140] This procedure constituted the company as agent for the sale of shares once a transfer notice had been given in accordance with the section and provided for the company to receive the purchase money and to register the name of the transferee in the event of failure by the transferor to transfer the shares. It is submitted that severance of the company from the contract rendered clause 4 ineffective and that therefore when the contract is examined as a whole, the test for severance was not satisfied.

A finding that the shareholders' agreement in this case was invalid would not necessarily have been meant the plaintiff would always be unable to prevent a new share issue. On the facts, the new shares were to be issued in order to capitalize the company's reserves, and were to be distributed *pro rata* according to the parties' shareholdings. The plaintiff made it clear that he had no objection to the proposed resolutions in themselves, but merely wished to establish that he would be able to prevent a future rights issue which could weaken his position in relation to the other shareholders if he did not have the necessary cash to take it up. Relief ought to be available to the plaintiff in the event of a future rights issue which he could not afford to take up if it were made for an improper purpose[141] or were unfairly prejudicial,[142] and the expression of the parties' expectations in the

---

*Attwood* v. *Lamont* [1920] 3 KB 571 (CA), *Brooks* v. *Burns Philp Trustee Co. Ltd.* (1969) 121 CLR 432 (HC), *T. Lucas & Co. Ltd.* v. *Mitchell* [1972] 1 WLR 938, *Re Davstone Estates Ltd.'s Leases*; *Manprop Ltd.* v. *O'Dell* [1969] 2 Ch. 378, *Stenhouse Australia Ltd.* v. *Phillips* [1974] AC 391 (PC). But cf., the criticisms of the inflexibility of the blue pencil test by Lord Nicholls of Birkenhead, 'Inequity in Equity', Seminar delivered at the Leo Cussen Institute, Melbourne, 1 March 1995.

[140] Cf., the more usual procedure of incorporating the pre-emption provisions in the articles, and merely protecting them from alteration by the shareholders' agreement.

[141] See e.g. *Howard Smith Ltd.* v. *Ampol Petroleum Ltd.* [1974] AC 821 (PC) and *Whitehouse* v. *Carlton House Pty. Ltd.* (1987) 162 CLR 285 (HC).

[142] See e.g. *Re Dalkeith Investments Pty. Ltd.* (1984) 9 ACLR 247; 3 ACLC 74, *Re a Company (No. 005134 of 1986)*; *Ex parte Harries* [1989] BCLC 383 also reported as *Re D. R. Chemicals Ltd.* (1989) 5 BCC 39 and *Re a Company (No. 007623 of 1984)* [1986] BCLC 362; (1986) 2 BCC 99,191.

shareholders' agreement would be likely to be regarded as a relevant factor in those proceedings.[143]

Perhaps the more important feature of *Russell's* case is not whether it was an appropriate case for severance, but rather the fact that the court declined to give effect to the consequences of finding that the contractual provision was illegal. Despite (or perhaps because of) the fact that the parties could have achieved the result by legal means,[144] the decision can be ranked alongside the equally controversial decision of the House of Lords in *Bushell* v. *Faith*[145] where again the court overcame potential illegality in order to give effect to the parties' attempt to formalize their expectations.

*Punt's* case and *Russell's* case posed a relatively clear conflict between an agreement to which the company was a party and the statutory power to alter the corporate constitution. However, the same question arises in a more indirect way where provisions of the articles of association are also embodied in an independent contact.

### (ii) External contracts based on the corporate constitution

This situation arose in *British Murac Syndicate Ltd.* v. *Alperton Rubber Co. Ltd.*[146] where the company entered into an agreement giving the plaintiff the right to nominate two directors to the board, provided it held a certain number of shares. A clause to the same effect was contained in article 88 of the articles of association. The plaintiff exercised its right of nomination, but the company objected to the nominees and requisitioned a meeting to delete article 88. Sargant J interpreted the extrinsic contract as involving as one of its terms that article 88 was not to be altered.[147] However, acting on the mistaken view that *Punt's* case had been overruled by *Bailey* v. *British Equitable Assurance Co.*,[148] his Lordship was prepared to grant an injunction to prevent the company from altering its articles to remove article 88.[149]

This case has attracted academic criticism because of its mistaken reading of *Bailey's* case.[150] It is submitted that the interpretation of the contract as involving a term that article 88 would not be altered is also open

---

[143] See Ch. 6 section 2(5) and section 2(8)(b)(ii).

[144] For example, if they had entrenched the provision via the memorandum or in *Russell's* case if they had ensured that the company was not a party to clause 3.

[145] Above n 108.    [146] [1915] 2 Ch. 186.    [147] Ibid., at 194.

[148] Above n 34. In fact, the only relief sought in *Bailey's* case was a declaration that the company was not entitled to break its contract merely because it had altered its articles.

[149] The order made was a declaration that the plaintiff's nominees were directors of the defendant company with liberty to apply from injunction if it became necessary.

[150] See e.g. D. Rice 'Terms of an Issue' (1958) 22 *Convey* 282 at 288 and Trebilcock, above n 34 at 113.

to criticism, and that the better view is that put forward by counsel for the defendant in that case,[151] namely that the company was free to alter the articles to delete article 88, but that this would not affect the plaintiff's independent contractual right to nominate two directors or the obligation on the company to accept those nominees. On this view, the independent contract would be valid, and the effect of the alteration of the articles would be merely to bring about the means for the company to commit a breach of it.

It is submitted that the quite different facts of *Southern Foundries (1926) Ltd. v. Shirlaw*[152] also fall within the same category as those in the *British Murac* case.[153] In *Shirlaw*'s case, the plaintiff challenged the ability of the company to remove him from his position as managing director pursuant to the articles of association. The plaintiff's contract of employment incorporated the articles which from the outset included a power to remove him before the expiration of his period of office. The company then altered its articles to empower Federated Foundries Ltd. to remove a director from office. The alteration of the articles enabled the plaintiff to be removed from office by a different procedure. But the alteration of the articles did not result in a breach of contract until the director was actually removed.

Where an alteration to articles of association facilitates a breach of contract, the other party is entitled to damages.[154] Declarations have also been made as to the terms of independent contracts in the face of proposals to alter the corporate constitution.[155] But where the remedy sought is an injunction to prevent breach of the contract, the argument may be raised that to grant an injunction would so far negate the exercise of the power to alter the articles that it almost negates the power itself.[156]

However, as Farrar points out,[157] the injunction does not stop the company acting on the article in respect of a person other than the party to the particular contract. There should therefore be no absolute bar to obtaining an injunction from acting upon altered articles in breach of contract.[158] Trebilcock[159] argues that there is no reason why the remedy of injunction should not also be available to prevent a threatened breach of contract before alteration of the articles.[160] Further, it is submitted that

---

[151] Above n 146 at 193.   [152] [1940] AC 701 (HL).

[153] Above n 146. See also McGlynn, above n 133.

[154] *Southern Foundries (1926) Ltd. v. Shirlaw*, above n 152.

[155] *Bailey* v. *British Equitable Assurance Co.*, above n 34.

[156] Farrar above n 71, at 136.   [157] Ibid.

[158] M. J. Trebilcock, above n 34 at 115 and L. S. Sealy, above n 21 at 110. But cf., H. A. J. Ford, *Principles of Company Law* (Sydney, Butterworths, 1974) at 178.

[159] Ibid.

[160] And this argument appears to receive some support from an obiter dictum of Scott J in *Cumbrian*'s case, above n 36. See also Gower, above n 30, at 546–7.

the cases where injunctions have been granted in terms which do interfere with the power of alteration of articles can be justified on grounds which need not conflict with the prohibition on contracting not to alter the articles. The two main cases in this category are the *British Murac* case[161] and the Australian case of *Fischer* v. *Easthaven*.[162]

Damages would have been of little assistance to the plaintiff in the *British Murac* case, in that what he wanted to ensure was the appointment of his nominees to the board. In the result, Sargant J granted an injunction to restrain the holding of the meeting and a declaration that the plaintiff's nominees were the directors of the company. In light of *Cumbrian*'s case,[163] if a case similar to the *British Murac* case were brought today, article 88 would be regarded as conferring a class right on the plaintiff, so that his consent would be required for an alteration to that article. In an appropriate case, similar relief might also be available under the oppression/unfair prejudice remedy.[164]

*Fischer*'s case,[165] concerned a home-unit company. Shares were divided into groups designated by a letter and a number. The plaintiffs owned shares designated M14 which entitled them to occupation of garage 14. The company proposed to delete group M14 from the articles which would have had the effect of depriving the plaintiffs of their right to use the garage. An injunction was granted preventing the passing of a resolution altering the articles on the ground that the company was under a contractual duty not to exercise its power of alteration.[166] Trebilcock[167] criticizes this decision on the ground that it is difficult to find 'anything between the shareholder and the company which on normal contractual principles could be regarded as a contract'. But it is submitted that the injunction could now also have been granted on the alternative ground that the alteration would vary class rights and that the necessary class consent had not be obtained.[168]

## 3. SHAREHOLDERS' AGREEMENTS[169]

The above discussion illustrates the way in which shareholders' voting

---

[161] Above n 146.          [162] Above n 44.          [163] Above n 36.
[164] See Ch. 6.            [165] Above n 44.          [166] Ibid., at 265.
[167] Above n 34, at 112.

[168] Although the court rejected this argument in *Fischer*'s case, it has been adopted in subsequent cases. See *Crumpton* v. *Morrine Hall Pty. Ltd.* above n 44, *Simon* v. *HPM Industries Pty. Ltd.* above n 51 and *Buckland* v. *Johnstone* (1991) 5 ACSR 404; 9 ACLC 1,193. See also R. Baxt, 'The Variation of Class Rights' (1968) 41 *Austl LJ* 490.

[169] See, generally, G. Stedman and J. Jones, *Shareholders' Agreements* (2nd edn., London, Longman Group UK Ltd., 1990), Finn, above n 130, and R. Baxt, 'Shareholders Voting Arrangements: American Sophistication or Recognized English Practice' 12 *Commercial Law Association Bulletin* 117.

agreements can be used to protect the provisions in the articles from alteration. They can also play a useful role in ensuring enforceability of the terms of the articles, for example if the shareholders enter into a separate agreement either in respect of particular provisions of the articles or generally, in terms that the articles will be enforceable by them in whatever capacity.[170] It is therefore appropriate to undertake a more detailed discussion of shareholders' agreements as a medium for the expression of the parties' expectations.[171]

Shareholders' agreements provide an alternative and in many respects preferable medium by which the parties can make detailed provision as to their rights and obligations. Voting agreements[172] may ensure that the company is set up in the way the parties intended[173] and may also be useful to control the balance of power during the life of the company.[174] Further, not only can the expression of the parties' expectations minimize the potential for disputes and hence the necessity for recourse to litigation, but express provision may be made as to the relief which will be available in respect of breach of specific provisions[175] or for alternative dispute resolution methods such as arbitration. Provision can also be made for exit from the company in the form of an express right to be bought out, or by specifying circumstances justifying a winding up.

## (1) Comparison with articles[176]

### (a) Parties

Shareholders' agreements may be between some or all of the shareholders and may also include the company as a party. In the above discussion of the

---

[170] For an example of such a clause see Stedman and Jones, ibid., at 6.

[171] There are two further extra-constitutional devices for augmenting the voting power of minority shareholders which it is not proposed to discuss but which are mentioned here for the sake of completeness, namely voting trusts and irrevocable proxies. By a voting trust, the shareholders transfer the title of their shares to trustees to then vote in accordance with the trust instrument. In the case of an irrevocable proxy, the owner retains the title to the shares but transfers the voting power to other persons. See further M. A. Pickering, 'Shareholders' Voting Rights and Company Control' (1965) 81 *Law Q Rev* 248, F. H. O'Neal, *Close Corporations* (2nd edn., Mundelein Illinois, Callaghan, 1971) §5.31 and Farrar, above n 71 at 142–3.

[172] Sometimes called 'pooling' agreements: see further S. Krüger, 'Pooling Agreements under English Company Law' (1978) 94 *Law Q Rev* 557 and 'Corporate Pooling Agreements and Restriction-of-Directors Agreements' (1981) 10 *Anglo-Am L Rev* 73.

[173] See further regarding formation agreements, *Encyclopaedia of Forms and Precedents*, Vol. 5 (5th edn., London, Butterworths, 1994 reissue).

[174] See e.g. *Ringuet* v. *Bergeron* (1960) 24 DLR (2d) 449; [1960] SCR·672 (SCC).

[175] For example in *Ringuet* v. *Bergeron*, ibid., the agreement provided that on a breach by one of the parties to the agreement, his shares were to be transferred to the others in equal parts.

[176] See *Shalfoon* v. *Cheddar Valley Co-operative Dairy Co. Ltd.* [1924] NZLR 561 *per* Salmond J.

prohibition on a company from altering its articles we have seen that the inclusion of the company as a party may render a shareholders' agreement invalid. There may however be advantages to the inclusion of the company if the agreement does not restrict alteration of the company's constitution, for example if it is sought to bind the company to agreements dealing with such matters as restrictions on borrowing, share transfers and purchase of shares. It may also bind the directors (indirectly) to give effect to arrangements in the agreement which could not be achieved directly because of the prohibition on fettering of directors' discretion.[177] If it is decided to include the company as a party, however, the question of consideration should be addressed. Mutual promises would provide sufficient consideration to make a binding agreement,[178] but where these are not present, the agreement will need to be under seal.

Unanimous shareholders' agreements have a special significance in that such an agreement is treated at common law as being equivalent to a resolution[179] and may even be effective as a special resolution altering or overriding the articles.[180] In *Cane* v. *Jones*[181] the plaintiff was able to obtain a declaration that a unanimous but informal shareholders' agreement overrode the articles so that the chairman was no longer entitled to a casting vote. However, there are limitations on the ability of a unanimous shareholders' agreement to overcome the lack of a resolution at common law,[182] and it would appear that the operation of the doctrine in so far as it

---

[177] See *Northern Counties Securities Ltd.* v. *Jackson & Steeple Ltd.* [1974] 1 WLR 1133, and see discussion below, section 3(2).

[178] In England and Australia. Cf., the occasional uncertainty surrounding this issue in the US. See H. Gelb, 'Close Corporation Control and the Voting Agreement' (1981) 16 *Land and Water L Rev* 225 at 234 and O'Neal, above n 171, §5.11.

[179] *Re Duomatic* [1969] 2 Ch. 365 and *Re P. W. Saddington & Sons Pty. Ltd.* (1990) 19 NSWLR 674. In *Re Duomatic Ltd.* which concerned unanimous consent to a matter requiring an ordinary resolution, Buckley J held that the agreement between the shareholders was sufficient to bind 2 additional shareholders who became members subsequent to the agreement.

[180] Cf., s. 255, CL (Aust) which provides that if all the members of an exempt proprietary company have signed a document containing a statement that they are in favour of a resolution in the terms set out in the document, a resolution in those terms is deemed to have been passed at a general meeting. Resolutions requiring special notice or to be passed by a majority other than a simple majority are not covered by the section. Note that the First Corporate Law Simplification Bill 1994 proposes to extend the operation of this section to all proprietary companies.

[181] [1980] 1 WLR 1451. See also *Re Home Treat Ltd.* [1991] BCLC 705; [1991] BCC 165.

[182] These limitations apply where the legislation can be interpreted as prescribing a procedure (such as the passing of a special resolution, a notice procedure or disclosure of certain matters either prior to or at a meeting) which must be complied with as the only method by which a particular matter may be achieved. See *M. Dalley & Co. Pty. Ltd.* v. *Sims* (1968) 120 CLR 603 at 614 *per* Barwick CJ (HC), *Re Duomatic Ltd.*, above n 179, *Guinness plc* v. *Saunders* [1990] 2 AC 663 (HL), *Re Barry Artist Ltd.* [1985] 1 WLR 1305 and *Re Compaction*

applies to written resolutions is limited in England by the statutory written resolutions procedure.[183]

Agreements may also usefully be entered into by only some of the shareholders. This was the case in *Ringuet* v. *Bergeron*[184] where the majority shareholders entered into an agreement designed to ensure that the parties would be elected to controlling board positions. The only limitation on the effectiveness of agreements to which not all members are parties is that where a majority of the shareholders are parties their conduct may result in a fraud on the minority or unfairly prejudicial conduct, in which case the shareholders who are not parties may be able to seek relief under the various minority protection remedies.[185]

### (b) Privity of contract

Unlike the statutory contract created by the articles, new members who acquire shares either by transfer or consequent on an allotment of shares will not automatically be bound by a shareholders' agreement. This is illustrated by the case of *Greenhalgh* v. *Mallard*.[186] Here the appellant agreed to invest capital in the company on terms that the three directors should vote with him, thereby giving him control of sufficient votes to carry an ordinary resolution. Subsequently the directors transferred some of their shares, and it was held that they had contracted to support the appellant only in respect of the shares which they held at any time.

It is possible to attempt to perpetuate a shareholders' agreement by making it a condition of transfer that the transferee become a party to the agreement. This may be reinforced by requiring the directors to ensure that the succeeding transferee has entered into an identical agreement

---

*Systems Pty. Ltd.* [1976] 2 NSWLR 477 at 484. See also Farrar, above n 71, at 338, Sealy, above n 21, at 168–9, and Ford and Austin, above n 43, para. 1818. Cf., R. Grantham, 'The Unanimous Consent Rule in Company Law' [1993] *Cambridge LJ* 245.

[183] Sections 381A–C, CA 1985 (UK) provide a procedure for 'written resolutions' for private companies. This procedure is free from the various common law limitations in that it applies even when the Act specifically requires a general meeting, it applies to special, extraordinary, elective and ordinary resolutions and is effective without any notice being given. However, it contains its own limitations in that the resolution is only effective if it is vetted by the auditors and they notify the company that the resolution does not concern them or need not be considered at a meeting or 7 days elapse. Section 381C(2) preserves the common law rule. But where the resolution is in writing, it would appear that auditors clearance (or the lapse of 7 days) is still required. See D. A. Bennett, 'The Companies Act 1989: Part II' *Journal of the Law Society of Scotland*, November 1990 at 469 and H. W. Higginson, 'Written Resolutions of Private Companies' (1993) 109 *Law Q Rev* 16. Note also the proposal to remove the requirement to involve auditors in the written resolution procedure. Department of Trade and Industry, *Resolutions of Private Companies* (February 1995).     [184] Above n 174.     [185] See Ch. 6–8.
[186] [1943] 2 All ER 234 (CA).

before the share transfer is registered. This procedure may, however, become unwieldy if the number of shareholders is large.[187]

The distinction between the articles and a shareholders' agreement in this regard may in some cases become blurred. If the agreement is unanimous and has the effect of altering the articles of association, then it may be that it binds subsequent members.[188] And even in cases where the company is not a party to a shareholders' agreement, there appear to be some circumstances where it can nevertheless rely on its terms. This highly unusual situation arose in *Snelling* v. *John G. Snelling Ltd.*[189] where all three shareholders who were also the directors of a family company had entered into an agreement which provided that in the event of a director voluntarily resigning, he would immediately forfeit all moneys due to him from the company. The directors fell out and the plaintiff resigned as a director. He then issued a writ against the company claiming moneys due to him as at the date of his resignation. The plaintiff's claim was dismissed on the basis that all the promisees under the agreement and the party to be benefited by the agreement (namely the company) were before the court.

### (c) Alterability

By contrast with the complexity involved in entrenching provisions of the articles of association, the agreement of all parties is needed to alter a shareholders' agreement.

### (d) Confidentiality

A further advantage which may be particularly attractive to commercial joint ventures is that a shareholders' agreement is confidential. There are, however, two limitations on the privacy of shareholders' agreements. The first is that in both jurisdictions there are some documents which require registration. In England, a unanimous agreement which is effective as a special or extraordinary resolution must be registered.[190] It may, however, be possible to avoid the necessity for registration by framing the agreement in terms that it does not override or amend the articles, but is instead an agreement to vote in a favour of a special resolution at a general meeting. In Australia, a document 'affecting the memorandum of a company' must

---

[187] It also poses problems of enforceability. See further Riley, above n 120, at 39–40.
[188] See above n 179.                                    [189] [1973] QB 87.
[190] Section 380(4)(c), CA 1985 (UK). Failure to do so constitutes a criminal offence (s. 380(5)) but does not render the agreement invalid as an amendment to the articles, although it may prevent the company from relying on it against other persons: see Farrar, above n 71, at 335. Cf., s. 256, CL (Aust).

be lodged within 14 days of execution,[191] and certain documents and agreements relating to class rights must be lodged within one month of being made.[192]

The second qualification which applies in England is that the Restrictive Trade Practices Acts 1976 and 1977 may require the agreement to be registered with the Director General of Fair Trading.[193]

### (e) Enforceability

Perhaps the greatest advantage offered by a shareholders' agreement is its enforceability. None of the complications of the *'qua* member' requirement are relevant, and the parties to the agreement are bound by and can enforce the agreement without reference to the capacity in which they entered the contract. Thus effective and binding provision can be made as to the composition of the board and the appointment, tenure, and removal of directors.

### (i) Voting agreements

Apart from setting out the parties' rights and obligations, a shareholders' agreement may either directly or indirectly require a shareholder to vote in a particular way at a company meeting. It has been held that such agreements are lawful,[194] and they have been enforced by the courts applying the authorities to the effect that the right to vote is a right of property which may be exercised in a shareholder's self interest.[195] A shareholders' voting agreement was first successfully enforced in 1902 in *Greenwell* v. *Porter.*[196] As part of the consideration for the sale of a block of shares, the plaintiff was granted the right to nominate two directors and the defendants agreed to vote for the re-election of the nominated directors on their retirement by rotation. When the defendants subsequently threatened to oppose the re-election of one of the nominee

---

[191] Section 171(2), CL (Aust).    [192] Section 256, CL (Aust).

[193] See further, M. Godfrey, 'Shareholder Agreements for Minority Shareholders' in College of Law Lectures, *Minority Shareholder Protection and Company Buy Backs* (Guildford, The College of Law, 1990) at 14–5.

[194] *Welton* v. *Saffery* above n 131 at 331 per Lord Davey, *Greenhalgh* v. *Mallard*, above n 186, *Russell* v. *Northern Bank Development Corporation Ltd.*, above n 1, and *Arnotts Ltd.* v. *Campbell Investment (Aust.) Pty. Ltd.* (1993) 9 ACSR 675 (CA NSW). Cf., Riley, above n 120, who argues that limits should be placed on voting agreements.

[195] *Pender* v. *Lushington*, above n 17, *North-West Transportation Co. Ltd.* v. *Beatty* (1887) 12 App. Cas. 589 (PC) and *Burland* v. *Earle* [1902] AC 83 at 94 (PC). Of course, the potential always exists for the court to intervene if there is minority oppression. Further, in *Walker* v. *Standard Chartered Bank plc* [1992] BCLC 535 (CA) the court granted an injunction to prevent a shareholder from voting his shares where the conduct of the shareholder was manifestly injurious to the interests of the company, and would destroy property over which the company's creditors had security.    [196] [1902] 1 Ch. 530.

directors who was about to retire, the plaintiff was able to obtain an injunction to restrain them from voting contrary to their agreement.

The enforcement of voting agreements was taken one stage further in *Puddephatt* v. *Leith*[197] where a mandatory injunction was granted to compel a shareholder to vote in accordance with his agreement.

### (ii) Available remedies

A shareholders' agreement is an ordinary contract and is therefore enforceable by all the customary contractual remedies including rectification,[198] injunction, and damages. Specific provision may also be made in an agreement as to the appropriate remedy in respect of breach of specific provisions of the agreement, which may avoid the necessity to take a dispute to the courts.

Further, it may be possible in some cases to enforce the terms of a shareholders' agreement via statutory minority protection remedies, such as the statutory remedy against unfairly prejudicial conduct.[199] This will be of advantage where the shareholders' agreement does not prescribe any or an appropriate remedy. For example, a shareholder may have breached a voting agreement. Clearly injunctive relief will be of no avail (except in respect of potential future breaches) and damages too may not provide an adequate remedy, since it may be difficult for the aggrieved party to produce sufficient evidence of loss.[200] It may be that, under the unfair prejudice provision, relief could take the form of a setting aside of the resolution.[201] Or to take another example, relations between the parties may have deteriorated to such an extent that the petitioner wishes to be bought out or for the company to be wound up. The availability of relief under the unfair prejudice remedy in these circumstances may be very valuable.

However, it is not to be assumed that enforcement via the unfair prejudice provision will always be preferable to contractual remedies. If the agreement does provide a penalty for breach such as the compulsory share transfer provision in *Ringuet* v. *Bergeron*[202] then if breach is proved, the plaintiff will be entitled to the remedy without any inquiry as to his or

---

[197] [1916] 1 Ch. 200.

[198] *Inge* v. *Inge* (1990) 3 ACSR 63; 8 ACLC 943 and *GPI Leisure Corporation Ltd.* v. *Herdsman Investments Pty. Ltd.* (unreported decision of Young J, 24 November 1989, NSW).

[199] The factors which would make it appropriate for a shareholder to proceed via the unfair prejudice provision rather than pursuing a remedy in contract are discussed in detail in Ch. 9, section 2(1).

[200] B. Gomard, 'Shareholders' Agreements in Danish Law' (1972) 16 *Scandinavian Studies in Law* 97, 126.

[201] Gomard, ibid., at 129–33, canvasses the question whether the setting aside of a resolution could be obtained in an contractual action against the company.

[202] Above n 174.

her conduct. The second advantage of contractual remedies is the ease of availability of injunctive relief. Although the court has power to grant injunctive relief under the unfair prejudice provision, it may be more difficult to demonstrate an arguable case[203] of unfairly prejudicial conduct, than a threatened breach of a shareholders' agreement. And, of course, it will not always be the case that a dispute arising out of a shareholders' agreement involves unfairly prejudicial conduct.[204]

### (iii) Conflict with statute

In common with both ordinary agreements and the statutory contract based on the articles of association, a shareholders' agreement will be invalid if it conflicts with statute, not only where it directly contravenes the provisions of an Act[205] but also where it is against the policy of an Act. This rule has been applied to shareholders' agreements in several contexts.

### (A) Contracts not to alter the articles

In *Russell*'s case[206] a contract under which a company contracted not to alter its articles of association was held to be invalid and unenforceable on the basis that it was contrary to the statutory power of amendment (although it was able to be saved by severance).[207]

### (B) Restraining the transferability of property

In *Reuthlinger* v. *MacDonald*[208] Needham J considered that an agreement by a shareholder not to transfer his shares unless certain conditions were satisfied could be void as a restraint on alienation.

### (C) Ousting the jurisdiction of the court

The law does not impose a blanket prohibition on a party relinquishing statutory rights or the right to bring legal proceedings.[209] Rather,

---

[203] *Re Posgate & Denby (Agencies) Ltd.* [1987] BCLC 8 at 15; (1986) 2 BCC 99,352 at 99,358.

[204] For example, where there is a dispute as to the correct interpretation to be given to a particular term. For cases where declarations have been made as to the correct interpretation of a term in a shareholders' agreement see: *Associated Products & Distribution Pty. Ltd.* v. *Sunkist Holdings Ltd.* (1967) 41 ALJR 61 (HC) and *Feiersinger* v. *Transfield (Australia) Pty. Ltd.* (unreported decision of Giles J, 3 November 1988, NSW). Another example of where relief would have been unavailable under the unfair prejudice provision is *Russell* v. *Northern Bank Development Corporation Ltd.* discussed in section 2(e)(i) above, where the complaining shareholder stated that he had no objection to the proposed resolutions but was rather concerned to test the validity of the agreement.

[205] There is much greater scope for this ground for invalidity in the US where legislation expresses corporate norms, e.g. that the business of a corporation shall be managed by its board of directors. See further O'Neal, above n 171, §5.06.     [206] Above n 1.

[207] See discussion above, section 2(e).     [208] [1976] 1 NSWLR 88

[209] *Brooks* v. *Burns Philp Trustee Co. Ltd.*, above n 139, at 452–3 and 456 *per* Windeyer J (HC), *Felton* v. *Mulligan* (1971) 124 CLR 367 at 385–6 *per* Windeyer J (HC).

the determination of whether a contract not to take particular legal proceedings is contrary to a particular statute depends upon:

(1) whether the language of the Act indicates that any such contract is ineffective;[210]
(2) whether the provisions of a statute read as a whole are inconsistent with the power to forego its benefits; and
(3) whether the scope and policy of the Act indicates that it has been passed wholly or partly for the benefit of the public as well as for the benefit of individual litigants and therefore is not capable of being renounced.

Thus, for example, separation agreements whereby a wife agreed not to apply to the court for a maintenance order have been held to be invalid.[211]

In *Re Peveril Gold Mines Ltd.*[212] the articles purported to limit the right given by section 82 of the Companies Act 1862 (UK) to petition for a winding up, by providing that a member could not present a petition without satisfying one of three conditions, namely: the consent in writing of two of the directors, a resolution passed by a general meeting, or a holding of at least one-fifth of the issued capital. An attempt to stay a petition brought in defiance of these requirements was unsuccessful. The Court of Appeal affirmed the first instance decision of Byrne J that the statutory right to petition could not be excluded or limited by the articles of association.[213]

Byrne J had based his decision on two grounds.[214] First, as a matter of statutory interpretation, section 82 was not expressed to be subject to any regulation in the articles to the contrary. This could be contrasted with the statutory provisions dealing with voting and summoning meetings. The

---

[210] See e.g. *Admiralty Commissioner* v. *Valverda* [1938] AC 173 (HL). The statute stated that 'No claim shall be allowed' and this was held to be an imperative enactment precluding an inconsistent contract.

[211] Usually this was on the third ground listed above, on the basis that the jurisdiction to make an award for maintenance has been held to exist not only for the benefit of the wife but also to prevent the burden of supporting her being thrown onto society. An additional ground for holding such agreements to be ineffective was that they substituted the agreement of the parties for the ability of the court to fix, vary or discharge an order for maintenance (an argument in terms of the second ground listed above). See e.g. *Davies* v. *Davies* (1919) 26 CLR 348 (HC), *Brooks* v. *Burns Philp Trustee Co. Ltd.*, above n 139, *Hyman* v. *Hyman* [1929] AC 601 (HL), *Felton* v. *Mulligan*, above n 209, at 375–7 *per* Barwick CJ and *Bennett* v. *Bennett* [1952] 1 KB 249 at 262 (CA). Statutory changes to the relevant Australian legislation now specifically require court approval of a maintenance agreement before it has any effect. See further *In the Marriage of Wright* (1979) 29 FLR 10.

[212] [1898] 1 Ch. 122 (CA).

[213] See also *Payne* v. *The Cork Company Ltd.* [1900] 1 Ch. 308 where articles which purported to deprive dissentient shareholders of certain statutory rights granted to them in a winding up were held to be *ultra vires*.                          [214] Above n 212, at 124.

second ground was that because the terms of the articles would bind future shareholders, and because intending shareholders were quite likely not to read the articles before applying for or accepting a transfer of shares, the articles could not be regarded as a special contract waiving their statutory rights. Byrne J did, however, appear to accept that a separate or distinct bargain excluding the right to petition might be made between the company and an individual prospective shareholder. As noted above, Byrne J's decision was affirmed by the Court of Appeal. However, that court was more noncommittal regarding the validity of waiver of the right to petition by an individual contributory, expressly leaving the question open.[215]

*(D) Vote purchasing*

In *Elliott* v. *Richardson*[216] there was an agreement between two share-holders of a company which was in the process of being compulsorily wound up. One of the shareholders, R, was also a creditor of the company. The agreement was that E would use his influence to obtain the postponement of a call which was about to be made, and would support R's claim against the company. R, in consideration, agreed to pay calls made on E's shares. R failed to pay the calls and in an action by E to enforce the agreement R successfully argued that the agreement was void.

All three members of the Court of Common Pleas regarded the fact that the agreement was secret both from the Court of Chancery and from the other shareholders and creditors as being contrary to the policy of the Winding-up Acts, since the process set up by the Acts was designed to be under the direction of the court and to do complete justice to all the parties. Keating J[217] regarded the object of the Acts as being that '. . . the process of winding up should be governed by all the parties in a free and unfettered manner'. Similarly, Montague Smith J found an expression of the policy of the winding up provisions in section 91 of the Companies Act 1862 which empowers the court to have regard to and give effect to the wishes of shareholders where they can do so with justice to the creditors.[218] In that context, he said, with regard to the agreements:[219]

One consequence of such an agreement is that the whole body of creditors and shareholders may be deceived, and think when one shareholder gives advice that a call shall be postponed that he is exercising his own judgment and sense of equity;

---

[215] Ibid., at 131 *per* Lindley MR and at 131–2 *per* Chitty LJ.
[216] (1870) LR 5 CP 744.                                                      [217] Ibid., at 750.
[218] Willes J (ibid., at 749) also regarded the agreement to delay proceedings as contrary to an implied intention on the part of the legislature that the process of winding up should be brought to conclusion within a reasonable time.                    [219] Ibid., at 751.

and when he supports the claim of another he may be similarly thought to be exercising his own judgment; and if his support has been really purchased, as here, the other shareholders may be deceived.[220]

This decision is understandable in light of the established jurisprudence regarding fraud on the creditors in a winding up.[221] However, the difficulty lies in drawing the line between permissible uses of the right to vote as an item of personal property, and impermissible vote purchasing.

Finn[222] argues on the basis of *Elliott*'s case[223] that a voting agreement will be struck down as illegal whenever the consideration takes the form of a purely personal pecuniary benefit. Farrar, however, points out[224] that agreements to vote in a particular way as consideration for a sale of shares[225] or a mortgage advance,[226] or which provided for a compulsory share transfer as a penalty for not voting in a particular way have all been upheld.[227] He therefore argues that the mere passing of a money consideration should not invalidate a voting agreement in a situation where there is no winding up. Additional support for the argument that the fact of money consideration should not of itself invalidate a voting agreement, can be found in the cases where the courts have given effect to agreements whereby shares have been transferred to nominees with the object of circumventing voting limitations in articles of association. These cases were decided on the basis of the classification of a right to vote as a right to property, so that the motives inducing its exercise are irrelevant.[228]

---

[220] Interestingly, very similar reasoning was initially adopted in the US, to strike down even the simplest stockholders' agreements and voting trusts as fraudulent, namely that each stockholder had a right to expect every other stockholder to exercise an independent judgment. Today, however, voting agreements are generally regarded as unobjectionable. See E. T. Delaney, 'The Corporate Director: Can His Hands be Tied in Advance' (1950) 50 *Colum L Rev* 52 at 53–4, L. C. B. Gower, 'Some Contrasts Between British and American Corporation Law' (1956) 69 *Harv L Rev* 1369 at 1376, F. H. Easterbrook and D. R. Fischel, 'Close Corporations and Agency Costs' (1986) 38 *Stan L Rev* 271 at 280–1, S. N. Bulloch, 'Shareholder Agreements in Closely Held Corporations: Is Sterilization an Issue?' (1986) 59 *Temp L Q* 61 and O'Neal, above n 171, §5.04. Gomard, above n 200, at 100 contrasts the position in France and Italy where voting agreements are still regarded as invalid on the basis that the full benefit of the free interchange of opinions at general meetings is obtainable only provided that the shareholders have complete freedom to exercise their voting rights.

[221] For examples of applications of a similar principle in the context of personal insolvency see *Hall* v. *Dyson* (1852) 17 QB 785; 117 ER 1481 and *Ex parte Baum; Re Baum* (1878) 7 Ch. D 719 (CA). [222] Above n 130, at 99. [223] Above n 216.

[224] Above n 71, at 140–1.

[225] *Coronation Syndicate Ltd.* v. *Lilienfeld and New Fortuna Co. Ltd.* 1903 TS 489 at 497 (Transvaal).

[226] *Puddephatt* v. *Leith*, above n 197.

[227] *Ringuet* v. *Bergeron*, above n 174.

[228] *Pender* v. *Lushington*, above n 17, and *Shears* v. *Phosphate Co-Operative Company of Australia Ltd.* (1988) 14 ACLR 747; 7 ACLC 812 (Full Ct, Vic).

## (2) Fetter of directors' discretion

Shareholders are free to enter into agreements which bind them to vote in a particular way, subject only to the constraints of conflict with statutory provisions, fraud on the minority, and the statutory minority protection remedies. This is an application of the rule that ownership of a share is a property right.[229] However, directors are in a different position. They are fiduciaries, and must therefore cast their votes at board meetings *bona fide* in the best interests of the company as a whole. That is not to say that a director can never enter into a contract which is to be performed at a later date.[230] As Kitto J stated in *Thorby* v. *Goldberg*:[231]

> There are many kinds of transactions in which the proper time for the exercise of the directors' discretion is the time of the negotiation of a contract, and not the time at which the contract is to be performed. A sale of land is a familiar example . . . If at the former time they are bona fide of opinion that it is in the interests of the company that the transaction should be entered into and carried into effect, I see no reason in law why they should not bind themselves to do whatever under the transaction is to be done by the board.

If at the time for performance of a contract, the directors no longer consider it to be in the company's interests, then the court will not enforce the contract by specific performance, although the directors may nevertheless be liable for damages if this will involve a breach of a personal undertaking.[232]

In determining whether directors have committed such a breach it appears that where the obligation is not absolute, but is in the form of a 'best endeavours' undertaking, it will be treated as being subject to the directors' fiduciary duty to act in the interests of the company. In two English cases, *John Crowther Group plc* v. *Carpets International plc*[233] and *Rackham* v. *Peek Foods Ltd.*[234] the directors' ability to bind the company was limited by Stock Exchange listing rules, so that in each case contracts were entered into conditional on shareholder approval. After entering into the contracts, circumstances changed so that the directors no longer

---

[229] See Ch. 8, section 4.

[230] Such an agreement may, however, be unconstitutional if it defeats the shareholder's right to appoint the directors: *Lee Panavision Ltd.* v. *Lee Lighting Ltd.* [1992] BCLC 22; [1991] BCC 620 (CA).

[231] (1964) 112 CLR 597 at 605–6 (HC). McTiernan and Windeyer JJ agreed in the judgment of Kitto J. Owen J delivered a separate but similar opinion at 617–8 but also agreed with Menzies J, as to which see text accompanying nn 239–42.

[232] *Coronation Syndicate Ltd.* v. *Lilienfeld*, above n 225.

[233] [1990] BCLC 460.

[234] [1990] BCLC 895.

considered the transactions to be in the companies' best interests, and in both cases it was held that the directors had not breached their undertakings to use their best endeavours to obtain the necessary approval and recommend the contracts to shareholders.[235]

The 'fetter' rule has been specifically applied in the case of shareholders' agreements.[236] However, the rule may be disapplied where the company consents.[237] It has been held that such consent can take the form of a unanimous shareholders' agreement.[238] This was the ground on which Menzies J reached his decision in *Thorby* v. *Goldberg*,[239] and this has since been applied in *Davidson* v. *Smith*[240] where Ipp J said:[241]

The beneficiaries, having instructed the fiduciaries to carry out their duties in a particular way, cannot complain when the fiduciaries so carry out those instructions. Therefore, despite the fact that the directors' discretion is fettered in regard to the internal management of the company, and despite the provision in the articles requiring the directors to exercise their discretion at any appropriate time in the future, in my opinion, the agreement to the fettering of the directors' discretion by all the relevant interested parties is valid, and specific performance thereof is capable of being enforced.

Mahon J in *Berlei Hestia (NZ) Ltd.* v. *Fernyhough*[242] supports this approach, saying: '. . . it seems not unreasonable for all the corporators to be able to agree upon an adjusted form of fiduciary liability, limited to circumstances where the rights of third parties vis-à-vis the company will not be prejudiced.'

Complications might, however, arise when the composition of the shareholders changed. Unless the new members also executed the shareholders' agreement, the potential could arise for prejudice to the minority,[243] and depending on the facts there may be cases where this could justify relief under one of the minority protection remedies.

---

[235] See also *Dawson International plc* v. *Coats Patons plc* 1988 SLT 854, affd. 1989 SLT 655 and A. Griffiths, 'The best interests of Fulham FC: Directors' fiduciary duties in giving contractual undertakings' [1993] *J Bus L* 576.

[236] See *Coronation Syndicate Ltd.* v. *Lilienfeld and the New Fortuna Co. Ltd.*, above n 225, and *Ringuet* v. *Bergeron*, above n 174.

[237] *Kregor* v. *Hollins* (1913) 109 LT 225 (CA).

[238] See Sealy, above n 11, at 109, and also at 110 as to the necessity to distinguish between forgiving directors' breaches of duty and binding the company to accept all or any delinquent acts that its directors might commit.            [239] Above n 231, at 616.

[240] (1989) 15 ACLR 732. See also *ANZ Executors & Trustee Company Ltd.* v. *Qintex Australia Ltd. (Recs and Mgrs apptd)* [1991] 2 Qd R 360 (Full Ct, Qld).

[241] Ibid., at 736.            [242] [1980] 2 NZLR 150 at 166.

[243] See Companies and Securities Law Review Committee (Australia) *Nominee Directors and Alternate Directors* Report No 8 (1989) at 29–30 who accordingly recommend against allowing a relaxation of the duty of directors to act in the best interests of the company as a whole to be made in the constituent documents of the company, unless the company is an exempt proprietary company or a non-commercial company.

Nevertheless, a director who is also a shareholder is still free as an individual shareholder to enter into a voting agreement binding him or her in that capacity.[244] And it may therefore be possible to bypass the 'fetter' rule if powers are not given by the articles to the directors, but rather are reserved to the general meeting. This raises the question whether, to the extent that an agreement gives power to shareholders to make management decisions, such powers may be exercised in the shareholders' self-interest or whether they attract fiduciary obligations similar to those imposed on directors. The courts have strongly resisted any attempt to characterize the equitable obligations placed on a majority of shareholders in exercising their voting power as fiduciary,[245] and as Finn points out[246] these two strands have quite separate origins.[247] But even if shareholders do not thereby become fiduciaries,[248] this device may have other consequences for shareholders.

Power to manage the company can be vested in the general meeting, but it is still not possible under English or Australian law to do away with the board of directors. Presumably the board would continue to act in the limited role of agent of the general meeting. Both the United Kingdom[249] and the Australian[250] legislation define the term 'director' to include a person occupying the position of director by whatever name called. It is not clear that this definition would extend to shareholders exercising powers which had been vested in the company in general meeting. But there is a greater potential for shareholders to be caught within the expression of 'a person in accordance with whose directions and instructions the directors . . . are accustomed to act'.[251] The consequences of this are particularly far-reaching in Australia, since directors' duties to act honestly and with reasonable care and diligence have been codified, and breach of these duties may attract criminal as well as civil penalties.[252] The consequences of coming within this definition in the United Kingdom legislation are more restricted, since provisions applying to shadow directors are limited to consideration of the interests of employees, certain

---

[244] See e.g. *Greenwell* v. *Porter*, above n 196, *Ringuet* v. *Bergeron*, above n 174 and *Davidson* v. *Smith*, above n 240. [245] See Ch. 8.
[246] P. D. Finn, *Fiduciary Obligations* (Sydney, The Law Book Company Ltd., 1977) para. 139.
[247] See Ch. 8 regarding the voting obligations of majority shareholders.
[248] Cf., R. J. Hay and L. A. Smith 'The Unanimous Shareholder Agreement: A New Device for Shareholder Control' (1985) 10 *Can Bus L J* 440 regarding the Canadian position.
[249] Section 741(1), CA 1985 (UK).
[250] Section 60(1), CL (Aust).
[251] The definition of 'director' in the Australian legislation extends to this category of person: s. 60(1), CL (Aust). The UK legislation classifies such a person as a 'shadow director': s.741(2), CA 1985 (UK). [252] Section 232, CL (Aust).

disclosure requirements and provisions regulating certain types of trans-action, and potential liability in the event of insolvency for wrongful trading.[253]

## 4. APPLICATION TO IDENTIFIED COMPLAINTS

In most cases a combination of provisions in the articles of association (possibly including class rights, weighted voting or quorum requirements) and a separate shareholders' agreement will be required in order to protect shareholders against the recurring problems identified in Chapter 2. Some examples of the measures which are able to be taken are as follows:[254]

### (1) Alteration of the articles

Provisions in the articles can be protected from alteration as described above[255] by entrenchment using the memorandum, or by a separate agreement under which shareholders agree to vote against a resolution to alter the articles unless all of the parties are in favour of it.

### (2) Dilution of equity stake or voting rights

Shareholders may similarly contract to vote against a new share issue or reconstruction unless all agree to it. Pre-emption rights in respect of new share issues may also be set out in the articles (and then separately protected from alteration).

### (3) Self-interested transactions by controllers

Restrictive covenants in a separate agreement may prohibit the majority shareholders competing with the business of the company or diverting work from it, and require them to devote all their time to the company.

### (4) Negligent or inefficient management

To limit the potential for mismanagement, express undertakings may be obtained requiring, for example, that the assets of the company be disposed of only at the best price obtainable.

### (5) Participation in profits

The articles may provide for the application of profits in a certain way, without the need for a dividend to be declared. However, to be effective

[253] See Pennington, above n 84, at 531 for the complete list. See also Ch. 3, section 3 (2)(e).
[254] More detailed descriptions of these self-help measures and precedents can be found in Stedman and Jones, above n 169.                                    [255] In section 2(2).

this would need to be complemented by controls over directors' remuneration in a separate agreement.

### (6) Information about the company's affairs

An express right to access to information may be obtained by agreement or provided for in the articles. Alternatively, provision may be made for transfer of information by nominated directors.

### (7) Illiquidity

One way of dealing with the problem is for shares to be made redeemable in order to ensure a market for them. Transfers to nominated categories of persons may also be expressly permitted.

### (8) Exclusion from management

Management participation may be secured by a class right to appoint and remove one or more directors, supplemented by quorum requirements, provisions dealing with the maximum board size, notice and location of and advance provision of papers for meetings, and possibly also the consent of the nominee(s) in respect of certain identified matters.

### (9) Compulsory acquisition

When the relationship between quasi-partners or joint venturers breaks down, the remedy usually sought by the minority shareholder is for his or her shares to be purchased by the majority, and compulsory acquisition does not arise as a problem. Where it may become a source for complaint is where there are pre-emption provisions in the company's articles or a separate shareholders' agreement which provide for valuation of the departing shareholder's shares on a discounted basis to reflect the fact that it is a minority holding.[256] This problem can be overcome if the articles or agreement provide for the shares to be valued on a *pro rata* basis.

### (10) Other complaints

One other complaint identified in Chapter 2 is disregard of rights granted by statute or the articles. There is no specific self-help measure which will prevent the majority disregarding the minority's rights. Once this happens, litigation may be the only remedy.

Self-help measures cannot prevent the relationship between the parties breaking down nor can they prevent oppressive conduct. But they can

---

[256] As to the availability of relief under the unfair prejudice remedy or the winding-up remedy in this situation see Ch. 6 section 2(8)(b)(i) and Ch. 7 section 2(4)(c).

minimize the scope for disputes, and if it is necessary to resort to the courts, they do put the minority shareholders in a significantly stronger position. Specific provisions in the agreement may enhance its enforceability by minority shareholders.[257] Further, if a shareholders' agreement exists, the courts will go to extreme lengths to enforce it.

For example, in *Breckland Group Holdings Ltd.* v. *London & Suffolk Properties Ltd.*[258] the two shareholders in the defendant company were B Ltd. and C Ltd. A shareholders' agreement provided that B Ltd. should appoint one and C Ltd. should appoint two directors to the board. The agreement also provided that in relation to specified matters, which included the institution of legal proceedings, the affirmative vote or consent in writing of the B Ltd. director and at least one C Ltd. director was required. Proceedings were instituted against the B Ltd. director without the requisite consent, and B Ltd. moved to restrain the action. Despite the obvious conflict of interest which would be faced by the B Ltd. director in deciding whether the proceedings should be instituted, the court granted the injunction. Even more striking are cases such as *Bushell* v. *Faith*,[259] *Cumbrian*'s case[260] and *Russell*'s case,[261] where the courts adopted innovative strategies in order to hold that the relevant provisions were enforceable. Each of these cases is open to criticism. Arguably what they demonstrate is a policy of giving effect to the parties' expressed intentions.

---

[257] For example, the minority shareholders can be put in control of bringing proceedings in respect of breach of duty to the company: Stedman and Jones, above n 169, at 119. Further, in Australia, where it is not clear that damages are available as a remedy for breach of the articles, their availability could be secured by agreement.

[258] [1989] BCLC 100; (1988) 4 BCC 542.

[259] Above n 108.

[260] Above n 36.

[261] Above n 1.

## — 5 —

# Self-Help in Other Companies

This chapter deals with a wide spectrum of different types of company. However, by virtue of their omission from the previous two chapters they have some common features. First, there is no ready market for their shares. Secondly, some at least of the shareholders are passive investors, so that there is a separation between ownership and control.

Depending upon where they fall in the spectrum, it may be that some of the devices described in the previous two chapters may be available to the minority shareholders in these companies. However, in the vast majority of cases, the membership will not be sufficiently large to enable a power base to form which would rival that of the management and, conversely, the fact that the shareholders are not actively contributing to the company will mean that they do not have sufficient bargaining power to secure the adoption of the self-help measures described in the context of quasi-partnership and joint venture companies. Of course in some cases one or more minority protection devices may already exist, since many of the companies falling within this residual group will be the successors of quasi-partnerships or second- or third generation family companies where shareholders have obtained their shares involuntarily by gift or inheritance, and where shareholders' agreements or specially drafted articles of association are in place. But even so, there is no guarantee that the expectations of the company's founders will coincide with those of the current shareholders.

Therefore, in the majority of companies falling within this residual category, minority shareholders will not be able to take steps to protect themselves, and they will be forced back onto litigious remedies where these are available.

The next part of this book examines these litigious remedies in detail.

# PART III

---

# *Remedy*

# 6

# The Oppression/Unfair Prejudice Remedy

1. History of the Remedy                                                              113
   (1) Limitations of the oppression remedy                                           116
       (a) Relationship with winding up                                               116
           (i) England                                                                116
           (ii) Australia                                                             116
       (b) Meaning of oppression                                                      117
       (c) The *qua* member requirement                                               118
   (2) Amendments consequent on the Jenkins Committee report                          119
   (3) 'Some part' of the members                                                     120

2. The Modern Remedy                                                                  121
   (1) *Locus standi*                                                                 122
       (a) Confined to 'members'                                                      122
       (b) Former members                                                             123
       (c) Conduct predating membership                                              123
   (2) Parties to the petition                                                        124
       (a) Joinder of all petitioners                                                 124
       (b) Persons who may be affected by the relief                                  124
       (c) Persons involved in the alleged misconduct                                 125
   (3) Conduct of the company's affairs                                               125
       (a) Conduct of shareholders distinguished                                      125
       (b) Isolated conduct and proposed acts or omissions                            127
   (4) The *qua* member requirement                                                   128
       (a) England                                                                    128
       (b) Australia                                                                  131
   (5) The influence of Lord Wilberforce's dictum in *Ebrahimi* v.
       *Westbourne Galleries Ltd.* on the grounds for jurisdiction                    132
   (6) An objective test                                                              133
   (7) 'Legitimate expectations' and 'fairness'                                       135
   (8) Application of the 'legitimate expectations' test                              137
       (a) Universal expectations                                                     137
       (b) Personal expectations                                                      139
           (i) The relevance of the articles of association                           141
           (ii) The relevance of a shareholders' agreement                            149

(9)  The relevance of the petitioner's conduct                         152
   (a)  Misconduct by the petitioner                    152
   (b)  Collateral purpose                               154
(10) Remedies                                                          154
   (a)  Winding up                                      154
   (b)  Regulating the company's affairs                 155
   (c)  Purchase order                                   155
      (i)  Valuation method                156
      (ii)  Appropriateness of a discount  157
      (iii)  Valuation date               157
      (iv)  Relevance of respondent's financial position  157
      (v)  Compulsory acquisition          157
      (vi)  Trustee companies              158
   (d)  Proceedings by or on behalf of the company       158
   (e)  Appointment of a receiver                        161
   (f)  Order restraining conduct                        162
   (g)  Order requiring conduct                          162
   (h)  Supervening appointment of an administrative
      receiver, administrator or liquidator 162
   (i)  Interim and interlocutory relief                 163
   (j)  Interest                                         163
   (k)  Costs                                            164
      (i)  Indemnity from company          164
      (ii)  Security for costs             165

## SUMMARY

*Both jurisdictions offer a statutory remedy to shareholders in respect of unfairly prejudicial conduct of a company's affairs. The traditional reluctance of the courts to interfere in management decisions meant that the remedy was initially interpreted restrictively. More recently, statutory amendments to remove these restrictions and a greater willingness on the part of the courts to assist oppressed minority shareholders have combined to make the unfair prejudice remedy an important source of relief for minority shareholders.*

*Influenced by the House of Lords' decision in* Ebrahimi v. Westbourne Galleries Ltd., *unfairly prejudicial conduct has been equated with an unfair departure from the member's legitimate expectations as to the way in which the company would be run, in light of the history and structure of the company. The effect of the conduct on the petitioner is assessed objectively, so that it is not necessary to show that the respondent has acted in bad faith. It is also unnecessary for the petitioner to come to court with clean hands.*

*Rather, factors such as these are taken into account in the exercise of the court's wide discretion to determine the appropriate relief.*

## 1. HISTORY OF THE REMEDY

The common law offers certain avenues of redress for minority shareholders. These avenues continue to play a role in minority protection in some recognized situations, but are deficient in significant respects.[1]

The deficiencies were filled in part by a statutory remedy borrowed from partnership law, namely that of winding up on the just and equitable ground.[2] Under this remedy, the courts are prepared to exercise their discretion in favour of granting a winding-up order in three main situations:[3]

(1) in cases of serious fraud, misconduct or oppression in regard to the affairs of the company, or other conduct giving rise to a justifiable lack of confidence;[4]

(2) where it has become impossible to carry on the company's business because of an irretrievable breakdown in the relationship between quasi-partners;[5] and

(3) in cases of failure of substratum, that is where it has become impossible to achieve the objects for which the company was formed.[6]

---

[1] See further Ch. 8.

[2] This provision derives from the Joint Stock Companies Winding-up Act 1848 (UK), s. 5(8). It was introduced in its present form by s. 79(5) of the Companies Act 1862 (UK). See now s. 122(1)(g), Insolvency Act 1986 (UK) and s. 461(k), CL (Aust). See further Ch. 7.

[3] Attempts to create categories or headings under which cases must be brought if the clause is to apply have been criticized: *Ebrahimi* v. *Westbourne Galleries Ltd.* [1973] AC 360 at 374 (HL), *Re Tivoli Freeholds Ltd.* [1972] VR 445, *Re Straw Products Pty. Ltd.* [1942] VLR 222 at 223. Nevertheless the classification has been justified by commentators as an aid to discussion (B. H. McPherson, 'Winding Up on the "Just and Equitable" Ground' (1964) 27 *Mod L Rev* 282 at 285) and as indispensable to the justice which requires like cases to be treated alike (F. H. Callaway, *Winding Up on the Just and Equitable Ground* (Sydney, Law Book Company Ltd., 1978) at 4).

[4] Situations where this ground has been applied include misappropriating company property, and failing to conduct the company's business in accordance with procedural requirements as a means of deliberately depriving shareholders of their rights or purchasing their shares at an undervalue. See: *Loch* v. *John Blackwood Ltd.* [1924] AC 783 (PC), *Re the Newbridge Sanitary Steam Laundry Ltd.* [1917] 1 IR 67, *Thomson* v. *Drysdale* 1925 SC 311, *Re Martello & Sons Ltd.* [1945] 3 DLR 626 (CA, Ontario), *Re Blériot Manufacturing Air Craft Co. Ltd.* (1916) 32 TLR 253, *Re Waipuna Investments Pty. Ltd.* [1956] VLR 115, *Re William Brooks & Co. Ltd.* [1962] NSWR 142, *Re Wondoflex Textiles Pty. Ltd.* [1951] VLR 458 and *Abeles* v. *Fuller Holdings Pty. Ltd.* (1977–1978) ACLC ¶40–329.

[5] See *Re Yenidje Tobacco Co. Ltd.* [1916] 2 Ch. 426 (CA) and *Re Davis and Collett Ltd.* [1935] Ch. 693.

[6] See *Re Suburban Hotel Co.* (1867) 2 Ch. App. 737, *Re Haven Gold Mining Co.* (1882) 20 Ch. D 151 (CA), *Re Red Rock Gold Mining Co. Ltd.* (1889) 61 LT 785, *Re Baku Consolidated*

In the landmark decision of *Ebrahimi* v. *Westbourne Galleries Ltd.*,[7] the winding-up remedy was extended to situations where the conduct of the majority represented a departure from the common assumptions and understandings upon which the company was based.[8] The facts of this case are well-known, and concerned a private company which was formed to take over the business carried on in partnership by E and N. E and N were the first directors, but soon afterwards N's son G was made a director. All profits were distributed as directors' remuneration and no dividends were ever paid. After a disagreement between E and N, N and G used their majority of votes in a general meeting to remove E as a director. Although both the articles and companies legislation gave N and G power to do this, the House of Lords held that the 'just and equitable' provision enabled the court to subject the exercise of legal rights to equitable considerations of a personal character arising between individuals which might make it inequitable to insist on legal rights or to exercise them in a particular way. Here E and N had joined in the formation of the company on the basis that the character of the association would remain the same as it had been when they were partners, that is, that it would remain a personal relationship involving trust and confidence and that E would be entitled to participate in management.[9] N repudiated that relationship and E thereby lost his right to a share in the profits and was in that respect at the mercy of N and G. Since there were restrictions on the transfer of shares which prevented E disposing of his interest without N and G's consent, the House of Lords held that the proper course was to dissolve the association by winding up the company.

Consistently with the origins of the remedy, Lord Wilberforce stated[10] that equitable considerations would not be superimposed on the terms of the articles where the association was a purely commercial one, and that in order to be an appropriate case for the court's intervention the company might typically include:

---

*Oilfields Ltd.* [1944] 1 All ER 24, *Re Kitson & Co. Ltd.* [1946] 1 All ER 435 (CA), *Galbraith* v. *Merito Shipping Co. Ltd.* 1947 SC 446, *Re Crown Bank* (1890) 44 Ch D 634, *Re Pacific Fisheries Ltd.* (1909) 26 WN (NSW) 127, *Re Southland Woollen-Mills Ltd.* [1929] NZLR 289. The significance of this ground has been reduced by the practice of drawing objects clauses extremely widely, and in Australia by the removal in 1984 of the requirement to specify objects (s. 117(2), CL (Aust)). Note that in England, s. 3A, CA 1985 (UK) permits a short-form objects clause.

[7] [1973] AC 360 (HL).

[8] Drawing on the earlier cases of *Re Wondoflex Textiles Pty. Ltd.*, above n 4, *Re Tivoli Freeholds Ltd.*, above n 3, and *Re Fildes Bros Ltd.* [1970] 1 WLR 592.

[9] Cf., M. R. Chesterman, 'The "Just and Equitable" Winding Up of Small Private Companies' (1973) 36 *Mod L Rev* 129 at 143–9 as to the evidence for the House of Lords' finding that E was in a position to build up expectations regarding equal status in management.     [10] Above n 3, at 379 *per* Lord Wilberforce.

. . . one, or probably more of the following elements: (i) an association formed or continued on the basis of a personal relationship, involving mutual confidence . . . (ii) an agreement, or understanding, that all or some . . . of the shareholders shall participate in the conduct of the business; (iii) restriction upon the transfer of the members' interest in the company—so that if confidence is lost, or one member is removed from management, he cannot take out his stake and go elsewhere.

In two respects, the House of Lords' decision represented a significant departure from the approach taken in some earlier cases.[11] First, the court recognized that the members of a company may have rights, obligations, or expectations not embodied in the company's constitutional documents which the court will protect in certain circumstances. Secondly, both Lord Wilberforce[12] and Lord Cross of Chelsea[13] emphasized that the availability of a winding-up order was not determined by whether N held a *bona fide* belief that removing E was in the best interests of the company.

From that point it was perhaps a relatively small step to the introduction of a specific provision enabling the court to grant a more sensitive range of remedies against oppressive conduct. The Lord President, Lord Cooper, described the reason for the introduction of the 'oppression' provision in *Elder* v. *Elder & Watson Ltd.*:[14]

Previous practice had shown that, wide as were the powers of the Court to order a winding-up under the 'just and equitable' clause (which dates back to 1862), strong grounds were normally insisted upon before the Court would afford a form of relief which tended to be regarded as only available in the last resort, and in the absence of feasible alternative remedies. In many such cases, moreover, the cure would have been worse than the disease, owing to the prejudice likely to be inflicted upon the applicants for relief as a result of a compulsory liquidation of the company. In that situation the new Act has empowered the Court in certain circumstances to afford relief by various methods falling far short of the extreme expedient of a winding-up.[15]

The Cohen Committee in conceiving the remedy recommended:[16]

. . . that the Court should have . . . the power to impose upon the parties to a dispute whatever settlement the Court considers just and equitable. This discretion

[11] These cases confined the parties' expectations to their constitutional rights, or failing that, to establishing want of *bona fides*. Lord Cross considered that both *Re Cuthbert Cooper & Sons Ltd.* [1937] Ch. 392 and *Re K/9 Meat Supplies (Guildford) Ltd.* [1966] 1 WLR 1112 were wrongly decided on this basis.
[12] Above n 3, at 381, with whom Viscount Dilhorne and Lord Pearson agreed.
[13] Ibid., at 386. [14] 1952 SC 49 at 54.
[15] For an Australian dictum to similar effect see *Re Dernacourt Investments Pty. Ltd.* (1990) 20 NSWLR 588 at 619–20.
[16] *Report of the Committee on Company Law Amendment* 1945 (Cmd. 6659) (UK), para. 60.

must be unfettered, for it is impossible to lay down a general guide to the solution of what are essentially individual cases. We do not think that the Court can be expected in every case to find and impose a solution; but our proposal will give the Court a jurisdiction which it at present lacks, and thereby at least empower it to impose a solution in those cases where one exists.

However, the Cohen Committee's aspiration that the court should have an unfettered discretion to impose upon the parties whatever settlement it considered just and equitable was not initially realized. Instead, the provision was interpreted strictly. Limitations were placed on its operation in four main situations, all of which have since been removed by legislation. However, they are outlined below, because an awareness of these limitations assists in understanding of the present form of the remedy.

### (1) Limitations of the oppression remedy

#### (a) Relationship with winding up

##### (i) England

Because of its origins as an alternative to the extreme expedient of winding up, the original drafting of the United Kingdom oppression provision was in terms that relief was available in circumstances which would otherwise justify an order to wind up the company on the just and equitable ground. This imported with it all the limitations of the just and equitable winding-up provision in terms of standing, and, in particular, the requirement that the petitioner have a tangible interest in a winding up. Thus, in *Re Bellador Silk Ltd.*[17] the petitioner was held not to be entitled to relief under the oppression remedy on the ground[18] that the financial position of the company was such that, on a winding up, the assets would not realize enough to leave anything for the contributories after creditors' claims were met.[19]

##### (ii) Australia

Even in Australia, where there was no requirement to show that the oppressive conduct would justify the making of a winding-up order,[20] the

---

[17] [1965] 1 All ER 667.

[18] This was one of two grounds for the decision. The other was that the petition had been presented to achieve a collateral purpose and was therefore an abuse of the process of the court. See discussion below in section 2(9)(b).

[19] This was premised on the view that the oppression provision was not intended to extend the class of possible petitioners, but to extend the possible relief to be given to contributories within an existing class: above n 17, at 673.

[20] See *Re Bright Pine Mills Pty. Ltd.* [1969] VR 1002 (Full Ct, Vic), *Re Ingleburn Horse and Pony Club Ltd.* [1973] 1 NSWLR 641, *Re Broadcasting Station 2GB Pty. Ltd.* [1964–5]

potential of the provision to offer a more sensitive range of remedies was not always achieved. An order for winding up on the just and equitable ground was still regarded as the primary remedy for an oppressed shareholder. Any alternative claim for relief under the oppression remedy was not even considered once it had been determined that there was sufficient evidence to justify a winding-up order,[21] and the practice which had developed as a result of the drastic nature of the remedy, namely to adjourn the matter before making the winding-up order[22] to enable the parties to reach an agreement among themselves, persisted.[23]

### (b) Meaning of oppression

Another major impediment to the effectiveness of the provision was the restrictive definition given to the term 'oppression', particularly by the English courts. A potentially wide interpretation was given in *Elder* v. *Elder & Watson Ltd.*[24] broadly equating 'oppression' with lack of 'fair dealing'. However, the more restrictive construction by Viscount Simonds in *Scottish Co-operative Wholesale Society Ltd.* v. *Meyer,*[25] equating 'oppression' with conduct which was 'burdensome, harsh and wrongful' was the one which was adopted in subsequent English cases.[26] By contrast, in Australia, although Viscount Simonds' dictum was applied in a number of cases, reference was also made to the broader definition proposed in *Elder*'s case[27] and greater emphasis was placed on the wide discretion given to the court.[28] Indeed, in the true spirit of the Cohen Committee,[29]

---

NSWR 1648. This distinction appears not to have been appreciated in the earlier decision of *Re Associated Tool Industries Ltd.* (1963) 5 FLR 55. See R. Baxt, 'Oppression of Shareholders—The Australian Remedy' (1971) 8 *Melb U L Rev* 91 at 96.

[21] See e.g., *Re City Meat Co. Pty. Ltd.* (1984) 8 ACLR 673; 2 ACLC 149.

[22] Cf., *Re Westbourne Galleries Ltd.* [1970] 1 WLR 1378 where Plowman J (at first instance) instead stayed a winding-up order. In a postscript to the later case of *Re A. & B. C. Chewing Gum Ltd.* [1975] 1 WLR 579 at 592, Plowman J explained that his granting of a stay had been a departure from the usual and correct practice.

[23] See *Re Caratti Holding Co. Pty. Ltd.* (1975) 1 ACLR 87, *Re City Meat Co. Pty. Ltd.*, above n 21, *Re Ingleburn Horse and Pony Club Ltd.*, above n 20, and *Re Tivoli Freeholds Ltd.* above n 3. This is described as a regular practice in England in *Re R. A. Noble & Sons (Clothing) Ltd.* [1983] BCLC 273 at 292.

[24] Above n 14. Lord Cooper said (at 55) that the term involved 'a visible departure from the standards of fair dealing, and a violation of the conditions of fair play' and Lord Keith (at 60) said that 'oppression involves, I think, at least an element of lack of probity or fair dealing to a member in the matter of his proprietary rights as a shareholder'.

[25] [1959] AC 324 at 342 (HL).

[26] *Re H. R. Harmer Ltd.* [1959] 1 WLR 62 (CA), *Re Five Minute Car Wash Service Ltd.* [1966] 1 WLR 745, *Re Lundie Brothers Ltd.* [1965] 1 WLR 1051, *Re Jermyn Street Turkish Baths Ltd.* [1971] 1 WLR 1042 (CA).

[27] Above n 14. See e.g., *Re Broadcasting Station 2GB Pty. Ltd.* and *Re Associated Tool Industries Ltd.*, both above n 20.

[28] See e.g., *Re Bright Pine Mills Pty. Ltd.*, above n 20.    [29] Above n 16, para. 60.

Lush J took the view in *Re M. Dalley & Co. Pty. Ltd.*[30] that: 'Section 186, is, upon the authorities, a wide remedial section not to be narrowed in the manner contended for by an interpretation of the first judicial observations made upon it.'

Although a slightly more expansive approach to the meaning of 'oppression' may have been taken in Australia, a further restriction imported into the provision and one which was common to both jurisdictions was the fact that the provision was expressed in terms that a member might make application to the court where the affairs of the company 'are being conducted' in an oppressive manner. The use of the present continuous tense was interpreted to require that the oppressive conduct continue up to the date of the petition, so that isolated acts in the past did not come within the ambit of the section.[31]

### (c) The *qua* member requirement

In addition to the limitations outlined above, the approach of the courts in interpreting the section was to subject it to the qualification placed on the ability of a member to enforce the articles of association, namely that the provision must concern the rights of a member *qua* member. This limitation has its origins in *Elder*'s case[32] which concerned the successor to a partnership which had been carried on by the fathers of the parties. The petitioners had been removed from their offices as directors and also from their employment with the company,[33] with the result that the remaining members gained control of the company. The petitioners were denied redress since the matters complained of affected them merely as directors and officers of the company but not as members. It was recognized by Lord Keith that such conduct might be relevant to an oppression application '. . . if it is part and parcel of conduct designed to react on the rights of members as such or to further a scheme whereby the rights of a section of members may be prejudiced'.[34] But oppressive conduct towards a member in his capacity as director could not *per se* justify an application under the section,[35] and the fact that the respondents thereby gained control of the

---

[30] (1968) 1 ACLR 489 at 492.

[31] *Re H. R. Harmer Ltd.*, above n 26, at 75 *per* Jenkins LJ, adopted in Australia in *Re Bright Pine Mills Pty. Ltd.*, above n 20, at 1012, *Re Ingleburn Horse & Pony Club Ltd.*, above n 20, at 645 and *Spicer* v. *Mytrent Pty. Ltd.* (1984) 8 ACLR 711; 2 ACLC 214.

[32] Above n 14.

[33] As secretary in one case and factory manager in the other.

[34] Above n 14, at 58.

[35] Cf., *Re H. R. Harmer Ltd.*, above n 26, where the respondent director and majority shareholder was running the company without regard to board decisions. It was held that the shareholders (who were also among the disregarded directors) had an interest as shareholders in the proper procedure being followed.

company was not regarded as prejudicial to the petitioners' rights as members.

### (2) Amendments consequent on the Jenkins Committee report

The combined effect of the various restrictive approaches to interpreting the provision was that there were very few successful petitions,[36] and the situation attracted considerable academic criticism.[37] As a consequence of these deficiencies, substantial amendments were made to the provisions in both jurisdictions.[38] The availability of a winding-up order was removed as a necessary precondition,[39] the tenses were changed to make it clear that the provision covered isolated acts as well as a course of conduct and the provisions were extended to proposed acts or omissions.[40] The amendments also added to the original remedies the ability to grant injunctions (both prohibitory and mandatory) and to authorize civil proceedings to be brought in the name of or on behalf of the company. However, the most substantial amendments made were those to the wording of the grounds of jurisdiction.

The word 'oppressive' was abandoned altogether in the United Kingdom, in favour of the expression 'unfairly prejudicial'. In Australia the expressions 'unfairly prejudicial' and 'unfairly discriminatory' were added to 'oppressive' conduct as grounds for jurisdiction, and relief may also be sought where conduct is contrary to the interests of the members as a whole. Further, under the Australian provision there appears to be no requirement that the member must have been one of those affected.[41]

---

[36] There were only two successful petitions in the UK prior to the 1980 amendments: *Scottish Co-operative Wholesale Society Ltd.* v. *Meyer*, above n 25, and *Re H. R. Harmer Ltd.*, above n 26. There were a few Australian cases where oppressive conduct was found to exist and orders made: *Re Associated Tool Industries Ltd.*, above n 20, *Re Bright Pine Mills Pty. Ltd.*, above n 20 and *Re M. Dalley & Co. Pty. Ltd.*, above n 30.

[37] See e.g. B. H. McPherson, 'Oppression of Minority Shareholders, Part II: Statutory Relief' (1963) 36 *Austl LJ* 427, K. W. Wedderburn, 'Oppression of Minority Shareholders' (1966) 29 *Mod L Rev* 321, H. Rajak, 'The Oppression of Minority Shareholders' (1972) 35 *Mod L Rev* 156, D. Prentice, 'Protection of Minority Shareholders: Section 210 of the Companies Act 1948' (1972) 25 *Current Legal Problems* 124.

[38] In the UK, in response to the Jenkins Committee report (*Report of the Company Law Committee* 1962 Cmnd. 1749 paras. 199–212) s. 210, CA 1948 was amended and replaced by s. 75, CA 1980, which later became s. 459, CA 1985. In Australia, with the introduction of the National Companies Code, the provision (s.320) was re-drafted. More substantial changes, mostly along the lines recommended by the Jenkins Committee, were made by the Companies and Securities Legislation (Miscellaneous Amendments) Act 1983 (s. 89). The modern version of the provision is now contained in s. 260, CL (Aust).

[39] See *Mincom Pty. Ltd.* v. *Murphy* [1983] 1 Qd. R 297 in this regard.

[40] The Australian provision also expressly applies to a resolution or proposed resolution of a class of members: s. 260(1)(a)(ii), CL (Aust).

[41] See *Re Spargos Mining NL* (1990) 3 WAR 166. The significance of the differences between the provisions in the two jurisdictions is discussed in greater detail in section 2 below.

These amendments substantially overcame many of the limitations which had been implied into the provision. However, the English courts subsequently gave a narrow construction to the provision in one further respect. This was a literal interpretation of the words 'some part' of the members of the company.

## (3) 'Some part' of the members

This qualification emerged at a relatively late stage in the history of the remedy[42] and was applied only by the English courts.[43] The approach can be traced back to an obiter dictum of Vinelott J in *Re Carrington Viyella plc*[44] to the effect that even if the directors in that case had acted in breach of their fiduciary duties,[45] no relief could be sought under the unfair prejudice remedy since the breach would have affected all members equally, and the remedy was available only where the conduct affected 'part' of the members. This interpretation was endorsed (although, on the facts, this test was found to be satisfied) in a series of actions concerning the company Cumana Ltd. where it was held that a *pari passu* rights issue was capable of being unfairly prejudicial if it was known that some of the shareholders were unable to take up their rights.[46] It was then applied as the basis for dismissing a petition in *Re a Company (No. 00370 of 1987); Ex parte Glossop*.[47] The issue in this case was whether leave should be granted to amend the petition to include an allegation of unfair prejudice based on inadequate dividends. Harman J distinguished cases where it was shown that the board intended to discriminate and knew that it was able to discriminate by making an offer purportedly to all which it well knew was unable to be accepted by all.[48] By contrast, in this case the low dividend policy affected all the shareholders equally, and the conduct of the directors was therefore not unfairly prejudicial to 'some part of the members' for the purpose of founding a petition under the provision.[49]

---

[42] No such approach had been adopted under the old oppression provision. See *Scottish Co-operative Wholesale Society Ltd.* v. *Meyer*, above n 25.

[43] This problem never arose in Australia because the section was worded differently from the outset.

[44] (1983) 1 BCC 98,951 at 98,959. But cf., the extra-judicial comments of Vinelott J regarding this case: (1985) 6 *Company Lawyer* 21 at 30.

[45] By entering into a disadvantageous service contract with the company's chief executive.

[46] *Re a Company (No. 002612 of 1984)* (1985) 2 BCC 99,453 affd. (1986) 2 BCC 99,495 and sub nom *Re Cumana Ltd.* [1986] BCLC 430 (CA.).

[47] [1988] 1 WLR 1068.

[48] His Lordship cited *Re Cumana Ltd.* above n 46, and *Re a Company* [1986] BCLC 362 also reported as *Re a Company (No. 007623 of 1984)* (1986) 2 BCC 99,199.

[49] Note also *Re a Company (No. 00789 of 1987); Ex parte Shooter* [1990] BCLC 384, also reported as *Re a Company No. 00789 of 1987 (Nuneaton Borough AFC Ltd.)* (1989) 5 BCC

This development was, however, disapproved in *Re Sam Weller & Sons Ltd.*[50] where an application to strike out parts of a petition relating to the company's dividend policy on the ground that it affected all the members equally was dismissed. Peter Gibson J held that Harman J's approach in *Glossop*'s case[51] gave insufficient emphasis to the changed wording of the section and was also out of line with the earlier authority of the Court of Session in *Meyer* v. *Scottish Textile and Manufacturing Co. Ltd.*[52] where Lord Cooper, the Lord President observed that: 'The most dangerous type of "oppressor" is the person who, having other fish to fry, can afford deliberately to curtail or even destroy the business of a company in which he holds perhaps the majority of the shares.' The status of this interpretation was therefore uncertain. The United Kingdom provision has since been amended[53] to make it clear that the provision applies even where all the members are equally affected by the conduct, thus reversing the result in *Glossop*'s case.

## 2. THE MODERN REMEDY

The following discussion examines the underlying basis for and the limitations on the court's intervention in company affairs under its expanded jurisdiction. The current version of the English remedy is contained in sections 459–461 of the Companies Act 1985. In Australia, the remedy is set out in section 260 of the Corporations Law. The wording differs slightly between the jurisdictions. In England, the legislation provides a remedy against conduct which is 'unfairly prejudicial to the interests of its members generally or of some part of its members'. In Australia, the remedy is available where conduct is 'oppressive or unfairly prejudicial to or unfairly discriminatory against a member or members'. There is also an alternative ground for relief in Australia where conduct is

---

792. In this case the repeated failure of the chief respondent to hold AGMs or to lay accounts before members, depriving the company of any proper board, any properly appointed auditors and any opportunity to consider the state of the company was held to be conduct prejudicial to the members, but since affecting all members equally, not within the section. (The petitioner did, however, succeed by showing individual prejudice).

[50] [1990] Ch. 682. See also A. J. Boyle, 'The Judicial Interpretation of Part XVII of the Companies Act 1985' in B. G.Pettet (ed.) *Company Law in Change: Current Legal Problems* (London, Stevens & Sons, 1987) at 27, and A. Boyle, 'The Companies Act 1980 (4)' (1980) 1 *Company Lawyer* 280.                                        [51] Above n 47.

[52] 1954 SC 381 at 392 (whose decision was upheld by the House of Lords).

[53] By Sch. 19 para. 11, Companies Act 1989 (UK). The Australian provision has as an alternative ground for jurisdiction where the affairs of the company are being conducted 'in a manner that is contrary to the interests of the members as a whole'. See further discussion below Ch. 9 section 5(1).

'contrary to the interests of the members as a whole'. For convenience, and in light of the interpretation of the Australian grounds for jurisdiction as a compound expression,[54] the current provision will in both cases be referred to in the following discussion as the 'unfair prejudice' provision. The extent to which the alternative ground for relief in Australia broadens the scope of the remedy is considered in Chapter 9.[55]

### (1) *Locus standi*

#### (a) Confined to 'members'

Standing to bring unfair prejudice proceedings is granted to a 'member'. Both the United Kingdom[56] and the Australian[57] legislation define 'member' as a person who agrees to become a member of a company and whose name is entered in its register of members.[58]

There was formerly some doubt as to the standing of the legal representative of a deceased shareholder.[59] Standing to such representatives has since been ensured by statutory amendment in both jurisdictions,[60] which defines the term 'member' to embrace legal personal representatives and persons to whom shares have been transmitted by operation of law. This statutory extension of the definition of 'member' has been interpreted strictly, and it has been held that an agreement to acquire shares does not satisfy it.[61] Some flexibility is, however, offered by the approach of Hoffman J who said, obiter, in *Re a Company (No. 003160 of 1986)*[62] that a member who held shares in the capacity of a trustee could obtain relief under the section in respect of departures from the expectation of the holder of the beneficial interest that the nominee shareholder would participate in management.

The English courts have taken a more restrictive approach than the Australian in respect of complaints of omission of a shareholder's name

---

[54] *Wayde* v. *New South Wales Rugby League Ltd.* (1985) 10 ACLR 87; 3 ACLC 799 (HC).
[55] Ch. 9 section 5(1).                                   [56] Section 22(2), CA 1985 (UK).
[57] Section 184, CL (Aust).
[58] The word 'agrees' was given a liberal interpretation in *Re Nuneaton Borough Association Football Club Ltd.* ([1989] BCLC 454; (1989) 5 BCC 792 (CA)) to include a person whose name appeared on the register of members and who had assented to taking shares in the company even though he had not entered into a contract to acquire shares.
[59] Cf., *Re Meyer Douglas Pty. Ltd.* [1965] VR 638 with the obiter dictum of Pennycuick J in *Re Jermyn Street Turkish Baths Ltd.*, above n 26.
[60] Section 459(2), CA 1985 (UK) and s. 260(5), CL (Aust).
[61] *Re a Company (No. 007828 of 1985)* (1986) 2 BCC 98,951, *Re Quickdome Ltd.* [1988] BCLC 370; (1988) 4 BCC 296, *Niord Pty. Ltd.* v. *Adelaide Petroleum NL* (1990) 54 SASR 87, *Leaney* v. *Olmstead Pty. Ltd.* (1994) 12 ACLC 520 (Extract).
[62] [1986] BCLC 391; (1986) 2 BCC 99,276.

from the register. In England, it has been held that the conclusiveness of the register means that the alleged member must first bring an action for rectification of the register.[63]

By contrast, in the Australian case of *Re Independent Quarries Pty. Ltd.*[64] an applicant for relief was held to have standing under the unfair prejudice provision where it had been issued with share certificates in respect of shares transferred to it, but its name had not been entered in the register of members, in circumstances where the reason for non-entry of the applicant's name on the register was that the register was in the control of a rival faction of the company. Williams J held that a holder of share certificates duly sealed by the company, which had been issued upon lodgment of a valid transfer form, and where the consideration for the transfer has been fully paid, was a member of the company for the purposes of the unfair prejudice provision, notwithstanding that the holder's name has not been entered in the register of members.

### (b) Former members

One other lacuna in relation to standing is that no *locus standi* is accorded to former members of the company. It has been persuasively argued that the statutory requirement should be expanded to include this class of persons, since unfairly prejudicial conduct may arise out of circumstances in which a person ceases to be a member,[65] or have occurred while the former members were still members but have come to light only after they ceased to be so.[66]

### (c) Conduct pre-dating membership

The converse question is whether the provision extends to conduct which pre-dates membership. Standing has been accorded to petitioners in this situation in Australia[67] and the prospects of success are significantly enhanced by the fact that the statutory wording in Australia does not require the petitioner to be among those who have suffered the unfairly prejudicial conduct. Prentice[68] argues in a similar vein that the wording of the English provision does not necessarily preclude a petition being

---

[63] Pursuant to s. 359, CA 1985 (UK), s. 212, CL (Aust), or to bring a claim based on estoppel by convention: *Jaber* v. *Science & Information Technology Ltd.* [1992] BCLC 764.
[64] (1993) 12 ACSR 188; 12 ACLC 159
[65] See, e.g., the fact situation described by A. Marsden, 'Prejudicial relief?' (1994) 15 *Company Lawyer* 178.
[66] D. D. Prentice, 'The Theory Of The Firm: Minority Shareholder Oppression: Sections 459–61 of the Companies Act 1985' (1988) 8 *Oxford J Legal Stud* 55 at 64.
[67] *Re Spargos Mining NL*, above n 41.     [68] Above n 66, at 62.

brought in these circumstances, but concedes that such a petitioner would face difficulty in showing that he or she has been unfairly prejudiced by acts antedating his or her membership. However, this would not usually be an obstacle to a petitioner complaining of conduct which occurred before he or she was registered as a member, but at a time when he or she was entitled to rectification of the register.[69]

(2) Parties to the petition

### (a) Joinder of all petitioners

The importance of joining all potential petitioners as parties to a petition is emphasized by *Morgan* v. *45 Flers Avenue Pty. Ltd.*[70] Here one share was held by each of the Morgan brothers and their wives and 100 shares by each of their family trusts. One of the brothers brought an action claiming to represent not only himself but also his family trusts. Young J stated, obiter,[71] that any relief in favour of the plaintiff would have to be restricted to the plaintiff's one legally owned share.

### (b) Persons who may be affected by the relief

It was held in a *Re a Company (No. 007281 of 1986)*[72] that in the case of a small private company all the members should be joined in the action even though no wrongdoing was alleged against them, as they might be affected by the making of the order, for example by the overriding of their pre-emption rights.[73]

However, in *Re Little Olympian Each-Ways Ltd.*[74] leave to add the owner of the company against whom relief was sought as a respondent to a petition was refused. This was on the grounds that there was no substantive relief sought against the owner, except that it should be a joint purchaser of the petitioner's shares and no court would order the owner to purchase the petitioner's shares.

---

[69] See *Re Quickdome Ltd.*, above n 61, and R. Hollington, *Minority Shareholders' Rights* (2nd edn., London, Sweet & Maxwell, 1994) at 48.

[70] (1986) 10 ACLR 692; 5 ACLC 222.

[71] In the result the petition was unsuccessful.

[72] [1987] BCLC 593.

[73] In *John J. Starr (Real Estate) Pty. Ltd.* v. *Robert R. Andrew (A'asia) Pty. Ltd.* ((1991) 6 ACSR 63; 9 ACLC 1372) an order that the plaintiff purchase the shares of the other members was held to be precluded by the fact that the other shareholders were not parties. See also *Re Hailey Group Ltd.* [1993] BCLC 459 also reported as *Re a Company No. 008126 of 1989* [1992] BCC 542.

[74] [1994] 2 BCLC 420; also reported as *Supreme Travels Ltd.* v. *Little Olympian Each-Ways Ltd.* [1994] BCC 947.

## (c) Persons involved in alleged misconduct

The persons against whom relief may be obtained under the unfair prejudice remedy are not confined to other members. Thus, in *Re a Company (No. 005287 of 1985)*[75] an application to strike out a claim against a former member was refused.

In *Re BSB Holdings Ltd.*[76] BSkyB was held to be a proper party to a petition, even though no relief was sought against it. Vinelott J considered that it was clearly affected by the relief sought (namely that there should be a transfer and registration of its shares) and that in such a complex case, the possibility that the court might make an order for the issue of BSkyB shares should not be precluded. His Lordship also considered that the joinder of BSkyB could be justified on the alternative ground that it was directly concerned in the transactions of which complaint was made, and its presence was necessary to ensure that all matters in dispute were determined.[77]

However, similar arguments failed to persuade the court that joinder of alleged wrongdoers was appropriate in *Re Baltic Real Estate Ltd. (No. 1)*.[78] Here, the persons whose conduct was alleged to have been unfairly prejudicial, but who had transferred their shares, were struck out as respondents. This was on the basis that the only relief sought was an order to purchase the shares, and this was sought against the transferees.

### (3) Conduct of the company's affairs

## (a) Conduct of shareholders distinguished

In both England and Australia, the unfair prejudice remedy applies only where the conduct complained of is conduct of the affairs of the company or is a proposed act or omission by or on behalf of the company. The effect of this choice of words was explained by Harman J in *Re Unisoft Group Ltd. (No. 3)*:[79]

In my judgment, it is vitally important to hold that shareholders' disputes concerning dealings with their shares are not the same as unfair conduct of the company's business. Shareholders must be kept distinct from the company so far as their private position as shareholders is concerned.

---

[75] [1986] 1 WLR 281.      [76] [1993] BCLC 246; [1992] BCC 915.
[77] A subsequent application seeking directions permitting BSkyB actively to participate in the petition and the costs it would thus incur was refused: *Re a Company (No. 001126 of 1992)* [1994] 2 BCLC 146; [1993] BCC 325.
[78] [1993] BCLC 498.
[79] [1994] 1 BCLC 609 at 623, also reported as *Re Unisoft Group Ltd. (No. 2)* [1994] BCC 766 at 777.

It is of course obvious that a company may act or conduct itself in a manner affecting a shareholder's rights in respect of his shares, for example the board may refuse to sanction a transfer of shares for improper reasons. The action of the board is conduct of the affairs of the company and so, if damage is alleged, may raise the ground of 'unfair' prejudice, and a petition . . . may be presented to the court. Further, a shareholder by exercising his own private right to vote his shares may cause the company to act, by the passing of some resolution in general meeting, in a matter alleged to be unfairly prejudicial to some members. Again it is not the act of the shareholder in voting that will found a petition but the result of that act if it produces action, or inaction, by the company. In my judgment the vital distinction between acts or conduct of the company and the acts or conduct of the shareholder in his private capacity must be kept clear. The first type of act will found a petition under [the unfair prejudice provision]; the second type of act will not.

Generally, the requirement is interpreted liberally. For example, it was held to be satisfied in *Nicholas* v. *Soundcraft Electronics Ltd.*[80] in respect of conduct by the company's 75 per cent shareholder (which was also incorporated) in treating the financial affairs of the two companies as that of a single enterprise and withholding payment from the company of amounts received by it on account of the company.[81] Diversion of corporate opportunities has also been held to be conduct in the affairs of the deprived company.[82]

Further, in *Re Norvabron Pty. Ltd. (No. 2)*[83] an argument that the oppressive conduct was confined to a subsidiary and was not conduct of the affairs of the company in respect of which relief was sought was rejected as 'artificial in the extreme'. Derrington J said:[84]

The technical answer is that the directors of Norvabron knew very well what was happening in respect of [the subsidiary] because they were the persons involved. By their omission to take action as directors of Norvabron to prevent their own conduct as directors of [the subsidiary], which of course was open to them and was their duty, they were guilty of an omission to remedy the situation. In the application of [the unfair prejudice remedy], this has equal validity in these circumstances with their conduct as directors of [the subsidiary]. The section refers to an omission as well as an act, and the nature of the section and its terms discountenance such a technical argument as is advanced here.

However, in *Morgan* v. *45 Flers Avenue Pty. Ltd.*,[85] it was held that a nominee director taking part in a board meeting was not acting in the

---

[80] [1993] BCLC 360, also reported as *Re a Company (No. 002470 of 1988); Ex parte Nicholas* [1992] BCC 895 (CA).

[81] Reversing the first instance decision on this point.

[82] *Scottish Co-operative Wholesale Society Ltd.* v. *Meyer*, above n 25, *Re BSB Holdings Ltd.* above n 76, *Re Stewarts (Brixton) Ltd.* [1985] BCLC 4.

[83] (1986) 11 ACLR 279; 5 ACLC 184.          [84] Ibid., at 292; 214.

[85] Above n 70.

'affairs' of the appointor company within the meaning of the unfair prejudice provision.

This requirement was also held not to be satisfied in *Re Macro (Ipswich) Ltd.*[86] Here, the petition complained of the failure of the majority shareholder to transfer shares to the petitioner, contrary to the understanding that the shares would be held equally by the two parties once the company was in a sound financial position. Arden J held that this was not an act or omission of the company.[87]

Further, this limitation operated to preclude relief in the Canadian case of *Johnston* v. *West Fraser Timber Co. Ltd.*[88] Here, an undertaking was given to the applicant by the majority shareholders that in consideration of the applicant agreeing to remain as president they would cause the company to go public and so create a market for his shares. At first instance, the respondent's failure to honour the undertakings to the applicant was held to be unfairly prejudicial. On appeal, this first instance decision was reversed. The Court of Appeal held that the oral policy assurances given to the petitioner were not given in conducting the affairs of the company, but in making a deal with the petitioner regarding the shares of two United States shareholders.[89] The breach was therefore not oppressive or unfairly prejudicial conduct of the company's affairs, but rather breach of a private arrangement and the statutory provision was not a remedy for breach of such an agreement.[90]

## (b) Isolated conduct and proposed acts or omissions

Under the current versions of the legislation in both jurisdictions, relief is available in respect of past instances of unfairly prejudicial conduct and proposed acts or omissions. The courts may nevertheless be more hesitant to grant relief in these situations. In *Re Norvabron Pty. Ltd. (No. 2)*[91] Derrington J said regarding past acts:

Obviously, in order to invoke the exercise of the court's discretion, the single past act would need to be so serious as to equate a continuing present state of affairs, but a series of past acts may be cumulative and may be considered in respect of their present and future effect. A single act in the past may not be so serious as to support the remedy or having been corrected may not support it, . . . but of course everything depends upon the circumstances of the particular case.

---

[86] [1994] 2 BCLC 354; [1994] BCC 781.

[87] However, this was not fatal to the petition, since T's conduct as sole director was held to be unfairly prejudicial.

[88] (1981) 29 BCLR 379, revsd (1982) 37 BCLR 360 (CA BC).      [89] Ibid., at 386.

[90] See also *Scottish Co-operative Wholesale Society Ltd.* v. *Meyer*, above n 25 and *Re a Company (No. 1761 of 1986)* [1987] BCLC 141.

[91] Above n 83 at 289; 212.

Similarly, in *Re Gorwyn Holdings Ltd.*[92] relief was refused in respect of a petition brought in relation to proposed conduct, on the basis that there was only a potential that the conduct would be carried out. However, in *Re Kenyon Swansea Ltd.*[93] an application to strike out a petition which related to proposed unfairly prejudicial conduct was refused.

(4) The qua member requirement

**(a) England**

Initially the requirement was applied under the re-worded provision as it had been under the oppression remedy. Thus, in *Re a Company (No. 004475 of 1982)*[94] Lord Grantchester QC struck out a petition brought by the trustees of infant shareholders wishing to sell the shares to finance the children's education. His Lordship considered that the company's failure to provide a scheme to purchase the shares did not prejudice the shareholders as members.

However, in more recent cases, the courts have drawn on the authority of the *Westbourne Galleries* case[95] with the result of substantially restricting the field of operation of the requirement.

The first inroad on the '*qua* member' requirement was the decision of Hoffmann J in *Re a Company (No. 008699 of 1985)*.[96] Here two competing offers were made for the shares of a private company. A petition was brought, based on the conduct of the chairman of the target company in sending a circular to the shareholders urging them to accept the lower offer but failing to state that it was made by a company promoted by the directors. Although accepting that the section required the petitioner to have suffered prejudice to his interests as a member of the company and not in some other capacity, Hoffmann J held that this requirement was satisfied on the facts, since one of the interests of a shareholder is being able to sell his or her shares at the best price. He went on expressly to reject the distinction made by Lord Grantchester QC in *Re a Company (No. 004475 of 1982)*[97] between a shareholder's capacity as a vendor as opposed to that as a member.[98]

The confinement of the '*qua* member' requirement was taken one stage

---

[92] (1985) 1 BCC 99,479 (CA).      [93] [1987] BCLC 514; (1987) 3 BCC 259.
[94] [1983] Ch. 178.      [95] Above n 3.
[96] [1986] BCLC 382; (1986) 2 BCC 99,024.
[97] Above n 94.
[98] His Lordship nevertheless regarded that case as having been correctly decided, on the basis that the refusal to propound the scheme, though prejudicial to the minority because they did not get their cash, was not unfair as a board decision supported by a majority of shareholders.

further by Hoffmann J in *Re a Company (No. 00477 of 1986).*[99] Here Mr and Mrs S, the two shareholders of a private company, A Ltd., sold all the shares to O plc on the basis that O plc would invest 'substantial sums' in its business, that Mr S would be employed as managing director, and that the association would be one of partnership. Mr and Mrs S alleged that O plc had stripped the assets of the company and terminated Mr S's employment as managing director. The respondents applied to strike out the petition on the basis that the alleged wrongs, if true, were wrongs to the petitioners in their capacity as defrauded vendors of the shares in A Ltd. or to Mr S as a dismissed employee. However, the application to strike out was refused. Although again accepting the proposition that the unfairly prejudicial conduct must affect a member in the capacity of a member, Hoffmann J drew an analogy with the approach adopted in the winding-up context in the *Westbourne Galleries case.*[100] His Lordship considered that the use of the word 'unfairly' enabled the court to have regard to wider equitable considerations, and that in the case of a small private company a shareholder's interest as a member might well include a legitimate expectation that he would continue in management, saying:[101]

Thus in the case of the managing director of a large public company who is also the owner of a small holding in the company's shares it is easy to see the distinction between his interests as a managing director employed under a service contract and his interests as a member. In the case of a small private company in which two or three members have invested their capital by subscribing for shares on the footing that dividends are unlikely but that each will earn his living by working for the company as a director, the distinction may be more elusive. The member's interest as a member who has ventured his capital in the company's business may include a legitimate expectation that he will continue to be employed as a director and his dismissal from that office and exclusion from the management of the company may therefore be unfairly prejudicial to his interests as a member.

Although O plc did not have the attributes of a quasi-partnership company identified by Lord Wilberforce, in that it was a public company in which shares were freely transferable, the combination of the factors that the association was to be one of 'partnership' and that there was in practice no market in which the shares in O plc could be sold led Hoffmann J to the conclusion that the petition should not be struck out.

The significance of the '*qua* member' requirement was further lessened by an *obiter dictum* of Hoffman J in *Re a Company (No. 003160 of 1986)*[102] that a member who held shares in the capacity of a trustee could obtain relief under the section in respect of departures from the expectation of the

---

[99] [1986] BCLC 376; (1986) 2 BCC 99,171.      [100] Above n 3.
[101] Above n 99 at 379; 99,174.      [102] Above n 62.

holder of the beneficial interest that the nominee shareholder would participate in management. However, there are limits to this approach.

In *Jaber* v. *Science & Information Technology Ltd.*[103] the petitioner's claim that he had an expectation that the company would be run as a co-operative, and therefore that he had suffered unfair prejudice in the majority shareholders' failure to recognize the voting rights of eight employees who claimed to be members was rejected.

Further, claims which have only a coincidental connection with the fact that the petitioner is a member of the company have been held to lie outside the unfair prejudice jurisdiction.[104]

A case where the '*qua* member' requirement was fatal to one of the pleas for relief is *Re J. E. Cade & Son Ltd.*[105] Here, the family farming business had been terminated with the various properties being divided *in specie*. The value of one property represented more than the share in the partnership of its occupier, John, and an arrangement was therefore reached whereby the petitioner purchased this property and then granted a five-year licence to a limited company to farm the land. The shareholders of the company were the petitioner, who was a minority shareholder, and his brother John who continued to live on the property. At the end of the five year period John refused to give up possession and sought an order for possession of the farm under the unfair prejudice petition. His argument was that he became a shareholder in the company as part of the arrangements which were made to give effect to their agreements and understandings, so that it was his expectations as a shareholder that he was seeking to protect. This argument was promptly rejected by Warner J[106] who held that the petitioner was clearly pursuing his interests as a freeholder of the farm and not his interests as a member of the company, which interests were in fact in opposition.

The '*qua* member' requirement was also invoked, albeit obiter, by Millett J as an alternative ground for staying a petition in *Re a Company (No. 003843 of 1986).*[107] In this case, Mr and Mrs D founded a company and were content that the company's affairs should be managed by their elder son. They did, however, intend that the company would be a source of income for Mr D who would act as its consultant (if and when required). This understanding was later replaced by an agreement whereby Mr D was to receive remuneration from the company for five years in return for which he was to have no involvement with the company. The company

[103] Above n 63.                    [104] See e.g., *Re Unisoft Group Ltd. (No. 3)*, above n 79.
[105] [1992] BCLC 213; [1991] BCC 360.                    [106] Ibid., at 228–30; 372–4.
[107] [1987] BCLC 562; (1987) 3 BCC 624.

reneged on the agreement on the ground that it was invalid. Mr and Mrs D and their younger son S petitioned under the unfair prejudice provision seeking orders that they be appointed directors. The petition was stayed on the ground that there was never any intention that they should participate in management. Millett J considered that there was much force in the argument that the petition was in any case demurrable on the basis that Mr D was petitioning not as a member but as a creditor or consultant. Thus, even in a small 'family' company, it may be possible to distinguish a member's interest *'qua* member' combined with any legitimate expectations flowing from that status, from an interest in another capacity.

### (b) Australia

In Australia the *'qua* member' requirement was expressly removed by what is now section 260(5)(b) of the Corporations Law which makes it clear that the section applies whether the conduct affects the member in his capacity as a member *or in any other capacity*.[108] Corkery[109] suggests that a member who was also a creditor might therefore be able to bring an action under the unfair prejudice provision in relation to prejudice suffered in that capacity as a result of inefficient or negligent management.

But despite the statutory wording, a form of *'qua* member' requirement continues to be recognized in Australia in a similar manner to England.[110] In *John J. Starr (Real Estate) Pty. Ltd.* v. *Robert R. Andrew (A'asia) Pty. Ltd.*[111] the petitioner was both a minority shareholder in the company and a franchisee of it. The conduct complained of included: bringing forward matters at board meetings which concerned the interests of franchisees without sufficient notice, restricting the time to speak at board meetings considering a proposed member, and holding mini-board meetings prior to actual meetings at which the respondent's faction would decide its view on matters to be dealt with at the next board meeting. Young J stated that the court would decline to give relief if the only effect of the conduct complained of was on the plaintiff in his capacity as a franchisee, but held that this was not the case. Rather the cumulative effect of the respondent's conduct was held to preclude the plaintiff from being able fully to participate in meetings, and he was accordingly entitled to relief under the unfair prejudice provision.

---

[108] Emphasis added.
[109] J. F. Corkery, 'Oppression or Unfairness by Controllers—What Can a Shareholder Do About It? An Analysis of s. 320 of the Companies Code' (1985) 9 *Adel L Rev* 437 at 447.
[110] See H. A. J. Ford and R. P. Austin, *Principles of Company Law* (6th edn, Sydney, Butterworths, 1990) para. 1748 and R. P. Austin, 'Companies and Securities Legislation—The 1983 Bill' Notes of a Seminar held by the Committee for Postgraduate Studies in the Department of Law, University of Sydney on 7 December 1983, at 116-7.
[111] Above n 73.

### (5) The influence of Lord Wilberforce's dictum in *Ebrahimi* v. *Westbourne Galleries Ltd.* on the grounds for jurisdiction

It was acknowledged from the start that the change in wording from oppression to unfair prejudice had the intended effect of widening the circumstances in which the court could intervene.[112] Lord Wilberforce's dictum in *Ebrahimi* v. *Westbourne Galleries Ltd.*[113] has been influential in both jurisdictions in shaping the interpretation of the new grounds for jurisdiction.[114]

For example, in *Re Posgate and Denby (Agencies) Ltd.*[115] Hoffmann J said:

> . . . the concept of unfair prejudice which forms the basis of the jurisdiction . . . enables the court to take into account not only the rights of members under the company's constitution, but also their legitimate expectations arising from the agreements or understandings of the members inter se. There is an analogy in Lord Wilberforce's analysis of the concept of what is 'just and equitable' in *Ebrahimi* v. *Westbourne Galleries Ltd.* . . . The common case of such expectations being superimposed on a member's rights under the articles is the corporate quasi-partnership, in which members frequently have expectations of participating in the management and profits of the company, which arise from the understanding on which the company was formed and which it may be unfair for the other members to ignore.

Dicta to similar effect may be found in numerous other cases, both in England[116] and Australia.[117]

The leading authority on the interpretation of the expanded Australian provision is *Wayde* v. *New South Wales Rugby League Ltd.*[118] There, the High Court adopted the approach taken in the earlier New Zealand case of *Thomas* v. *H. W. Thomas*,[119] in which Richardson J[120] quoted extensively from Lord Wilberforce's opinion in the *Westbourne Galleries* case[121] and concluded that the expressions 'oppressive', 'unfairly prejudicial' and

---

[112] *Re Bovey Hotel Ventures Ltd.* 31 July 1981, unreported, approved in *Re R. A. Noble & Sons (Clothing) Ltd.* above n 23, at 290 and *Re Sam Weller & Sons Ltd.* above n 50, at 692.

[113] Above n 3.

[114] Although Lord Wilberforce's dictum has been influential in shaping the unfair prejudice remedy, there have nevertheless been a few instances where conduct has been held not to be unfairly prejudicial, and yet to ground an order for winding up the company on the just and equitable ground. These are examined in Ch. 7.

[115] [1987] BCLC 8 at 14; (1986) 2 BCC 99,352 at 99,357–99,358.

[116] See e.g., *Re a Company (No. 00477 of 1986)* above n 99, *Re a Company (No. 003160 of 1986)* above n 62, *Burr* v. *Harrison*; *Re Saul D. Harrison & Sons plc* [1994] BCC 475 (CA).

[117] See *Re Norvabron Pty. Ltd. (No. 2)* above n 83, and *Re Dalkeith Investments Pty. Ltd.* (1984) 9 ACLR 247; 3 ACLC 74.

[118] Above n 54.

[119] [1984] 1 NZLR 686 (CA NZ).

[120] Richardson J delivered the leading judgment.

[121] Above n 3.

'unfairly discriminatory' should not be considered as alternatives, but rather as a compound expression, the essence of which is an unjustly detrimental effect on the interests of a member or members in the light of the history and structure of the particular company and the reasonable expectations of members. Brennan J, who delivered the leading judgment in *Wayde*'s case,[122] considered that the critical enquiry in determining whether relief is available under the provision is whether the decision is 'unfair'.

In the subsequent Australian case of *Morgan* v. *45 Flers Avenue Pty. Ltd.*[123] Young J drew a parallel between the Australian provision and the equivalent English and New Zealand provisions, citing authorities from all three jurisdictions in the course of his analysis. His Honour concluded:[124] 'In my view a court now looks at sub-s 2 (a) as a composite whole and the individual elements mentioned in the section should be considered merely as different aspects of the essential criterion, namely commercial unfairness.'[125]

## (6) An objective test

The emphasis in both jurisdictions in interpreting the provision is on the concept of objective 'unfairness', as judged by departure from the 'legitimate' expectations of the members. In assessing whether there has been an unfair departure from the petitioner's legitimate expectations, the court adopts an objective approach, and examines the impact of the decision upon the member, as judged by a reasonable bystander.[126] At the same time, at least in Australia, there is a subjective element to the test in that the reasonable bystander is imbued with any special skills or knowledge possessed by the oppressors.[127]

An example of the objective nature of the test can be seen in *Re M. Dalley & Co. Pty. Ltd.*[128] Here the company and its directors expropriated

---

[122] Above n 54.
[123] Above n 70. To similar effect are Shears v. *Phosphate Co-operative Company of Australia Ltd.* (1988) 14 ACLR 747; 7 ACLC 812, *Re Dernacourt Investments Pty. Ltd.* (1990) above n 15, and *McWilliam* v. *L. J. R. McWilliam Estates Pty. Ltd.* (1990) 20 NSWLR 703.
[124] Above n 70, at 704; 233.
[125] In this regard Young J expressly disapproved the test applied although not the result reached in the earlier cases of *Re a Company (No. 004475 of 1982)* above n 94, and *Re G. Jeffery (Mens Store) Pty. Ltd.* (1984) 9 ACLR 193; 2 ACLC 421. In the latter case the three elements of the provision were examined separately, with 'oppression' being interpreted in the same way as prior to the amendment of the provision.
[126] *Re Bovey Hotel Ventures Ltd.* (31 July 1981, unreported decision of Slade J) approved in *Re R. A. Noble & Sons (Clothing) Ltd.* above n 23, at 290–1, and in *Re Sam Weller & Sons Ltd.* above n 50, at 690.     [127] *Wayde*'s case, above n 54, at 96; 806–7.
[128] (1968) 1 ACLR 489.

the petitioner's shares, erroneously claiming that they were employee shares. Lush J held that the fact that the respondents were acting on the advice of their solicitors and accountants was irrelevant, saying:[129] 'One person may "subject another to continual injustice" by insisting, however honestly, on a proposition that is wrong or by using his strength to maintain, however honestly, a position unjustified in law.'[130]

However, to say that conduct may be unfairly prejudicial, despite being in good faith[131] is not to say that the intention of the oppressor is irrelevant. The oppressor's purpose in exercising a particular power may well be a relevant factor in determining whether prejudicial conduct is unfair. For example, in *Wayde* v. *New South Wales Rugby League Ltd.*[132] the articles gave the board an express power to determine which clubs should be entitled to participate in competitions conducted by the league. In good faith the board decided to reduce the number of teams in the competition and consequently excluded the team 'Wests'.

The High Court held that the exercise of the power under the articles must necessarily be prejudicial either to the league as a whole or to Wests. In that situation, the court would intervene under the unfair prejudice provision only if the directors' decision was so unfair that 'reasonable directors, possessing any special skill, knowledge or acumen possessed by the directors and having in mind the importance of furthering the corporate object on the one hand and the disadvantage, disability or burden which their decision will impose on a member on the other, would have decided that it was unfair to make that decision'.[133] On the facts, the court decided that the board's decision was not manifestly unfair.

Similar reasoning underlay the refusal of relief under the unfair prejudice provision in *Re R. A. Noble & Sons (Clothing) Ltd.*[134] and *Jesner* v. *Jarrad Properties Ltd.*[135] In both cases, the respondent's conduct was held to be prejudicial. However, in light of the history of the relationship between the parties and the acquiescence of the petitioner in the conduct, it was held not to be unfair.

The oppressor's intention may also be material to the question of what relief is to be accorded. For example, in *Re H. R. Harmer Ltd.*[136] the fact

---

[129] (1968) 1 ACLR 489 at 492.

[130] But cf., *Chase Corporation (Australia) Pty. Ltd.* v. *North Sydney Brick and Tile Co. Ltd.* (1994) 14 ACSR 586; 12 ACLC 997 where Cohen J considered the fairness should be judged by reference to what is known at the time, so that to take a step in the honest belief of it being a correct one would not amount to acting unfairly. However, the discussion of oppression in this case was brief, and is open to criticism on the basis that it applies a subjective rather than an objective test.

[131] As for example in *Thomas* v. *H. W. Thomas Ltd.*, above n 119, and *Wayde*'s case, above n 54.                                                                          [132] Ibid.

[133] Ibid., at 96; 806–7 *per* Brennan J. See also the joint majority judgment at 92; 803–4.

[134] Above n 23.                              [135] [1993] BCLC 1032; [1992] BCC 807 (CS(IH)).

[136] Above n 26.

that the respondent persisted in his conduct well knowing it to be wrong necessitated a more stringent order to protect the interests of the shareholders.

### (7) 'Legitimate expectations' and 'fairness'

Company law assumes that the members intend the company's business to be governed by the companies legislation and by the terms of the memorandum and articles of association. It also assumes a separation between ownership and management, that the majority view will predominate, and that a contribution to the company's capital is intended to remain in the company while its substratum subsists.[137]

There is a traditional reluctance on the part of the courts to depart from these assumptions. Thus, non-interference in the management of companies is a strong theme in the cases, which is translated from the pre-existing common law and is expressed in the first petition under the oppression provision, *Elder* v. *Elder & Watson Ltd.*[138] It has continued to be re-iterated under the amended unfair prejudice provision, so that for example the New South Wales Court of Appeal said in *Wayde* v. *New South Wales Rugby League Ltd.*:[139] 'Notwithstanding the adoption in Australia, as in New Zealand, of the wider language of "unfair prejudice" to supplement the traditional criterion of oppression, courts should exercise care in invading the traditional roles of directors and shareholders of companies to determine the management of the corporation.'[140]

A related consideration, which is also embodied in that dictum, is that the courts will strive where possible to uphold the principle of majority rule. The fact that the minority may consistently be outvoted does not form the basis for an unfair prejudice action. As Luch J said in *Re M. Dalley & Co. Pty. Ltd.*:[141] 'In assessing the facts of the present case it is necessary to remember that the petitioner is a minority shareholder. There are in the position of such a shareholder in a proprietary company many grave

---

[137] *McWilliam* v. *L. J. R. McWilliam Estates Pty. Ltd.*, above n 123, at 707. Exceptions of course exist: In the case of majority rule, this principle is ousted by statute in certain situations. Contrary provision may be made in the articles. Statute also now makes provision for reductions of capital during the life of the company.

[138] Above n 14. See also *Re Bright Pine Mills Pty. Ltd.* above n 20, at 1011.

[139] [1985] 1 NSWLR 86 at 102 (CA NSW).

[140] Similar cautions against an unwarranted assumption of management are expressed in the High Court decision in the joint judgment: above n 54, at 92; 804. See also *Reid House Pty. Ltd.* v. *Beneke & Ors* (1986) 5 ACLC 451 and *Re Dernacourt Investments Pty. Ltd.* above n 15. Perhaps the most striking example of this approach can be seen in *Zephyr Holdings Pty. Ltd.* v. *Jack Chia (Australia) Ltd. & Ors* (1988) 14 ACLR 30 at 37–8; 7 ACLC 239 at 246 where Brooking J stated that he considered that the proposed option issue was antipathetic to the interests of the company, but nevertheless declined to grant relief since he was not prepared to say that the inclination of his own opinion should prevail over the view formed by the board of directors. [141] Above n 128, at 492.

disadvantages but however galling and even financially damaging these may be they do not in themselves constitute oppression of the shareholder within s. 186.'[142]

It is up to the petitioner to establish any legitimate expectations overriding these assumptions. This is well illustrated by *Wayde*'s case[143] where the joint majority judges pointed out:[144]

. . . no amount of sympathy for Wests can obscure the fact that the League was expressly constituted to promote the best interests of the sport and empowered to determine which clubs should be entitled to participate in competitions conducted by it. It was upon this basis that the clubs, including Wests, chose to incorporate. Indeed, the 1984 correspondence between Wests and the League which is in evidence plainly shows that Wests itself fully appreciated that it had no secure right to participate in the premiership competition.

But as Corkery observes,[145] the provision 'is all about interference in internal management'.[146] He says: 'Now we see reflected increasingly in the legislation the belief that while usually the majority should be able to vote as it wishes and prevail in company decision making, no longer should it do so unfairly.'[147]

Other commentators have, however, greeted the concept of a test based on 'fairness' with dismay on the basis that it does not provide an environment of sufficient certainty for business to operate.[148] But arguably, it is not an abstract concept of fairness which is being applied under the provision. This point was made firmly by Cosgrove J in *Re Richard Pitt & Sons Pty. Ltd.*[149] who said:

. . . we are not considering questions of abstract morality, nor how properly understanding and generous members of a family might be expected to behave towards one another, but whether those in de facto control of the company are abusing their power so as to deny to other members their just rights or legitimate expectations from the company.

The point was emphasized most recently in another case concerning a family farming business, *Re J. E. Cade & Sons Ltd.*,[150] where Warner J

---

[142] See also *Re G. Jeffery (Mens Store) Pty. Ltd.* above n 125, at 195; 423 *per* Crockett J.

[143] Above n 54. The same point is made by Hoffmann J in *Re Posgate & Denby (Agencies) Ltd.* above n 115.

[144] Ibid., at 92; 803 *per* Mason ACJ, Wilson, Deane and Dawson JJ.

[145] Above n 109, at 449.

[146] This is particularly so in Australia where the expression 'the affairs of a body corporate' is defined by s. 53(c) CL to include inter alia 'the internal management and proceedings of the body'.　　　　　　　　[147] Above n 109, at 439.

[148] D. A. Wishart, 'Fairness in Company Law' (1990) 4 *Canterbury L Rev* 284.

[149] (1979) 4 ACLR 459 at 481–2 (Full Ct, Tas).

[150] Above n 105, at 227; 372.

rejected a submission that the court could ignore the effect of what the parties had agreed if fairness demanded it, saying, 'The court . . . has a very wide discretion, but it does not sit under a palm tree.'

The question then arises whether it is possible to give more substance to this concept of 'fairness' or 'legitimate expectations' which enables the court to disturb the will of the majority. In seeking to answer this question, it is submitted that legitimate expectations fall into two distinct categories, and that it is necessary to deal with them separately. One category derives from *Ebrahimi* v. *Westbourne Galleries Ltd.*[151] It is personal to the parties and consists of their mutual expectations as to their rights and obligations. Legitimate expectations as to standards of fair dealing are, however, not confined to companies formed on the basis of a special understanding, but can also be founded in a universal standard of acceptable commercial practice. It is submitted further, that it is important to recognize the significance of the nature of the company in terms of the establishment of relevant expectations.[152] Moreover, specific content is given to the operation of the 'legitimate expectations' test when it is applied to particular identified grievances.[153]

(8) Application of the 'legitimate expectations' test

**(a) Universal expectations**

Universal expectations are (by definition) common to all companies and can be equated with external standards of fair dealing.[154] It is submitted that the common law fleshes out the potentially vague concept of 'fair dealing' in this context, and serves in many cases to identify the situations where there is a dormant claim in respect of unfairness to the petitioner. Thus, although it has been held[155] that allegations of unlawful conduct are neither necessary nor sufficient to sustain an unfair prejudice petition, it is significant that in successful unfair prejudice petitions based on universal expectations, there usually exists the potential for an overlapping action at common law for breach of directors' duties, breach of statute, or interference with the petitioner's personal rights.[156]

---

[151] Above n 3.

[152] This latter factor is dismissed by Wishart, above n 148, at 286 who 'hesitates to place too much meaning on it'. [153] See Ch. 9.

[154] Relief under the unfair prejudice provision is compared with a derivative action in Ch. 9, especially in section 5.

[155] *Re a Company (No. 8699 of 1985)* above n 96, at 388; 99,029, *Re Charnley Davies Ltd. (No. 2)* [1990] BCLC 760 at 783; [1990] BCC 605 at 624, and *ASC* v. *Multiple Sclerosis Society of Tasmania* (1993) 10 ACSR 489; 11 ACLC 461.

[156] See e.g., *Scottish Co-operative Wholesale Society Ltd.* v. *Meyer* above n 25, *McGuinness* v. *Bremner plc* 1988 SLT 891, affd. 1988 SLT 898n, *Re Spargos Mining NL* above n 41, and *Jenkins* v. *Enterprise Gold Mines NL* (1992) 6 ACSR 539; 10 ACLC 136 (Full Ct, WA) (all of

There are, however, certain features of an action under the unfair prejudice provision which distinguish it from a common law action, and which may make it a preferable alternative.[157] Under the unfair prejudice provision, the court is concerned with whether on an objective assessment the conduct complained of is unfairly prejudicial to the petitioner's interests rather than with the motivation of the wrongdoers or any wrong to the company. Another important distinction is that the cumulative effect of the respondents' conduct may be unfairly prejudicial to the petitioner, even though no one instance would successfully ground an action.[158] Moreover, the unfair prejudice provision offers a much wider range of remedies and, significantly, is not fraught with any of the difficulties in establishing standing which exist at common law.

The well-known case of *Scottish Co-operative Wholesale Society Ltd.* v. *Meyer*[159] provides an example of an unfair prejudice petition based on universal expectations in a joint venture company. The conduct complained of amounted to a breach of directors' duty, but the wide range of remedies available under the unfair prejudice provision enabled the petitioners to be bought out at a price which included an element of compensation for the injury they had suffered at the hands of the parent company.

An example of the operation of the unfair prejudice provision in the context of a small private company, but one which was a purely commercial venture can be seen in *Re a Company (No. 00314 of 1989)*[160] where a petitioner sought relief in respect of proposals to remove her as a director, to appoint other directors, to alter the memorandum and articles of association and to purchase her shares without providing her with information relevant to ascertaining their value or to the running of the company. Despite the finding that the company was set up on a purely commercial basis, it was held that the unfair prejudice claim was not so clearly unarguable that it should be struck out.

There are very few cases where it has been sought to bring an unfair prejudice petition in respect of a listed company. Even assuming the petitioner is able to establish unfairly prejudicial conduct, the further obstacle to relief in the case of a listed company is the unwillingness of the

which could also have given rise to derivative actions in respect of breach of directors' duties). See also *Re a Company (No. 00314 of 1989)* [1991] BCLC 154; [1990] BCC 221 (There is insufficient information in the report to be certain, but the facts here may well have founded a personal action in respect of alteration of the memorandum and articles) and *Re M. Dalley & Co. Pty. Ltd.* above n 30 (where the alternative of an action to rectify the register was open to the petitioner).

[157] See more detailed discussion in Ch. 9 regarding the interrelationship between the unfair prejudice provision and the common law.
[158] See e.g., *ASC* v. *Multiple Sclerosis Society of Tasmania*, above n 155.
[159] Above n 25.                                        [160] Above n 156.

courts to assist a petitioner where a remedy exists in the form of sale of shares by the petitioner on the open market.[161] But that is not to say that an unfair prejudice petition regarding a listed company can never succeed.[162]

One illustration both of a successful petition concerning a listed company and of the focus of the unfair prejudice jurisdiction upon the effect of the conduct on the petitioner can be seen in the Scottish case of *McGuinness* v. *Bremner plc.*[163] Here, the petitioners had deposited a requisition[164] requiring the directors to convene an extraordinary general meeting in order to replace the board. A date was set for the meeting more than six months away. Although there was no breach of statute, the delay was held to be wholly unreasonable and to constitute unfair prejudice.

There are also two recent Australian examples of successful petitions concerning listed companies, *Re Spargos Mining NL*[165] and *Jenkins* v. *Enterprise Gold Mines NL.*[166] These cases concerned companies which were part of the same group, and the conduct complained of in both cases concerned a history of transactions of dubious commercial value which also involved subordination of the interests of the company to the perceived interests of the group.

### (b) Personal expectations

A petition based on universal expectations is based on grounds unrelated to the nature of the company. However, there is also a second type of petition (and this has formed the basis of the majority of unfair prejudice petitions) where it is sought to enforce mutual understandings or 'personal expectations' as to the way the company is to be run which have not been formally expressed. In purely commercial ventures, be they listed public companies or, as in *Re a Company (No. 00314 of 1989)*,[167] small private companies, petitioners will effectively be limited to petitions based on universal expectations, since it will seldom, if ever, be possible to establish personal expectations of the kind referred to by Lord Wilberforce in the *Westbourne Galleries* case.[168] This is illustrated by *Re Blue Arrow plc.*[169] Here the petitioner built up a number of businesses which she later sold to a public company. Under the arrangement, she took a 45 per cent shareholding in the new company, B subscribed cash for the remaining shares, the petitioner became an executive director and took the title of

---

[161] See e.g., *Re Kornblums Furnishings Ltd.* [1982] VR 123.
[162] See G. P. Stapledon, 'Use of the Oppression Provision in Listed Companies in Australia and the United Kingdom' (1993) 67 *Austl LJ* 575. 　　[163] Above n 156.
[164] Under s. 368, CA 1985 (UK). 　　[165] Above n 41. 　　[166] Above n 156.
[167] Above n 156. 　　　　　　　　　　　　　　　　　　[168] Above n 3.
[169] [1987] BCLC 585; (1987) 3 BCC 618.

president, B took the title of chairman. Later, the company was floated[170] and the proportionate shareholding of the two major shareholders was consequently reduced. Although the petitioner initially remained as a director, she later agreed to resign her directorships while remaining as president. The petitioner subsequently wanted to resume as a director, but the other directors resisted and came to the view that it would be damaging if she continued even as president. They therefore convened a meeting to amend the articles so that the president would be removable by the directors (rather than by resolution in general meeting). One of the petitioner's claims was that in light of the history and mutual intentions of B and herself, she had a legitimate expectation that she would remain as president unless removed by the machinery provided. Vinelott J rejected[171] this argument for the reason that this was a large public listed company, and outside investors were entitled to assume that the whole of the company's constitution was contained in the articles. There was thus no room for a legitimate expectation founded on some agreement between the directors and not disclosed to those placing shares with the public.

Petitions based on 'personal expectations' will therefore effectively be confined to quasi-partnership companies. But there are certain features of personal expectations which should be noted. The first is that they are not static. Thus, even in a company which was originally formed as a quasi-partnership, the courts recognize that the parties' expectations may change over time. For example,[172] in *Morgan* v. *45 Flers Avenue Pty. Ltd.*[173] the share capital of a company was initially held in equal proportions by two brothers. Then additional shares were allotted and the brothers' share-holding diluted. Later still, one brother resigned from his position as director of the company and virtually traded his 'right' to exercise any directive control over the company to his brother in consideration of acquiring for himself a part of the business previously carried on by the company.[174] In these circumstances, Young J held that although the company may initially have come within the category of companies where equitable obligations between the parties could be superimposed on the legal rights and duties arising out of the articles of association and the law of companies, no such equitable obligations existed as at the date of the summons.

But it is not only the expectations of the founders which may change over time, the company's membership may also change. Where new

---

[170] On the unlisted securities market.

[171] Above n 169, at 590; 623.

[172] See also *Re a Company (No. 005134 of 1986); Ex parte Harries* [1989] BCLC 383, also reported as *Re D. R. Chemicals Ltd. (Re a Company (No. 005134 of 1986)* (1989) 5 BCC 39.

[173] Above n 70.

[174] Ibid., at 707; 235–6.

members obtain their shares by purchase, they may be in a position to establish new expectations with the existing members. But where members obtain their shares involuntarily, for example by inheritance or gift they have no similar bargaining power. This can be seen in *Re G. Jeffrey (Mens Store) Pty. Ltd.*[175] and *Thomas* v. *H. W. Thomas Ltd.*[176] which respectively concerned second- and third-generation family companies. In both cases, the petitioners had inherited minority stakes and their complaint was that the dividends which were being distributed were too low. As a consequence of the manner in which they had obtained their shares the petitioners were effectively precluded from establishing any personal expectation overriding majority rule. It has also been held that a shareholder's legitimate expectations in a company do not transmit to a judicial factor (or legal personal representative) appointed to wind up the shareholder's estate.[177]

### (i) The relevance of the articles of association

In protecting personal expectations, the courts often adopt a contractual analogy to justify the basis of their intervention. Sometimes the parties are described as having entered into an 'implied arrangement' that the affairs of the company would not be governed by a strict application of the rules of the company.[178]

The enforcement of an implicit rather than explicit contract may pose evidentiary problems for a petitioner. The risk inherent in not formalizing the arrangement is that as a matter of evidence it may not be possible to establish that those expectations were mutually held. Further, as in *Re R. A. Noble & Sons (Clothing) Ltd.*,[179] such petitioners leave themselves particularly vulnerable to the finding that disregard of those expectations is not unfair in light of the evolution of the running of the company over time and the conduct of the parties.[180]

But it also raises the question of whether all of the articles are equally vulnerable to being overridden by the parties' legitimate expectations. This

---

[175] Above n 125.

[176] Above n 119.

[177] *Murray's Judicial Factor, Petitioner* [1993] BCLC 1437; [1992] BCC 596 (CS (IH)).

[178] See e.g. *Re Dalkeith Investments Pty. Ltd.* above n 117, at 252; 79. See also J. Hill, 'Protecting Minority Shareholders and Reasonable Expectations' (1992) 10 *Company & Sec LJ* 86. As noted in the above discussion, in ascertaining the terms of the parties' arrangement, the court looks not only to the circumstances surrounding the formation of the company, but also to the manner in which it is subsequently conducted. An example of a winding-up case which expressly uses the language of contract is *Re Fildes Bros Ltd.* above n 8, at 596. Commentators writing in relation to the winding-up remedy have drawn an analogy between the underlying principle governing the making of orders on the just and equitable ground and the contractual doctrines of discharge by frustration and discharge by breach: see e.g., Callaway, above n 3, at 6–12.                                      [179] Above n 23.

[180] As to the relevance of the petitioner's conduct, see below section 2(9).

issue does not arise when the parties' legitimate expectations merely flesh out gaps in the articles of association. It is the function of the articles of association to set out the rights and obligations of the parties, and by statute those provisions are given contractual effect.[181] There is, however, no obligation on persons wishing to conduct their business through a company limited by shares to register special articles of association appropriate to their intended company.[182] Whether the standard form articles or purpose-drafted articles are adopted, there exists the possibility that they will be silent as to the conduct complained of by the petitioner, and the parties' legitimate expectations will then assume importance.

The alternative problem which may face the petitioner, particularly where standard form articles apply, is that the impugned conduct may be expressly permitted by the articles, but be contrary to the petitioner's legitimate expectations. Historically, the corollary of the contractual effect given to the articles of association by statute was that the parties were nevertheless bound by their terms. The certainty of this approach was abandoned in the *Westbourne Galleries* case.[183] But the concept of the articles as a binding contract between the parties was not completely forsaken. In the *Westbourne Galleries* case[184] itself the court stressed that the parties' relationship would ordinarily be governed by the terms of the company's articles. And, as we have seen in *Wayde*'s case,[185] they remain the starting point for any analysis of unfair prejudice. On the facts of that case there was held to be no basis for a legitimate expectation overriding the terms of the articles, since there was correspondence between Wests and the league which showed that Wests 'fully appreciated that it had no secure right to participate in the premiership competition'.[186]

The legitimate expectations analysis is, however, to be contrasted with a series of cases,[187] of which *Re XYZ Ltd.*[188] is perhaps the leading authority, which appear to revert to the former view that the parties are bound by the terms of the articles, at least in respect of pre-emption provisions which provide a means for a shareholder in a quasi-partnership type company to extract his or her investment after a breakdown of relations.

---

[181] Section 14, CA 1985 (UK), s. 180(1), CL (Australia). See discussion of statutory contract in Ch. 4.

[182] By virtue of statute a model set of articles applies to the extent that it is not excluded or modified by special articles: s. 8, CA 1985 (UK), s. 175, CL (Aust).

[183] Above n 3.                                                                                         [184] Ibid.

[185] Above n 54. See also *Re Posgate & Denby (Agencies) Ltd.* above n 115, *Re a Company; Ex parte Burr* [1992] BCLC 724; affd. sub nom. *Burr* v. *Harrison* above n 116.

[186] Above n 54, at 92; 803 *per* Mason ACJ, Wilson, Deane and Dawson JJ.

[187] *Re a Company (No. 007623 of 1984)* above n 48, *Re XYZ Ltd.* (*Re a Company (No. 004377 of 1986)* [1987] 1 WLR 102, *Re a Company (No. 006834 of 1988). Ex Parte Kremer* [1989] BCLC 365; [1980] BCC 218, *Re Castleburn Ltd.* [1991] BCLC 89; (1989) BCC 652, and the first instance decision of Hoffmann J in *Re Abbey Leisure Ltd.* [1989] BCLC 619; (1989) 5 BCC 183.                                                                          [188] Ibid.

This approach, of course, assumes that the relationship has broken down in circumstances where no clear cut blame can be apportioned. Where there has been unfairly prejudicial conduct in the form of impropriety by the respondent, and, *a fortiori* where that conduct diminishes the value of the shares, the courts have in most cases[189] shown a willingness to override the provisions in the articles and value the shares on an appropriate basis. An Australian example is provided by *Sanford* v. *Sanford Courier Services Pty. Ltd.*[190] where the defendants were found to have awarded themselves excessive salaries and emoluments. Pre-emption provisions existed requiring the plaintiff to offer his shares to the other shareholders at a price to be fixed by the company's auditors. However, the court was prepared to intervene and value the shares on the assumption that emoluments provided for the second defendants as directors had been and would be on a commercial basis.

The proposition which emerges from the *Re XYZ* line of cases is that the exclusion of one participant in a quasi-partnership once relations have broken down is not necessarily unfairly prejudicial. It depends upon whether it is reasonable for that party to leave and, more importantly, upon the terms on which he or she is asked to go. Thus, a petitioner cannot complain of unfairly prejudicial conduct if it is reasonable for the petitioner to leave and he or she is offered a 'fair' price for his or her shares. In each of the cases applying this approach, the articles contained pre-emption provisions which provided for the auditor to value the holding of a member desiring to sell his or her shares. The court took the view that provided the petitioner was the appropriate party to be bought out and he or she was offered a price calculated in accordance with that formula, there was no basis for a complaint of unfairly prejudicial conduct.

Such pre-emption provisions typically provide that if a member wishes to transfer his or her shares the company's auditors will certify[191] a 'fair' value or an 'open market' value as on a sale between a 'willing vendor and a willing purchaser'. These expressions have generally been interpreted to contemplate that a discount will be applied to a minority holding.[192] On the

---

[189] See e.g., *Meyer* v. *Scottish Co-operative Wholesale Society Ltd.* above n 52, *Re Bird Precision Bellows Ltd.* [1984] Ch. 419, affd. [1986] Ch. 658 (CA) and *Re a Company (No. 005134 of 1986); Ex parte Harries* above n 172. See also the comments of Hoffmann J in *Kremer's* case, above n 187, at 368; 221. But cf., *Re a Company (No. 007623 of 1984)* above n 48.                                                                                         [190] (1986) 10 ACLR 549; 5 ACLC 394.
[191] Usually in default of agreement.
[192] And conversely that a premium will attach to a majority holding. See e.g., *Howie* v. *Crawford* [1990] BCLC 686; [1990] BCC 330. But cf., *Holt* v. *Cox* (1994) 15 ACSR 313, where the opposite decision was reached on similar facts to *Howie's* case. In *Holt's* case, the articles provided for a compulsory sale of shares acquired as a result of an incentive scheme on termination of the shareholder's employment. Having regard to the issue of the shares as a share incentive, and to the element of expropriation, Santow J held that to discount the price rather than giving it a liberal estimate would not be 'fair'.

facts of the cases referred to, there was evidence supporting the finding that there was no legitimate expectation that such a discount would not be applied.[193] However, the broad terms in which the grounds for decision were expressed effectively precluded a petitioner from setting up a legitimate expectation, which would be a feature of many quasi-partnerships, namely that no such discount would be applied.

The effect of this approach was that a valuation made in terms of the articles was treated as *ipso facto* fair and therefore not able to be challenged in proceedings under the unfair prejudice provision,[194] unless it could be shown that the valuer was not independent of the respondents.[195]

More recently, however, there has been a move away from the approach outlined above. The source of the counter movement is a case concerning an application for winding up on the just and equitable ground, *Re Abbey Leisure Ltd.*[196] Here the Court of Appeal overruled the first instance decision which had been based on the approach outlined above, and held that equitable considerations rendered it not unreasonable for the petitioner to refuse to submit to a valuation of his shares pursuant to the articles. The understanding that the company had been formed for a single venture which had since been completed formed the basis for a finding that the petitioner was entitled to an order that the company be wound up, and that he receive a proportion of the proceeds relative to his shareholding, as opposed to the discount which would have been applied to any valuation of his shareholding under the pre-emption provisions in the articles.

Balcombe LJ, who delivered the leading judgment, said:[197]

---

[193] Thus, e.g., in *Re XYZ Ltd.*, above n 187, the petitioner voted in favour of inserting the pre-emptive rights and provisions triggering them into the articles after a clear conflict in management style had arisen, in *Re a Company (No. 007623 of 1984)*, above n 48, Hoffmann J indicated the valuation he would have placed on the shares had he had jurisdiction to do so, and considered that a discount was appropriate, in *Kremer*'s case, above n 187, the petitioner bought into an existing business, presumably paying an open market value for his shares, in *Re a Company (No. 003096 of 1987)* (1987) 4 BCC 80 the petitioners conceded that the offer made by the respondents was fair, and in *Re Castleburn Ltd.* above n 187, where the facts perhaps most lent themselves to an argument based on such a legitimate expectation, the petitioners appear instead to have relied on the articles, arguing that on their true construction no discount should have been applied.

[194] *Re Castleburn Ltd.* above n 187. As to the circumstances in which a valuation may be challenged in other proceedings see *Jones v. Sherwood Computer Services plc* [1992] 1 WLR 277 (CA), *Legal & General Life of Australia Ltd. v. A. Hudson Pty. Ltd.* (1985) 1 NSWLR 314 (CA, NSW), *Strang Patrick Stevedoring Pty. Ltd. v. James Patrick & Co. Pty. Ltd.* (1993) 32 NSWLR 583, *Holt v. Cox*, above n 192 and *McConochie v. Derrawee Pastoral Co. Pty. Ltd.* (1994) 15 ACSR 126.

[195] See e.g., *Re Norvabron Pty. Ltd. (No. 2)* above n 83, where it was held that the applicant was not obliged to use the put option in the articles, since the auditor was found to have manifested a distinct bias towards the respondents. See also *Re Boswell & Co. (Steels) Ltd.*; *(Re a Company No. 001567 of 1987)* (1989) 5 BCC 145.

[196] [1989] BCLC 619; (1989) 5 BCC 183, revsd [1990] BCC 60 and sub nom. *Virdi v. Abbey Leisure Ltd.* [1990] BCLC 342 (CA).     [197] Ibid., at 68; 350.

The House of Lords in *Ebrahimi* v. *Westbourne Galleries Ltd.* . . . . made it clear that on a petition for the winding up of a company on just and equitable grounds, the legal rights and obligations conferred or imposed on shareholders by the constitution of the company may be subjected to equitable considerations. If in the present case it may be equitable to ignore the provisions of the company's constitution which prima facie entitle the directors to carry on the business of the company after the sale of the Pavilion, I do not see why it would not be equally equitable, if this had been a case where Mr Virdi was bound by art. 27 to sell his shares to the majority at whatever price the accountant might fix, to ignore those provisions also.

It should be noted that the Court of Appeal's decision in *Re Abbey Leisure Ltd.*[198] was not a final determination of whether the petitioner had established such a legitimate expectation. Rather it was a decision not to strike out the petition as an abuse of the process of the court. For this purpose, the petitioner's allegation that there was an agreement that the company should not undertake any ventures other than the Pavilion nightclub was assumed to be true. In his capacity as the company's solicitor, the petitioner had in fact drafted the articles which contained not only the pre-emption provisions but also an objects clause which expressed the company's objects as extending to various activities within the entertainment industry and gave no indication of the understanding that the sole project to be undertaken was in fact the acquisition and management of the Pavilion nightclub. It is submitted that this may well have involved sufficient conscious agreement to prevent a petitioner setting up any legitimate expectation overriding their terms at the trial of the action. However, the important part of the decision for the purposes of this discussion is the rejection of the proposition that the existence of a valuation procedure in a pre-emption provision cannot be overridden by establishment of a contrary legitimate expectation.

*Re Abbey Leisure Ltd.*[199] is distinguishable from the usual unfair prejudice petition, since it was essentially a case of alleged failure of substratum, that is, a case of compulsory inclusion rather than compulsory exclusion. Nor was the Court of Appeal's decision directed towards unfair prejudice petitions. Indeed, Balcombe LJ expressly left open the applicability of the decision to an unfair prejudice provision for a future case in which the point was clearly in issue.[200] However, in light of the earlier discussion as to the influence of the *Westbourne Galleries* case[201] on the shaping of the unfair prejudice provision Balcombe LJ's[202] reasons for disregarding provisions in the articles for determining the fair value of shares should be equally applicable to a legitimate expectations test.

---

[198] Ibid.      [199] Ibid.      [200] Ibid., at 68; 350.      [201] Above n 3.
[202] Above n 196, at 65; 347 with which Sir George Waller agreed.

The approach taken by the Court of Appeal in *Re Abbey Leisure Ltd.* is in line with that adopted in Australian and New Zealand cases. For example in *Re Norvabron Pty. Ltd. (No. 2* Derrington J said regarding a put option in the articles entitling the petitioner to require the other two shareholders to purchase his shares:[203]

It requires little in the way of real proof of probable disadvantage to a party under such an existing remedy before the court will disregard it in favour of the application of [the unfair prejudice remedy] where the other circumstances are suitable. This reflects the view that the alternative remedy may not be entirely satisfactory because, if the valuation is wrong, there is seldom any satisfactory means of challenging or rectifying it: *Re Dalkeith Investments Pty. Ltd.* . . . Conversely, however, the existence of the put option in the articles lends some support to the application to the extent that it demonstrates that, given the presence of oppression or unfair prejudice, it is a suitable case for a purchase order.

This is also the approach which appears to have been taken in the recent English case of *Re a Company (No. 00330 of 1991); Ex parte Holden.*[204] Here the petitioner's complaint did not relate to the possibility of the value of his shares being wrongly discounted. Rather it related to difficulties in the method of valuation and, in particular, the three factors that: the articles did not require the expert to explain the method of valuation, that there was no provision for representations to be made to the expert, and that there were claims against the company requiring evaluation which might or might not be taken into account in the valuation. Referring to *Re Abbey Leisure Ltd.*[205] Harman J said:[206]

That decision . . . has altered the balance against the view that shareholders who enter into a company with articles allowing for compulsory transfer are bound to go through compulsory transfer provisions rather than exercising their statutory rights and are unreasonable if they do not accept the transfer provisions . . . There must be questions of fact. In some cases a petitioner may be held to be unreasonable because it can be seen that it would be unreasonable to refuse to follow the contractual term; in other cases it will not. But the broad brush approach that it is always reasonable to insist upon the articles and it is always unreasonable to refuse so to do is no longer, as I understand *Abbey Leisure*, the law as it must be applied.

---

[203] Above n 83, at 292–3; 214. See also *Re Dalkeith Investments Pty. Ltd.* above n 117, *Coombs* v. *Dynasty Pty. Ltd.* (1994) 14 ACSR 60; digested (1994) 12 ACLC 915 (in this case there was both a finding of unfair prejudice and a history of information being withheld from the minority shareholder and from the auditor), *Shadgett* v. *Appellor Fisheries Ltd.* (1992) 6 NZCLC 68,166, *Re Rongo-ma-tane Farms Ltd.* (1987) 3 NZCLC 100,145. But cf., *Kizquari Pty. Ltd.* v. *Prestoo Pty. Ltd.* (1993) 10 ACSR 606; 11 ACLC 568, although in this case a purchase order was not considered appropriate.
[204] [1991] BCLC 597; [1991] BCC 241.                    [205] Above n 196.
[206] Above n 204, at 604; 247.

Hoffmann J in any event specifically excluded from the proposition set out in *Re XYZ*[207] the situation where the articles provided an arbitrary or artificial method of valuation[208] and it may therefore be possible to reconcile the *Re XYZ* line of cases with *Holden*'s case.[209] However, the above dictum of Harman J seeks to base the decision not merely upon the deficiencies in the valuation method, but also on the wider approach embodied in *Re Abbey Leisure Ltd.*[210] In doing so, it represents a change in direction, and it is therefore worthwhile to digress into the policy arguments in favour of the two approaches.

Hoffmann J's reasons for giving supremacy to the pre-emption provisions in *Re XYZ*[211] revolved around a concern as to the potential for the presentation of an unfair prejudice petition to operate as a powerful negotiating tactic to induce the respondents to pay the petitioner the price he asks for his shares. The pressures on a company identified by Hoffmann J were twofold. The first related to the likelihood of the company's bank account being frozen on the bank getting to hear of the petition, because the court could allow an amendment which would result in a winding up being deemed to have commenced at the date of presentation. His Lordship's second concern was as to the crippling burden of legal costs and expenditure of management time involved in the litigation process. In *Re a Company (No. 006834 of 1988); Ex parte Kremer*[212] Hoffmann J added as a justification for this approach the fact that the respondent has un-expectedly to find the funds in order to pay out the petitioner.

Since those cases were decided, there have however been some changes to the background against which such petitions are brought. A recent Practice Direction in England attempts to remove the potentially damaging effects to the company of the inclusion of an alternative winding-up prayer in a petition, by discouraging the unnecessary inclusion of an alternative claim for winding up and by providing a procedure to ensure the validity of financial transactions between the date of presentation of the petition and the date of judgment.[213] Arguably therefore, an alternative solution has

---

[207] Above n 187.
[208] And where bad faith or impropriety had a detrimental effect on the value of the shares. See also *Re Rongo-Ma-Tane Farms Ltd.* above n 203.      [209] Above n 204.
[210] Above n 196.      [211] Above n 187, at 110.
[212] Above n 187, at 369; 222.
[213] The Practice Direction (Chancery 1/90 [1990] 1 All ER 1056) provides that a prayer for winding up as an alternative to an order under the unfair prejudice provision should be included only if that is the relief which the petitioner prefers or if it is considered that it may be the only relief to which he is entitled. Further, when a prayer for winding up is included in a petition, the petitioner must state whether he consents to an order under s. 127, IA 1986 (UK) which provides that dispositions between the date of presentation of the petition and the date of judgment shall not be void in the event of an order for winding up being made. Further, if the petitioner objects to the order, the company may apply (in cases of urgency *ex parte*) to the judge for an order.

now been found to Hoffmann J's first concern. No such practice direction exists in Australia. However, it has been held that improper use of legal proceedings which causes damage to a company, such as where it is damaged by an announcement about its possible winding up amounts to an actionable tort.[214]

His Lordship's other concerns which related to the potential for oppression of the majority remain valid. There are, however, counter-vailing policy arguments. One such argument was voiced by counsel in the winding-up case of *Re a Company (No. 002567 of 1982)*,[215] namely that if the petitioner were to be denied the remedy 'the court will, in effect, expose any minority shareholder in a company of this kind to the hazard that the majority will be able to exclude him from participation in the affairs of the company, contrary to the understanding which underlay the formation of the company and then compulsorily acquire his shares, notwithstanding the absence of any power in the articles to do so'. These sentiments are endorsed by Prentice[216] who criticizes Hoffmann J's approach on the basis that it enables the majority to oust a minority shareholder provided the price offered for his shares is in accordance with the valuation provisions of a company's articles thus making the interest of the shareholder effectively defeasible. Prentice also raises the point that Hoffmann J's approach equates a shareholder forced to leave the company with one who is a voluntary seller, since provisions in articles dealing with the valuation of shares in connection with pre-emption provisions are directed towards voluntary sales whereas a sale effected under the unfair prejudice provision is seen as being coercive.[217] These arguments were also employed by the Court of Appeal in *Re Abbey Leisure Ltd.*[218]

It is submitted that no special case should be made in respect of pre-emption provisions, and that the general approach should be taken, namely to ascertain whether the petitioner has a legitimate expectation that the articles will be applied. This is largely a question of fact as to what the parties mutually agreed. However, there is also an element of value judgment by the court. It has been argued above that had there been a trial on the facts of *Re Abbey Leisure Ltd.*, the petitioner, who actually drafted the company's constitutional documents, should have found it difficult to establish a contrary legitimate expectation.[219] A more finely balanced fact situation was presented by *Re XYZ Ltd.*[220] In that case, the pre-emption

---

[214] *QIW Retailers Ltd.* v. *Felview Pty. Ltd.* [1989] 2 Qd. R 245. See also Ch. 7, section 3(4)(a).

[215] [1983] 1 WLR 927 at 936.

[216] D. D. Prentice, above n 66.

[217] Prentice also raises the further argument that Hoffmann J's approach places a shareholder in a company which contains a valuation provision in its articles in a worse position than a shareholder in a company whose articles do not contain such a provision.

[218] Above n 196.     [219] See text accompanying n 198.     [220] Above n 187.

provisions and article 10 which set out the circumstances in which a person would become bound to give a transfer notice under the pre-emption provisions did not form part of the company's original articles, but rather had been inserted after the breakdown in relations between the parties. Counsel for the petitioner, arguing that these articles were not binding on the petitioner, raised the objections that the petitioner had had neither adequate notice of the new articles nor adequate opportunity at the meeting to consider them in any depth, and that the respondent owed a duty to the petitioner to explain the effect of the new articles or allow him time for consideration. This argument was rejected by Hoffmann J who observed[221] that there was no suggestion that the petitioner had been misled or that he had asked for explanation or further time, and that the new articles could not have been adopted if he had voted against them.

Such pre-emption provisions do not form part of the model articles in Table A, and it might be argued on that basis that a petitioner should not easily be able to establish a contrary legitimate expectation.[222] By the very nature of a legitimate expectation test it is submitted that it is not possible to draw a line at which a petitioner must take responsibility for his or her own protection. However, on facts such as those in *Re XYZ Ltd.*[223] where the adoption of the relevant article involved the conscious act of voting, there is a great deal of force in the argument that the petitioner should be bound by that vote. The situation may be different where, for example, the company was purchased 'off the shelf' with the pre-emption provisions already incorporated in the articles.

### (ii) The relevance of a shareholders' agreement

The above discussion raises a further point as to the means by which the parties choose to set out their rights and obligations. Although traditionally one might have expected such matters to be contained exclusively in the articles, shareholders today sometimes (and indeed routinely in the case of joint ventures) enter into a separate shareholders' agreement regarding certain matters.[224] The question therefore arises whether a private contract entered into consensually by the members stands on any different footing from the contract imposed by statute. *Re a Company (No. 005686 of 1988); Ex parte Schwarcz (No. 2)*[225] suggests that it may.[226]

The facts of that case were that S's family companies merged with

---

[221] Ibid., at 107.

[222] A. Clark, 'Unfair Prejudice and the Corporate Quasi-Partnership' (1989) 10 *Company Lawyer* 153 at 155.                                          [223] Above n 187.

[224] The relative merits of each approach are discussed in Ch. 4.

[225] [1989] BCLC 427, also reported as *Re Ringtower Holdings plc (Re a Company No. 005686 of 1988 (No. 2))* (1989) 5 BCC 82.

[226] See also *Re Elgindata Ltd.* [1991] BCLC 959.

another group of companies through Ringtower Ltd. ('R Ltd.'). The documentation surrounding the acquisition by R Ltd. of the Aeresta group of companies extended to 115 documents. The agreements expressly stated that they contained all the terms agreed. Part of the documentation consisted of service agreements between S and R Ltd. In accordance with the terms of the service agreement, S's employment was terminated for misconduct. An unfair prejudice petition brought by S based in part on a claim that his dismissal was in breach of his legitimate expectations to participate in management was struck out. Peter Gibson J held that the detailed documentation surrounding the acquisition of the company by R Ltd. precluded any such claim, saying:[227]

This submission is nothing if not bold. What the petitioners are asserting in this case is that at the very same time as the petitioners were entering into massively detailed and professionally drawn agreements governing the sale of the Aeresta group and the acquisition by them of very small shareholdings in Ringtower they were entering into unspoken and unrecorded mutual obligations intended to govern their relationship with each other inconsistent with the express terms of the service agreements, providing as they did for limits to the term of their employment, including the ability of Ringtower to terminate the agreements, and that the terms therein contained were the entire terms of their employment.

This is not inconsistent with Prentice's comments,[228] since his arguments are based on the assumption that 'many shareholders do not fully appreciate the implications of the provisions in a company's articles of association and it would be stretching the meaning of the word agreement to say that they had agreed to them'.[229] Admittedly there may also be cases where shareholders do not fully appreciate (or even read) the terms of an agreement. But, like voting, the act of entering into an agreement involves a conscious step which does not necessarily exist in the case of articles of association by virtue of the contractual effect given to them by statute.

Nevertheless, it is difficult to extrapolate a general approach from *Schwarcz*'s case.[230] The facts of that case were relatively straightforward, since the alleged expectation was in direct contradiction with the express terms of the contemporaneous agreements. A rather more difficult question is posed where the agreements between the parties are less comprehensive, and the expectation relied upon relates to a matter for which there is no express provision. In this situation, should a shareholder be confined to a contractual remedy or should the shareholder be able to enforce such expectations via the unfair prejudice remedy? Under contractual remedies additional terms will be implied only if they are

---

[227] Above n 225.                    [228] Above n 66.
[229] Ibid., at 89.                    [230] Above n 225.

necessary to give business efficacy to the arrangement. They may be easier to establish under the unfair prejudice jurisdiction.[231] In *Re Elgindata Ltd.*[232] Warner J said that:

In general members of a company have no legitimate expectations going beyond the legal rights conferred on them by the constitution of the company, that is to say its memorandum and articles of association. None the less, legitimate expectations superimposed on a member's legal rights may arise from agreements or understandings between the members. Where, however, the acquisition of shares in a company is one of the results of a complex set of formal written agreements it is a question of construction of those agreements whether any such superimposed legitimate expectations can arise.

A related question is whether a petitioner should be able to establish unfair prejudice by departure from a legitimate expectation which has arisen over the passage of time, overtaking the written contractual terms, or whether instead this should be done by proving an oral variation of contract.

On the one hand it would seem illogical that a shareholder who is party to an out-of-date, incomplete, or poorly drafted shareholders' agreement should be in a more vulnerable position than a shareholder with no agreement at all. On the other hand, it can be argued that there ought to be a point at which the law provides a positive incentive for parties to formalize the terms of their business arrangements accurately. *Schwarcz*'s case[233] embodies this policy element in precluding the assertion of a legitimate expectation contrary to contemporaneous and detailed agreements. However, in other contexts the courts have recognized that legitimate expectations may alter during the life of a company, and have been prepared to give effect to the expectations existing at the time of the disputed conduct.[234] In a similar vein, it is submitted that relief under the unfair prejudice provision should potentially be available in respect of expectations which were not anticipated at the time of entering into the agreement or have emerged since that date. However, where a party seeks to assert legitimate expectations arising from a settled course of conduct or from a change in circumstance arising since the drafting of an agreement

---

[231] M. C. Ahrens, 'Incorporated Joint Ventures' in R. P. Austin and R. Vann (eds) *The Law of Public Company Finance* (Sydney, The Law Book Company Ltd., 1986) 450 at 483–6. Cf., *Greenhlagh* v. *Arderne Cinemas Ltd.* [1946] 1 All ER 512 (CA) where Greenhalgh alleged a breach of an implied term of a voting agreement to the effect that the company would be precluded from acting in any way which would interfere with the voting control which it conferred. The Court of Appeal, however, refused to imply such a term.

[232] Above n 226, at 985.  [233] Above n 225.

[234] See text accompanying nn 172–4.

and conflicting with its terms, the petitioner should face a heavy burden of proof.[235]

## (9) The relevance of the petitioner's conduct

The conduct of the petitioner may have a bearing on the success of a petition in two distinct respects. The first consideration is whether the petitioner has behaved in such a way as to encourage the conduct of the respondent. The second is whether the petitioner has some collateral purpose in bringing the actual petition. Each of these issues is considered below.

### (a) Misconduct by the petitioner

Here it is appropriate to digress in order to consider the position under the just and equitable winding-up remedy. It is stated in a number of cases that a 'petitioner who relies on the "just and equitable" clause must come to court with clean hands, and if the breakdown in confidence between him and the other parties to the dispute appears to have been due to his misconduct he cannot insist on the company being wound up if they wish it to continue'.[236]

However, the courts recognize that there may be a breakdown in relations without any identifiable misconduct by any party, or in circumstances where a clear-cut apportionment of blame is impossible,[237] and will be prepared to find, as on the facts in the *Westbourne Galleries* case[238] '. . . that the respondents' loss of confidence in the petitioner might have been due to a tragic and inexplicable misunderstanding'.[239] Even, in cases of proven misconduct by the petitioner, this will not bar a winding-up order if it is not causative of the breakdown in relations.[240]

Under the unfair prejudice provision, Nourse J in *Re London School of Electronics Ltd.*[241] made it clear that there is no independent or overriding requirement that the petitioner should come to the court with clean hands. The question of 'clean hands' has since been considered in an Australian

---

[235] M. Ahrens, 'Joint Venture Structures—The Corporate Form' in *Public Company Finance*, Papers and Commentaries Delivered on 18 and 25 November 1982 to the Committee for Post-Graduate Studies in the Department of Law, University of Sydney at 300.

[236] *Per* Lord Cross in *Ebrahimi* v. *Westbourne Galleries Ltd.*, above n 3, at 387. See also *Re F. Hall & Sons Ltd.* [1939] NZLR 408 (CA NZ), *Menard* v. *Horwood* (1922) 31 CLR 20 (HC), *Re Martello & Sons Ltd.* above n 4.

[237] *Re Rongo-Ma-Tane Farms Ltd.* above n 203.    [238] Above n 3.

[239] Ibid., at 387 *per* Lord Cross.

[240] *Vuynovich* v. *Vuynovich* [1988] 2 NZLR 129 (CA NZ), affd. [1989] 3 NZLR 513 (PC). In that case the respondent diverted business away from the company long after the breakdown in confidence on which the petition was based.

[241] [1986] Ch. 211.

unfair prejudice petition, *Morgan* v. *45 Flers Avenue Pty. Ltd.*,[242] where Young J applied the approach of Nourse J in *Re London School of Electronics Ltd.*[243] With respect to an alternative claim for a winding-up order on the just and equitable ground, Young J went on to say,[244] obiter, that he preferred the view that the plaintiff's conduct should be taken into account in the same way as in relation to an unfair prejudice provision, making it unnecessary to consider the plaintiff's conduct again as a matter of defence.

What then is the relevance of the petitioner's conduct to an unfair prejudice petition? In *Re R. A. Nonle & Sons (Clothing) Ltd.*[245] the petitioner's disinterest in the company's affairs led to a finding that N's failure to consult him was not unfair, and this was fatal to the petition.[246] Similarly, in *Jesner* v. *Jarrad Properties Ltd.*,[247] the petitioner's acquiescence in the conduct complained of over a number of years was held to render conduct which was accepted to be prejudicial not unfair.[248] Nourse J endorsed this approach in *Re London School of Electronics Ltd.*[249] His Lordship went on to say[250] that the petitioner's conduct may also be material in determining the relief granted by the court. This is consistent with the approach taken in earlier cases regarding valuation of shares, where the presumption in favour of a *pro rata* valuation of the shares of a quasi-partner may be displaced not only by reference to the circumstances of purchase of the shares but also in light of the petitioner's conduct.[251] On the facts of *Re London School of Electronics Ltd.*[252] Nourse J held that the petitioner's traits of being unreliable, difficult, and lazy in the discharge of his duties did not render the respondent's conduct in appropriating the company's students not unfair. Nor were the petitioner's breaches of duty subsequent to the respondent's unfairly prejudicial conduct relevant to the question of unfair prejudice, although they did give rise to a liability to account to the company. However, his Lordship considered that the petitioner's conduct should be taken into account in determining not only the basis for but also the date of the valuation.[253]

---

[242] Above n 70.      [243] Above n 241.      [244] Above n 70, at 708; 236.

[245] Above n 23.

[246] Cf., discussion below in Ch. 7 regarding the residual role of the winding-up remedy.

[247] Above n 135.

[248] In both *Noble*'s case and *Jesner*'s case a winding-up order was granted on the basis that there had been a breakdown in the relationship between quasi-partners.

[249] Above n 241.      [250] Ibid., at 222.

[251] *Re Bird Precision Bellows Ltd.* above n 189.      [252] Above n 241.

[253] See further, D. D. Prentice, 'Minority Shareholder Oppression: Valuation of Shares' (1986) 102 *Law Q Rev* 179.

### (b) Collateral purpose

Although misconduct by a petitioner in the course of the parties' relationship will not necessarily bar relief, the petitioner's reason for bringing the petition is nevertheless an important factor in terms of whether the court is prepared to grant relief.

In *Re Bellador Silk Ltd.*[254] it appeared in cross examination that the real object of presenting the petition was to get repayment of a loan owed by the company to the petitioner's group of companies. One of the grounds for refusing relief was that the petition had been brought to achieve a collateral purpose and was therefore an abuse of the process of the court.[255] In *Jaber* v. *Science & Information Technology Ltd.*[256] identical allegations were made in an action commenced by writ and an unfair prejudice petition, so that it would have been appropriate for them to be tried together. In these circumstances, the unfair prejudice petition was struck out as the only relief sought was relief pending trial of the writ action.[257]

### (10) Remedies

The legislation in both the United Kingdom and Australia gives a wide discretion to the court to grant the relief best suited to deal with the conduct complained of, although in both cases, examples of the types of relief which may be ordered are also listed.

### (a) Winding up

One difference between the legislation in the two countries is the greater overlap between the winding-up remedy and the unfair prejudice remedy in Australia. The list of possible remedies in the Australian unfair prejudice provision specifically includes an order that the company be wound up. Conversely, unfairly prejudicial conduct is expressly listed in the Australian winding-up provision as a ground for making an order.[258] Section 260(4) of the Corporations Law prohibits the court from making a winding-up order under the unfair prejudice provision if it is of the opinion that the winding up of the company would unfairly prejudice the oppressed member or members. Nevertheless, there are instances where the power to

---

[254] Above n 17.
[255] The other ground related to standing requirements. See discussion above at section 1(1)(a)(i).  [256] Above n 63.
[257] See Ch. 9 regarding the overlap between actions at common law and unfair prejudice petitions.  [258] Section 461(f) and (g), CL (Aust).

make a winding-up order has been exercised as a remedy for unfairly prejudicial conduct.[259]

Although it would be open to an English court make an order for the winding up of a company under the unfair prejudice provision, this has not yet been done, and a practice direction discourages the unnecessary inclusion of an alternative claim for winding up or the just and equitable ground unless it is genuinely the remedy sought.[260]

## (b) Regulating the company's affairs

An order of this type was made under the old oppression provision in *Re H. R. Harmer Ltd.*[261] Here the founder of the company had continued to run the business as if it were still his own after incorporation, disregarding board decisions and the wishes of the shareholders. The court ordered that the founder be appointed president of the company for life and that the company should contract for his services as a consultant, but that he should not interfere in the affairs of the company otherwise than in accordance with the valid decisions of the board.

In *Re Spargos*[262] where the other board had approved transactions which were for the benefit of the other members of the group but were not in the interests of the company, Murray J made orders replacing the existing board with one of his own choosing, protecting the new board from removal and giving the directors discretion to carry out certain investigations and institute certain proceedings.

In *Roberts* v. *Walter Developments Pty. Ltd. (No. 2)*[263] the court ordered payment to the plaintiff of the dividend which should have been payable to him (but for the payment of excessive directors' fees) and an amendment to the articles of association whereby directors' remuneration was to be determined by a unanimous shareholder resolution or, failing that, determined by an independent 'remuneration expert'.

## (c) Purchase order

The most commonly sought and awarded remedy is an order that one of the parties (usually the respondents) purchase the other's shares.[264] It will often be the most appropriate remedy where a breakdown in relations between quasi-partners results in unfairly prejudicial conduct. However, in cases where the petitioner has elected to become an ordinary minority

---

[259] See e.g., *Wallington* v. *Kokotovich Constructions Pty. Ltd.* (1993) 11 ACSR 759; 11 ACLC 1207.      [260] See discussion above at text accompanying n 213.
[261] Above n 26.      [262] Above n 41.      [263] (1992) 10 ACLC 1734.
[264] See e.g., *Re Ghyll Beck Driving Range Ltd.* [1993] BCLC 1126.

shareholder prior to the conduct complained of, applications for purchase orders have been refused, with the court instead making orders designed to put the company back on the rails. For example, in *Kizquari Pty. Ltd.* v. *Prestoo Pty. Ltd.*[265] the court made an order for reimbursement of moneys improperly paid out in directors' salaries, in the expectation that repetition of the conduct was unlikely.[266]

Where a purchase order is considered appropriate, the question then arises as to the appropriate basis for valuation of the shares. Valuation of shares is a specialized area, and a detailed treatment of it is beyond the scope of this book. Rather, the purpose of the following discussion is to highlight some of the issues which have arisen in the decided cases.[267]

### (i) Valuation method

The appropriate valuation method will depend on the type of company, and the way in which it has been run.[268] It may also depend upon the conduct complained of. For example, in *Re Bodaibo Pty. Ltd.*[269] a valuation method was chosen which would compensate the applicant for the fact that he was forced by the respondent's conduct to sell his interest in an extremely unfavourable economic environment.

The court also has wide powers to make appropriate orders regarding how the parties' conduct should be taken into account in the context of the valuation process. Thus, the court may order the valuation to be made on the footing that unfairly prejudicial conduct had not occurred, where the conduct has diminished the value of the shares.[270] The general approach to the question of valuation is described by Vincent J in *Re Bodaibo Pty. Ltd.*[271] Referring to the decision of the House of Lords in *Scottish Co-operative Wholesale Society Ltd.* v. *Meyer*,[272] Vincent J said:

The court is clearly endowed with a wide discretion in order that justice can be achieved in the variety of circumstances encompassed by the statute. As Lord Denning pointed out, in some situations an element of compensation is integral to the determination of a fair price. Certainly, in the ascertainment of a fair price, consideration must be given to the selection of the most appropriate method of valuation in the particular circumstances of the matter before the court, and to the

---

[265] Above n 203.

[266] See also *Roberts* v. *Walter Developments Pty. Ltd. (No. 2)*, above n 263.

[267] See generally, Prentice, above n 253.

[268] See e.g. *Re Macro (Ipswich) Ltd.*, above n 86, *Re a company (No. 00789 of 1987); Ex parte Shooter*, above n 49, *Sanford* v. *Sanford Courier Service Pty. Ltd.*, above n 190, *Sanford* v. *Sanford Courier Service Pty. Ltd. (No. 2)* (1986) 11 ACLR 373, and *Re Ghyll Beck Driving Range Ltd.*, above n 264.      [269] (1992) 6 ACSR 509; 10 ACLC 351.

[270] See e.g., *Re Dalkeith Investments Pty. Ltd.* above n 117, *Re Bagot Well Pastoral Co. Pty. Ltd*; *Shannon* v. *Reid* (1992) 9 ACSR 129; 11 ACLC 1; affd sub nom *Re Bagot Well Pastoral Co Pty Ltd* (1993) 61 SASR 165 (Full Ct, SA).

[271] Above n 269, at 513; 354.      [272] Above n 25.

possible necessity that some adjustment should be made to the figure arrived at in order to offset the effects of the oppressive behaviour. In other words, as far as reasonably practicable, the court must endeavour to achieve equity between the parties and to ensure that an oppressor does not profit from the wrongful behaviour in which that party engaged to the detriment of those against whom it has so acted.

### (ii) Appropriateness of a discount

Where a purchase order is made consequent on a finding of unfair prejudice in a quasi-partnership company, *Re Bird Precision Bellows Ltd.*[273] is authority that the price should generally be fixed *pro rata* according to the value of the shares as a whole and not discounted for the fact that it is a minority holding. Further, it has been considered relevant to take into account the advantage to the respondent of having complete control of the company in the future.[274] A discount will, however, generally be appropriate if the petitioner is an ordinary minority share-holder[275] or deserves his or her exclusion.[276]

### (iii) Valuation date

The facts of the case will also be taken into account in determining an appropriate date on which the shares should be valued. For example, in *Re London School of Electronics Ltd.*[277] a date was chosen which was calculated to compensate the petitioner for the respondent's appropriation of students from the company, but did not entitle him to share in subsequent profits which were entirely referable to the efforts of the respondents.[278]

### (iv) Relevance of respondent's financial position

Where a purchase order is made after a finding of unfair prejudice, the order is in the nature of compensation, so that it should not be affected by the fact that the respondent is impecunious.[279]

### (v) Compulsory acquisition

Generally, where a purchase order is sought, it is the petitioner who is seeking to be bought out. However, in *Re a Company (No. 00789 of 1987);*

---

[273] [1984] Ch. 419, affd. [1986] Ch. 658 (CA). See also discussion above in section 8(b)(i).
[274] *Sanford* v. *Sanford Courier Service Pty. Ltd.*, above n 190 and *Reid* v. *Bagot Well Pastoral Co. Pty. Ltd.*; *Shannon* v. *Reid*, above n 270. See also *Re Macro (Ipswich) Ltd.*, above n 86, regarding the allocation of a control premium.
[275] *Re a Company (No. 005134 of 1986); Ex parte Harries* above n 172.
[276] *Re Bird Precision Bellows Ltd.*, above n 189.  [277] Above n 241.
[278] See further regarding the choice of valuation date: *Re OC (Transport) Services* [1984] BCLC 251, *Re a Company (No. 002612 of 1984)* (1985) 2 BCC 99,453 affd. (1986) 2 BCC 99,495 and sub nom. *Re Cumana Ltd.* [1986] BCLC 430 (CA), and *Re Quest Exploration Pty. Ltd.* (1992) 6 ACSR 659.
[279] *Re Cumana*, ibid. See also *Re Norvabron Pty. Ltd. (No. 2)* above n 83.

*Ex parte Shooter*[280] the court ordered that the respondent should divest his shares in favour of the petitioner in circumstances where the respondent had been conducting the company's affairs without regard to company law formalities.

### (vi) Trustee companies

Trustee companies pose complicated valuation problems. In *Bodaibo*'s case[281] Vincent J took into account the assets of a trust in valuing shares in a trustee company. However, dicta in two subsequent cases have disapproved this approach where oppression has occurred in relation to the operation of a trust, but has not affected the value of the shares of the trustee company.[282]

### (d) Proceedings by or on behalf of the company

The power to authorize proceedings to be brought on behalf of the company has been exercised in only one reported case, *Re Overton Holdings Pty. Ltd.*[283] The conduct complained of amounted to a breach of directors' duties. The respondent, F, had caused the company to borrow money it did not require and to lend it at commercially unrealistic terms without adequate security to a company in which the company had no financial interest and which F controlled.

There was little consideration in that case of the nature of the action, except to say that the power to authorize such proceedings gave 'statutory force to the exception to the rule in *Foss* v. *Harbottle*'.[284] This assimilation between conduct which amounts to breach of directors' duties and conduct for which the unfair prejudice provision provides a remedy has not been adopted in subsequent cases, although breach of duty has been considered to be a relevant factor in determining whether unfairness has been established.[285] The Companies and Securities Law Review Committee[286] took the view that the Australian unfair prejudice provision in its present form does not necessarily provide standing to a member to bring an action in respect of a breach of duty which is owed solely to the company in the absence of any evidence of unfair prejudice to a member or members. On this view, there is an inherent conflict in the unfair prejudice provisions in both the United Kingdom and Australia. On the one hand the court's jurisdiction is grounded on conduct which is unfairly prejudicial to

---

[280] Above n 49.                                                    [281] Above n 269.

[282] *Kizquari Pty. Ltd.* v. *Prestoo Pty. Ltd.* above n 203, and *Re Bountiful Pty. Ltd.* (1994) ACLC 902.                    [283] [1985] WAR 224.                    [284] Ibid., at 230.

[285] See e.g. *Jenkins* v. *Enterprise Gold Mines NL* above n 156 and Stapledon, above n 162.

[286] *Report No 12: Enforcement of the Duties of Directors and Officers of a Company by Means of a Statutory Derivative Action* (November 1990, Australia).

members. But on the other hand, the court is expressly empowered to authorize the petitioner to institute proceedings in the name of and on behalf of the company.

The committee dealt with this conflict by recommending the introduction of a statutory derivative action provision along Canadian lines.[287] The Companies and Securities Advisory Committee has subsequently endorsed this recommendation, but recommended some modifications to the proposed legislation.[288]

Although the introduction of a statutory derivative action would eliminate the problems associated with the derivative action at common law, it would not resolve the inherent conflict involved in the court's power under the unfair prejudice provision to grant leave to sue in the name of and on behalf of the company. Writing in relation to the Canadian provisions, MacIntosh[289] observes that no clear resolution of this ambiguity can be discerned either from the legislation or the interpretation given to it in the courts. Regrettably, the Australian Companies and Securities Law Review Committee[290] elected not to make any specific provision regarding this issue. Nor did that committee or the Companies and Securities Advisory Committee address the relationship of a statutory derivative action with the already existing statutory provisions in Australia which provide a form of derivative action.

In any event, law reform proposals in this area have been overtaken to some extent by case law developments in Australia. Although there are no other cases where actions have been authorized to be brought on behalf of the company, the unfair prejudice remedy has been used to obtain relief in situations where breach of directors' duties had adversely affected the company, but where it would have been difficult to show unfair prejudice to the applicant, since he had purchased his shares after the impugned conduct, at a price which reflected the diminution in value. In *Re Spargos Mining NL*[291] Murray J considered that an order directing the company to

---

[287] Ibid., at 7. The introduction of a statutory derivative action in Australia is also recommended by the House of Representatives Standing Committee on Legal and Constitutional Affairs (Lavarch Committee) in its report, *Corporate Practices and the Rights of Shareholders*, 28 November 1991, Recommendation 26, para. 6.3.33. English commentators favouring the introduction of a statutory derivative suit according to the Canadian model or the alternative approach contained in Art. 16 of the draft EC 5th Directive (which grants standing to shareholders holding a qualifying percentage of the share capital—currently 10%) include A. J. Boyle, 'The Judicial Interpretation of part XVII of the Companies Act 1985' in B. G. Pettet, (ed.) *Company Law in Change: Current Legal Problems* (London, Stevens & Sons, 1987) at 34, A. Boyle, 'The Companies Act 1980 (4)' (1981) 1 *Company Lawyer* 280, 283. A statutory derivative action has recently been introduced in New Zealand: ss. 165–8, Companies Act 1993 (NZ).

[288] See discussion in Ch. 8 section 6(2).

[289] J. G. MacIntosh 'The Oppression Remedy: Personal or Derivative?' (1991) 70 *Can B Rev* 29.　　　[290] Above n 286, paras 250–3.　　　[291] Above n 41.

institute specified proceedings would be premature, but granted relief which was,[292] '. . . designed to secure independent and disinterested management to this company dedicated to the taking of future decisions for the benefit of the company and the investigation of and pursuit of available remedies in respect of any past transactions such as, but not limited to those raised by the petitioner, where relevant causes of action are found to exist'. On the other hand, in *Parker* v. *National Roads and Motorists' Association*[293] the court refused authorization to the plaintiff to bring proceedings on behalf of the company.[294] In this case, the plaintiff complained that payments had been made to the board members of the National Roads and Motorists' Association ('NRMA') in their capacity as members of an Insurance Liaison Committee, and as directors of two companies, NRMA Finance Ltd. and NRMA Life Ltd., purely to circumvent the remuneration limitations in the articles. The plaintiff also challenged the payment of expenses to the president and vice-president of the NRMA without proper documentation or authorization. The plaintiff claimed that failure to investigate and pursue recovery of the remuneration and unauthorized expenses amounted to unfairly prejudicial conduct.

Hodgson J considered that one of the objectives of setting up the Insurance Liaison Committee was probably to achieve reasonable remuneration for board members, and that in formulating the directors' fees in NRMA Finance Ltd. and NRMA Life Ltd., regard was had to membership of the board of management. Although his Honour considered that there could be a *prima facie* case against the payments, he regarded it as a matter on which minds could reasonably differ, so that the decision not to pursue recovery of the payments was not oppressive.

In respect of the unauthorized expenses, Hodgson J regarded the council and directors' attitude which prevented any investigation of the non-disclosed allowances as oppressive. But he merely ordered the council and directors to consider whether anything should be done either about past non-disclosures or future practices for payment of allowances. Hodgson J's decision was affirmed by a majority of the New South Wales Court of Appeal.

In a strong dissent, Kirby P would have granted relief to the plaintiff on both substantive and procedural grounds. In addition, his Honour would have awarded indemnity costs to the plaintiff, on the basis that he had brought the proceedings in the public interest and without any motivation of personal gain, saying that courts[295] '. . . should support corporate

---

[292] Above n 41 at 193.
[293] (1989) 1 ACSR 227, affd. (1993) 11 ACSR 370; 11 ACLC 866 (CA NSW).
[294] See discussion of this case in Ch. 9 section 5(1).
[295] Above n 293 at 384; 878.

gadflies when their cause is the correction of apparently unlawful and self-interested action by directors, defended by oppressive conduct'.

It is difficult to speculate whether the existence of a statutory derivative action would have altered the outcome of this litigation. If regard is had only to the basis for decision of Hodgson J and the majority of the Court of Appeal, then the answer is that it probably would not have. However, it is possible that the fact of introduction of such a provision may alter judicial perceptions in favour of a minority shareholder in the position of the plaintiff in that case.

### (e) Appointment of a receiver

The courts (especially in England) are reluctant to appoint a receiver because of the slur it will cast on the company.[296]

Similarly, when the appointment of a receiver and manager was sought by the petitioner in *Re Spargos Mining NL*[297] and *Re Enterprise Gold Mines NL*,[298] it was refused by Murray J in both cases, because it would involve the company defaulting on agreements and because there was no suggestion that the company should proceed to an ultimate winding up. In *Re Spargos* his Honour nevertheless made far-reaching relief designed to place the company on a sound footing and pursue remedies in respect of past defaults. In *Re Enterprise* Murray J made the more limited order that until the next annual general meeting the company should not pay, transfer, sell, convey, or otherwise dispose of any money or other property to or in favour of a director of the company or Independent Resources Ltd. ('IRL') (a company controlled by the same persons as controlled Enterprise Gold Mines NL) or to any subsidiary or associate of IRL without the prior approval of the shareholders in general meeting at which neither the beneficiary nor its associates should be entitled to vote. On appeal, from the decision in *Re Enterprise*, this conservative approach was disapproved and a receiver and manager was appointed with full powers to investigate the transactions. The Full Court said:[299]

The respondent submitted that the appointment of a receiver and manager at the time when his Honour was giving consideration to the appropriate remedy could have had a prejudicial effect on certain securities. We were told that that prejudice no longer exists. However, even were that not the case, the relief proposed by his Honour was in our view inadequate and based on a wrong premise. It was based on a conservative view that the shareholders in annual general meeting could

---

[296] See *Jaber* v. *Science & Information Technology Ltd.*, above n 63, and *Re Mountforest Ltd.* [1993] BCC 565. [297] Above n 41. [298] (1991) 3 ACSR 531.
[299] Above n 156, at 563; 155–6.

overcome any unfairness to minority shareholders. Objectively that does not follow and in the present case has been shown to be wrong. As well, the order proposed by his Honour did not give any relief to the appellant which would enable the earlier transactions to be fully investigated.

### (f) Order restraining conduct

In *Re Mountforest*[300] (where the petition was based on allegations of exclusion from management) the court declined to appoint a receiver and manager. However, because the transaction was a self-dealing transaction, and there was a complete lack of disclosure,[301] it granted an injunction restraining the sale of the company's business. Injunctions were also ordered in *Whyte, petitioner*[302] to prevent the removal of a director and in *Re a Company (No. 002612 of 1984)*[303] to prevent an allotment of shares which would have diluted the petitioner's holding.

### (g) Order requiring conduct

In addition to the other relief granted in *Re Spargos*,[304] the court ordered deletion of certain articles. In *McGuinness* v. *Bremner plc*[305] the court ordered the convening of an extraordinary general meeting on a specified date, and the appointment of a named firm of accountants to act as independent scrutineers to be responsible for counting all the votes cast at the meeting.

### (h) Supervening appointment of an administrative receiver, administrator or liquidator

In *Re Hailey Group Ltd.; Re a Company (No. 008126 of 1989)*[306] the petition complained of sums being improperly paid out from the company. When presented, the petition sought an order that the majority shareholders sell their shares to the petitioner. An administrative receiver was subsequently appointed, after which the petitioner sought instead for the majority shareholders to purchase the petitioner's shares, repayment of the various sums allegedly improperly paid out and, in default of repayment, authorization for the petitioner to bring civil proceedings on behalf of the company. Richard Sykes QC held that the appointment of the administrative receiver meant that there was no longer any order appropriate for

---

[300] Above n 296.
[301] The court distinguished *Re Posgate and Denby (Agencies) Ltd.* above n 115, in this regard. An injunction was also granted restraining a winding up, since as there was to be no sale, there should be no resolution for liquidation.                [302] 1984 SLT 330.
[303] [1985] BCLC 80; (1984) 1 BCC 99,262.
[304] See above at n 262 and accompanying text.                [306] Above n 73.
[305] Above n 156.

giving relief in respect of the matters complained of. His Honour considered that to require the respondents to purchase the petitioner's shares would be tantamount to imposing a fine on them, since there was nothing of any value for them to purchase. Further, the petitioner no longer needed to dispose of his shares in order to obtain relief in respect of the matters complained of. Nevertheless his Honour considered[307] that relief under the unfair prejudice provision might be appropriate, despite the appointment of an administrative receiver (or administrator or liquidator) in a case where unfairly prejudicial conduct had prevented the petitioner selling his or her shares at a proper price prior to the insolvency, or where the relief sought at a time when the company was solvent was for a purchase of the petitioner's shares by the respondents.

### (i) Interim and interlocutory relief

In *Re a Company (No. 004175 of 1986)*[308] Scott J refused to make an interim payment order, on the basis that the jurisdiction to order a payment to be made by the respondents to the petition did not arise until the unfair prejudice had been established.[309]

However, interim and interlocutory relief has been granted on general principles to regulate the position pending the hearing of the petition,[310] for example by an injunction to preserve the status quo,[311] or otherwise protect the company's position pending the hearing of the petition.[312] A provisional liquidator was appointed in *Re Back 2 Bay 6 Pty. Ltd.*,[313] where the court was satisfied that failure to do so would expose the applicant to an unacceptable risk of damage that could not effectively be later reversed. And, in *Re a Company (No. 00596 of 1986)*[314] a receiver was appointed to manage the company's affairs pending the resolution of a winding-up petition by analogy with the circumstances in which a receiver would be appointed in a partnership context.

### (j) Interest

A claim for equitable interest on the purchase price of the shares of a petitioner who had been excluded from management was unsuccessful in

---

[307] Ibid., at 473; 554–5.   [308] [1987] 1 WLR 585.
[309] Cf., the situation where this has been conceded: *Ferguson* v. *Maclennan Salmon Co. Ltd.* [1990] BCC 702 (CS (IH)).
[310] See e.g., *Jaber* v. *Science & Information Technology Ltd.* above n 63, *Currie* v. *Cowdenbeath Football Club* [1992] BCLC 1029.
[311] *Tullamore Holdings Ltd.* v. *The Selby Shoe Company Ltd.* (1986) 3 NZCLC 99,759. Cf., *Rutherford, Petitioner; Re Lawrie & Symington Ltd.* [1994] BCC 876.
[312] *Re a Company (No. 003061 of 1993); Safinia* v. *Comet Enterprises Ltd.* [1994] BCC 883.
[313] (1994) 12 ACSR 614; 12 ACLC 253.
[314] [1987] BCLC 133; (1986) 2 BCC 99,063.

*Harrison* v. *Thompson*,[315] although Knox J, at first instance, left open the possibility of an award of equitable interest where it was consistent with the intention of the parties.

## (k) Costs[316]

### (i) *Indemnity from company*

Most disputes concerning quasi-partnership companies stem from a breakdown in the relations between the parties, and are essentially personal, rather than relating to some injury to the company. This fact has been recognized by the courts, and applications for indemnification based on the procedure in *Wallersteiner* v. *Moir (No. 2)*[317] have been refused where the substance of the complaint is personal. For example, in *Re a Company (No. 005136 of 1986)*[318] Hoffmann J refused to make an order indemnifying the petitioner for his costs in an action concerning an improper allotment of shares. His Lordship held that although the action gave rise to a breach of fiduciary duty, the substance of the petitioner's complaint was an infringement of his personal rights. It has also been held that the company's funds should not be used to finance a majority shareholders' defence to an action by a minority shareholder where the action is essentially a dispute between the shareholders.[319]

However, it is submitted that the *Wallersteiner* procedure has the potential to be applied in the unfair prejudice context where, as in *Re Spargos*,[320] the action is brought in respect of a wrongs done to the company. In *Parker* v. *National Roads and Motorists' Association*[321] the majority of the New South Wales Court of Appeal declined to award costs on an indemnity basis to a petitioner who unsuccessfully sought authorization to bring proceedings on behalf of the company.[322] However, the strong dissent of Kirby P should be noted. His Honour said:[323]

Where a director, alerted to what are considered to be suspicious or dubious circumstances of payments made by a company (particularly by way of fees to

---

[315] [1992] BCLC 833; [1992] BCC 67; affd. [1993] BCLC 784; [1992] BCC 962 (CA).

[316] See generally *Re Elgindata Ltd. (No. 2)* [1992] 1 WLR 1,207 (CA) and *Re a Company (No. 001126 of 1992)* above n 77.

[317] [1975] QB 373 (CA). See further Ch. 8, section 3(1)(e).

[318] [1987] BCLC 82, also reported as *Re Sherborne Park Residents Co. Ltd.* (1986) 2 BCC 99,528.

[319] *Re Crossmore Electrical & Civil Engineering Ltd.* [1989] BCLC 137; (1989) 5 BCC 37. *Re Milgate Developments Ltd.* [1993] BCLC 291; [1991] BCC 24, *Re a Company (No. 004502 of 1988); Ex parte Johnson* [1992] BCLC 701; [1991] BCC 234, *Re a Company (No. 001126 of 1992)* above n 77.          [320] Above n 41.                    [321] Above n 293.

[322] Affirming the first instance decision of Hodgson J.

[323] Above n 293, at 382–3; 877, citing *Wallersteiner* v. *Moir (No. 2)* above n 317, at 391 ff, 403, *Prudential Insurance Co. Ltd.* v. *Newman Industries (No. 2)* [1982] Ch. 204 (CA) at 221, and H. A.J. Ford *Company Law*, (5th edn., Butterworths, Sydney 1990) para. 1731.

directors or officers) brings such circumstances to public attention in a court, it is contrary to the public interest that such director should do so only at a substantial burden in costs which must then be privately borne. If the proceedings effectively vindicate the director's conduct—or even if they do not procure the order sought but demonstrate the genuineness and arguability of the claim made and concern expressed—a court may order the company to pay the director's costs on an indemnity basis. It will do so, in proper cases, in order to uphold the effectiveness of company law and the part which directors must necessarily play in bringing suspected infractions to the notice, first, of their colleagues and (absent satisfaction) eventually to the authorities and the courts. The provision of indemnity costs in such cases has been described in terms analogous to the protection which courts give to trustees, who also owe fiduciary duties, in bringing proceedings in the interests of the object of the trust.

Further, despite the uncertainty as to the extent to which an action which is derivative in nature can be pursued via the unfair prejudice provision, and consequently whether the substance of the claim is personal or is brought to remedy a wrong to the company, there ought to be some scope for the application of *Marx* v. *Estates and General Investments Ltd.*[324] in this context.[325]

It was held in *Re Hailey Group Ltd.*; *Re a Company (No. 008126 of 1989)*[326] that there was no jurisdiction to order an indemnity out of assets charged to a creditor.

### *(ii) Security for costs*

It has been held in England that a petitioner in an unfair prejudice provision can be ordered to give security for costs.[327]

---

[324] [1976] 1 WLR 380.   [325] See Ch. 8 section 3(1)(e).
[326] Above n 73.
[327] *Re Unisoft Group Ltd. (No. 1)* [1993] BCLC 528; [1992] BCC 494; affd. [1993] BCLC 1292; [1994] BCC 11 (CA). See *Re Unisoft Group Ltd. (No. 2)* [1993] BCLC 532 regarding the exercise of the discretion to make such an order. See also *Re Little Olympian Each-Ways Ltd.* [1994] BCC 959.

$$\longrightarrow 7 \longrightarrow$$

# Winding Up

1. Introduction    167

2. Independent Operation of the Winding-up Remedy    168
   (1) Where a winding-up order is considered more
       appropriate    169
       (a) No ongoing business    169
       (b) Deadlock    170
   (2) Where relief was unavailable under the unfair prejudice
       provision    171

3. Wider Scope of the Unfair Prejudice Remedy    172
   (1) *Locus standi*    172
       (a) England    173
       (b) Australia    173
   (2) Commercial companies    173
       (a) England    174
       (b) Australia    175
   (3) Clean hands    175
   (4) Alternative relief    176
       (a) An action under the unfair prejudice remedy    176
       (b) A personal action at common law    177
       (c) An offer to purchase the petitioner's shares    177

## SUMMARY

*The decision of the House of Lords in* Ebrahimi v. Westbourne Galleries Ltd. *was a landmark in the development of minority shareholders' remedies. Its influence has extended beyond the context of winding-up petitions, and has helped to shape the present form of the unfair prejudice remedy. As a consequence of:*

*(1) the development of the unfair prejudice remedy into a viable alternative to seeking a winding-up order;*
*(2) the wider range of remedies available under the unfair prejudice remedy; and*

*(3) the requirement that the court decline to make a winding-up order on the just and equitable ground if it is of opinion that some other remedy is available and the petitioner is acting unreasonably in pursuing the winding-up remedy,*

*the scope of operation of the winding-up remedy has diminished in recent times.*

*However, it continues to play a role where the company is insolvent or has ceased trading, in some cases of irretrievable deadlock and where the petitioner's conduct means that prejudicial conduct on the part of the respondent cannot be regarded as unfair.*

## 1. INTRODUCTION

Legislation in both countries empowers the court to wind up a company on the ground that it is just and equitable to do so.[1]

In Australia, section 461 of the Corporations Law (which governs the court's power to wind up a company compulsorily) includes in the list of grounds for making a winding-up order the same grounds on which the court may make an order under the unfair prejudice remedy.[2] A winding up may also be ordered in Australia if directors have acted in the affairs of the company in their own interests rather than in the interests of the members as a whole, or in any other manner whatsoever that appears to be unfair or unjust to other members.[3]

In the following discussion, the power to make a winding-up order on the just and equitable ground is referred to generally as 'the winding-up remedy', and specific reference is made to the additional grounds for making an order under the Australian legislation in the course of the discussion as appropriate.

The history of the winding-up remedy has been examined in Chapter 6, and is therefore not be covered again here. As discussed in that chapter,[4] the landmark decision of the House of Lords in *Ebrahimi* v. *Westbourne Galleries Ltd.*[5] swept away the tendency to categorize the situations which would justify the court's intervention, and a winding-up order was granted where there had been a departure from the common assumptions and understandings upon which the company had been formed. This approach was later drawn upon in the development of the unfair prejudice remedy.

---

[1] Section 122(1)(g), IA 1986 (UK) and s. 461(k), CL (Aust). See *Re Kalblue Pty. Ltd.* (1994) 12 ACLC 1057 regarding the court's inherent power to wind up a company where it is just and equitable to do so.　　　　　　　　　　　　　[2] Section 461(f) and (g), CL (Aust).
[3] Section 461(e), CL (Aust).　　　　　　　　　　　　　　　　　[4] Ch. 6 section 1.
[5] [1973] AC 360 (HL).

It is argued in this chapter that a large part of the function formerly performed by the winding-up remedy has been taken over by the unfair prejudice remedy. Thus, instead of discussing the winding-up remedy in the abstract, this chapter examines the extent to which the winding-up remedy continues to play an independent role in minority shareholder protection and the interrelationship between it and the unfair prejudice remedy.

## 2. INDEPENDENT OPERATION OF THE WINDING-UP REMEDY

During the development of the unfair prejudice remedy, the courts interpreted the remedy restrictively, and so petitioners continued to seek a winding-up order as an alternative form of relief, despite the potentially wider range of remedies available under the unfair prejudice provision.[6] *Ebrahimi* v. *Westbourne Galleries Ltd.*[7] provides a notable example of the role played by the winding-up remedy both in stopping the gaps in the oppression provision and highlighting the deficiencies of that provision. Recourse to the winding-up remedy continued to provide an important safety net in England where minority shareholders complained of conduct which affected all members equally until the unfair prejudice provision was amended by the Companies Act 1989.[8]

However, as a result of statutory amendments, and a gradual shift towards a more expansive interpretation, the unfair prejudice remedy has taken over much of the ground initially covered by the winding-up remedy. This shift is particularly noticeable in the more liberal interpretation of the reference to 'interests' of members which appears in the United Kingdom provision, where there has been a movement towards assimilation of the grounds justifying relief under the two remedies.[9] A recent statement confirming this trend is that of Warner J in *Re J. E. Cade & Son Ltd.*[10] that:

---

[6] See Ch. 6 section 1.   [7] Above n 5.

[8] Section 145, sch. 19 para. 11. See *Re a Company (No. 00370 of 1987); Ex parte Glossop* [1988] 1 WLR 1068 but cf., the more liberal approach taken in *Re Sam Weller & Sons Ltd.* [1990] Ch. 682 at 693–4. See discussion in Ch. 6, section 1(3). But cf., D. Bouchier, 'The Companies Act 1989—Yet Another Attempt to Remedy Unfair Prejudice' [1991] *J Bus L* 132 at 143, who recommends a further amendment to the unfair prejudice provision to base the court's jurisdiction on the 'just and equitable' ground so that judges will not be tempted to interpret the words.

[9] *Re a Company (No. 00477 of 1986)* [1986] BCLC 376; (1986) 2 BCC 99,171, *Re a Company (No. 003160 of 1986)* [1986] BCLC 391; (1986) 2 BCC 99,276, *Re Posgate and Denby (Agencies) Ltd.* [1987] BCLC 8; (1986) 2 BCC 99,352.

[10] [1992] BCLC 213 at 233–4; [1991] BCC 360 at 377.

'It would be quite illogical . . . to hold that a shareholder was entitled to seek a winding-up order on the just and equitable ground for the purpose of protecting a wider range of interests of his than he could seek to protect by means of proceedings under [the unfair prejudice provision].' This dictum suggests that the winding-up remedy has been subsumed within and surpassed by the unfair prejudice provision. However, there have been orders made for a winding up on the just and equitable ground subsequent to the evolution of the unfair prejudice provision into a workable remedy, and it is therefore necessary to consider the residual role of the winding-up remedy.

### (1) Where a winding-up order is considered more appropriate

In the cases where the interrelationship of the two remedies has been expressly considered, the finality of a winding-up order is often emphasized, as is the consequent reluctance on the part of the court to make such an order against the wishes of the majority of the shareholders in a successful, solvent company,[11] or where it would achieve by way of return much less than if the business were sold.[12]

### (a) No ongoing business

Winding-up orders made subsequent to the expansion of the unfair prejudice remedy have largely been restricted to cases where the company had ceased trading or was insolvent[13] or where there had been a failure of the company's substratum.[14] *Wallington* v. *Kokotovich Constructions Pty Ltd.*[15] (although not a true case of failure of substratum) can also be placed in this category, since the company's main business had been sold, and its only ongoing activity was to let land which it owned to other companies in the group. In the absence of an offer from either side to buy out the other at a fair price, Young J considered that a liquidator would get a fair price

---

[11] See e.g., *Cumberland Holdings Ltd.* v. *Washington H. Soul Pattinson & Co. Ltd.* (1977) 2 ACLR 307 (PC), *John J. Starr (Real Estate) Pty. Ltd.* v. *Robert R. Andrew (A'Asia) Pty. Ltd.* (1991) 6 ACSR 63; 9 ACLC 1372 and *Re a Company (No. 00314 of 1989)* [1991] BCLC 154; 1990] BCC 221.

[12] *Lusk* v. *Archive Security Ltd.* (1991) 5 NZCLC 66,979.

[13] *Re Bransfield Engineering Ltd.* (1985) 1 BCC 99,409, *Re East West Promotions Pty. Ltd.* (1986) 10 ACLR 222; 4 ACLC 84, *Re Zinotty Properties Ltd.* [1984] 1 WLR 1249 and *Re Perfectair Holdings Ltd.* [1990] BCLC 423; (1989) 5 BCC 837.

[14] *Re Checker Holdings Pty. Ltd.* (1985) 3 ACLC 565, *Bernhardt* v. *Beau Rivage Pty. Ltd.* (1989) 15 ACLR 160; 7 ACLC 639, *Re Rongo-Ma-Tane Farms Ltd.* (1987) 3 NZCLC 100 at 145 and *Re Abbey Leisure Ltd.* [1989] BCLC 619; (1989) 5 BCC 183, rvsd. [1990] BCC 60 and sub. nom. *Virdi* v. *Abbey Leisure Ltd.* [1990] BCLC 342 (CA).

[15] (1993) 11 ACSR 759; 11 ACLC 1207.

for the company's assets and that a winding up was as good a way of resolving the conflict as any other.[16]

## (b) Deadlock

A winding-up order was made in *Vuynovich* v. *Vuynovich*[17] where there was a deadlock in the relationship between three brothers. One of the brothers, Tony, had progressively taken a greater role in the management of the company and there had been a corresponding diminution in the contribution of the other brothers. Tony sought orders under the unfair prejudice provision allowing him to acquire the shares of his brothers and, in the alternative, a winding-up order, based on complaints of: failure by his brothers to work, obstructive and improper conduct, and failure to respond constructively to his proposals to resolve the deadlock. At first instance,[18] Henry J made a winding-up order, expressing regret that relief was not available under the unfair prejudice provision. The New Zealand Court of Appeal[19] rejected Henry J's restrictive interpretation of the unfair prejudice provision, but also accepted the validity of the other brothers' cross-allegations that Tony was putting unfair pressure on them to force them to sell and that he had diverted corporate opportunities to his family company. The Court of Appeal considered that these incidents were symptoms rather than the cause of the collapse of the underlying partnership, and in light of the mutual oppression were not prepared to make an order against the wishes of one party for the sale of his shares. They therefore affirmed the winding-up order. The Court of Appeal decision was subsequently affirmed by the Privy Council on the basis that there was no error in the way in which the Court of Appeal had exercised its discretion.[20]

As Shapira observes,[21] the facts of this case were highly unusual: first, because the minority had not been excluded from participation; on the contrary they had managerial control, and secondly, because both sides were seeking not to be bought out but to buy out. An additional unusual feature is that the court was unwilling to determine which of the parties should be bought out. It may be that in this highly atypical situation the

---

[16] See also *Rural Industries Co-operative Society Ltd.* v. *Porky Pigs Pty. Ltd.* (1988) 12 ACLR 794; 6 ACLC 383, where winding-up on the just and equitable ground was held to be inevitable because the business for which the company had been formed had come to an end and the relationship between the two groups of shareholders was diametrically opposed. A provisional liquidator was appointed to evaluate the minority shareholders' complaints against the former directors.

[17] [1988] 2 NZLR 129, affd. [1989] 3 NZLR 513 (PC).

[18] [1988] 2 NZLR 129.        [19] Ibid., from 150.        [20] Above n 17.

[21] G. Shapira, 'Deadlock in the Domestic Company: Buyout or Winding Up?' [1989] *NZLJ* 178 at 182.

winding-up remedy should continue to have a role. However, Henry J suggested[22] the alternative of a private auction for a cash sale to the highest bidder. This possibility was not explored by the Court of Appeal, and in line with Shapira,[23] it is submitted that this was unfortunate in light of the fact that the company was otherwise viable.

Whatever the merits of the decision in *Vuynovich*'s case,[24] the other cases referred to above where a winding-up order has been made since the deficiencies in the unfair prejudice remedy have been remedied are not instances of the winding-up remedy plugging the gaps left by the other remedies, but rather situations where winding-up was genuinely the remedy sought. *Vuynovich*'s case can on one level be included with these cases, since the appeal court held that relief under the unfair prejudice provision was potentially available in cases of irretrievable deadlock, but considered a winding-up order to be the appropriate remedy. The same cannot be said of the two cases to be discussed under the next heading.

### (2) Where relief was unavailable under the unfair prejudice provision

*Re R. A. Noble & Sons Ltd.*[25] concerned a breakdown in relations in a two-man company which had been formed to take over N's business. B was to inject cash and to become an equal shareholder and director. It was tacitly agreed that although B would not be involved in the day-to-day running of the business he would be consulted on all major decisions. In fact N did not consult him. Applying the *Westbourne Galleries* case,[26] Nourse J would have been prepared to grant a winding-up order on the basis that there had been a destruction of the mutual confidence on which the company had been formed.[27] His Lordship, however, went on to hold that B's disinterest was decisive in precluding relief under the unfair prejudice provision as it rendered N's failure to consult him not 'unfair'.[28]

It is clear from *Re London School of Electronics Ltd.*[29] that the fact that the petitioner's conduct is not exemplary will not always bar relief. In that case, the petitioner's traits of being unreliable, difficult and lazy in the discharge of his teaching duties were held not to justify the respondent's conduct in appropriating the company's students (the company's substantial source of income).[30]

---

[22] Above n 18, at 149–50.      [23] Above n 21, at 183.      [24] Above n 17.
[25] [1983] BCLC 273.                                             [26] Above n 5.
[27] Nourse J did not in fact make the order, but rather adjourned the petition to enable the parties to reach an agreement which would make an order unnecessary.
[28] His Lordship did not regard B's conduct in demanding early repayment of the loans to the company and notable disinterest in the affairs of the company as barring relief on the just and equitable ground, since the substantial cause of the destruction of mutual confidence was N's conduct.      [29] [1986] Ch. 211.      [30] Ibid., at 222.

However, the approach taken in *Noble*'s case[31] was also adopted, with the same result, in the Scottish case of *Jesner* v. *Jarrad Properties Ltd.*[32]

In *Jesner*'s case, two companies ('Jarrad' and 'Jesner') had been run as a single family business since they were set up in 1963 for the purpose of investing money for the benefit of the children of three brothers. The petitioner complained of interest-free loans between the two companies, amendments to the memorandum of Jarrad to enable credit arrangements to be made without the guarantee of the respondents, and a threat by one of the respondents to use Jarrad's assets to pay the debts of Jesner. At first instance, the sheriff accepted that the conduct was prejudicial but did not consider it unfair, because the two companies had historically been run as one with the acquiescence of the petitioner, until a proposed sale of property had brought matters to a head. The sheriff also refused relief to make a winding-up order 'for the same reasons for which . . . a share purchase order is not appropriate'. On appeal, the decision regarding the unfair prejudice provision was affirmed. However, the Inner House of the Court of Session granted relief on the just and equitable ground, on the basis that it was unnecessary for the appellants to establish more than that there had been a genuine breakdown of mutual confidence due to actions of the respondents for which the appellants were not responsible, since it was of the essence of a quasi-partnership that mutual confidence should exist.[33]

## 3. WIDER SCOPE OF THE UNFAIR PREJUDICE REMEDY

Given that the winding-up remedy continues to play a role in minority protection, it is necessary to consider the limitations on its availability.

### (1) *Locus standi*

The standing requirements for a winding-up order are in some respects wider but in other respects narrower than those for the unfair prejudice remedy. In both England and Australia, a minority shareholder seeking a winding-up order would generally apply to the court as a 'contributory'.[34]

---

[31] Above n 25.

[32] [1993] BCLC 1032; [1992] BCC 807 (CS (IH)).

[33] Ibid., at 1043; 816.

[34] Standing is also given to other categories of persons including the company itself and creditors. The provisions vary as between jurisdictions: see s. 124, IA 1986 (UK) and s. 462, CL (Aust).

## (a) England

'Contributory' is defined in the United Kingdom legislation[35] to mean every person liable to contribute to the assets of the company in the event of its being wound up. This clearly gives standing to a partly paid-up shareholder. However, the effect of this definition as regards a fully paid shareholder, is that in order to petition for a compulsory winding up, he or she must show a tangible interest in the winding up. In general, this will require the petitioner to establish a *prima facie* case that there would be assets available for distribution if the company were wound up,[36] although a petition was allowed to proceed in *Re Wessex Computer Stationers Ltd.*[37] where one of the reasons for bringing the petition was a failure to provide proper accounts or accurate financial information, so that the petitioner was prevented from ascertaining whether or not there would be a surplus. In England, standing is also dependent upon the petitioner having held shares in the company for at least six months during the 18 months preceding the commencement of the winding up, although there are some limited exceptions to this requirement.[38]

## (b) Australia

In Australia the definition of 'contributory'[39] specifically extends to a holder of fully paid-up shares in a company. In addition, section 467(2) of the Corporations Law provides that the court shall not refuse to make a winding-up order merely because the company's property has been mortgaged to an amount equal or greater than the value of the property or the company has no property.[40]

### (2) Commercial companies

There is an argument that, at least in England, the winding-up remedy is not available in respect of purely commercial companies.

---

[35] Section 79, IA 1986 (UK).

[36] *Re Othery Construction Ltd.* [1966] 1 WLR 69, *Re a Company (No. 002470 of 1988); Ex parte Nicholas* [1991] BCLC 480, affd. [1992] BCC 895 and sub nom. *Nicholas* v. *Soundcraft Electronics Ltd.* [1993] BCLC 360 (CA). See further J. H. Farrar et al., *Farrar's Company Law* (3rd edn., London, Butterworths, 1991) at 455.

[37] [1992] BCLC 366.      [38] Section 124, IA 1986 (UK).

[39] Section 9, CL (Aust).

[40] But see H. A. J. Ford and R. P. Austin, *Ford's Principles of Corporations Law* (6th edn., Sydney, Butterworths, 1992) para. 2205 regarding the necessity for holders of fully-paid shares to show that their interest is at some way at stake.

## (a) England

We have seen in Chapter 6 that the court's jurisdiction under the unfair prejudice remedy extends not only to quasi-partnership companies but also to commercial ventures.[41] Whether the winding-up remedy would be available in these circumstances is unclear. Lord Wilberforce in the *Westbourne Galleries* case[42] stated that equitable considerations would not be superimposed on the terms of the articles where the association was a purely commercial one. However, in *Re A. & B. C. Chewing Gum Ltd.*[43] a winding-up order was made in respect of a commercial company, on the basis of failure by the respondents to give effect to legal rights embodied in the articles and also in a shareholders' agreement. The making of a winding-up order in this latter case has been the subject of criticism by Womack[44] on several grounds, one of which was that the company fell within the category of 'purely commercial' association mentioned by Lord Wilberforce.[45]

In the more recent case of *Re a Company (No. 00314 of 1989)*[46] the petitioner sought relief alternatively under the winding-up remedy and the unfair prejudice provision in respect of proposals to remove her as a director, to appoint other directors, to alter the memorandum and articles of association and to purchase her shares without providing her with information relevant to ascertaining their value or to the running of the company. The winding-up petition was struck out because there was no allegation that the company had been formed out of any special relationship of mutual confidence nor was there any special obligation entitling the petitioner to continue to participate in management. By contrast, despite the finding that the company was set up on a purely commercial basis, it was held that the unfair prejudice claim was not so clearly unarguable that it should be struck out. Mummery J said:[47]

[The unfair prejudice provision] refers in the most general terms to conduct, acts or omissions which have the character of actually or potentially causing unfair prejudice to the interests of some of the members, including the petitioner. I see no good reason, either on the wording of the statutory provisions or on the authorities, for confining protection of shareholders from this kind of conduct to cases in which the company is of the *Westbourne Galleries* type.

Even assuming that a court may consider it appropriate to make a winding-up order on the just and equitable ground in the case of some purely

---

[41] *Re a Company (No. 00314 of 1989)* above n 11.  [42] Above n 5.
[43] [1975] 1 WLR 579.  [44] J. Womack [1975] *Cambridge LJ* 209.
[45] Ibid., at 210–1.  [46] Above n 11.  [47] Ibid., at 161; 227.

commercial companies, the wide discretion in the court to determine the appropriate relief (as illustrated in the relief granted in respect of a listed company in *McGuinness* v. *Bremner plc*[48]) means that the unfair prejudice remedy inevitably has a much wider field of operation than the winding-up remedy.

### (b) Australia

The question whether the unfair prejudice remedy is wider in scope than the just and equitable winding-up remedy (in that it is available in respect of purely commercial companies) is of little practical significance in Australia, because the Australian winding-up provision reproduces the terms of the unfair prejudice provision as alternative grounds for a court to make a winding-up order.[49] Despite the fact that a court could instead make a winding-up order on these grounds under the unfair prejudice provision, this reproduction is not superfluous, because a wider range of persons have standing to apply to the court under the winding-up remedy than under the unfair prejudice provision; for example a contributory who was not a member could apply for relief under the winding-up remedy, but not under the unfair prejudice provision.

### (3) Clean hands

It is stated in a number of cases that a petitioner who relies on the just and equitable clause must come to court with clean hands, so that if a breakdown in relations between quasi-partners results from the petitioner's misconduct, he or she cannot insist on the company being wound up.[50] At least in Australia,[51] the status of this proposition is unclear as Young J considered, obiter, in *Morgan* v. *45 Flers Avenue*[52] that the petitioner's conduct should not constitute an absolute bar. On the other hand, it is clear that under the unfair prejudice provision the petitioner's conduct does not operate as a bar to relief although it may be taken into account in determining whether prejudicial conduct is unfair and in deciding what relief should be granted.[53]

---

[48] 1988 SLT 891, affd. 1988 SLT 898n.

[49] Section 461 (f) and (g), CL (Aust).

[50] *Per* Lord Cross in *Ebrahimi* v. *Westbourne Galleries Ltd.* above n 5, at 387. See also *Re F. Hall & Sons Ltd.* [1939] NZLR 408 (CA NZ), *Menard* v. *Horwood & Co. Ltd.* (1922) 31 CLR 20 (HC) and *Re Martello & Sons Ltd.* [1945] 3 DLR 626 (CA Ontario).

[51] See also in this regard the comments of Beldam LJ in *Barrett* v. *Duckett* [1995] BCC 362 (CA).

[52] (1986) 10 ACLR 692; 5 ACLC 222.

[53] See *Re R. A. Noble & Sons (Clothing) Ltd.* above n 25, *Re London School of Electronics Ltd.* above n 29 and discussion in Ch. 6, section 2(9)(a).

### (4) Alternative relief

There is a statutory requirement in both jurisdictions (for which there is no equivalent in respect of the unfair prejudice remedy) that the court decline to make a winding-up order on the just and equitable ground if it is of opinion that some other remedy is available to the petitioners and that they are acting unreasonably in seeking to have the company wound up instead of pursuing that other remedy.[54] In Australia, the same limitation applies where a winding-up order is sought on the ground that the directors have acted in affairs of the company in their own interests rather than in the interests of the members as a whole, or in any other manner whatsoever that appears to be unfair or unjust to members.[55] The application of this statutory limitation to various forms of alternative relief is considered in greater detail below.

### (a) An action under the unfair prejudice remedy

In interpreting that discretion the courts consider that relief under the unfair prejudice provision is an alternative remedy which should generally be pursued in preference to the more drastic remedy of winding-up.[56]

In England, the preference for the unfair prejudice remedy is further promoted by a Practice Direction[57] which states that an alternative prayer for a winding up of the company should be included in an unfair prejudice petition only 'if that is the relief which the petitioner prefers or if it is considered that it may be the only relief to which he is entitled'.[58]

No equivalent direction exists in Australia. However, in *QIW Retailers Ltd.* v. *Felview Pty. Ltd.*,[59] it was held that a winding-up petition had been instituted not to obtain the winding up of the company, but to force its board of directors to negotiate with the defendants in order to obtain control of the company. Immediately prior to the filing of the winding-up application the defendants had contacted a trade magazine circulating in the trade in which the company was engaged and arranged the publication

---

[54] Section 125, IA 1986 (UK), s. 467(4), CL (Aust).

[55] Section 461(e), CL (Aust). See *Re William Brooks & Co. Ltd.* [1962] NSWR 142.

[56] *Re Norvabron Pty. Ltd. (No. 2)* (1986) 11 ACLR 279; 5 ACLC 184, *Re Dalkeith Investments Pty. Ltd.* (1984) 9 ACLR 247 at 252; 3 ACLC 74 at 79, *Mincom Pty. Ltd.* v. *Murphy* [1983] 1 Qd. R 297 at 306, *Morgan* v. *45 Flers Avenue Pty. Ltd.* above n 52, *Re a Company (No. 002567 of 1982)* [1983] 1 WLR 927, *Gammack, Petitioner* 1983 SLT 246, *Re a Company (No. 3096 of 1987)* (1988) 4 BCC 80. It would appear, however, that the court will not necessarily strike out a winding-up petition on this ground: *Re a Company (No. 001363 of 1988)*; *Ex parte S-P* [1989] BCLC 579 at 586; (1989) 5 BCC 18 at 25.

[57] Chancery 1/90 [1990] 1 All ER 1056.

[58] Cf., Bouchier, above n 8, at 137 in this regard.

[59] [1989] 2 Qd. R 245.

of an article in relation to the winding-up application. The company was held to have proved actionable damage by showing the facts relating to the making of the winding-up application and the publication of the article.[60]

Further, the Australian version of the unfair prejudice provision includes an additional prohibition on the court from making a winding-up order if it is of the opinion that the winding up of the company would unfairly prejudice the oppressed member or members.[61]

### (b) A personal action at common law

Where the alternative relief is a remedy at common law, such as a personal action to enforce the provisions of the articles of association, or a derivative action in respect of a wrong to the company, then, generally, the feature which would make it reasonable for the petitioner to pursue the winding-up remedy is the fact that the majority's conduct is more than an isolated incident, but rather has implications for the future management of the company's affairs.[62] As was stated by Laidlaw JA in *Re Martello & Sons Ltd.*:[63]

An action in the Courts would not provide means of protection against future misconduct on the part of the person or persons in control of the management of the company business. It would not restore the confidence of the petitioner in such persons, nor enable him satisfactorily to exercise his voting power in respect of company affairs. It appears to me likely that the company will never be able to carry on in an orderly, regulated and controlled manner, but on the contrary the affairs of the corporate body will be conducted in such a way as to cause injustice and inequity to the petitioner.[64]

### (c) An offer to purchase the petitioner's shares

In the case of a public company, an alternative to applying to wind up the company may be for the dissatisfied shareholder simply to sell his or her

---

[60] In addition, the court has an inherent power to prevent abuse of its process, which would enable it summarily to grant an injunction restraining the presentation of a petition, or if it had already been presented to dismiss the petition if its presentation would constitute an abuse of process. Abuse of process might arise where a petition has no chance of success, or where the existence of a genuine cross-claim by the company based on substantial grounds makes it likely that the petition, if presented, would either be dismissed or adjourned to await the outcome of the cross-claim: see *Mincom Pty. Ltd.* v. *Murphy* above n 56, at 305–8, discussed below in text following n 68. [61] Section 260(4), CL (Aust).

[62] Cf., *Menard* v. *Horwood and Co. Ltd.* above n 50, where relief was refused *inter alia* on the ground that the circumstances surrounding the acts complained of did not justify an inference of systematic or recurring dishonesty on the part of the governing director.

[63] Above n 50, at 628.

[64] See Ch. 9 regarding the relationship of the unfair prejudice remedy and common law relief.

shares.[65] However, winding-up orders have been granted in respect of companies which although public in form, are essentially 'domestic' in nature[66] or where the misconduct of the majority has depressed the Stock Exchange price for the shares.[67]

There has been some controversy as to whether an offer to purchase a petitioner's shares in a private company constitutes alternative relief such that the pursuit of a winding-up petition is unreasonable.

In *Mincom Pty. Ltd. v. Murphy*[68] G. N. Williams J restrained the presentation of a winding-up petition as an abuse of process, on the basis that the petitioner had chosen a procedure which might do irreputable harm to the company, rather than a suitable alternative procedure in the form of the procedure for the sale of shares set out in the articles.[69] That case is, however, complicated by the fact that his Honour considered that the petition was in any event unlikely to succeed.

The issue is more difficult where this element is not present. In *Re a Company (No. 002567 of 1982)*,[70] Vinelott J held that 'some other remedy' in terms of the section included not only other statutory remedies, but any alternative course reasonably open to the petitioner, including an offer to purchase his shares. Thus, the question the court had to consider was whether the petitioner was acting unreasonably in refusing the offer. One argument put by counsel for the petitioner in this regard was that:[71]

. . . if [the petitioner] is denied the remedy of a winding-up order on the ground that the respondents have made a reasonable offer to purchase his shares, the court will, in effect, expose any minority shareholder in a company of this kind to the hazard that the majority will be able to exclude him from participation in the affairs of the company, contrary to the understanding which underlay the formation of the company and then compulsorily acquire his shares, notwithstanding the absence of any power in the articles to do so.

Vinelott J rejected this argument on the particular facts of the case, since the petitioner had not insisted upon a winding up rather than a sale of his shares, but had from the start been willing to sell his shares if a fair price could be negotiated. Having encouraged the respondents to continue to run the company in the expectation that a fair machinery for ascertaining

---

[65] This is not usually possible in a private company where the combination of wrongdoer control and provisions restricting the transfer of shares commonly prevent petitioners extricating their investment at a reasonable price.

[66] *Loch* v. *John Blackwood Ltd.* [1924] AC 783 (PC). Here 50% of the shares were held by associated parties. Of the remainder, just under 25% were held by each of two shareholders. The three remaining shares were held by nominees of those two shareholders.

[67] *Re William Brooks & Co. Ltd.* above n 55.                    [68] Above n 56.

[69] See further: B. H. McPherson, *The Law of Company Liquidation* (3rd edn. by J. O'Donovan, Sydney, The Law Book Company Limited, 1987) at 138–9.

[70] Above n 56.                                              [71] Ibid., at 936.

the price of his shares could be agreed and having now been offered a price for his shares reached by machinery which met all his reasonable objections, he was held not to be entitled to a winding-up order.

Similarly, when this issue next arose before Millett J in *Re a Company (No. 003843 of 1986)*,[72] a winding-up petition was struck out as an abuse of process in the face of an offer to buy out the petitioners at a reasonable price. On the facts of that case a winding-up order would have resulted in a later payment of a lesser sum to the petitioners. In response to the petitioners' argument that because there was suspicion of misfeasance and misappropriation of the company's assets, it was not possible to say that they had been made a fair offer Millett J said:[73] 'In my judgment, there is nothing in that point. The terms of the offer that I have read ensure that both sides will have an opportunity to have access to all the company's books and papers and to make whatever representations they wish to make to the independent accountants.'

These two English decisions are to be compared with the Australian case of *Bernhardt* v. *Beau Rivage Pty. Ltd.*[74] This was an application to wind up a company on the just and equitable ground on the basis that the company had been formed as a quasi-partnership to purchase a motel which had since been sold and the proceeds invested in bank bills which had not yet matured. Here again, the respondents argued that the order should not be made since they had made offers on various terms to purchase the applicants' shares or to pay them an amount equal to a certain percentage of the net asset backing of their shares. Young J declined to follow the two earlier English decisions, considering that the words 'some other remedy' meant 'other cause of action' whether general law or statutory, and should not include an out-of-court offer to purchase the applicants' shares or to pay the applicants an amount equal to the value of their shares.[75]

Nevertheless, his Honour went on to consider the reasonableness of the applicants' conduct on the assumption that the English position was correct, namely that an offer to purchase shares could constitute 'some other remedy'. Young J did not regard the offer in this case as a viable alternative to what the applicants would receive in a winding up. This was for two reasons. First, his Honour referred[76] to the fact that the respondents had not agreed to meet the plaintiff's costs out of the assets of the company. Secondly, by contrast with Millett J in *Re a Company (No. 003843 of 1986)*[77] his Honour considered[78] that the valuation of the applicants' shares by an accountant over whose appointment they would

---

[72] [1987] BCLC 562; (1987) 3 BCC 624.        [73] Ibid., at 571; 632.
[74] Above n 14.        [75] Cf., *Mincom Pty. Ltd.* v. *Murphy*, above n 56.
[76] Above n 14, at 165; 644.        [77] Above n 72.
[78] Above n 14, at 165; 644.

have no say, relying on experts in whose choice the applicants would also have no say, presented great uncertainties as compared with the alternative of the appointment of a liquidator with attendant rights of review to the court. He also referred to the fact that any valuation would have to assess the validity of a claim by a Mr Vago based on his exclusion from the company that the company held 20 per cent of its assets on trust for him, saying:[79] 'Almost certainly one would need to have senior barristers involved in the assessment and even they, without actually seeing the witnesses in the witness box, would have difficulty at doing more than assessing a range of percentage of success that the company may have in that litigation.' In light of these factors, Young J did not regard the offer as providing a viable alternative to what the applicants would receive in a winding-up and granted the winding-up order.

The disadvantage to the petitioner of a valuation being carried out by an accountant as opposed to the court was also a factor in the decision of the Court of Appeal in the most recent English decision to discuss this issue, *Re Abbey Leisure Ltd.*[80] Further, this case takes up the argument raised by the petitioner in *Re a Company (No. 002567 of 1982)*[81] as to the importance in winding-up proceedings of the understandings underlying the formation of the company in the face of provisions in the articles granting pre-emption rights and providing a machinery for the valuation of shares.

In this case a company was formed with the objects: to construct, acquire, equip, maintain, manage, and carry on business as proprietors of dance halls, discothèques, ballrooms and other 'leisure industry' activities. The petitioner was a 40 per cent shareholder of, and solicitor to the company. The other two shareholders were the directors of the company and held respectively 40 per cent and 20 per cent of the share capital. The petitioner's case[82] was that it was agreed and understood at the time the company was formed that the sole project to be undertaken was the acquisition and management of the Pavilion nightclub. Upon the sale of the nightclub, the petitioner claimed 40 per cent of the proceeds in exchange for his shares. Instead, the directors offered to purchase his shares in accordance with the pre-emption provisions in the articles which provided for an independent accountant to determine a fair value 'as between a willing seller and a willing buyer'. The substance of the petitioner's claim was that the directors were intending to procure the company to acquire a new business in which the petitioner did not wish and was not obliged to participate, because of the understanding not to commit his capital to any new venture without his consent, and that in these

---

[79] Ibid.                    [80] Above n 14.                    [81] Above n 56.
[82] Which was denied by the respondents, but assumed to be true for the purposes of the respondents' application to strike out the petition.

circumstances it was just and equitable that the company be wound up.[83] The motivation for his complaint was that the valuation procedures would be likely to result in the value of his shares being discounted for the fact that they represented a minority holding.

Hoffmann J held that the petitioner was acting unreasonably in refusing the offer and struck out the petition. His Lordship referred to the fact that the purpose of such provisions is to provide a quick and cheap method by which the parties can go their separate ways as opposed to the much more expensive alternative of petitioning under the unfair prejudice remedy or for a winding up. He took into account[84] the potential damage which a winding-up order could do to the company and to the interests of those shareholders who wished it to carry on in business and the fact that the petitioner not only submitted to but actually drafted the terms of the articles in question. Hoffmann J also drew support[85] from his own earlier decision in the context of an unfair prejudice petition[86] that where there is a mechanism for determining a fair price a party should not be entitled to petition under the unfair prejudice provision unless he has invoked or offered to invoke that mechanism and the majority have refused to buy at that price.[87] His Lordship considered that submissions regarding the appropriateness of a discount could equally well be made to the accountant as to the court.

The Court of Appeal[88] expressly disagreed with all the grounds upon which the first instance decision was based. First, Balcombe LJ[89] did not regard the pre-emption procedure as appropriate to the petitioner. The petitioner was not a member desiring to transfer his shares. Further, even if he were to initiate the procedure, this would impose no obligation upon the other members to purchase the shares, and was therefore 'a somewhat empty remedy'. Secondly, as regards the respondents' offer to purchase the shares at a price fixed in the manner provided for the articles, Balcombe LJ saw nothing unreasonable in the petitioner refusing to accept the risk of a discount being applied to the valuation of his interest in the company.[90]

Thirdly, he rejected the contention that a winding up would necessarily

---

[83] The petitioner also claimed in the alternative relief under the unfair prejudice remedy that the directors or the company should be ordered to buy his shares. However, the case was dealt with both at first instance and on appeal on the basis that the petitioner's primary claim was for a winding-up order.

[84] [1989] BCLC 619 at 624; (1989) 5 BCC 183 at 187.

[85] Ibid., at 624; 187–8.

[86] *Re a Company (No. 007623 of 1984)* [1986] BCLC 362 at 367; (1986) 2 BCC 99,191 at 99,195–6.       [87] See discussion above Ch. 6 section 2(8)(b)(i).

[88] Above n 14.

[89] Ibid., at 347; 65. Sir George Waller agreed with Balcombe LJ.

[90] Ibid., at 350; 68.

be more expensive than an estimation of the worth of the petitioner's shares by an accountant since the assets were largely cash,[91] and regarded the machinery available in a winding up for the proper determination of these claims as preferable to an accountant's estimation.

Finally, the Court of Appeal was prepared to give effect to any agreement (if proved) as to the way in which the company was to be run in determining whether it was reasonable for a petitioner to reject an offer to purchase his or her shares.

Thus, certainly in England and possibly in Australia, a purchase offer will be regarded as an alternative form of relief which may make it unreasonable for a petitioner to pursue a winding-up order. But only if this would cause no unfairness to the petitioner, either in the method of valuation or by departure from the petitioner's legitimate expectations.

[91] See also Sir George Waller, ibid., at 351; 69.

# ⌒ 8 ⌒

# *Common Law Relief*

1. Introduction                                                           184

2. Personal Actions                                                       185
   (1) Enforcement of rights granted by contract                          185
   (2) *Ultra vires* acts                                                 186
       (a) England                                                        186
       (b) Australia                                                      186
   (3) Illegal acts                                                       186
   (4) Special majorities                                                 187
   (5) Enforcement of other provisions of the memorandum or
       articles                                                           187
   (6) Enforcement of rights conferred by the companies legislation       188
   (7) Allotments of shares                                               188

3. Derivative Actions                                                     189
   (1) Limitations on the ability to bring derivative proceedings         189
       (a) Relevance of membership                                        189
       (b) Companies in liquidation                                       190
       (c) Procedural requirements                                        190
       (d) Equitable restrictions                                         190
       (e) Costs                                                          191
   (2) Wrongdoer control                                                  192
   (3) Fraud                                                              193

4. Limitations on Majority Voting Power                                   194
   (1) Appropriation of the company's property                            195
   (2) Release of directors' breach of duty                               196
       (a) Misappropriation distinguished from excusable
           profit-making                                                  196
       (b) Requiring ratification by independent shareholders             198
       (c) Allotments of shares for an improper purpose                   199
           (i) England                                                    199
           (ii) Australia                                                 200
   (3) Alteration of articles                                             203
   (4) Equitable considerations                                          209

5. Section 1324 of the Corporation Law                                    213

6. Law Reform Proposals                                                   215
   (1) United Kingdom                                                     215
   (2) Australia                                                          215

## SUMMARY

*Shareholders can sue at common law to enforce personal rights. The sources of personal rights include private agreements, legislation and the memorandum and articles of association. However, when suing to enforce a provision of the memorandum or articles of association there is a risk that the court will decline to accord the shareholder standing on the basis that the breach is merely a procedural irregularity.*

*If a wrong has been done to the company, for example as a result of a breach of directors' duties, then generally the company should bring proceedings to challenge it. However, an individual shareholder will have standing to bring proceedings on behalf of the company (derivative proceedings) if he or she can establish that the wrongdoers are in control of the company and are preventing it from suing, and that the wrong is not capable of being ratified.*

*The cases where wrongs have been held to be ratifiable are difficult to reconcile. One approach to reconciling the cases is to say that ratification will not be possible if the majority are appropriating the company's property, or are releasing the directors from a breach of duty involving dishonesty, or as a result of which directors benefit themselves at the expense of the company.*

*Outside the context of ratification, the courts have also limited the power of the majority to bind the minority in respect of alterations to the articles of association where no reasonable person could regard the alteration as beneficial to the company. There are also several isolated instances where the court has limited majority voting power in respect of other resolutions on the basis of equitable considerations, although it may be that similar cases would now be brought under the unfair prejudice remedy.*

## 1. INTRODUCTION

A shareholder seeking to sue at common law must establish either that a personal right has been infringed or that he or she has standing to sue in respect of a wrong that has been done to the company.

Allowing individual shareholders unrestricted standing to sue in respect of wrongs done to the company raises two potential problems: multiplicity of actions and vexatious litigation. The Rule in *Foss* v. *Harbottle*[1] addresses these two concerns. The classic statement of the Rule is by Jenkins LJ in *Edwards* v. *Halliwell*:[2]

First, the proper plaintiff in an action in respect of a wrong alleged to be done to a company or association of persons is *prima facie* the company or association of persons itself. Secondly, where the alleged wrong is a transaction which might be made binding on the company or association and on all its members by a simple majority of the members, no individual member of the company is allowed to maintain an action in respect of that matter for the simple reason that, if a mere majority of the members of the company or association is in favour of what has been done, then *cadit quaestio* [there is an end to the argument].

However, in recognition of the fact that the persons responsible for a wrong to the company may also be in a position to prevent proceedings being brought against them, standing is given to individual shareholders to sue on behalf of the company (in exception to the Rule in *Foss* v. *Harbottle*) where there is a 'fraud on the minority'. This type of action is known as a derivative action, and is discussed in greater detail in section 3 below.

In addition, there are certain situations where individual shareholders have been recognized to have personal standing as exceptions to the Rule in *Foss* v. *Harbottle*, but more accurately on the basis that the Rule does not apply, namely in respect of *ultra vires* or illegal acts and where a special majority is required in order to effect a transaction. Both are considered in section 2 below.

## 2. PERSONAL ACTIONS[3]

### (1) Enforcement of rights granted by contract

Where personal rights arise under an agreement,[4] they will be readily identifiable as such. There will generally therefore be no dispute as to a shareholder's standing to enforce them, and the matter will be decided on its merits.

---

[1] (1843) 2 Hare 461; 67 ER 189.
[2] [1950] 2 All ER 1064 at 1066 (CA).
[3] A fiduciary relationship may also arise between a director and a shareholder on special facts, breach of which would give rise to a personal action. See Ch. 10 section 2(5).
[4] See Ch. 4, section 3(1)(e) regarding enforceability of shareholders' agreements, and section 2(2)(e) of the same chapter regarding external contracts based on the corporate constitution.

## (2)  *Ultra vires* acts

### (a)  England

It was held in *Smith* v. *Croft (No. 2)*[5] that an individual shareholder can bring a personal action to restrain a company from taking action which would be *ultra vires* (in the sense that it is beyond the company's capacity as set out in its memorandum). That proposition has since been qualified by section 35(2) of the Companies Act 1985, which provides that no such proceedings shall lie in respect of an *ultra vires* act to be done in fulfilment of a legal obligation arising from a previous act of the company.

*Smith* v. *Croft (No. 2)* also decided that an action for compensation to the company for loss caused by an *ultra vires* or illegal transaction must be a derivative one.[6] Derivative actions are discussed in greater detail in section 3 below. However, it should be noted that the ability to bring such an action is limited by section 35(3) of the Companies Act 1985 which enables the company to ratify the *ultra vires* act and to relieve the directors from personal liability arising from an *ultra vires* transaction. In each case, a special resolution is required.

### (b)  Australia

The doctrine of *ultra vires* has been abolished in Australia by a legislative provision stating that a company has the legal capacity of a natural person.[7] However, it is still possible for a company to place restrictions on the exercise of powers contained in the memorandum or articles or to elect to state objects, and if a company contravenes these limitations an individual shareholder has standing to sue to restrain the action.[8] As in England, an action to recover funds improperly expended would still need to be brought as a derivative action.[9]

## (3)  Illegal acts

A member's individual standing to sue to restrain illegal acts is generally regarded as being the same as the common law position regarding *ultra vires* acts.[10] However, in the recent Australian case of *Australian*

---

[5] [1988] Ch. 114 at 167.                         [6] Ibid., at 170.
[7] Section 161, CL (Aust).                          [8] Section 162, CL (Aust).
[9] *Hawkesbury Development Co. Ltd.* v. *Landmark Finance Pty. Ltd.* [1969] 2 NSWR 782 at 794, *Nankivell* v. *Benjamin* (1892) 18 VLR 543. But cf., *FAI Insurances Ltd.* v. *Urquhart (No. 2)*, (1986) 11 ACLR 38, where the court regarded an action to recover money spent by the directors in *ultra vires* acts as ancillary to injunctive relief.
[10] See J. H. Farrar *et al.*, *Farrar's Company Law* (3rd edn., London, Butterworths, 1991) at 446 and H. A. J. Ford and R. P. Austin, *Ford's Principles of Corporations Law* (6th edn., Sydney, Butterworths, 1992) para. 1725.

*Agricultural Company* v. *Oatmont Pty. Ltd.*[11] the Northern Territory Court of Appeal considered that it would be oppressive to permit an individual shareholder to seek declaratory relief that conduct proposed by the company would be contrary to section 38A of the Crown Lands Act (Northern Territory), and accordingly denied the shareholding standing. The facts of the case were, however, complicated by the fact that the Crown did not assert that the conduct was unlawful, the Attorney-General had refused his *fiat*, and the probability of proceedings being brought against the company for the alleged offence was practically non-existent. Another factor considered relevant by the court was that the plaintiff had purchased a small number of shares in the company at a time when it was aware of the unlawfulness of the proposed transaction purely in order to obtain standing.

### (4) Special majorities

Standing has been accorded to individual shareholders where a matter is one which requires the sanction of some special majority of shareholders. Thus in *Edwards* v. *Halliwell*[12] two members of a trade union obtained a declaration that a resolution increasing members' contributions was invalid because the rules required a two-thirds majority for such resolutions.

### (5) Enforcement of other provisions of the memorandum or articles

Shareholders seeking to enforce provisions in the memorandum or articles face two obstacles. The first is the uncertainty which surrounds the enforceability of 'outsider rights'. This limitation is discussed in Chapter 4[13] and will not be covered further here. The second obstacle is that the courts have sometimes declined to enforce a particular article on the basis that the breach is a mere irregularity, and therefore a wrong to the company rather than to the individual.[14]

This distinction between irregularities of substance and mere irregularities of form is easier to state than to apply. The classic contrast is between *Pender* v. *Lushington*[15] where it was held that a member had a personal right to have his or her vote recorded, and *MacDougall* v. *Gardiner*[16] where it was held that a member did not have a right to have a poll taken.[17]

---

[11] (1992) 8 ACSR 255; 10 ACLC 1220 (CA NT).     [12] Above n 2.
[13] Ch. 4 section 2(1)(a).     [14] *Edwards* v. *Halliwell* above n 2.
[15] (1877) 6 Ch. D 70.     [16] (1875) 1 Ch. D 13 (CA).
[17] For a more extensive list of those articles which have been held to be enforceable and those which have not see K. W. Wedderburn, 'Shareholders' Rights and the Rule in *Foss* v. *Harbottle*' [1957] *Cambridge LJ* 194 and R. J. Smith 'Minority Shareholders and Corporate Irregularities' (1978) 41 *Mod L Rev* 147. For further Australian examples see Ford and Austin, above n 10, paras 1710 and 1721.

The irregularity in the conduct of the meeting in the latter case was classified as a wrong to the company rather than to the individual shareholder.

Various attempts have been made to rationalize these inconsistencies, and it is not proposed to traverse that ground again here.[18] Despite notable arguments to the contrary[19] it appears that a member does not have a right to have all the articles observed, and it will often be impossible to determine in advance whether a particular act or omission will be regarded as a wrong which affects the company or individual shareholders.[20]

However, despite this theoretical uncertainty, there has been a tendency in Australia for the courts to rule on complaints of procedural irregularities without considering the question of standing in detail.[21]

### (6) Enforcement of rights conferred by the companies legislation

Ford and Austin suggest that the same limitations may apply to a shareholder's ability to enforce rights conferred by legislation as to the memorandum and articles, depending on the construction of the legislation.[22]

Support for this approach can be found in the recent case of *National Roads & Motorists' Association* v. *Parker*[23] where the Motorists' Association was able to obtain a declaration that it was not obliged to hold an extraordinary general meeting, despite having received a requisition which complied with the formal requirements of the companies legislation and the articles. The resolutions set out in the requisition concerned matters vested exclusively in the directors. Since the directors' exercise of these powers could not be effectively controlled or interfered with by a resolution of members in general meeting, the directors were able to decline to act on the requisition.

### (7) Allotments of shares

There has been a growing recognition in recent cases in both England and Australia that an allotment of shares for an improper purpose may not only

---

[18] See the articles listed at n 30 of Ch. 4.      [19] Wedderburn, above n 17.

[20] E.g., cf., *Prudential Assurance Co. Ltd.* v. *Newman Industries Ltd. (No. 2)* [1982] Ch. 204 (CA) with *Wilson* v. *Jones* (1867) LR 2 Exch. 139, *Nurcombe* v. *Nurcombe* [1985] 1 WLR 370 (CA) and *Marx* v. *Estates and General Investments Ltd.* [1976] 1 WLR 380. See also *Kraus* v. *J. G. Lloyd Pty. Ltd.* [1965] VR 232 and M. J. Sterling, 'The Theory and Policy of Shareholder Actions in Tort' (1987) 50 *Mod L Rev* 468, C. Baxter, 'The Role of the Judge in Enforcing Shareholder Rights' [1983] *Cambridge LJ* 96, 111 and L. S. Sealy, 'Problems of Standing, Pleading and Proof in Corporate Litigation' in B. G. Pettet (ed.) *Company Law in Change: Current Legal Problems* (London, Stevens & Sons, 1987) 1 at 8.

[21] See Sealy 'The Rule in *Foss* v. *Harbottle*: The Australian Experience' (1989) 10 *Company Lawyer* 52.      [22] Ford and Austin, above n 10, para. 1721.

[23] (1986) 6 NSWLR 517.

be a wrong to the company but may also infringe shareholders' personal rights.[24] This issue is discussed in greater detail in below.[25]

## 3. DERIVATIVE ACTIONS

One aspect of the Rule in *Foss* v. *Harbottle* is that the company is generally the only proper plaintiff in a cause of action for a wrong to the company (such as a breach of directors' duties).

However, unless there is a change of control (either through variation in the composition of the board of directors or appointment of a liquidator) or only a minority of the directors is involved in the breach, the board is unlikely to bring proceedings to remedy it. Shareholders are therefore accorded standing to sue on the company's behalf in cases of 'fraud on the minority' provided that the majority of the minority shareholders wish the action to go ahead.[26] 'Fraud on the minority' will be established where the conduct amounts to a fraud on the company and the wrongdoers are in control of the company, and are preventing the company from taking action itself. An additional limitation imposed by *Smith* v. *Croft (No. 2)*[27] is that the claim may not be pursued if an independent majority of the minority shareholders does not wish the claim to go ahead. The elements of 'fraud' and 'control' are examined in greater detail below.[28] But first it is appropriate to consider the limitations on bringing a derivative action.

### (1) Limitations on the ability to bring derivative proceedings[29]

#### (a) Relevance of membership

If a shareholder is registered as a member, it is no bar to bringing a derivative action that he or she became a member after the wrong was done to the company.[30] It has been held in Australia that a person who is merely an equitable owner of shares is not permitted to bring a derivative action.[31] The position in England on this issue is less clear.[32]

---

[24] See *Howard Smith Ltd.* v. *Ampol Petroleum Ltd.* [1974] AC 821 (PC), *Re a Company (No. 005136 of 1986)* [1987] BCLC 82, also reported as *Re Sherborne Park Residents Co. Ltd.* (1986) 2 BCC 99,528, *Eromanga Hydrocarbons NL* v. *Australis Mining NL* (1988) 14 ACLR 486; 6 ACLC 906 and *Residues Treatment and Trading Co. Ltd.* v. *Southern Resources (No. 4* (1988) 51 SASR 196 (Full Ct, SA). [25] See section 4(2)(c).
[26] *Smith* v. *Croft (No. 2)* above n 5. [27] Ibid.
[28] See sections 3(2) and 3(3).
[29] See further R. R. Pennington, *Company Law* (6th edn., London, Butterworths, 1990) at 653–5. [30] *Seaton* v. *Grant* (1867) LR 2 Ch. App. 459.
[31] *Maas* v. *McIntosh* (1928) 28 SR (NSW) 441, *Hooker Investments Pty. Ltd.* v. *Email Ltd.* (1986) 10 ACLR 443.
[32] Cf., the interpretation given to the cases of *Bagshaw* v. *Eastern Union Railway Co.* (1849) 7 Hare 114, affd. (1850) 2 Mac & G 389 and *Binney* v. *Ince Hall Coal and Cannel Co.* (1866) 35 LJ Ch. 363 by Pennington above n 29, at 654, with that of Master White in *Fulloon* v. *Radley* [1992] 2 Qd. R 290.

### (b) Companies in liquidation

Once a company goes into liquidation, it is up to the liquidator to decide whether to bring or continue proceedings on behalf of the company, and a dissatisfied shareholder must use the statutory remedies under the liquidation regime to seek an order that the liquidator bring the action or the right to bring the action in the name of the company.[33]

However, in *Farrow* v. *Registrar of Building Societies*[34] the plaintiffs were able to bring a derivative action after appointment of an administrator, seeking the removal of the administrator, alleging that he had not been properly appointed and had misconducted the administration.[35]

### (c) Procedural requirements

In England, an additional procedural hurdle confronts minority shareholders in that their standing to bring a derivative action must be established as a preliminary issue before the case can be heard on its merits.[36] By contrast, the Australian courts have preferred to not to lay down an inflexible procedure for determination of the plaintiff's standing, and usually consider it inappropriate for the question of standing to be tried as a preliminary issue.[37] A statutory innovation in Australia in terms of procedure has been the introduction of a procedure for 'opt out' class actions.[38]

### (d) Equitable restrictions

A shareholder seeking to bring a derivative action must establish that he or she 'comes to court with clean hands'. In *Nurcombe* v. *Nurcombe*[39] the

---

[33] *Cape Breton Co.* v. *Fenn* (1881) 17 Ch. D 198 (CA), *Fargro Ltd.* v. *Godfroy* [1986] 1 WLR 1134, *Scarel Pty. Ltd.* v. *City Loan & Credit Corporation Pty. Ltd.* (1988) 12 ACLR 730; 6 ACLC 219, *Zempilas* v. *J. N. Taylor Holdings Ltd. (in liq.) (No. 6)* (1991) 5 ACSR 28. Another possibility referred to in *Scarel*'s case at 737; 225 (citing *Garden Mews—St. Leonards Pty. Ltd.* v. *Butler Pollnow Pty. Ltd.* (1984) 9 ACLR 91 at 95) is the appointment of a receiver of the company's right of action to enforce it in the name of the company. This course was also adopted in *Aloridge Pty. Ltd.* v. *West Australian Gem Exporters Pty. Ltd.* (1995) 15 ACSR 645; 13 ACLC 196 where the company was in provisional liquidation.
[34] [1991] 2 VR 589.
[35] See *Watts* v. *Midland Bank plc* [1986] BCLC 15 regarding the bringing of a derivative action in respect of a company in receivership.
[36] *Prudential* v. *Newman (No. 2)*, above n 20.
[37] *Hurley* v. *BGH Nominees Pty. Ltd.* (1982) 31 SASR 250 (Full Ct, SA), *Dempster* v. *Biala Pty. Ltd.* (1989) 1 WAR 266 (Full Ct, WA), *Eromanga Hydrocarbons NL* v. *Australis Mining NL & Ors* above n 24, and *Biala Pty. Ltd.* v. *Mallina Holdings Ltd.* (1993) 11 ACLC 757.
[38] Federal Court of Australia Amendment Act 1991. But see R. Baxt, 'Class Actions Legislation—A Mirage for the Consumer?' (1992) 66 *Austl LJ* 223. As the title of the article suggests, Baxt questions the impact of this legislation.          [39] Above n 20.

plaintiff had benefited from the wrongdoing, in that it had been taken into account in calculating maintenance awarded to the plaintiff in matrimonial proceedings between the same parties. The court considered that she was not qualified to bring derivative proceedings to recover the profits for the company. Lawton LJ said:[40] 'In this action she is in effect saying: although I have shared with the first defendant his ill-gotten gains, I want the court to order that he should pay over to [the company] his share of them plus my share so that I can have a chance of getting some more because of my status as a shareholder. In my judgment, the court should not countenance such conduct.'

In a similar vein, the majority of the Court of Appeal in *Barrett* v. *Duckett*[41] considered that personal rather than financial reasons were motivating the plaintiff, and this was one of the grounds on which the derivative action was struck out.[42]

## (e) Costs

Because a derivative action is brought on the company's behalf, the company obtains any benefit from the action. The plaintiff has no right to obtain his or her solicitor-client costs without an order from the court. However, any costs of the action not recovered from the defendants will generally be ordered to be paid by the company. Further, in *Marx* v. *Estates and General Investments Ltd.*[43] Brightman J awarded the plaintiffs their costs on a common fund basis as the plaintiffs had done a great service to the members of the company.

An order may be made indemnifying the minority shareholder for his or her costs from the company at an early stage of derivative proceedings using a procedure developed in *Wallersteiner* v. *Moir (No. 2)*.[44] Restrictions were placed on this procedure in *Smith* v. *Croft*[45] where Walton J considered that such orders might cause injustice if made before discovery, and that they should only be made if the plaintiffs genuinely needed an indemnity in order to proceed. However, the latter limitation was not applied in *Jaybird Group Ltd.* v. *Greenwood*.[46]

A liberal approach was also taken in Australia in *Farrow* v. *Registrar of*

---

[40] Ibid., at 377.

[41] [1995] BCC 362 (CA).

[42] The other ground (and the sole ground for Beldam LJ's decision) was that the winding-up petition presented by the other shareholder before the derivative action was commenced was an effective alternative remedy for the complaining shareholder.

[43] Above n 20.

[44] [1975] QB 373 (CA). See further A. Boyle 'Minority Shareholders' Suits for Breach of Directors' Duties' (1980) 1 *Company Lawyer* 3.

[45] [1986] 1 WLR 580. See further D. D. Prentice, 'Wallersteiner v Moir: A Decade Later' [1987] *Conv & Prop Law (ns)* 167.   [46] [1986] BCLC 319.

*Building Societies*[47] where Marks J rejected a submission that an order should not be made unless it appeared that the plaintiffs were destitute or so financially handicapped that the case otherwise could not continue.[48]

## (2) Wrongdoer control

Control exists where the wrongdoers own more than 50 per cent of the company's shares. Further, in *Barrett* v. *Duckett*[49] a 50 per cent shareholder was treated as being under the same disability as a minority shareholder in that as a practical matter it would not have been possible for her to set the company in motion to bring an action.[50]

Vinelott J at first instance in *Prudential Assurance Co* v. *Newman Industries Ltd. (No. 2)*[51] was prepared to recognize that the directors who had only a small shareholding were in a position to ensure that the issue of whether the company should proceed or not would never be put to the shareholders in a way which would enable them to exercise a proper judgment. His Lordship therefore considered that Prudential had shown that the interests of justice required that a minority action should be permitted. On appeal, the Court of Appeal[52] did not accept that there is a general exception to the Rule in *Foss* v. *Harbottle* if the interests of justice require it,[53] but did seem to agree that the majority could be made up not only of the votes of the wrongdoer, but also of those likely to vote with the wrongdoer as a result of influence or apathy.

By contrast, Vinelott J's approach was adopted in the Australian case of *Biala Pty Ltd.* v. *Mallina Holdings Ltd. (No. 2)*.[54] Ipp J held that the plaintiff had not established that more than 50 per cent of the shareholders would have voted against commencing or proceeding with an action, so that the fraud on the minority exception was not made out.[55] However, his Honour considered that the interests of justice favoured allowing the plaintiff to bring a derivative action.[56] This was on the basis that, in

---

[47] Above n 34.

[48] But cf., the approach of the majority of the CA NSW towards indemnity costs in the context of proceedings under the unfair prejudice provision in *Parker* v. *National Roads and Motorists' Association* (1993) 11 ACSR 370; 11 ACLC 866 (CA NSW).

[49] Above n 41.

[50] *Per* Peter Gibson LJ with whom Russell LJ agreed. The derivative action was, however, struck out on other grounds.          [51] [1981] Ch. 257 at 326–7.

[52] Above n 20.

[53] See also *Estmanco (Kilner House) Ltd.* v. *Greater London Council* [1982] 1 WLR 2 at 10–11.

[54] (1993) 11 ACSR 785; 11 ACLC 1,082, affd. sub nom. *Dempster* v. *Mallina Holdings Ltd.* (1994) 15 ACSR 1 (Full Ct, WA).

[55] See also *Shears* v. *Chisholm* (1992) 9 ACSR 691.

[56] Cf., the earlier conflicting Australian dicta regarding the 'interests of justice' exception in *Scarel Pty. Ltd.* v. *City Loan and Credit Corporation Pty. Ltd.* above n 33 and *Eromanga Hydrocarbons NL* v. *Australis Mining NL* (1988) 14 ACLR 486; 6 ACLC 906.

practice, the prospect of the company bringing an action was remote, and it was only because the defendant had disposed of his shares between the commencement of the writ and the trial of the action that the fraud on the minority exception was not made out.[57]

In all the above cases, the test for control focuses on the general meeting. However, most companies vest the power to manage the business of the company in the directors, so that the board is the appropriate body to institute proceedings on behalf of the company, and the general meeting may not interfere.[58] Of course, the articles may, for example, permit directions to be given to the directors by special resolution, in which case the general meeting is able to direct the directors to institute proceedings (among other things) in accordance with the article.[59] In the Australian case of *Shears* v. *Chisholm*[60] J. D. Phillips J considered, obiter, whether the establishment of control of the board might be sufficient to establish standing in a case where the articles commit the commencement of proceedings expressly to the board. However, it was not necessary to reach a decision on this question since fraud was not established.

## (3) Fraud

'Fraud' in this context does not necessarily connote dishonesty. Rather it has been interpreted as extending to abuse or misuse of power.[61] 'It merely means that the power has been exercised for a purpose, or with an intention, beyond the scope of or not justified by the instrument creating the power',[62] and is sometimes translated into the stipulation that majority shareholders must act '*bona fide* in the interests of the company'.

Generally, the courts will not permit a derivative action to be brought if the conduct could be ratified by an ordinary resolution.[63] Thus, to

---

[57] Ipp J held that while generally the date on which 'control' is determined for the purposes of deciding whether there has been a fraud on the minority is the date on which the writ is issued, events had occurred and been pleaded which were relevant to the question of control, so that it would have been artificial and not conducive to justice to determine the question of fraud as at the date of issue of the writ.

[58] *Quin & Axtens Ltd.* v. *Salmon* [1909] AC 442 (HL), *John Shaw & Sons (Salford) Ltd.* v. *Shaw* [1935] 2 KB 113 (CA), *Breckland Group Holdings Ltd.* v. *London & Suffolk Properties Ltd.* [1989] BCLC 100; (1988) 4 BCC 542, *Kraus* v. *J. G. Lloyd Pty. Ltd.* above n 20. See further L. S. Sealy, *Cases and Materials in Company Law* (5th edn., London, Butterworths, 1992) at 189–90. [59] See e.g., Art. 70 Table A (UK).

[60] Above n 55 at 788–90.

[61] See Dixon J in *Peters' American Delicacy Co. Ltd.* v. *Heath* (1939) 61 CLR 457 (HC) and Megarry V-C in *Estmanco (Kilner House) Ltd.* v. *Greater London Council* above n 53, at 12. See also L. C. B. Gower, *Principles of Modern Company Law* (5th edn, London, Sweet & Maxwell, 1992) at 593, Ford and Austin, above n 10, para. 1703, Farrar, above n 10, at 449 and P. G. Xuereb, 'The Limitation on the Exercise of Majority Power' (1985) 6 *Company Lawyer* 199. [62] *Per* Lord Parker in *Vatcher* v. *Paull* [1915] AC 372 at 378 (PC).

[63] Where the complaint relates to an issue of shares for an improper purpose, the standing of an individual shareholder to sue derivatively has been recognized even though proceedings

determine whether the conduct amounts to 'fraud' such as to form the basis of a derivative action, it is necessary to examine the limitations which the courts have placed on majority voting power.[64]

## 4. LIMITATIONS ON MAJORITY VOTING POWER

Complaints of abuse of majority voting power cut across the distinction between personal and derivative actions. For example, a shareholder's action to complain about a resolution which alters the articles of association will be personal. Whereas, if a resolution purports to ratify a breach of fiduciary duty by the directors, a minority shareholder's action would be derivative. But the principles which the court applies in determining whether to intervene to disturb the shareholders' resolution are the same in each case.

It is established as a general rule that a share is a right of property, and the holder is entitled to exercise the voting right attached to it in his or her own self interest, irrespective of the interests of the company as a whole.[65] 'The shareholders are not trustees for one another, and, unlike directors, they occupy no fiduciary position and are under no fiduciary duties.'[66] One of the classic dicta establishing this proposition is that of Sir Richard Baggallay delivering the judgment of the Privy Council in *North-West Transportation Co. Ltd.* v. *Beatty*[67] where he said:

The general principles applicable to cases of this kind are well established. Unless some provision to the contrary is to be found in the charter or other instrument by which the company is incorporated, the resolution of a majority of the shareholders, duly convened, upon any question with which the company is legally competent to deal, is binding upon the minority, and consequently upon the company, and every shareholder has a perfect right to vote upon any such question, although he may have a personal interest in the subject-matter opposed to, or different from, the general or particular interests of the company.

---

were adjourned to enable the impugned allotment to be ratified: *Hogg* v. *Cramphorn Ltd.* [1967] Ch. 254. This anomaly is of less significance in light of the recent recognition of a personal right to challenge improper allotments. See G. P. Stapledon, 'Locus standi of shareholders to enforce the duty of company directors to exercise the share issue power for proper purposes' (1990) 8 *Company & Sec LJ* 213 and discussion at nn 128–9 and accompanying text.

[64] Note, however, that an unfair prejudice action may be available irrespective of ratification.

[65] See e.g., *Pender* v. *Lushington* above n 15.

[66] *Per* Dixon J in *Peters' American Delicacy Co. Ltd.* v. *Heath* above n 61, at 504.

[67] (1887) 12 App. Cas. 589 at 593 (PC).

But although this is the general rule, in recognition of the potential for abuse inherent in the power to control a general meeting, qualifications to the power of shareholders to vote in their own interests have been recognized. Certain categories of conduct have consistently been the focus of intervention by the courts, namely appropriation of the company's property, release of directors from breach of duty, and alterations of the company's constituent documents. Each of these categories is examined separately below, and it is then considered whether there is scope for equitable intervention with majority voting power in circumstances not falling within these recognized categories.

### (1) Appropriation of the company's property[68]

The minority can maintain an action to complain of a resolution[69] '. . . where the majority are endeavouring directly or indirectly to appropriate to themselves money, property, or advantages which belong to the company, or in which the other shareholders are entitled to participate'.[70]

An early[71] example of this qualification is *Menier* v. *Hooper's Telegraph Works*[72] where Hooper's company, the majority shareholder, used its voting influence to procure the company to abandon certain legal proceedings, enabling Hooper's to sell a telegraph cable it was making for the company to another company. Sir G. Mellish LJ said:[73] 'I am of opinion that although it may be quite true that the shareholders of a company may vote as they please, and for the purpose of their own interests, yet that the majority of shareholders cannot sell the assets of the company and keep the consideration, but must allow the minority to have their share of any consideration which may come to them.'

This principle was applied in *Cook* v. *Deeks*[74] where the directors had obtained a construction contract in their own names to the exclusion of the company, and then sought to use their votes to pass a resolution at a general meeting declaring that the company had no interest in the contract. The Privy Council decided that the wrongdoers could not use their voting power in this way since they were dealing with property which belonged in

---

[68] Note that in respect of listed companies there is now less acceptance that interested directors should be able to vote their shares: London Stock Exchange, *Listing Rules* rr. 11.4 and 11.5, ASX Listing Rule 3J(3) (Aust). Note also that statutory provisions now govern approval of certain transactions involving directors. See ss. 312, 313, 319, 320 and 337, CA 1985 (UK) and s. 237 and Part 3.2A, CL (Aust).

[69] In exception to the Rule in *Foss* v. *Harbottle* above n 1.

[70] *Per* Lord Davey in *Burland* v. *Earle* [1902] AC 83 at 93 (PC).

[71] For a recent example of a majority attempting to use its voting power to prevent proceedings being brought against it in the name of the company see *Estmanco (Kilner House) Ltd.* v. *Greater London Council* above n 53.

[72] (1874) LR 9 Ch. App. 350.  [73] Ibid., at 354.

[74] [1916] 1 AC 554 (PC).

equity to the company. Lord Buckmaster LC delivering the judgment of the board said:[75]

> . . . if directors have acquired for themselves property or rights which they must be regarded as holding on behalf of the company, a resolution that the rights of the company should be disregarded in the matter would amount to forfeiting the interest and property of the minority of shareholders in favour of the majority, and that by the votes of those who are interested in securing the property for themselves. Such use of voting power has never been sanctioned by the Courts.

This case raises the perplexing[76] question of what exactly are the limitations on the power of the majority to excuse conduct of the directors which is in breach of duty.[77]

### (2) Release of directors' breach of duty

Sir Richard Baggallay stated in *Beatty*'s case[78] that the power to affirm or ratify a voidable transaction is subject to the proviso that 'such affirmance or adoption is not brought about by unfair or improper means, and is not illegal or fraudulent or oppressive towards those shareholders who oppose it.' Attempts to obtain absolution have failed on the grounds of 'unfair or improper means' where the disclosure given to the general meeting has been regarded as insufficient.[79] The difficulty has lain in drawing the line at which conduct will be regarded as illegal, fraudulent or oppressive. Several approaches to this question can be identified.

### (a) Misappropriation distinguished from excusable profit-making

Gower[80] reconciles *Cook* v. *Deeks*[81] with *Regal (Hastings) Ltd.* v. *Gulliver*[82] by regarding the former as a case of inexcusable misappropriation of corporate assets and the latter as a case of excusable profit-making. In *Regal*'s case, the directors profited from taking up an opportunity on their own account which had first been offered to the company, but which it was unable to take up because of lack of funds, and because the directors

---

[75] [1916] 1 AC 554 (PC) 564.

[76] The task of reconciling the cases in this area has been described as 'one of the most difficult in company law': S. M. Beck, 'The Saga of Peso Silver Mines: Corporate Opportunity Reconsidered' (1971) 49 *Can B Rev* 80 at 114. See also Gower, above n 61, at 595 who describes it as 'difficult (and perhaps impossible)'.

[77] See generally, R. Baxt, 'Judges in Their Own Cause: The Ratification of Directors' Breaches of Duty' (1978) 5 *Monash UL Rev* 16.      [78] Above n 67 at 594.

[79] See e.g., *Winthrop Investments Ltd.* v. *Winns Ltd.* [1975] 2 NSWLR 666 (CA NSW).

[80] Gower, above n 61, at 595. See also Beck, above n 76, at 116–7, Sealy, above n 58, at 269 and B. H. McPherson, 'Duties of Directors and the Powers of Shareholders' (1977) 51 *Austl LJ* 460 at 464.      [81] Above n 74.      [82] [1967] 2 AC 134n (HL).

declined to give personal guarantees on its behalf. The directors were held liable to account to the company, but the court considered that they could have protected themselves from this by ratification.

On this basis, it might be generalized[83] that the general meeting may validate a transaction which is voidable because of directors' conflict of interest[84] and may excuse breaches of the duty to exercise care and skill.[85] It may not excuse breaches involving dishonesty,[86] or conflicts of interest in circumstances where, as a result of the breach, the directors benefit themselves at the expense of the company.[87]

As many commentators have observed, this distinction is a very difficult one to draw. Beck[88] rejects the distinction because in both cases the directors in the course of acting for the company personally acquired property which it was their duty to acquire for the company. He argues that the *bona fides* of the directors in *Regal*'s case may be the distinguishing factor between the cases. Sealy[89] suggests that the nature of the claim brought may be relevant, since in *Regal*'s case the directors were held severally liable in proceedings for money had and received, whereas, in *Cook* v. *Deeks* the directors were held jointly and severally liable as constructive trustees.

Even accepting that the distinction proposed by Gower can be made and is palatable on the facts of *Regal*'s case[90] where the company could not

[83] Recently, an additional rider has begun to emerge, namely that where the company is insolvent shareholders cannot ratify breaches of duty which affect creditors adversely. See *Kinsela* v. *Russell Kinsela Pty. Ltd. (in liq.)* (1986) 4 NSWLR 722 (CA NSW). Street CJ left open the possibility of this limitation applying in cases of financial instability failling short of insolvency, depending upon whether in the circumstances it was plain that the creditors' money was at risk. See too, the more cautious English dicta in *Re Horsley & Weight Ltd.* [1982] Ch. 442 at 454–6 and *Multinational Gas and Petrochemical Co.* v. *Multinational Gas and Petrochemical Services Ltd.* [1983] Ch. 258 at 268–9, 280–2, 288 ff, and L. S. Sealy, 'Directors "Wider" Responsibilities—Problems Conceptual, Practical and Procedural' (1987) 13 *Monash UL Rev* 164 at 182.

[84] *Beatty*'s case, above n 67, *Boulting* v. *Association of Cinematograph, Television and Allied Technicians* [1963] 2 QB 606 (CA).

[85] *Pavlides* v. *Jensen* [1956] Ch. 565.

[86] *Atwool* v. *Merryweather* (1867) LR 5 Eq 464n. The bald proposition that breaches of the duty of good faith are not ratifiable may be regarded as inconsistent with the Court of Appeal decision in *Bamford* v. *Bamford* [1970] Ch. 212 (CA) where ratification was allowed of an allotment of shares which was assumed to be *mala fide*. However, although the Court of Appeal decision proceeded on this basis Plowman J at first instance decided the case on the basis that the directors were acting in good faith but for an improper purpose: [1970] Ch. 212 at 216. See K. W. Wedderburn, 'Going the whole Hogg v Cramphorn?' (1968) 31 *Mod L Rev* 688 at 689 and 'Unreformed Company Law' (1969) 32 *Mod L Rev* 563.

[87] The question of ratification of directors' negligence was not discussed by Templeman J in *Daniels* v. *Daniels* [1978] Ch. 406 but arguably it may be implied from his citation of *Cook* v. *Deeks*, above n 74, that it would not have been possible on the facts of that case, namely where the directors were profiting from their negligence at the expense of the company. See further Baxt, above n 77, at 25.                                    [88] Above n 76 at 116–7.

[89] Above n 58, at 269.                                                          [90] Above n 82.

have taken up the opportunity which resulted in the directors' profit, the same cannot be said of the facts of the Australian case of *Furs Ltd.* v. *Tomkies.*[91] In that case Tomkies was negotiating the sale of the company's tanning and dyeing business and at the same time (with the blessing of the company's board) arranging his own future employment with the purchaser. Unbeknown to the board, Tomkies was to receive £5,000 in addition to his salary in consideration for disclosing the company's secret formulae. This would make the formulae valueless to the company. The High Court stated, obiter,[92] that a properly informed general meeting could have ratified the transaction enabling Tomkies to retain his secret profit. Although it may be argued that the form of the action and the scope of the dicta were confined to an account of profits, '[s]urely it is a misappropriation of property to sell the company's business for a low price and, in effect, to pocket the balance of its worth.'[93]

### (b) Requiring ratification by independent shareholders

An alternative approach is to regard all breaches of duty as ratifiable, provided the interested shareholders do not vote.

Vinelott J at first instance in *Prudential Assurance Co Ltd.* v. *Newman Industries Ltd. (No. 2)*[94] would have allowed ratification only by an independent body of shareholders.[95] This approach removes the objection of wrongdoers being judges in their own cause, but even some of its proponents acknowledge that the implementation of such a system would be daunting from a practical point of view. Nevertheless, an Australian court has been prepared to undertake a detailed examination of how major shareholders acquired their shares, and to find that a number of apparently independent shareholders were not disinterested and would have voted against a motion to institute an action against a director.[96]

---

[91] (1936) 54 CLR 583 (HC).

[92] Ibid., at 590–1 *per* Latham CJ, and at 592, 599 *per* Rich, Dixon and Evatt JJ (joint judgment).

[93] J. F. Corkery, *Directors' Powers and Duties* (Melbourne, Longman Cheshire Pty. Ltd., 1987) at 95. See also the criticisms by G. R. Sullivan, 'Restating the Scope of the Derivative Action' [1985] *Cambridge LJ* 236 at 240–3 of the distinction between proprietary and non-proprietary claims as a basis for the availability of ratification.

[94] Above n 51, at 307, 323.

[95] Contrast *Mason* v. *Harris* (1879) 11 Ch. D 97 at 109 (CA) *per* James LJ. But for academic support for this approach see Beck, above n 76, at 118–9, Baxt, above n 77, at 49, and Sullivan, above n 93, at 245 ff. For strong criticisms of this approach see K. W. Wedderburn, 'Derivative Actions and Foss v Harbottle' (1981) 44 *Mod L Rev* 202 at 208, and L. S. Sealy, '*Foss* v. *Harbottle*—A Marathon Where Nobody Wins' [1981] *Cambridge LJ* 29 at 32. See also K. Yeung, 'Disentangling the Tangled Skein: The Ratification of Directors' Actions' (1992) 66 *Austl LJ* 343 who advocates a disinterested vote on a resolution to release a director from civil liability, but allowing directors to vote on a separate resolution to validate and adopt a transaction.

[96] *Biala Pty. Ltd.* v. *Mallina Holdings Limited (No. 2)* above n 54.

There are echoes of this approach in *Smith* v. *Croft (No. 2)*[97] where it was held that a derivative action could not proceed where the majority of independent shareholders did not wish the action to continue, although in that case no question of ratification arose, since an *ultra vires* act was involved.

There are no Australian cases where this approach has been taken in the context of ratification, although law reform along these lines has been recommended.[98] A parallel can perhaps be drawn in recent cases concerning reductions of capital, where shareholders who stand to benefit from the reduction (and their associates) customarily refrain from voting on the basis that it will be difficult to persuade a court that a reduction is fair if those who stand to benefit from the reduction have dominated the voting.[99]

Australian cases concerning allotments of shares for an improper purpose have taken a completely different approach towards limiting the opportunity for ratification, and this is discussed in detail in the next section.

### (c) Allotments of shares for an improper purpose

#### (i) England

The position in relation to ratification of allotments of shares is governed by *Hogg* v. *Cramphorn*[100] and *Bamford* v. *Bamford*,[101] the latter being a decision of the Court of Appeal, which decided that an allotment made for an improper purpose and therefore voidable, can be validated by the majority of shareholders in general meeting.[102]

---

[97] Above n 5.

[98] The Companies and Securities Law Review Committee recommended that 'Fairness requires that the person who will be relieved should not consent to his or her own wrong. Interested directors, their associates and relatives should not be able to vote'. *Company Directors and Officers: Indemnification, Relief and Insurance*, Report No. 10, May 1990, para. 60.

[99] See *Nicron Resources Ltd.* v. *Catto & Ors* (1992) 8 ACSR 219 at 223 and 238; 10 ACLC 1186 at 1189 and 1200, *Re Shine Fisheries Ltd.* (1994) 12 ACSR 627 at 636; 12 ACLC 223 at 229 and discussion in Ch. 10, section 4(2). Note also that Part 3.2A of the Corporations Law which deals with certain related party transactions, and allows financial benefits to be given to related parties if there is shareholder approval, precludes a related party to whom the benefit may or will be given or an associate of the related party from voting to approve the benefit, unless the ASC permits them to vote: s. 243ZF, CL (Aust).          [100] Above n 63.

[101] Above n 86.

[102] See generally three articles by K. W. Wedderburn, 'Shareholders' Control of Directors' Powers: A Judicial Innovation?' (1967) 30 *Mod L Rev* 77, 'Going the Whole Hogg v Cramphorn?' above n 86, 'Unreformed Company Law' above n 86, and B. A. K. Rider, 'Amiable Lunatics and the Rule in Foss v Harbottle' [1978] *Cambridge LJ* 270. But note the potential for a personal action to be brought in these circumstances: see above n 24.

### (ii) Australia

In *Ngurli Ltd.* v. *McCann*[103] a decision which predates *Hogg's*[104] case and *Bamford's* case,[105] the High Court applied[106] the doctrine of fraud on a power to impose an obligation on shareholders not to use the powers conferred on them in general meeting for an improper purpose. Although recognizing[107] that shareholders are not trustees for their votes, and can therefore, as individuals, exercise their votes for their own benefit, this was subjected to the obligation on the majority of shareholders in general meeting to use their powers *bona fide* for the benefit of the company as a whole in the sense of the corporators as a general body,[108] and a prohibition on exercising this power so as to commit a fraud on a minority, in the sense of appropriating to themselves or to some of themselves, property, advantages, or rights which belong to the company.[109] Williams ACJ, Fullagar and Kitto JJ in a joint judgment went on to classify the right to issue new capital as an advantage belonging to the company, so that an attempt to exercise this right not for the benefit of the company as a whole[110] could be restrained in a suit brought by the minority applying the principle in *Cook* v. *Deeks*.[111] Thus, in relation to ratification of an issue of shares for an improper purpose they concluded:[112] 'Attempts were made by the trustee company . . . to have the issues confirmed in general meeting . . . But even in general meeting a majority of shareholders cannot exercise their votes for the purpose of appropriating to themselves property or advantages which belong to the company for that would be for the majority to oppress the minority.'

When subsequently to *Bamford's* case[113] the question of ratification of an allotment of shares for improper purposes was considered by the New South Wales Court of Appeal in *Winthrop Investments Ltd.* v. *Winns Ltd.*[114] the majority judges based their opinions upon the insufficiency of the disclosure made to the general meeting, so that their discussion of the question of ratification was obiter. Unlike *Ngurli Ltd.* v. *McCann*,[115] this case involved an allotment of shares to a third company in part-payment for the purchase of retail stores from subsidiaries of the third company. Thus, it was not argued that the exercise of power by the general meeting

---

[103] (1953) 90 CLR 425 (HC).     [104] Above n 63.     [105] Above n 86.
[106] Above n 103 at 438.     [107] Ibid., at 438–9.
[108] The court relied on the first paragraph of Evershed MR's famous dictum in *Greenhalgh* v. *Arderne Cinemas Ltd.* [1951] Ch. 286 at 291 (CA) in support of this proposition.
[109] The court referred to *Cook* v. *Deeks* above n 74, and *Menier* v. *Hooper's Telegraph Works* above n 72, in support of this proposition.
[110] In this case for the improper purpose of ensuring that the director maintained his controlling power over the company.     [111] Above n 74.
[112] Above n 103, at 447.     [113] Above n 86.     [114] Above n 79.
[115] Above n 103.

operated fraudulently so as to appropriate to the majority of shareholders rights belonging to the company. Although the majority judges assumed, in line with *Bamford*'s case,[116] that a majority of shareholders in a general meeting had power to affirm an otherwise voidable decision of the directors in this context, Samuels JA expressly did not base his decision on this point[117] and Mahoney JA made various references[118] to the fact that it was not necessary to lay down general principles on an interlocutory application.[119] Assuming that such ratification was possible, Mahoney JA attempted to steer a middle ground[120] between *Bamford*'s case[121] and *Ngurli Ltd.* v. *McCann*.[122] He distinguished *Bamford*'s case in the following terms:[123] '*Bamford* v. *Bamford* . . . decides that, in an exercise by the shareholders of the power of the company to avoid a transaction voidable on that ground, a resolution may be valid to affirm the transaction; it decides . . . nothing as to whether that resolution may be ineffective, because the majority had the same purpose.'

His Honour went on to state[124] that a purported ratification of an allotment of shares otherwise voidable as in breach of fiduciary duty may be ineffective where the shareholders have the same collateral purpose as the directors.[125] This was on the basis that the resolution may not be for the purposes of the company as a whole as explained in *Ngurli Ltd.* v. *McCann*.[126] He described this[127] as a serious question which remained to be argued, if evidence were led at trial so as to raise the question.

It has since been held in single judge decisions in both England[128] and Australia[129] on the authority of the decision of the Privy Council in *Howard Smith Ltd.* v. *Ampol Petroleum Ltd.*[130] that shareholders have standing to bring a personal action to challenge an allotment of shares for an improper purpose.[131] Further, in the recent decision of the Full Court of the Supreme Court of South Australia, *Residues Treatment and Trading*

---

[116] Above n 86.     [117] Above n 79, at 681.     [118] Ibid., at 700–1 and 702.

[119] See A. G. Diethelm, 'Impugned Share Allotments and the Rule in *Foss* v. *Harbottle*' (1989) 5 *Austl B Rev* 262 at 273.

[120] See further: H. Mason, 'Ratification of the Directors' Acts: An Anglo-Australian Comparison' (1978) 41 *Mod L Rev* 161.     [121] Above n 86.

[122] Above n 103.     [123] Above n 79, at 707.     [124] Ibid.

[125] For a recent Australian example of an obligation being placed on a shareholder to exercise a power for the purpose for which it was given see *BWN Industries Pty. Ltd.* v. *Downey* (1993) 11 ACSR 777; 11 ACLC 1191.

[126] Above n 103, at 438–9.     [127] Above n 79, at 707.

[128] *Re a Company (No. 005136 of 1986)* above n 24.

[129] *Eromanga Hydrocarbons NL* v. *Australis Mining NL* above n 24.

[130] Above n 24. In that case an action to challenge an allotment of shares for an improper purpose appears to have been brought by the plaintiff in its individual capacity, although the plaintiff's standing was not expressly discussed.

[131] On the basis that this is a breach of their contractual rights under the articles. See R. J. Smith, 'Minority Shareholders and Corporate Irregularities' (1978) 41 *Mod L Rev* 147.

*Co. Ltd.* v. *Southern Resources Ltd. (No. 4)*,[132] unequivocal recognition was given to the existence of a personal right in a shareholder founded in equity[133] to have the voting power of his or her shares undiminished by improper actions on the part of the directors, and of his or her *locus standi* to institute and prosecute proceedings to protect that right.

As regards the possibility of ratification of such an improper allotment, King CJ[134] doubted the authority of *Bamford*'s case, noting[135] that the statement by the New South Wales Court of Appeal in *Winthrop Investments Ltd.* v. *Winns Ltd.* that a general meeting could ratify an allotment made for an improper purpose was made at a time when that court felt constrained to follow *Bamford*'s case as a decision of the English Court of Appeal and that that constraint is no longer recognized to apply to the Supreme Courts of Australian States. He therefore stated:[136] 'If . . . such an allotment infringes the personal rights of shareholders, it is difficult to see how the potential for ratification can deprive the wronged shareholder of locus standi while the infringement continues.'[137]

King CJ, however, acknowledged[138] the possibility of an argument that although a shareholder has *locus standi* to challenge an *improper* share allotment, the action might be defeated if the issue were made lawful by ratification of the allotment and it could therefore be said that the infringement ceased. In this regard, he referred[139] to the dictum of the High Court in *Ngurli Ltd.* v. *McCann*[140] that 'voting powers conferred on shareholders and powers conferred on directors by the articles of association of companies must be used *bona fide* for the benefit of the company as a whole' and continued: 'If it is correct that a shareholder has a personal right to have the voting power of his shares undiminished by an allotment of shares made for an improper purpose, there is to my mind a substantial argument that an exercise of the voting power of the majority to ratify such an allotment would be beyond the scope of the purpose for which that power exists.'

---

[132] Above n 24, at 210–2. See: A. Beck, 'Minority Shareholders and Allotments for an Improper Purpose' (1989) 17 *Austl Bus L Rev* 321 and R. Baxt 'Has the Rule in *Foss* v. *Harbottle* Been Put to Rest in Corporate Takeover Litigation' (1989) 17 *Austl Bus L Rev* 224.

[133] Although King CJ drew additional support from the decisions in *Re a Company (No. 005136 of 1986)* above n 24, and *Eromanga Hydrocarbons NL* v. *Australis Mining NL* above n 24, he did not base this right on the statutory contract but in equity. He regarded it as a right to have the say in the company which accrues to a shareholder by virtue of the voting rights which are attached to his or her shares by the contract with the company, preserved against improper actions by the company or the directors who manage its affairs: above n 24, at 201–2.

[134] With whom the other members of the Full Court of the South Australian Supreme Court agreed.                 [135] Above n 24, at 204.                 [136] Ibid., at 205.

[137] See C. J. H. Thomson, 'Share Issues and the Rule in *Foss* v. *Harbottle*' (1975) 49 *Austl LJ* 134 and Diethelm, above n 119, at 276. See also *Nash* v. *Lancegaye Safety Glass (Ireland) Ltd.* (1958) 92 Ir LTR 11 at 26 and *Pender* v. *Lushington* above n 15.

[138] Above n 24, at 205.                 [139] Ibid., at 204–5.                 [140] Above n 103, at 438.

At one level, the Australian cases can be reconciled with *Hogg*'s case[141] and *Bamford*'s case,[142] since King CJ appears to accept that a shareholder's personal standing to challenge an improper allotment may be defeated by a valid ratification.[143] But the proviso which has not been expressly recognized in England is that the ratification may be ineffective as a fraud on a power if the shareholders are motivated by an improper purpose in passing the resolution. King CJ arguably goes one stage further in suggesting that a ratification of an allotment which diminishes the voting power of a minority will always be for an improper purpose. This assumption has been criticized by commentators.[144] Nevertheless, it has since been applied to disregard a purported ratification of an improper allotment in *Colarc Pty. Ltd.* v. *Donarc Pty. Ltd.*[145]

### (3) Alteration of articles

The courts have sought to strike a balance between the interests of majority and minority shareholders in the context of resolutions to alter the articles, acknowledging on the one hand that a share is a right of property giving the owner the ability to exercise the right to vote attached to the share in his or her own interests, and on the other hand that the exercise of this individual right has the potential to affect the rights of others. The difficulty has lain '. . . in attempting to discover and fasten upon some element the presence of which will always vitiate a resolution for the alteration of articles of association'.[146] An early expression of this limitation and an appropriate starting point for discussion (despite the rejection of this test in Australia)[147] is a dictum of Lindley MR in *Allen* v. *Gold Reefs of West Africa Ltd.*[148] that:

The power thus conferred on companies to alter the regulations contained in their articles is limited only by the provisions contained in the statute and the conditions contained in the company's memorandum of association. Wide, however, as the

---

[141] Above n 63.  [142] Above n 86.

[143] Although *Hogg* and *Bamford* themselves represent a departure from the orthodox position represented by *MacDougall* v. *Gardiner* that the mere potential for ratification should deprive the plaintiffs of standing in that they grant standing to a minority shareholder pending such ratification. Cf., Diethelm, above n 119, at 276, who argues that the shareholders' personal right makes no sense unless immune from extinguishment by the majority.

[144] Cf., Yeung, above n 95, at 353, who argues that the inference that because the directors have acted for improper purposes, then the general meeting must also have acted for improper purposes cannot be justified. See also L. S. Sealy, ' "Bona Fides" and "Proper Purposes" in Corporate Decisions' (1989) 15 *Monash UL Rev* 265, at 273.

[145] (1991) 4 ACSR 155.

[146] *Peters' American Delicacy Co. Ltd.* v. *Heath*, above n 61, at 507 *per* Dixon J.

[147] See discussion below at nn 180–8 and accompanying text.

[148] [1900] 1 Ch. 656 at 671 (CA) emphasis added.

language of s. 50 is, the power conferred by it must, like all other powers, be exercised subject to those general principles of law and equity which are applicable to all powers conferred on majorities and enabling them to bind minorities. It must be exercised, not only in the manner required by law, but also *bonâ fide for the benefit of the company as a whole*, and it must not be exceeded. These conditions are always implied, and are seldom, if ever, expressed.

The same test has been applied not only to alterations of the articles of association but also to resolutions altering the rights of a class of shareholders[149] or bondholders,[150] although in this context as well, the test has been rejected as inappropriate in more recent authorities.[151]

From the outset, difficulties arose in interpreting and applying the 'bona fide for the benefit of the company' test. Two attempts[152] to consider separately the questions of the good faith of the alteration and its tendency to benefit the company as a whole were rejected.[153] Also rejected was the approach inherent in the twofold test that the court could substitute its opinion as to what is in fact for the benefit of the company for that of the members. Rather the test has been interpreted[154] as being whether the alteration is in the subjective opinion of the shareholders for the benefit of the company, with the proviso that the alteration may be so oppressive as to cast suspicion on the honesty of the person responsible for it, or so extravagant that no reasonable person could really consider it for the benefit of the company.

In the leading Australian case of *Peters' American Delicacy Co. Ltd. v. Heath*[155] Dixon J interpreted Lindley MR's reference to the benefit of the company as a whole in *Allen*'s case[156] as 'a very general expression negativing purposes foreign to the company's operations, affairs and organizations'.[157] His Honour drew support from Lord Lindley's later statement in *British Equitable Assurance Co. Ltd. v. Baily*[158] that 'Of course, the powers of altering by-laws, like other powers, must be exercised bona fide, and having regard to the purposes for which they are created, and to the rights of persons affected by them'.

---

[149] *Re Holders Investment Trust Ltd.* [1971] 1 WLR 583. But see text accompanying nn 284–6 in Ch. 3.

[150] *British America Nickel Corporation Ltd. v. O'Brien* [1927] AC 369 (PC).

[151] See *Re Leigh Estates (UK) Ltd.* [1994] BCC 292 and *Nicron Resources Ltd. v. Catto* (1992) 8 ACSR 219; 10 ACLC 1186 at 232; 1196.

[152] *Brown v. British Abrasive Wheel Co. Ltd.* [1919] 1 Ch. 290 and *Dafen Tinplate Co. Ltd. v. Llanelly Steel Co. (1907) Ltd.* [1920] 2 Ch. 124.

[153] *Sidebottom v. Kershaw, Leese & Co. Ltd.* [1920] 1 Ch. 154 (CA) and *Shuttleworth v. Cox Brothers and Co. (Maidenhead) Ltd.* [1927] 2 KB 9 (CA). See also *Greenhalgh v. Arderne Cinemas Ltd.* above n 108.

[154] See e.g., *Shuttleworth v. Cox Brothers & Co. (Maidenhead) Ltd.* ibid., at 18 *per* Bankes LJ and at 23 *per* Scrutton LJ.   [155] Above n 61.   [156] Above n 148.

[157] Above n 61 at 512.   [158] [1906] AC 35 at 42 (HL).

Latham CJ, Dixon J and Rich J all made the point that the case before them was not a case of oppression or appropriation of an unjust or reprehensible nature. Rather the alteration of the articles was one which simply involved a conflict between the interests of the majority and the minority.[159] Thus, Latham CJ observed:[160] 'In cases where the question which arises is simply a question as to the relative rights of different classes of shareholders the problem cannot be solved by regarding merely the benefit of the corporation.' Dixon J said in stronger terms: 'No-one supposes that in voting each shareholder is to assume an inhuman altruism and consider only the intangible notion of the benefit of the vague abstraction called . . . "the company as an institution".'[161] Perhaps the clearest is Rich J who stated, after reviewing the authorities:[162]

Where the very problem which arises contains as inherent in itself all the elements of a conflict of interests between classes of shareholders these authorities do not mean that the power of alteration is paralysed, they mean only that the purpose of bringing forward the resolution must not be simply the enrichment of the majority at the expense of the minority. The resolution in the present case was brought forward to solve a difficulty and make possible a capitalization. It can hardly be supposed that the only solution of such a difficulty which can be lawfully adopted is that which gives the minority an advantage at the expense of the majority.

The application of Dixon J's 'fraud on a power' test to facts involving a simple conflict between the majority and minority interests appears to be that the will of the majority should prevail except where no reasonable person could regard the alteration as a fair one to be made.[163] A similar approach to the relevance of the interests of the company as a corporate entity to a resolution which essentially involves a conflict between the interests of the majority and minority shareholders was taken

---

[159] This point is taken up by F. G. Rixon, 'Competing Interests and Conflicting Principles: An Examination of the Power of Alteration of Articles of Association' (1986) 49 *Mod L Rev* 446, who discusses the concept of 'the benefit of the company as a whole' and distinguishes between alterations of the articles which involve a conflict between the company and a member or group of members, and those which involve an adjustment of the rights of members *inter se*. He argues that only in the former case can the interests of the company as a whole be identified with those of the company as a corporate entity. See also B. H. McPherson, 'Oppression of Minority Shareholders, Part I: Common Law Relief' (1963) 36 *Austl LJ* 404 at 410 who observes that Evershed MR's interpretation of the benefit to the company test in *Greenhalgh* v. *Arderne Cinemas Ltd.*, above n 108, in terms of 'the corporators as a general body' is inappropriate to cases of fraud on the company, and see D. D. Prentice, 'Winding Up on the Just and Equitable Ground: The Partnership Analogy' (1973) 89 *Law Q Rev* 107 at 116.　　　　　　　　　　　　　　　　[160] Above n 61, at 481.
[161] Ibid., at 512.　　　　　　　　　　　　　　　　　　　　　　　　　　[162] Ibid., at 495.
[163] Certainly, Dixon J, ibid., at 512, did not envisage an examination of the purpose of the resolution as involving an examination of the motives of the each shareholder voting with the majority. This he describes as an 'impossible proceeding'.

in the leading English case on alteration of articles of association, *Greenhalgh* v. *Arderne Cinemas Ltd.*[164] Here, Evershed MR reviewed the authorities and concluded that:[165]

. . . the phrase, 'the company as a whole' does not (at any rate in such a case as the present) mean the company as a commercial entity, distinct from the corporators: it means the corporators as a general body. That is to say, the case may be taken of an individual hypothetical member and it may be asked whether what is proposed is, in the honest opinion of those who voted in its favour, for that person's benefit.

I think that the matter can, in practice, be more accurately and precisely stated by looking at the converse and by saying that a special resolution of this kind would be liable to be impeached if the effect of it were to discriminate between the majority shareholders and the minority shareholders, so as to give to the former an advantage of which the latter were deprived. . . . It is therefore not necessary to require that persons voting for a special resolution should, so to speak, dissociate themselves altogether from their own prospects and consider whether what is thought to be for the benefit of the company as a going concern.

The first paragraph[166] of this formulation echoes the approach taken in *Peters'* case and, as mentioned earlier, was adopted by the Australian High Court in *Ngurli Ltd.* v. *McCann.*[167] However, the second paragraph which adopts discrimination between majority and minority shareholders so as to give an advantage to the majority as the test of invalidity appears to be inconsistent with *Peters'* case where Latham CJ stated:[168] 'It is plainly not the law that the fact that an alteration of articles alters the rights or prejudices the rights of some shareholders is sufficient to prevent the alteration from being validly made.'[169] It is also, as commentators have pointed out,[170] difficult to reconcile with the actual decision in *Greenhalgh's* case.[171] In that case the resolution removed pre-emption rights to allow sales of shares to non members (with the sanction of an ordinary resolution passed at a general meeting). The minority argued that the effect of the resolution was discriminatory on the dual bases that they lost the right on a sale to tender for the majority holding of shares, and also that the majority would be able to sell their shares on the open market and thus obtain a

---

[164] Above n 108.                                              [165] Ibid., at 291.
[166] The third paragraph is in a similar vein.                 [167] Above n 103.
[168] Above n 61, at 480.
[169] In a similar vein, Dixon J, ibid., at 507, said: 'To base the application of the epithets [fraudulent, oppressive, or unjust] upon the circumstance that the majority obtain a benefit by the change seems to involve some departure from the principle that the vote attached to a share is an incident of property which may be used as the shareholders' interests may dictate.'
[170] L. C. B. Gower *et al.*, *Gower's Principles of Modern Company Law* (4th edn., London, Stevens & Sons, 1979) at 627. See also H. A. J. Ford, *Principles of Company Law* (4th edn., Sydney, Butterworths, 1986) at 471 and Rixon, above n 159 at 462.
[171] Above n 108.

higher price for them, whereas the minority shareholders would only be able to sell to other shareholders. Despite these consequences, the Court of Appeal held that the proposed resolution was not unfairly discriminatory so as to fall within the principle stated.

This brings us to the point arrived at by Jacobs J in *Crumpton* v. *Morrine Hall Pty. Ltd.*[172] where he said:

The questions which are raised in this regard are of no little difficulty, and the difficulty is made no less, I feel, by the fact that, as I see it, no text-writer or single judgment has succeeded in reconciling or resolving the various approaches which appear in the various decisions which have been given on this subject-matter. It seems to me that the truth is that the courts in each generation or in each decade have set a line up to which shareholders have been allowed to go in affecting the rights of other shareholders by alterations of Articles of Association, and beyond which they have not been allowed to go. It seems to me that no amount of legal analysis or analytical reasoning can conceal the fact that the decision has in the past turned, and must turn ultimately, on a value judgment formed in respect of the conduct of the majority—a judgment formed not by any strict process of reasoning or bare principle of law but upon the view taken of the conduct.

That case concerned a special resolution altering the articles of association of a home-unit company restricting the right to sub-lease and enabling determination of the right to use the unit in the event of failure to pay maintenance or to take proper care of the unit. The justification for this alteration advanced by the majority was that owner occupancy would result in a better standard of care of the units and a better relationship between the various occupants. The alteration was successfully challenged by the minority. In cases such as this where, although applicable generally, the resolution would affect one or a minority in particular, Jacobs J did not regard it as sufficient to say that it was considered that the property of the company would benefit as a result of the alteration of the articles.[173] He said:[174]

I think that the taking away of the rights peculiarly attached to shares, or substantially affecting those rights, is a fraud on the holder of those rights unless good reasons for so doing are established very clearly indeed. The weightiness of the reasons may depend on the degree of interference with the rights. For instance, it might be thought that very strong and exceptional circumstances would have to exist before preference shareholders should become subject to any reduction in the dividend payable to them on their shares.

Here, since the shares were purchased on the basis of rights of occupancy, subletting and licensing and the provision of such rights was stated as the

---

[172] [1965] NSWR 240 at 243–4.     [173] Ibid., at 244.     [174] Ibid.

first object of the company, Jacobs J considered that very strong reasons would have to be advanced in order validly to interfere with those rights. The drastic interference with the right to sublet or grant licences was not justified by the wish of the majority to see owner-occupancy of the units.[175]

One stage more drastic still is an alteration to the articles which enables the shares of the minority to be expropriated.[176] An alteration of this kind was allowed in *Sidebottom* v. *Kershaw, Leese & Co Ltd.*[177] where the minority shareholder was competing with the company, and the alteration limited expropriation to that situation. However, the implication from cases such as *Re Bugle Press Ltd.*[178] is that the inference of bad faith would arise unless the shareholders to be expropriated were acting in a manner destructive or highly damaging to the company's interests.[179]

This issue has recently been considered by the Australian High Court in *Gambotto* v. *WCP Ltd.*[180] All five members of the High Court held that the '*bona fide* for the benefit of the company as a whole' test of Lindley MR in *Allen* v. *Gold Reefs of West Africa Ltd.*[181] was inappropriate to determine the validity of an alteration which gives rise to a conflict of interests and advantages between the majority and minority shareholders. Where the alteration does not involve an actual or effective expropriation of shares or valuable property rights attaching to shares, the majority judges[182] considered that a special resolution to alter the articles which was regularly passed would be valid unless it was '. . . ultra vires, beyond any purpose contemplated by the articles or oppressive as that expression is understood in the law relating to corporations'.[183] The majority judges also held that, of itself, the conferral of a power to acquire compulsorily the property of the minority shareholders or shareholders was not within the contemplated objects of the power to amend the articles. A proper purpose for an alteration involving expropriation would be established only where it was reasonably apprehended that the continued shareholding of the minority was deterimental to the company and expropriation was a reasonable means of eliminating that detriment.[184] The further stipulation

---

[175] Ibid., at 244, 245.
[176] This issue is discussed in detail in Ch. 10.                    [177] Above n 153.
[178] [1961] Ch. 270 at 287 *per* Lord Evershed MR (CA).
[179] Cf., Rixon, above n 159, at 461–2.
[180] (1995) 16 ACSR 1; 12 ACLC 342 (HC).                    [181] Above n 148.
[182] Mason CJ, Brennan, Deane and Dawson JJ.
[183] Above n 180, at 8–9; 348.
[184] Cf., McHugh J who considered that no distinction should be drawn between an expropriation that would enable a company to pursue a beneficial course of action that would otherwise be denied to it and an expropriation that avoids a detriment to the existing interests of the company: above n 180, at 16–7; 354.

that the alteration should not be oppressive required that the expropriation should be fair in the circumstances.[185]

The shift to a proper purposes test represents a departure from the essentially subjective nature of the '*bona fide* for the benefit of the company' test.[186] As such, *Gambotto*'s case appears to bring the grounds for challenging an alteration to the articles at common law closer to those which would apply under the statutory remedy against oppressive or unfairly prejudicial conduct.[187] The approach taken by the majority judges also diverges from earlier expropriation cases[188] by placing the onus on those supporting expropriation to show that the power has been validly exercised.

### (4) Equitable considerations

Accepting that the common law imposes restrictions on the exercise of majority voting power in cases of misappropriation of company property, alteration of the constituent documents of the company and release of directors' breach of duty, the question then arises as to whether such common law intervention is confined to these recognized categories of resolution or whether it extends to other resolutions. Certainly Lindley MR's dictum in *Allen*'s case[189] based as it is on '. . . general principles of law and equity which are applicable to all powers conferred on majorities and enabling them to bind minorities'[190] admits of a wider interpretation, and it is not only by alteration of the articles of association that the rights of shareholders may be affected.[191] Although the test contained in this dictum was not applied in *Gambotto*'s case[192] it was the formulation of the test rather than its potential sphere of operation with which the court took issue.

In the Australian cases of *Ngurli Ltd.* v. *McCann*,[193] *Residues Treatment and Trading Co. Ltd.* v. *Southern Resources Ltd. (No. 4)*[194] and Mahoney JA's judgment in *Winthrop Investments Ltd.* v. *Winns Ltd.*[195] there is a willingness to extend the operation of equitable intervention to shareholder resolutions authorizing or ratifying directors' actions in breach of the duty to exercise powers for proper purposes. And in the *Southern Resources* case King CJ said[196] with reference to *Peters'*[197] case and *Allen*'s case:[198] 'Those cases were concerned with alterations to the articles of

---

[185] For a more detailed discussion of *Gambotto*'s case and of compulsory acquisition generally see Ch. 10.      [186] See above nn 152-4, and accompanying text.
[187] See further Ch. 9, section 3.
[188] See above nn 177-9, and accompanying text.      [189] Above n 148.
[190] Ibid., at 671.      [191] See McPherson, above n 159, at 405.
[192] Above n 180.      [193] Above n 103.      [194] Above n 24.      [195] Above n 79.
[196] Above n 24, at 204.      [197] Above n 61.      [198] Above n 148.

association but there appears to be no reason why a similar restraint on the exercise of majority voting power should not exist in relation to other resolutions.'

This development was extended to a resolution appointing directors in *Theseus Exploration NL* v. *Mining and Associated Industries Ltd.*[199] where Hoare J relied on Evershed MR's dictum in *Greenhalgh*'s case[200] to grant an interlocutory injunction restraining the majority shareholders from electing directors of their choice when it was known to them that the directors would not act in the interests of the company generally, but in the interests only of the major shareholder.[201]

These cases have been concerned with the situation where directors in breach of fiduciary duty can be identified with the majority shareholders whose voting power will be instrumental in effectuating or perpetuating the breach. No parallel development has yet been seen in the English cases.[202] There has, however, been a willingness in both jurisdictions to extend equitable intervention to corporate quasi-partnerships.[203]

For example, in *Re Medefield Pty. Ltd.*[204] two groups agreed to form a company in which they would have an equal shareholding. The implication from the agreement was that there would be no provision for the exercise of a casting vote. Unbeknown to the parties, the articles of association of the shelf company they had purchased gave a casting vote to the chairman of directors when acting as chairman of a general meeting. H assumed the position of chairman of directors for administrative reasons at a time when neither party was aware of the right to a casting vote. On discovering it, H purported to exercise the right at an extraordinary general meeting. Needham J referred to the fact that the circumstances would justify an application to wind up the company on the just and equitable ground. In granting an interlocutory application to restrain H from exercising the casting vote[205] he said:[206] 'In reliance upon [the pre-incorporation agreement] the Field Group has entered into this incorporated partnership, and it would be I think most unjust and inequitable if the other group were permitted by a mere accident . . . to destroy entirely the incorporating

---

[199] [1973] Qd. R 81.                                    [200] Above n 108.

[201] But cf., *Abraham* v. *Tunalex Pty. Ltd.* (1987) 5 ACLC 888 where Needham J declined to restrain a major shareholder from exercising his voting power to replace the company's directors so as to terminate an action against him by the company, reaffirming the ability of a shareholder to exercise his vote in his own interests.

[202] Xuereb, above n 61, at 200 argues that there are powerful reasons for extending Lindley MR's dictum in *Allen*'s case to exercise of majority power to ratify directors' breach of duty.

[203] See generally B. A. K. Rider, 'Partnership Law and Its Impact on "Domestic Companies" ' [1979] *Cambridge LJ* 148.

[204] (1977) 2 ACLR 406; (1977–1978) ACLC ¶40–325.

[205] In the context of proceedings brought by H against F regarding ownership of formulae held by H.                                    [206] Above n 204, at 410; 29,393.

agreement and place complete control of the company in the hands of one of the groups.'

The initial attitude to such an approach in England was unfavourable. In *Bentley-Stevens* v. *Jones*[207] all the shares were held by three shareholders who were also the three directors. The two defendants purported to remove the plaintiff as a director, but the notice convening the general meeting was irregular. The plaintiff sought to rely on *Ebrahimi* v. *Westbourne Galleries Ltd.*[208] to argue that the court should restrain the two 'partners' from expelling the third. That argument was firmly refused by Plowman J who confined such application of equitable principles to petitions for winding up on the just and equitable ground. This is, however, to be contrasted with two subsequent English single judge decisions, *Clemens* v. *Clemens Brothers Ltd.*[209] and *Pennell* v. *Venida Investments.*[210]

In *Pennell's* case,[211] Templeman J granted an interlocutory injunction to restrain a breach of an 'understanding' between the shareholder factions that there would be no increase in the company's share capital without the consent of the plaintiff.

The well-known case of *Clemens* v. *Clemens Bros. Ltd.*[212] involved a resolution by the company in general meeting to allot shares partly to directors of the company and partly to set up a trust for the company's employees. The effect of the scheme on the plaintiff was that her 45 per cent shareholding would be reduced to below 25 per cent. After quoting from the various authorities regarding the exercise of majority voting power to alter the articles of association and, in particular Evershed MR's dictum in *Greenhalgh's* case,[213] Foster J continued:[214] 'If that is right, the question in the instant case which must be posed is this: did Miss Clemens, when voting for the resolutions, honestly believe that those resolutions, when passed, would be for the benefit of the plaintiff?' Foster J also placed reliance on the approach adopted in cases concerning statutory remedies for minority shareholders, referring to *Meyer* v. *Scottish Textile and Manufacturing Co. Ltd.*, *Scottish Cooperative Wholesale Society Ltd.*[215] and *Ebrahimi* v. *Westbourne Galleries Ltd.*,[216] and continued:[217]

I think that one thing which emerges from the cases to which I have referred is that in such a case as the present Miss Clemens is not entitled to exercise her majority

---

[207] [1974] 1 WLR 638.　　　　　　　　　　　[208] [1973] AC 360 (HL).
[209] [1976] 2 All ER 268.
[210] Unreported decision of Templeman J, 25 July 1974, noted by S. J. Burridge, 'Wrongful Rights Issues' (1981) 44 *Mod L Rev* 40, and 'Minority Shareholders: A Further Ray of Hope' (1981) 2 *Company Lawyer* 107.　　　　　　　　　　　　　　　　　　[211] Ibid.
[212] Above n 209.　　　[213] Above n 108 at 291.　　　[214] Above n 209 at 281.
[215] 1954 SC 381 at 392.　　[216] Above n 208 at 379.　　[217] Above n 209 at 282.

vote in whatever way she pleases. The difficulty is in finding a principle, and obviously expressions such as 'bona fide for the benefit of the company as a whole', 'fraud on a minority' and 'oppressive' do not assist in formulating a principle.

I have come to the conclusion that it would be unwise to try to produce a principle since the circumstances of each case are infinitely varied. It would not, I think, assist to say more than that in my judgment Miss Clemens is not entitled as of right to exercise her votes as an ordinary shareholder in any way she pleases. To use the phrase of Lord Wilberforce,[218] that right is 'subject . . . to equitable considerations . . . which may make it unjust . . . to exercise [it] in a particular way'.

Foster J's equation of the interests of the individual hypothetical shareholder with those of the plaintiff has been attacked on the basis that this destroys the ability of a shareholder to take account of his or her own interests and displaces majority rule.[219]

The application of *Ebrahimi* v. *Westbourne Galleries* outside the context of proceedings for a just and equitable winding up has also been criticized[220] as neglecting the distinction between the jurisdiction of shareholders to effect a particular transaction and matters merely triggering the right to discretionary relief.[221]

Further, as commentators note,[222] the authority of *Clemens'* case[223] is diminished by the failure of the court to address the contrary decision on comparable facts in *Greenhalgh's* case,[224] and by the fact that the judge was not referred to *Bentley-Stevens* v. *Jones*.[225] But despite these doubts and criticisms, many commentators have welcomed the actual decisions reached.[226]

These cases were all decided at a time when the only other alternative to seeking a winding-up order was the pre-amendment oppression provision. It is submitted that similar results to those in *Clemens'* case,[227] *Pennell's* case[228] and *Medefield's* case[229] can now be achieved by a less controversial means via the unfair prejudice provision.

---

[218] [1972] 2 All ER at 500, [1973] AC at 379.

[219] V. Joffe, 'Majority Rule Undermined?' (1977) 40 *Mod L Rev* 71 and L. S. Sealy, 'Equitable and Other Fetters on the Shareholder's Freedom to Vote' published as Ch, 10 of N. E. Eastham and B. Krivy (eds) *Cambridge Lectures 1981* (Toronto, Butterworths, 1982) and Gower, above n 61, at 603.

[220] Joffe, ibid., Burridge, above n 210. See also G. R. Sullivan, 'Protection of the Minority Shareholder—Another Advance' (1977) 41 *Convey* 169. But for an article which argues that this is a recognition by Foster J of a thread of authority sanctioning the imposition of equitable considerations on the exercise of legal rights in 'domestic' companies see Rider, above n 196.

[221] D.D. Prentice, 'Restraints on the Exercise of Majority Shareholders Power' (1976) 92 *Law Q Rev* 502. [222] See e.g., Rider, above n 203 at 152.

[223] Above n 209. [224] Above n 108. [225] Above n 207.

[226] See e.g., Sullivan, above n 210 and Prentice, above n 221.

[227] Above n 209. [228] Above n 210. [229] Above n 204.

## 5. SECTION 1324 OF THE CORPORATIONS LAW

In Australia, section 1324 of the Corporations Law gives standing to a person whose interests have been, are, or would be affected by conduct that constitutes or would constitute a breach of the Corporations Law to seek injunctive relief (both mandatory and prohibitory) and damages in the alternative or in addition.[230]

A liberal interpretation has been given to the expression 'a person whose interests have been, are or would be affected by the conduct'. Standing has been granted to a company the shares in which were the subject of a takeover offer,[231] and it has been regarded as arguable that the section gives standing to a creditor.[232] In light of this approach it is unlikely that a shareholder would not be able to satisfy this requirement.[233]

The codification of directors' duties in Australia in the Corporations Law[234] means that the section provides an alternative remedy in many situations which would fall within the scope of a derivative action, although it is not available if there is no breach of the Corporations Law (as, for example, where the company has a cause of action against a person who is not one of its directors or officers).

Commentators have regarded this remedy as having immense potential in terms of minority protection[235] by eliminating many of the procedural problems resulting from the Rule in *Foss* v. *Harbottle*. However, the section has not yet formed the basis for a statutory alternative to a derivative action. One reason for this is the uncertainty which exists as to whether the court's jurisdiction is dependent on its ability to make an order for an injunction, so that the section would not apply to completed conduct. This question was adverted to in *Biala Pty. Ltd.* v. *Mallina*

---

[230] Section 1324(10), CL (Aust).

[231] *Broken Hill Proprietary Co. Ltd.* v. *Bell Resources Ltd.* (1984) 8 ACLR 609; 2 ACLC 157.

[232] *Allen* v. *Atalay* (1993) 11 ACSR 753; 12 ACLC 7.

[233] Standing is also granted to the ASC. Although beyond the scope of this book it should be noted that under s. 50 Australian Securities Commission Act 1989 (Aust) the ASC is empowered to bring civil proceedings in the name of any person where (as a result of an investigation or examination) it believes it to be in the public interest for that person to bring civil proceedings. Further, under s. 1325(3), CL (Aust) where the ASC has instituted proceedings for an injunction to restrain a contravention of the Act, it may make an application for an order for compensation on behalf of identified consenting persons who have suffered or are likely to suffer loss by virtue of the contravention. This enables the ASC to conduct something akin to a class action.

[234] Section 232, CL (Aust).

[235] Sealy, above n 21, at 57, R. Baxt, 'Will Section 574 of the Companies Code Please Stand Up!' (1989) 7 *Company & Sec LJ* 388. But cf., the reservations of the Companies and Securities Law Review Committee, *Discussion Paper No 11: Enforcement of the Duties of Directors and Officers of a Company by Means of a Statutory Derivative Action* July 1990 at 8.

*Holdings Ltd.*[236] where relief was sought under section 1324 in the alternative to a derivative action at common law. But at the trial of the action[237] compensation was awarded at common law without exploring the statutory remedy. However, in *Permanent Trustee Australia Ltd.* v. *Perpetual Trustee Co. Ltd.*[238] Cohen J was prepared to make an award of damages under the predecessor of section 1324 despite the fact that the conduct was completed. This was on the basis that although the power to order a person to pay damages under the section was conditional on the power to grant an injunction, the terms in which the legislation was drafted[239] enabled a person to seek a mandatory injunction even though there was no prospect of a further offence or contravention of the legislation, and irrespective of whether there had been a previous offence or contravention.

There is also uncertainty as to the relationship between relief under section 1324 and at common law. In *Re Southern Resources Ltd.*,[240] as in *Biala*'s case, both grounds were pleaded, but relief again was granted purely on equitable grounds. In the *Southern Resources* case, it was on the basis that it would be inappropriate to grant relief under the predecessor of section 1324 when there was an entitlement to similar relief in equity.

Further, it is unclear whether any of the baggage of the Rule in *Foss* v. *Harbottle* is relevant in an action brought under the section. Some hope that this may be avoided is offered by the obiter suggestions that ratification should not prevent a shareholder bringing proceedings under section 1324 in respect of a breach of directors' duties,[241] and that standing may exist under section 1324 irrespective of the limitations which would apply to a common law action.[242]

However, as appears from *Premier Gold NL* v. *Ocean Resources NL*[243] the court still has a discretion whether to grant relief under the section. In that case directors had failed to convene a meeting when requisitioned by a shareholder in accordance with the companies legislation.[244] Nevertheless the court declined to grant a mandatory injunction under section 1324 on the basis that the shareholders had not demonstrated urgency or a threat to

---

[236] Above n 37. This question was also considered but left open in *Eastern Petroleum Australia Ltd.* v. *Horseshoe Lights Gold Pty. Ltd.* (1985) 9 ACLR 980; 3 ACLC 594 .

[237] *Biala Pty. Ltd.* v. *Mallina Holdings Ltd. (No. 2)* above n 54.

[238] (1994) 15 ACSR 722; 13 ACLC 66.

[239] Specifically, ss. 574(5) and (6) of the Companies Code which were the precursors of and are broadly equivalent to ss. 1324 (6) and (7), CL (Aust.)

[240] (1989) 15 ACLR 770, affd. sub nom. *Southern Resources Ltd.* v. *Residues Treatment and Trading Co. Ltd.* (1990) 56 SASR 445 (Full Ct, SA).

[241] *Scarel Pty. Ltd.* v. *City Loan and Credit Corporation Pty. Ltd.* above n 33.

[242] *Re Southern Resources Ltd.* above n 231. But cf., Ford and Austin, above n 10, para. 1729 who suggest that it would be open to a court to interpret the reference to 'interests' in s. 1324, so that a member has standing only where the member has an individual membership right to be vindicated or is relying on an exception to the Rule in *Foss* v. *Harbottle*.

[243] (1994) 15 ACSR 695; 12 ACLC 931.            [244] Section 246 CL (Aust).

the assets or interests of the company, nor any prejudice which would follow from the delay occasioned by having to make a fresh requisition.[245] This case was, however, complicated by the fact that when the company failed to act, the beneficial owner of the shares had dispatched notices convening a general meeting in the company's name, and Commissioner Heenan AC considered that to grant an injunction in these circumstances would amount to condoning that misconduct.

One case where the remedy has been of assistance to a minority shareholder is *Darvall* v. *North Sydney Brick & Tile Co. Ltd. (No. 2)*.[246] Here, the court ordered that resolutions be put to a general meeting to consider whether to authorize the plaintiff to give notice avoiding an agreement which had been entered into in contravention of section 205 of the Corporations Law.[247]

## 6. LAW REFORM PROPOSALS

### (1) United Kingdom

The Draft Fifth EC Directive on Company Law contains proposals on various aspects of the law relating to public limited companies. Particularly relevant in this context is Article 16, which would permit an action to be brought on behalf of the company against directors in breach of duty by one or more shareholders holding 10 per cent of the subscribed capital of a public company.

In light of the considerable extension to minority shareholder rights embodied in this proposal, the United Kingdom has argued in favour of limiting this right to illegal and *ultra vires* acts.[248]

### (2) Australia

In Australia, several law reform bodies have recommended the introduction of a statutory derivative action,[249] based on similar developments in

---

[245] The directors had offered an unconditional undertaking to convene a general meeting within the next few weeks.                                    [246] (1987) 16 NSWLR 212.

[247] The plaintiff had satisfied the court that there was a situation of concern as to whether the agreement should be avoided, and whether the matter should simply be left to the company's directors. However, it was not satisfied that the plaintiff was a person who could properly be regarded as representing the shareholders of the company.

[248] See *Amended Proposal for a Fifth Directive on the Harmonisation of Company Law in the European Community, A Consultative Document,* January 1990. The Directive has been the subject of prolonged consideration because of the controversial nature of its proposals relating to employee participation and board structure.

[249] See Ch. 6 section 2(10)(d), and see generally I. M. Ramsay, 'Corporate Governance, Shareholder Litigation and the Prospects for a Statutory Derivative Action' (1992) 15 *UNSW LJ* 149, and J. Kluver, 'Derivative Actions and the Rule in *Foss* v. *Harbottle*: Do we Need a Statutory Remedy?" ' (1993) 11 *Company & Sec LJ* 7.

Canada and New Zealand.[250] Such a system would enable *locus standi* to be determined in a preliminary application and would grant standing to applicants who could satisfy the court they were acting in good faith and had a *prima facie* reasonable cause of action on behalf of the company.[251]

The most recent proposal is that of the Companies and Securities Advisory Committee ('CASAC') in 1993.[252] The essential features of its proposal are:

(1) derivative actions at common law should be abolished and replaced with a statutory regime;

(2) the ASC, current members, directors and other officers[253] and persons entitled to be registered as members should be able to apply to the court for leave to bring a statutory derivative action;

(3) Fourteen days' advance notice should be given to the corporation of the applicant's intention to apply to the court and of the applicant's complaint (but provision should be made for *ex parte* hearings in cases of urgency);

(4) the court should not grant leave to bring the proceedings unless satisfied:

(i) it is probable that the corporation will not take proceedings;

(ii) the applicant is acting in good faith with a view to the best interests of the corporation;

(iii) it appears to be in the best interests of the corporation that proceedings be taken; and

(iv) there is a serious question to be tried;

(5) the court should have power to order the applicant's costs to be paid by the corporation, but with a discretion to rescind or vary any such order, and to require the applicant to meet some or all of the defendant's costs. The court should also have power to order the applicant and the company to give security for costs;

(6) the court should have power to authorize an independent body, such as the company auditor, to investigate a complaint and to report to the court for the purposes of determining the merits of a proposed action,

---

[250] *Report No 12: Enforcement of the Duties of Directors and Officers of a Company by Means of a Statutory Derivative Action* (November 1990, Australia), House of Representatives Standing Committee on Legal and Constitutional Affairs (Lavarch Committee), *Corporate Practices and the Rights of Shareholders*, 28 November 1991, Recommendation 26, para. 6.3.33 and CASAC, *Report on a Statutory Derivative Action*, July 1993.

[251] The recommended provision for derivative procedure is modelled on a similar provision in the Ontario Business Corporations Act 1982, ss. 245–8.

[252] Above n 250.

[253] As defined in s. 232(1), CL (Aust).

with absolute discretion in the court regarding orders for the costs of the investigation;

(7) ratification should not be a reason for staying or dismissing an application, but evidence of it may be taken into account where the court is satisfied that the approval has been given by fully informed independent shareholders; and

(8) actions brought or taken under the procedure should be disclosed in the company's annual report.

These proposals are complemented by proposed extensions to the court's power under section 319 of the Corporations Law to authorize inspection of a company's books.[254]

---

[254] See Ch. 9 section 8(2)(b)(v).

## 9

# *Application of Litigious Remedies to Identified Complaints*

1. Introduction                                                                                 220

2. Disregard of Rights                                                                           221
   (1) Enforcement of contractual rights                                                         221
   (2) Enforcement of statutory rights                                                           224
   (3) Enforcement of the articles                                                               225

3. Alteration of the Articles and Majority Voting                                                226
   (1) Unfair prejudice                                                                          226
   (2) Common law                                                                                227

4. Dilution of Equity Stake or Voting Rights                                                     227
   (1) Unfair prejudice                                                                          227
   (2) Common law                                                                                228
   (3) Relevance of the articles of association                                                  229

5. Self-Interested Transactions by Controllers                                                   231
   (1) Unfair prejudice                                                                          231
   (2) Common law                                                                                237
   (3) Section 1324 of the Corporations Law                                                       237

6. Negligent or Inefficient Management                                                           238
   (1) Unfair prejudice                                                                          238
   (2) Common law                                                                                239
       (a) Financial competence                                                                  240
           (i) England                                                                           240
           (ii) Australia                                                                        240
       (b) Delegation                                                                            241
   (3) Section 1324 of the Corporations Law                                                       242
   (4) United Kingdom reform proposals                                                           242

7. Little or No Participation in Profits                                                         242

8. Limited Access to Information about the Company's Affairs                                      245
   (1) General statutory rights                                                                  245

(2) Rights to information relating to disputes 246
    (a) Common law 246
    (b) Additional statutory rights in Australia 246
        (i) A special interest requirement? 247
        (ii) Good faith and proper purpose 248
        (iii) Board minutes 249
        (iv) Reform proposals 250
(3) The unfair prejudice provision 251
    (a) Australia 251
    (b) England 252

9. Illiquidity 252

10. Exclusion from Management 254
    (1) Legitimate expectation of participation in management 255
    (2) Buy-out on a breakdown of relations 256

11. Compulsory Acquisition 258

## SUMMARY

*The unfair prejudice provision now plays an important role in remedying the majority of the complaints identified in Chapter 2.*

*In most cases, it complements rather than supersedes the common law, with each remedy offering relief in some situations where the other does not assist. However, where shareholders are complaining of exclusion from management, the unfair prejudice provision is the main source of relief. The other potentially significant contribution of the unfair prejudice provision is as an alternative to a common law derivative action.*

*In the latter context, the unfair prejudice remedy eliminates many of the difficulties associated with standing and the effect of ratification. On the other hand, a common law derivative action may be preferred where standing can be established, since it avoids the far-reaching inquiry involved in establishing unfair prejudice.*

*There is also some uncertainty as to whether the unfair prejudice remedy as presently drafted can fully replace the derivative action. Australian courts have shown a willingness to interpret the unfair prejudice provision in a way which could supersede the derivative action. An expansive interpretation of the United Kingdom provision is encouraged by the recent amendment clarifying that the section extends to conduct which affects the members generally. However, the United Kingdom provision is still limited by the requirement that the petitioner be one of the members affected.*

## 1. INTRODUCTION

It can been seen from Chapter 8, that there are various deficiencies in the relief available to a minority shareholder at common law. The dividing line between those situations where standing is accorded to an individual shareholder to bring an action on his or her own behalf and those where it is not is, to say the least, difficult to predict. As regards derivative actions, the ability of the shareholders to release directors from breaches of duty may operate to preclude a shareholder suing on the company's behalf in respect of some breaches; in any event there may be little financial incentive for a shareholder to bring such an action since the company receives the benefit of it. Further, the remedies available at common law are directed towards making good a particular wrong. They focus on a single act or transaction, rather than on a course of conduct over a period of time. Moreover, the common law does not enable a shareholder to complain where he or she suffers a wrong in a capacity other than as a shareholder. Finally, considerable uncertainty surrounds the potential for relief where the company's constitutional documents, which will frequently be either a standard form word-processed document or drafted for a shelf company, do not accurately reflect the understanding on which the company was formed or carried on. Proceeding instead under the unfair prejudice provision removes most of these obstacles.

An unfair prejudice petition is not confined to the situation where there is no other remedy available.[1] On the contrary, it has been held that the existence of an unfair prejudice petition should be taken into account by the court in deciding whether to exercise its jurisdiction to order a company meeting to be held.[2]

This chapter considers the extent to which the unfair prejudice remedy and (to the extent that they still have a role to play) the common law and any other specific statutory rights can overcome the commonly expressed grievances of minority shareholders identified in Chapter 2. Further, by examining the application of the unfair prejudice remedy to specific situations, more precise content is given to the 'legitimate expectations' test.

The winding-up remedy is not specifically referred to in the following discussion. As described in Chapter 7, there has been a virtual assimilation between the grounds justifying relief under the winding-up remedy and those applied in respect of the unfair prejudice remedy. As a consequence,

---

[1] *Re a Company (No. 005287 of 1985)* [1986] 1 WLR 281, *Re Macro (Ipswich) Ltd.* [1994] 2 BCLC 354; [1994] BCC 781.
[2] *Harman* v. *BML Group Ltd.* [1994] 1 WLR 893.

the winding-up remedy will have very little operation unless it is genuinely the remedy sought (as, for example, in cases where the company is no longer trading or the purpose for which it was formed has come to an end), or the petitioner's conduct is such that the respondent's conduct is not considered unfair.

## 2. DISREGARD OF RIGHTS

### (1) Enforcement of contractual rights

If a contract is breached, contract law provides a range of remedies. The conduct may also potentially satisfy the requirements for an action under the unfair prejudice provision,[3] and the question therefore arises whether a petitioner can enforce contractual rights under that provision. The limitations discussed in Chapter 6,[4] that the petitioner must be suing *'qua member'* and that the conduct complained of must be conduct in the affairs of the company or proposed conduct by or on behalf of the company will clearly restrict the circumstances in which relief under the unfair prejudice provision will be available in a contractual dispute. However, assuming that the conduct satisfies these tests, an authority which would suggest that a petitioner could obtain relief under the unfair prejudice provision in respect of a breach of contract is a case which concerned a petition for winding-up on the just and equitable ground (decided before the unfair prejudice provision provided a viable alternative), *Re A. & B.C. Chewing Gum Ltd.*[5] Here, repudiation of a shareholders' agreement prescribing consent levels for certain policy and management decisions formed the basis of the making of a winding-up order.[6]

That decision must, however, be contrasted with the comments of Vinelott J in *Re Kenyon Swansea Ltd.*[7] In the latter case, the company and the two shareholders (K and M) entered into an agreement giving the company and M options to acquire K's shares at a certain date for a certain sum.[8] K later became dissatisfied with the terms of the agreement and unwilling to transfer his shares. Nevertheless the company purported to exercise the option. K then proposed that one of these shares be transferred to his wife, and that the pre-emption provisions be removed from the articles, and eventually requisitioned a general meeting to consider these proposals. K was in a position to secure the passing of the

---

[3] But cf., *Re Tottenham Hotspur plc* [1994] 1 BCLC 655.
[4] Ch. 6 sections 2(3) and 2(4).            [5] [1975] 1 WLR 579.
[6] Cf., the criticism of this case by J. Womack [1975] *Cambridge LJ* 209 and see Ch. 7 section 3(2)(a).        [7] [1987] BCLC 514; (1987) 3 BCC 259.
[8] £350,000 (which was later increased by agreement to £360,000 to be paid by instalments).

proposed resolutions. Before the meeting to consider K's proposals was held, M presented an unfair prejudice petition alleging that passing the resolutions would be unfairly prejudicial since M reasonably expected to acquire control of the company and had acted in reliance on that assumption. Vinelott J observed[9] that the difficulty faced by the petition was that on the one hand an unfair prejudice petition was not an appropriate proceeding to enforce an alleged contract, and on the other hand, the court could not make an order for the purchase of K's shares by M or the company as sought in the petition so long as a claim by the company to be entitled to enforce an agreement for the purchase of certain of those shares was asserted. Although remarking that the contractual claim in any event faced formidable difficulties,[10] Vinelott J was not prepared to brush it aside entirely, and therefore indicated that if M wished to assert a contractual right on behalf of the company to purchase any of K's shares, the petition would have to be stayed until appropriate proceedings had been commenced and the issue determined. Counsel then elected to abandon that claim.

In Australia, the only judicial pronouncement on the question is an obiter dictum of Cosgrove J in *Re Richard Pitt & Sons Pty. Ltd.*[11] that departure from the terms of a contract might form the basis for a petition under the old Australian oppression provision.[12]

Various academic views have been expressed on this question. Referring to *Johnston v. West Fraser Timber Co. Ltd.*,[13] (where the conduct was held not to have involved conduct of the affairs of the company)[14] Austin[15] argues that in such a case the court should, in the exercise of its discretion, decline to interfere with the normal contractual consequences unless intervention was very clearly justified.

Prentice[16] regards the critical factor to be whether the agreement is unanimous. If it is, then he argues that a failure to implement it should not be seen purely as a breach of contract between shareholders but rather as affecting the way in which the affairs of the company are to be conducted and as having constitutional implications.

---

[9] Above n 7 at 519–20; 263–4.

[10] Because of the ambiguity of the terms of the contract, and because it was in breach of various statutory provisions.

[11] (1979) 4 ACLR 459 at 481–2 (Full Ct, Tas).

[12] Equally equivocal is the only New Zealand dictum on this topic in *Re The Great Outdoors Co. Ltd.* (1984) 2 NZCLC 99,260.

[13] (1981) 29 BCLC 379, revsd. (1982) 37 BCLR 360 (CA BC).

[14] See Ch. 6 section 2(3).

[15] R. P. Austin, 'Companies and Securities Legislation—The 1983 Bill' Notes of a Seminar held by the Committee for Postgraduate Studies in the Department of Law, University of Sydney on 7 December 1983.

[16] D. Prentice, 'The Closely-held Company and Minority Oppression' (1983) 3 *Oxford J Legal Stud* 417 at 420.

Shapira[17] concedes the advantage to the court in being able to take an overall view and prescribe an appropriate remedy in cases where a contractual dispute is tied in with other intra-corporate disputes. He also acknowledges the particular advantage to the petitioner in being potentially able to obtain the remedy of a purchase order under the unfair prejudice provision which is not available in other actions. Nevertheless, he considers that the unfair prejudice jurisdiction should not be extended to claims based essentially in contract or tort. He suggests a broad test of whether the particular capacity in which the member has been prejudiced was, in part or in whole, the reason for his subscribing to, or remaining a member of the company. Applying this test to the hypothetical example of a petitioner who has entered into a franchise agreement with the company, he would allow the enforcement of the contract by means of the unfair prejudice remedy where the agreement was the petitioner's prime reason for investing in the company.

A common thread in the arguments of all three commentators (and one with which the writer agrees) is that it is preferable for purely contractual claims to be pursued by means of an ordinary contractual action. However, where, as is often the case, the contractual dispute is interrelated with other intra-corporate disputes then, as Shapira observes, there is an advantage in the court being able to take an overall view. Although breach of a unanimous agreement will usually be a symptom rather than the cause of intra-corporate problems (as was the case in *Re A. & B. C. Chewing Gum Ltd.*)[18] and therefore a case where relief under the unfair prejudice provision may be appropriate, recourse to the unfair prejudice provision should not be confined to this situation.[19] Conversely, a test based on the reason for becoming a member of the company would not necessarily exclude cases such as *Re J. E. Cade & Son Ltd.*[20] from the ambit of the unfair prejudice jurisdiction.[21] In that case, relief was refused under the unfair prejudice provision because the petitioner was pursuing his interests as a freeholder of a farm rather than his interests as a member, which interests were in fact in opposition.[22] The *qua* member requirement (which appears still to have some operation in Australia, contrary to the clear wording of the section)[23] and the requirement that the conduct complained of be conduct in the affairs of the company will exclude many contractual claims from the ambit of the section. Further, the test for unfair prejudice

---

[17] G. Shapira, 'Minority Shareholders' Protection—Recent Developments' (1982) 10 *NZUL Rev* 134 at 154–6. See also G. Shapira, 'Statutory Protection of Minority Shareholders: Towards the "Squeeze Out"?' in J. H. Farrar, (ed.) *Contemporary Issues in Company Law* (Auckland, CCH (NZ) 1987) 205 at 214–5.   [18] Above n 5.
[19] Cf., Prentice, above n 16.   [20] [1992] BCLC 213; [1991] BCC 360.
[21] Cf., Shapira, above n 17.   [22] See Ch. 6 section 2(4).
[23] Ibid.

itself will limit the opportunity to seek relief under the provision. Since the test looks at the effect of the conduct on the petitioner in the wider context of the way in which the company is conducted, it may be that a breach of contract is held not to be unfair. On the other hand, if a breach of contract does amount to unfairly prejudicial conduct in the affairs of the company, the petitioner should have access to the wider range of remedies offered by the section.

### (2) Enforcement of statutory rights

There is a clear potential for overlap between the unfair prejudice remedy and other specific rights contained in the companies legislation.[24] The range of remedies available under these specific provisions is, however, much more limited than that available under the unfair prejudice remedy. For example in the case of resolutions altering class rights or the objects of the company, the specific remedy merely cancels the resolution. Where the conduct complained of is symptomatic of unfairly prejudicial conduct, there is, in the writer's view, no reason to confine the complainant to the specific procedures.[25] Support for this approach[26] can be found in *Re M. Dalley & Co. Pty. Ltd.*[27] where Lush J considered that the conduct of the respondents was oppressive despite the fact that the petitioner could have brought the dispute to a head soon after it developed by proceedings to rectify the register, since there was nothing to justify the stand taken by the respondents which was dictated by their self-interest and obdurately maintained.[28]

A rather more complicated question is posed by Austin,[29] namely whether relief should be available under the unfair prejudice provision to plug an alleged gap in more specific legislation. The example which Austin gives is of a purchase by a shareholder in X Ltd. of shares in Y Ltd., from X Ltd. when X Ltd. is in possession of price-sensitive information about Y Ltd., but in circumstances where there is no breach of the insider trading legislation. He suggests that, at least where the section in question creates a criminal offence, the unfair prejudice provision should not be used to

---

[24] E.g., s. 5, CA 1985 (UK) enables a member to apply to the court for a cancellation of a change of objects and special procedures exist to challenge a resolution varying class rights: s. 127, CA 1985 (UK), ss. 197–9, CL (Aust). A shareholder can also bring proceedings to rectify the register: s. 359, CA 1985 (UK), s. 212, CL (Aust).

[25] In Australia, the position regarding a resolution or proposed resolution is clarified by s. 260(1)(a)(ii) which expressly contemplates an unfair prejudice action being brought in this situation. [26] See also Austin, above n 15, at 109.

[27] (1968) 1 ACLR 489 at 494.

[28] See also *ASC* v. *Multiple Sclerosis Society of Tasmania* (1993) 10 ACSR 489; 11 ACLC 461 and *Re Bagot Well Pastoral Co. Pty Ltd*; *Shannon* v. *Reid* (1992) 9 ACSR 129; 11 ACLC 1; affd sub nom (1993) 61 SASR 165 (Full Ct, SA).

[29] Austin, above n 15, at 115.

plug up alleged gaps in the law. With respect, it is submitted that a preferable approach to such an overlap is that adopted by Millett J in *Re Charnley Davies Ltd. (No. 2)*,[30] namely to acknowledge that although the same conduct may potentially found various claims for relief, the appropriate relief will be indicated by the gist of the complaint. Although the purpose of insider trading legislation is far from non-controversial, a desire to maintain confidence in the market is at the least a major rationale of that legislation. On the other hand, the purpose of the unfair prejudice provision is to grant relief where the controllers' conduct unfairly prejudices a member or members. If a shareholder is able to demonstrate that the conduct was unfairly prejudicial, then whether or not the conduct is proscribed by statute should not determine the availability of relief.

### (3) Enforcement of the articles

The difficulty in predicting whether a particular article will be enforceable by personal action at common law is discussed in Chapters 4 and 8.[31] A shareholder seeking to bring an action of this kind faces the possibility that the right will be interpreted as being enjoyed otherwise than as a member, or that its non-observance will be regarded as a wrong to the company rather than to the shareholder. These obstacles are avoided under the unfair prejudice provision.

However, even under the latter remedy the court will not grant relief against all departures from procedural requirements. Many instances have been held to be trivial and hence incapable of amounting to unfair prejudice.[32] But at least the circumstances where the court is prepared to intervene are more readily identifiable under the unfair prejudice remedy. Where irregularities are persistent and prevent the shareholders participating in meetings, this has been held to be unfairly prejudicial.[33] The other

---

[30] [1990] BCLC 760 at 784; [1990] BCC 605 at 624.

[31] Ch. 4 section 2(1)(a) and Ch. 8 section 2(5).

[32] E.g.: filing accounts late and laying them late before the company in general meeting: *Re a Company (No. 005685 of 1988); Ex parte Schwarcz (No. 2)* [1989] BCLC 427, also reported as *Re Ringtower Holdings plc (No. 2)* (1989) 5 BCC 82, fixing directors' bonuses in an unconstitutional manner: *Morgan v. 45 Flers Avenue Pty. Ltd.* (1986) 10 ACLR 692; 5 ACLC 222, irregular maintenance of records: *J & E Holdings Pty. Ltd. v. Bourke* (1994) 13 ACSR 83 and refusing to allow access to the register of members: *ASC v. Multiple Sclerosis Society of Tasmania* above n 28.

[33] *Re H. R. Harmer Ltd.* [1959] 1 WLR 62 (CA), *John J. Starr (Real Estate) Pty. Ltd. v. Robert R. Andrew (A'Asia) Pty. Ltd.* (1991) 6 ACSR 63; 9 ACLC 1372, *Re a Company (No. 00789 of 1987); Ex parte Shooter* [1990] BCLC 384, also reported as *Re a Company (No. 00789 of 1987) (Nuneaton Borough AFC Ltd.)* (1989) 5 BCC 792. This last case was decided before the amendment to the UK legislation which makes it clear that conduct which affects all members equally may amount to unfairly prejudicial conduct, with the result that the complaints relating as to the failure to hold AGMs were held not to justify relief under the section. However, Harman J did consider that the facts would otherwise have founded an

major advantage of the unfair prejudice remedy is that it is not restricted to complaints of irregularity or invasion of legal rights[34] but can also be relied on in cases of departure from the parties' legitimate expectations. It may, however, be preferable to seek to enforce personal rights at common law where it is sought to narrow the focus of the court's enquiry.[35]

## 3. ALTERATION OF THE ARTICLES AND MAJORITY VOTING

### (1) Unfair prejudice

The unfair prejudice remedy provides alternative relief in respect of alterations to the memorandum and articles. An example of the overlap between the two remedies is provided by *Shears* v. *Phosphate Co-operative of Australia Ltd.*[36] The plaintiff in that case was held to be entitled to relief in the form of a declaration that a resolution altering the articles of association was void, both at common law because the person responsible for introducing the alteration could not reasonably have thought that it was for the benefit of the company as a whole,[37] and under the unfair prejudice provision because it constituted a considerable burden on the petitioner by diluting his voting power relative to those opposed to him.

However, the different emphasis of the unfair prejudice provision means that relief would potentially be available in a wider range of cases. For example, *Greenhalgh* v. *Arderne Cinemas Ltd.*[38] may be decided differently if the case were to be brought again today under the unfair prejudice provision, especially since this particular case was not an isolated one, but rather the seventh in a row![39] Further, court intervention under the unfair

---

unfair prejudice petition, and in the result relief was granted; the holding of the extraordinary meetings were held to be unfairly prejudicial to the petitioner since he paid the company a substantial sum for shares which did not exist.

[34] *Thomas* v. *H. W. Thomas Ltd.* [1984] 1 NZLR 686 at 693 (CA NZ) *per* Richardson J, *Wayde* v. *New South Wales Rugby League Ltd.* (1985) 10 ACLR 87; 3 ACLC 799 (HC), *Re a Company (No. 008699 of 1985)* [1986] BCLC 382 at 387–8; (1986) 2 BCC 99,024 at 99,029 and *Ashburton Veterinary Club Incorporated* v. *South Island Dairy Association Ltd.* (1991) 5 NZCLC 67,296.

[35] H. A. J. Ford and R. P. Austin, *Ford's Principles of Corporations Law* (6th edn., Sydney, Butterworths, 1992) para. 1726.

[36] (1988) 14 ACLR 747; 7 ACLC 812 (Full Ct, Vic).

[37] Note that the Australian High Court has subsequently held that the '*bona fide* for the benefit of the company' test is inappropriate in this context: *Gambotto* v. *WCP Ltd.* (1995) 16 ACSR 1; 13 ACLC 342 (HC.) See further, Ch. 8 section 4(3) and below, section 3(2).

[38] [1951] Ch. 286 (CA). See text following n 171 in Ch. 8.

[39] L. C. B. Gower, *Gower's Principles of Modern Company Law* (4th edn., London, Stevens & Sons, 1979) at 624–6.

prejudice remedy is on the basis that there has been a departure from the parties' legitimate expectations in light of the history and structure of the company. This remedy may therefore be of greater assistance than the common law to a minority shareholder seeking to challenge an alteration to the articles of association where he or she has a stake in the company other than merely as a passive investor.

In addition, the unfair prejudice provision provides a less controversial remedy where it is sought to challenge a shareholder resolution in a situation which does not fall within the categories where standing is clearly recognized. For example, on similar facts to those in *Pennell* v. *Venida Investments Ltd.*[40] and *Clemens* v. *Clemens Bros Ltd.*,[41] where proposed allotments of shares were challenged at common law on the ground that they would constitute a breach of the understanding between the shareholders, a shareholder could instead bring an action under the unfair prejudice provision in respect of a departure from the parties' legitimate expectations.

### (2) Common law

In *Gambotto* v. *WCP Ltd.*,[42] a proposed alteration to the articles to permit the expropriation of the minority shareholdings was successfully challenged at common law. The common law therefore clearly continues to provide a valuable minority shareholder remedy in this context in Australia. In England, the unfair prejudice provision has substantially supplanted the common law personal action[43] and it is likely that an action challenging such an alteration would now be brought under that provision.

## 4. DILUTION OF EQUITY STAKE OR VOTING RIGHTS

### (1) Unfair prejudice

Relief has been granted in respect of allotments of shares made to dilute a minority shareholder's stake under the unfair prejudice provision in numerous cases.[44] The great advantage of proceeding under the unfair

---

[40] Unreported decision of Templeman J, 25 July 1974 (England).
[41] [1976] 2 All ER 268.
[42] Above n 37. The facts and result of this case are discussed in Ch. 8 section 4(3), Ch. 10 section 5(3).
[43] See L. C. B. Gower, *Principles of Modern Company Law* (5th edn., London, Sweet & Maxwell, 1992) at 603.
[44] See *Re Dalkeith Investments Pty. Ltd.* (1984) 9 ACLR 247; 3 ACLC 74, *Re a Company (No. 005134 of 1986); Ex parte Harries* [1989] BCLC 383, also reported as *Re D. R. Chemicals Ltd.* (1989) 5 BCC 39, *Coombs* v. *Dynasty Pty. Ltd.* (1994) 14 ACSR 60; digested (1994) 12

prejudice provision is that ratification does not preclude the proceedings being brought, and may in fact compound the unfair prejudice.[45] In *Re a Company (No. 005136 of 1986)*[46] it was necessary to consider whether the basis for the complaint was that the directors had exercised their powers for an improper purpose or whether the petitioner was seeking to assert a personal right because he was seeking indemnification from the company in respect of his costs. Hoffmann J held that the substance of the complaint before him was an improper (and unfairly prejudicial) infringement of the petitioner's personal rights, rather than the wrong to the company, and that an indemnity was not appropriate.

### (2) Common law

In a number of Australian cases decided since the unfair prejudice provision became a workable remedy, shareholders have nevertheless continued to challenge allotments of shares at common law on the ground that they were not made for proper purposes.[47] That shareholders persist in bringing actions at common law in respect of this complaint is not so surprising in light of the growing support for the proposition that shareholders have standing to bring a personal action to challenge an allotment of shares made for an improper purpose,[48] and that ratification should not deprive a shareholder of standing to bring such an action.[49] Where the only relief sought is the setting aside of the allotment, it may be easier to prove improper purpose than to undertake the more wide ranging

---

ACLC 915 and *Wallington v. Kokotovich Constructions Pty. Ltd.* (1993) 11 ACSR 759; 11 ACLC 1207. This approach has also been applied to *pari passu* rights issues where their effect is to reduce the other shareholder's stake: *Re a Company (No. 007623 of 1984)* [1986] BCLC 362; (1986) 2 BCC 99,191, and *Re a Company (No. 002612 of 1984)* (1985) 2 BCC 99,453, affd. (1986) 2 BCC 99,495 and sub nom. *Re Cumana Ltd.* [1986] BCLC 430 (CA). See further, B. Hannigan, 'Section 459 of the Companies Act 1985—A Code of Conduct for the Corporate Quasi-Partnership' (1988) *Lloyd's Mar & Com LQ* 60 at 71–4.

[45] This was found to have occurred in *Jenkins v. Enterprise Gold Mines NL* (1992) 6 ACSR 539; 10 ACLC 136 (Full Ct, WA).

[46] [1987] BCLC 82, also reported as *Re Sherborne Park Residents Co. Ltd.* (1986) 2 BCC 99,528.

[47] See e.g., *Whitehouse v. Carlton Hotel Pty. Ltd.* (1987) 162 CLR 285 (HC), *Eromanga Hydrocarbons NL v. Australis Mining NL & Ors* (1988) 14 ACLR 486, *McGuire v. Ralph McKay Ltd. & Ors* (1987) 12 ACLR 107 (Full Ct, Vic), *T. C. Newman (Qld) Pty. Ltd. v. D. H. A. Rural (Qld) Pty. Ltd.* [1988] 1 Qd R 308, *Bailey v. Mandala Private Hospital Pty. Ltd.* (1987) 12 ACLR 641; 6 ACLC 43, *Doncon v. Doncon & Ors* (1990) 2 ACSR 385; 8 ACLC 860, *Lorenzi v. Lorenzi Holdings Pty. Ltd.* (1993) 12 ACSR 398.

[48] *Re a Company (No. 005136 of 1986)* above n 46 and *Eromanga Hydrocarbons NL v. Australis Mining NL* ibid. See also *Nash v. Lancegaye Safety Glass (Ireland) Ltd.* (1958) 92 Ir LTR 11 and *Howard Smith Ltd. v. Ampol Petroleum Ltd.* [1974] AC 821 (PC).

[49] *Residues Treatment and Trading Co. Ltd. v. Southern Resources Ltd. (No. 4)* (1988) 51 SASR 196 (Full Ct, SA), *Colarc Pty. Ltd. v. Donarc Pty. Ltd.* (1991) 4 ACSR 155. See Ch. 8 section 4(2)(c).

task of demonstrating unfairly prejudicial conduct.[50] However, in many of those cases relief under the unfair prejudice provision was sought in the alternative. Failure to take this precaution may have deprived the plaintiff of relief in *Doncon* v. *Doncon*.[51] The company here was a family farming company. The parents and their son G all held life governing shares in the company. There were also ordinary shares which were held either by G or by the trustee of G's family trust. Subsequently, G died and his wife inherited his ordinary shares. The parents intended to issue a further life governing share (in all probability to their other son K) to take away from the plaintiff as the holder of the ordinary shares the control of the company she would otherwise have on their death. One ground for the plaintiff's action was that the allotment constituted a breach by the directors of their fiduciary duties. However, Pidgeon J interpreted the general meeting as having specifically requested the allotment to be made. His Honour considered that since the directors were acting pursuant to that request they were acting within the constitution of the company so that there could not be any abuse of the exercise of a fiduciary power.

Pidgeon J's decision that shareholders are able to ratify or prospectively to authorize directors' breaches of duty where the shareholders are motivated by the same purpose as the directors is out of line with other recent cases concerning ratification of allotments made for an improper purpose.[52] But arguably this is just the type of situation where the unfair prejudice remedy has advantages over a common law action, since under the unfair prejudice remedy, whether the oppressors act in their capacity as directors or majority shareholders is irrelevant.[53]

### (3) Relevance of the articles of association

The articles will be relevant in determining the purposes for which an allotment may properly be made for the purposes of a common law action challenging an allotment of shares. They will also be relevant to an unfair prejudice action, unless a contrary legitimate expectation can be established.

In *J. D. Hannes* v. *M. J. H. Pty. Ltd.*[54] the respondent argued that the

---

[50] See e.g., *Bailey* v. *Mandala Private Hospital Pty. Ltd.* above n 47 and *Re Southern Resources Ltd.* (1989) 15 ACLR 770, affd. sub nom. *Southern Resources* v. *Residues Treatment and Trading Co. Ltd.* (1990) 56 SASR 455 (Full Ct, SA).

[51] Above n 47.

[52] See *Ngurli Ltd.* v. *McCann* (1953) 90 CLR 425 (HC), *Winthrop Investments Ltd.* v. *Winns Ltd.* [1975] 2 NSWLR 666 (CA, NSW), and L. S. Sealy, ' "Bona Fides" and "Proper Purposes" in Corporate Decisions' (1989) 15 *Monash UL Rev* 265, especially at 272–3. See also Ch. 8 section 4(2)(c)(ii).

[53] See e.g., *Re Dalkeith Investments Pty. Ltd.* above n 44 where it was held that the phrase 'the affairs of the company' extends the ambit of the provision to a resolution of a general meeting.                                            [54] (1992) 7 ACSR 8; 10 ACLC 400 (CA, NSW).

conferral upon him as governing director of wide authority to exercise powers which might otherwise be vested on the board freed him from the restraints otherwise imposed on directors or shareholders in the exercise of their powers. Although accepting that the articles might be framed to authorize, expressly or impliedly, the exercise of the power of allotment of unissued shares for what would otherwise be a vitiating purpose, the New South Wales Court of Appeal held that the articles had not changed the nature of this power on the facts. The respondent's conduct in alloting shares in the company to another company in which he and his wife were the only shareholders and procuring the company to execute a service agreement which provided for him to be paid a large salary and to receive other benefits were held to amount to a breach of fiduciary duty which was not capable of ratification by a majority of shareholders and also entitled the court to make orders under the unfair prejudice provision.

An argument that the power of allotment had been freed from restraints was, however, successful in *Buche* v. *Box Pty. Ltd.*[55] Two companies had been formed, 'Pastoral' which owned the family farming property, and a holding company, 'Box' which held the entire beneficial shareholding in Pastoral. The articles of Box placed the voting rights and dividend entitlements of the shares allotted to the founder's children entirely in the discretion of the directors and gave the governing director all the powers of the board. The petitioner was one of the founder's children. Relations between the petitioner and her father had deteriorated because he wished to leave control and ownership of the property to his sons. Her action was based in part on allotments of shares which diluted her shareholding in Box.[56] Brownie J distinguished the company from an ordinary commercial enterprise where such allotments might well justify relief, on the basis that the formation of the company as a device to avoid death and estate duties and minimize income tax modified the fiduciary duty which would normally be owed. Here, the plaintiff conceded that an allotment of shares to one of her siblings would be appropriate in some extraordinary event, such as if he or she became paraplegic, but said that otherwise allotments should only be made to the children on equal terms. In light of:

(1) the plaintiff's concession;
(2) the fact that the shares had initially been allotted unequally, and
(3) the fact that the dilution of the plaintiff's shareholding had little real

---

[55] (1993) 31 NSWLR 368.
[56] Another aspect of the action concerned changes to the capital structure of Pastoral which reduced Box's interest from 100% beneficial ownership to the position of a minority shareholder with effective control of the company residing with the founder's sons. These allotments were set aside.

meaning, since her only rights were to attend meetings, but not to vote, and to receive whatever dividends the governing director or the directors chose to have the company pay to her,

his Honour held that the allotments did not amount to a breach of fiduciary duty or justify relief under the statutory remedies.

Similarly, in *Re Bagot Well Pastoral Co. Pty. Ltd.*[57] it was held that the ability of the holder of the Life Governor's Share to request the allotment of unissued shares was a special right conferred by the articles on a particular privileged shareholder and was not affected by the fiduciary restraints applicable to persons acting as directors of a company.

## 5. SELF-INTERESTED TRANSACTIONS BY CONTROLLERS

### (1) Unfair prejudice

The technicalities of establishing standing which are confronted by shareholders bringing a derivative action are eradicated under the unfair prejudice remedy. It is enough that the petitioner is a shareholder at the time that the suit is brought.[58] It is not necessary for a member to show a lack of probity or want of good faith towards him or her on the part of those in control of the company.[59] There is no absolute requirement that the petitioner come to court with clean hands.[60] Further, the possibility of advance release or subsequent ratification of breaches of directors' duties which poses a major obstacle to the bringing of a derivative action at common law is of considerably reduced significance, since such release or ratification does not alter the focus of the court's enquiry, namely whether the conduct is unfairly prejudicial to the petitioner. Indeed, ratification may be found to exacerbate the unfairly prejudicial conduct.[61]

Relief has been granted under the unfair prejudice provision in cases of diversion of corporate opportunity,[62] in various instances where controllers

---

[57]  *Shannon* v. *Reid* (1992) 9 ACSR 129; 11 ACLC 1, affd. (1993) 61 SASR 165 (Full Ct, SA).

[58]  Standing also extends to a person who is not a member, but to whom shares have been transferred or transmitted by operation of law: s. 459(2), CA 1985 (UK), s. 260(5), CL (Aust). See further, Ch. 6 section 2(1)(a).

[59]  *Thomas* v. *H. W. Thomas Ltd.* above n 34, at 693, *Wayde* v. *New South Wales Rugby League Ltd.* above n 34, at 94; 805 *per* Brennan J, *Re Bovey Hotel Ventures Ltd.* (31 July 1981, unreported decision of Slade J) approved in *Re R. A. Noble & Sons (Clothing) Ltd.* [1983] BCLC 273 at 290–1 and in *Re Sam Weller & Sons Ltd.* [1990] Ch. 682 at 690, *Re a Company (No. 005134 of 1986); Ex parte Harries* above n 44.

[60]  See Ch. 6 2(9)(a). Cf., the position at common law: *Nurcombe* v. *Nurcombe* [1985] 1 WLR 370 (CA).          [61]  See *Jenkins* v. *Enterprise Gold Mines NL* above n 45.

[62]  *Scottish Co-operative Wholesale Society Ltd.* v. *Meyer* [1959] AC 324 (HL), *Re Bright Pine Mills Pty. Ltd.* [1969] VR 1002 (Full Ct, Vic), *Sanford* v. *Sanford Courier Service Pty. Ltd.* (1986) 10 ACLR 549; 5 ACLC 394 and *Re London School of Electronics Ltd.* [1986] Ch 211.

have made secret profits,[63] misapplied company assets,[64] awarded themselves excessive remuneration,[65] exercised their powers for an improper purpose,[66] sought to procure the company to abandon legal proceedings against them,[67] or to frustrate a takeover offer.[68] It has also been accepted that a decision by directors to continue to trade when a company was failing to make a profit could, if influenced by a desire to remain in office, constitute grounds for relief under the unfair prejudice provision.[69] In many of these cases, an express parallel has been drawn between the principles developed in the cases dealing with the obligations of directors and majority shareholders in determining whether conduct is unfairly prejudicial.[70]

However, as discussed in the context of enforcement of personal rights via the unfair prejudice provision, there is a distinction in the basis for intervention. The emphasis of the enquiry under the unfair prejudice provision is on the impact of the decision on the member, as judged by a reasonable bystander.[71] This is an objective test and is to be contrasted with the courts' approach to setting aside company decisions on the basis of breach of directors' duties where the test focuses on the whether the director has acted *bona fide* in the best interests of the company as a whole

[63] *Re a Company (No. 005287 of 1985)* above n 1, *Re Associated Tool Industries Ltd.* (1963) 5 FLR 55, *Re East West Promotions Pty. Ltd.; Cheetham* v. *McCoy* (1986) 10 ACLR 222; 4 ACLC 84, and *Coombs* v. *Dynasty Pty. Ltd.* above n 44.

[64] *Re Elgindata Ltd.* [1991] BCLC 959.

[65] *Re Cumana Ltd.* above n 44, *Tullamore Holdings Ltd.* v. *The Selby Shoe Company Ltd.* (1986) 3 NZCLC 99,759, *Sanford* v. *Sanford Courier Service Pty. Ltd.*, above n 62, *Roberts* v. *Walter Developments Pty. Ltd.* (1992) 10 ACLC 804, and *J. D. Hannes* v. *M. J. H. Pty. Ltd.* above n 54 (in combination with an allotment for an improper purpose). But cf., *Parker* v. *National Roads and Motorists' Association* (1989) 1 ACSR 227, affd. (1993) 11 ACSR 370; 11 ACLC 866 (CA NSW) and *Smith* v. *Croft* [1986] 1 WLR 580.

[66] *Re Cumana*, above n 44, *Re a Company (No. 00370 of 1987); Ex parte Glossop* [1988] 1 WLR 1068, and *Re Bagot Well Pastoral Co. Pty. Ltd.* above n 28 at 224.

[67] *Whyte, Petitioner* 1984 SLT 330.

[68] *Re a Company (No. 008699 of 1985)* above n 34. In this case the directors' recommendation to shareholders to accept the lower of two offers for the shares of the company without revealing that they were the promoters of the company making the lower bid was held to have impaired the chances of the minority shareholders to sell their shares to the highest bidder.

[69] *Re a Company; Ex parte Burr* [1992] BCLC 724, also reported as *Re Saul D. Harrison & Sons plc* [1994] BCC 475, affd. sub nom. *Burr* v. *Harrison; Re Saul D. Harrison & Sons plc* [1994] BCC 475 (CA). However, the petition was struck out on the facts.

[70] *Re Broadcasting Station 2GB Pty. Ltd.* [1964–5] NSWR 1648 at 1662, a case decided under the old oppression remedy. See also *J. D. Hannes* v. *M. J. H. Pty. Ltd.* above n 54, *Re a Company (No. 002612 of 1984)* (1984) 1 BCC 99,262 and *Re a Company (No. 00370 of 1987); Ex parte Glossop* above n 66.

[71] *Re Bovey Hotel Ventures Ltd.* (31 July 1981, unreported decision of Slade J) approved in *Re R. A. Noble & Sons (Clothing) Ltd.* above n 59, at 290–1 and in *Re Sam Weller & Sons Ltd.* above n 59, at 690.

and for proper purposes.[72] The '*bona fide* for the benefit of the company' test is also applied to impugned shareholder resolutions, although in the latter context the test is frequently acknowledged to be inappropriate. In both contexts, and particularly in respect of shareholder resolutions, the test may be applied negatively (and consequently more objectively) by asking whether any reasonable person could regard the resolution as for the company's benefit.[73] Nevertheless, the emphasis is still on the intention of the oppressor rather than on the effect on the minority.

The different focus of the court's inquiry under the unfair prejudice provision means that a petitioner may be able to establish unfairly prejudicial conduct in respect of self-interested transactions by controllers which fall short of breach of fiduciary duty or would not otherwise ground an action at common law. As Brennan J observed in *Wayde* v. *New South Wales Rugby League Ltd.*,[74] the operation of the unfair prejudice provision may be attracted to a decision made by directors which is made in good faith and for a purpose within the power but which reasonable directors would think to be unfair.

In *McGuinness* v. *Bremner plc*[75] a six month delay in convening an extraordinary general meeting requisitioned by the petitioners was held to be wholly unreasonable and to constitute unfairly prejudicial conduct, even though it did not breach the statute. The directors had an interest in procrastinating, since the purpose of the meeting was to be their replacement. In a similar vein, in *Re Ashby Bergh & Co. Ltd.*[76] the New Zealand High Court refused to strike out a petition under the unfair prejudice provision in respect of allegations of insufficient premium, insufficient consideration and insufficient information in the context of a reverse takeover, even though it was accepted that the defendants' conduct might not amount to breach of fiduciary duty.[77]

Conversely, there may be conduct which amounts to a breach of fiduciary duty, but is not unfairly prejudicial. Although not a case where fiduciary duty was considered, *Nicholas* v. *Soundcraft Electronics Ltd.*[78]

---

[72] See *Re Charnley Davies Ltd. (No. 2)* above n 30, and *Re Halt Garage (1964) Ltd.* [1982] 3 All ER 1016.

[73] *Shuttleworth* v. *Cox Brothers & Co. (Maidenhead) Ltd.* [1927] 2 KB 9 AT 23 (CA), *Charterbridge Corporation Ltd.* v. *Lloyds Bank Ltd.* [1970] Ch. 62 at 74.

[74] Above n 34, although Brennan J delivered a separate judgment from the joint majority judgment delivered by Mason ACJ, Wilson, Deane and Dawson JJ, Brennan J's judgment has come to be regarded as the leading judgment. See *Shears* v. *Phosphate Co-operative of Australia Ltd.* above n 37 at 755; 820 *per* O'Bryan J (Full Ct, Vic) and *Re Dernacourt Investments Pty. Ltd.* (1990) 20 NSWLR 588 at 620 *per* Powell J.

[75] 1988 SLT 891, affd. 1988 SLT 898n.     [76] (1988) 4 NZCLC 64,131.

[77] Referring to *Gething* v. *Kilner* [1972] 1 WLR 337. See also *Re a Company (No. 008699 of 1985)* above n 34.

[78] [1993] BCLC 360, also reported as *Re a Company (No. 002470 of 1988); Ex parte Nicholas* [1992] BCC 895 (CA).

gives an indication of the type of situation where this may arise. The company's majority shareholder ('Electronics') administered the company's financial affairs in return for a management charge. Electronics' financial situation deteriorated, and it used its control of the company's cheques to withhold payments received by it from foreign customers on behalf of the company. The Court of Appeal held that it was in the interests of the company that Electronics should not go into liquidation, and that the attempt to keep the group afloat by recourse to the assets of both companies was a reasonable commercial judgment in the circumstances, and was not unfair, although it caused harm to the company.[79]

One suggested loophole in the unfair prejudice provision, in terms of its ability to supersede the derivative action, is that it is limited to acts or omissions *by or on behalf of the company*. It does not refer to acts or omissions *by or on behalf of persons* conducting the affairs of the company. As such it could be argued that it is not wide enough to catch objectionable conduct of directors or controllers other than on behalf of the company, such as where they favour a competitor by passing on corporate information, or where they establish a business competing with that of the company.[80] The omission of this additional ground from the Australian provision is particularly noteworthy since the fact that the 'directors have acted in affairs of the company in their own interests rather than in the interests of the members as a whole, or in any other manner whatsoever that appears to be unfair or unjust to other members' is specifically listed as a ground on which the company may be wound up by the court.[81] However, no such restrictive interpretation was given to the former oppression provision in *Scottish Co-operative Wholesale Society Ltd.* v. *Meyer*,[82] and the unfair prejudice provision has also been interpreted to extend to such conduct.[83]

It is also clear that it will be easier to establish unfair prejudice to shareholders arising from conduct which affects all shareholders equally than it would be to establish a personal right at common law. In *Re Macro (Ipswich) Ltd.*[84] Arden J held that mismanagement which was financially damaging to the company was necessarily unfairly prejudicial to the interests of the plaintiffs as shareholders. This approach can be contrasted

---

[79] See also *Parker* v. *National Roads and Motorists' Association* (1993) 11 ACSR 370; 11 ACLC 866 (CA NSW) and discussion in Ch. 6 section 2(10)(d).

[80] These loopholes are identified by Austin above n 15, at 108 and 118 and A. B. Afterman 'Statutory Protection for Oppressed Minority Shareholders: A Model for Reform' (1969) 55 *Va L Rev* 1043 at 1055.                                    [81] Section 461(e), CL (Aust).

[82] Above n 62, at 326.

[83] *Re BSB Holdings Ltd.* [1993] BCLC 246; [1992] BCC 915, *Re Stewarts (Brixton) Ltd.* [1985] BCLC 4, *Sanford* v. *Sanford Courier Service Pty. Ltd.* above n 62.

[84] Above n 1.

with the restrictive attitude taken in the context of common law proceedings where it was held in *Prudential Assurance Co. Ltd.* v. *Newman Industries Ltd. (No. 2)*[85] that the individual plaintiff's personal action based on the fact that the company in which the plaintiffs were interested has suffered damage was misconceived. This was because the plaintiff's right as a shareholder was merely a right of participation in the company on the terms of the articles of association, and any damage done to the company had not affected that right. Further, in smaller companies, and particularly in quasi-partnership companies, it will seldom be difficult to find the requisite element of unfairness to members in order to bring the conduct within the scope of the unfair prejudice provision, since, as MacIntosh observes, it frequently reflects an underlying dispute between corporate constituents.[86]

The question then arises whether it is necessary to identify unfairness to shareholders (whether or not there is also a concurrent wrong to the company) in order to bring a claim under the provision.[87] There are cases in England where petitioners have been unsuccessful because they failed to do so. In *Re Charnley Davies (No. 2)*[88] relief was refused under the unfair prejudice provision, in circumstances where Millett J considered[89] that the evidence, if proved, would found a simple action for professional negligence.[90] And, in *Re Blue Arrow plc*[91] it was held that an unfair prejudice petition was an inappropriate procedure through which to challenge the good faith of directors in sending out a notice convening a meeting.

There is scope for the argument that a distinction can be drawn between the United Kingdom and Australian provisions in this regard. Although the United Kingdom provision has been amended to clarify that it applies where conduct is unfairly prejudicial to the interests of the members generally as well as to some part of the members,[92] in the Australian provision conduct which is 'contrary to the interests of the members as a whole' provides an alternative ground for relief to conduct which is oppressive, unfairly prejudicial to, or unfairly discriminatory against a

---

[85] [1982] Ch. 204, 222–3 (CA). But cf., the situation where the plaintiff (rather than the company) has a right of action against the defendant for breach of contract, in which case diminution in the value of shares is a potential head of damage: *George Fischer (Great Britain) Ltd.* v. *Multi-Construction Ltd.*, [1995] BCC 310 (CA).
[86] J. G. MacIntosh, 'The Oppression Remedy: Personal or Derivative? (1991) 70 *Can B Rev* 29 at 46.       [87] See also Ch. 6 section 2(10)(d).
[88] Above n 30.       [89] Ibid., at 784; 625.
[90] Cf., J. F. Corkery, 'Oppression or Unfairness by Controllers—What can a Shareholder Do About It? An Analysis of s. 320 of the Companies Code' (1985) 9 *Adel L Rev* 437 at 459.
[91] [1987] BCLC 585; (1987) 3 BCC 618.
[92] Sch. 19, para. 11, CA 1989 (UK).

member or members. There has been some discussion in the recent cases of *Re Spargos Mining NL*[93] and *Zephyr Holdings Pty. Ltd. v. Jack Chia (Australia) Ltd. & Ors*[94] as to whether all elements of the Australian section should be viewed as different aspects of a fundamental yardstick of 'commercial unfairness' as was decided in *Morgan* v. *45 Flers Avenue Pty. Ltd.*[95] or whether conduct which is 'contrary to the interests of the members as a whole' establishes a separate ground for intervention. In neither case was it found necessary to decide this question, although tentative support was expressed in both cases for the view that this is a separate ground.[96]

It appears to have been assumed that it provides a separate ground for intervention in *Re Overton Holdings Pty. Ltd.*[97] where an order was made authorizing the plaintiff to institute proceedings in the name of and on behalf of the company.[98] The facts were that the respondent had committed a breach of fiduciary duty to Overton Holdings by causing it to borrow money for the purpose of lending onward to companies controlled by the respondent to the detriment of Overton Holdings. Rowland J said:[99] 'It seems to me that the powers given to the court by [the unfair prejudice provision] are extremely wide and now give statutory force to the exception to the rule in *Foss* v. *Harbottle* . . .'

An additional point of distinction between the two jurisdictions and one which also arguably provides greater scope for the derivative action to be subsumed within the Australian unfair prejudice provision is that, by contrast with the United Kingdom provision, the unfairly prejudicial conduct need not affect the member who brings the action. Thus, in *Re Spargos Mining NL*[100] a minority shareholder was able to bring a successful petition even though almost all of the impugned conduct and transactions had occurred prior to his becoming a shareholder and the price paid by him for his shares reflected any corresponding depression in their value, so that he could not be said to have suffered any prejudice. Murray J disposed of the argument that the shareholder had no standing saying that the 'operative' unfairness may be with respect to any member or group of members to which the applicant need not belong and that, for similar reasons, if oppression to the members as a whole were established, relief could not be denied on the basis that the applicant's shareholding was so small as to be minimal.

By contrast, a minority shareholder who did not seek to gain from the

---

[93] (1990) 3 WAR 166.          [94] (1988) 14 ACLR 30 at 37; 7 ACLC 239 at 245–6.
[95] Above n 32.
[96] See also *Re Bagot Well Pastoral Co. Pty. Ltd.* above n 28, at 224.
[97] [1985] WAR 224.
[98] The possibility of this kind of order was considered but rejected in *Re Spargos Mining NL*, above n 93.          [99] Above n 97, at 230.          [100] Above n 93.

proceedings was unsuccessful in his application for authorization to bring proceedings on behalf of a company in respect of improperly paid remuneration and unauthorized expenses in *Parker* v. *National Roads and Motorists' Association.*[101] However, this application failed on the facts.[102]

### (2) Common law

*Re Spargos Mining NL*[103] and *Jenkins* v. *Enterprise Gold Mines NL*[104] show the potential for the oppression remedy to bypass, and possibly supersede, the derivative action, even in listed companies. However, derivative actions have been brought in Australia since those cases were decided. A recent example of a successful derivative action is *Biala Pty. Ltd.* v. *Mallina Holdings Ltd. (No. 2).*[105] Here, the plaintiffs were held to have standing on the basis of the 'interests of justice' exception to the Rule in *Foss* v. *Harbottle,*[106] and equitable compensation was awarded against the defaulting director. Ipp J held that the potential for an action to be brought under the unfair prejudice remedy did not affect the justice of the plaintiff's case.

Derivative actions also continue to be brought in England. In *Barrett* v. *Duckett*[107] a derivative action was commenced in a company with two shareholders, each with a 50 per cent holding. Standing was refused on the basis that the plaintiff was bringing the action for an ulterior motive, and that, in the unusual circumstances of that case, alternative relief existed in the form of a liquidation, which made a derivative action inappropriate. By the time that the derivative proceedings were commenced, the company was insolvent and an action under the unfair prejudice remedy was likely to have led to the same result. However, Peter Gibson LJ said that a plain and obvious remedy available to the plaintiff when negotiations for the sale of her shares broke down would have been a petition under the unfair prejudice provision seeking the purchase of her shares or, alternatively, authorization to bring proceedings in the name of or on behalf of the company.

### (3) Section 1324 of the Corporations Law

In Australia relief is, potentially, also available under section 1324 of the Corporations Law where the directors' conduct breaches the codified

---

[101] Above n 65.     [102] See discussion of this case in Ch. 6 section 2(10)(d).
[103] Above n 93.     [104] Above n 45.
[105] (1993) 11 ACSR 785; 11 ACLC 1082 (digest only) affd. sub nom. *Dempster* v. *Mallina Holdings Ltd.* (1994) 15 ACSR 1 (Full Ct, WA).
[106] (1843) 2 Hare 461; 67 ER 189. See Ch. 8 section 3(2).
[107] [1993] BCC 778 revsd. [1995] BCC 362 (CA).

directors' duties in section 232 of the Corporations Law. Section 1324 has not yet formed the basis of a successful action in these circumstances. It was an alternative ground for the plaintiff's action in *Biala Pty. Ltd.* v. *Mallina Holdings Ltd.*[108] Uncertainty as to the power of the court to award damages under this section where the conduct is completed meant that the ultimate damages award was based on purely equitable grounds. However, Cohen J was prepared to make an award of damages under the predecessor of section 1324 despite the fact that the conduct was completed in the later case of *Permanent Trustee Australia Ltd* v. *Perpetual Trustee Co. Ltd.*[109]

## 6. NEGLIGENT OR INEFFICIENT MANAGEMENT[110]

### (1) Unfair prejudice

The reluctance of courts to become involved in management decisions comes to the fore when they are faced with complaints of negligent management, and, despite two statutory amendments,[111] this charge has founded only one successful petition under the unfair prejudice provision, in the recent English case of *Re Macro (Ipswich) Ltd.*[112] In the earlier case of *Re Elgindata Ltd.*[113] Warner J considered[114] that unfair prejudice could be established by a breach of a director's duty of skill and care or by serious mismanagement which caused real economic harm to the company's business and therefore to the value of the petitioners' shares. But neither of these gauges of unfairly prejudicial conduct was satisfied on the facts. Similar views, and results, can be found in other cases.[115] However, in *Re Macro (Ipswich) Ltd.*[116] Arden J distinguished *Re Elgindata*,[117] saying:[118]

> . . . this is not a case where what happened was merely that quality of management turned out to be poor . . . This is a case where there were specific acts of mismanagement by Thompsons, which Mr Thompson failed to prevent or rectify. Moreover, several of the acts of mismanagement which the plaintiffs have

---

[108] (1993) 11 ACLC 757.

[109] (1994) 15 ACSR 722; 13 ACLC 66. See Ch. 8 section 5.

[110] See generally, V. Finch, 'Company Directors: Who Cares About Skill and Care?' (1992) 55 *Mod L Rev* 179.

[111] The Jenkins Committee appeared to intend that the change to 'unfairly prejudicial' conduct would extend the provision to complaints of negligence: Cmnd. 1749 para. 207. The other change was the clarification that conduct which affects all members can amount to unfair prejudice: Companies Act 1989 Sch. 19 para. 11. These amendments were intended to overcome the implication arising from *Re Five Minute Car Wash Service Ltd.* [1966] 1 WLR 745 that negligence did not amount to oppression.       [112] Above n 1.

[113] Above n 64.       [114] Ibid., at 993–4.

[115] See e.g., *Re Charnley Davies Ltd. (No. 2)* above n 30.       [116] Above n 1.

[117] Above n 64.       [118] Above n 1 at 406; 834.

identified were repeated over many years, as for example in relation to the failure to inspect repairs. In my judgement, viewed overall, those acts (and Mr Thompson's failure to prevent or rectify them) are sufficiently significant and serious to justify intervention by the court under [the unfair prejudice provision].

This case is significant as an instance where mismanagement was held on the facts to constitute unfair prejudice. However, it also reflects the earlier suggestions by commentators that such actions are more likely to succeed if the petition is based on a refusal to take action in the face of negligence by directors, rather than on the negligence itself as the source of unfair prejudice.[119]

## (2) Common law

There is virtually no prospect of a shareholder[120] being able to bring a derivative action to enforce directors' duties of care and diligence, since mere negligence, in the absence of any benefit to the directors, has been held not to amount to fraud on the minority.[121] Nevertheless, it is relevant to examine the cases where common law actions have been successfully brought since *Re Elgindata*[122] suggests that the same facts would also found an unfair prejudice petition.

Historically, the courts have imposed very low standards of care and skill on directors and have found them liable only in cases of 'gross negligence'.[123] Three propositions were articulated by Romer J in the leading case of *Re City Equitable Fire Insurance Co. Ltd.*[124] First, the degree of care and skill to be exercised by a director is that which can reasonably be expected from a person with the director's knowledge and experience. Secondly, a director is not required to give continuous attention to the company's affairs, and is therefore not negligent merely because he or she fails to attend board meetings. Finally, directors are entitled to delegate responsibility to other company officials,[125] provided they are justified in trusting those officials to perform those duties

---

[119] R. R. Pennington, *Company Law* (6th edn., London, Butterworths, 1990) at 670.
[120] As opposed to the company, or, more usually, a liquidator.
[121] *Pavlides* v. *Jensen* [1965] Ch. 565. Cf., *Daniels* v. *Daniels* [1978] Ch. 406 *Re* self-serving negligence.
[122] Above n 64.
[123] See e.g., *Lagunas Nitrate Co.* v. *Lagunas Syndicate* [1899] 2 Ch. 392 at 435 (CA), *Overend & Gurney Co.* v. *Gibb* (1872) LR 5 HL 480 at 487, *Re Brazilian Rubber Plantations & Estates Ltd.* [1911] 1 Ch. 425 at 436–7, *Re National Bank of Wales Ltd.* [1899] 2 Ch. 629 at 672 (HL) and *Re Faure Electric Accumulator Co.* (1888) 40 Ch. D 141 at 152.
[124] [1925] Ch. 407 (CA).
[125] Cf., the statement of the UK Panel on Takeovers and Mergers (30 July 1987) that although the day-to-day conduct of a takeover may be delegated, the full board must maintain an active involvement in monitoring the conduct of the offer.

honestly.[126] Trebilcock has summarized the effect of these propositions, saying:[127] '. . . the fewer a director's qualifications for office, the less time and attention he devotes to his office, and the greater the reliance he places on others, legally the less responsible he is.'

More recently, cases generated by the excesses of the 1980s (particularly in Australia) have re-examined the propositions set out in the *City Equitable*[128] case and, in particular the required levels of financial competence and involvement in company affairs.

### (a) Financial competence

#### (i) England

In the United Kingdom insolvency legislation, 'wrongful trading' is judged by reference to a minimum objective standard of knowledge, skill and experience for a person carrying out the director's functions and can be augmented by reference to the director's actual knowledge, skill and experience.[129] In *Norman* v. *Theodore Goddard*[130] Hoffmann J was prepared to assume the correctness of an argument based on the wrongful trading provisions that directors should exercise their duties of care and skill according to a minimum objective standard which might be increased by the subjective knowledge, skill and experience of the director.

#### (ii) Australia

Similarly, in Australia, cases decided in the insolvency context[131] have adopted an objective interpretation of the standard of financial competence required of directors, and have held that a director cannot rely on self-imposed ignorance of a company's financial position as a defence to liability for insolvent trading.[132] This approach has subsequently been

---

[126] In Australia, it will be an implied term of the service contract of an executive director that the director has the skills of a reasonably competent person appointed to that position and that he or she will act with reasonable care, diligence and skill. Strangely, the implication of such terms is excluded in England by the Supply of Goods (Exclusion of Implied Terms) Order 1982 (SI 1982 No 1771). It is, of course, still possible to incorporate express terms to this effect. Another term which is normally expressly imposed is a requirement that the director give exclusive attention to the company's affairs.

[127] M. J. Trebilcock, 'The Liability of Company Directors for Negligence' (1969) 32 *Mod L Rev* 499 at 508–9.     [128] Above n 124.

[129] Section 214, IA 1986 (UK).     [130] [1991] BCLC 1908; [1992] BCC 14.

[131] *Metal Manufacturers Pty. Ltd.* v. *Lewis* (1988) 13 NSWLR 315 (CA NSW) *per* Kirby P dissenting, *Morley* v. *Statewide Tobacco Services Ltd.* [1993] 1 VR 423 (Full Ct, Vic), *Commonwealth Bank of Australia* v. *Friedrich* (1991) 5 ACSR 115; 9 ACLC 946, *Group Four Industries Pty. Ltd.* v. *Brosnan* (1992) 59 SASR 22 (Full Ct, SA) and *Rema Industries and Services Pty. Ltd.* v. *Coad; Re Taspac Thermoforming Pty. Ltd.* (1992) 7 ACSR 251; 10 ACLC 530.

[132] Those cases related to s. 592, CL (Aust). See now s. 588G, CL (Aust) which has a wider operation than its predecessor.

applied in the context of actions against directors for breach of the duty of care and diligence.[133]

## (b) Delegation

The ability of directors to delegate their duties has been considered in a number of recent cases. In both England and Australia directors who have acted *bona fide* but whose inactivity assisted another director to misapply company funds have been held liable for the consequent losses on the basis that they should have made reasonable efforts to acquaint themselves with the affairs of the company.[134]

These cases are, however, outnumbered by those where directors were held to have discharged their responsibilities in circumstances where they had relied on their colleagues, in the absence of anything which would put them on alert.[135] Notably, in *Biala Pty. Ltd.* v. *Mallina Holdings Ltd. (No. 2)*,[136] an executive director was held not to be negligent in trusting the chairman and managing director, in light of their long relationship, even though the correct position could have been ascertained by a mere telephone call. Further, *Hurley* v. *NCSC*[137] is authority that a director does not have a duty to attempt to take action if it would be doomed to failure.

On the other hand, it was held in *Permanent Building Society (in liq.)* v. *Wheeler*[138] that the chief executive and managing director of a company was not able to avoid his obligation to ensure that the other directors appreciated the potential harm inherent in the relevant transaction and to point out steps that could be taken to reduce the possibility of that harm by 'metaphorically speaking, burying his head in the sand'.[139] It was held that the director had either failed to make enquires which he should have made or was satisfied with superficial and inadequate answers in circumstances requiring further investigation, and that he had failed to exercise a reasonable degree of care, skill and diligence.

These decisions refine the third proposition in the *Re City Equitable* case[140] but do not overrule it.

---

[133] *AWA Ltd.* v. *Daniels* (1992) 7 ACSR 759; 10 ACLC 933.

[134] *Re Australasian Venezolana Pty. Ltd.* (1962) 4 FLR 60 and *Dorchester Finance Co. Ltd.* v. *Stebbing* [1989] BCLC 498.

[135] See *Norman* v. *Theodore Goddard* above n 130, where this monitoring obligation was held to be satisfied. The defendant director had in fact queried the unusual transactions and had received answers which it was held reasonable for him to accept as true. See also *AWA Ltd.* v. *Daniels*, above n 133, *Australian Securities Commission* v. *Gallagher* (1993) 10 ACSR 43; 11 ACLC 286 (Full Ct, WA) and *Vrisakis* v. *Australian Securities Commission* (1993) 9 WAR 395 (Full Ct, WA). [136] Above n 105.

[137] (1993) 11 ACLC 443.

[138] (1994) 11 WAR 187, noted by R. Baxt (1995) 69 *Aust L J* 20.

[139] Ibid., at 160; 682. [140] Above n 124.

### (3) Section 1324 of the Corporations Law

The codification of the duty of care in diligence in section 232(4) of the Corporations Law has been amended to reflect the more objective standard of care required in the insolvency context,[141] so that directors are required to exercise the care and diligence that a reasonable person in a like position in a corporation would exercise in the corporation's circumstances. The test is an objective one, in that it looks to what could be expected of a reasonable person. But it has subjective elements which relate both to the attributes of the particular director and the allocation of functions in the particular corporation.

Breach of this section could potentially be actionable by a minority shareholder under section 1324.[142]

### (4) United Kingdom reform proposals

Article 14 of the proposed Fifth EEC Directive would make directors jointly and severally liable for damage to the company that results from breaches of duty by one or more of them. Directors would be able to exonerate themselves from liability by proving that no fault was attributable to them personally, but the fact that the act giving rise to damage did not fall within a director's assigned field of competence would not suffice for this purpose. This proposal reverses the present position under English law in relation to fault.[143] Further, under Article 16, shareholders would have standing to bring proceedings on behalf of a company to enforce that liability, subject to a qualification of not more than a 10 per cent holding.[144]

## 7. LITTLE OR NO PARTICIPATION IN PROFITS[145]

In line with the pre-existing common law,[146] the courts have been prepared to make a finding of unfairly prejudicial conduct where the decision to

---

[141] The explanatory memorandum to the Corporate Law Reform Act 1994 states that the amendments to s. 232(4), CL (Aust) are intended to confirm the approach evidenced in *Morely*'s case, *Brosnan*'s case, *Coad*'s case (all above n 131) and the *AWA* case (above n 133).

[142] But see section 5(3) above and Ch. 8 section 5.

[143] DTI Consultative Document, *Amended Proposal for a Fifth Directive on the Harmonisation of Company Law in the European Community* January 1990, para. 15.2. The DTI indicates that Art. 14 is opposed by a number of member states including the UK.

[144] OJ Vol. 26, C 240, 9 September 1983, pages 2–38, amended in 1989 raising the maximum qualification from 5%.

[145] See generally, S. Sievers, 'Failure to Pay Dividends—Oppression or a Ground for Winding Up' (1989) 7 *Company & Sec LJ* 65.

[146] *Miles* v. *The Sydney Meat Preserving Co. Ltd.* (1913) 17 CLR 639 (PC) and *Dodge* v. *Ford Motor Co.* 204 Mich 459; 170 NW 668 (1919).

distribute low dividends has been made on the basis of considerations extraneous to the best interests of the company, and which operate to the detriment of minority shareholders.[147] The main advantage of the unfair prejudice remedy in this context lies in the range of available remedies.[148]

Unfair prejudice may also result where the controllers persistently withdraw profits in the form of directors' emoluments to the detriment of minority shareholders.[149] For example, in *Re Sam Weller & Sons Ltd.*[150] the same low dividend had been paid for 37 years despite the company being profitable and despite significant reserves having been built up. At the same time the sole director and his sons were taking income from the company in other forms and were therefore unaffected by the low dividends. Peter Gibson J considered that the court would view allegations of unfair prejudice on this ground with great caution, but nevertheless refused an application to strike out the parts of a petition relating to the low dividend policy. In *Morgan v. 45 Flers Avenue Pty. Ltd.*[151] the same approach was adopted by an Australian court. Here the board had for a number of years adopted a policy of declaring low dividends while granting high bonuses and directors fees.[152] The petitioner had formerly been a member of the board but had fallen out with his brother, the other major protagonist, and now complained that the dividend policy operated to his disadvantage. On the facts, the plaintiff did not make out a case for relief. Young J had particular regard to the fact that the plaintiff had benefited from this policy in previous years.[153] Nevertheless, his Honour left open the possibility that the petitioner might be successful if this policy were to be adopted in future years, saying:[154] 'Obviously if the policy was extended in future years so that there would be a significant diversion of the funds of [the company] from the shareholders to the executives there would be a legitimate matter of complaint as to its probity, but the facts do not satisfy me that this has occurred to date.'

The more difficult situation is where there is no question of diversion of funds away from shareholders, but rather a question of whether the company's profits should be retained or distributed. Different answers appear to have been given in different jurisdictions to the question of

---

[147] *Re Waitikiri Links Ltd.* (1989) 4 NZCLC 64,922 and *Re City Meat Co. Pty. Ltd.* (1984) 8 ACLR 673; 2 ACLC 149.  [148] See *Re Waitikiri Links Ltd.*, ibid.

[149] See e.g., *Roberts v. Walter Developments Pty. Ltd.*, above n 65.

[150] Above n 59.  [151] Above n 32.

[152] The dividends paid were the minimum necessary to avoid a liability under Division 7 of the Income Tax Assessment Act 1936.

[153] Cf., the approach taken on similar facts in *Sanford v. Sanford Courier Service Pty. Ltd.* above n 62 where, once the plaintiff was no longer a director, Waddell CJ in Eq. considered (at 559; 403) that the question of the fairness of the means taken to distribute the company's profits should be completely reconsidered.

[154] Above n 32 at 706; 234–5.

whether this is capable of amounting to unfairly prejudicial conduct. In Australia and New Zealand, the courts have applied the same approach under the unfair prejudice provision as at common law. Thus, they have been reluctant to base a finding of unfair prejudice on low dividend yields alone without any accompanying allegations of impropriety, regarding this as an unwarranted interference with the directors' management powers.[155] This attitude has the most significant consequences for minority shareholders in unlisted companies who have obtained their shares involuntarily (for example by gift or inheritance), and so have neither a market for their shares nor the negotiating strength to establish personal expectations regarding the distribution of profits.

These Australasian decisions can be contrasted with the English case of *Re a Company (No. 00370 of 1987); Ex parte Glossop*[156] which concerned a low dividend policy adopted over a period of 12 years. Here Harman J considered that relief was potentially available on the basis of the company's failure to meet the members' legitimate expectation to receive reasonable dividends. This was so, irrespective of the considerations that the directors were not influenced by any motive of personal gain and that they honestly believed that the policy was in the best interests of the company. His Lordship drew support from *Howard Smith Ltd.* v. *Ampol Petroleum Ltd.*[157] and *Associated Provincial Picture Houses Ltd.* v. *Wednesbury Corporation*[158] for the proposition that if the directors habitually exercised their powers for 'bye-motives', their decision would be open to challenge. He referred to changes in the system of taxation of dividends, restoring the position that one of the prime purposes of a company is a vehicle to earn profits which should be distributed by way of dividends to its members. The effect of this change was to give the members a corresponding right to have profits distributed so far as commercially possible. His Lordship therefore considered that the directors would be exercising their power to recommend dividends for a 'bye-motive' if their motive was to keep the money within the company so as to build a larger company in the future.

The relief which Harman J was prepared to grant was leave to amend the petition to include the allegations as to inadequate dividends as a ground for a winding-up order. His Lordship refused to allow an amendment to the petition to claim relief under the unfair prejudice provision. However, this was on the basis that relief under that provision was limited to conduct which affected 'some part of the members'. That aspect of the decision has

---

[155] *Re G. Jeffery (Mens Store) Pty. Ltd.* (1984) 9 ACLR 193; 2 ACLC 421, *Thomas* v. *H. W. Thomas Ltd.* above n 34, *McWilliam* v. *L. J. R. McWilliam Estates Pty. Ltd.* (1990) 20 NSWLR 703, and *Re Bagot Well Pastoral Co. Pty. Ltd.* above n 28 at 224.
[156] Above n 66.          [157] Above n 48.                    [158] [1948] 1 KB 223 (CA).

since been altered by statute, and it is submitted that his Lordship's comments as regards the winding-up remedy can now be regarded as relevant to the availability of relief under the unfair prejudice provision.[159]

The question then arises how far *Glossop*'s case[160] represents a departure from the common law approach which continues to be reflected in the Australian decisions. In terms of legal theory as opposed to actual result, the gulf between the reasoning adopted in the two jurisdictions may not be as wide as it first appears. In the context of complaints as to low dividends the courts in both jurisdictions have openly considered not only the impact of the conduct on the petitioners but also the reasonableness of the motivation of the respondents. Further, in making the determination of whether the directors were acting reasonably in deciding to invest profits back into the company or to pay out the profits as dividends to shareholders, the courts have referred not only to the company's own short-term and long-term plans, but also to the influence of external factors such as the prevailing economic conditions and the applicable taxation legislation. The taxation regime was particularly influential both in the Australian decision in *McWilliam* v. *L. J. R. McWilliam Estates Pty. Ltd.*[161] that the dividend policy was reasonable and in the English decision in *Glossop*'s case[162] that the policy was unreasonable.

Although it is possible to reconcile the decisions in this way, it is submitted that *Glossop*'s case[163] does involve a new development, namely the express recognition of a legitimate expectation to have profits distributed as far as commercially possible.

## 8. LIMITED ACCESS TO INFORMATION ABOUT THE COMPANY'S AFFAIRS

### (1) General statutory rights

Shareholders are given various statutory rights: to receive copies of accounts and reports,[164] to receive disclosure of, and in many cases to approve (or disapprove) transactions between the company and directors,[165] to inspect registers and records which the company is required

---

[159] Support for this submission can be found in *Re Sam Weller & Sons Ltd.* above n 59.
[160] Above n 66.  [161] Above n 155.  [162] Above n 66.
[163] Ibid.
[164] See ss. 238–9, and 251–3, CA 1985 (UK), s. 315, CL (Aust), but note the proposal in the First Corporate Law Simplification Bill 1994 to require small proprietary companies to prepare annual financial statements only if required to do so by members holding 5% of the shares or by the ASC.
[165] Sections 312, 313, 319, 320, CA 1985 (UK), s. 237 and Pt 3.2A, CL (Aust).

to keep, including minute books of general meetings,[166] and to receive written notice of meetings.[167] There are also special provisions in both jurisdictions regarding takeovers which are designed to ensure that shareholders have sufficient information, advice and time to reach a properly informed decision, although in England these are not statutorily based.[168]

A detailed examination of these provisions reveals numerous minor divergences between the statutory provisions in the two jurisdictions where there are gaps in the specific rights to information. Further, shareholders do not have the right to inspect the minutes of directors' meetings. Indeed, it has been held that even where the articles provide that 'the books of the minutes of the proceedings of the . . . Company' should be open to shareholder inspection, such a clause gives shareholders the power to inspect only the minutes of the proceedings at general meetings and not the minutes of the directors' meetings.[169]

### (2) Rights to information relating to disputes

#### (a) Common law

Where matters have progressed to the stage of a dispute, the common law provides some assistance. Shareholders may apply to the court for an order allowing them to inspect any company document to the extent that the inspection is necessary for an existing action or some specific dispute or question in which the applicant is interested.[170] This has been interpreted as requiring that the applicant have some 'special interest different from that of his fellow members'. Inspection will therefore potentially be available where the applicant is engaged in a personal dispute, but not where the action is derivative in nature. Thus applications have been refused where the applicants were concerned about the possibility of mismanagement and misappropriation by the directors.[171]

#### (b) Additional statutory rights in Australia

In Australia, the common law position has been augmented by a specific

---

[166] Section 383, CA 1985 (UK), s. 259(1), CL (Aust).

[167] Section 369, CA 1985 (UK), ss. 247 and 253, CL (Aust).

[168] City Code, general principle 4 and r. 23 ff (UK), Ch. 6, and in particular s. 750, CL (Aust).

[169] *R v. The Mariquita and New Granada Mining Company* (1858) 1 El & El 289; 120 ER 917.

[170] *Bank of Bombay* v. *Suleman Somji* (1908) 99 LT 62 (PC). See also *Edman* v. *Ross* (1922) 22 SR (NSW) 351.

[171] *R v. Merchant Tailors' Company* (1831) 2 B & Ad 115; 109 ER 1086.

statutory provision[172] which enables shareholders to apply for inspection of the company's books[173] on their behalf by a qualified legal practitioner or registered company auditor.[174] In exercising its discretion to make an order under the section, the court must be satisfied that the member is acting in good faith and that the inspection is to be for a proper purpose.

### (i) A special interest requirement?

One controversial question in the interpretation of the section has been whether it incorporates the common law requirement that the order must be necessary to protect some specific personal right of the applicant. It has been emphasized in all the cases decided under the section that the creation of the statutory right of inspection should not affect 'the basic rule of company law . . . that a shareholder ought not ordinarily to have recourse to the courts to challenge a managerial decision made by or with the approval of its directors'.[175] In some cases it has been considered to be a necessary corollary of this proposition that the personal interest requirement apply.[176] Nevertheless in a number of cases[177] a special interest has been found in the fact that the applicants had a substantial shareholding in the company, and were seeking to protect their investment. Although these cases purport not to enlarge the pre-existing common law position, it submitted that this interpretation of 'special interest' is much more liberal than that at common law. Moreover, in *Re Claremont Petroleum NL*,[178] the Full Court of the Supreme Court of Queensland expressly rejected the argument that it was necessary for an applicant under the section to demonstrate a special interest not shared by other shareholders to obtain an order. Endorsing the remarks made by McPherson J at first instance as to the enlargement of shareholder remedies under the companies legislation their Honours said:[179]

---

[172] Section 319, CL (Aust).

[173] Section 9, CL (Aust) defines 'books' as including a register or other record of information, accounts or accounting records, however compiled, recorded or stored, and documents.

[174] Despite the wording of the statue, the section has been interpreted to allow inspection by both a qualified legal practitioner and a registered company auditor, not merely by one or the other: *Unity APA Ltd.* v. *Humes Ltd. (No. 2)* [1987] VR 474 and *Gibson* v. *Opalspectrum Pty. Ltd.*, unreported decision of Moore J, 10 November 1994, Federal Court (NSW).

[175] *Re Augold NL* [1987] 2 Qd. R 297 at 308, *Unity APA Ltd.* v. *Humes Ltd. (No. 2)*, ibid.

[176] *Re Augold NL* ibid., and *Barrack Mines Ltd.* v. *Grants Patch Mining Ltd.* [1988] 1 Qd. R 606 (Full Ct, Qld).

[177] *Quinlan* v. *Vital Technology Australia Ltd.* (1987) 5 ACLC 389, *Barrack Mines Ltd.* v. *Grants Patch Mining Ltd.* ibid, *Intercapital Holdings Ltd.* v. *MEH Ltd.* (1988) 13 ACLR 595; 6 ACLC 1068 and *Biala Pty. Ltd.* v. *Mallina Holdings Ltd.* (1990) 2 WAR 381.

[178] (1989) 1 ACSR 494; 8 ACLC 56, affd. [1990] 2 Qd. R 31 (Full Ct, Qld).

[179] Ibid., at 34.

One can readily understand that it is a relevant consideration that there is a specific dispute rather than general dissatisfaction with management; likewise that the applicant is personally interested, as also the extent and value of his interest; but to insist that his interest be separate and distinct from that of the general body of members is to treat the statutory discretion as confined to one only of the well recognised exceptions to the rule in *Foss* v. *Harbottle*. So to restrict the application of [section 319] would be to ignore the very great extent to which the rights of shareholders have been enlarged under the companies legislation and the great inroads which have been made by statute upon that famous rule.

This decision paves the way of the section to be used where any proceedings brought as a result of the inspection would be likely to be derivative in nature, as well as where personal rights are affected.

### (ii) Good faith and proper purpose

It is also clear that the section significantly liberalizes the common law position in that it enables inspection to be made before proceedings are commenced. Indeed, it is not necessary that there be any immediate prospect of bringing proceedings. Proper purposes extend to exercising rights as a shareholder, for example: to ask proper questions at a general meeting, to convene a meeting, to remove the directors,[180] to protect an investment in a company[181] or to ascertain the value of shares.[182]

There are nevertheless some restrictions on the circumstances in which inspection may be granted. Inspection was refused in *Quinlan* v. *Vital Technology Australia Ltd.*[183] where a managing director who had been dismissed for dishonesty acquired 100 shares in the company in order to bring the inspection application. Inspection was also refused in *Re Augold NL*[184] where it was held that the applicant's real purpose for seeking the inspection was to improve its prospects of making a successful takeover bid for the company. But it is clear that where an applicant is able to establish a proper purpose, the fact that he or she may also have an improper purpose, such as to obtain assistance in a takeover offer, will not be fatal to the application.[185]

Similarly, if a proper purpose is established, the fact that the information is confidential or that the applicant is in competition with the company will

---

[180] *Intercapital Holdings Ltd.* v. *MEH Ltd.* above n 177, *Cescastle Pty. Ltd.* v. *Renak Holdings Ltd.* (1991) 6 ACSR 115; 9 ACLC 1333.

[181] *Re Claremont Petroleum NL*, above n 178.

[182] *Tinios* v. *French Caledonia Travel Service Pty. Ltd.* (1994) 13 ACSR 658; 12 ACLC 622 and *Gibson* v. *Opalspectrum Pty. Ltd.*, above n 174.                     [183] Above n 177.

[184] Above n 175.

[185] *Unity APA Ltd.* v. *Humes (No. 2)* above n 174, *Barrack Mines Ltd.* v. *Grants Patch Mining Ltd.* above n 176, *Intercapital Holdings Ltd.* v. *MEH Ltd. & Ors* above n 175 and *Cescastle Pty. Ltd.* v. *Renak Holdings Ltd.* above n 180.

not preclude an order for inspection. This is illustrated by *Tinios* v. *French Caledonia Travel Service Pty. Ltd.*[186] where an order was granted for inspection of the company's books, to enable the applicant to give notice in accordance with pre-emption provisions in the articles which required him to state what he considered to be the fair value of his shares. The applicant was in competition with the company, and the respondent had asked that the inspection be by a registered company auditor chosen by the court who would not be allowed to communicate anything to the applicant other than his opinion as to the value of the shares. However, the court considered that the applicant should be free to select his own advisers, since the value of a share was a matter of opinion.

The proper purpose requirement has, however, been interpreted to import a '*qua* member' requirement.[187] Thus, an application was refused where the plaintiff sought access to the company's books for use in litigation with the company's receiver and manager and a debenture holder. It was held that it was not a proper purpose to seek access to documents required for litigation to which the companies were not parties and did not concern the plaintiff's shares or rights and duties as a shareholder.[188]

### (iii) Board minutes

McPherson J declined to order inspection of minutes of board meetings in *Re Claremont Petroleum NL (No. 2)*.[189] stating that:

> The procedure under [s 319] is not intended as a form of or substitute for inspection of documents after discovery on affidavit or answers to interrogatories in pending litigation. I therefore consider that in many circumstances a shareholder ought not to be assisted by an order under [s 319] to examine decisions of directors, or the reports or records leading to those decisions; but I think that in a case like this he is entitled by inspection of books to find out what the results of those decisions are; that is to say, whether the company has entered into agreements, and with whom, disposing of corporate assets of value, and for what consideration, and what has happened to those assets or the consideration given in return for them.

However, inspection of board minutes was ordered in the recent case of *Gibson* v. *Opalspectrum Pty. Ltd.*[190] The facts were that the applicant's

---

[186] Above n 182.

[187] *Knightswood Nominees Pty. Ltd.* v. *Sherwin Pastoral Company Ltd.* (1989) 15 ACLR 151; 7 ACLC 536.

[188] *Bride* v. *Commissioner for Corporate Affairs* (1989) 1 ACSR 36; 7 ACLC 1202. This limitation may prove to be significant where the applicant for inspection is a director who has been removed from office, unless a liberal interpretation of the '*qua* member' requirement is adopted. [189] (1990) 2 ACSR 84 at 89; 8 ACLC 548 at 552.

[190] Above n 174.

employment with the company had been terminated on the basis of alleged misconduct. The termination triggered a provision in the applicant's service agreement which provided for the applicant's shares to be repurchased at 50 cents per share if his employment had been validly terminated but, if the applicant ceased to be an employee in other circumstances, the price to be paid for the shares was to be the higher of 50 cents per share and the fair market value of the shares determined by the board on the advice of the auditors. Following the termination of his employment, the applicant was also removed as a director.

The applicant sought access to a wide range of documents on two grounds: to determine the value of his shares, and to ascertain whether there were grounds for bringing an action for unfair prejudice. Moore J rejected the argument that the value of the shares would only be of relevance to the applicant if his termination was found to be invalid, and made an order for inspection of certain categories of documents. Further, his Honour considered that the applicant had established that he might reasonably entertain concerns about the management of the company as it related to his interests as a shareholder and director and authorized inspection of further categories of documents including minutes of directors' meetings held after his termination.[191]

### (iv) Reform proposals

Both the Companies and Securities Law Review Committee[192] and the Companies and Securities Advisory Committee[193] have recommended amendments to section 319, among them an express provision that the court's discretion extends to authorizing inspection of the records of boards of directors and their delegates, and a widening of the categories of persons entitled to inspect books to include any person whom the court thinks is a proper person to undertake the inspection.[194]

However, the need for the first of these amendments has been substantially diminished by the decision in *Gibson*'s case.[195]

---

[191] His Honour reserved to the respondents liberty to seek to have that order limited so as to preclude inspection of the minutes of the board of directors that related directly to the litigation being adjudicated on.

[192] *Enforcement of the Duties of Directors and Officers of a Company by Means of a Statutory Derivative Action*, Report No. 12, November 1990.

[193] *Report on a Statutory Derivative Action*, July 1993.

[194] Cf., the more far-reaching provision in s. 178 of the New Zealand Companies Act 1993. This requires the company to provide any information requested by a shareholder within 10 working days of receiving a written request. Reasons for a refusal must be given, and are limited to the situations where disclosure would or would be likely to prejudice the company's commercial position, or the commercial position of a third person, or the request for the information is frivolous or vexatious.                              [195] Above n 174.

## (3) The unfair prejudice provision

Although a complaint of lack of access to information has formed one of the grounds for some successful unfair prejudice petitions,[196] it is not possible to generalize from these cases since there were other grounds for complaint such as diversion of corporate opportunity, removal of the petitioner as a director,[197] alteration of the articles of association[198] and failure to declare dividends in order to build up the company's assets for the respondent's benefit.[199]

### (a) Australia

In one recent Australian case where access to the company's records was the sole basis for an unfair prejudice petition, *Re Dernacourt Investments Pty Ltd.*,[200] the application was refused. Powell J considered[201] that the refusal of the plaintiff's request was not unfair. This was for three reasons: first that the court should be loath to interfere with matters of management; secondly, that the plaintiff's concerns related to possible lack of efficiency, rather than lack of probity; thirdly, that the proposed inspection (which extended to records for a period of at least six years) would be likely to be burdensome and disruptive of the company's business.

Given the courts' general reluctance to regard negligent management as unfairly prejudicial conduct, it is perhaps not surprising that a far-reaching request for information which at most was expected to expose possible mismanagement was refused. However, Powell J went on to say[202] that since the provision was directed towards remedying unfairly prejudicial conduct, it was not available to enable a potential litigant to have pre-trial discovery with a view to determining whether to commence proceedings under the provision. In this regard he drew added support from the fact that a separate provision (section 319 of the Corporations Law)[203] existed specifically granting a potential litigant a right in certain cases to apply for preliminary discovery,[204] and that once unfair prejudice proceedings had

---

[196] See e.g., *Re Federated Fashions (NZ) Ltd.* (1981) NZCLC 98,109 and *Re a Company (No. 00314 of 1989)* [1991] BCLC 154; [1990] BCC 221.

[197] Both these other grounds for complaint were present in *Re Federated Fashions (NZ) Ltd.* ibid.

[198] This ground was combined with complaints of proposals to remove the petitioner as a director and appoint other directors in *Re a Company (No. 00314 of 1989)* above n 196.

[199] *Re Bagot Well Pastoral Co. Pty. Ltd.* above n 28 at 224.          [200] Above n 74.

[201] Ibid., at 618–9.          [202] Ibid., at 619–20.          [203] See above discussion.

[204] See also *Swane v. Swane Bros Pty. Ltd.* (1992) 10 ACLC 904 where the existence of s. 319 was regarded as a reason for refusing relief under the unfair prejudice provision in respect of complaints of lack of information about how the company's affairs were being conducted.

been commenced, a plaintiff would have recourse to the usual interlocutory procedures for obtaining discovery.[205]

## (b) England

No equivalent to section 319 of the Corporations Law exists in England,
although discovery is available as an interlocutory procedure once
proceedings have been commenced.[206] Nevertheless, it is submitted that it
is likely that a similar negative decision would be reached in relation to an
application for access to documents in order to determine whether a case
could be brought under the unfair prejudice provision. In the Scottish case
of *Murray's Judicial Factor, Petitioner*,[207] it was held not to be unfairly
prejudicial to refuse the judicial factor's request for information as to the
name of the valuer or the basis on which the valuation of its shares had
been made.

One situation where the unfair prejudice provision has, however, been
useful to shareholders in obtaining information is in the takeover context.
In *Re a Company (No. 008699 of 1985)*[208] the directors' failure to
recommend the highest bid in a take-over bid was held to be capable of
amounting to unfairly prejudicial conduct. Hoffmann J held that although
directors are not under a duty to advise shareholders on the merits of
competing bids, where they decide to do so they must provide sufficient
information and advice to enable shareholders to reach an informed
decision, and must refrain from giving misleading advice or exercising their
fiduciary powers in ways which would prevent shareholders from being
able to make an uninhibited choice.[209]

## 9. ILLIQUIDITY

Claims by minority shareholders in unlisted companies as to insufficient
dividends or excessive director remuneration are often combined with
complaints that they are 'locked in'.[210] Typically, the dissatisfied minority

---

[205] See *Re Australian Marinas (A'asia) Pty. Ltd.* [1975] VR 372 and *Re ABT Holdings Pty.
Ltd.* (1979) 4 ACLR 40. But cf., *Sypkes Securities* v. *Jeugny Pty. Ltd.* (1991) 4 ACSR 668
where the applicant had obtained copies of company accounts under the unfair prejudice
provision, and further incidental relief was granted. However, in this case, the parties
mutually conceded jurisdiction.
[206] See e.g. *Re Hydrosan Ltd.* [1991] BCLC 418; [1991] BCC 19.
[207] [1993] BCLC 1437; [1992] BCC 596 (CS(IH)).          [208] Above n 34.
[209] See also *Cotterall* v. *Fidelity Life Assurance Co. Ltd.* (1987) 3 NZCLC 100,054, where it
was accepted that a petitioner could obtain relief under the unfair prejudice provision after a
director and major shareholder had bought her shares without disclosing the existence of a
significantly higher offer by another buyer.
[210] Illiquidity is not generally a problem which affects shareholders in listed companies.

shareholder wishes to replace his or her investment in the company with one providing a greater rate of return, but is either unable to find a purchaser or able to find one only at an unacceptable price. Unfair prejudice petitions brought in this situation have been consistently rejected: A person does not make out a case of commercial unfairness merely because he or she cannot dispose of shares in a proprietary company.[211] Nor is it relevant that the company has sufficient resources to purchase the shares without prejudicing its activities.[212]

An example, although a variation on the usual fact situation, is *Re a Company (No. 004475 of 1982)*[213] where the trustees of minority (infant) shareholders wanted to sell their shares to finance the children's education. On the open market, the trustees would have been able to sell the shares only at an undervalue relative to their asset-backing because they constituted a minority holding. Their petition arguing that the fact that the company did not provide a scheme to purchase the shares was unfairly prejudicial was struck out. Although the basis for the decision[214] was disapproved in a subsequent case,[215] the actual decision was affirmed on the basis that the refusal to propound the scheme, though prejudicial to the minority because they did not get their cash, was not unfair as a board decision supported by a majority of shareholders.

A more typical fact situation, but one leading to the same result, is the Australian case of *McWilliam* v. *L. J. R. McWilliam Estates Pty Ltd.*[216] Young J held that the ordinary rule is that once money is committed to a company, it is to remain as part of the joint stock while the company's substratum is still there, until there is a winding up or at least a reduction of capital.[217] This was subject to the proviso that if the minority shareholders' attempts to dispose of shares are frustrated by the actions of the majority, there may be a case for relief under the section. But without more, the mere fact that the member cannot dispose of his shares is not sufficient.

Although in that case there were pre-emption provisions which provided a means for valuing the shares, they were not of much assistance to the plaintiffs, since the other members of the company were not prepared to buy the shares at the price reached by the valuation procedure.

The unwillingness to assist a locked-in minority shareholder to withdraw his or her investment from a company was taken a stage further in *Kizquari Pty Ltd.* v. *Prestoo Pty Ltd.*[218] Young J found that excessive salaries were

---

[211] *Re G. Jeffery (Mens Store) Pty. Ltd.* above n 155. See also *Swane* v. *Swane Bros Pty. Ltd.* above n 204.
[212] *Thomas* v. *H. W. Thomas Ltd.* above n 34, at 696 *per* Richardson J (CA NZ).
[213] [1983] Ch. 178.
[214] Namely an application of the '*qua* member' requirement.
[215] *Re a Company (No. 008699 of 1985)* above n 34.      [216] Above n 155.
[217] Ibid., at 707 and 711.      [218] (1993) 10 ACSR 606; 11 ACLC 568.

being paid to the defendants as employees of the company, and that this conduct was unfairly prejudicial, but considered that an order for reimbursement was a sufficient remedy.

The above cases all concerned locked-in minority shareholders who were not actively involved in the management of the company's business. Where a quasi-partner is excluded from management, the unfair prejudice remedy may assist that person to realize his or her investment. The operation of the unfair prejudice remedy in this context is examined in the following section.


## 10. EXCLUSION FROM MANAGEMENT

A director who is removed from that position may be able to bring an action for breach of contract.[219] However, in order to bring an action under the unfair prejudice remedy, the excluded director will need to establish a legitimate expectation of management participation. This will be very difficult in a company where there are outside investors.[220] Thus, complaints of this kind are essentially limited to quasi-partnership companies.

There is growing recognition of the quasi-partnership as a company type in which the parties will often have personal expectations which are in direct contrast with the expectations which the law generally assumes to exist in other types of company. One of these is an expectation of participation in management. This contrasts with the general theory of the shareholders as passive investors putting their money into a pool of funds to be managed by the board of directors. Related to this there may be other expectations as to the means of extracting profits from the company. In a typical quasi-partnership, this is often achieved by means of directors' remuneration rather than in the form of dividends.[221] The second expectation relates to what is to happen if the relationship between the quasi-partners breaks down. The general assumption that money, once committed to the company, is to remain in it is modified in the case of quasi-partnerships. Rather, there is an expectation that if the relationship between the parties breaks down but the company is still viable as a going concern, then[222] one of the quasi-partners will buy the other out, and that the value of the bought-out member's shares will be proportionate to his or

---

[219] See Ch. 4 section 2(1)(a)(i).

[220] See *Re Blue Arrow plc* above n 91 and *Re Warrick Howard (Aust) Pty. Ltd.* (1982) 7 ACLR 441.

[221] The tax incentive for this practice has, however, now been removed in both England and Australia.

[222] Assuming their financial means are sufficient to do so.

her shareholding.[223] It is therefore on these two categories of personal expectation that we shall focus.

### (1) Legitimate expectation of participation in management

The initial barrier to granting relief against exclusion from management was the '*qua* member' requirement.[224] This requirement has been expressly removed from the Australian version of the provision. Although it remains a part of the interpretation of the United Kingdom provision, and although debate continues as to whether some form of '*qua* member' requirement persists in Australia[225] the combination of the statutory amendments and a more liberal interpretation mean that in both England and Australia the courts now recognize that members may have legitimate expectations of participating in the management and profits of the company, which arise from the understanding on which the company was formed and which it may be unfair for the other members to ignore.[226] That is not to say that such expectations will exist in every case. It is always up to the petitioner to establish that the expectation exists on the facts. This will be very difficult where there is an express agreement to the contrary, as in *Re a Company (No. 005685 of 1988); Ex parte Schwarcz (No. 2)*.[227] Further, in *Re a Company (No. 003843 of 1986)*[228] it was held that there was no legitimate expectation that the petitioner would participate in management notwithstanding that the case concerned a small 'family' company.[229] Conversely, it may be possible to establish an expectation to participate in management even in a company which does not possess all the typical attributes of quasi-partnership. In *Re a Company (No. 00477 of 1986)*[230] Hoffmann J considered that the petitioners might have been able to establish such a legitimate expectation even though the company was a public one, and therefore declined to strike out the petition. His Lordship was persuaded by the factors that the association was to be one of 'partnership' and that there was in practice no market in which the shares

---

[223] That is, without any discount or premium being applied to reflect whether or not the shareholding is a controlling one. See *Re Bird Precision Bellows* [1984] Ch. 419, affd. [1986] Ch 658 (CA) and Ch. 6 section 2(10)(c)(ii).

[224] See e.g., *Elder v. Elder & Watson Ltd.* 1952 SC 49.

[225] See discussion in Ch. 6 section 2(4)(b).

[226] See e.g., *Re Posgate and Denby (Agencies) Ltd.* [1987] BCLC 8 at 14; (1986) 2 BCC 99,352 at 99,357–99,358, *Re Bird Precision Bellows Ltd.* above n 223, *Re a Company (No. 002612 of 1984)* above n 44, *Re London School of Electronics Ltd.* above n 63 and *Coombs v. Dynasty Pty. Ltd.* above n 44.

[227] Above n 32.

[228] [1987] BCLC 562; (1987) 3 BCC 624.

[229] See also *Re Warrick Howard (Aust) Pty. Ltd.* above n 220, where again the contention that the company was a quasi-partnership was rejected and it was held that the shareholders were perfectly entitled to use their numbers to remove the petitioner as a director.

[230] [1986] BCLC 376; (1986) 2 BCC 99,171.

in the company could be sold. Nevertheless, '[t]he common case of such expectations being superimposed on a member's rights under the articles is the corporate quasi-partnership'.[231]

It has been mentioned above that the profits in a quasi-partnership company may be distributed by way of directors' emoluments rather than in the form of dividends. Where all of the quasi-partners participate in management, this bookkeeping arrangement is of little importance. However, where the relationship between the shareholders breaks down and one quasi-partner is excluded from participation in management, the method of distribution of profits assumes considerable importance. For although the excluded shareholder retains his or her shareholding, there is effectively no return on his or her investment. And, as we have seen,[232] if the remaining directors persist in this method of profit distribution, this may amount to unfairly prejudicial conduct.

### (2) Buy-out on a breakdown of relations

Where the excluded shareholder is able to show a legitimate expectation to participate in management, this exclusion may well constitute unfairly prejudicial conduct. There is, however, a proviso to this statement which can be traced to a dictum of Hoffmann J in *Re a Company (No. 007623 of 1984)*:[233]

> There are many cases in which it becomes in practice impossible for two people to work together without obvious fault on either side . . . In those circumstances the only solution is for them to part company. If one of them asks the other to leave the business, I cannot accept that the former must automatically be regarded as having acted in a manner unfairly prejudicial to the interests of the latter. It must depend upon whether it is reasonable that one should leave rather than the other and, even more important, on the terms on which he is asked to go.

Applying this to the facts of that case Hoffmann J held that there was no unfairly prejudicial conduct. 'The petitioner was in a minority, he was an employee rather than an entrepreneur and he was nearly 60 years old. There was never any suggestion from him that he should take over the company'.[234] It was therefore reasonable that he should leave. Furthermore, in this case, the company's articles contained pre-emption provisions which contemplated the sale of shares by one shareholder to another at a fair valuation certified by the company's auditors. Hoffmann J considered that the petitioner could not complain of unfairly prejudicial conduct until

---

[231] *Re Posgate and Denby (Agencies) Ltd.* above n 226.
[232] See discussion above, section 7.          [233] Above n 44 at 366; 99,194.
[234] Ibid.

he had tested the majority's willingness to pay a fair price for his shares.

We have already discussed[235] the question of what is a 'fair' price in this context. In particular we have examined the question of whether valuation provisions in pre-emption clauses should be applied to the case of a sale of shares consequent on a breakdown in relations between quasi-partners, and it has been submitted that this should itself be a question of the parties' legitimate expectations. Nevertheless, it remains good law that a petitioner cannot complain of unfair prejudice in circumstances where the relationship between quasi-partners has broken down without obvious fault on either side, it is clear which should be the party to leave, and he or she has been offered a fair price for his or her shares.

Assuming an excluded quasi-partner can complain of unfair prejudice where he or she is not offered a fair price for his or her shares, is he or she entitled to a purchase order by way of relief or is this subject to the financial means of the respondents? This is a question which appears to have arisen directly in only one case, *Re a Company (No. 002612 of 1984)*.[236] In all the other reported cases the respondents have made an offer or are prepared to purchase the petitioner's shares and the issue is the 'fairness' of any offer. Here, the respondent submitted that an order compelling him to purchase the petitioner's shares would be unfair since he could not afford to do so and would therefore be forced to join with the petitioner in selling the company. He therefore argued that the right course was either that the company be compulsorily wound up or that an order be made giving the respondent an option to purchase the petitioner's shares, and, in default of exercise of the option, giving the petitioner the right to purchase the respondent's shares, and providing in default of exercise of either option for the compulsory winding up of the company. Vinelott J rejected these submissions. His Lordship considered that if the company were wound up, the respondent would be in a position to appropriate substantially the whole of the business of the company to himself, since he had always dealt with the company's suppliers and customers, the senior members of staff would follow him and there would be no-one to outbid him if he made an offer to the liquidator for the right to use the company's name and logo. Vinelott J continued:[237] 'The result, it seems to me, would be far more unfair to Mr Lewis than a compulsory order for the acquisition of the shares by Mr Bolton. It would be unfair that he should be deprived of a share in the "going concern" value of a company in the formation of which he participated and to the establishment of the business of which he made a significant if not indispensable contribution.' His Lordship considered that the alternative order would be equivalent to making a winding-up order,

---

[235] Above, Ch. 6 section 2(8)(b)(i),        [236] (1985) 2 BCC 99,453.
[237] Ibid., at 99,483.

since the petitioner did not have the resources to buy the respondent's shares.

Vinelott J's approach was endorsed by the Court of Appeal.[238] Relying on the decision of the House of Lords in *Scottish Co-operative Wholesale Society Ltd.* v. *Meyer*,[239] Lawton LJ regarded the purchase order as compensatory in nature.[240] As such, the fact that the wrongdoer was impecunious was not a reason why judgment should not be given against him for the amount due to his victim.

However, the facts of this case were not those of a breakdown in relations without obvious fault on either side. The respondent had diverted business to another company, procured the company to make a rights issue so as to reduce the petitioner's proportional holding and paid himself an excessive salary. It was therefore appropriate to regard the order as compensatory in nature. Arguably the financial resources of the respondent could be a relevant factor in a different case. As Nicholls LJ said:[241]

Of course, in considering whether to make a purchase order, the court will have regard to the means of the respondent and also, if he will need to have recourse to the property which is the subject of the purchase order, or other property, to obtain the purchase price, to the likelihood of him being able to realise or obtain money on the security of that property. But these are questions of degree, and the weight to be attached to these considerations will depend on all the circumstances of the case. They are matters for the discretion of the trial judge.

## 11. COMPULSORY ACQUISITION

The proposition outlined in the previous section that a minority shareholder cannot complain of unfair prejudice where:

(1) the relationship between quasi-partners has broken down without obvious fault on either side;
(2) it is clear which should be the party to leave; and
(3) he or she has been offered a fair price for his or her shares,

merits further discussion. On the one hand, as discussed above, it prevents a minority shareholder in this situation being compelled to remain as a locked-in minority shareholder, contrary to the expectations with which

---

[238] *Re Cumana Ltd.* [1986] BCLC 430 (CA).
[239] Above n 62, at 369 *per* Lord Denning.
[240] Above n 238, at 437. See also Nicholls LJ at 443–5.
[241] Ibid., at 444.

the company was formed. On the other hand, the unavailability of relief under the unfair prejudice provision or the winding-up remedy in this situation may be viewed as sanctioning a form of compulsory acquisition. This is really only a problem for a minority shareholder if a 'fair' price incorporates a discount to reflect the fact that a minority holding is being sold. However, as noted above, the starting point in valuing the shares of a quasi-partner is that no such discount should be applied, and it has been submitted[242] that the parties' expectations regarding *pro rata* valuation should be able to override a contrary provision in the company's articles of association in an appropriate case.

There are, however, several direct methods by which the shares of a minority shareholder may be expropriated, and these are examined in detail in the next chapter.

[242] Ch. 6 section 2(8)(b)(i).

## 10

# *Compulsory Acquisition*

1. Introduction                                                     262

2. Takeovers                                                        263
   (1) Procedure                                                    263
       (a) England                                                  264
           (i) Acceptance threshold                                 264
           (ii) Other features                                      264
       (b) Australia                                                266
           (i) Takeovers not regulated by statute                   266
               (A) Acceptance threshold                             266
               (B) Other features                                   267
           (ii) Takeovers regulated by statute                      267
               (A) Acceptance threshold – first limb                268
               (B) Acceptance threshold – second limb               270
               (C) Other features                                   270
   (2) Independence of Majority                                     271
       (a) England                                                  271
       (b) Australia                                                272
           (i) Takeovers not regulated by statute                   272
           (ii) Takeovers regulated by statute                      273
   (3) The role of the court                                        274
   (4) Consideration                                                276
   (5) Shareholder information                                      277
   (6) Restrictions                                                 281

3. Schemes of Arrangement                                           281
   (1) Procedure                                                    283
   (2) Independence of majority                                     284
       (a) England                                                  284
       (b) Australia                                                285
   (3) The role of the court                                        286
   (4) Consideration                                                287
   (5) Shareholder information                                      287
   (6) Restrictions                                                 290

4. Reductions of Capital 290
   (1) Procedure 291
   (2) Independence of majority 291
   (3) The role of the court 293
   (4) Consideration 295
   (5) Shareholder information 296
   (6) Restrictions 297

5. Amendment of the Articles 298
   (1) Procedure 298
   (2) Independence of majority 298
   (3) The role of the court 299
      (a) Proper purpose 302
      (b) Oppression 302
   (4) Consideration 303
   (5) Shareholder information 303
   (6) Restrictions 305

6. Policy Issues 305
   (1) Takeovers 305
   (2) Schemes of arrangement 308
      (a) England 308
      (b) Australia 309
   (3) Reductions of capital 311
   (4) Amendment of the articles 314
   (5) General 315

## SUMMARY

*There are four main methods by which the shares of a minority shareholder may be compulsorily acquired;*

*(1) under the statutory procedure which applies where a takeover has been accepted by a large majority of shareholders;*
*(2) under a scheme of arrangement;*
*(3) pursuant to a selective reduction of capital; and*
*(4) by altering the company's articles of association to add a power of expropriation.*

*Each of these methods has its own procedural requirements and offers a varying level of protection to the minority shareholders whose shares are to be compulsorily acquired.*

*The takeover provisions have the most onerous procedural requirements and there is little scope for resisting compulsory acquisition if all these requirements have been observed. The lower approval threshold in the scheme of arrangement procedure is counterbalanced by specific disclosure obligations, class consent requirements and the necessity to obtain court approval. Although the reduction of capital procedure offers much less protection, it still requires court approval. When considering whether to confirm a reduction, the English courts have disapproved the use of the reduction procedure to effect a takeover. In Australia the courts have instead sought to ensure that a comparable level of protection is given to minority shareholders irrespective of the method of expropriation adopted. It is not generally possible to circumvent the protections provided by these three methods of expropriation by altering the company's articles of association to include an expropriation power unless the substantial purpose of the alteration is to secure the company from significant detriment or harm, and the alteration would not be oppressive to the minority shareholders.*

## 1. INTRODUCTION

Section 10 of Chapter 9 refers to an indirect form of compulsory acquisition which may arise as a result of the unavailability of the unfair prejudice remedy where the relationship between quasi-partners has broken down, one of the parties has been excluded and a fair offer has been made for his or her shares. That issue is not discussed further in this chapter. Instead, this chapter examines the methods by which the shares of a minority shareholder may be compulsorily acquired by direct means.

In the absence of a provision in a company's articles of association permitting compulsory acquisition of a member's shares,[1] there are various ways in which the shares of minority shareholders may be acquired against their wishes. In the context of takeovers, there is a specific statutory procedure for compulsory acquisition which applies where a takeover offer has been accepted by a large majority of shareholders. Other methods which may also be used but which do not exist solely for the purpose of compulsory acquisition include:[2]

---

[1] *Phillips* v. *Manufacturer's Securities Ltd.* (1917) 116 LT 290 (CA) is authority that such a provision is valid and enforceable if included in the articles at the time of the company's formation.

[2] Alternative methods of excluding minority shareholders which do not involve acquisition of their shares and which are therefore beyond the scope of this chapter are sale of the company's assets and/or winding up. See further regarding winding up C. R. Galbraith,

(1) acquiring the shares of the minority under a scheme of arrangement;
(2) selectively reducing the company's capital; and
(3) altering the articles to introduce a provision permitting expropriation.[3]

In this chapter the above methods are compared and contrasted, by examining the following issues:

(1) the procedural requirements of the relevant statutory provisions[4] and the level of majority approval required;
(2) whether there is a requirement that those approving expropriation of the minority are independent, and the methods by which this independence is sought to be achieved;
(3) what controls exist for ensuring the fairness of the consideration received by the expropriated shareholders;
(4) what controls exist for ensuring that shareholders voting on the expropriation are fully informed;
(5) the role of the court in the procedure; and
(6) any restrictions on the use of the procedure.

## 2. TAKEOVERS

### (1) Procedure

The basic feature of the statutory provisions in both the United Kingdom and Australia[5] is that a takeover offeror who has achieved a very high level

---

'Other "Creative Approaches" ' in *Recent Developments in Takeovers* (Melbourne, Business Law Education Centre, 1985) and see generally Q. Digby, 'Eliminating Minority Shareholdings' (1992) 10 *Company & Sec LJ* 105.

[3] More detailed discussion of all of these topics can be found in: I. A. Renard and J. G. Santamaria, *Takeovers and Reconstructions in Australia* (Sydney, Butterworths, 1990, looseleaf) regarding the Australian provisions and M. A. Weinberg, (Consulting Ed.) *Weinberg & Blank on Take-overs and Mergers* (5th edn. by L. Rabinowitz, London, Sweet & Maxwell, 1990, looseleaf) regarding the English position. See also I. A. Renard, 'Takeovers and Acquisitions of Companies with Energy Resources' [1983] *AMPLA Yearbook* 402 with respect to the Australian scheme of arrangement provisions.

[4] In Australia, the Legal Committee of CASAC has identified compulsory acquisition of shares as an area for law reform. Various policy and procedural issues relevant to this topic are set out in its Issues Paper entitled *Compulsory Acquisitions*, March 1994.

[5] The provisions were first enacted in the UK in s. 50 Companies Act, 1928, following the recommendation of the Greene Committee, *Company Law Amendment Committee 1925–1926* Cmd. 2657. The current UK provisions were introduced by the Financial Services Act 1986, s. 172, sch. 12 based substantially on the recommendations of the Law Society's Standing Committee on Company Law, November 1984, and are contained in Part XIIIA, CA 1985 (UK). In Australia, the relevant provisions are ss. 411 and 701–3, CL (Aust).

*Remedy*

of acceptances is able compulsorily to acquire the remaining shares, subject to the right of dissenting shareholders to apply to the court. Although the impetus for the provisions was to introduce a procedure for acquiring the shares of a dissenting minority, complementary provisions have since been added[6] entitling minority shareholders to be notified once the requisite level of acceptances has been obtained and enabling them to compel the offeror to purchase their shares. These complementary provisions are certainly desirable in preventing shareholders having to remain as a 'locked-in' minority.[7] However, it is the compulsory acquisition aspect of the legislation with which this chapter is concerned.[8]

The detailed provisions in the two jurisdictions diverge in many respects, and they will therefore be described separately.

### (a) England

#### (i) Acceptance threshold

Where a takeover offer is made for all the shares (or all the shares of any class or classes of shares) and an offeror has acquired nine-tenths of the shares (or nine-tenths of the shares of any class to which the offer relates), the offeror is able to acquire the shares of the dissenting minority shareholders on the same terms as the offer, subject to the right of dissenting shareholders to apply to the court.

#### (ii) Other features

Earlier versions of these provisions applied to 'a scheme or contract involving the transfer of shares'. This choice of words attracted criticism,[9] and in the current provisions, the wording has been changed so that it applies to a 'takeover offer for all the shares, or all the shares of any class'.

---

[6] Following the recommendation of the Cohen Committee, *Report of the Committee on Company Law Amendment*, Cmd. 6659 (1945).

[7] Note that this right only applies in the takeover context, and does not provide a general remedy for a locked-in minority shareholder.

[8] See further regarding the complementary provision (in England): Weinberg, above n 3, especially para. 3–881 (and in Australia): *Kingston* v. *Keprose Pty. Ltd.* (1987) 11 NSWLR 404 (CA NSW), *Mercantile Mutual life Insurance Co. Ltd. & Ors* v. *Actraint No. 85 Pty. Ltd. (No. 2)* (1990) 52 SASR 506, Renard and Santamaria, above n 3, para. 1212, H. A. J. Ford and R. P. Austin, *Ford's Principles of Corporations Law* (6th edn., Sydney, Butterworths, 1992) para. 2060 and D. Grave, 'Compulsory Share Acquisitions: Practical and Policy Considerations' (1994) 12 *Company & Sec LJ* 240 at 254–5.

[9] *Australian Consolidated Press Ltd.* v. *Australian Newsprint Mills Holdings Ltd.* (1960) 105 CLR 473 at 479 (HC) *per* Dixon CJ and *Re Simo Securities Trust Ltd.* [1971] 1 WLR 1455 at 1464.

This amendment clarifies that the procedure does not apply to partial offers. Further, in *Re Chez Nico (Restaurants) Ltd.*[10] an invitation to shareholders to offer their shares for sale was held not to be an 'offer' within the terms of the section, with the result that the respondents were not able to take advantage of the compulsory acquisition procedure.[11]

Special provision is made to preserve, as far as possible, the ability of dissentient shareholders to take advantage of any choice of consideration which was available within the offer period,[12] and at the same time enabling the offeror to specify the consideration which will apply if the shareholder fails to make an election.

The procedure has also been extended to offers made by individuals and to joint offers,[13] reversing the decision of the Privy Council in *Blue Metal Industries Ltd.* v. *R. W. Dilley*[14] that the compulsory acquisition power was not available where an offer was made by two or more companies jointly.

Several former obstacles to reaching the 90 per cent threshold were: the exclusion of on-market purchases, the treatment of revised offers, and the problem of untraceable shareholders.

Under the current provisions, market purchases may be counted if the consideration does not exceed that specified in the terms of the offer, or if the offer price is revised accordingly.[15] A revised offer is treated as an extension of the original offer if the terms of the offer make provision for their revision.[16] The court also has a discretion, if it considers it just and equitable to do so in light of the number of actively dissenting shareholders, to authorize an offeror to give compulsory acquisition notices where it has received less than nine-tenths acceptances. However, the court must be satisfied that shareholders necessary to achieve the minimum level of acceptances cannot be traced and the consideration offered is fair and reasonable.[17]

---

[10] [1992] BCLC 192; [1991] BCC 736.

[11] For the implications of this decision on the ability of minority shareholders to compel purchase of their shares see L. C. B. Gower, *Gower's Principles of Modern Company Law* (5th edn., London, Sweet & Maxwell, 1992) at 733. Gower suggests that a minority shareholder may nevertheless have a remedy under s. 459, CA 1985 (UK): see Ch. 6. A similar issue arises in relation to the clarification in the recent amendments that the takeover offer must (with limited exceptions in relation to overseas offers) be on terms which are the same in relation to all the shares to which the offer relates: see Gower at 734 and D. Ll. Morgan, 'Compulsory Acquisition of Shares' [1988] *J Bus L* 486 at 486–7.

[12] Section 430(3) and (4), CA 1985 (UK). This gives legislative effect to the decision in *Re Carlton Holdings Ltd.* [1971] 1 WLR 918. However, it has been suggested that it may be possible to circumvent the protection this offers to minority shareholders if the alternative consideration is offered by a third party. See Morgan, ibid., at 492 and Gower, ibid., at 736.

[13] Section 430D, CA 1985 (UK), and see discussion below at nn 294–5 and accompanying text.                                                    [14] [1970] AC 827 (PC).

[15] Section 429(8), CA 1985 (UK).            [16] Section 428(7), CA 1985 (UK).

[17] Section 430C(5), CA 1985 (UK).

Specific provision is also made regarding securities which are convertible into shares, or entitle the holder to subscribe for shares.[18] These are treated as a separate class of shares (separate even from the class of shares to which they may be converted). This alters the result in *Re Simo Securities Trust Ltd.*[19] where debentures which were converted into shares during the offer period were included in calculating the threshold for compulsory purchase of the relevant shares, whereas debentures which could have been but which were not converted were ignored.

### (b) Australia

In Australia, there are two sets of provisions for compulsory acquisition: one which applies to a takeover which is effected by 'takeover scheme' or 'takeover announcement' in accordance with the statutory provisions regulating takeovers contained in Chapter 6 of the Corporations Law, and the other which applies to unregulated takeovers.[20]

### (i) Takeovers not regulated by statute

The main situations in which the statutory takeover provisions do not apply[21] are where a bid:

(1) is made for the shares of a company with 15 or fewer members;
(2) is for a class of non-voting shares;[22]
(3) is made by an offeror who is already 'entitled' to 90 per cent or more of the target's voting shares;[23] or
(4) is exempted from section 615 of the Corporations Law either by regulation or by the written approval of the ASC.[24]

In cases where a formal takeover bid under Chapter 6 is not required or is not possible,[25] the compulsory acquisition procedure set out in section 414 of the Corporations Law applies.

### (A) Acceptance threshold

Section 414 is similar to the provisions which applied in England prior to the 1986 amendments. Where a takeover offer is accepted in respect of

---

[18] Section 430F, CA 1985 (UK).                                    [19] Above n 9.

[20] Cf., the position in England, where Part XIIIA applies irrespective of whether the takeover is regulated by the City Code on Takeovers and Mergers. As to the applicability of the City Code see below n 112.

[21] Exceptions also exist in the case of acquisitions of no more than 3% of the voting shares of the target in a 6-month period and acquisitions after shareholder approval.

[22] Although in this situation a bidder may nevertheless choose to bring the acquisition within the statutory procedure: ASC Practice Note 8.

[23] See text following n 35 regarding 'entitlement' to shares. See also *North Sydney Brick & Tile Co. Ltd.* v. *Darvall & Anor*(1986) 5 NSWLR 681 (CA NSW).

[24] Section 633, CL (Aust).                              [25] See text preceding n 45.

90 per cent of the shares to which it relates (excluding shares held by the offeror's nominees or subsidiaries) the offeror may compulsorily acquire the remaining shares of that class (or those classes). Consent must be obtained from 90 per cent of shareholders of each class where an offer is made in respect of more than one class of shares.[26] A further acceptance threshold (introduced following the Cohen Committee's recommendation[27] but since removed from the United Kingdom legislation) applies where the offeror initially holds more than 10 per cent of the relevant shares and requires that acceptances be received from at least 75 per cent in number of shareholders in the relevant class (as well as 90 per cent in value).

### (B) Other features

Section 414 extends to offers by individuals,[28] although not to joint offers,[29] and preserves the choice of dissenting shareholders where alternative consideration is offered under the takeover.[30] It also has an additional feature not present in the United Kingdom provision, in that when a compulsory acquisition notice is given to a non-assenting shareholder, he or she may obtain the names and addresses of all other dissenting shareholders.[31]

There are, however, several unfortunate features in the drafting of section 414. Some of these, such as the 'scheme or contract' wording have been overcome by interpretation.[32] However, others continue to produce anomalous results. For example, the express requirement that an offer be made on the same terms to all shareholders where an offeror (and/or its nominee or subsidiary) already holds more than 10 per cent of the shares to which the offer relates leaves open the argument that offers made on differential terms do not preclude compulsory acquisition in other cases. The section makes no express provision to enable compulsory acquisition of options and convertible securities, so that the common law as expressed in *Re Simco Securities Trust Ltd.*[33] would presumbaly apply.

### (ii) Takeovers regulated by statute

In regulating the conduct of takeovers, the Corporations Law relies on the concept of 'entitlement' to voting shares. In broad terms, a person is

---

[26] Section 414(2), CL (Aust). Cf., *Australian Consolidated Press Mills Ltd.* v. *Australian Newsprint Mills Holdings Ltd.*, above n 9.     [27] Above n 6.

[28] The extension to individuals implements the recommendation of the Eggleston Committee, *Report of the Company Law Advisory Committee to the Standing Committee of Attorneys-General on Disclosure of Substantial Shareholdings and Takeovers* (1969), Vic, para. 51.     [29] *Blue Metal Industries Ltd.* v. *Dilley*, above n 14.

[30] Section 414(10), CL (Aust).     [31] Sections 414(7) and (8), CL (Aust).

[32] See *Australian Consolidated Press Ltd.* v. *Australian Newsprint Mills Holdings Ltd.*, above n 9.     [33] Above n 9, and see text accompanying n 19.

prohibited from acquiring shares in a company if the acquisition would lead to the person becoming entitled to more than 20 per cent of the voting shares of the company, unless that person makes a takeover offer under a takeover scheme in accordance with Part 6.3 of the Corporations Law or takeover announcement in accordance with Part 6.4. The prohibition does not, however, apply if the person is already entitled to 90 per cent or more of the company's shares.[34]

In general terms,[35] shares to which a person is 'entitled' include shares in respect of which that person or an 'associate' of that person[36] has the power to exercise the right to vote or power to dispose or exercise control over disposal.[37] It also includes shares in respect of which that person has entered or proposes to enter into certain agreements relating to voting, disposal or acquisition.[38]

If the person, is a body corporate, its 'associates'[39] automatically include its directors and secretary, related bodies corporate and their directors and secretary.[40] Associateship may also arise in this context as a result of agreements, arrangements or understandings for controlling the board or the conduct of the affairs of a body corporate, by acting in concert or by an informal association.[41]

The wide definition of 'entitlement' may frustrate an offeror seeking to obtain 100 per cent ownership via section 701 because shares held by an associate of the offeror at the commencement of the bid are excluded from compulsory acquisition, regardless of whether:

(1) the offeror has any control over those shares;
(2) the association continues; or
(3) the shares are retained, or sold by the associate to a third party during the bid.[42]

### (A) Acceptance threshold—first limb

The concept of 'entitlement' is also used in the compulsory acquisition procedure when a takeover has proceeded by way of takeover scheme or announcement, and this has influenced the drafting of the procedure as it operates in this context. Thus, whereas the United Kingdom provision and

---

[34] See also the situations listed above at nn 21–4 and accompanying text.

[35] See further Ford and Austin, above n 8 paras 2017 and 2018.

[36] Other than a nominee body corporate approved by the ASC.

[37] I.e., shares in which the person or its associate has a 'relevant interest' as defined in Pt. 1.2, Div. 5, CL (Aust): s. 609, CL (Aust).

[38] Section 609(2), CL (Aust). 'Agreement' is widely defined in s. 9, CL (Aust).

[39] 'Associate' is defined in Pt. 1.2, Div. 2, CL (Aust).

[40] Section 11, CL (Aust).  [41] Sections 609, 11, 12 and 15, CL (Aust).

[42] CASAC Issues Paper, above n 4 at 5.

the alternative Australian provision require acceptances to be obtained in respect of 90 per cent of the shares subject to the offer in order to enable the offeror to acquire the shares of the dissentients, section 701 requires instead that the offeror has, during the takeover period, become 'entitled' to at least 90 per cent in value of the shares in the class to which the offer relates; that is, the 90 per cent entitlement is measured in respect of total rather than outstanding shares in the relevant class.

There is no equivalent of section 430C(5) of the United Kingdom legislation which enables an offeror who has not achieved the minimum level of acceptances to apply to the court for a compulsory acquisition order, if it can establish that the shortfall consists of uncontactable shareholders and that the bid consideration is fair and reasonable. This is perhaps less likely to arise as an issue in Australia because of the wide operation of the concept of 'entitlement'.[43] In any event, it is possible for the ASC to grant relief from this requirement under section 730 of the Corporations Law.[44]

Ironically, a greater problem is likely to be faced by offerors entitled to more than 90 per cent of the voting shares, as they are unable to use section 701 to acquire the balance of the voting shares by making a further bid that complies with Part 6.3 or Part 6.4 of the Corporations Law unless the 90 per cent threshold requirement is modified by the Commission under section 730.[45] The NCSC rejected an application by TNT Ltd. seeking a modification of the legislation along these lines on the basis that it was loath to extend the power of expropriation at the expense of certainty as to property rights. However, the Victorian Supreme Court allowed an appeal[46] against the NCSC's decision[47] and held that the dissentients' interest in certainty as to their property rights was outweighed by the combination of:

(1) the inconvenience being suffered by TNT;
(2) the apathy of the non-assenting shareholders;

---

[43] See *North Sydney Brick & Tile Co. Ltd.* v. *Darvall & Anor* above n 23, where a company which held 16.99% of the target company's shares was not required to comply with the takeover regime because the existence of pre-emption rights in the company's articles had the effect that it was 'entitled' to 100% of the target company's shares by virtue of the fact that the definition of 'relevant interest' includes power to 'exercise control over the disposal of that share'.

[44] See CASAC Issues Paper, above n 4, at 6. See also discussion below at text accompanying n 51 regarding exercise of this power in the context of the second limb of the acceptance threshold.

[45] See ASC Practice Note 8 para. 4 and CASAC report at 5.

[46] Note that the right of appeal to a court in this context has been replaced by Administrative Review under Part 9.4A CL.

[47] *TNT Ltd.* v. *NCSC* (1986) 11 ACLR 59; 4 ACLC 624.

(3) the cost of servicing them;
(4) the inhibition on commercial planning arising from the uncertainty of the situation;
(5) the expert opinion that the price offered was generous; and
(6) the impracticability of alternative solutions to these disadvantages.

### (B) Acceptance threshold—second limb

Where a bidder starts with an entitlement of more than 10 per cent of the shares (in the class or classes to which the offer relates), then a further threshold must be satisfied in addition to the 90 per cent test. Either 75 per cent of the offerees must have disposed of their shares to the offeror, or at least 75 per cent of the shareholders registered on the day before the takeover offer must no longer be registered one month after the close of the offer period.

The latter alternative was introduced on the recommendation of the Edwards Committee[48] who noted that the provision had been found to be ambiguous as the number of offerees was difficult to determine, particularly where a target was listed and where there was extensive market activity in the target shares during the course of a takeover bid.[49] However, like the former alternative, it is potentially open to manipulation by vote splitting, since it looks to the number of shareholders and not the value of their shareholding.[50]

It has already been noted that the 75 per cent requirement has been abandoned in England. In *Brierley* v. *Dextran Pty. Ltd.*[51] the NCSC exercised its discretion to extend the time of the offer to enable sufficient acceptances to be obtained in order to satisfy the 75 per cent requirement.

### (C) Other features

As in the section 414 procedure, dissenting shareholders are able to obtain the names and addresses of all other dissenting shareholders.[52] Further,

---

[48] *Report of the Joint Select Committee on Corporations Legislation* (April 1989) para 13.32 ff.
[49] The difficulty arises because under s. 649, CL (Aust), persons who acquire shares in the target company during the period of the bid are counted as offerees, while the transferor also remains an offeree, at least until the time of the transfer, making it impossible to keep track of the proportion of offerees accepting a takeover offer. See further, NCSC Policy Statement Release 139 para. 5, Attorney General's Department submission to the Edwards Committee, ibid., para. 13.43, Digby, above n 2, at 109 and CASAC Issues Paper, above n 4, at 8.
[50] CASAC Issues Paper, above n 4, at 8 ff. See also Renard and Santamaria, above n 3, para 1203, M. A. Weinberg *et al.*, *Weinberg & Blank on Take-overs and Mergers* (4th edn., London, Sweet & Maxwell, 1979) para. 1445 and W. Kent and L. Vary, 'Compulsory Acquisition of Shares' (1991) 9 *Company & Sec LJ* 261 at 264.
[51] (1990) 3 ACSR 455; 9 ACLC 30.
[52] Section 701(9), CL (Aust), although the CASAC Issues Paper, above n 4, at 12–3 points out that there are deficiencies in the drafting of this provision.

many of the uncertainties related to the drafting of section 414 of the Corporations Law and the pre-1986 United Kingdom legislation have been removed from section 701. Thus, for example, it is clear that the offer must be for all of the shares in the relevant class,[53] provision is made to enable dissenting shareholders to choose between alternative consideration offered,[54] the minimum level of acceptances is required in respect of each class,[55] and it is irrelevant whether the level of entitlement arises through on-market acquisitions or from acceptances of the takeover offer.

However, there are still several matters which cause difficulty. The procedure does not enable shares issued subsequent to the relevant date[56] to be compulsorily acquired.[57] Further, in common with section 414, section 710 does not enable a bidder compulsorily to acquire options or convertible notes[58] or any other form of security convertible into equity (although if the takeover takes place via a formal takeover scheme or takeover announcement, the holders of these interests have the power to compel compulsory acquisition).[59] This may encourage a target company to issue shares or convertible securities as a takeover defence.[60]

## (2) Independence of majority

### (a) England

The most recent amendments to the United Kingdom legislation introduce the concept of 'associate'. 'Associate' is expansively defined[61] to include nominees of the offeror, companies in the same group as the offeror, bodies corporate in which the offeror is substantially interested,[62] and any

---

[53] Section 701(2)(a) refers to a 'full takeover scheme': see s. 635(a), CL (Aust). Partial bids cannot be made under the alternative procedure of a takeover announcement.

[54] Section 701(7) and (8), CL (Aust).

[55] Section 701(2)(b), CL (Aust).

[56] In the case of a takeover scheme, the date of service of the Part A statement and, in the case of a takeover announcement, the date of the announcement.

[57] This is because the notice given pursuant to s. 701(2) entitles and binds the offeror to acquire the 'outstanding shares' which is defined to mean shares in respect of which the offers were made.

[58] See e.g., *ANZ Executors & Trustees Ltd.* v. *Humes Ltd.* (1989) 15 ACLR 392.

[59] Section 703, CL (Aust). See *Kingston* v. *Keprose Pty. Ltd.*, above n 8, Edwards Committee Report, above n 48 para 13.48, and CASAC Issues Paper, above n 4, at 5.

[60] See further Renard and Santamaria, above n 3, para. 1213, N. O'Bryan, 'Takeover Offers and Prospectus Requirements under the Companies Code' (1985) 3 *Company & Sec LJ* 3 and T. Steel, 'Defensive Tactics in Company Takeovers' (1986) 4 *Company & Sec I.J* 30. But note the limitations on the issue of equity securities or securities convertible to equity within three months from notice of an actual or proposed takeover offer or announcement in ASX Listing Rule 3R(3).         [61] Section 430E(4), CA 1985 (UK).

[62] An offeror has a 'substantial interest' in another body corporate if the latter company or its directors are accustomed to act in accordance with the offeror's directions or instructions;

person[63] who is a party to an agreement with the offeror for the acquisition of shares or in an interest in shares.[64] In the case of an offeror who is an individual, his or her associates also include his or her spouse and any minor child or step-child.[65]

Shares held or contracted to be acquired by this expanded range of persons are excluded[66] when calculating whether the minimum acceptance requirements have been satisfied, except where they have been purchased on-market during the offer period at a consideration equal to or below the offer price.[67] The introduction of this provision goes a long way to ensuring that the acceptances which trigger the compulsory acquisition power are independent of the offeror.

### (b) Australia

#### (i) Takeovers not regulated by statute

Section 414 of the Corporations Law shares the philosophy underlying the current United Kingdom provision, namely that it is the very high percentage of acceptances, combined with the fact that those acceptances are independent from the offeror which provides the *prima facie* justification for overriding the property rights of the minority share-holders.[68] However, the method of ensuring that only acceptances from genuinely independent shareholders are counted has certain defects. Although section 414 excludes shares held by nominees or subsidiaries of the offeror when calculating whether the minimum level of acceptances have been achieved, it does not exclude acceptances from a holding company of an offeror or by the other categories of persons falling within the definition of 'associate' in the United Kingdom provision. A dissenting shareholder would need to apply to the court to defeat compulsory acquisition in these circumstances.

---

or the offeror is entitled to exercise or control the exercise of one-third or more of the voting power at general meetings of that body: s. 430E(6). The circumstances where a person will be taken to be 'entitled to exercise or control the exercise of voting power' are further expanded by virtue of ss. 430E(7), 203(3) and (4), CA 1985 (UK).

[63] Or nominee of that person.

[64] The agreement must include provisions imposing obligations or restrictions on one or more of the parties to it with respect to their use, retention or disposal of their interests in that company's shares acquired in pursuance of the agreement. 'Agreement' in this context includes a binding agreement or arrangement or one involving mutuality in the undertakings, expectations or understandings of the parties: ss. 430E(7), 204(5) and (6), CA 1985 (UK).

[65] Section 430E(8), CA 1985 (UK).

[66] Section 430E(1) and (2), CA 1985 (UK).

[67] Conversely, they are included when calculating whether the offeror has acquired sufficient shares to give the minority shareholder a right to be bought out by the offeror: s. 430E (3), CA 1985 (UK).

[68] See *Re Bugle Press Ltd.* [1961] Ch. 270 (CA).

In *Re Bugle Press Ltd.*[69] a company had three shareholders, two of which between them held 90 per cent of the issued shares. They formed a separate company which made an offer for the company's shares and, having accepted it, sought to acquire the shares of the third shareholder compulsorily. At first instance, Buckley J found in favour of the dissenting shareholder on the basis that there could be no presumption as to the fairness of the offer where the acceptances where not independent of the offeror. The onus of proof was therefore on the offeror to demonstrate that the offer was fair, and on the facts this onus was held not to have been discharged.

The Court of Appeal also found in favour of the applicant, but on the slightly different ground that the offeror was using the section not for a true scheme or contract but for the purpose of enabling majority shareholders to expropriate the minority. This raised a *prima facie* presumption that the court ought to refuse compulsory acquisition. The court suggested that in order to discharge the onus of showing fairness, the majority would need to show 'that there was some good reason in the interests of the company' for allowing the acquisition, such as that the minority shareholder was 'acting in a manner destructive or highly damaging to the interests of the company from some motives entirely of his own'.[70] In reaching its decision, the court placed emphasis on the fact that the section only enabled an offer to be made by a company and not by an individual.

*Re Bugle Press Ltd.*[71] was applied in the Australian case[72] of *Re Rees' Application*[73] where a similar strategy was attempted (although the facts were slightly more complicated). The dissenting shareholders were also successful in this case.

Since these cases were decided, the compulsory acquisition power has been made available to individuals in both jurisdictions, effectively removing the basis for the Court of Appeal's decision in *Re Bugle Press Ltd.*[74] However, a similar decision may well still be reached applying Buckley J's reasoning that the presumption of fairness which arises from 90 per cent acceptance cannot apply where those acceptances come from persons connected with the offeror.

### (ii) Takeovers regulated by statute

It is more difficult to find an underlying philosophy in section 701 that acceptances should be received from persons independent of the offeror. This is because the pre-requisite for compulsory acquisition does not depend on the level of acceptances of the offer, but rather on whether the

---

[69] Ibid.  [70] Ibid., at 287 *per* Lord Evershed MR.  [71] Ibid.
[72] For a Canadian example see *Esso Standard (Inter-America) Inc* v. *J. W. Enterprises Inc. and Morrisroe* (1963) 37 DLR (2d) 598 (SCC).  [73] [1972] QWN 47.
[74] Above n 68.

offeror's 'entitlement' to shares has reached a certain level during the course of a takeover offer. The wide ambit of the concept of entitlement militates against the argument that acceptances by persons connected with the offeror should be disregarded.

### (3) The role of the court

Dissenting shareholders who wish to resist compulsory acquisition are given an express right to apply to the court. It has been consistently held that in the absence of special circumstances (such as existed in *Re Bugle Press Ltd.*)[75] the onus of proof is on the applicant to establish a reason (other than the mere fact that the sale or exchange is compulsory) why his or her shares should not be acquired.[76]

There is repeated comfirmation in case-law of the weight of this onus.[77] Perhaps the most extreme is the dictum of Vaisey J in *Re Sussex Brick Co. Ltd.* that:[78]

It must be affirmatively established that, notwithstanding the view of the majority, the scheme is unfair, and that is a different thing from saying that it must be established that the scheme is not a very fair one or not a fair one: a scheme has to be shown affirmatively patently, obviously and convincingly to be unfair.

Hardie Boys J in the New Zealand case of *Re Deans*[79] considered that dictum to be a 'rather enthusiastic overstatement' of what is required, saying 'I am sure that the applicant does not need to show that the majority were morons.' Nevertheless, a common theme in the cases is: the higher the level of acceptances, the greater the burden on the applicants.[80]

In discharging the onus, the applicants must prove unfairness to the body of shareholders and not to individuals.[81] Thus, for example, in *Re Grierson, Oldham & Adams Ltd.*[82] a complaint by dissenting shareholders that they would be compelled to sell their shares at a loss which would not be deductible for capital gains tax could not be used as a basis for challenging compulsory acquisition.[83]

---

[75] Above n 68. [76] *Re Hoare & Co. Ltd.* (1933) 150 LT 374 at 375.
[77] See e.g., *Re Grierson, Oldham & Adams Ltd.* [1968] Ch. 17.
[78] [1961] Ch. 289 at 293. [79] [1986] 2 NZLR 271 at 274.
[80] *Eddy v. W. R. Carpenter Holdings Ltd.* (1985) 10 ACLR 316; 4 ACLC 101.
[81] See the criticism of this approach by P. Spender, 'Compulsory Acquisition of Minority Shareholders' (1993) 11 *Company & Sec LJ* 83 at 99. [82] Above n 77.
[83] See also *Manning v. Harris Steel Group Inc.* (1989) 63 DLR (4th) 125 (CA BC), *Cockle v. Carlingford Nominees Ltd.* (1989) 4 NZCLC 65,120, *Elkington v. Shell Australia Ltd.* (1993) 32 NSWLR 11 (CA NSW) and *Re Shoppers City Ltd. and M. Loeb Ltd.* (1968) 3 DLR (3d) 35. In the last case, the fact that other shareholders had accepted the offer, relegated the dissentient's evidence as to the insufficiency of the price into the category of individual unfairness rather than unfairness to the body of shareholders. Cf., schemes of arrangement in this regard: see below at nn 172–3 and accompanying text.

In cases where shareholders are able to establish unfairness, the court's powers vary according to the jurisdiction. The United Kingdom provision empowers the court to make an order varying the terms of the offer where an application is being made by a shareholder seeking to resist compulsory acquisition.[84]

It seems that the Australian courts are restricted to ordering that the offeror is not entitled to acquire the dissentient's shares.[85] The express power granted to the court to vary the terms on which shares are to be acquired where a shareholder applies to the court after requiring acquisition of his or her shares[86] seems to imply that the court does not have this power where a shareholder is seeking to resist compulsory acquisition. However, in the New Zealand case of *Plaza Fabrics (Tauranga) Ltd.* v. *National Airlines Co. Ltd.*[87] Henry J considered, obiter, that the court had power to vary the terms of acquisition in the latter situation, on the basis that there was no reason why the shareholder's entitlement should differ depending upon which procedure happens to be invoked.[88]

Despite the uncertainty as to the extent of its powers, the courts have been prepared to award interest to unsuccessful dissentients in order to equate the consideration they receive with that received by those who accepted the offer.[89] However, Hardie Boys J in *Re Deans*[90] found this difficult to reconcile with the principle that the court may interfere only if the scheme is unfair to the shareholders as a body.

In order to encourage dissenting shareholders to submit the matter to the court, the English courts have been generous to dissenting shareholders in their costs orders. In *Re Hoare & Co. Ltd.*[91] Maugham J ordered that the company should pay the costs of the application despite finding that the applicants had not established grounds for avoiding compulsory acquisition.[92] In subsequent English cases, the practice has instead been to make no order as to costs in the case of unsuccessful

---

[84] Section 430C(1), CA 1985 (UK). See the Jenkins Committee, *Report of the Company Law Committee*, Cmnd. 1749, (1962) UK, para. 287.

[85] Sections 414(3) and 701(6), CL (Aust).

[86] For examples of exercises of the court's discretion to fix the consideration when an applicant is requiring his or her shares to be purchased, see *Mercantile Mutual life Insurance Co. Ltd.* v. *Actraint No. 85 Pty. Ltd. (No. 2)*, above n 8, (preference shares) and for a case relating to options see *Kingston* v. *Keprose Pty. Ltd. (No. 2)* (1987) 12 ACLR 599; 6 ACLC 111. See also Renard and Santamaria, above n 3, para. 1214.

[87] (1991) 5 NZCLC 67,288.

[88] Relying on dicta to this effect in *Re Deans*, above n 79.

[89] *Re Hoare & Co. Ltd.*, above n 76, *Re Grierson Oldham & Adams Ltd.*, above n 77, and *Re Carlton Holdings*, above n 12, at 926. [90] Above n 79, at 278.

[91] Above n 76, at 376.

[92] The company was also ordered to pay costs in *Re Fras Hinde & Sons Ltd. The Times*, 23 April 1966 at 8 on the basis of the unusual facts of that case.

applications.[93] Specific provision now exists in section 430C(4) Companies Act 1985 (UK) which provides that no order for costs shall be made against a shareholder applying to the court unless the court considers that the application was 'unnecessary, improper or vexatious' or there has been unreasonable delay in making the application or unreasonable conduct on the shareholder's part in conducting the proceedings on the application. The liberal interpretation of this new section in *Re Britoil plc*[94] suggests that it may, if anything, augment the bias in favour of the dissenting shareholder in respect to costs.

In Australia, it is usual for no order to be made as to costs. Two exceptions are *Williams v. United Dairies Ltd.*[95] and *Brierley v. Dextran Pty. Ltd.*[96] where costs orders were made against dissenting shareholders. In *Elkington v. Shell Australia Ltd.*[97] the dissenting shareholder was ordered to pay the costs of an appeal to the New South Wales Court of Appeal on the basis that he had had his opportunity to air his complaints before McLelland J and no error had been shown in McLelland J's judgment.

## (4) Consideration

In the case of companies whose shares are quoted, the market price has been taken to be a *prima facie* indication of the value of the shares in question, so that an offer price in excess of the market price will *prima facie* be regarded as fair.[98] Further, in the absence of evidence that the market price was distorted or manipulated, the market price has been taken as a more reliable guide to fairness than an expert's report.[99] However, the court will be prepared to examine the conduct of the offeror in the period preceding the making of the offer in order to determine whether the market price has been distorted.[100]

Courts have been similarly unsympathetic to complaints regarding the consideration offered in private companies. For example, in *Re Dad's Cookie Co. (BC) Ltd.*[101] Macdonald J acknowledged that the dissenting

---

[93] *Re Evertite Locknuts Ltd.* [1945] Ch. 220 and *Re Grierson, Oldham & Adams Ltd.*, above n 77. See also *Re Deans*, above n 79, and the Canadian case of *Re Sayvette Ltd.* (1975) 65 DLR (3d) 596. Cf., *Blue Metal Industries Ltd. v. R. W. Dilley*, above n 14. In that case the applicants were successful and the respondents were ordered to pay their costs of the appeals as between solicitor and client.                                    [94] [1990] BCC 70 (CA).
[95] (1986) 10 ACLR 406; 4 ACLC 275.                          [96] Above n 51.
[97] Above n 83.
[98] *Re Press Caps Ltd.* [1949] Ch. 434 (CA), *Re Western Manufacturing (Reading) Ltd.* [1956] Ch. 436, *Eddy v. W. R. Carpenter Holdings Ltd.*, above n 80, and *Re Sheldon* (1987) 3 NZCLC 100,058.                          [99] *Elkington v. Shell Australia Ltd.*, above n 83.
[100] *Elkington v. Vockbay Pty. Ltd.* (1993) 10 ACSR 785; 11 ACLC 591 citing *Catto v. Ampol Ltd.* (1989) 16 NSWLR 342. See discussion of this case below in section 4(4).
[101] (1969) 7 DLR (3d) 243 at 255.

shareholder 'may be right in what he says about the value of the shares', but nevertheless did not consider the evidence led to be sufficient to overcome the presumption of fairness established by the acceptance of the offer by 90 per cent of the shareholders.

It has also been held that unfairness is not established by showing that the consideration offered does not include any amount attributable to the benefit of control of the company which would accrue to the respondents from the acquisition of all the company's shares,[102] even where the applicant was able to demonstrate that the total shareholding of the target company was subsequently sold by the offeror at a profit.[103]

Thus, as regards consideration, the greatest protection of individual shareholders generally lies in the view taken by the majority.[104]

## (5) Shareholder information

Until very recently, complaints of lack of information and hence uncertainty as to the fairness of the offer were viewed less than sympathetically by the English and Australian courts,[105] even in *Re Evertite Locknuts Ltd.*[106] where the court acknowledged that the information supplied was 'a little meagre'. A similar attitude was taken to discovery, which was refused in *Re Press Caps Ltd.*[107] Again, this was not on the basis that the complaint was without merit, but in view of[108] '. . . the serious consequences which might follow if the holder of one per cent. of the shares of a company should in any large number of cases become entitled by making an application under this section to obtain an extensive investigation of the company's affairs.'

Shareholders seeking to challenge the consideration offered for their shares were therefore left in the position of pointing to inconsistencies between the price offered and previous announcements as to the company's prospects. However, raising doubts of this kind was considered insufficient to discharge the heavy onus of showing unfairness.[109] The only

---

[102] *Re Grierson, Oldham & Adams Ltd.*, above n 77 and *Manning* v. *Harris Steel Group Inc* above n 83.

[103] *Re Sheldon*, above n 98. But cf., McHugh J's judgment in *Gambotto* v. *WCP Ltd.* (1995) 16 ACSR 1; 13 ACLC 342 (HC), where his Honour noted that minority shareholders whose shares are being expropriated have no say in the timing of the expropriation, and considered that *Re Sheldon* should not be followed in Australia.

[104] The unwillingness of the courts to listen to complaints of inadequate terms is criticized by commentators: See e.g., Weinberg, above n 3, para. 3–888 and H. Bond, 'The Statutory Protection of Minority Shareholders' (1984) 5 *Company Lawyer* 155.

[105] A more lenient approach was taken in the Canadian case of *Re John Labatt Ltd. and Lucky Lager Breweries Ltd.* (1959) 20 DLR (2d) 159, where the court considered, obiter, that failure by the offeror to make full disclosure of its intentions would provide grounds for ordering against compulsory acquisition. [106] Above n 93.

[107] [1948] 2 All ER 638. [108] Ibid., at 639.

[109] *Nidditch* v. *The Calico Printers' Association Ltd.* 1961 SLT 282.

concession to minority shareholders in this regard was that if information were given to shareholders, it was considered that it should not be untrue in any material respect by reason of what was stated in or omitted from it.[110]

A similarly unsympathetic approach was taken in the Australian case of *Eddy* v. *W. R. Carpenter Holdings Ltd.*[111] where the dissenting shareholder established that the valuations relied on might well be out of date and made on an inappropriate basis, yet the court did not consider this to be the 'hard evidence' required to discharge the heavy onus of establishing unfairness.

However, more recent decisions reflect the fact that in the situations where takeovers are regulated,[112] there are now comprehensive disclosure obligations in the City Code on Takeovers and Mergers in England[113] and in the Corporations Law in Australia,[114] designed to ensure that shareholders are able to make a fully-informed decision whether to accept a takeover offer.

Further, Rule 3.1 of the City Code requires the board of the target company to obtain competent independent advice and pass on the substance of that advice to shareholders, and Note 1 to that rule emphasizes the importance to shareholders of independent advice in a management buy-out or similar situations. Similarly, in Australia, where an offeror is entitled to 30 per cent more of the voting shares in a class of the target company or where a director of the target company is or is on the board of the offeror, the target company must obtain and provide to shareholders an independent expert's report stating whether in the expert's

---

[110] *Sammel* v. *President Brand Gold Mining Co. Ltd.* 1969 (3) SA 629. In Australia s. 52 of the Trade Practices Act 1974 (Cth) and ss. 995 and 999, CL (Aust) will also be relevant. Section 52 prohibits false and misleading conduct or conduct which is likely to mislead or deceive in general terms: see *Fraser* v. *NRMA Holdings Ltd.* (1994) 14 ACSR 656; 12 ACLC 855 affd. (1995) 15 ACSR 590; 13 ACLC 132 (Full Fed Ct). The Corporations Law provisions prohibit conduct that is misleading or deceptive or is likely to mislead or deceive in connection with dealings in securities, and false or misleading statements in relation to securities. See also ss. 704–5, CL (Aust) regarding liability for mis-statements in takeover documents, public statements and advertisements.

[111] Above n 80.

[112] In England, obligations are imposed mainly by the City Code on Takeovers and Mergers which applies to public companies, whether listed or unlisted and to private companies if during the previous 10 years: their equity capital has been listed on the Stock Exchange; dealings in their equity capital have been advertised on a regular basis for at least six months; their equity capital has been afforded facilities for dealings on the Unlisted Securities Market or other investment exchange; or they have filed a prospectus for the issue of their equity shares. In Australia, takeovers are regulated by Chapter 6 of the Corporations Law: see discussion in text preceding n 34 regarding the applicability of this regime. Additional obligations contained in the listing rules in both jurisdictions may be relevant.

[113] See especially, General Principle 4 and Rules 23 ff.

[114] See s. 750, CL (Aust).

opinion the takeover offer is fair and reasonable and setting out the reasons for forming that opinion.[115]

As noted above, this regulatory emphasis on full and fair information to shareholders has not proved to be of assistance to dissenting shareholders who merely raise questions as to the information provided, such as whether valuations were made on an appropriate basis.[116] However, a more receptive approach to complaints of insufficient disclosure seems to be reflected in more recent English decisions. For example, in *Re Lifecare International plc*[117] discovery was ordered to enable a shareholder to demonstrate that the advice received by the board on the basis of which it made its recommendation was flawed. Hoffmann J distinguished *Re Press Caps Ltd.*[118] noting that the Supreme Court Rules had been altered since that case was decided with the effect that discovery will ordinarily be ordered in originating summons proceedings unless the court is satisfied that it is not necessary.[119] His Lordship also rejected the 'flood-gates' argument relied on in the earlier case, saying:[120]

The question is, 'Am I satisfied in this case that discovery of the limited kind sought by the applicant [*viz* limited to the documents relevant to the board's decision to recommend the offer] is not necessary?' I am not so satisfied, because, in my view, the whole issue in the case is going to be whether the advice said to have been given to the board by Greg Middleton & Co Ltd was good advice or not, and I find it difficult to see how the judge hearing the summons could form a view on that matter without seeing the documents which reflect exactly what that advice was.

Further, in *Re Chez Nico (Restaurants) Ltd.*,[121] Browne-Wikinson V-C considered that the level of information provided to shareholders was particularly relevant where the bidder was already a director and shareholder in the target company. He said, obiter,[122] that failure to comply with the City Code's provisions as to disclosure was a very major factor operating against compulsory acquisition of non-assenting shareholders' shares, and regarded the non-compliance as evidence negativing any presumption that the offer was fair because 90 per cent of shareholders had accepted. His Lordship distinguished *Re Evertite Locknuts Ltd.*[123] as a

---

[115] Section 648, CL (Aust). See also ASC Policy Statement 75 and Practice Note 43.

[116] *Eddy* v. *W. R. Carpenter Holdings Ltd.*, above n 80.

[117] [1990] BCLC 222; (1989) 5 BCC 755.  [118] Above n 107.

[119] The applicability of this decision in Australia will depend upon the court rules in the relevant jurisdiction. It should also be noted that shareholders in Australia have an alternative means to obtain information as a result of the statutory rights granted in s. 319, CL: See discussion in Ch. 9 section 8(2)(b).

[120] Above n 117, at 225; 757.  [121] Above n 10.

[122] The compulsory acquisition power was held not to be available because there was no 'takeover offer' within the terms of Part XIIIA.

[123] Above n 93.

case where the bidder was an outsider and, importantly, as predating the City Code.

In *Chez Nico*'s case[124] the lack of disclosure was particularly significant, since the bidders knew that the financial position of the company was not the same as that disclosed in the accounts, and that rather than making a loss, the company was in fact trading profitably, despite large increases in the directors' emoluments. By contrast, in the Australian case of *Elkington* v. *Vockbay Pty. Ltd.*,[125] a dissenting shareholder seeking to rely on lack of disclosure to resist compulsory acquisition was unsuccessful as he was unable to establish that the disclosure was inadequate for determining whether the consideration offered was fair and reasonable.

This raises the question of whether the courts will be equally responsive to complaints of lack of information in a case where takeovers are unregulated so that there are no specific disclosure obligations.

It may be that on the facts of a particular case, the directors will be in a fiduciary position *vis-à-vis* the shareholders which carries with it a duty of disclosure, as was the case in *Coleman* v. *Myers*.[126] Woodhouse J[127] in that case identified as factors relevant to whether a fiduciary relationship would arise on the facts: dependence upon information and advice, the existence of a relationship of confidence, the significance of some particular transaction for the parties and the extent of any positive action taken by or on behalf of the director or directors to promote it.[128]

Quite apart from special fact fiduciary relationships, Brightman J considered, obiter, in *Gething* v. *Kilner*[129] that compulsory acquisition might be resisted if shareholders had been misled into accepting a takeover offer. In that case the directors had recommended acceptance of a takeover offer in the face of advice from their stockbrokers that the offer was too low.

Finally, an alternative avenue of relief in cases where shareholders may have been misled is an action based on unfairly prejudicial conduct.[130] In *Re a Company (No. 008699 of 1985)*[131] there were two competing takeover

---

[124] Above n 10.

[125] Above n 100. Cf., the disclosure obligations imposed by the Australian High Court in *Gambotto*'s case, above n 103, in the context of an expropriation effected by alteration of the articles. See further below, sections 5(3)(b) and 5(5).

[126] [1977] 2 NZLR 225 (CA NZ).                     [127] Ibid., at 325.

[128] For Australian and English authorities approving the finding that the directors may in special circumstances owe fiduciary duties (including disclosure obligations) directly to shareholders see: *Re Chez Nico (Restaurants) Ltd.* above n 10, at 750, *Darvall* v. *North Sydney Brick & Tile Co. Ltd.* (1989) 16 NSWLR 260 at 317 (CA NSW) and *Glandon Pty. Ltd.* v. *Strata Consolidated Pty. Ltd.* (1993) 11 ACSR 543; 11 ACLC 895 (CA NSW). For a case recognising the possibility of a fiduciary duty arising between a director and a co-director in his capacity as guarantor of the company's debts see *Elliott* v. *Wheeldon* [1993] BCLC 53; [1992] BCC 489 (CA).

[129] [1972] 1 WLR 337.                     [130] See Ch. 6.

[131] [1986] BCLC 382; (1986) 2 BCC 99,024.

offers for the shares of a private company not governed by the City Code. One offer was promoted by the directors and the other, at a substantially higher figure, came from a trade competitor. The petitioners complained that a circular sent to shareholders by the directors recommending the lower offer was misleading, and that if the circular had dissuaded shareholders from accepting the higher offer, it had unfairly prejudiced their interests. Hoffmann J referred to the obligation in General Principle 4 of the City Code to provide shareholders with sufficient information and advice to enable them to reach a properly informed decision and equated it with the directors' obligation of fairness for the purposes of section 459.[132] His Lordship did not consider that the detailed provisions of the Code necessarily coincided with the requirements of fairness, noting that in a private company there may be cases where the board's duty to provide sufficient information and advice is satisfied by doing nothing. However, in that case the board had not done nothing and Hoffmann J was not prepared to strike out the petition.

## (6) Restrictions

The availability of the statutory compulsory acquisition procedure depends upon the number of shareholders and the sizes of their holdings. In Australia, in a company where the offeror holds 10 per cent and there are fewer than four other shareholders, the 75 per cent requirement precludes the operation of the procedure. In both England and Australia, a shareholder with 90 per cent or more of the shares may have difficulty in obtaining the required levels of consent.

There are also two major drawbacks which apply only to the Australian provision. First, neither section 414 nor section 701 permits compulsory acquisition of options, convertible notes or other interests convertible into shares. Secondly, in the case of section 701 it is not possible to use the procedure to acquire shares issued after the takeover period has commenced.

## 3. SCHEMES OF ARRANGEMENT

A scheme of arrangement may be made between a company and its creditors or any class of them and/or between a company and its members or any class of them. The scheme of arrangement procedure permits a dissenting minority to be bound by an arrangement after certain conditions have been complied with, which are designed to ensure that proper

---

[132] Ibid., at 389; 99,030.

consideration is given to the interests of various classes of members and/or creditors.

A common method by which a takeover may be achieved using the scheme of arrangement procedure[133] is by a 'cancellation and reduction scheme'.[134] There are several variations on this theme. It will usually involve cancellation of all the issued shares in the target company (or all those not held by the 'offeror')[135] by way of a reduction of capital. The scheme may also provide for the issue of new shares in the target company to the offeror from the reserve created. The consideration to the expropriated shareholders may be in the form of cash,[136] shares in the offeror,[137] a combination of cash and shares[138] or a choice between shares and a cash payment.[139]

An alternative method is a 'transfer scheme'[140] which provides for the acquisition by the offeror of the whole of the issued capital of the target company, other than shares already owned by it and payment to the expropriated shareholder, again either in cash and/or shares in itself.[141]

The ability to include creditors in the arrangement offers distinct advantages to an offeror in Australia seeking to obtain 100 per cent ownership in a company which has issued options or convertible securities, since in Australia,[142] the compulsory acquisition procedures which apply to takeovers do not enable an offeror to acquire those interests.[143]

---

[133] A scheme of arrangement offers various options for achieving a 100% takeover. Since this chapter is concerned with expropriation of shares, one method which will not be examined is a scheme under which a company's undertaking is transferred to another company.

[134] This terminology derives from *Re Savoy Hotel Ltd.* [1981] Ch. 351 at 357. As this type of scheme involves a reduction of capital, the specific statutory procedure for a reduction of capital will also have to be complied with. See discussion below in section 4.

[135] The term 'offeror' is used in the following discussion to describe the person who will obtain ownership of the company as a result of the scheme.

[136] See e.g., *Re Hellenic & General Trust Ltd.* [1976] 1 WLR 123.

[137] See e.g., *Re the Bank of Adelaide* (1979) 22 SASR 481 (Full Ct, SA)

[138] See e.g., *Re ACM Gold Ltd.* (1992) 7 ACSR 231; 10 ACLC 573.

[139] See e.g., *Re Wallace Dairy Co. Ltd.* [1980] VR 588, *Re Stockbridge Ltd.* (1993) 9 ACSR 637; 11 ACLC 201.

[140] Again, this is the terminology used in *Re Savoy Hotel Ltd.*, above n 134, at 356.

[141] See e.g., *Singer Manufacturing Co.* v. *Robinow* 1971 SC 11 and *Re Savoy Hotel Ltd.*, ibid.

[142] Cf., the English position. See discussion above at n 18 and accompanying text.

[143] Convertible noteholders will be regarded as creditors of the company, and there is Australian authority favouring the view that option holders who are entitled to an award of damages if shares are not issued following the exercise of the option should be regarded as 'contingent creditors': *Re Austamax Resources Ltd.* (1985) 10 ACLR 194; 4 ACLC 76, *Re Asia Oil & Minerals Ltd.* (1986) 5 NSWLR 42, *Re BDC Investments Ltd.* (1988) 13 ACLR 201; 6 ACLC 1196 and *Re US Masters Ltd.* (1991) 4 ACSR 462.

## (i) Procedure

The main features of the legislation[144] in both England and Australia are very similar.[145] In both jurisdictions, the statutory procedure is in three stages. The first stage is an application to the court for class meetings to be ordered. This application will usually be made by the company.[146] It is up to the applicant (and not the court) to identify the relevant classes.[147]

Class meetings are then held, at which approval must be obtained from a majority in number and three-fourths in value of the members or class of members present and voting either in person or by proxy.[148] The approval requirement is therefore much lower under a scheme of arrangement than under the specific compulsory acquisition procedure where acceptances are required from 90 per cent in value (and, in certain cases in Australia, 75 per cent in number). Not only are the approval thresholds lower, but the calculation is made by reference to shareholders 'present and voting either in person or by proxy', so that a much lower percentage than 75 per cent of all class members may in fact be required. On the other hand, the requirement for a 'majority in number' of shareholders to approve the scheme is calculated in the same way, so that a well organized minority could veto of the scheme,[149] although the majority may be able to overcome this problem by vote splitting.[150]

Once the resolutions have been passed by the requisite class majorities, a further application is made to the court for approval. If obtained, the scheme is binding on all members or creditors (or the relevant class of them), provided that the additional procedural requirement of registration of the court's order is complied with.[151]

One distinction between the two jurisdictions is that in Australia the ASC is also involved in the process of obtaining approval for the scheme. Fourteen days' notice (or a lesser period if permitted by the court or the ASC) must be given to the ASC of the hearing of the initial application to

---

[144] In England, formal schemes are governed by ss. 425–27A, CA 1985 (UK) and in Australia by ss. 411–3, CL (Aust).

[145] Some of the differences in detail are outlined below. There is also detailed provision in the Australian provision to enable consolidated meetings to be held: s. 411(1A)–(1C), CL (Aust).

[146] It may also be made by a member or a creditor and, in the case of a company being wound up, by a liquidator (or, in England an administrator): s. 425(1), CA 1985 (UK), s. 411(1), CL (Aust).

[147] See Practice Note [1934] WN 142. The determination of 'classes' in this context is discussed in section 3(2).

[148] Section 425(2), CA 1985 (UK), s. 411(4)(a)(ii), CL (Aust).

[149] Renard and Santamaria, above n 3, para. 1674.

[150] See e.g., *Re Direct Acceptance Corporation Ltd.* (1987) 5 ACLC 1037.

[151] In England the order is to be delivered to the Registrar of Companies for registration: s. 425(3), CA 1985 (UK). In Australia it is to be lodged with the ASC: s. 411(10), CL (Aust).

the court, and the court is not permitted to order class meetings to be held unless it is satisfied that the ASC has had a reasonable opportunity to study the terms of the proposed compromise or arrangement and the draft explanatory statement[152] and to make submissions to the court in relation to them.[153] Secondly, where a scheme does not involve creditors, the statement must be registered with the ASC before being despatched to members.[154]

### (2) Independence of majority

The requirement that the scheme be separately approved by each class of members is one of the protections offered to minority shareholders. The classic test for determining who should belong to a particular class is a dictum of Bowen LJ in *Sovereign Life Assurance Co.* v. *Dodd*[155] that: 'It seems plain that we must give such a meaning to the term "class" as will prevent the section being so worked as to result in confiscation and injustice, and that it must be confined to those persons whose rights are not so dissimilar as to make it impossible for them to consult together with a view to their common interest.'

The test in *Dodd*'s case is used as the basis for determining whether separate class meetings should be ordered in both England and Australia. However, it has been interpreted differently in the two countries.

### (a) England

In England, the leading authority is *Re Hellenic & General Trust Ltd.*[156] In this case Hambros, the offeror, had a subsidiary which already owned 53.01 per cent of the ordinary shares of the target company, and exercised that voting power in favour of the scheme at the meeting convened to consider it. The minority shareholders successfully argued that the purchaser's wholly-owned subsidiary was in a different class from the other ordinary shareholders, and the court declined to sanction the scheme. Academic views are divided on the merits of this approach. Although the case of a subsidiary presents a relatively clear conflict of interest, once strict legal rights are abandoned, it may be difficult in other cases to be confident of the boundaries of a class. For example, it would appear that in some cases directors of the offeror or significant shareholders in the offeror should be excluded from the class which is to approve the scheme.[157]

---

[152] See discussion in section 3(5) and subsequent text.
[153] Section 411(2), CL (Aust).　　　　　　　　　[154] Section 412(6) and (8), CL (Aust).
[155] [1892] 2 QB 573 at 583 (CA).　　　　　　　　[156] Above n 136.
[157] See Weinberg, above n 3, para. 2–072. The approach is criticized by J. A. Hornby, 'Class Membership in a Company's Scheme of Arrangement' (1976) 39 *Mod L Rev* 207. Cf.,

## (b) Australia

By contrast, in Australia, in the context of creditors' schemes the courts have preferred to examine the motives of class members in the exercise of their discretion when considering whether to sanction the scheme, rather than finding that separate class meetings should have been ordered.[158] In the cases where separate class meetings have been ordered, it has been on the basis that the legal relationship between the creditor and the company can be distinguished.[159] But despite the reluctance of the Australian courts to call separate class meetings, the fact that some members of the class have interests opposed to those of the class as a whole has been regarded as providing a substantial basis for supposing that the scheme might operate in a manner prejudicial to non-associated members. As Street J explained in *Re Jax Marine Pty. Ltd.*[160] (which again concerned a creditors' scheme):

To say that the Smithson group's interests do not preclude their being members of the class is, of course, far from saying that their vote will, if and when a petition is subsequently presented, carry equal weight to that of an unsecured creditor who is not shown to have any special interest. When the petition, if there be a petition, comes before the Court there is ample room within the Court's statutory discretion to decide the petition in accordance with the requirements of justice and equity as those requirements appear to affect the rights of the class and its members. Quite frequently it is necessary to discount, even to the point of discarding from consideration, the vote of a creditor, who, although a member of a class, may have such personal or special interest as to render his view a self-centred view rather than a class-promoting view.

If the same approach were to be taken to the determination of class membership in a members' scheme,[161] it is submitted that in an Australian

---

D. D. Prentice, 'Corporate Arrangements—Protecting Minority Shareholders' (1976) 92 *Law Q Rev* 13 who defends the approach taken on the facts in *Re Hellenic & General Trust Ltd.*, above n 136, but argues that it may cause difficulties where a subsidiary is not wholly owned.

[158] *Re Chevron (Sydney) Ltd.* [1963] VR 249, *Re Jax Marine Pty. Ltd.* [1967] 1 NSWR 145, *Re Landmark Corporation Ltd.* [1968] 1 NSWR 759, *Re Direct Acceptance Corporation Ltd.*, above n 150, *Nordic Bank plc* v. *International Harvester Australia Ltd.* [1983] 2 VR 298 at 301 (Full Ct, Vic). Note that Templeman J in *Re Hellenic & General Trust Ltd.*, above n 136, remarked, obiter, that he would in any event have refused to approve the scheme in the exercise of this discretion, on the basis that the votes of the subsidiary would not have been able to count towards the 90% acceptance threshold for compulsory acquisition if the take-over had proceeded by way of a bid.

[159] See *Re Gazelle Constructions Pty. Ltd.* (1984) 10 ACLR 140; 2 ACLC 680 and *Re Bond Corporation Holdings Ltd.* (1991) 5 WAR 143.

[160] Above n 158, at 148.

[161] This would be consistent with the rights-based approach taken to class membership reflected in ASC Practice Note 32.

case with similar facts to *Re Hellenic & General Trust Ltd.*[162] any votes cast
by a subsidiary in favour of the scheme would almost inevitably be
disregarded by the court. The ASC's Policy Statement 60 should be noted
in this regard. It states that the interests of interested parties should be
fully disclosed, and that interested parties should decline to vote on the
resolution to approve the acquisition,[163] or if they do, their votes should be
separately recorded to assist the court in determining whether or not to
approve the scheme.

### (3) The role of the court

The fact that the court has already convened class meetings, does not
foreclose the right of a shareholder to oppose approval of the scheme by
the court at the subsequent hearing.[164] Nor does it constrain the discretion
of the court in considering the objection.[165]

At the hearing for approval of the scheme, the court must be satisfied of
two things: first, that the resolutions are passed by the statutory majority in
value and number at properly convened meetings,[166] and secondly that the
proposal is such that an intelligent and honest member of the class
concerned acting in his or her own interest might reasonably approve.[167]
There is, nevertheless, an assumption that if creditors or members 'are
acting on sufficient information and with time to consider what they
are about, and are acting honestly, they are . . . much better judges of
what is to their commercial advantage than the Court can be'.[168]

Commentators have noted a reluctance on the part of the courts to
intervene in the exercise of their discretion (as opposed to failure
to comply with procedural requirements).[169] As Weinberg observes,[170] it

---

[162] Above n 136.

[163] The majority shareholder abstained from voting in *Nicron Resources Ltd.* v. *Catto*
(1992) 8 ACSR 219; 10 ACLC 1186.

[164] There are some Australian dicta to the effect that the court will generally not convene
class meetings unless it is satisfied that the arrangement is such that a court would be likely to
approve it on the hearing of an unopposed petition: *F. T. Eastment & Sons Pty. Ltd.* v. *Metal
Roof Decking Supplies Pty. Ltd.* (1977) 3 ACLR 69; (1977–78) CLC ¶40–368 (CA NSW), *Re
Linter Textiles Corporation Ltd. (Recs and Mgrs apptd.)* [1991] 2 VR 561. However, Renard,
above n 3, at 427 notes that the attitude taken by courts at the initial hearing differs markedly
from State to State.

[165] *Re Austamax Resources Ltd.*, above n 143. See also *Re Bond Corporation Holdings
Ltd.*, above n 159. Nor does it amount to a determination that the proposed arrangement is
one which falls within the scope of the section: *ASC* v. *Marlborough Gold Mines Ltd.* (1993)
177 CLR 485 (HC).

[166] *Re Dorman Long & Co.* [1934] Ch. 635 at 655. The courts have not looked favourably
on irregularities in complying with procedural requirements: see e.g., *Re W. Coogan & Co.
Pty. Ltd.* (1993) 10 ACSR 461; 11 ACLC 388.

[167] *Re Dorman, Long & Co. Ltd.*, ibid., at 657.

[168] *Per* Lindley LJ in *Re English, Scottish & Australian Chartered Bank* [1893] 3 Ch. 385 at
409 (CA).                                                   [169] See e.g., Gower, above n 11, at 697.

[170] Above n 3, para. 2–072.

'. . . makes the second function of the court a duplication of the first and renders the discretion vested in the court (which would, if vigorously exercised, provide the justification for the lower percentages required under [the scheme of arrangement procedure] than under [the takeover procedure]) nugatory.'

However, the courts have been prepared to withhold confirmation of a scheme where the information circulated to members to explain the scheme is insufficient or misleading.[171]

Further, it would appear that the courts will have regard to the unfairness of a scheme to the interests of individual dissenting shareholders, in determining whether to approve a scheme. Courts in both England[172] and Australia[173] have regarded potential capital gains tax liability as a substantial factor weighing against the court approving a scheme. It should be noted that in both those cases, associates of the offeror had been included among those voting in favour of the schemes, providing substantial grounds for withholding confirmation. Nevertheless, these comments are to be compared with the judicial attitude to 'unfairness' in the context of the compulsory acquisition procedure which applies in respect of takeovers. There, the courts have considered that adverse consequences of the scheme which are limited to particular shareholders (such as a liability for capital gains tax) do not provide grounds for exercising their discretion to prevent the acquisition, on the basis that the alleged unfairness must affect the shareholders as a body.[174]

## (4) Consideration

As in the context of compulsory acquisitions, the courts have been reluctant to intervene on the ground that the consideration offered is inadequate. The protection offered to shareholders in this regard therefore boils down to the information provided to them and the judgement of the majority.

## (5) Shareholder information

When summoning the class meetings, a statement must be provided[175] to each member or creditor[176] which explains the effect of the compromise or

---

[171] Ibid. See discussion below section 3(5).

[172] *Re Hellenic & General Trust Ltd.*, above n 136. This aspect of the decision is questioned by Prentice, above n 157, at 17.

[173] *Re Direct Acceptance Corporation Ltd.*, above n 150, at 1044.

[174] Cf., *Re Grierson, Oldham & Adams Ltd.*, above n 77 and text accompanying n 82.

[175] Or in the case of a notice summoning the meeting which is given by advertisement, members or creditors should be notified of how to obtain a copy of the statement, which is to be provided to them free of charge: s. 426(3) and (5), CA 1985 (UK), s. 412(1)(b) and (4), CL (Aust). In Australia, creditors owed $200 or less need only be advised of the place where a copy of the statement may be inspected: s. 412(2), CL (Aust).

[176] Section 426(2), CA 1985 (UK), s. 412(1)(a), CL (Aust).

arrangement and, in particular, states any material interests of the directors (whether as directors, members, creditors, or otherwise) and the effect of the scheme on those interests, in so far as it is different from the effect of the interests of others.[177] Directors are required to provide information to the company to enable these disclosures to be made.[178]

In England, the wide definition of 'offer' in the City Code on Takeovers and Mergers means that the disclosure obligations in the Code will also apply to a scheme, if it is otherwise within the Code's sphere of operation.[179]

In Australia, schemes of arrangement are separately regulated from takeovers, and the statute sets out specific disclosure requirements in addition to the requirement for an explanatory statement which are similar but not identical to those which apply to takeovers.[180] First, there is a statutory obligation[181] to set out prescribed information[182] and any other information material to the making of a decision by a member whether or not to agree to the arrangement within the knowledge of the directors which has not previously been disclosed. Secondly, in a scheme affecting members, where the other party to the scheme is entitled to at least 30 per cent of the voting shares or is a corporation with a director common to the scheme company, an independent expert's report is required, stating whether implementation of the scheme is in the best interests of members and setting out the reasons for that opinion.[183] A general meeting can also instruct named accountants and/or solicitors to report on the scheme.[184] In addition, Listing Rule 3N requires that shareholders of listed companies be advised, among other things, of the effect of the reconstruction on the par and paid-up value of shares.

Importance is placed on provision of accurate information to shareholders in both England and Australia. Even in schemes which predate the introduction of express requirement for an explanatory statement (or any

---

[177] Failure to comply with the requirement resulted in an order that the meetings be reconvened in *City Property Investment Trust Corporation Ltd., Petitioners* 1951 SLT 371.
[178] Section 426(7), CA 1985 (UK), s. 412(5), CL (Aust).
[179] See above discussion at n 112 and subsequent text.
[180] See discussion at nn 114–5.                [181] Section 412(1)(a)(ii), CL (Aust).
[182] Reg. 5.1.01 and sch, 8 Corporations Regulations 1990 (Aust). The ASC may dispense with any of the requirements of reg. 5.1.01.
[183] Sch. 8, Pt. 3, cl. 3, Corporations Regulations 1990 (Aust). See *Phosphate Co-operative Co. of Aust Ltd.* v. *Shears & Anor (No. 3)* [1989] VR 665. See also Ford and Austin, above n 8 para. 2032 and R. Nicholson, 'The Pivot Case—New Standards for Schemes of Arrangement' (1989) 7 *Company & Sec LJ* 277. Cf., the takeover procedure where a report is required in broadly similar circumstances but is instead required to state whether the offer is fair and reasonable: s. 648, CL (Aust).
[184] Section 411(13), CL (Aust). The court also has power under s. 415(2), CL (Aust), to require a report.

other express disclosure requirements) provision of full information to shareholders was regarded as a pre-requisite for approval of a scheme by the court. In *Re Dorman Long & Co. Ltd.* Maugham J said in this regard:[185] '. . . the Court takes the view that it is essential to see that the explanatory circulars sent out by the board of the company are perfectly fair and, as far as possible, give all the information reasonably necessary to enable the recipients to determine how to vote.' The court in that case declined to approve the scheme on the basis that the information provided to shareholders was insufficient and misleading, in not explaining the conflict of interest faced by the trustees for debenture holders who stood to gain from the scheme[186] and in failing to state the amount of revaluation of the company's undertaking and assets. A strict insistence of full and fair disclosure can be seen in subsequent cases, and approval for schemes has consistently been withheld where the information provided to shareholders has been regarded as misleading or insufficient,[187] even in cases where the votes in favour of a scheme were almost unanimous.[188] The test is whether a reasonable shareholder would change his or her decision as to how to act on the scheme if the information had been disclosed.[189]

However, there appears to be a divergence between the two jurisdictions as to the appropriate action to be taken to inform shareholders or creditors if the circumstances change after despatch of the explanatory statements, but prior to the holding of class meetings.

The English authorities have consistently required that all members who received the initial explanatory statement be advised of the new information if it were reasonable to suppose that the change might have influenced the way in which the members voted at the meetings or abstained from voting.[190]

---

[185] Above n 166, at 657.

[186] This information is now expressly required to be provided by virtue of s. 426(4), CA 1985 (UK) and s. 412(3), CL (Aust).

[187] See *Rankin & Blackmore Ltd., Petitioners* 1950 SLT 160 (petition sent to shareholders instead of explanatory statement), *Coltness Iron Company Ltd., Petitioners* 1951 SLT 344 (failure to disclose extent of directors' interests), *Re Old Silkstone Collieries Ltd.* [1954] 1 Ch. 169 (CA) (misleading circular), *Re Pheon Pty. Ltd.* (1986) 47 SASR 427 (non-disclosure of financial information which was necessary to determine whether more was to be gained from the scheme or a winding up) and *Phosphate Co-operative Co. of Aust Ltd.* v. *Shears & Anor (No. 3)*, above n 183 (misleading expert's report).

[188] *Metropolitan Life Assurance Co. of NZ Ltd.* v. *Triple M Ltd.* (1989) 4 NZCLC 64,821

[189] See e.g., *Re Minster Assets plc* [1985] BCLC 200; (1984) 1 BCC 99,299. Note also the extensive disclosure obligations imposed by the Australian High Court in *Gambotto*'s case, above n 103, in the context of an expropriation effected by alteration of the articles. See further below, sections 5(3)(b) and 5(5).

[190] *Re Jessel Trust Ltd.* [1985] BCLC 119, *Re Minster Assets plc*, ibid., and *Re MB Group plc* [1989] BCLC 672; (1989) 5 BCC 684. See also N. J. L. Doran, 'Explanatory statements in schemes of arrangement: if in doubt, disclose!' (1991) 12 *Company Lawyer* 62 and R. Pliner, 'Arranging a Take-over—A Scheme Around the Code?' (1979) 7 *Austl Bus L Rev* 51.

By contrast, in the Australian case of *Re Australian Foundation Investment Company Ltd.*,[191] Gowans J considered that it was sufficient if the new information was conveyed at class meetings, and held that it was not necessary for the meetings to be adjourned in order to inform those who did not attend the meetings or had committed themselves to proxies. In light of the fact that many members will vote by proxy, (for example in *Re Jessel Trust Ltd.*[192] only one of the 7 per cent preference shareholders attended and voted in person at the relevant class meeting) it is submitted that the approach taken in the English cases is to be preferred. Gowans J's decision is also inconsistent with the approach generally taken to notice of meetings, where it has been held that the person to be protected is not the dissentient but the absent shareholder who, having received and with more or less care looked at the circular, considers that he can leave the matter to the majority.[193]

## (6) Restrictions

One restriction on the use of the procedure is that it requires the co-operation of the company. Although any shareholder or creditor can apply to the court to convene class meetings, the court in *Re Savoy Hotel Ltd.*[194] declined to order that meetings be convened where a scheme was proposed in order to effect a hostile take-over, on the basis that the approval of the company to the scheme was essential. A further feature of a scheme which has both positive and negative aspects is that the questions of control and 100 per cent ownership are finally resolved at one time. This has the advantage over the takeover procedure that there is no delay in ascertaining if there is opposition. However, it has the disadvantage that the offeror cannot take advantage of control at an earlier stage than the filing of the court order.[195]

## 4. REDUCTIONS OF CAPITAL

Rather than implementing a cancellation and reduction scheme it is possible in some cases to effect a 100 per cent takeover simply by cancelling all the issued shares in a company (other than those held by the 'offeror') by way of a reduction of capital.

---

[191] [1974] VR 331 at 338–9                                    [192] Above n 190.
[193] *Tiessen* v. *Henderson* [1899] 1 Ch. 861 at 870, *Bulfin* v. *Bebarfald's Ltd.* (1938) 38 SR (NSW) 423 at 432–8 and *Fraser* v. *NRMA Holdings Ltd.*, above n 110.
[194] Above n 134.
[195] See further Weinberg, above n 3, paras 2–068, 2–069 and 2–021. See also the discussion of s. 411(17) CL (Aust) in section 6(2)(b) below.

## (1) Procedure[196]

In order to effect a formal reduction of capital,[197] there must be: permission in the company's articles, a special resolution of the company (that is, approval by a 75 per cent majority and the requisite notice period), court confirmation, and registration of the court order confirming the reduction.[198] In Australia, the resolution for reduction must also be registered.[199]

Unless the reduction also involves a variation of class rights, there is no equivalent of the class consent requirement which applies to schemes of arrangement.[200]

## (2) Independence of majority

The weight given by the court to the votes of shareholders who stand to benefit from the reduction or are associated with the instigator of the proposal depends upon the purpose with which they have voted. Thus, in *Carruth* v. *Imperial Chemical Industries Ltd.*[201] the House of Lords stated that little attention should be paid by the court to the votes of the majority shareholders in considering whether a scheme was fair 'when it is proved that the majority of a class have voted or may have voted in the way they did because of their interests as shareholders in another class.' Nevertheless, the House of Lords confirmed the reduction as fair. More recently, in *Re Holders Investment Trust Ltd.*[202] the court refused to confirm a reduction of capital where the majority preference shareholders had considered their own interests without regard to what was best for the preference shareholders as a class.[203]

---

[196] The Corporations Law Simplification Task Force has proposed changes to the reduction of capital procedure in Australia: *Share Capital Rules: Proposal for Simplification*, November 1994. If implemented, the most significant impact of the proposed changes (as far as shareholders are concerned) would be replacement of the procedure for court confirmation with a right to apply to the court to oppose the reduction in certain circumstances.

[197] Exceptions to the formal reduction of capital procedure are provided to enable companies to purchase their own shares in certain circumstances which are not relevant in this context. The formal reduction of capital procedure applies in all other cases.

[198] Sections 135–41, CA 1985 (UK), s. 195, CL (Aust).

[199] In England, the court order confirming the reduction and a minute with details of the reduction are registered with the Registrar of Companies, and the resolution for reduction takes effect on registration: s. 138(1) and (2), CA 1985 (UK). In Australia, the resolution for reduction cannot take effect until a certified copy of the resolution and an office copy of the court order are lodged with the ASC, although the resolution may specify a date earlier than the date of registration from which the reduction is to have effect: s. 195(7), CL (Aust).

[200] See discussion below in section 4(3).

[201] [1937] AC 707 at 769 (HL) *per* Lord Maugham.

[202] [1971] 1 WLR 583. See also *British America Nickel Corpn Ltd.* v. *O'Brien* [1927] AC 369 (PC).

[203] The failure of the majority to consider the interests of the class as a whole was held to reverse the onus of proof, so that the court would confirm the reduction only if it was proved

On one view, *Holders'* case[204] may be regarded as placing a positive obligation on shareholders to exercise their votes at class meetings in the best interests of the class. An alternative interpretation, which attracts some support from *Re Leigh Estates (UK) Ltd.*[205] is that the court in *Holders'* case considered it appropriate to disregard the votes of the majority of preference shareholders in determining whether the reduction was fair.[206]

The latter approach has been adopted in recent Australian cases concerning selective reductions of capital. Referring to *Holders'* case[207] Bryson J said in *Nicron Resources Ltd. v. Catto*:[208] 'It would in my opinion be vain to attribute legal consequences to a purpose held by a shareholder at a general meeting that he should cast his vote for the benefit of the class as a whole, because a shareholder has no duty to behave in that way or govern himself by any such purpose, and there is little likelihood that a shareholder would.'

In light of the court's discretion to disregard the votes of interested shareholders, it is usual in Australia for shareholders who stand to benefit from a reduction to abstain from voting. As Bryson J observed in *Nicron Resources Ltd. v. Catto*:[209] 'Aztec was in a position to control or cast votes in respect of more than three-quarters of the issued shares and hence to carry a special resolution against all possible opposition, but decided in advance not to do so, and I infer that this was done on the view that it would be difficult to persuade the Court that the result was fair if Aztec had dominated the voting.' Later in the same case, after referring to the cases which use legal rights as the basis for the division of shareholders into classes,[210] Bryson J said:[211] 'In relation to these resolutions there is such a sharp distinction between the effects produced by the resolutions on Aztec and the effects produced by them on all others that reliance on conformity with the articles would not be appropriate, and it was only common prudence for Aztec to decide not to cast votes and to make that decision known in advance.'

The same approach was taken in *Re Shine Fisheries Ltd.*[212] where Master Adams said: 'The principle of fairness requires that only those share-holders whose shares are to be cancelled should be entitled to vote at the

---

to be fair. However, this case was decided before the enactment of statutory provisions protecting class rights. See discussion below in section 4(3) regarding protection of class rights in this context.

[204] Above n 202.                                        [205] [1994] BCC 292.
[206] See also D. Harding, 'Do Institutional Investors in Australia have a Fiduciary Responsibility to Vote?' *Proxy Voting Conference Convened by the AIMA and the Institute of Corporate Managers, Secretaries and Administrators Ltd.*, 7 September 1994.
[207] Above n 202.                                        [208] Above n 163, at 232; 1196.
[209] Ibid., at 223; 1189.                                [210] See discussion above in section 3(2).
[211] Above n 163, at 238; 1200.
[212] (1994) 12 ACSR 627 at 636; 12 ACLC 223 at 229.

meeting and that any parties related to the Lombardo interests or associated in any way with them should not vote. This seems to me to be a fundamental aspect of fairness as otherwise those who stand to benefit from the transaction could overwhelmingly carry the resolution by virtue of their majority holding.'

This view is also echoed in the ASC's Practice Note 29 entitled 'Selective Capital Reductions' which states that the instigator of the reduction should not vote on the resolution, and that it will help the court if the company retains ballots or an audited record of the voting for the court to inspect if it wishes.

### (3) The role of the court

There are two aspects to the court's role in confirming a reduction of capital. First, since reductions of capital may adversely affect creditors, the statute contains various measures designed to protect their interests.[213] The other part of the court's role is to ensure that the reduction treats shareholders fairly. As noted above, this may involve determining what weight, if any, should be given to the votes cast in favour of the scheme by shareholders who are in some way associated with the instigator of the scheme or otherwise stand to benefit from it. It also requires a consideration of whether the reduction varies class rights and, if so, whether the appropriate variation procedure has been complied with.

As we have seen in the discussion of class rights,[214] a very restrictive attitude has been taken in determining whether class rights will be altered by a reduction. For example, a reduction of capital which involves repayment of paid-up share capital on preference shares which have a right to prior return of capital on a winding up has been considered simply to be a fulfilment of the rights of the preference shareholders. Accordingly it has been held that no separate class meetings are necessary to approve the reduction.[215] Millett LJ described the unfortunate position of preference shareholders in the following terms:[216] 'In the absence of special provision in the company's articles of association, therefore, preference shareholders are in an unenviable position. Locked into their investment when the general level of interest rates is higher than the fixed yield of their shares,

---

[213] A discussion of these measures is beyond the scope of this book.

[214] In Ch. 4 section 2(2)(b)(iii).

[215] *Re Saltdean Estate Co. Ltd.* [1968] 1 WLR 1844 and *House of Fraser plc* v. *ACGE Investments Ltd.* [1987] AC 387 (HL). Cf., the criticism of this approach by S. Lindsay, 'The Position of Preference Shareholders in a Reduction of Capital' (1987) 5 *Company & Sec LJ* 77.

[216] *Re Northern Engineering Industries plc* [1994] 2 BCLC 704 at 706; [1994] BCC 618 at 620 (CA).

they could find themselves bought out by the company against their will when interest rates fall below it.'

Listed companies will often lessen this disadvantage by inserting a provision in the articles adopting the Spens formula, which ensures that preference shareholders at least receive the market value of their shares in a reduction of capital, and gives them voting rights on the special resolution required to approve the reduction. It is also possible for a reduction of capital to be deemed in the articles of association to constitute a variation of class rights, and if this is done, class consent must be obtained for the reduction.[217] There are some authorities where it has been held that the court has a discretion to approve a reduction which it regards as fair even if it does not treat classes of shareholders in accordance with their rights.[218] However, these decisions are inconsistent with *Re Old Silkstone Collieries Ltd.*[219] and with the more recent case of *Re Northern Engineering Industries plc*,[220] and have been superseded by statutory provisions protecting class rights.[221]

A reduction which does not involve a variation of class rights and under which capital is repaid in the order in which the different classes would rank in a winding up will generally be regarded as fair.[222] And it has been held in both jurisdictions that the court has power to confirm a reduction of capital in which certain, but not all of the issued shares are paid off and cancelled.[223] The *prima facie* position of the court is that whether the proposal is good or bad is a question for the commercial judgment of the shareholders.[224]

The non-interventionist attitude of the courts in this context has been

---

[217] *Re Northern Engineering Industries plc* ibid.

[218] See e.g., *Re Holders Investment Trust Ltd.* above n 202, where the fact that no effectual class consent was obtained was held to reverse the onus of proof rather than precluding confirmation of the reduction. See also D. G. Rice, 'Capital Reduction and its Effect on Class Rights' (1959) 23 *Convey* 244 at 253–4 and Gower, above n 11, at 692. Cf., J. H. Telfer and R. J. Mitchell, 'Reductions of Capital and the Rights of Minority Classes of Shareholders: A New Approach to Section 64' (1981) 55 *Austl LJ* 249.          [219] Above n 187.

[220] Above n 216.          [221] Section 125, CA 1985 (UK), ss. 197–9, CL (Aust).

[222] *Prudential Assurance Co. Ltd.* v. *Chatterley-Whitfield Collieries Co. Ltd.* [1949] AC 512 (HL), *Re Saltdean Estate Co. Ltd.*, above n 215, *House of Fraser plc* v. *ACGE Investments Ltd.*, above n 215, *Re Fowlers Vacola Manufacturing Co. Ltd.* [1966] VR 97. But cf., *Scottish Insurance Corp. Ltd.* v. *Wilsons & Clyde Coal Ltd.* [1949] AC 462 (HL) with *Re William Jones & Sons Ltd.* [1969] 1 WLR 146 as to the fairness of a reduction where there is also a right to participate in any surplus on a winding up. See Rice, above n 218 at 251, as to whether repayment otherwise than in accordance with priorities in a winding up amounts to a variation of class rights.

[223] See e.g., *British and American Trustee and Finance Corpn. Ltd. and Reduced* v. *Couper* [1894] AC 399 (HL) and *Thornett* v. *Federal Commissioner of Taxation* (1938) 59 CLR 787 at 800 (HC).

[224] *Re English, Scottish and Australian Chartered Bank*, above n 168, *Re Deniliquin Corp. Ltd.* (1994) 12 ACSR 623; 12 ACLC 261.

criticized by commentators,[225] and by some judges. Lord President Cooper said in *Wilsons & Clyde Coal Company* v. *Scottish Insurance Corpn.*[226] 'Nothing could be clearer and more reassuring than these formulations of the duties of the Court. Nothing could be more disappointing than the reported instances of their subsequent exercise. Examples abound of the refusal of the Courts to entertain a plea that a scheme was not fair or equitable, but it is very hard to find in recent times any clear and instructive instance of the acceptance of such an objection.'

A low point in the court's unwillingness to intervene is *Re MacKenzie & Co. Ltd.*[227] where the effect of the special resolution was to reduce the amount payable as a preferential dividend to the benefit of ordinary shareholders. In *Holders'* case[228] the court was prepared to take a more interventionist role. But, in that case and the other English cases where court confirmation has been withheld, it has been on the basis that the requisite class consent was not obtained, rather than purely on the basis that the reduction was unfair.[229]

By contrast, in three recent Australian cases courts have refused to confirm proposed reductions on the basis that the price offered was not fair.[230]

### (4) Consideration

The English courts have disapproved the use of the reduction procedure to effect a takeover because of the lower protections offered to minority shareholders.[231] In Australia, the judicial tendency is instead to seek to ensure that shareholders have similar protection if the reduction procedure is used to that which they would have had if the transaction had proceeded as a scheme of arrangement or as a takeover bid. Accordingly, the Australian courts have been prepared to consider not only the market price of the shares at the time of the proposed reduction, but also the wider circumstances surrounding and preceding the proposed reduction.

In *Catto* v. *Ampol Ltd.*,[232] the effect of confirming the proposed reduction was that Pioneer would have acquired all the preference shares of the company. In these circumstances, the New South Wales Court of Appeal considered that it should have regard to the principles underlying the regulation of takeovers, and in particular the concept that all shareholders should share equally in any premium brought into existence

---

[225] See especially Gower, above n 11, at 691–2.     [226] 1948 SC 360 at 376.
[227] [1916] 2 Ch. 450.     [228] Above n 202.
[229] *Re Old Silkstone Collieries Ltd.*, above n 187 and *Re Holders Investment Trust Ltd.*, ibid.
[230] *Catto* v. *Ampol Ltd.*, above n 100, *Re Shine Fisheries Ltd.*, above n 212 and *Melcann Ltd.* v. *Super John Pty. Ltd.* (1994) 13 ACLC 92. See discussion in next section.
[231] See discussion below in section 6(3).     [232] Above n 100.

by the rights attached to that class of shares. The court considered it appropriate to interpret its discretion under the reduction of capital provisions to 'endeavour to provide an interpretation . . . which affords a harmonious, practical and mutually supportive operation to each.'[233] It therefore placed emphasis on two factors: first, although the price offered was in excess of the market price, the market price had been depressed because the large majority of preference shares was held by Pioneer and because the valuable right to participate fully in the election of a nominee director had disappeared in a commercial sense. Secondly, Pioneer had been prepared to pay considerably more for the preference shares than was being offered in the reduction in order to obtain a controlling holding of the preference shares. In these circumstances the court considered that the consideration offered was unfair, and withheld approval for the reduction.

Similarly, in *Re Shine Fisheries Ltd.*,[234] confirmation for a reduction of capital was withheld where the price which shareholders were to receive for their shares was below the range identified by an independent expert. This decision was reached despite the fact that opposition to confirmation came only from the ASC, and none of the shareholders to be expropriated appeared to oppose the petition.

Further, in *Melcann Ltd.* v. *Super John Pty. Ltd.*,[235] confirmation of a reduction of capital was refused on the basis that the valuation of the shares by an independent expert failed to take into account the synergy benefits which would accrue to the majority shareholders when they acquired 100 per cent of the company's shares. The benefits from merging the company's business with that of the majority shareholders was estimated to produce marketing savings in the order of $A100,000 to $A200,000 annually.

### (5) Shareholder information

By contrast with takeovers and schemes of arrangement, there are no specific disclosure requirements for a reduction of capital. However, it has been held that the proposals should be properly explained to shareholders at the general meeting, so that they can exercise an informed judgement on them.[236] When additional information is circulated to shareholders, the court will examine it to ensure that it fairly represents the position. As Clauson J stated in *Re Imperial Chemical Industries Ltd*:[237]

---

[233] Ibid., at 345 *per* Kirby P.        [234] Above n 212.        [235] Above n 230.
[236] *Re Ratners Group plc* [1988] BCLC 685; (1988) 4 BCC 293. See also *Re Thorn EMI plc* [1989] BCLC 612; (1988) 4 BCC 698. In relation to listed companies in the UK, Listing Rule 14.10 states that a circular in connection with a resolution proposing to reduce the company's capital must include a statement of the reasons for and the effects of the proposal.
[237] [1936] Ch. 587 at 618 and approved in *Carruth* v. *Imperial Chemical Industries Ltd.*, above n 201, at 768.

Where the matter is one of difficulty, the Court will always scrutinise such a circular very carefully; but where, as in this case, there is no suggestion that the directors were doing otherwise than honestly putting forward to the best of their skill and ability a fair picture of the company's position, the question is not whether the circular might not have been differently framed, but whether there is any reasonable ground for supposing that such imperfections as may be found in the circular have had, with or without other circumstances, the result that the majority (who have approved the proposal placed before them) have done so under some serious misapprehension of the position.

This approach does not appear to add anything to the level of information or scrutiny by the court which would accompany a special resolution in any other context.[238] Nevertheless, it has provided the basis for refusal of confirmation in several Australian cases.

In *Re Campaign Holdings Pty. Ltd.*,[239] confirmation of a reduction of capital which treated fully paid and partly paid shareholders differently was refused because the directors had not made sufficient disclosure of the benefits that would flow to partly paid shareholders by not having any of their shares cancelled, and had not disclosed the interest they had in the cancellation and the planned reconstruction. Fullagar J referred to *Re Robert Stephen Holdings Ltd.*[240] and echoed the comments made by Plowman J in that case that it was regrettable that the reduction did not proceed as a scheme of arrangement under which the directors would have been required to make full disclosure.

Similarly, in *Re Prime Group Holdings Ltd.*[241] it was held that incorrect information contained in an expert's report provided to shareholders meant that the majority who voted for the resolution did so 'under a serious misapprehension of the position' and the application for confirmation of the reduction of capital was accordingly refused.

### (6) Restrictions

One practical disadvantage of the reduction of capital procedure as a method of compulsory acquisition is the ability of creditors to object,[242] unless the court orders otherwise.[243] In common with schemes of arrangement, effecting a takeover by means of a reduction of capital

---

[238] Note, however, the extensive disclosure obligations imposed by the Australian High Court in *Gambotto*'s case, above n 103, in the context of an expropriation effected by alteration of the articles. See further below, sections 5(3)(b) and 5(5).

[239] (1989) 15 ACLR 762; 8 ACLC 64.

[240] [1968] 1 WLR 522.

[241] (1994) 13 ACSR 357; 12 ACLC 308

[242] Section 136(3)—(5), CA 1985 (UK), s. 195(3), CL (Aust).

[243] Section 136(6), CA 1985 (UK), s. 195(4), CL (Aust). See Digby, above n 2, at 115.

requires the co-operation of the target company. Moreover, the consideration received by expropriated shareholders must be provided by the target company, although it may be possible to overcome this restriction by the 'offeror' providing the target company with the consideration, for example through a loan or gift to the company or a subscription for new shares.[244] In Australia, Listing Rule 3J(32) may also affect the company's ability to reduce its capital.

## 5. AMENDMENT OF THE ARTICLES

### (1) Procedure

The courts have been prepared to give effect to provisions in the articles which permit minority shareholders to be expropriated if those provisions have been in the articles since the company's inception,[245] although the exercise of the expropriation power may still potentially give rise to an action either at common law or under the unfair prejudice provision. In order to insert a provision to this effect into the articles at a later date, the only procedural requirement is the passing of a special resolution. Thus, 21 days' written notice must be given of the meeting and of the intention to propose the resolution as a special resolution, and it must be passed by a 75 per cent majority of members attending and voting in person or by proxy.[246]

### (2) Independence of majority

There is no legal requirement that interested shareholders abstain from voting, although they may elect to abstain, as happened in the recent case of *WCP Ltd.* v. *Gambotto*.[247] The majority of the High Court in that case expressly left open the question whether failure to refrain from voting would be oppressive to the minority.

---

[244] *Re Hunter Resources Ltd.* (1992) 7 ACSR 436; 10 ACLC 538. See Digby, ibid., and discussion at n 323 and subsequent text.

[245] *Phillips* v. *Manufacturers Securities Ltd.*, above n 1. As regards expulsion clauses in companies limited by guarantee cf., *Gaiman* v. *National Association for Mental Health* [1971] Ch. 317 with *ASC* v. *The Multiple Sclerosis Society of Tasmania* (1993) 10 ACSR 489; 11 ACLC 461.

[246] Section 378(2), CA 1985 (UK), s. 253, CL (Aust). Under s. 378(3), CA 1985 (UK), s. 253(4), CL (Aust), 95% of members may consent to a shorter notice period. The percentage may be reduced to not less than 90% in a private company in England by elective resolution.

[247] *Gambotto* v. *WCP Ltd.* (1992) 8 ACSR 141; 10 ACLC 1046, on appeal *WCP Ltd.* v. *Gambotto* (1993) 30 NSWLR 385 (CA NSW), reversed sub nom. *Gambotto* v. *WCP Ltd.* above n 103.

## (3) The role of the court

There is no involvement of the court in the procedure unless a dissenting shareholder brings an action complaining of infringement of his or her personal rights at common law and/or of unfairly prejudicial conduct. All the reported cases concerning actions of this type have been brought at common law.

The English cases concerning this question predate the introduction of the unfair prejudice remedy, and were decided by asking whether the alteration was '*bona fide* for the benefit of the company as a whole'. The earliest reported case where this issue arose is *Brown* v. *British Abrasive Wheel Co. Ltd.*[248] Here, the majority held 98 per cent of the company's shares. The company was in great need of further capital, and the majority shareholders were prepared to make the necessary investment, but only on the basis of 100 per cent ownership. When attempts to obtain the shares of the remaining five small shareholders by agreement failed, a resolution was passed altering the articles to enable the majority to purchase the shares of the minority compulsorily on certain terms. The minority shareholders successfully challenged the alteration on the basis that it was not made *bona fide* for the company as a whole. Astbury J considered that although it would be for the benefit of the company if the further capital were provided, the proposed alteration did nothing to ensure that this would happen.

The next case where an expropriating article was considered and one where the expropriation was successful is *Sidebottom* v. *Kershaw, Leese & Co. Ltd.*[249] Here a special resolution was passed altering the articles to introduce a power for the directors to require any shareholder who was competing with the company's business to transfer his or her shares at their fair value to nominees of the directors. The plaintiff (a minority shareholder who carried on a competing business) challenged the resolution. The Court of Appeal held that it had been passed *bona fide* for the benefit of the company as a whole as it was designed to protect the company's trade secrets, and was therefore valid and enforceable. The court disapproved the approach taken by Astbury J in *Brown*'s case of treating '*bona fides*' and 'the benefit of the company' as if they were two separate tests. It nevertheless approved the result in *Brown*'s case on the basis that the majority had voted not in the interests of the company at large but entirely for their own benefit and in their own interests.

The third case in the series is *Dafen Tinplate Co. Ltd.* v. *Llanelly Steel Co. (1907) Ltd.*[250] This again concerned a shareholder who was competing with the company. The company had been formed on the understanding

---

[248] [1919] 1 Ch. 290.    [249] [1920] 1 Ch. 154 (CA).    [250] [1920] 2 Ch. 124.

that the members would purchase steel bars from it, although there was no binding obligation on them to do so. The plaintiff had taken its custom to a rival steel company which it had been instrumental in forming. The company passed a resolution altering the articles to introduce a power enabling the majority to determine that the shares of any member (with one exception) should be offered for sale by the directors to the directors' nominee at their fair value. The resolution was struck down as going much further than was necessary for the protection of the company, since it enabled the expropriation of shareholders who were not doing anything to the detriment of the company, and therefore was not *bona fide* for the benefit of the company as a whole. This case reverted to the test propounded in *Brown*'s case, that the court should consider separately the questions of whether the resolution was passed in good faith and whether it was objectively for the benefit of the company. But in the subsequent case of *Shuttleworth* v. *Cox Brothers & Co. (Maidenhead) Ltd.*[251] (which was not an expropriation case) the court re-affirmed the subjective test, namely that the court will only intervene if the members are acting in bad faith. However, it accepted that this might be shown if the proposal to amend the articles was either incapable of being for the benefit of the company or such that no reasonable person could consider it for the benefit of the company.

The three English expropriation cases discussed above were decided between 1919 and 1920, and it was widely assumed since then that in order to justify expropriation by alteration of the articles, the minority shareholder must be acting in a manner destructive or highly damaging to the company's interests or for some motive entirely his or her own.[252]

Recently, this assumption was tested in Australia in *Gambotto* v. *WCP Ltd.*[253] Here, the majority shareholders (which were all wholly owned subsidiaries of Industrial Equity Ltd) held 99.7 per cent of the company's shares. A resolution was passed altering the company's articles to insert a new article 20A empowering any member who was 'entitled for the purposes of the Corporations Law to 90 per cent or more of the issued shares' to acquire the other issued shares prior to a specified date at a stated price. The plaintiff did not attend the meeting. The resolution was passed on a poll at which only the three minority shareholders voted, all voting in favour of the resolution.

At first instance, McLelland J held that since the immediate purpose and effect of the amendment was expropriation, it amounted to unjust oppression of the objecting minority. His Honour also referred to the fact

---

[251] [1927] 2 KB 9 (CA).
[252] See *Re Bugle Press Ltd.*, above n 68 at 287 *per* Lord Evershed MR.
[253] Above n 247.

that the express power of expropriation in sections 414 and 701 of the Corporations Law would be unnecessary if it were possible simply to amend the articles to achieve the same result.

McLelland J's decision was reversed by the New South Wales Court of Appeal which applied and, it is submitted, extended[254] the non-interventionist approach taken in *Shuttleworth's* case,[255] holding that where it was arguable that the resolution was beneficial for the company, the court should simply decline to interfere. This decision was, in turn, reversed by the High Court.[256]

A theme common to the judgments at all three levels (despite their differing outcomes) was that expression '*bona fide* for the benefit of the company as a whole' laid down by Lindley MR in *Allen* v. *Gold Reefs of West Africa Ltd.*[257] was inappropriate to test the validity of a special resolution altering the articles and giving rise to a conflict of interests and advantages between majority and minority shareholders. All three courts referred to *Peters' American Delicacy Co. Ltd.* v. *Heath*[258] in this regard and, in particular, to Dixon J's statement that:[259]

If the challenged alteration relates to an article which does or may affect an individual, as, for instance, a director appointed for life or a shareholder whom it is desired to expropriate, or to an article affecting the mutual rights and liabilities *inter se* of shareholders or different classes or descriptions of shareholders, the very subject matter involves a conflict of interests and advantages. To say that the shareholders forming the majority must consider the advantage of the company as a whole in relation to such a question seems inappropriate, if not meaningless, and at all events starts an impossible inquiry.

The majority of the High Court (consisting of Mason CJ, Brennan, Deane and Dawson JJ) went on to hold that an alteration of the articles to confer a power in the majority to expropriate shares or valuable proprietary rights attaching to the shares of a minority does not lie within the contemplated objects of the power to amend the articles,[260] and may be introduced only if:

(1) it is exercisable for a proper purpose; and
(2) its exercise will not operate oppressively in relation to minority shareholders.

---

[254] See above n 252 and preceding paragraph.     [255] Above n 251.
[256] Above n 103.     [257] [1900] 1 Ch. 656 at 671 (CA).
[258] (1939) 61 CLR 457 (HC). McLelland J also referred to *Crumpton* v. *Morrine Hall Pty. Ltd.* [1965] NSWR 240.     [259] Ibid., at 512.
[260] Above n 103, at 9; 348.

Further, the onus of establishing that the power is validly exercised lies on those supporting expropriation.

### (a) Proper purpose

The majority of the High Court considered that a proper purpose might exist where it was reasonably apprehended that the continued shareholding of the minority was detrimental to the company, its undertaking or the conduct of its affairs, and expropriation was a reasonable means of eliminating or mitigating that detriment. However, the majority shareholders could not expropriate the minority merely in order to secure for themselves the benefit of a corporate structure that could derive some new commercial advantage.[261] Their Honours gave as examples of proper purposes for introduction of such an article the case where a shareholder was competing with the company or where expropriation of foreign shareholders was necessary to enable a broadcasting company to obtain renewal of a television licence.

They accordingly held that the taxation and administrative savings which would result from the elimination of minority shareholders did not provide a sufficient justification for expropriation. They noted in this regard that it was difficult to conceive of circumstances in which financial and administrative benefits would not be a consequence of the expropriation of minority shareholdings by a majority shareholder, and that to allow expropriation for this reason would open the way to circumventing the protection which the Corporations Law gives to minorities who resist compromises, amalgamations and reconstructions, schemes of arrangement and takeover offers.[262]

### (b) Oppression

In addition to being made for a proper purpose, the court held that an amendment permitting the expropriation of shares must also be fair, both procedurally and substantively. Procedural fairness required disclosure of all relevant information, and presumably valuation by an independent expert. As noted above, the majority of the High Court left open the question whether it also required the majority shareholders to refrain from voting on the proposed amendment. Substantive fairness required that the terms of expropriation (and particularly the price) must be fair.[263]

McHugh J delivered a separate judgment allowing the appeal against the decision of the New South Wales Court of Appeal but for different

---

[261] Above n 103, at 9; 349.    [262] Above n 103, at 10; 349.
[263] See discussion in section 5(4) below.

reasons. His Honour rejected the distinction drawn by the majority judges between an expropriation that would enable a company to pursue a beneficial course of action that would otherwise be denied to it and an expropriation that would avoid a detriment to the existing interests of the company. Instead, he held that a company could alter its articles to enable a shareholder to acquire the shares of existing shareholders only when the acquisition was necessary to protect or promote the interests of the company and would not be oppressive to those shareholders.[264] As a result, McHugh J considered that the saving to the company of over $A4 million in taxes which would be the result of the expropriation was a legitimate business objective and one that would justify expropriation. However, he allowed the appeal on the basis that the company had failed to prove that the price was fair, that the appellants had been dealt with fairly and that full disclosure of all matters in relation to the alteration and expropriation had been made. The minority shareholders had not challenged the alteration on these grounds. However, in common with the other members of the court, McHugh J regarded these matters as having to be affirmatively proved by the majority shareholders.

## (4) Consideration

In the decided cases where compulsory acquisition has been permitted, there has been no objection taken to the price which has been offered. However, all members of the High Court in *Gambotto*'s case[265] held that there was an onus on the majority to establish that the price was fair, and that this would usually require an independent expert valuation to be obtained. Their Honours considered that the market price was a cogent factor in determining the fairness of the price, but adopted the approach taken by the Delaware Supreme Court in *Weinberger* v. *UOP Inc.*[266] that a shareholder's interest cannot be valued solely by the current market value, and that the fairness of the price also depends on factors such as assets, market value, dividends and the nature of the corporation and its likely future.

## (5) Shareholder information

Certain disclosure obligations have been held to apply generally to special resolutions. The notice convening the meeting must contain a general statement of the purposes of the resolution so that shareholders may make

[264] Above n 103, at 15; 352.
[265] Ibid., at 10–11; 349 *per* Mason CJ, Brennan, Deane and Dawson JJ and at 17–19; 354–6 *per* McHugh J.
[266] 457 A 2d 701 at 711 (1983).

a reasonably informed decision whether to attend.[267] The notice must set out the text or the entire substance of the resolution.[268] It must also fully and clearly disclose the nature and extent of any personal interest of the directors.[269] Any comments on the resolution which are given in the form of a circular or memorandum from the board of directors must fully and fairly inform and instruct the shareholders on what is proposed to be done.[270] The notice will be ineffective if it could mislead shareholders.[271]

These disclosure requirements, although not insubstantial, fall short of the detailed information which is required to be provided to shareholders in the context of a regulated takeover or a scheme of arrangement.

The majority of the High Court in *Gambotto*'s case[272] stated that the requirement of procedural fairness required the majority shareholders to disclose all relevant information leading up to the alteration, but did not discuss the extent to which this augmented the disclosure obligations generally applying to special resolutions. However, McHugh J stated[273] that full disclosure:

. . . will usually mean the disclosure of the purpose of the transaction, the giving of full reasons for rejecting alternative means of achieving that purpose and for concluding that the compensation offered will be fair to those affected, and the obtaining of an independent valuation for the shareholders. In most cases, full disclosure will also require information concerning the current and historical market prices of the shares where they are applicable, the net book value of the assets, and the value of the company both as a going concern and on a liquidation together with any reports or appraisals prepared in relation to the alteration and any firm offers for, or serious inquiries about the purchase of, the assets of the company.

---

[267] *Residues Treatment & Trading Co. Ltd.* v. *Southern Resources Ltd.* (1988) 14 ACLR 375 at 378 *per* White J, *Devereaux Holdings Pty. Ltd.* v. *Pelsart Resources NL (No. 2)* (1985) 9 ACLR 956 at 958 and *Bulfin* v. *Bebarfald's Ltd.*, above n 193 at 432–8.
[268] *MacConnell* v. *E. Prill & Co. Ltd.* [1916] 2 Ch. 57, *Re Moorgate Mercantile Holdings Ltd.* [1980] 1 WLR 227.
[269] *Kaye* v. *Croydon Tramways Co.* [1898] 1 Ch. 358 at 373 (CA), *Tiessen* v. *Henderson*, above n 193 at 870, *Baillie* v. *Oriental Telephone & Electric Co. Ltd.* [1915] 1 Ch. 503 (CA), *Chequepoint Securities Ltd.* v. *Claremont Petroleum NL* (1986) 11 ACLR 94; 4 ACLC 711.
[270] *Bancorp Investments Ltd.* v. *Primac Holdings Ltd.* (1984) 9 ACLR 263; 3 ACLC 69 and *Chequepoint Securities Ltd.* v. *Claremont Petroleum NL*, ibid., at 96; 713.
[271] *Bain & Company Nominees Pty. Ltd.* v. *Grace Bros Holdings Ltd.* (1983) 1 ACLR 816. See also *Fraser* v. *NRMA Holdings Ltd.* above n 110, regarding the potential application of the Trade Practices Act 1974 (Cth) in this context in Australia.
[272] Above n 103, at 10; 349.
[273] Ibid., at 19; 355. His Honour compared the disclosure requirements in s. 672(3), CL (Aust) (which relate to alteration of the articles to include a takeover approval provision) in this regard.

### (6) Restrictions

As mentioned above, the only limitation on the procedure is a successful action brought by a minority shareholder.

## 6. POLICY ISSUES

### (1) Takeovers

In the absence of legislation permitting shares to be compulsorily acquired, the expectation of a shareholder is taken to be that his or her investment in a company will remain in that company for the life of the venture. It may be possible to establish a contrary expectation, and this is most likely to be possible in a quasi-partnership or joint venture company.[274] But in other companies, in the absence of attempts by majority shareholders to frustrate the minority from selling their shares or other oppressive conduct, complaints by minority shareholders that they are 'locked-in' are met with the response that:[275] 'Where parties have entered into a joint stock company, they have agreed that their contribution to capital together with all the other contributions to capital that will be put in as part of the joint stock with which the company will trade will remain in the company whilst its substratum is there until there is a winding up or at least a reduction of capital.' Apart from authority, Young J regarded this as 'consonant with first principles'.[276]

This expectation may be displaced where the company's articles of association have provided since the company's formation for compulsory acquisition of a member's shares,[277] or where, for example, shares are issued which are redeemable preference shares.

However, it was against the expectation of an indefinite investment that the legislation permitting compulsory acquisition after a successful take-over was introduced, and this can be seen in the judicial response to the introduction of the procedure. Maugham J in the first reported case on the provision said:[278] 'I confess I have some sympathy with people in the position of the applicants. I am myself not quite able to understand why the Legislature should ever have passed sect. 155 at all, and therefore I am not

---

[274] See Ch. 9 section 10(2).

[275] *McWilliam* v. *L. J. R. McWilliam Estates Pty. Ltd.* (1990) 20 NSWLR 703 *per* Young J at 707 citing *Re G. Jeffery (Mens Store) Pty. Ltd.* (1984) 9 ACLR 193; 2 ACLC 421. See also *Re a Company (No. 004475 of 1982)* [1983] Ch. 178, *Swane* v. *Swane Bros Pty Ltd.* (1992) 10 ACLC 904 and *Kizquari Pty. Ltd.* v. *Prestoo Pty. Ltd.* (1993) 10 ACSR 606; 11 ACLC 568.

[276] *McWilliam* v. *L. J. R. McWilliam Estates Pty. Ltd.*, ibid.

[277] *Phillips* v. *Manufacturers Securities Ltd.*, above n 1.

[278] *Re Hoare & Co. Ltd.*, above n 76 at 376.

at all indisposed to consider the objections of such applicants as I have before me.'

An even stronger view was expressed by Rand J in *Rathie* v. *Montreal Trust Co.* who said:[279] 'Here is the exercise of a power by which an individual's property may be taken from him, possibly by a fellow shareholder, and a more complete negation of the terms upon which originally, at least, individuals entered into the association of company membership can hardly be imagined.'

The background to law reform in this field has been a premise that takeovers are beneficial, and should be encouraged.[280] It has also been recognized that an offeror will often not be prepared to proceed with an acquisition unless it is able to gain 100 per cent ownership of the target company. There are various reasons for this:

### (1) *Intended investment by the majority*

The offeror may intend to invest large sums in the company, in the expectation that the company will become more profitable. Where the minority shareholders will not be making a proportionate investment, the majority may not wish to share the return of the investment with the minority.[281]

### (2) *Transfer of funds between group companies*

Subject to directors' duties to the target company,[282] 100 per cent ownership of a subsidiary enables a holding company more easily to operate its subsidiaries in the interests of the group as a whole without needing to consider the interests of minority shareholders, for example by transferring funds between group companies.[283]

### (3) *Administrative savings*

One hundred per cent ownership simplifies administrative control, enables rationalization of the use of inter-company personnel and

[279] [1953] 4 DLR 289 at 299 (SCC) .

[280] Commentators are divided as to the economic benefits of takeovers. On the one hand, it is argued that takeovers bring assets under more productive management to the overall benefit of society. A counter-argument is made that the threat of takeovers forces management to focus on short-term goals, and that takeovers are an expensive way of encouraging managerial efficiency. See further: J. H. Farrar *et al.*, *Farrar's Company Law* (3rd edn., London, Butterworths, 1991) at 605 ff, Ford and Austin, above n 8, para. 2005, and references cited in these works and J. P. Charkham, *Keeping Good Company: A Study of Corporate Governance in Five Countries* (Oxford, Clarendon Press, 1994) at 309–14.

[281] *Brown* v. *British Abrasive Wheel Co. Ltd.*, above n 248, and Farrar, ibid., at 623.

[282] See e.g., *Charterbridge Corp Ltd.* v. *Lloyds Bank Ltd.* [1970] Ch. 62 and *Equiticorp Finance Ltd. (in liq.)* v. *Bank of New Zealand (*1993) 32 NSWLR 50 (CA NSW).

[283] Farrar, above n 280, at 623, and Kent and Vary, above n 50.

resources,[284] and results in savings in company secretarial and share registry expenses.[285]

### (4) *Confidentiality*

It protects the confidentiality of the company's business plans and product developments.[286]

### (5) *Tax savings*

In Australia, section 80G of the Income Tax Assessment Act 1936 (Cth) enables allowable deductions in a subsidiary company to be offset against assessment income of the parent company or other wholly-owned subsidiaries.[287] In *ANZ Executors & Trustees Ltd.* v. *Humes Ltd.*[288] the group tax relief savings were estimated to be between six million and 28 million Australian dollars per year.

On the other hand, the factors standing in the way of an offeror achieving 100 per cent ownership include:[289]

(1) apathy on the party of minority shareholders, or a desire to extract better terms than those being offered (greenmail);[290]
(2) untraceable shareholders; and
(3) executors and trustees who do not have authority or are at the time not yet empowered to accept the bid.[291]

An implied but less frequently mentioned[292] premise for legislation in this area is that many shareholders have no personal attachment to the companies in which they invest.

However, if the benefits of 100 per cent ownership are accepted as justifying a compulsory acquisition procedure, there are certain features of the procedure which are anomalous. Principal among these is the fact that an offeror may choose to acquire the shares of some but not all dissenting shareholders. Equally anomalous is the second limb of the acceptance criterion which applies to takeovers regulated by statute in Australia. This

---

[284] *Elkington* v. *Shell Australia Ltd.*, above n 83, at 16–17 *per* Kirby ACJ.

[285] *TNT Ltd.* v. *NCSC* above n 47, at 62; 627.

[286] CASAC Issues Paper, above n 4, at 1.

[287] See Taxation Ruling IT2465 and Digby, above n 2, at 107. Cf., the UK position where group relief is not dependent upon 100% ownership: s. 413 Income and Corporation Taxes Act 1988 (UK).                                                    [288] Above n 58 at 395.

[289] Weinberg, above n 3, para. 3.872.

[290] Greene Committee, above n 5, para. 84–5. See also *Elkington* v. *Shell Australia Ltd.*, above n 83, at 16–17 *per* Kirby ACJ.                          [291] Weinberg, above n 3, para. 3–872.

[292] But cf., Weinberg, ibid.

requirement may be satisfied whether the shares have been transferred to the offeree or to a rival bidder or simply in the ordinary course of trading.[293]

Extension of the procedure to individual and joint offerors also departs from the original impetus for the introduction of the provision which was to facilitate the merger of companies, rather than to concentrate property interests.[294] To that extent, it may be seen as a step detrimental to the interests of minority shareholders.[295]

It is relevant to consider whether anything has changed since Baxt described the protection offered to the minority shareholder by an application to the court as 'illusory'[296] in 1970. One factor which has changed in the intervening years is the greater importance now placed on full and fair disclosure to shareholders in the takeover context. Another is the recognition that the conduct of the offeror may depress the share price and potentially render compulsory acquisition unfair. Otherwise, the only meaningful protection offered to the minority by the section is the high acceptance threshold.

The question then arises whether an offeror who cannot meet the acceptance thresholds in the compulsory acquisition procedure should be able to expropriate minority shareholders by an alternative route.

## (2) Schemes of arrangement

### (a) England

The courts have consistently rejected the argument that a scheme of arrangement cannot be used to expropriate dissenting minority share-holders in what is essentially a takeover. This has been on the dual grounds that:

(1) there is nothing in the language of the section which necessarily requires the scope of the arrangement procedure to be limited;[297] and

---

[293] See Kent and Vary, above n 50.

[294] See *Blue Metal Industries Ltd.* v. *R. W. Dilley*, above n 14. The desire of the Greene Committee, (above n 5), had been to facilitate the merger of companies, and the Jenkins Committee, (above n 84, para. 283) affirmed this rationale for the procedure and accordingly opposed its extension to individuals.

[295] On the other hand, the complementary right given to a locked-in minority shareholder to compel purchase of his or her shares is also extended: see K. Kolodny, 'Protection of Minority Shareholders After a Take-over Bid: The UK and Ontario Compared' (1986) 7 *Company Lawyer* 17.

[296] R. Baxt, 'The Unprotected Shareholder and the Compulsory Acquisition of Shares' [1970] *J Bus L* 86, at 87.

[297] But cf., s. 411(17), CL (Aust). See discussion below at n 307 and subsequent text.

(2) different considerations are involved in the compulsory acquisition procedure as compared with the court's function in approving a scheme of arrangement.

Plowman J said in *Re National Bank Ltd*:[298]

Under [the scheme of arrangement procedure] an arrangement can only be sanctioned if the question of its fairness has first of all been submitted to the court. Under [the takeover procedure], on the other hand, the matter may never come to the court at all. If it does come to the court, then the onus is cast on the dissenting minority to demonstrate the unfairness of the scheme. There are, therefore, good reasons for requiring a smaller majority in favour of a scheme under [a scheme of arrangement] than the majority which is required under [the takeover procedure] if the minority is to be expropriated.

*Re National Bank Ltd.*[299] was applied in *Singer Manufacturing Co.* v. *Robinow*[300] to enable a straightforward takeover by way of transfer of shares to proceed under a scheme of arrangement.[301] However, Templeman J in *Re Hellenic & General Trust Ltd.*[302] considered that there must be a very high standard of proof on the part of the petitioner to justify obtaining by a scheme of arrangement what could not be obtained by the takeover procedure.

## (b) Australia

This question arises against a different background in Australia, because takeovers are regulated by statute in certain circumstances, and there is authority that a transaction cannot be carried out under a scheme where an alternative specific procedure exists.[303] This formed the basis for White J's dissenting judgment in *Re the Bank of Adelaide*[304] that a takeover could not be achieved under a scheme of arrangement. However, the majority in that case relied on a combination of literal statutory interpretation and the element of reduction of capital involved in the scheme to follow *Re National Bank Ltd.*,[305] and the same decision was reached in the later case of *Re Wallace Dairy Co. Ltd.*[306]

Since those cases were decided a new provision has been inserted into the Australian legislation[307] which prohibits a court from approving a scheme unless:

---

[298] [1966] 1 WLR 819 at 829–30.    [299] Ibid.    [300] Above n 141.
[301] See also *Re Savoy Hotel Ltd.*, above n 134.    [302] Above n 136, at 129.
[303] See e.g., *Re International Harvester Co. of Australia Pty. Ltd.* [1953] VLR 669 (Full Ct, Vic) and *Re Anglo-Continental Supply Company Ltd.* [1922] 2 Ch. 723.
[304] Above n 137.    [305] Above n 298.    [306] Above n 139.
[307] Section 411(17) CL, (Aust).

(1) it is satisfied that the scheme has not been proposed for the purpose of enabling a person to avoid the operation of any of the provisions of Chapter 6 of the Corporations Law (which regulates takeovers); or

(2) the ASC produces a written statement to the court that it has no objection to the scheme.

The legislation also provides that the court is not obliged to approve the scheme merely because it receives a written statement from the ASC.

The ASC intervened (unsuccessfully) in two recent cases, both of which were cases where a 100 per cent acquisition was achieved by a cancellation and reduction scheme. In the first case, *Re ACM Gold Ltd.*,[308] the consideration to shareholders was to be 10 cents per share from the target company, and shares in the new parent company; in *Re Stockbridge Ltd.*,[309] shareholders were offered a choice of cash or shares in the offeror company. Two additional elements in *Re Stockbridge Ltd.*,[310] were the company's arguments that it was a necessary condition that the entire ownership of the target company be resolved in favour of the offeror (or not) at one time and the fact that the company had also issued options which could not be acquired under a takeover scheme.

In each case it was held that as long as the scheme had the hallmarks of a commercial enterprise and there was nothing which pointed to a contrivance of an element which was unreal or unnecessary, the scheme was to be assessed at face value. Since in each case the scheme involved a reduction of capital, it could not have been achieved under Chapter 6. Accordingly the court considered that section 411(17) had not been contravened and ordered class meetings to be convened.

In the wake of *Re ACM* and *Re Stockbridge* the ASC released Policy Statement 60, in which it indicates that it will provide a written statement under section 411(17)(b) if the specific disclosure provisions relating to schemes of arrangement are complied with and the standard of disclosure to and equal treatment of shareholders is commensurate with that which would be required in a takeover under Chapter 6.

The ASC's aim is to endeavour to ensure that minority shareholders are not disadvantaged by the use of the scheme of arrangement procedure. However, there are two respects in which the statement may not have its intended effect. First, no distinction is made by the ASC between a straightforward transfer scheme[311] and a takeover which cannot be achieved under the Chapter 6 procedure, for example because it concerns options or convertible interests or involves a reduction of capital. If, as seems to be the case, the ASC will provide a written statement in either

---

[308] Above n 138.          [309] Above n 139.          [310] Ibid.
[311] See above n 140 and accompanying text.

case, then this goes further than the decisions in *Re ACM* and *Re Stockbridge*, and significantly reduces the potential role of the ASC under section 411(17).

Secondly, under a regulated takeover, information is provided both by the offeror and the target company. The policy statement requires that commensurate information be provided under a scheme, but in cases of inconsistency between those provisions this will not be possible.[312] More importantly, the policy statement does not indicate who has the obligation to provide information regarding the offeror. Unlike the directors of the target company,[313] there is no express obligation in the scheme provisions for the offeror to supply the necessary information to the target company. However, it is the target company which will normally be the applicant in respect of the scheme. Although this factor is of limited significance if the scheme involves a simple reduction of capital where the expropriated shareholders receive cash in consideration for their shares, it will become important if they are to be offered shares in the 'offeror'.

Both *Re Stockbridge* and *Re ACM* were hearings to convene class meetings. In light of the lower approval threshold and the fact that shareholders may not be as well-informed regarding the offeror under a scheme of arrangement as under a takeover bid, if and when the schemes returned to the court for approval, Templeman J's dictum to the effect that a high standard of proof would be required to justify obtaining by a scheme of arrangement what could not be obtained under the takeover procedure would have been relevant.[314] In addition to examining the consideration offered and the information provided to shareholders, the higher standard of proof may be reflected, as it was in *Re Hellenic & General Trust Ltd.*[315] and *Re Direct Acceptance Corporation Ltd.*[316] in placing a greater emphasis on how the scheme will affect the interests of an individual shareholder, rather than focusing on unfairness to shareholders as a body.[317]

### (3) Reductions of capital

The approval and disclosure requirements for a reduction of capital are less stringent than those applying to a regulated takeover. Further, selective reductions of capital provide less protection to minority shareholders when effected outside the scheme of arrangement procedure because of the

---

[312] E.g.,the distinction between an expert's determination of whether an offer is fair and reasonable as opposed to whether a scheme is in the best interests of members.
[313] Section 412(5), CL (Aust).
[314] *Re Hellenic & General Trust Ltd.*, above n 136, at 129.     [315] Ibid.
[316] Above n 150.          [317] See discussion at nn 172–3 and accompanying text.

absence of a requirement for class meetings[318] as part of the approval process. Moreover, unlike the scheme of arrangement and takeover provisions, there is no legislative requirement for provision of an independent expert's report to shareholders in the context of a reduction of capital.

In *Re Robert Stephen Holdings Ltd.*,[319] the court adverted to the fact that shareholders who are to be paid off are better protected under the scheme of arrangement procedure. The petition seeking confirmation of the reduction in that case was unopposed (even though votes were cast against the special resolution at the meeting), and the court confirmed the reduction.[320] However, it criticized the use of the reduction of capital procedure to eliminate the minority shareholdings, implying that it may not have been prepared to confirm the reduction if it had been opposed. The effect of this case is therefore to channel English shareholders seeking to acquire control of a company into using the scheme of arrangement procedure.

It has been argued in Australia, where there is a specific statutory regime applying to takeovers, that the court should refuse to confirm a selective reduction of capital on the basis that the procedure is being used to avoid complying with statutory provisions. This argument has consistently been rejected[321] despite the court's acknowledgement in one case[322] that the reason for using the procedure was that the 'offeror' had not acquired enough shares to use the compulsory powers of acquisition in Chapter 6 of the Corporations Law. Although the courts have not sought to direct applicants to use a procedure which provides greater protection to the minority shareholders, they have considered it relevant when deciding whether to approve a reduction to have regard to the requirements which would have applied had the matter proceeded as a regulated takeover. One underlying feature of the takeover provisions is that all members of the minority are given the opportunity to share equally in any control premium or any other premium which the rights attached to their shares bring into existence. Thus, in *Catto v. Ampol Ltd.*[323] approval of a reduction was withheld where in order to achieve its majority position, Pioneer had paid $A4 per share, whereas the price at which the preference shares were to be repaid was $A2.78. The same approach was applied in *Nicron Resources Ltd. v. Catto*.[324] However, since in this case the 'offeror' already had control, Bryson J considered that the only difference to shareholders if the

---

[318] In the wide sense in which the term 'class' is interpreted in the scheme of arrangement context.                                                                    [319] Above n 240, at 524–5.
[320] See also *Re Rank Radio and Television Ltd., The Times*, 19 November 1963 at 5.
[321] *Ramsay Health Care Ltd. v. Elkington* (1992) 7 ACSR 73; 10 ACLC 421 and *Nicron Resources Ltd. v. Catto*, above n 163.                    [322] *Nicron Resources Ltd. v. Catto* ibid.
[323] Above n 100.                                                                    [324] Above n 163.

Chapter 6 takeover procedure had been used was that the procedure would have been more elaborate and less certain. His Honour accordingly approved the reduction of capital.

A further practical limitation on the use of the reduction of capital procedure as a means of effecting a takeover in Australia is the intervention of the ASC. Unlike the scheme of arrangement procedure, the ASC does not have a specific statutorily based role in the process of confirmation by the court. However, the ASC has stated[325] that it may intervene to oppose the confirmation of a capital reduction if there has not been full and frank disclosure of all material information to shareholders at a level comparable to that which would apply under a takeover or a scheme of arrangement, or if there is evidence to suggest that the proposal is not fair to expropriated or to continuing shareholders. The Practice Note emphasizes the desirability of providing an independent expert's report, and of interested shareholders making full disclosure of their interests and abstaining from voting on the resolution.

*Re Hunter Resources Ltd.*[326] imposes a further limitation on the use of the reduction of capital procedure as a means of effecting a takeover. Here, an application for confirmation of a reduction was refused on the basis that the Chapter 6 takeover procedure should have been used. Instead of receiving cash for their shares, the expropriated shareholders were to receive shares in the parent company. The fact that this 'consideration' was not consideration from the company at all but rather came from the parent company was important to the court's finding that this was not a true reduction of capital.[327] The court said:[328] 'If the company wishes to achieve its objective it should invoke the provisions of the Corporations Law concerning schemes of arrangement or takeover schemes which have special procedures designed for cases such as the present and which protect the interests of minority shareholders.'

Although the Australian courts have been prepared to countenance the use of a reduction of capital to achieve a takeover provided that comparable safeguards are applied, it is interesting to note that even in the most recent cases, there is a recognition that the power of compulsory acquisition which is provided by statute runs counter to the expectations which shareholders would otherwise have. As Bryson J stated in *Nicron Resources Ltd.* v. *Catto*:[329]

---

[325] Practice Note 29.   [326] Above n 244.
[327] Ibid., at 443. An alternative ground for decision in that case based on s. 184, CL (Aust) (which is equivalent to s.22(2), CA 1985 (UK)) was that the section requires the agreement of a person before he or she can become a member of a company.
[328] Ibid., at 444.   [329] Above n 163, at 228–9; 1193.

It could be thought inconsistent with the nature of a company that this should happen. When a number of persons join [*sic*] together and contribute to a joint stock of capital with which to carry on a venture, the ordinary contemplation is that the venture will go on indefinitely while it is a success. It has struck me as an anomaly that any one member should be in a position to tell the others that their membership of the company and their association in its affairs are no longer required, and that they will be given an objectively determined fair sum of money and dismissed or expelled. An event like that could be interpreted as according less than appropriate value to the standing of shares as property which should be respected and not subjected to expropriations, even with compensation, unless there is lawful authority; and also less than appropriate value to continuing membership of an association and freedom from expulsion; and also less than appropriate value to the continuation, except on pre-established grounds, of reasonable and legitimate expectations which have been relied on for serious commercial conduct.'

His Honour nevertheless considered himself bound by the long-standing authority permitting a selective reduction of capital provided that it was fair and equitable to all concerned. Later in the same case he stated:[330]

The fairness and equity of a reduction is primarily a matter of the treatment of the minority shareholder's economic interests. If he is expelled with a cheque for a fair sum, his feelings of attachment to his property and his decision to invest in it and his wish to continue with the investment are not the test of fairness. I say 'primarily' because the decision is discretionary and there could I suppose be some circumstances in which an exclusively economic conspectus was not appropriate because of some personal dealings among those involved or for some other reason. But in this case and on its facts, the economic conspectus confines my appraisal of the fairness and equity of the reduction, as it does in most cases.

### (4) Amendment of the articles

In Australia, the decision of the majority of the High Court in *Gambotto*'s case[331] effectively eliminates the potential for the minority shareholder protections in the statutory methods of compulsory acquisition to be circumvented by the insertion of an expropriation power into the company's articles of association. However, the majority decision permits this method of compulsory acquisition to be used where the minority shareholder's continued membership of the company poses a threat to the company's business or to its confidential information.

Although there is no recent English authority on this specific question, it is likely that an English court would take a similar approach to that of the Australian High Court. Indirect support for this submission can be found in the discouragement given to the use of the reduction of capital

---

[330] Above n 163, at 231; 1195.      [331] Above n 103.

procedure as a compulsory acquisition method in *Re Robert Stephen Holdings Ltd.*,[332] on the grounds that it offers a low level of protection to minority shareholders.

## (5) General

Compulsory acquisition cuts across the expectations with which shareholders become members of a company. The legislature has made a conscious decision to do this, after balancing the advantages of takeovers to the company concerned and the wider community over the disadvantages to shareholders in having their property expropriated, bearing in mind the disproportionate power which minority shareholders would have to demand an excessive price for their shares if some form of compulsory acquisition power did not exist. The express power which is given in the takeover context is, however, accompanied by safeguards designed to protect the interests of the minority, one of which is a high acceptance threshold. The justification for enabling expropriation to take place by alternative means which involve a lower approval threshold in the context of schemes of arrangement has been the fact that the procedure is scrutinized by the court, which can ensure that the expropriation takes place on terms which are fair.[333] Further, as is borne out by the cases, the courts have been prepared to take on that role and have interpreted the concept of 'unfairness' more liberally than when exercising their discretion on the application of a dissenting shareholder under the takeover procedure. For the same reason, English courts have shied away from sanctioning a reduction of capital as a permissible means of effecting a takeover, and although the Australian courts have taken the opposite view, this has been on the basis that the level of protection given to the minority shareholders is not compromised as a result.

It is not possible to ensure that shareholders are protected to the same degree in an expropriation which arises from alteration of the company's articles as under the other means of compulsory acquisition. An alteration involves a lower approval threshold and no legal impediment to the resolution being carried by the votes of interested shareholders. Moreover, there is no supervision by the court of the procedure unless a minority shareholder brings an action seeking to strike down the resolution. All the obstacles which lie in the path of the minority shareholder in terms of time and financial resources militate against such actions being brought. Accordingly, the courts have not permitted this method of expropriation to be used unless the shareholder to be expropriated poses a threat to the company.

Most of the cases mentioned in the above discussion concern listed

---

[332] Above n 240.     [333] *Re National Bank Ltd.* above n 298.

companies where, even though some shareholders may have a certain level of attachment to their shares,[334] they are generally passive investors in the company. Although an argument can be made for equating shareholding in a listed company with a purely economic interest, this situation is distinguishable from that where the shareholder to be expropriated would otherwise have participated actively in the company's business. The approval requirements for all of the above methods of compulsory acquisition mean that the procedure will seldom be available in a quasi-partnership or other unlisted company. However, in cases where they would enable the majority compulsorily to acquire the shares of a minority shareholder who is not merely a passive investor, the expropriation would potentially provide grounds for an action by the minority shareholder, either at common law or under the unfair prejudice provision.

[334] Cf., *Re Shoppers City Ltd.* v. *M. Loeb Ltd.*, above n 83, at 40 where an argument that the shares to be expropriated had been a Christmas present from the shareholder's wife and that he had planned to present them to his three-year-old son on his 21st birthday was not regarded as relevant.

# PART IV

*Conclusions*

# Overview and Conclusions

1. Listed Companies                                                319

2. Quasi-Partnership Companies                                     320
   (1) Over-protection of the minority                             321
   (2) Inappropriateness of corporate norms                        322
       (a) A special code                                          325
       (b) Other approaches                                        326

3. Other Companies                                                 328

4. Comparison between Jurisdictions                                328

This book began by dividing companies into three broad categories, and identifying the most commonly expressed complaints of minority shareholders in each category of company. It is therefore appropriate to end by examining the extent to which solutions can be found to those complaints.

## 1. LISTED COMPANIES

As regards listed companies, institutional shareholders can be distinguished from other categories of minority shareholder because although no single institution may have a controlling shareholding in a company, collectively institutions will usually own a substantial majority of its shares. This creates opportunities for self-help in the form of collective institutional pressure.

The influence of the institutions has the potential to combat all of the identified complaints, either by direct action or by the introduction of structural changes. To the extent that these measures are successful, they generally benefit all shareholders, except that the institutions' very success in establishing better lines of communication with the companies in which they invest has arguably weakened the channels of information which are available to all shareholders. The area in which institutional activism has probably had least success is in preventing self-interested conduct by the directors, particularly in respect of remuneration. This is at least partly because the non-executive directors on whom the institutions have placed the responsibility for monitoring company boards are often unable to perform that role, either because they are not sufficiently independent of social and hierarchical constraints or because they require the board's co-operation. The challenge of establishing effective monitoring structures has, however, been recognized and a lively debate continues as to the best way forward.

Litigation is not extensively resorted to in listed companies because there is always the possibility of selling the shares on the open market. Where proceedings have been brought, the potential of the unfair prejudice remedy has been slow to be realized. An action in respect of mere negligence still faces difficulties, even under the unfair prejudice provision. But for shareholders who are confronted by more serious cases of breach of fiduciary duty or other self-interested transactions by the directors, the elimination of standing problems and the range of remedies offered by the unfair prejudice provision represent a real advance on (although not a total overlap with) the common law alternative. The unfair prejudice remedy has been used to advantage in two recent Australian cases concerning listed companies,[1] and statutory amendments have paved the way for a similar approach to be taken in England. An indication that the courts may move in this direction can be seen in a Scottish case which predates the amendments and where the unfair prejudice provision provided a remedy to some of the shareholders in a listed company who were particularly affected by the directors' self-interested conduct.[2]

One complaint which has, however, been a fruitful source of litigation in listed companies (and other widely held companies) is compulsory acquisition of minority shareholdings. The statutory procedure which applies in the context of a successful takeover reflects a policy decision as to the appropriate balance between majority and minority interests in this context, and has been used as a guide by the courts when adjudicating on challenges to compulsory acquisition by other means.

## 2. QUASI-PARTNERSHIP COMPANIES

Quasi-partners are at the same time vulnerable to the greatest range of oppressive conduct and most able to do something about it.

By devices such as weighted voting, class rights and shareholders' agreements, provision can be made to limit the potential for all of the

---

[1] *Re Spargos Mining NL* (1990) 3 WAR 166 and *Jenkins* v. *Enterprise Gold Mines NL* (1992) 6 ACSR 539; 10 ACLC 136 (Full Ct, WA).
[2] *McGuinness* v. *Bremner plc* 1988 SLT 891, affd. 1988 SLT 898n.

identified complaints. Such provision not only confines the areas of possible dispute, but also places minority shareholders in a very strong position should recourse to the courts become necessary. If the parties commit their expectations to writing, the courts will bend over backwards to give effect to them, even if it necessitates major innovations in the substantive law or in interpretative techniques.[3]

But if quasi-partners do not take advantage of the opportunities available to them to formalize their arrangement, all is not lost. The lack of formalities may pose difficulties in ascertaining the parties' expectations,[4] but the courts will still strive to give effect to the arrangement even if this means overriding the terms of the articles. It is submitted that the unfair prejudice provision is now the remedy of first resort in this context. It puts the enforcement of members' personal expectations on a secure footing, thereby effectively confining the winding-up remedy to situations where it is an appropriate remedy, and avoiding the uncertainty of relying on the tentative steps towards recognition of equitable obligations between quasi-partners outside the statutory framework.[5] Further, there is now a developing jurisprudence in the context of unfair prejudice petitions regarding expectations of participation in management, distribution of profits and buy-out on a breakdown of relations.

However, these developments do raise two further issues. The first is the potential for over-protection of the minority, or indeed oppression of the majority. The second is the desirability or otherwise of enacting legislation specifically designed to meet the needs of quasi-partnerships.

### (1) Over-protection of the minority

Protection of the minority creates the potential for deadlock and for consequent oppression of the majority, and these are issues which should be addressed by those drafting minority protection devices.

It is possible to include various deadlock-breaking mechanisms, such as casting votes, arbitration clauses and buy-out clauses.[6] Alternatively, a positive decision may be taken not to include any express provision. This is

---

[3] See *Bushell* v. *Faith* [1970] AC 1099 (HL), *Cumbrian Newspapers Group Ltd.* v. *Cumberland and Westmorland Herald Newspaper and Printing Co. Ltd.* [1987] Ch. 1, and *Russell* v. *Northern Bank Development Corporation Ltd.* [1992] 1 WLR 588 (HL).

[4] See *Re R. A. Noble & Sons (Clothing) Ltd.* [1983] BCLC 273 at 288.

[5] *Re Medefield Pty. Ltd.* (1977) 2 ACLR 406; (1977–1978) ACLC ¶40–325, *Pennell* v. *Venida Investments Ltd.*, unreported decision of Templeman J, 25 July 1974, noted by S. J. Burridge, 'Wrongful Rights Issues' (1981) 44 *Mod L Rev* 40 and *Clemens* v. *Clemens Bros Ltd.* [1976] 2 All ER 268.

[6] See further P. C. Heerey, 'The Company Law Framework for Resolving Deadlocks' in *Deadlock in Your Company: What Can You Salvage?* (Melbourne, Faculty of Law, Monash University, 1982) at 1.

perhaps more likely to be the case in a large commercial joint venture, since the parties' conduct and the decision whether to bring litigation will effectively be determined by political, economic and commercial factors which may be more far-reaching than the actual venture.

If no provision is made, then the granting of veto powers to minority shareholders may bring management to a standstill.[7] This raises the question whether what have been described as 'minority protection remedies' are available to majority shareholders. A flexible approach has been taken to the establishment of wrongdoer control for the purposes of a common law derivative action in several cases.[8] In *Barrett v. Duckett*[9] a 50 per cent shareholder was treated as being in an equivalent position to a minority shareholder for practical reasons, although the Court of Appeal struck out the proceedings on other grounds.[10] Similarly, arguments that an unfair prejudice petition could not be brought by a majority shareholder have been rejected by both the English and Australian courts,[11] and relief was granted to a shareholder with a 50 per cent holding who was able to show that he did not have voting control of the company in the South African case of *Benjamin v. Elysium Investments*.[12]

### (2) Inappropriateness of corporate norms

Perhaps the most striking feature of quasi-partnerships is the limited advantage which is taken of the extensive possibilities for the parties to express and thereby protect their expectations as to their rights and obligations. This contrasts starkly with the attitude of the parties to commercial joint ventures who almost invariably formalize their understandings.[13] Prentice[14] suggests this may be attributable to the fact that parties forming an incorporated partnership are poorly advised, or in the case of parties who choose to minimize their formation costs by purchasing an off-the-shelf company they may not be advised at all. Even with the

---

[7] See R. Baxt 'The Variation of Class Rights' (1968) 41 *Austl LJ* 490 at 496.
[8] *Prudential Assurance Co. Ltd. v. Newman Industries (No. 2)* [1981] Ch. 257, rvsd. [1982] Ch. 204 (CA), *Barrett v. Duckett* [1995] BCC 362 (CA) and *Biala Pty. Ltd. v. Mallina Holdings Limited (No. 2)* (1993) 11 ACSR 785; 11 ACLC 1082 (digest only), affd. sub nom *Dempster v. Mallina Holdings Ltd.* (1994) 15 ACSR 1 (Full Ct, (WA)).
[9] [1993] BCC 778.
[10] Above n 8.
[11] *Re Associated Tool Industries* (1963) 5 FLR 55 and *Re Stewarts (Brixton) Ltd.* [1985] BCLC 4 at 7. Note that in *Re H. R. Harmer Ltd.* [1959] 1 WLR 62 (CA) the father was a minority shareholder but (with his wife) held the majority of the voting shares.
[12] 1960 (3) SA 467.
[13] See F. Wooldridge, 'A New Form of Incorporation—Responding to the Gower Proposals' (1982) 3 *Company Lawyer* 58.
[14] D. D. Prentice, 'Winding up on the Just and Equitable Ground: The Partnership Analogy' (1973) 89 *Law Q Rev* 107 at 118.

benefit of legal advice, it may be that detailed planning is perceived to be too expensive compared with the risk of a serious dispute, or that too much negotiation might sour a peaceful relationship,[15] or that since the relationship is intended to be ongoing, entrenched rights may become a nuisance.[16] It may also be that because of the essentially personal relationship of quasi-partners it is considered to be unnecessary.

The fact remains, however, that although relations between the parties may be harmonious for the early life of the business, some recurring situations will inevitably generate conflict. Chesterman[17] recounts some of the more common of these circumstances: a dominant founder-entrepreneur may wish to get rid of a 'partner' who was useful in the firm's early days but is now a drag on his independence, the offspring of a founder may resent the domination of the parent, sleeping 'partners' may dispute with active parties if expansion is taking predominance over distributing income, and there may be disputes over allocating investment to faithful employees or adhering to a single product or style of service. In the absence of express protection in the articles or a shareholders' agreement, the corporate form and, in particular, its features of majority rule, demarcation between the roles of directors and shareholders, free transferability of shares and perpetual existence may result in a structure which does not give effect to the parties' intentions and which renders minority shareholders vulnerable to abuses of power.

Although the conflicts described above may be an inevitable fact of human nature, the consequences of such disagreements are not inevitable. Had the parties conducted their business as partners rather than corporators the scope for such abuses would have been severely curtailed:[18]

The inherent characteristics of the partnership form of business preclude many of the corporate squeeze-out techniques. Partners ordinarily do not depend on salaries or dividends for a return on their investment but receive a share of the profits of the enterprise. Additionally, a partner, as a co-owner of the business, is entitled to continued employment by the firm. In consequence, there is no partnership counter-part of the corporate squeeze technique of terminating a shareholder's employment and withholding dividends.

Further, the fall-back position adopted in the Partnership Acts in the event that parties do not provide to the contrary, is that the parties are bound to

---

[15] See e.g., H. Beale and T. Dugdale, 'Contracts between Businessmen: Planning and the use of Contractual Remedies' (1975) 2 *British Journal of Law and Society* 45.

[16] M. Chesterman, *Small Businesses* (2nd edn., London, Sweet & Maxwell, 1982).

[17] Ibid.

[18] O'Neill and Derwin, *Expulsion or Oppression of Business Associates* (1961) at 143, cited by Prentice, above n 14, at 115.

act with the utmost good faith,[19] that decisions on basic matters such as the composition of the partnership and alterations to the agreement must be unanimous,[20] that every partner has the right to participate in management decisions,[21] to inspect the books and accounts,[22] to obtain information from the other partners,[23] as well as the obligation to account for use of the partnership assets,[24] and that no partner may compete with the partnership.[25] Moreover, a partner can in some situations unilaterally terminate the partnership relationship.[26]

But despite the quite serious disadvantages of the corporate form to quasi-partners, and despite the fact that the main advantage of incorporation, namely limited liability, is in reality severely curtailed because most credit providers and landlords require directors to act as guarantors for the company, and in cases of negligence and other torts the individuals who have acted for the company can be sued as well as or instead of the company, nevertheless, as Gower observes:[27] '. . . if businessmen are provided with the choice of limited liability with complications or simple incorporation without it they are likely to opt for the former.'

The courts have recognized the special features of the quasi-partnership[28] and have striven to give effect to the expectations of the parties. However, the ever-increasing number of cases where relief is sought in respect of unfairly prejudicial conduct[29] does raise the question of whether the corporate form as it presently stands is an appropriate medium for the conduct of quasi-partnership businesses,[30] and suggest the potential

---

[19] This is achieved by the provision in the Acts that the rules of equity and common law are to apply, except where they are inconsistent with the express provisions of the Acts: Partnership Act (UK) s. 46, (NSW) s. 46, (Qld) s. 48, (SA) s. 46, (Tas) s. 5, (Vic) s. 4, (WA) s. 6 Partnership Ordinance (ACT) s. 5: K. L. Fletcher, *The Law of Partnership in Australia and New Zealand* (6th edn., The Law Book Company Limited, Sydney, 1991) at 10.

[20] Partnership Act (UK) s. 24, (NSW) s. 24, (Qld) s. 27, (SA) s. 24, (Tas) s. 29, (Vic) s. 28, (WA) s. 34, Partnership Ordinance (ACT) s. 29.      [21] Ibid.      [22] Ibid.

[23] Partnership Act (UK) s. 28, (NSW) s. 28, (Qld) s. 31, (SA) s. 28, (Tas) s. 33, (Vic) s. 32, (WA) s. 39, Partnership Ordinance (ACT) s. 33.

[24] Partnership Act (UK) s. 29, (NSW) s. 29, (Qld) s. 32, (SA) s. 29, (Tas) s. 34, (Vic) s. 33, (WA) s. 40, Partnership Ordinance (ACT) s. 34.

[25] Partnership Act (UK) s. 30, (NSW) s. 30, (Qld) s. 33, (SA) s. 30, (Tas) s. 35, (Vic) s. 34, (WA) s. 41, Partnership Ordinance (ACT) s. 35.

[26] Chesterman, above n 16, and Prentice, above n 14, at 119.

[27] Department of Trade Green Paper, *A New Form of Incorporation for Small Firms—A Consultative Document* February 1981 (Cmnd. 8171) (UK). Reproduced as Annex A to the Green Paper is Professor Gower's proposal, 'A Code for Incorporated Firms?' para. 9.

[28] See further B. A. K. Rider, 'Partnership Law and its Impact on "Domestic Companies" ' [1979] *Cambridge LJ* 148.

[29] See Law Commission, *Reform of the Law Applicable to Private Companies: A Feasibility Study* para. 5.45 in Department of Trade and Industry, *Company Law Review: The Law Applicable to Private Companies*, A Consultative Document, November 1994.

[30] For detailed discussion of the disadvantages of incorporation for small businesses see M. Chesterman, above n 16.

usefulness of a code more closely suited to the needs of quasi-partners than Table A.

## (a) A special code

There have been law reform proposals in both England[31] and Australia[32] recommending the creation of a new legal entity which would combine the perceived benefits of the corporate form with a framework similar to that adopted by partners as regards the parties' *inter se* relations without the need for the parties to make detailed provision in the articles of association and/or a separate shareholders' agreement.

One of the essential points of distinction between a partnership and a company is that a company has perpetual existence.[33] This is brought into sharp focus not only in relation to the addition of new members but also when a member retires or dies, or if for any other reason (including a breakdown of relations) one or more of the members wishes to leave the quasi-partnership. Partnership law deals with these situations by providing for the dissolution of the partnership[34] in the event of death[35] or retirement.[36] There is consequently less need to address the problems posed by the changing nature of the parties' relationship over time.

The friction between the corporate norm of perpetual existence and the

[31] Above n 27. Legislation based substantially on Professor Gower's Proposal has been introduced in South Africa: Close Corporations Act, No. 69 1984. See further, D. S. Ribbens, *In Quest of the Appropriate Code for the Ideal Legal Form for the Proprietary Business Enterprise* (1986) Cambridge University Ph.D. 14620.

[32] See Companies and Securities Law Review Committee Discussion Paper No. 1, *Forms of Legal Organization for Small Business Enterprises* 1984, Companies and Securities Law Review Committee, Report to the Ministerial Council on *Forms of Legal Organisation for Small Business Enterprises*, September 1985, Close Corporations Act 1989 (this Act was assented to on 14 July 1989 but has not been proclaimed) and Discussion Paper, *Report of the Joint Parliamentary Committee on Corporations and Securities: Close Corporations Act 1989*, July 1993.

[33] See the radical US proposals which have sought to address this issue: F. H. Easterbrook and D. R. Fischel 'Close Corporations and Agency Costs (1986) 38 *Stan L Rev* 271 at 288 discuss the proposals of A. B. Afterman, 'Statutory Protection for Oppression Minority Shareholders: A Model for Reform' (1969) 55 *Va L Rev* 1043 at 1063–1064, who has advocated involuntary dissolution whenever a minority shareholder's reasonable expectations have been frustrated; and J. A. C. Hetherington and M. P. Dooley 'Illiquidity and Exploitation: A Proposed Statutory Solution to the Remaining Close Corporation Problem' (1977) 63 *Va L Rev* 1, who have argued that minority shareholders in close corporations should have the absolute right to force the buyout of their shares at an agreed price or in default a price fixed by the court.

[34] Although a partnership deed will usually make provision for the partnership to last for a specific term of years, impliedly restricting withdrawal before the expiration of the period unless the partner can show good legal cause why the partnership should be wound up earlier.

[35] Partnership Act (UK) s. 33, (NSW) s. 33, (Qld) s. 36, (SA) s. 33, (Tas) s. 38, (Vic) s. 37, (WA) s. 44, Partnership Ordinance (ACT) s. 38.

[36] Partnership Act (UK) s. 32, (NSW) s. 32, (Qld) s. 35, (SA) s. 32, (Tas) s. 37, (Vic) s. 36, (WA) s. 43, Partnership Ordinance (ACT) s. 37.

expectations of quasi-partners is addressed in the Gower proposals,[37] where it was recommended that on the death or retirement of a member the firm should have first option to purchase his or her shares at a valuation to be agreed or, failing agreement, determined by arbitration. A second option would be granted to members in the proportions to which they were entitled as between themselves or as otherwise agreed. If none was prepared to buy the firm, it would be wound up unless the continuing members were prepared to admit to membership an outside purchaser or legatee of the shares.

By contrast the only attempt to address this issue in the Australian Close Corporations Act 1989 (and the subsequent discussion paper on the Act)[38] was a limit of 10 members.[39] This type of provision cannot ensure that a close corporation retains its essential nature as a quasi-partnership if, for example, the shares of one co-founder are transferred to or inherited by a member who has no ability to participate in management.

### (b) Other approaches

The question nevertheless remains whether the enactment of special legislation for quasi-partnerships is the best solution to the fact that the assumptions inherent in the companies legislation will not always reflect the parties' expectations.[40] A number of counter-arguments can be made.

First, reference may be made to the diversity of closely-held companies, thereby making it difficult to construct a scheme which could encompass them all and at the same time avoid imposing complex requirements.[41] Secondly, the creation of a new form of incorporation will not prevent parties failing to adopt it.[42] A further argument is that not only do different quasi-partnerships have different needs, but the needs of a particular quasi-partnership company will change. Thus, even though a company may be formed on the basis of joint ownership and management, there is no guarantee that it will continue to function on that basis.

Reforms in England have instead focused on reducing the administrative burdens on small business.[43] This has taken the form of a more lenient

---

[37] Above n 27, para. 19.  [38] Above n 32.

[39] Section 60 Close Corporations Act 1989 (Aust). Gower, above n 27, at para. 14 also favours this number.

[40] See Sealy, above n 33, and Wooldridge, above n 13, who consider it unlikely that there would be widespread use of a new form of incorporation along the lines of the Gower Proposals unless the private limited company were made less attractive to quasi-partners.

[41] K. H. Dickinson, 'Partners in a Corporate Cloak: The Emergence and Legitimacy of the Incorporated Partnership' (1984) 33 *Am U L Rev* 559 at 597.  [42] Ibid.

[43] Several commentators have advocated giving such reforms a higher priority than a new legal structure. See R. Baxt, 'Forms of Legal Organisation for Small Business Enterprises— An Initial Response' (1984) 2 *Company & Sec LJ* 248, J. Birds, 'The Consolidation of the Companies Act' (1985) 6 *Company Lawyer* 151, Chesterman, above n 16 and L. Sealy, 'The New Form of Incorporation: A Personal View' (1981) 2 *Company Lawyer* 128.

regime for small and medium-sized companies as regards the filing of accounts, the introduction of a procedure for written resolutions and relaxation of other formal requirements[44] by 'elective resolutions'.[45] A similar approach is proposed in Australia.[46]

These reforms do not address the internal relationship between quasi-partners. Scope to address this issue is offered by section 128 of the Companies Act 1989 (United Kingdom) which would insert a new section 8A into the Companies Act 1985. Section 8A would enable companies limited by shares to adopt standard form articles suitable for a partnership company which would be contained in a new Table G. However, section 128 has not yet come into force. Further, the definition of 'partnership company' in section 8A refers to companies whose shares are intended to be held at a substantial extent by or on behalf of employees, and this reform does not appear to be directed at the domestic quasi-partnership company. Nevertheless, the approach of providing one or more forms of standard articles designed to meet the needs of quasi-partnership companies, suggests a fruitful direction for future reform.[47]

In the absence of such a reform, the present system in England and Australia at least has the advantage that it is to a large degree capable of manipulation to reflect the parties' expectations. Even though the distinction between shareholders and directors cannot be removed, it is possible to make all the shareholders directors and/or to confine the directors' powers to effectively acting as agents of the general meeting.

What then of those shareholders who fail to take advantage of such devices? Hill[48] considers that since members of such companies are sufficiently knowledgeable to prefer incorporation over partnership, they should be sufficiently knowledgeable to protect themselves by contract. Perhaps a re-education process for those who advise quasi-partners is the answer?

---

[44] Namely: duration of authority to allot shares, the majority required to consent to short notice of meetings, dispensing with laying of accounts and reports before a general meeting, dispensing with annual general meetings and with annual appointment of auditors.

[45] More recently, the Law Commission (above n 29) has doubted whether a new incorporated limited liability structure would be of significant assistance to small business and suggested that a reform of partnership law may be more beneficial.

[46] The First Corporate Law Simplification Bill 1994 will, if enacted, repeal the Close Corporations Act 1989 (and related legislation). The Bill distinguishes between small and large proprietary companies and exempts small proprietary companies from preparation of annual financial statements unless required to do so by five per cent of members or the ASC. It also proposes removal of the requirement for proprietary companies to hold an annual general meeting.

[47] See J. Freedman, 'Small Businesses and the Corporate Form: Burden or Privilege?' (1994) 57 *Mod L Rev* 555.

[48] J. Hill, 'Close Corporations in Australia—The Close Corporation Bill 1988' (1989) 15 *Can Bus LJ* 43.

In the mean time, it is submitted that the next best method to give effect to the reasonable expectations of the parties is by judicial development in granting relief against unfairly prejudicial conduct.

## 3. OTHER COMPANIES

Companies in this third category are defined only by their exclusion from the previous two groups. Within this wide category, those who have most often sought the aid of the courts have been shareholders who have obtained their shares by gift or inheritance. Shareholders who choose to become minority shareholders at least have the option to accept that position and possibly to take steps to protect their position. But those who have obtained their shares involuntarily have very little prospect of being able to do so. Often there is no market for their shares (except perhaps to the other members). Further, the unfair prejudice remedy does little to alleviate their complaints which are typically of low dividends and illiquidity. However, in common with shareholders in other types of company, they may take advantage of the benefits offered by the unfair prejudice remedy in some situations.

## 4. COMPARISON BETWEEN JURISDICTIONS

Finally, some observations should be made regarding the comparison between English and Australian law. As regards self-help measures, there is little to distinguish the two jurisdictions. In listed companies, there are parallels both in the concentration of share ownership in the hands of institutional investors and in the economic factors which have arguably stimulated a more active use of that power. If a distinction can be drawn, it is that shares in blue-chip companies in Australia are more likely to be concentrated in the hands of only a few institutions, who consequently play a dominant role in those companies. In the case of quasi-partnership companies, the only divergences are those which have been taken in drafting the legislative provisions giving contractual effect to the memorandum and articles and giving protection to class rights. However, the effects of these differences can be neutralized by an appropriate combination of the articles and a separate shareholders' agreement.

Greater differences between the two jurisdictions can be seen in the availability and interpretation of litigious remedies. Sealy[49] has noted the

---

[49] L. S. Sealy, 'The rule in *Foss* v. *Harbottle*: The Australian Experience' (1989) 10 *Company Lawyer* 52 and 'Problems of Standing, Pleading and Proof in Corporate Litigation'

willingness of Australian judges to minimize the procedural obstacles of the Rule in *Foss* v. *Harbottle*.[50] However, this factor is now of reduced significance in light of the development of the unfair prejudice remedy. To the extent that the unfair prejudice remedy takes over the ground covered by the common law, it eliminates many of the difficulties associated with: establishing standing, the effect of ratification and the operation of the test requiring majority shareholders to exercise their powers '*bona fide* for the benefit of the company as a whole'. And although the English courts were slower than their Australian counterparts to take full advantage of their jurisdiction under the unfair prejudice provision, changes in judicial attitude and statutory amendments have closed the gap. There is, however, one proviso to this statement, in that it is submitted that even if a liberal interpretation is adopted to the recent amendments to the United Kingdom unfair prejudice provision, the requirement that the petitioner be one of the members affected will still preclude an action being brought on similar facts to those in *Re Spargos Mining NL*.[51] As a consequence, the derivative action (with all its attendant complications) will continue to have a potentially greater sphere of operation in England than in Australia.

The other major distinguishing feature between the two countries, arguably one which offers a tangible advantage to minority shareholders in Australia, is the ability to apply to the court for information regarding the company's affairs.[52]

As for the future, law reform proposals in Australia are increasingly drawing their inspiration from North American developments[53] whereas the European Community is having a growing influence on the shape and direction of United Kingdom company law. It therefore remains to be seen whether the relatively close correspondence in the law in the two countries will continue.

in B. G. Pettet, (ed.) *Company Law in Change: Current Legal Problems* (London, Stevens & Sons, 1987) 1.

[50] (1863) 2 Hare 461; 67 ER 189.     [51] Above n 1. See Ch. 9 section 5(1).
[52] See Ch. 9 section 8(2)(b).
[53] E.g., the proposals for a statutory derivative action: see Ch. 8 section 6.

# Index

**abuse of power**
majority voting power 194–5
potential for 5
**administrative receiver**
unfair prejudice/oppression petition,
supervening appointment 162–3
**administrator**
derivative action to remove 190
unfair prejudice oppression petition,
supervening appointment 162–3
**annual general meeting**
conduct of 60
institutions and other shareholders,
resolution of conflicts between 61–2
**articles of association**
alteration
benefit of company, for 204, 208
class members, conferring rights on
75–81 *see also* **class rights**
common law proceedings 227
conflict of interests in 205–6
expropriation of shares, for *see*
**expropriation of shares, provision for,**
and **compulsory acquisition of shares,**
amendment of articles for, *below*
external contracts based on constitution,
effect of 88–90
fraud on holder of rights, as 207–8
general principles of law, subject to 204
majority voting power, limitations on
203–9
proper purposes test 208–9
protection from 104
removal of director, to allow 89
restrictions on 74 et seq
rights of shareholders, prejudicing 206
shareholders' agreement, restriction by
means of 83–90, 97
shares of minority, allowing
appropriation of 208, 298–305
unfair prejudice/oppression 226–7
weighted voting on 81–2
compulsory acquisition/transfer,
provisions on 105, 146–7, 262, 298
constitution, containing 66–7
contract not to alter 84–8
contractual effect 68, 71
disregard of rights 105–6
enforcement of
damages 73
declaration, remedy of 72–3
injunction, remedy of 72–3
outsider rights 67–72
personal action, by 87–8, 225–6
remedies 72–3
shareholders' agreement, use of 91
enforcement of provisions, personal action
for 187–8
expropriation of shares, amendment for
consideration 303
court, role of 299–303
justification 315
majority, independence of 298
oppression 302–3
policy issues 314
procedure 298
proper purpose 302
protection of shareholders 315–16
shareholder information 303–4
statutory procedure, restrictions on
availability 305
illiquidity, dealing with 105
impugned conduct permitted by 142
information about company affairs,
provision for 105
legitimate expectations, relevance to
141–9
management participation, securing
105
model set of 67, 325–7
new members bound by 93
outsider rights
Australia, in 70–2
England, in 68–70
*qua* member rights distinguished 68–9,
71–2
participation in profits, provision for
104
parties to 91–3
pre-emption provisions in 105, 142–9
quorum requirements in 83
shareholders' agreement, advantage over
67
**audit committees**
Australia, listing rules in 27
establishment, failure of legislation
concerning 23–4
increase in 50
recommendations for 23, 26, 28
**Australian Investment Managers'**
**Association**
formation of 25

**beneficial share ownership**
Australian companies 16, 18–20
UK companies 17, 19–20
**board minutes**
information, obtaining 249–50
**breach of contract**
as unfair prejudice/oppression 221–4

**class rights**
alteration
construction of 79–81
procedure for 76–9
governing director, special rights
conferred on 78
reduction of capital 80–1
remedies 79
articles, in 76
categories of 76
creation of 75
memorandum, variation clause in 77–8
quorum for reduction of capital, on a 293
statutory provisions 75–9
weighted voting 81–2
**common law remedies**
articles, alteration of 227
Australian Corporations Law, alternative
remedies under 213–15, 237, 242
controllers, self interested transactions by
237
derivative action *see* **derivative action**
equity stake or voting rights, dilution
of 228–9
information, rights to 246
majority voting power, limitations on *see*
**majority voting power**
negligent or inefficient management,
actions involving
care and skill, standard of 239
delegation of duty 241
financial competence, as to 240
personal rights, action to enforce *see*
**personal action**
relief available, deficiencies in 220
unfair prejudice/oppression remedy
complementing 219
**companies**
corporate quasi-partnerships *see* **quasi
partnership companies**
joint venture *see* **joint venture companies**
listed public *see* **listed companies**
private *see* **private company**
types of 3
**company affairs, information about**
articles of association, provision in 105
Australia, in
additional statutory rights 246–50
board minutes 249–50
good faith and proper purpose 248–9

reform proposals 250
special interest requirement 247–8
complaints 7
institutional activism 52–3
disputes, concerning
common law rights 246
English and Australian law compared 329
expropriation of shares, amendment of
articles for 303–4
listed companies
annual general meetings 60
briefings 59
continuous disclosure requirement 56–9
frequency of reporting 61
individual shareholders, implications of
activism for 56–61
institutional activism 52–3
listing rules 56
London Stock Exchange guidance 57
reduction of capital, on 296–7
schemes of arrangement, on 287–90
shareholders' agreement, provision in 105
statutory rights 245–6
Australia, in 246–50
takeovers, on 277–81
unfair prejudice provision/oppression
remedy
Australia, in 251
cases of 251
England, in 252
**company law**
majority rule, principle of 5
**complaints**
common 3
company, nature of 4
corporate quasi-partnerships, relating to 6
lack of information, as to 7
listed public companies, relating to 5
top 10 7–8
**compulsory acquisition of shares/
expropriation**
amendment of articles, for
common law, relief for 208–9, 227
consideration 303
court, role of 299–303
justification 315
majority, independence of 298
oppression 302–3
policy issues 314
procedure 298
proper purpose 302
protection of shareholders 315–16
shareholder information 303–4
statutory procedure, restrictions on
availability 305
articles of association, provisions of 105,
298
complaints, institutional activism 53–4

corporate quasi-partnerships 6–7
indirect form of 262
joint venture company 6–7
methods of 261
policy issues 305–15
private company, in 6–7
purchase order, order for 157–8
reduction of capital *see* **reductions of capital**
scheme of arrangement *see* **scheme of arrangement**
shareholders' agreement, provisions of 105
takeovers *see* **takeover, acquisition of shares on**
unfair prejudice/oppression remedy 157–8, 258–9
**contract**
breach of, as unfair prejudice/oppression 221–4
**controllers, self interested transactions by**
Australian Corporations Law, action under 237–8
common law derivative actions 237
institutional activism regarding 42–8
executive remuneration 43–8
management buy-outs 42
related party transactions 48
scrip dividends, issue of 43
separate agreement, convenants in 104
unfair prejudice/oppression remedy 231–7
**corporate governance**
Australia, in 24–7
Bosch Committee, discussion paper from 25–6
Cadbury Code 22–3
corporate sector under-performance, responses to 21
enforcement 23–4, 26–7
institutional investors, role of 21 et seq
Australia, in 27
Institutional Shareholders' Committee *see* **Institutional Shareholders' Committee**
momentum, loss of 22
non-executive directors *see* **non-executive directors**
United Kingdom, in 21–4
**courts, recourse to**
discussion on 3–4

**derivative action**
Australian Corporations Law, alternative remedy under 213–15, 237, 242
breach of duty, release of directors from 196–203, 220
clean hands, requirement of 190–1
company obtaining benefit of 191

controllers, self interested transactions by 237
costs 191
fraud, requirement for 193
limitations on ability to bring
costs 191
equitable restrictions 190–1
liquidation, companies in 190
membership, relevance of 189
procedural requirements 190
negligent or inefficient management, actions involving 239
right to bring 184
standing to sue 189
statutory, proposal for 215–17
unfair prejudice/oppression remedy, replacement by 219
wrongdoer control, requirement for 192–3
**directors**
appointment and removal of, influence of institutional shareholders 50–2
Australian Corporations Law, codification of duties in 213
breach of contract, action for 254
breach of duty
allotment of shares for improper purpose 188, 199–203
misappropriation and excusable profit-making 196–8
ratification by independent share-holders 198–9
release of 196–203, 220
care and skill, standard of 239
delegation of duty 241
discretion, agreement fettering 101–4
financial competence 240
general meeting, as agent of 103
major shareholders, identification with 210
personal undertaking, breach of 101
shadow
meaning 34
potential liability of 34–5
voidable transactions, validation of 197
voting agreement, entering into as shareholder 103
**dividends**
policy 52
individual shareholders, implications of institutional activism for 56

**eligible officer**
company, of 71
**equity stake or voting rights, dilution of** 229–31
**European Union**
Fifth Company Law Directive, proposals in 215

**executive remuneration**
institutional shareholders, complaints of
company performance, linkage to 45–6
contracts, term of 45
disclosure of make-up 43–4
remuneration committees, encouragement of 47–8
total remuneration, curbing 46–7
remuneration committees 47–8
total, curbing 46–7
**expropriation/compulsory acquisition** *see* **compulsory acquisition of shares**

*Foss* v. *Harbottle*
Australian Corporations Law, relevance in action under 214
procedural obstacles, minimizing 329
rule in 185
**fraud on a power**
doctrine of 200, 205
**fraud on the minority**
derivative action *see* **derivative action**
establishment of 189
fraud, meaning 193
standing to sue 189

**general meeting**
annual
conduct of 60
institutions and other shareholders, resolution of conflicts between 61–2
director as agent of 103
extraordinary, delay in convening 233
quorum requirements 83

**half-yearly reports**
requirement for 61

**illegal acts**
restraint of 186–7
**illiquidity**
articles of association, provision in 105
minority shareholders, disadvantage to 6
shareholders' agreement, provisions of 105
unfair prejudice/oppression, and 252–4
**Independent Shareholder Services**
proxy advice from 37
**insider dealing**
enforcement of legislation 58
**insolvent trading**
penalties 35
**Institutional Shareholders' Committee**
formation of 21
initiatives of 22

**joint venture companies**
articles of association *see* **articles of association**

companies legislation, appropriateness of 66
compulsory acquisition of shares 6–7
corporate form, advantages of 65–6
definition 65
minority shareholders, bargaining power 65
universal expectations in 138
**jurisdiction**
court, of, ousting 97–9

**liquidator**
unfair prejudice/oppression petition, supervening appointment 162–3
derivative action by 190
**listed companies**
beneficial share ownership
Australian companies 16, 18–20
UK companies 17, 19–20
board structure and composition of 49–50
controllers, self interested transactions by
executive remuneration 43–8
management buy-outs 42
related party transactions 48
scrip dividends, issue of 43
corporate governance *see* **corporate governance**
disposal of shares in 5
half-yearly reports 61
individual shareholders, implications of activism for
detrimental 55
dividend policy 56
information, access to 56–61
pre-emption rights 55–6
information, access to
annual general meetings 60
briefings 59
continuous disclosure requirement 56–9
frequency of reporting 61
individual shareholders, implications of activism for 56–61
institutional activism 52–3
listing rules 56
London Stock Exchange guidance 57
institutional activism, examples of
appointment and removal of directors 50–2
board structure and composition 49
company affairs, information about 52–3
compulsory acquisition 53–4
controllers, self interested transactions by 42–8
disregard of rights 53
dividend policy, as to 52
equity stake, dilution of 39–42

negligent or inefficient management
    48–52
voting rights, dilution of 39–42
institutional activism, influences on
    collective institutional shareholding,
        size of 31
    competition 32
    conflicts of interest 32–3
    cost benefit 32
    disincentives 32–9
    incentives 31
    indexing 31
    recession, in 31
    shadow directors, potential liability as
        34–5
    short term horizons 33–4
    social pressure 31
    takeover legislation, in 38–9
    voting disincentives 36–9
institutional shareholders
    activism 15
        influences on *see* institutional
            activism, influences on, *above*
    control by 19
    corporate governance, role in 21
    differential voting rights, shares with
        40–2
    equity stake, dilution of 39–42
    external influences on 14–15
    influence of 319–20
    other minority shareholders
        distinguished 14
    pre-emption rights, disapplication of 40
    proportion of shares held by 16–20
    voting rights, dilution of 39–42
litigation, resort to 320
minority control 15
minority shareholders
    institutional shareholders distinguished
        14
    shareholders classified as 15
non-executive chairman, with 49
PRO NED Code of Recommended
    Practice, compliance with 24
shareholders, transformation in
    constituency of 15–16
unfair prejudice/oppression remedy 138–9
voting
    differential voting rights, shares with
        40–2
    disincentives to institutional activism
        relating to 36–9
    funds, power of 37–8
    legal obstacles to 37–9
    Pensions Investments Research
        Consultants, advice from 37
    practical obstacles to 36–7
    proxy service 37

regular basis, use of votes on 36
unit holders, approval from 38

**majority rule**
    principle of 5
**majority voting power**
    abuse of 194–5 et seq
    exercise of rights, entitlement to exercise
        194
    limitations on, common law
        alteration of articles 203–9 *see also*
            **articles of association**
        company's property, appropriation of
            195–6
        directors' breach of duty, release of
            196–203 *see also* **directors**
        equitable considerations 209–12
**management buy-outs**
    institutional shareholders, complaints of
        42
**management, participation in**
    breakdown in relations, buyout on 256–8
    class rights, secured by 105
    legitimate expectations 255–6
    personal expectations of 254
    *qua* member requirement 255
**meeting** *see also* **general meeting**
    delay in convening 233
    quorum requirements 83
**memorandum of association**
    constitution, containing 66
    enforcement of provisions, personal action
        for 187–8
    entrenchment via the 75
    variation of rights clause in 77–8
**minority shareholders**
    Australian Corporations Law, action
        under 213–15
    choosing to become 328
    common complaints of *see* **complaints**
    Fifth Company Law Directive, proposals
        in 215
    illiquidity, disadvantage of 6
    oppression/unfair prejudice remedy *see*
        **unfair prejudice/oppression remedy**
    participation in management, expectation
        of 6
    power base 107
    small private company, in 6

**negligent or inefficient management**
    Australian Corporations Law, action
        under 242
    common law actions
        care and skill, standard of 239
        delegation of duty 241
        financial competence, as to 240
        listed companies, of 48–52

negligent management (*cont.*):
  reform proposals 242
  separate agreement, undertakings
      104
  unfair prejudice/oppression remedy 238–9
**non-executive directors**
  appointment, failure of legislation
      concerning 23–4
  Australia, in 25–6
  company affairs, time spent on 29
  Fifth Company Law Directive, provisions
      of 27–8
  greater numbers, appointment of 27
  increasing proportion of 49
  independence 29
  PRO NED *see* **PRO NED**
  role of
      ideological objections 27–9
      monitoring 27–8
      practical objections 29
      reform proposals 30

**oppression/unfair prejudice remedy** *see*
    **unfair prejudice/oppression remedy**

**Pensions Investments Research Consultants**
  voting advice from 37
**personal action**
  allotment of shares, as to 188
  articles, enforcement of 225–6
  company suffering damage, based on 235
  illegal acts, restraint of 186–7
  memorandum or articles, enforcement of
      187–8
  multiplicity 185
  rights conferred by companies legislation,
      enforcement of 188
  rights granted by contract, enforcement
      of 185
  special majorities, matters requiring 187
  *ultra vires* acts, restraint of 186
  vexatious 185
  winding up remedy, alternative to 177
**personal rights**
  action to enforce *see* **personal action**
  allotment of shares, in relation to 188
  companies legislation, conferred by 188
  contract, granted by 185
  infringement, proof of 184–5
  sources of 184
  standing on 185
**pre-emption rights**
  disapplication of 40
  individual shareholders, implications of
      institutional activism for 55–6
  legitimate expectation in case of 143–9
  unfair prejudice/oppression petition,
      effect of presenting 147

valuation
  method of 146
  minority holding, discounting 143–4
**private company**
  compulsory purchase of shares 6–7
  isolated minority shareholder, position
      of 6
  personal relationship of participants,
      breakdown in 6
  return on investment in 6
  transfer of shares, restrictions on 6
**PRO NED**
  Code of Recommended Practice 22
  establishment of 21
  PRO-NED Australia 25
**professional negligence**
  action founding 235
**profits, participation in**
  articles of association, provision in 104
  low dividend policy 244
  retention or distribution 243–4
  unfairly prejudicial conduct/oppression
      242–4
**property**
  company, appropriation of 195–6

**quasi-partnership companies**
  articles of association *see* **articles of
      association**
  breakdown in relations, buyout on 256–8
  companies legislation, appropriateness
      of 66
  complaints, limiting potential for 320–1
  compulsory acquisition of shares 6–7
  conflicts in 323
  corporate form, advantages of 65–6
  corporate norms, inappropriateness of
      322–8
  decisions in 5–6
  exclusion of party from 143
  expectations of parties 324
  formalizing arrangement 321
  meaning 54–5
  minority shareholders
      bargaining power 65
      over-protection of 321–2
  participation in management
      legitimate expectations 255–6
      personal expectations of 254
      *qua* member requirement 255
  personal expectations, unfair prejudice/
      oppression petitions based on 140
  profits, distribution of 256
  *qua* member rights 68–9
  relations between parties 323
  relationship between partners compared
      327

special legislation for
  arguments against 326
  proposals for 325–6.
typical features of 65

**receiver**
  appointment of 161
**reductions of capital, compulsory acquisition by**
  ASC, intervention of 313
  consideration 295–6
  court, role of 293–5
  limitations on use of 313
  majority, independence of 291–3
  policy issues 311–14
  procedure 291
  shareholder information 296–7
  statutory procedure, restrictions on availability 297–8
  statutory provisions, avoiding compliance with 312
  takeover, effecting 262, 290
**remuneration committees**
  encouragement of 47–8
  increase in 50
**rights**
  contractual, enforcement of 221–4
  disregard of
    articles of association 67, 105–6, 187, 225–6
    institutional activism 53
    remedies 221–6
    shareholders' agreement 105–6
  statutory, enforcement of 224–5

**schemes of arrangement, compulsory acquisition by**
  alternative procedure existing, where 309
  approval of 283–4
  approval threshold 262
  cancellation and reduction scheme 282
  class meetings 283 et seq, 311
  commercial enterprise, as 310
  consideration 287
  court, role of 286–7
  information, provision of 311
  majority, independence of
    Australia, in 285–6
    England, in 284
  policy issues 308–11
  procedure 281–4
  shareholder information 287–90
  statutory procedure, restrictions on availability 290
  takeover, effecting 282
  transfer scheme 282

**scrip dividends**
  institutional shareholders, complaints of 43
**self-help**
  English and Australian law compared 328
  joint venture company *see* **joint venture companies**
  listed companies *see* **listed companies**
  prevention by 3
  quasi-partnerships *see* **quasi-partnership companies**
  remedies 107
**service contracts**
  term of 45
**shareholders**
  fiduciary position, not in 194
  information available to 7, 105, 246, 249–50
**shareholders' agreement**
  alteration of 94
  alteration of articles, restriction of 83–91
  articles of association, advantage of 67
  compulsory acquisition, provisions on 105
  confidentiality 94–5
  contract not to alter constitution 84–8
  contractual remedies, availability of 96
  disregard of rights 105–6
  enforceability
    advantage of 95
    directors' discretion, fettering 101–4
    injunctive relief 97
    remedies 96–7
    statute, conflict with 97–100
    statutory minority protection remedies 96
    unfair prejudice/oppression provision, under 96, 221–4
    voting agreements 95–100
  enforcement of articles, role in 91
  equity stake or voting rights, voting against dilution of 104
  information about company affairs, provision for 105
  legitimate expectations, relevance to 149–52
  majority shareholders, entered into by 93
  management participation, securing 105
  negligent or inefficient management, undertakings as to 104
  new share issue, prevention of 87
  parties to 91–3
  personal pecuniary benefit, consideration as 100
  privity of contract 93–4
  recourse to 64
  registration 94–5
  rights and obligations, provision as to 91

shareholders' agreement (*cont.*):
  self interested transactions by controllers,
    covenants against 104
  severance of clause 86–8
  statute, conflict with
    contract not to alter articles 97
    effect of 97
    jurisdiction of court, ousting 97–9
    transfer of property, restraint on 97
    vote purchasing 99–100
  unanimous 92
  voting 91
**shares**
  allotment
    common law action challenging 229–31
    improper purpose, for 199–203
    personal rights 188, 202
    ratification of 199–203
    reduction of holding by 211–12
  compulsory acquisition *see* **compulsory
    acquisition of shares/expropriation**
  equity stake, dilution of
    articles of association, relevance
      of 229–31
    common law, challenge at 228–9
    complaints, institutional activism 39–42
    shareholders' agreement 104
    unfair prejudice/oppression, relief for
      227–8
  transfer, restrictions on 6
  voting rights, dilution of
    articles of association, relevance
      of 229–31
    common law, challenge at 228–9
    complaints, institutional activism 39–42
    shareholders' agreement 104
    unfair prejudice/oppression, relief for
      227–8

**takeover, compulsory acquisition of shares on**
  administrative savings 306
  Australia, in
    acceptance threshold 266–70
    majority, independence of 272–4
    takeovers not regulated by statute 266–7
    takeovers regulated by statute 267–71
  confidentiality 307
  consideration
    challenging 277–8
    determining 276–7
  court, role of 274–6
  directors, fiduciary position of 280
  disclosure obligations 278–80
  England, in
    acceptance threshold 264
    associate, definition of 271–2
    majority, independence of 271–2
    procedure 264–6
  group companies, transfer of funds
    between 306
  law reform, background to 306
  majority, independence of
    Australia, in 272–4
    England, in 271–2
  majority, intended investment by 306
  policy issues 305–8
  procedural requirements 262 et seq
  procedure
    Australia, in 266–71
    England, in 264–6
    statutory provisions 263–4
  shareholders
    equal treatment of 58
    expectations of 305
    information 277–81
  statutory procedure, restrictions on
    availability 281
  tax savings 307
  unfairly prejudicial/oppressive conduct
    280–1

*ultra vires* **acts**
  restraint of 186
**unfair prejudice/oppression remedy**
  administrative receiver, administrator or
    liquidator, supervening appointment
  of 162–3
  alteration of memorandum and articles,
    relief in respect of 226–7
  alternative remedy, availability of 146
  assumptions 135
  breach of contract, for 221
  common law action distinguished 138
  common law, complementing 219
  company affairs, information about
    Australia, in 251
    England, in 252
  company's affairs, regulation of 155
  complaints, remedying 219–20
  conduct
    order requiring 162
    order restraining 162
  conduct of company's affairs
    conduct of shareholders distinguished
      125–7
    isolated 127
    proposed acts and omissions 127
    subsidiary, oppressive conduct confined
      to 126
    undertakings, failure to honour 127
  constitutional documents, rights on
    members not embodied in 115
  contract or tort, claims based in 223
  contractual rights, enforcement of 221–4
  controllers, self interested transactions by
    231–7

costs
  company, indemnity from 164–5
  security for 165
court's inquiry, focus of 233
derivative action, replacement of 219
effect of ratification, elimination of
  difficulties with 219
English and Australian law compared
  329
history of 113–21
impugned conduct permitted by articles,
  where 142
intention, immaterial 134
interest, claim for 163
interim and interlocutory relief 163
interpretation of 112
intervention, basis for 232–3
introduction of provision 115–16
Jenkins Committee report, amendments
  after 119
jurisdiction, grounds for 132–3
legitimate expectations
  articles of association, relevance
    of 141–9
  changing membership, of 140–1
  contractual analogy 141
  departure from arising over time 151
  establishment of 135–7
  fair dealing, concept of 137
  legal rights, going beyond 151
  participation in management, of 150
  personal 139–52
  shareholders' agreement, relevance
    of 149–52
  substratum, alleged failure of 145
  test, application of 137–52
  universal 137–9
limitations
  oppression, meaning 117–18
  *qua* member requirement 118
  winding up, relationship with 116–17
listed company, petition in respect
  of 138–9
*locus standi*
  conduct pre-dating membership, in
    relation to 123–4
  former members, of 123
  members, confined to 122–3
  shareholders, of 231
majority, oppression of 148
majority rule, upholding principle
  of 135–6
modern remedy 121 et seq
more specific legislation, plugging gaps
  in 224–5
negligent or inefficient management
  238–9
objective unfairness, test of 133–7

other remedies, availability of 220
participation in profits, in relation
  to 242–4
partnership law, borrowed from 113
persons conducting affairs of company,
  acts or omissions on behalf of 234
petition, parties to
  all petitioners, joinder of 124
  alleged misconduct, persons involved
    in 125
  relief, persons affected by 124
petitioner's conduct, relevance of
  clean hands, concept of 152–3
  collateral purpose 154
  disinterest in affairs 153
  misconduct 152–3
proceedings by or on behalf of company,
  authorization of 158–61
purchase order, order for
  appropriate remedy, where 155–6
  compulsory acquisition 157–8
  discount, appropriateness of 157
  respondent's financial position,
    relevance of 157
  trustee companies, valuation 158
  valuation date 157
  valuation methods 156
*qua* member requirement
  Australia, in 131
  coincidental connection 130
  England, in 128–31
  equitable considerations 129
  freeholder, petitioner pursuing interests
    as 130
  limitation, as 118
  nominee shareholder 130
  restriction of operation 128–30
  stay of petition on ground of 130–1
receiver, appointment of 161
reimbursement of money paid out, order
  for 156
shareholder resolution, challenging 227
some part of members, conduct affecting
  120–1
standing, elimination of difficulties
  with 219, 231
statutory derivative action 159–61
statutory provisions 121
statutory rights, enforcement of 224–5
taking advantage of 328
unfairly prejudicial, use of term 119
winding up
  alternative prayer for 147
  order for 154–5
winding up remedy more appropriate,
  where
  deadlock, in case of 170–1
  no on-going business 169

**unfairly prejudicial/oppressive conduct**
all shareholders, conduct affecting 234
breach of fiduciary duty, conduct
    amounting to 233–4
extraordinary general meeting, delay in
    convening 233
good faith, in 134
impropriety 143
intention, immaterial 134
interpretation of 112
member bringing action, not affecting
    236
objective unfairness, test of 133–7
permitted by articles, where 142
petitioner, effect on 112
pre-emption provisions, exercise of 143–9
professional negligence, action founding
    235
remedy *see* **unfair prejudice/oppression
remedy**
statutory remedy against 4
takeover, acquisition of shares on 280–1
UK and Australian provisions
    distinguished 235–6

**winding up**
creditors, fraud on 100
inadequate dividends as ground for 244–5
just and equitable ground, on 113–15,
    145, 167 *see also* **winding up remedy**
postponement of calls, agreement as to 99
scope of operation, diminishing 167
**winding up remedy**
abuse of process, as 178–9
alternative relief

out-of-court offer to purchase
    shares 179
personal action at common law 177
petitioner's share, offer to purchase
    177–82
statutory requirement 176
unfair prejudice/oppression remedy,
    action under 176–7
clean hands, petitioner with 175
commercial companies, availability
    for 173–5
common assumptions and understandings
    on which company based, departure
    from 167
contributory, application by 173
expense of 181–2
independent operation of 168–72
meaning 167
more appropriate than unfair prejudice/
    oppression remedy, where
    deadlock, in case of 170–1
    no on-going business 169
operation of 221
petitioner acting unreasonably, striking
    out for 181
petitioner's conduct, relevance of 171–2
unavailability of relief under unfair
    prejudice/oppression provision 171–2
unfair prejudice/oppression remedy
    development of 166–8
    overlap with 154–5
    relationship with 116–17
valuation of shares 180
wider scope of, *locus standi* 172–3
**wrongful trading**
care and skill, standard of 240